International Perspectives on

Environment, Development, and Health

Toward a Sustainable World

To Chuck –

With great respect and admiration for your contributions and commitment to environmental health.

Barry

Gurinder S. Shahi, MBBS, PhD, MPH, is a physician with degrees in environmental toxicology (National University of Singapore) and international health policy and management (Harvard University). He has helped organize major initiatives in environment, development, and health for several international agencies and nongovernmental organizations, including the Rockefeller Foundation, World Health Organization, and Management Sciences for Health. He is currently working with the United Nations Development Programme to establish a new international organization dedicated to the prevention of infectious disease through science, the International Vaccine Institute in Seoul, Korea.

Barry S. Levy, MD, MPH, is a public health physician who has worked in the field of environmental and occupational health for over 20 years as an educator, researcher, clinician, consultant, and program director in over 20 countries, including Africa and Central and Eastern Europe. He is an Adjunct Professor at Tufts University School of Medicine, the 1997 President of the American Public Health Association, author of over 100 publications, and coeditor of a leading textbook on occupational health.

Al Binger, PhD, is a chemical engineer, biophysicist, and agronomist. From 1985 to 1990, Dr. Binger served as President of the Biomass Users Network, a nonprofit international cooperative organization dedicated to promoting South-South cooperation in the sustainable development of natural resources. Since 1991 Dr. Binger has been the Director of the Rockefeller Foundation's Global Environment Divison. His responsibilities include management and implementation of several initiatives, including Leadership for Environment and Development (LEAD) which focuses on capacity-building in sustainable development issues in major developing and developed countries.

Tord Kjellström, MD, MEng, is an environmental and occupational health specialist with degrees in medicine and engineering from Stockholm, Sweden. Since 1994 he has been the Director of the Office of Global and Integrated Health within the Programme for the Promotion of Environmental Health at the World Health Organization.

Robert S. Lawrence, MD, is Associate Dean for Professional Education and Programs and Professor of Health Policy at the Johns Hopkins School of Hygiene and Public Health. As chair of the U.S. Preventive Services Task Force from 1984–1989 and member from 1990–1995, Dr. Lawrence helped shaped prevention policy using evidence-based decision rules.

International Perspectives on
Environment, Development, and Health
Toward a Sustainable World

A collaborative initiative of the World Health Organization, the United Nations Development Programme, and the Rockefeller Foundation

---

Gurinder S. Shahi, PhD, MBBS, MPH

Barry S. Levy, MD, MPH Al Binger, PhD

Tord Kjellström, MD Robert Lawrence, MD

Editors

SPRINGER PUBLISHING COMPANY

Springer Publishing Company, Inc.
536 Broadway
New York, NY 10012-3955

Cover design by Tomas Yabut and Margaret Dunin
Production Editors: Joyce Noulas and Louise Farkas

97 98 99 00 / 5 4 3 2 1

Library of Congress Cataloging-in-Publication Data

International perspectives in environment, development, and health: toward a sustainable world/Gurinder S. Shahi . . . [et al.].
p. cm.
Includes bibliographical references and index.
ISBN 0-8261-9190-8
1. Economic development—Health aspects. 2. Economic development—Environmental aspects. 3. Environmental health—Developing countries. 4. Sustainable development—Health aspects. I. Shahi, Gurinder S.
RA566. I555 1996
362.1—dc20 95-33678
CIP

Printed in the United States of America

To those who hear the drumbeat . . .
and to those who will inherit this Earth.

Contents

Contributors

Tomi Adekanye
Department of Agricultural Economics
University of Ibadan
Ibadan, Nigeria

Robert Beaglehole
Department of Community Health
University of Auckland
Auckland, New Zealand

Seth Berkley
Assistant Director
Health Sciences Division
The Rockefeller Foundation
New York, NY

Al Binger
Director
Global Environment Division
The Rockefeller Foundation
New York, NY

Dr. Martin H. Birley
Programme Manager
The Liverpool Health Impact Programme
Liverpool School of Tropical Medicine
Pembroke Place, Liverpool, England

Eugene Brantly
WASH Project
Arlington, VA

Donald Bundy
Scientific Coordinating Centre
Partnership for Child Development
West Beit, Imperial College
Prince Consort Road
London

Eric Chivian
Psychiatrist
Massachussetts Institute of Technology
Brookline, MA

Carlos Corvalán
Division of Environmental Health
World Health Organization
Geneva

Ila L. Cote
Associate Director
Health Effects Research Laboratory
United States Environmental Protection Agency
Research Triangle Park, NC

Nitin Desai
Under-Secretary-General for Policy Coordination and Sustainable Development
United Nations

Faye Duchin
Institute for Economic Analysis
New York University
New York, NY

Mohamed Mahmoud El Batanouny
Vice Director
Cairo University Hospitals
Department of Occupational Diseases and Environmental Medicine
Kasr El Aini Faculty of Medicine
Cairo University
Cairo

Gamal Hosni El Samra
Professor of Occupational Medicine
Kasr El Aini Faculty of Medicine
Cairo University
Cairo

Steven A. Esrey
Senior Project Officer
Water and Environmental Sanitation
UNICEF

Daniel B. Fishbein
International Branch
Division of Field Epidemiology
Centers for Disease Control and Prevention
Atlanta, GA

Gilles Forget
Director
Health Sciences Division
International Development Research Center (IDRC)
Ottawa, Ontario

Howard Frumkin
Director
Division of Environmental and Occupational Health
Emory University
School of Public Health
Atlanta, GA

Dr. Norman G. Gratz
Specialist in Vector Biology & Control
Commugny, Switzerland

Kenneth M. Green
Consultant,
Chevy Chase, MD

Andrew Hall
Scientific Coordinating Centre
Partnership for Child Development
West Beit, Imperial College
London

Scott Halstead
Associate Director
Health Sciences Division
The Rockefeller Foundation
New York, NY

Jorge E. Hardoy
(deceased)
President
IIED America Latina
Buenos Aires, Argentina

Frank Hartvelt
Deputy Director
Science, Technology and Private Sector Division (STAPSD)
United National Development Programme
New York, NY

Robert Hetes
Research Triangle Institute
Research Triangle Park, NC

Heidi Lyn Holt
International Branch,
Division of Field Epidemiology
Centers for Disease Control and Prevention
Atlanta, GA

C.J. Hong
Professor
Department of Environmental Health
Shanghai Medical University
Shanghai, People's Republic of China

J. Jeyaratnam
Head, Division of Occupational Medicine
Head, WHO Collaborating Centre for Occupational Health
National University Hospital
Singapore

Tord Kjellström
Director
Office of Global and Integrated Health (EHG)
World Health Organization
Geneva

Joseph LaDou
Director
Division of Occupational and Environmental Medicine
International Center for Occupational Medicine
University of California, San Francisco

Robert S. Lawrence
Associate Dean
Professional Education and Programs
Professor
Health Policy and Management
School of Hygiene and Public Health
The Johns Hopkins University
Baltimore, MD

Lee Chen
Consultant
Seoul, Korea

Barry S. Levy
Director
Barry S. Levy and Associates
Sherborn, MA

Jim Listorti
Senior Adviser
The World Bank
Washington, DC

Garrick E. Louis
Director
Development Implementation Agency
New York, NY

Roberto Luis Monte-Mor
CEDEPLAR/ECMVS
Minas Gerais, Brazil

Shabbir M. Moochhala
Senior Research Scientist/Toxicologist
Department of Surgery
National University Hospital
Singapore

Arturo Morillo
Executive Director
International Clinical Epidemiology Network (INCLEN)
Executive Office
Philadelphia, PA

Olu Oluwasola
Lead Fellow
Foundation for Environmental Development and Education in Nigeria (FEDEN)
Leadership for Environmental and Development Programme (LEAD)
Yaba, Lagos, Nigeria

Prof. Adeniyi Osuntogun
National Programme Director
Foundation for Environmental Development and Education in Nigeria (FEDEN)
Leadership for Environment and Development Programme (LEAD)
Yaba, Lagos, Nigeria

Jonathan A. Patz
Johns Hopkins School of Hygiene and Public Health
Baltimore, MD

Genandrialine L. Peralta
Assistant Professor
Environmental Engineering
National Engineering Center
University of the Philippines
Diliman, Quezon City
Philippines

Rebecca Peterson
Faculty of Environmental Studies
York University
North York, Ontario, Canada

Clydette Powell
Health First Medical Group
Memphis, TN

Kathleen Rest
Occupational Health Program
Department of Family and Community Medicine
University of Massachusetts Medical School
Worcester, MA

Rosalia Rodriguez-Garcia
Director
Center for International Health and Development
George Washington University
Washington, DC

Phillip W. Sarocco
Health Economist
Health Outcomes Research Division
International Pharmaceuticals Group
Pfizer Incorporated
New York, NY

David Satterthwaite
Senior Research Associate
Human Settlements Programme
International Institute for Environment and Development (IIED)
London

Gurinder S. Shahi
Coordinator
Operations Development
International Vaccine Institute Project
United Nations Development Programme
Seoul, Korea

Victor W. Sidel
Distinguished Professor of Social Medicine
Montefiore Medical Center
Albert Einstein School of Medicine
Bronx, NY

Kirk Smith
Senior Fellow
Coordinator, Risk and Development
Program on Environment
East-West Center
Honolulu, Hawaii

Carl E. Taylor
Professor Emeritus of International Health
Senior Adviser to UNICEF
School of Hygiene and Public Health
John Hopkins University
Baltimore, MD

Daniel Taylor-Ide
Senior Associate
School of Hygiene and Public Health
John Hopkins University
Baltimore, MD

Philomène A. Verlaan
United Nations Environment Programme
Nairobi, Kenya

Linda Whiteford
University of South Florida
Tampa, FL

Mary Yacoob
Research Triangle Institute
Research Triangle Park, NC

Foreword

This book performs an invaluable service by focusing attention on the close link between environment, health, and development. When talking of environment and development, our thoughts do not run automatically to the health sector. Nevertheless, concern for human health has been a key motivating force behind environmental activism as environmental quality has a profound impact on human health and well-being.

Some 2.5 million people in developing countries suffer from illnesses linked to contaminated water and poor sanitation, while nearly 4 million infants die each year from diarrheal diseases due to contaminated food or water. Infectious and parasitic diseases are still by far the leading causes of death in developing countries and represent a tremendous drain on the productivity of these countries, not to mention the toll in human suffering. On a global scale hundreds of million of people suffer from respiratory and other diseases caused by air pollution as well as chemical and biological agents. These and other health problems and risks related to the environment and their impact on development are well documented in this excellent collection.

One of the key difficulties of governments and international organizations is how to ensure that environmental considerations are fully integrated into decision-making structures at all levels, including decision making on health-related matters. In addition, full account has to be taken of the health implications of environment and development decisions. We must find new ways to integrate a multiplicity of factors into governmental decision-making processes and educate health professionals and policy makers through new methods of learning that stress interdependence of natural and man-made systems.

Although improved techniques of risk assessment can provide us with statistical measures of potential health risks for certain kinds of decisions, decision makers cannot afford to view these matters in purely abstract terms when the welfare of large populations is at stake. In short, all of our scientific techniques must be informed by a degree of critical scepticism and underlying concern for their impact on human beings.

I am convinced that the nongovernmental community has a pivotal role to play in ensuring that the "Spirit of Rio" remains a dynamic force in the world. Although NGOs are often critical of both governments and international organizations, their interest and commitment is a positive challenge to all of us to do better. Those NGOs that are devoted to health and human welfare have already played a key part in improving health and environmental standards worldwide. The gap, however, between goals and achievements remains large, and, in many cases, continues to grow.

The solution to our most difficult environment, development, and health problems will require a confluence of techniques, technologies, finance, knowledge, and moral commitment unprecedented in our history. I believe that this volume is an important contribution to our understanding of how this can be achieved.

NITIN DESAI
Under-Secretary-General
for Policy Coordination
and Sustainable Development
United Nations

Preface

Practitioners of public health have traditionally focused on the well-being of the individual and, more recently, on that of society, and on the impact of physical, chemical, biological, and social hazards on human health. The different ecosystems within which people live and interact tend to be viewed by health professionals in terms of the potential dangers and risks they might bring to human health and well-being.

Environmentalists and ecologists, on the other hand, have tended to focus on concerns of the impact of human society and human activities on the environment and global ecology. From their perspective, human lifestyles and economic activities are potentially detrimental to environmental and global sustainability.

Substantial bodies of evidence exist to support both perspectives. Increasingly, humankind is recognizing that these perspectives are, in fact, complementary and that better account of the stresses that we place on local and global life-support systems needs to be taken. Such stresses are clearly detrimental to ecological and environmental integrity and tend also, in the long term, to threaten human well-being.

In addition to recognizing the importance to health of where and how individuals live, what kind of work they do, the type and quantity of food they eat, and the source of water they drink, health professionals have found themselves having to consider the health implications of global environmental concerns. Such concerns include deforestation, urbanization, rapid population growth, emerging (and reemerging) diseases, global warming, ozone depletion, loss of biodiversity, and air and water pollution.

The extent and scope of human-generated environmental contamination and degradation and its direct and indirect implications for the health of the planet and, ultimately, ourselves, is becoming increasingly clear. A new appreciation of the interrelationships between socioeconomic activities (including development), the environment, and human health is therefore taking shape.

The key phrase of the 1990s has become "sustainable development," an idealized conception of development wherein increased economic and social well-being is brought about in a manner that does not degrade or destroy the environment and does not increase the options for the present generation at the expense of future generations.

The maintenance and promotion of increased human well-being is only possible where resources are available to meet human needs and where living conditions and the working environment are protected from life- and health-threatening pollutants, pathogens, and physical hazards (Report of WHO Commission on Health and Environment, 1992). Humankind cannot hope for sustainable development without first developing the capacity to identify, investigate, and eventually, prevent environmentally and occupationally related risks to human health and well-being.

The nature of environment- and development-related concerns is such that dealing with them requires a much broader perspective than is currently available in any one field of endeavor or geographical region. Thus, different sectors and disciplines need to be partners in analyzing and addressing these concerns. At the regional and local levels, we are recognizing that each country's or region's problems are not isolated but, in fact, have much in common with those of others, and that we have much to learn from each other. This monograph brings together examples from different parts of the world of health concerns and solutions related to environment and development issues. We hope that they will inspire and promote discussion, analysis, and action at local and global levels, involving professionals in all relevant disciplines and the communities involved.

Halfdan Mahler, the Director-General Emeritus, World Health Organization, and Secretary General, International Planned Parenthood Federation, has stated

> The global village has achieved a measure of interdependence requiring recognition by all concerned with the health of both individuals and communities that there is an urgent need to share our knowledge and deploy our resources in the best interests of people everywhere.

This broader perspective, representing a synthesis between cutting-edge thinking about public health and concern for sustainable and human development, may be characterized as sustainable public health. Achieving sustainable public health will require systemic changes in the way public health and development professionals think, teach, practice, and research.

This book builds on the contributions of the United Nations Conference on Environment and Development (UNCED), Agenda 21, and the WHO Commission on Health and Environment. Although the work presented here complements and supplements earlier contributions to thinking about environment and development, its focus is on elaborating a new appreciation of the environment-development-health interface.

Further, this book considers the implications of our new understanding of environment-development-health interactions in determining future research priorities and directions; it documents the experience of some important programs and projects at the forefront of integrated, multidisciplinary work; and it outlines a strategy for incorporating and implementing sustainable public health thinking and practices in our health systems.

Given the scope of issues and concerns considered, it is inevitable that not all subjects of interest will be covered to the depth they deserve. In a spririt of continuing dialogue and a desire to gain from your insights, perspectives, comments, and suggestions, the editors and chapter authors would be interested in receiving your feedback. Please write c/o Springer Publishing Co., 536 Broadway, New York, NY 10012-3955.

Acknowledgments

We are grateful for the support and assistance provided by the Rockefeller Foundation, World Health Organization, and the United Nations Development Programme, and for the interest and commitment shown by the innumerable colleagues who contributed their time, energy, and ideas to write or review the many manuscripts that were included in this work.

This book was conceived while Editor Gurinder Shahi was a Warren Weaver Fellow at the Rockefeller Foundation in 1992–1993. It has benefited from the collective wisdom of colleagues and friends associated with international organizations, governments, nongovernmental organizations, research and academic institutions, as well as other interested individuals throughout the world.

The views and perspectives expressed herein represent those of the respective chapter authors and editors and are not necessarily shared by the organizations and institutions with which they may be associated.

PART I
Introductory Overview

1

The Environment–Development–Health Interface

Gurinder S. Shahi, Barry S. Levy, Garrick E. Louis, Al Binger, Tord Kjellstrom, and Robert S. Lawrence

INTRODUCTION

Mahatma Gandhi once wrote: "[Hu]mankind is notoriously too dense to read the signs that God sends from time to time. We require drums to be beaten into our ears, before we should wake from our trance and hear the warning . . ."

The drums have been sounding for a long time now, warning us that the route we have taken to economic growth and development is flawed. Can we hear them beating? Listen:

- Widening income disparity and inequity among nations and within nations;
- Rapid population growth and substandard urbanization;
- Rising consumption—and overconsumption—of renewable and nonrenewable resources;
- Massive deforestation and destruction of natural environments;
- Loss of biodiversity at such rates that 25 percent of current species may be extinct within 50 years;
- Inappropriate agricultural techniques, resulting in declining soil fertility and the threat of declining agricultural yields;
- Pollution and waste generation at such rates that we now have to contend with hazardous contamination of many of our waterways and lakes;

The authors wish to express their gratitude to Frank Hartvelt, Lee Chen, Michael Sacks, Maninder Shahi, and Jacklyn Sims, for their helpful comments and suggestions.

- A gaping hole in the ozone layer;
- The potential for global warming and climate change, engendered by the stresses we have placed on global homeostatic and life-support systems.

Those who hear the drumbeat recognize the need to evolve holistic approaches to dealing with environmental and developmental concerns in a way that protects and promotes both environmental and human well-being. Evolving such approaches requires a sound understanding of the nature of interaction of environment, development, and health.

ENVIRONMENT

The "environment" can be viewed, from the perspective of the individual, as consisting of the internal environment (or, as Claude Bernard described it, the *milieu interieur*) and the external environment. This discussion, unless otherwise specified, refers to the external environment.

The external environment might be described in terms of the human-altered environment and the natural environment. Expanding human settlement and exploitation of natural resources has left few, if any, "natural" environments on the planet that are truly unaltered by the impact of human activities and waste products. We also think often in terms of such subsets of the environment as "indoor environments" and "work environments."

Another way to view the environment is in terms of such attributes as:

1. *The physical environment*, which refers to the physical aspects of the environment around us including, for example, the structures in which we live and work; the weather and climate; the soil and types of vegetation; water sources, water supply and sanitation networks; or roads and components of our transportation systems and facilities.
2. *The biological environment*, which refers to the sum total of biological life in the environment—the microorganisms (including bacteria, viruses, and fungi), the plants, and the animals—and the ecosystems which support them. Biological lifeforms provide much of the food we eat, the clothes we wear, and the energy that drives our modern lives (petroleum and coal, for example, are derived from ancient biological life forms). Interactions with the biological environment can impact greatly on health and well-being, as evidenced by ill health occurring when our bodies are infected with disease-causing organisms.

3. *The chemical environment,* which refers to the components in the environment around us which can interact chemically with the physiological systems that make up the *milieu interieur* of life forms and can potentially affect growth, development, and well-being. The chemical environment includes oxygen and carbon dioxide in the air we breathe, and pollutants, carcinogens, and toxic substances to which we may be exposed.[1]
4. *The human or "conceptual" environment.* Humankind is essentially a species that lives in groups. We have created societies and super-societies around ourselves that determine the languages we speak, the norms of our behavior, the nature of our interaction with each other, and the rules by which we live our lives. Hence, all aspects of human intercourse—including the social, cultural, political, legal, ethical, and economic environments—can be considered as constituting elements of the so-called human or "conceptual" environment (Dubos, 1973).

Any sub-classifications of the environment we make are simply tools for understanding. Clearly, environmental interactions are complex and multifaceted. Hence, forests, for example, cannot simply be placed in any one definitional compartment but are of significance in several different contexts—constituting important interactors of our physical, chemical, biological, social, and cultural environments.

Our lives are, to a large extent, greatly influenced by environmental factors. Our sleep–wake patterns, for example, are generally dictated by the cycles of light and dark that constitute day and night. We dress according to the weather and the seasons—sunny or rainy, cold or hot. Our behavior and attitudes are often modified to avoid infectious and other environmental exposure-related diseases—with profound impact our hygiene, feeding, drinking, and even sexual behavior.

DEVELOPMENT

In its broadest sense, development refers to change in the course of interaction of the individual and of human society with the environment—presumably (but not always) resulting in evolution and progress toward higher standards of living in terms of income, health, education, and increased freedom of choice. Human activities leading to "development"—including, for example, the exploitation and utilization of natural

[1] While individuals living in contemporary societies are exposed to as many as 80,000 different chemicals, we have characterized the health implications of exposure to only a few hundred of these chemicals.

Box 1.1—Human Impact on the Environment

Human intervention has done much to shape the environment. Many ecosystems we consider to be "natural" today were quite different in their original pristine state.

The olive tree is regarded today as being of Mediterranean origin. In fact, it was introduced from Iran (Dubos, 1973). The tulip, considered so much a part of the Dutch landscape today, was introduced into Holland from Turkey.

The English moors, much celebrated in poetry and literature, were once covered with forests. They were deforested through the farming and grazing practices of the medieval monks, and later again when tunnel construction for mining resulted in a large demand for timber (Dubos, 1973).

There is substantial archeological evidence that the ancient Sumerian and Babylonian civilizations thrived at the expense of degrading their land resource base so badly that they eventually brought about their own downfall. As recently as 7,000 B.C., the sites of these civilizations were covered with productive forests and grasslands (Tyler Miller, 1990). They established a sophisticated system of agriculture with elaborate networks of irrigation canals. But deforestation, soil erosion, and overgrazing led to the silting of the canals and were, in large part, responsible for the conversion of the previously fertile land in what is today modern Iraq and Iran into barren desert by 3,000 B.C. (Tyler Miller, 1990).

Are we in danger of repeating the same mistakes?

resources (renewable and nonrenewable), construction of industrial and economic infrastructure, or cultural and social change—cannot be pursued without positive and/or negative effects on the natural and/or human environments (see Box 1.1).

Until recently, development tended to be considered as synonymous with economic development. The Gross National Product (GNP) of a country or region was often taken as the principal indicator of development. Growing recognition, in the last decade, of the inadequacy of GNP as an indicator for development, has led to a major rethinking of how best to characterize development. Development is increasingly being seen in terms of human well-being, and in terms of the impact of social, cultural, economic, and environmental change on maximizing human potential. With this changing emphasis, such terms as "sustainable development," "human development," and "sustainable human development" have come increasingly into use.

HEALTH

The Constitution of the World Health Organization (WHO) states: "Health is a state of complete physical, mental and social well-being and not merely the absence of disease or infirmity." This definition of health has been an important one that has helped health-care providers expand their understanding of health and well-being of the individual.[2] Not only must the individual be free of disease, but she should also feel well and be in a state of harmony with herself, the people around her, and with the social environment in which she finds herself. These are seen as prerequisites for achieving a state of complete physical, mental, and social well-being.

Useful and important though this definition has been, there is need, as we approach the new millennium, to reevaluate our understanding of health, and perhaps redefine health in terms of a broader appreciation of individual and societal well-being within the dynamic context of developmental and environmental well-being (see Box 1.2).

Health in the Context of Environment and Development

Each individual has a unique genetic constitution (the genotype), with the possible exception of identical twins, and is equipped with certain mental, physical, and metabolic attributes—which are shaped largely by genetic as well as environmental influences (phenotype). Just as genetic abnormalities can result in ill health (for example, metabolic diseases such as the Lesch Nyhan syndrome), exposure to environmental influences can also have consequences on health and well-being.[3]

---

[2] It should be noted that some physicians and scientists find the WHO definition too idealistic, vague, and subjective. How, they ask, does one measure "well-being"? These critics prefer to use a more limited and objectively measurable definition, wherein health is the "absence of premature death, illness, impairment, disability, or any failure of growth or development" (Task Force Report, 1976).

[3] Environmental influences to which exposure occurs can be *physical*—as with temperature, humidity, or exposure to dusts; *chemical*—as is the case with exposure to toxins or carcinogens in food; or *biological*—as with exposure to viruses or bacteria.

Box 1.2—Should We Redefine Health?

How should we, as we approach the dawn of the 21st century, see ourselves and the way we interact with our environment? How should we define health and well-being—from a narrow "I, me, myself, my family" perspective? or a broader "global community" perspective? Our choice is very important, because it will shape the way we interact with ourselves and our environment. It may also have direct bearing on our future as a species and on the future (and form) of life on this planet.

We should not, for example, contemplate development and environmental interactions in which an individual may feel complete physical, mental, and social well-being at a particular moment in time without also considering the long-term implications of such interactions. Hence, if a person indulges in an activity which is unsustainable and leads eventually to degradation and destruction of the environment, that activity cannot be described as "healthy" because, in the long term, it is likely to result in consequences which are damaging to the health of the planet, to society, and to the individual.

Similarly, the wealthy in any society can purchase the resources to buffer themselves from the environment—the heat and the cold, the rain, the exposure to pests and pollutants. They also consume resources far out of proportion to their needs. Clearly, their affluence cannot absolve these individuals from the need to recognize that their activities, attitudes, and consumption patterns can have devastating consequences on the health and well-being of the planet.

It seems, therefore, relevant and important to expand the definition of health to include a recognition of the need for human cultural, economic, and social activities to be sustainable and health-promoting, rather than degrading. Also, when we think of health, it is important that we see it in a much broader and longer-range context than has generally been the case—health should refer not only to the health of persons but also to the health of global life-support systems, to the health of ecosystems, and to the sustainability of development and human interactions with the other inhabitants of this planet.

To take appropriate account of this broader understanding of the links between environment, development, and health, a more holistic definition of health is proposed: "Health is a state of complete physical, mental, social, ecological, and environmental well-being." Such a perspective would be fundamental to sustainable public health and sustainable human development.

Our interactions with other members of our ecosystems (whether we live in urban or rural communities) are also important in determining our state of health: how people treat animals and pets; the concern individuals show for greenery and the maintenance of plant life; how individuals deal with potentially disease-causing vermin and pests. All these have a fairly direct bearing on the health and well-being of the individual, and can provide strong indications of one's state of health and well-being. The same is true for our interactions with other ecosystems—human-centered as well as natural. The way we interact with other human societies is obviously also important—whether we live in peace or are at war with other communities, for example, would have a direct impact on health and well-being.

Should we strive for human development and the exploitation of natural resources without concern for the impact such exploitation might have on other ecosystems, on the future, or on our own livelihoods? What impact would ecosystem destruction due to overexploitation of resources or excessive waste generation have on our health? More and more, we are finding that our activities as a species can have a direct impact on the life-support system of this planet and greatly alter local ecosystems (see Box 1.3). The wastes we generate, the loss of species and biodiversity, and the local environmental destruction we have caused in the name of progress and development have all resulted in real and measurable changes—rising carbon dioxide levels, the hole in the ozone layer, rising pollution of our fisheries and waterways, and growing degradation of croplands. Perpetuating such stresses on the environment is likely to have dire consequences on our own health and well-being—and on our very survival.

POPULATION, ENVIRONMENT AND DEVELOPMENT

Casting an eye on the history of humankind's interaction with the environment, there have obviously been periods when changing conditions resulted in significant increases (and, from time to time, decreases) in carrying capacity—the upper limit of the population of any given species which an ecosystem can sustainably maintain.

Global human population during the caveman days was thought to be fairly stationary, with humans generally living at (or close to) the carrying capacity of their ecosystems. When populations got too high, increased competition, lack of food, and/or disease outbreaks would keep population numbers in check.

The wave of change from hunting and foraging to more settled agricultural and pastoral lifestyles about 10,000 years ago resulted in advances

Box 1.3—Ecological Health Concerns

The health and well-being of humankind and our future viability depend very much on whether we can develop mechanisms to respect and support the maintenance of biodiversity and the continued health of the various ecosystems and habitats—ecological health.

We are now beginning to see that we cannot—at least should not—continue to use and abuse natural ecosystems and replace them at will with systems generated to suit the needs of humankind. As we alter these ecosystems with our interventions and our pollutants, we also risk threatening the life-support systems that surround us. These life-support systems include the carbon cycle, the oxygen cycle, the nitrogen-fixation cycle, the photosynthetic pathways, the planetary homeostatic mechanisms which help maintain temperatures, atmospheric oxygen and carbon dioxide levels, and the ozone layer, which helps to prevent entry of hazardous ultraviolet rays into the atmosphere.

We are becoming increasingly aware of the interaction between humankind and the various ecosystems in which we live or with which we interfere. Sometimes, the entry of humans into a new ecosystem can result in the introduction of major disease and devastation as human-associated infectious agents and environmentally devastating behavior wreak havoc on the environment (as happened, for example, when human viruses spread to sea mammal populations).

At the same time, humans can cause disturbances to ecosystems that tend to favor the establishment of diseases that are damaging to human well-being—for example, the destruction of forests creates conditions favorable to colonization by mosquitos. If diseases such as malaria are endemic to a region in which such destruction occurs, the spread of these diseases to human communities settling in the region is very likely.

Hence, the interaction of humans with any ecosystem is fraught with dangers and threats—not only to humans but also to the flora and fauna of the ecosystem.

which permitted increases in carrying capacity and, hence, population growth. The ability to grow and produce their own food allowed our ancestors a certain measure of control over the environment and allowed significant increases in population—the human carrying capacity of an agricultural existence being much higher than that of hunting and gathering.

As the new lifestyles and knowledge of crop-growing technology and animal husbandry spread through much of the ancient world, there were associated rises in population in connection with the rising carrying capacity of these human-centered ecosystems. Each advance in agriculture—such as the use of animals to plow the land, or the utilization of the wheel to transport produce to the marketplace, or the introduction of irrigation systems—would have resulted in more effective use of the resources of the land (from a human-carrying-capacity perspective) and greater food production surpluses. This freed many individuals from having to grow or hunt their own food and provided the basis for greater division of labor. Eventually, these advances enabled the establishment of populous urban centers that continued, nevertheless, to depend on the agricultural hinterlands for food.

DEMOGRAPHIC TRANSITIONS

Human societies, throughout most of history, have generally had moderately high birth rates accompanied by high death rates. The result was that population growth occurred slowly, if at all. In other words, population remained essentially stationary at about the level of the carrying capacity. Infant and childhood mortality in these societies tended to be high, with life expectancy low. The incidence of infectious diseases was high, and it was not uncommon for epidemics of diseases like cholera or the plague to decimate entire communities.

Global population grew very slowly before the dawn of the industrial age. Hence, the total population has been estimated to have been between 250 and 400 million about 2,000 years ago (Carl Haub, personal communication) and was still only about 470 million in 1650 (Table 1.1).

With the acquisition of wealth and the dawn of the industrial age came more modern concepts of health, hygiene, and nutrition, as well as better tools for dealing with infectious and other diseases. As illustrated in Table 1.1 and Figure 1.1, the world's population started to rise initially in the more developed countries (MDCs) of today.

The MDCs experienced a modest population explosion of a little over 1.5 percent annually, as death rates fell and the benefits of modernization slowly accrued, with resulting increases in the carrying capacities of these societies. A reduction in fertility came with increased survival of offspring and changing norms, as societies adjusted to more urbanized lifestyles with greater individual freedoms and increased opportunities for female education and employment (to name a few factors).

TABLE 1.1 Estimated and Projected World Population (millions) Between 1650 and 2150

Year	World	MDC	(%)	LDC	(%)
1650	470	103	(21.9)	367	(78.1)
1750	760	180	(23.7)	568	(76.3)
1800	1,000	248	(24.8)	752	(75.2)
1850	1,211	340	(28.1)	871	(71.9)
1900	1,628	560	(34.4)	1,068	(65.6)
1950	2,517	833	(33.1)	1,684	(66.9)
2000	6,204	1,265	(20.4)	4,939	(79.6)
2050	10,035	1,319	(13.1)	8,716	(86.9)
2100	11,330	1,310	(11.6)	10,020	(88.4)
2150	11,499	1,314	(11.4)	10,185	(88.6)

MDC—more developed countries; LDC—less developed countries.
Sources: Carl Haub (1993) Population Reference Bureau, Washington, DC (personal communication). Bulatao et al. (1990) *World Population Projections*, The World Bank.

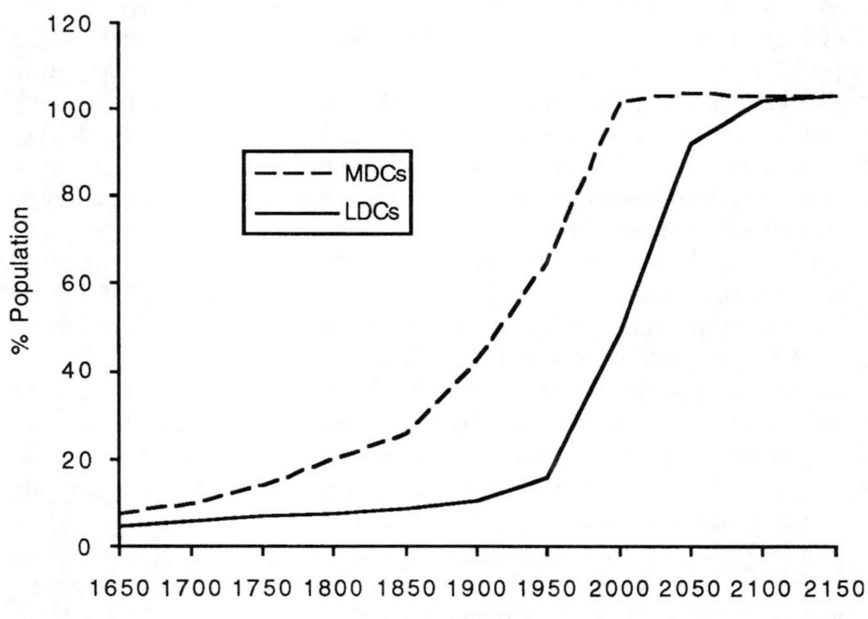

FIGURE 1.1 Population growth in more developed countries (MDCs) and less developed countries (LDCs). 1650–2150

N.B.—Data are derived from Table 1.1 using values for 2150 as 100%.

These societies eventually settled into a pattern of low birth and death rates. They have essentially completed what is called the *demographic transition* from high fertility, high death rates, to low fertility, low death rates.

After about 1900, the less developed countries (LDCs) also started to benefit from modern concepts of sanitation, hygiene, nutrition, and health care, and began to experience the beginnings of their own demographic transition (Table 1.1 and Figure 1.1).

While the introduction of improved approaches to sanitation, health, and nutrition came relatively late into these LDC societies, these innovations have been very effective in helping to rapidly bring down death rates—especially infant mortality rates. However, this decline in mortality was generally not accompanied by rising standards of living and the sort of social and cultural changes which brought lowered fertility in MDCs. Hence, until fairly recently, there has been a relatively small concomitant fall in birth rates, and population growth started to occur in these societies at rates far exceeding those seen in any MDC. Essentially, the difference between birth and death rates, or the rate of natural increase, has been much larger in LDCs than had previously occurred in MDCs (Figure 1.2).

The resulting phenomenal rate of population growth, with some countries experiencing growth rates as high as 3–4 percent annually, has largely fueled the rise in global population from less than a billion in 1800 to over 5.5 billion in 1993. Projections indicate continued rapid global population growth until well into the next century (Table 1.1 and Figure 1.1)—based on current mortality and fertility trends, projections suggest that global population may reach about 10 billion by 2050 and finally come to stationary levels of about 11.5 billion around 2150 (Bulatao et al., 1990).[4]

During the same period, the proportion of the world's population coming from MDCs has fluctuated dramatically. From less than a quarter of world population in 1800, it peaked at a little over one third between 1900 and 1950, and has since started a rapid slide which is expected to result in MDCs holding little more than a tenth of the world's population by 2150 (Table 1.1).

---

[4] The above figures are based on the mid-range of population projection estimates. Recent studies suggest that population trends are more likely to follow the low range of population projection figures because family planning programs and changing sociocultural norms are resulting in a faster decline in global total fertility rates than had previously been anticipated. Low-range projections point to global population levels stabilizing at approximately 9 billion people.

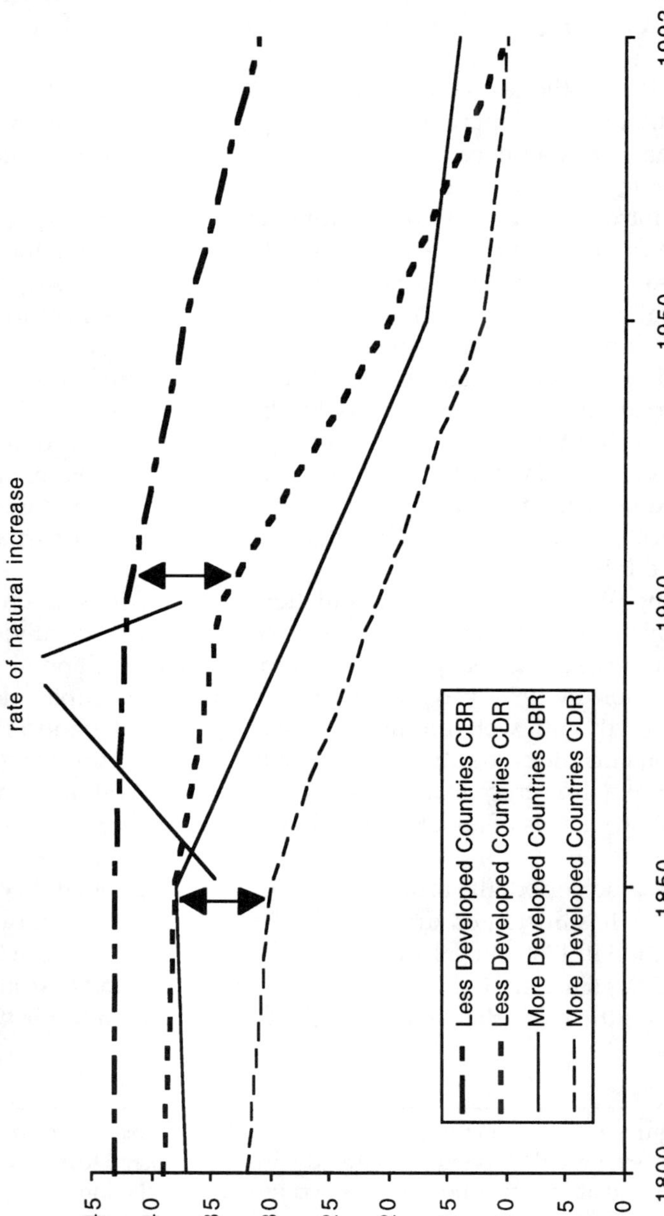

FIGURE 1.2 Changes in crude birth rate (CBR) and crude death rate (CDR) for more developed countries and less developed countries 1800–1993. (*Source*: Population Reference Bureau, Washington, DC).

DEVELOPMENT AND PUBLIC HEALTH

The major improvements in human health that have taken place in the last 200 years have had relatively little to do with improvements in health care delivery per se, but a lot to do with development. Development (in all its dimensions, encompassing, for example, technological, human, social, economic, and infrastructural development) has contributed to raising the ambient level of health and well-being of human society through such means as: improving access to food and better nutrition; encouraging education and literacy (especially of women); raising awareness of the relationship between nonhygienic conditions and disease; better housing; investment in water supply and sanitation; and increasing access to employment opportunities (Advisory Committee on Health Research, 1993). Additionally, concern for health and health-seeking behavior have tended to rise with the rising incomes and education levels associated with development.

Traditional societies tended to be characterized by the frequent occurrence of acute infectious diseases and epidemic outbreaks of disease associated with high mortality rates (especially of infants) and consequent low life expectancy. Societies which have undergone the demographic transition have generally also observed a transition in their pattern of disease and mortality—the so-called "health transition." Post-transitional societies generally have low mortality and morbidity associated with infectious diseases and diseases of childhood—they have low infant mortality and high life expectancy. Longevity in these societies has resulted in the unmasking and increased incidence of diseases of old age and chronic diseases such as cardiovascular diseases and malignancies.

While some societies, particularly the MDCs and the newly industrializing countries (NICs) of East Asia, have essentially completed their health transitions, the vast majority of LDCs are still "transitional" and are at different stages in their respective health transitions (Mosley, Bobadilla, & Jamison, 1993).

Table 1.2 provides a snapshot showing the health profiles in developing countries according to their level of human development (United Nations Development Programme, 1992). It can be strongly argued, even from a cursory examination of the data, that a positive correlation exists between human development and such parameters as life expectancy, female literacy, access to health care, and gross domestic product (GDP), while a negative correlation exists for human development versus childhood mortality and fertility.

The least developed countries—many of which are concentrated in sub-Saharan Africa and in South Asia—have been unable, for a variety of socioeconomic and geopolitical reasons, to invest adequately in human

TABLE 1.2 Health Indicators in Developing Countries in Relation to Their Levels of Human Development

	Life Expectancy (years) 1990	Under 5 Mortality Rate (/1000) 1990	Health Services Access (%) (R/U) 1987–89	Female Literacy Rate (%) 1990	Total Fertility Rate 1990	GDP per capita (PPP$) 1989
High Human Development	70.5	40	83 (?/?)	?	2.9	6,027
South Korea	70.1	30	94 (86/97)	94	1.7	6,117
Argentina	71.0	35	72 (?/80)	95	2.9	4,310
Kuwait	73.4	19	100 (?/?)	67	3.7	?
Mexico	69.7	49	78 (?/?)	85	3.3	5,691
Medium Human Development	68.6	55	81 (67/97)	66	2.9 3.8 (excluding China)	3,146
Brazil	65.6	83	? (?/?)	80	3.3	4,951
China	70.1	42	? (?/?)	62	2.4	2,656
Iran	66.2	59	80 (60/95)	43	5.0	3,120
South Africa	61.7	88	? (?/?)	?	4.3	4,958
Thailand	66.1	34	70 (?/?)	90	2.4	3,569
Low Human Development	56.8	152	56 (41/81)	39	5.0	1,115
Burkina Faso	36.2	228	49 (?/51)	9	6.5	617
Guatemala	63.4	94	34 (25/47)	47	5.6	2,531
India	59.1	142	? (?/?)	34	4.2	910
Nigeria	51.5	167	46 (30/75)	40	6.7	1,160
Zaire	53.0	130	26 (17/40)	61	6.1	380
Sub-Saharan Africa	51.8	175	48 (36/80)	40	6.5	1,187
All Developing Countries	62.8	112	64 (49/90)	54	3.9	2,296

Source: United Nations Development Programme (1992).

development. These societies are still at an early phase of their respective demographic and health transitions, and continue to experience a high incidence of infectious diseases and childhood mortality, coupled with high fertility.

It is important to recognize that societies are not homogeneous. Even in the most developed societies, one is likely to find pockets of individuals who have not yet completed their health transition (this is true, for example, in many inner-city populations in the United States). Conversely, even the poorest and least developed societies tend to have elites who have achieved relatively high levels of human development and who are relatively advanced in terms of completing their health transitions. The data presented in Table 1.2, hence, represent only the average situation in any society.

POPULATION GROWTH AND CARRYING CAPACITY

Populations living in MDC societies today are generally no longer limited or constrained by the carrying capacity. These societies have experienced a sustained divergence of potential human carrying capacity from actual population levels.

This dissociation represents what might be called the *population reserve capacity* of MDCs—which is, in other words, the safety margin that MDCs have built up between their actual populations and the maximum number of people they could possibly hold. Establishing population reserve capacities in any society would depend on achieving one or both of the following objectives:

1. Accelerating increases in human carrying capacity—through investment in development and technological innovation resulting in such improvements as increased food production, income-generation, or reduced disease mortality and morbidity.
2. Accelerating reduction in population growth rates—either directly, through investing in meeting the unmet need for access to family planning, or indirectly, through investing in development, in improving education and social status of women, and in changing sociocultural attitudes in favor of lowered fertility.

The stationary levels that populations in MDC societies are experiencing (Figure 1.1) are, for the first time in human history, not determined by the carrying capacity of their respective ecosystems. In these societies, the slowdown in population growth rates has been brought about, instead, by development, growing wealth, and associated changes in social and cultural norms which have promoted lower fertility and worked against rapid population growth.[5] These changes in population dynamics have been occurring at the same time that continuing improvements in technology and advances in agriculture and medicine are working, at an accelerating pace, to increase the potential carrying capacity of these societies. Hence, development has contributed immensely to the population reserve capacities these societies now enjoy—both by accelerating increases in potential carrying capacity, and by accelerating reductions in population growth rates.

---

[5] While initially thought of as a positive trend, this development-associated decline in fertility is being viewed with growing concern as societies consider the economic implications of "inverted" population pyramids as these societies age. Countries such as France and Singapore, for example, have initiated pronatalist population policies, aimed at raising fertility in their societies from current low levels.

That people living in MDC societies have, in large measure, been freed from the biological, chemical, and physical constraints that have regulated our lives and our numbers, is very significant. An analogous dissociation has already started to occur in the newly industrializing countries (NICs) where economic and social development have increased potential carrying capacity while increased access to family planning and changing social norms in favor of smaller families have accelerated reductions in population growth.

Still, as many as 1.5 billion people continue to live their lives in absolute poverty. These individuals, concentrated mainly in the least developed LDCs, are trapped at or near the carrying capacity of their respective societies. Their societies have failed to establish a significant population reserve capacity. They are, therefore, at great risk of death and disability when drought, famine, and other environmental and human-generated calamities lead to temporary or permanent reductions in the potential carrying capacities of their ecosystems. It remains to be seen if humankind has the foresight and wisdom to invest in appropriate development in LDCs that would enable these societies to establish sustainable population reserve capacities and the poor in these societies to escape the hopelessness and indignity of absolute poverty.

DISCUSSION

Sustainable Human Development and Sustainable Public Health

Completion of the demographic and health transitions in any society is closely linked to the level of human development which, in turn, tends to be closely linked to the level of economic development of that society.

It is becoming increasingly clear, however, that many of the industrial and commercial practices that have fueled economic development in MDCs, as well as the accepted norms of lifestyle and quality of life, are fundamentally unsustainable, in that they involve an excessive rate of consumption of valuable natural resources (nonrenewable resources are in danger of being depleted, and renewable resources are being harvested at rates which exceed their natural capacity for renewal). They also result in unacceptably high levels of environmental contamination and degradation.

There is need, if we are to achieve sustainability, for considerable changes in our economic and social expectations and norms, in our leisure activities, and our lifestyles. This is as true in the overconsuming MDCs, as it is in the still underconsuming, but striving to overconsume, NICs and LDCs.

"Sustainable human development" is a response to the problems and inequities in our current approaches to development. It seeks to balance the need to ensure that economic growth and development lead to a better life for all human beings, with the need to ensure that such development does not occur at the expense of environmental and ecological integrity. It recognizes also that short-term gain must not occur at the expense of long-term viability.

> Sustainable human development is development that doesn't merely generate growth, but distributes its benefits equitably; it regenerates the environment rather than destroying it; it empowers people rather than marginalizing them; it enlarges their choices and opportunities and provides for peoples' participation in decisions affecting their lives. Sustainable human development is development that is pro-poor, pro-nature, pro-jobs and pro-women. It stresses growth but growth with employment, growth with environment, growth with empowerment, growth with equity.
>
> James Gustave Speth

The fundamental goals of sustainable human development—more equitable economic growth, poverty alleviation, greater participation of people in making the decisions that affect their lives, and maintenance of environmental and ecological integrity—have been generally accepted by the United Nations system and by many major international agencies, national governments, and nongovernmental organizations. In the pursuit of sustainable human development, we will need, in each of our societies, to establish a common vision and to define the paradigms within which we choose to operate. Then we can work toward putting in place the enabling policy environment and the necessary institutional support and resources that would enable us to achieve our development vision.

"Sustainable public health" refers to public health thinking, practice, research, and teaching in the context of sustainable human development. What implications does sustainable human development have for practitioners of public health? Does the new thinking in relation to sustainable human development call for changes in the way we view health and well-being? Does it have implications for the way we provide health care, conduct research, and train future health workers? How might practitioners of public health contribute to sustainable human development? These are some of the important questions and issues which will need to be addressed by the global public health community. Evolving effective strategies for sustainable public health requires a good understanding of the many links between environment, development, and health, and how they interact. There is much need to evolve sound, effective public health responses to environmental and developmental concerns, and to the challenge of sustainable human development.

REFERENCES

Advisory Committee on Health Research (1993). Relevance of the Economic Environment to Health. In *Research for Health—Principles, Perspectives and Strategies* (pp. 20–23). Geneva: World Health Organization.

Bulatao, R. A., Bos, E., Stephens, P. W., & Vu, M. T. (1990). World Population Projections, 1989–1990 Edition—Short- and Long-term Estimates. From the Data Files of the World Bank. New York: Oxford University Press.

Dubos, R. (1973). Environment. In Philip P. Wiener (Ed.), *Dictionary of the History of Ideas—Studies of Selected Pivotal Ideas. Volume II* (pp. 120–127). New York: Charles Scribner's Sons.

Mosley, W. H., Bobadilla, J., & Jamison, D. T. (1993). The Health Transition: Implications for Health Policy in Developing Countries. In D. T. Jamison & W. H. Mosley (Eds.), *Disease Control Priorities in Developing Countries.* Oxford: Oxford University Press.

Task Force Report (1976). *Theory, Practice and Application of Prevention in Environmental Health Services—Social Determinants of Human Health.* New York: Prodist.

Tyler Miller, G., Jr. (1990). *Living in the Environment* (6th edition). Belmont, CA: Wadsworth.

United Nations Development Programme (1992). *Human Development Report 1992.* New York: Oxford University Press.

2

A Historical Perspective

Gurinder S. Shahi, Lee Chen, Barry S. Levy, Al Binger, Tord Kjellstrom, and Robert S. Lawrence

INTRODUCTION

> Progress, far from consisting in change, depends on retentiveness. When change is absolute there remains no being to improve and no direction set for possible improvement: and when experience is not retained, as among savages, infancy is perpetual. Those who cannot remember the past are condemned to repeat it.
>
> Santayana, *Life of Reason*

Humankind has always been acutely aware of our links to nature. In ages past, our ancestors were often completely at nature's mercy. They were awed by natural phenomena such as earthquakes, volcanic eruptions, thunder, and lightning. They prayed for good weather and often turned to the gods of nature for sustenance when things were difficult.

In recent centuries, however, there has been a growing tendency for human self-aggrandizement. As we began to understand the physical laws of nature, to find ways to lessen the impact of natural phenomena on our lives, and to harness nature's bounty for our own use (and profit), we also deluded ourselves into believing that somehow humankind was supposed to be the summit of the evolutionary process, and that the wealth and diversity of the world exists solely and exclusively for human use and exploitation.

Such thinking has led to rapid new advances in technology and economic productivity but has also contributed greatly to human-generated destruction of natural ecosystems, the extinction of many species of animals and plants, and stresses on global life-support systems that

The authors are extremely grateful to Michael Sacks, Garrick Louis, Jacklyn Sims, Maninder Shahi, and Misa Kishi for their helpful comments and suggestions.

threaten our very survival. We have devastated the environment in which we live and the plants and animals with which we live—all in the name of "progress" and "development." If we are to live in peace with ourselves and with the other inhabitants of this planet, and to assure health and well-being for all, we need to find ways to live more sustainably.

Ideas and paradigms constitute the framework within which we define ourselves as well as our relationships with the planet and its other inhabitants. The word "paradigm" and the concept of the "paradigm shift" have tended to be overused in recent years. It is important, nevertheless, not to underestimate the impact of our worldview and paradigms on shaping and coloring our perspectives and attitudes. Understanding how, historically, our paradigms have helped shape our actions and interpretations, and how changes in prevailing paradigms have tended to alter our interactions with nature and the environment, can help us to develop appropriate paradigms that are consistent with our needs and with ensuring that we learn from the experiences and mistakes of the past.

TRADITIONAL VIEWS ON HEALTH AND ENVIRONMENT

It is common for practitioners of modern medicine to trace the roots of medical practice, and our understanding of health and disease, to Hippocrates and the ancient Greeks. The significant contributions of ancient Chinese and Indian practices, the role played by the Arabs in integrating and expanding on these ancient traditions, as well as contributions from other cultures and thought patterns, tend too often to be forgotten. A close examination of three great traditions that have contributed substantively to our current understanding of health and well-being—the Greco-Arabic, the Indian, and the Chinese—reveals that they had far more in common with each other than differences. These traditions were remarkably similar, for example, in the way they viewed the relationships between humankind and the environment, and between health and disease.

Fundamentals of Greco-Arabic Practices and Beliefs

The roots of Greco-Arabic science can be traced to the ideas of the ancient Greeks, especially, Hippocrates. During the Dark Ages in Europe, the center of Greco-Arabic learning shifted into the Arabic world, where the ideas and practices of the Greeks were enriched with Arabic contributions before, eventually, finding their way back into Europe with the Crusades and the dawn of the Renaissance. The richness of Arabic and Islamic artistic, scientific, and cultural accomplishments of the era no doubt contributed to the intellectual ferment for which the Renaissance in Europe has since come to be recognized.

The Greco-Arabic tradition viewed the body and its state of health as being constituted of a balanced interaction of four humors: yellow bile, black bile, blood, and phlegm. Further, it was thought that all matter was constituted of four elements—earth, air, fire, and water (Leslie, 1988).

Fundamentals of Indian Practices and Beliefs

Ayurveda ("knowledge of longevity") is the Indian tradition of medical science. Its earliest text was the *Caraka Samhita,* a manual compiled by the physician Caraka in the 1st century B.C. This book discussed such issues of disease management as pathology, diagnostics, physiology, anatomy, prognosis, therapeutics, and pharmaceutics. A subsequent manual, *Sushruta Samhita,* is famed for its guidance on surgical treatment.

Ayurveda is based on the belief that the state of health of an individual consists of a balanced interaction between three humors (*dosha*)—wind, bile, and phlegm. Indian science further saw all matter as consisting of five elements (*bhuta*)—earth, water, fire, air, and ether.

Fundamentals of Chinese Practices and Beliefs

The earliest and most influential Chinese medical text was the *Huangdi Neijing* (The Yellow Emperor's Manual of Corporeal Medicine)—written between the 1st and 2nd centuries B.C. The Chinese used the analogy of rivers, canals, and reservoirs to develop the concept that health is sustained by the flow of pneuma or life force (*qi*) in the body as it accommodates to internal and environmental circumstances (Chen and Bunge, 1989). The application of needles (acupuncture) or heat (moxibustion—using tender from burning mugwort leaves) at specific therapeutic points was thought to help maintain flow of the pneuma in channels or meridians or to correct disruptions in such flow. The Chinese also believed that five elements were the fundamental building blocks of the world around them—earth, metal, water, fire, and wood.

They developed a system of understanding based on the idea that all matter had contrasting properties of *yin* and *yang* in interaction with each other. These properties can be characterized in terms of such dualities as femaleness (*yin*) and maleness (*yang*), quiescence and movement, dark and light, and cold and heat. The Chinese tradition saw all external influences (including, for example, environmental and dietary factors) in terms of their impact on the *yin–yang* interactions within an individual. An individual is seen as being in good health when internal *yin* and *yang* forces are well balanced and in harmony. On the other hand, ill health is thought to occur when gross imbalances in *yin* and *yang* forces result in disruption of the harmonious functioning of the body (Chen & Bunge, 1989).

Differences and Similarities Between the Great Traditions

Superficially it would appear that there are major irreconcilable differences between these three philosophical traditions. Chinese and Indian science were, for example, based on five elements while Greco-Arabic science recognized only four. All three traditions accepted earth, water, and fire as basic elements. Greco-Arabic and Indian science also considered air to be an element while the Indians further added ether.[1] The Chinese, on the other hand, recognized wood and metal as elements, but not air.

Greco-Arabic science saw health as being dependent upon the balanced interaction of four humors while the Indians recognized only three humors in balance—both systems viewing bile and phlegm as humors although the Greco-Arabic tradition recognized two types of bile (yellow and black) and added blood as a humor while the Indians added wind. To investigate the subtle differences in philosophy and worldview underlying these differences in belief, the reader is referred to the many excellent reference books on ancient medical practice.

The similarities between these ancient traditions of medicine far outweigh the differences. The Greco-Arabic, the Chinese, and the Indian traditions all had in common some notion of humors and the idea that equilibrium of these humors maintained health, while their disequilibrium caused illness (Leslie, 1988). Further, all three systems postulated that an individual's age, sex, and temperament all affected and regulated this humoral equilibrium in relation to such factors as the seasons, food consumption, and nutritional status.

All three systems were based on systems of correspondence that aligned the organization of the universe, society, the human body and other forms of life into an all embracing order of things combining such qualities as heat/coldness, moistness/dryness, lightness/darkness,

---

[1] It seems likely that the Indian concept of ether was essentially similar to pneuma (the life force or *qi*) that the Chinese believed flowed freely in channels or meridians in each healthy organism.

subtlety/materiality (which the Chinese characterized as *yin* and *yang*).[2] These systems also tried to take account of the impact of the seasons of the year, the directions of the compass, and the cycle of birth, growth, and death on health and well-being. They also viewed different places as having either good or bad constitutions—conditions of poverty, ignorance, filth, and squalor were, for instance, seen in all three traditions to be associated with bad constitutions and to be related to disease and ill-health. Because they provided a comprehensive way of perceiving patterns that ran through nature, these systems of understanding served as classifying and mnemonic frameworks for observing health and environmental interactions, and for reflecting upon, storing, and interpreting empirical knowledge.[3]

Therapy in all three systems depended mainly upon modifying the patient's diet and surroundings. They also used a wide range of medicaments and were often liberal in prescribing physical manipulations. The process of preparing for treatment was often seen to be as therapeutic as the treatment itself—it was, therefore, not uncommon for medicines to require elaborate preparation, and the use of such therapies as rare and difficult to obtain herbs gathered from distant mountains, or gold, precious stones, or parts of animals (Leslie, 1988).

Evidence exists of significant cross-fertilization between these three great humoral traditions of medicine, with the exchange of ideas and products. Hippocrates, for example, mentions drugs and herbal preparations from India in his texts; and medieval Arab scholars knew much about Chinese and Indian medicine. The influential Persian physician Ibn Sina (or Avicenna, as he came to be known in Europe) (980–1037) incorporated elements of Chinese and Indian medical practices in his *Al-qanun fi-al-tibb* (Canon of Medicine) which remains, today, the text of greatest authority among practitioners of humoral medicine. This work was, for

---

[2] The Chinese practice of geomancy (*feng shui*) takes the thinking on interactions between environmental influences and the individual to a level of practical significance not generally observed in other cultures or paradigms. Practitioners of geomancy will study the geography and location of any site and are often concerned with the positive and negative attributes of location and alignment (in terms of their implications for *yin–yang* balances). Places with "good" *feng shui* are associated with wealth, happiness and good health. On the other hand, locations with "bad" *feng shui* are considered to have the inverse effect.

[3] Unfortunately, practitioners of these systems were also subject to dogmatism and self-deception and, often, prevented the expression of new ideas and ways of viewing the world which could not be reconciled with their prevailing paradigms. The best minds then, as (unfortunately) many are compelled to do now, felt duty-bound to fit their observations in the clothes of the paradigms of their time and seldom ventured to consider different systems of thought.

many centuries, considered one of the great "oracles" of knowledge (Leslie, 1988). Still, each tradition maintained its distinctive character and continues today in modified but recognizable form.

HEALTH, ENVIRONMENT, AND DISEASE

Hippocrates (460–377 B.C.) advised those interested in becoming physicians, in investigating the state of health of their communities, or in predicting the common diseases within any community, to:

> . . . consider the seasons of the year, and what effects each of them produces . . . then the winds, the hot and the cold, especially such as are common to all countries, and then such as are peculiar to each locality . . . concerning the waters which people use, whether they be marshy and soft, or hard, and running from elevated and rocky situations, and then if saltish and unfit for cooking . . . and the mode in which the inhabitants live, and what are their pursuits, whether they are fond of drinking and eating to excess, and given to indolence, or are fond of exercise and labor . . .
>
> Hippocrates, *Airs, Waters, Places*

The views expressed by Hippocrates in *Airs, Waters, Places* (Hippocrates, 1977) indicate a remarkably "modern" appreciation of the relationship between health, the environment and behavior. A similar sophistication in appreciating the links between environment and health can be found in all the major traditions.

The Greco-Arabic, Chinese, and Indian traditions also had in common an understanding of three major mechanisms for the causation of disease:

1. *Humoral imbalances* (akin to the *yin–yang* imbalances in Chinese medical tradition)—wherein internal imbalances resulted in ill health. This was thought, for example, to account for illness in those afflicted with metabolic conditions such as gout.
2. *Unfavorable environmental constitutions*—wherein emanations from dead or decaying animal, human, and vegetable matter, or sulphurous emanations from the depths of the earth were thought to result in disease. Unfavorable environmental constitutions were thought to be responsible for such diseases as the plague or malaria.
3. *Unfavorable atmospheric constitutions*—where atmospheric conditions associated with weather, climate and seasons were seen as being causative in the occurrence of illness and periodic epidemics. Unfavorable atmospheric constitutions were thought to be responsible for outbreaks of pleurisy, or to account for such seasonal recurrences as the common cold.

Environmental and atmospheric constitutional factors were thought to cause disease by bringing about humoral imbalances within the individual—such imbalances being, as practitioners saw it, the final common pathway for disease.

These concepts of disease etiology continued to influence scientific thinking until at least the end of the 19th century.

POST-RENAISSANCE THINKING ON ENVIRONMENT AND DISEASE

Theories of Epidemic Spread

Epidemic outbreaks of infectious disease have been a major focus of attention in practically all societies and cultures since prehistoric times because they have been responsible for much death and human misery. It has been estimated, for example, that Europe's population fell by as much as 50 percent in the 100 years following the introduction of epidemic bubonic plague in the 1350s.[4]

The location at which an epidemic was in progress would often be described, by proponents of the humoral tradition, as having an "epidemic" constitution—which was seen to arise when environmental and atmospheric conditions (or constitutions) combined in particular "complexes" which were considered to favor the outbreak and spread of epidemics (Wilcocks, 1965). This belief in the role of complexes of atmospheric and environmental constitutions in the transmission of epidemic disease came to be known, in Europe in the 15th and 16th centuries, as the "miasmic" theory. The study of epidemic outbreaks and their possible links to emanations and atmospheric conditions came to be called "miasmatology" (now an obsolete term). Proponents of miasmatology believed, for example, that outbreaks of malaria occurred as a result of foul emanations from swamps, hence the name *mal aria* (which is Latin for "bad airs").

In a divergence from the ideas derived from the humoral and "miasmic" perspectives, Girolamo Fracastoro (1484–1553), in 16th-century Italy,

---

[4] The reasons for the great impact of the plague would not be difficult for a modern person to find—people living in Europe at this time lived in cities filled with farm animals, rats and other vermin. There were no drains, no sanitation, and drinking water from dirty wells (often with fecal contamination) was the normal state of affairs. Contrast this with the advanced irrigation and drainage systems constructed by such peoples as the Romans and the Indus valley civilization—it is no wonder that the period preceding the Renaissance and the Age of Enlightenment in Europe has come to be popularly known as the "Dark Ages."

suggested an alternative hypothesis that epidemic spread of disease occurred as a result of the transmission of minute infective agents or spores from person to person either directly, via intermediaries, or through the air (Rosen, 1958). This theory of the spread of disease, which came to be known as the "contagion" theory, was a remarkable insight into the eventual discovery that microorganisms were often responsible for disease. It became the dominant theory for the next century or so and provided, for the first time, a rational basis for such practices as quarantine and the idea that the isolation of diseased persons might reduce the likelihood of spread of diseases.[5]

In the 17th and 18th centuries, the "miasma" theory once again became prominent, as many investigators found the "contagion" theory lacking and felt that it did not offer a convincing explanation for epidemic spread of many diseases (Riley, 1987). While it was generally accepted, for example, that epidemic spread of some diseases such as smallpox could be explained on the basis of contagious transmission, investigators expressed concern that the "contagion" theory could not adequately account for other epidemics (Arbuthnot, 1733). It was observed, for example, that bubonic plague could occur in widely separate localities between which there were no known contacts. A "miasmic" explanation hypothesizing that any area could be susceptible to any constitution of the atmosphere and the environment and, therefore, to any disease was, hence, seen as more convincing for diseases such as the bubonic plague (Arbuthnot, 1733). Further, it was noted that seasonal and periodic changes of the atmospheric constitution (a "miasmic" explanation) provide a much more convincing basis for the often observed seasonal variations in the occurrence of certain diseases such as the common cold than the "contagion" theory could.

It became very much the conventional wisdom in the 17th and 18th centuries to accept a synthesis of the "miasma" and "contagion" theories

---

[5] Quarantine refers to the practice of preventing individuals who may be carrying a disease from entering a protected environment until it is clear that they do not carry disease. Some form of quarantine has been used throughout much of history as the primary means of preventing and slowing the spread of disease.

Individuals who suffered from easily identifiable diseases such as leprosy, for example, were often ostracized and forced to live in leper colonies—a practice that was already quite widespread in Biblical times (McNeill, 1976). The practice of mandatory quarantine became common during the 14th century as a means of isolating travellers who arrived by sea from suspected plague-infested ports, for example, until it was clear that they did not get sick and would not constitute a health risk (McNeill, 1976).

within which it was suggested that atmospheric and local environmental circumstances could either aid or hinder the epidemic propagation of a disease to different localities (a "miasmic" explanation), while propagation within any particular locality was generally thought to occur by a contagious process (Riley, 1987). Much scientific effort went, therefore, into investigation aimed at discovering the specific atmospheric and environmental complexes leading to epidemic constitutions favoring the spread of particular disease epidemics.

This reemergence and adaptation of the "miasma" theory led to interesting changes in quarantine practices. Whereas quarantine had started as the practice of isolating the already diseased from the still healthy, it became concerned in the 18th and 19th centuries with the isolation of the still healthy from the site of disease and the epidemic constitution. Instead of merely quarantining diseased individuals, physicians sought to reduce the likelihood of disease spread by quarantining or modifying the "pathogenic" site (Riley, 1987). Hence, such practices as burning the clothing of the sick person, and seeking to disinfect locations where disease occurred, became popular during this period.

Passivism vs. Activism

Prior to the 17th and 18th centuries, philosophers and physicians tended to take a passive attitude toward the environment and its impact on health—considering the environmental conditions in which an individual lived and worked as given and uncontrollable. They recognized that many diseases could be treated—by changing behavior and diet, for example—but did not generally consider that it might be feasible to alter or modify the environment to make it more conducive to well-being and health (Winslow, 1952).

During the 18th century, there was a definite move from this earlier passive fatalism toward a newer, more "activist" approach to thinking about and dealing with the relationship between humankind and the environment. In particular, it came increasingly to be recognized that human molding of the environment to serve humankind's wants and needs—what has since come to be called "development"—could result in exposures that are either deleterious or beneficial to human health and well-being, and that it was possible to modify the environment in ways which could be conducive to well-being and health.

This change in perspective seems to have had its roots in the philosophical Enlightenment that began in the 17th century. Prior to this time, nature was seen as being sometimes benign and sometimes malevolent but always beyond human influence (except, perhaps, through divine intervention). It came to be seen during the period of the Enlightenment as an object for manipulation (Riley, 1987).

Knowledge of physical laws and the ability to measure natural phenomena increased greatly during the Enlightenment (this was, after all, the era of such luminaries as Newton, Pascal, Huygens, Boyle, Descartes, Bacon, Hooke and Niewentijd). During this remarkable period, the fundamental laws of nature were discovered, explanations for many previously unexplained natural phenomena were provided, and new means for measuring natural phenomena were invented or perfected (including, for example, instruments for measuring temperature, atmospheric pressure, humidity, rainfall, wind speed and direction).

There was a sense that soon all would be revealed and that humankind, through science, would be able to explain all natural phenomena in terms of the rules of nature that regulated them. Investigators sought the beautiful and elegant mathematical formulations which they believed underlay God's order in the universe. The physicists, mathematicians, and physicians of this era sought also to uncover the links between particular environmental and atmospheric constitutions and complexes and the occurrence of epidemic or endemic disease. Seeking to understand the conditions under which outbreaks of disease occurred was a preoccupation of the time because disease commonly occurred in epidemics or even pandemics—with plague and other epidemic outbreaks (such as cholera) bringing death and devastation to entire cities at frequent but irregular intervals. Hence, for example, Robert Boyle, the great physicist and chemist who discovered many important characteristics of gases (including what has since come to be known as Boyle's Law) published papers which argued that weather in a locality could be linked to epidemics, and lent support to "miasmic" thinking with his belief that emanations from the earth and from diseased persons could transmit disease (Boyle, 1666).

Growing anthropocentricity during the age of Enlightenment, fueled often by Biblical interpretations suggesting God-given rights of human dominance over nature's bounty, led to the belief that all nature existed for humankind's comfort and exploitation. Changing from the passive acceptance of earlier understanding, there was a trend toward an "activist" seeking of ways to improve life and human well-being.

The "Social Hygiene" Movement

The new activism which came to be applied to public health can be described as the "social hygiene" movement. Abbé Claude Fleury (1640–1723), a lawyer and historian living in France, is generally acknowledged as the founder of the social hygiene movement (Riley, 1987).[6] Fleury's writing and activism led to efforts throughout 17th and 18th century Europe to "cleanse the environment, to reduce its pathogenic properties and its capacity to promote epidemics" (Riley, 1987). Massive infrastructural development and clean-up campaigns and projects were undertaken during this period to create environments that were favorable to health and well-being and which could help reduce the likelihood of epidemic constitutions developing.

Projects undertaken as a consequence of the social hygiene movement included:

- Providing drainage to prevent the accumulation of stagnant, dirty water in cities;
- Filling of marshes and swamps;
- Ensuring safe, uncontaminated drinking water and cleaner wells;
- Building massive city-wide sanitation and sewage systems;
- Improving the ventilation of homes and workplaces;
- Relocating waste-producing industries and waste sites;
- Burying of refuse (Riley, 1987).[7]

The social hygienists successfully used economic and social welfare arguments to persuade their respective governments to make the massive capital expenditure required for these major social-investment projects. A particularly persuasive argument used was that such investment would lead to improved health of workers and increased availability of rich farmland (when marshes and swamps were filled, for example), all of which would mean greater worker productivity, higher crop yields, and greater tax returns to fill government coffers. (Contemporary development professionals might well learn something from the experience and

---

[6] Riley (1987) describes this as the "environmentalist" movement. While there are many parallels between 18th century and present day environmentalism—the recognition that pollution could be deleterious to well-being, for example, there are many differences—such as the fact that current thinking is much less anthropocentric. To avoid unnecessary confusion, we have chosen to use the term "social hygiene"—a derivation of the 18th-century French term *"hygiène publique"*—to refer to the earlier "environmental" movement.

[7] It should be noted that many of the infrastructure development projects undertaken by the social hygiene movement in 17th and 18th century Europe were not new ideas—there is substantial archeological evidence to show, for example, that the Indus Valley, Inca and Roman civilizations invested heavily in major water and sanitation projects. It would appear that humankind had forgotten these technologies and that they had to await the social hygiene movement before they were rediscovered and received the wide-scale implementation these technologies now enjoy.

effectiveness of the social hygienists in mobilizing public interest and investment in environmental and infrastructural development!)

Writing in 1842, over a century after Fleury started the social hygiene movement, Edwin Chadwick, in his *Report on the Sanitary Conditions of the Labouring Population of Great Britain*, demonstrated a correlation between environmental variables—described as "insanitation," defective drainage, inadequate water supply, and overcrowded housing—and disease, high mortality rates, and low life expectancy (Chadwick, 1965).[8] Chadwick's work also clearly established that disease often was both a cause and a consequence of low levels of social and economic development (Weisbrod et al., 1973), and provided strong scientific support for the social and environmental improvements initiated decades earlier by the social hygienists.

ROOTS OF BIOSTATISTICAL AND EPIDEMIOLOGICAL INVESTIGATION

Environmental and health ideas came to be combined, in the 18th and 19th centuries, with new methodologies and tools for studying epidemic diseases and their spread. Mathematical approaches such as the study of probability, demographic statistics, and the analysis of meteorological data, were all applied to interpreting and seeking to explain the links between environmental and atmospheric conditions and disease.

However, it was not uncommon for data to be subjectively interpreted since no commonly accepted methodologies for experimental design and interpretation of results existed at the time. To demonstrate the effectiveness of measures taken to clean up the environment, for example, 18th- and 19th-century scientists would compare improved and unimproved sites and make such assessments as "greater healthiness" after improvement (Riley, 1987).

The approaches developed in this era led eventually to the establishment of the science of epidemiology. John Snow (1813–1858), often considered to be one of the earliest and finest epidemiologists, conducted landmark studies, which demonstrated, for example, that exposure to drinking water which had been contaminated by human excreta was linked to the incidence of diarrhea and to a cholera epidemic which was devastating London (Snow, 1965).

---

[8] Chadwick's great work is generally considered to be the first systematic attempt to link disease and health factors directly to economic, social, environmental and demographic variables.

CONTRIBUTIONS TO PUBLIC HEALTH OF HUMORAL- AND MIASMA-BASED SCIENCE

The humoral and miasmatological assumptions and hypotheses accepted by social hygienists as the basis for action were based on scientific paradigms which are no longer considered valid by practitioners of modern science and medicine. Nevertheless, such activism directly contributed to establishment of concepts of hygiene and sanitation which are taken for granted today in the more developed countries (MDCs) and the more developed parts of less developed countries (LDCs).

The efforts of the "social hygiene" movement helped to bring down death rates and promote improved health and quality of life. The development of new scientific approaches applied to dealing with poor environmental "constitutions," combined with significant advances in concepts regarding nutrition and health-promoting behavior, initiated the decline in mortality and morbidity that was observed throughout this period. Crude death rates, for example, declined with the gradual cleaning up of European cities from about 40 per 1,000 at the beginning of the 18th century to lower than 10 per 1,000 (Riley, 1987).

The relationship between the implementation of social hygiene approaches and the incidence of epidemic outbreaks is particularly striking. While epidemics were relatively frequent before the 18th century, epidemics in Europe were noted to occur less frequently and to be generally less severe as social and urban environmental conditions improved. Those epidemics that did occur, such as the mid-19th century cholera epidemics and the influenza pandemic of 1918, did not generally carry the heavy mortalities associated with, for example, the "Black Death," which occurred in Europe during the 14th century (Riley, 1987).

Improvements in quality of life, and in humankind's ability to prevent and treat infectious diseases and deficiencies of important nutrients, led to the health transition in the more developed countries (MDCs)—with infant and child mortality due primarily to infectious diseases decreasing in incidence; life expectancy rising; and chronic diseases, degenerative disease and malignancies becoming increasingly unmasked as major causes of mortality. The contrast between these countries and the LDCs became ever starker—diseases such as cholera, typhoid, tuberculosis, and bubonic plague, for example, became infrequent in the MDCs and came increasingly to be linked mostly with the filth and squalor that now tend to be associated with urban centers in less developed countries (LDCs).

The humoral paradigm emphasized the importance of the interaction of individuals with one another and with environmental factors to create healthy or unhealthy states. Edward Jenner, working at the end of the 18th century, developed an approach to preventing smallpox through vaccination with cowpox.[9] Working during the heyday of the era of the social hygienists and the humoral environment-human-disease paradigm, he was as concerned with the host's experience with disease as he was with the presumed disease agent itself. Jenner's work fitted well with the humoral ideas of his time—it emphasized the importance of considering the host's constitution (in this case, the immune status) in interaction with disease-causing environmental agents. And it gave birth to the fields of immunology and vaccinology.

ASCENDANCY OF "GERM" THEORY AND THE ERA OF SPECIFIC ETIOLOGY

The "miasmic" concept and humoral medicine fell into disrepute as "germ" theory and the connection between disease-causing microorganisms and illness became generally accepted in the 19th century.

In fact, the world had known of the existence of microorganisms since the time of Antonie van Leeuwenhoek (1623–1723) who invented the microscope, and provided the first detailed description of microorganisms in the 17th century. Van Leeuwenhoek did not, however, associate microorganisms with disease or ascribe particular significance to them.

It was not until 1849, when Ignaz Philipp Semmelweis (1818–1865) demonstrated the infectious nature of puerperal fever, its microbial source of infection, the mode of infectious transmission, and the means by which infection could be prevented, that the role of microorganisms in infectious disease causation came to be recognized. Semmelweis's efforts, together with substantial further evidence showing the link between microorganisms and disease through the work of other scientists (the most influential among whom was Louis Pasteur), led directly to the ascendancy of "germ" theory and what might be called the era of "specific etiology."

The dawn of the specific etiology era led to a major paradigm shift with very important consequences—the focus shifted from a holistic consideration of the interaction between the individual and the environment to a

[9] The practice of vaccination for smallpox was actually in use in Chinese, Indian, and Middle Eastern cultures for centuries before Jenner's time (McNeill, 1976). These cultures traditionally used the smallpox virus itself for vaccination during ritualized inoculations. Individuals so infected sometimes developed severe disease—with resultant morbidity and occasional mortality. Jenner's innovation allowed the prevention of smallpox with minimal morbidity and mortality because cowpox caused mild disease in humans yet, because of cross-immunity, provided protection against smallpox.

more restrictive but highly productive emphasis on seeking to identify specific etiological factors (particularly disease-causing microorganisms—germs) in the causation of disease. This paradigm shift led to great advances in bacteriology and immunology, facilitated the discovery of specific agents to counter specific disease-causing organisms (for example, antibiotics), and led to the organization of highly effective, disease-specific public health systems and services.

The benefits wrought by this paradigm shift cannot be overemphasized. As White (1991) noted:

> Formerly dreaded diseases that killed millions have been eliminated or brought under control—yellow fever, typhus, typhoid, diphtheria, poliomyelitis, rabies, scarlet fever, and smallpox are the most obvious. Other potentially noxious organisms have been identified, and efficacious immunization, vaccination, control measures and treatments developed. . . . Pasteur's contributions had a fundamental impact on the course of medicine and public health for many decades. . . .

The period since the era of specific etiology began has been, without question, the most productive era in the history of science and medicine. By seeking the root causes of public health concerns and diseases and developing targeted solutions, we have been able to develop highly effective and specific approaches to preventing and treating previously intractable problems.[10] These specific interventions, together with improvements in diet, nutrition, and living conditions, have all contributed to a massive decline in mortality and morbidity due to infectious diseases.

UNFORESEEN CONSEQUENCES OF THE ERA OF SPECIFIC ETIOLOGY

While the era of specific etiology has been highly productive and has contributed greatly to our current understanding of environment–development–health interactions, it has also led to potentially negative consequences which could not have been previously foreseen.

One unfortunate consequence of this era has been that a lot of sensible ideas seen to be associated with the miasmic theory (such as the need to take a holistic perspective in understanding the link between the individual and disease, or between the environment and health) came to be somewhat discredited. The use of statistical approaches to identify

---

[10] Smallpox, a major cause of disfigurement and mortality, was eradicated using such approaches. Over the next decade, it is anticipated that poliomyelitis and possibly measles will be eradicated.

and study disease causation and epidemics, which gave rise to the field of epidemiology, tended also to be pushed aside by the perceived power of bacteriology and microbiology to determine the "cause" of each disease.

We became so enraptured by the search for specific etiology that we have often "thrown the baby out with the bath water," as it were. We began to neglect the use of holistic, more comprehensive approaches to disease prevention in favor of highly specific, targeted approaches. Malaria, for example, is a parasitic disease transmitted by mosquitos which used to be prevented by what can be described as environmental-management approaches.[11] It was a disease which, in the 1960s, seemed very much on the way to being controlled. But the focus of our approach to dealing with malaria changed as highly specific and effective drugs that could eliminate malarial parasites in different phases of their development became available. We began to emphasize their use in prophylaxis and treatment of malaria, and neglected our earlier emphasis on environmental management.

The indiscriminate (ab)use of these anti-malarials has resulted in the development of drug-resistant malarial parasites and a resurgence in the importance of malaria as a public health concern with high mortality and morbidity. There has been, also, a belated rediscovery of the importance of environmental factors in the causation of malaria. The use of bednets to prevent biting (common in the early half of this century) is once again being encouraged, as are efforts directed at controlling populations of potentially disease-spreading mosquitos through environmental-management approaches—especially when outbreaks of disease occur.

What is true of malaria is even more true of bacterial infections, including tuberculosis. Essentially, we have allowed environmental control of disease to be replaced by laboratory control (Dubos, 1973). Our overreliance on "magic bullet" drugs has contributed to the development of multiple drug resistance and a belated realization that we need to use our tools and specific treatments much more sparingly than we have, and that it is often better to utilize multiple strategies for disease prevention rather than depending excessively on any specific approach.

The increased availability of antibiotics and vaccines aimed at dealing with specific disease-causing agents has led to major improvements in our ability to reduce death and disability. These new tools have served to

[11] Environmental-management approaches such as seeking to eliminate mosquito breeding sites and to prevent mosquito bites were effective strategies that contributed greatly to the elimination of malaria from most of Europe and North America in the 19th and early 20th centuries.

rapidly reduce mortality and morbidity associated with infectious disease—especially in infants. This led to remarkable declines in death rates, especially in developing countries which, unfortunately, were not, until recent years, accompanied by a corresponding decline in birth rates (see Table 1.1, chapter 1). The consequent population explosion which occurred in developing countries can be attributed largely to the fact that our investment in health interventions aimed at mortality reduction was not, until recently, accompanied by adequate investment aimed at improving quality of life, promoting human development, and dealing effectively with class and gender inequities—all of which are now recognized to be important determinants of fertility (Shahi & Lee, 1993). Hence, humanitarian efforts in the early 20th century—greatly facilitated by the dawning of the age of specific etiology, and aimed at halting death and disability arising from infectious diseases—have contributed to fueling the unprecedented rise in human populations we have witnessed during this century (see chapter 1). The well-meaning efforts of our predecessors in public health and international development to serve the common good contributed to creating one of the greatest crises confronting contemporary society—the threat of overpopulation. This experience illustrates the need to consider and understand the long-term implications of our activities—not just from the perspective of the individual or that of human society, but also more holistically in terms of the possible impact of our activities and interventions on environmental and developmental sustainability.

19TH- AND 20TH-CENTURY PARADIGMS AND THEIR IMPACT ON ENVIRONMENT, DEVELOPMENT, AND HEALTH

What is true of our approach to disease prevention and treatment is also true of society in general during the 20th century. As we invested in "knowing more and more about less and less," we found ourselves in a situation where people generally did not feel qualified to deal with broad societal concerns and problems—preferring to deal with specific, specialty areas in which they were trained.

While it has been considered the norm, in most societies, for educated intellectuals to maintain an interest in a wide range of different fields and endeavors, the phenomenal growth in new knowledge and 20th-century educational emphasis on detailed knowledge and specialization have meant that individuals could spend their entire careers focusing on very specific, narrow areas of interest. We have, in this century, witnessed the creation of ever more specialized areas of interest—not just medicine but internal medicine, not just internal medicine but gastroenterology, not just gastroenterology but proctology, and so on. Similarly, we have come to prize expertise in very specialized areas in other fields of endeavor—be it sociology, engineering, law, or pharmacology.

The Germans have a word for individuals who are so specialized that they know everything about a small area of specialized interest but little else—*Fachidioten* (specialist idiots). Such specialization has come with a tremendous cost—we have sacrificed breadth for depth. The educated individual who feels competent to engage in work in a variety of fields, so common in the 18th and 19th centuries, is today a rarity who exists in spite of the system and not because of it.

We have become so enamored of scientific and technological fixes to problems that we have often ignored simple, people-oriented approaches to problem solution—preferring instead to invest in research and development. In medicine, we have seen a growing affinity to high-tech approaches, a tendency to consider clinical sciences as being somehow more desirable than public health and prevention, and overemphasizing specialization and the creation of ever more circumscribed areas of specialty. This has resulted in the so-called "schism" between public health and clinical medicine (White, 1991).

Essentially, the holistic view of the link between humankind and the environment is no longer being adequately emphasized in our medical schools. The focus has become tertiary care and specialization—primary care is seen as simply not being exciting enough. The ascendancy of therapeutic medicine over preventive medicine can be traced to the early years of this century when medical schools started to earnestly look for "magic bullet" solutions to the ills that faced mankind.

Earlier advances had come from recognizing the links between various exposures and disease and seeking to avoid such exposures—as illustrated by the classical discoveries of Lister in relation to the spread of nosocomial infections and sepsis. The discovery of specific tools for eradicating or curing disease—the discovery of penicillin and its near-miraculous effect of wiping out mortality due to sepsis, the widespread use of quinine for prevention of malaria, the discovery of vaccines for treatment of smallpox (and its eventual eradication), the polio vaccine, and so forth—all helped promote the notion that the discovery of newer and better modalities for treating and eradicating disease should be the way to deal with such conditions.

Greater and greater value began to be placed on "high-tech" solutions and the low-tech (and commonsense) approaches espoused by preventive health and public health practitioners, essentially fell by the wayside. They were undervalued because theirs were not perceived as being the

Box 2.1—A Modern Parable?*

Imagine that you are one of a class of medical students who have come together to meet after having completed their residencies. In the class are many brilliant, promising individuals who fully intend to dedicate their lives to medicine and science. Your youthful enthusiasm is infectious.

Now imagine that you come together again after 30 years. You are now nearing retirement. Many have fulfilled their promise and have gone on to become famous professors and highly respected innovators in their chosen field. One by one, each stands up to describe her or his achievements and they are very impressive—one has written several textbooks in orthopedic surgery, another has pioneered a new technique for pancreatectomy, a third has started a world-famous institute for the management of psychosexual dysfunctions. This is indeed a very distinguished cohort of peers.

Then, someone stands up and asks her colleagues: "In the 30 years that we have contributed to our careers and distinguished ourselves as specialists and academics, infant mortality has continued to be over 50/1000 live births, children are still dying from largely preventable causes such as diarrhea and acute respiratory infections, mothers continue to hemorrhage to death during childbirth after living lives of absolute poverty. We have grown rich and famous in our well-insulated oases of intellectual ferment while others suffered and died. What have we really achieved?"

The moral? We need to view the world more holistically—always considering how our efforts fit within the overall scheme of things.

* Adapted from a speech given by Ken Prewitt, Senior Vice-President, The Rockefeller Foundation, at the first International Leadership for Environment and Development (LEAD) session in Chiangmai, Thailand. March, 1993.

most advanced or "state-of-the-art" approaches.[12] Generations of students of medicine and of science were raised on the notion that specialization was somehow a higher calling—the best minds would train in such subspecialties as cardiology, endocrinology, and neurosurgery (see Box 2.1).

[12] Public health professionals have tended to be among the lowest earners in the health field. More and more, a physician's ability to generate income for his or her

While such values and attitudes might be understandable in medical schools in the MDCs where the epidemiological transition (from infectious diseases and high, early-childhood mortality to long life expectancy and an increase in the importance of chronic diseases as the eventual cause of death) was nearly complete, they were completely out of place in the medical schools of most LDCs, where simple preventive measures would have been far more effective than the high-tech, high-specialization approach espoused by MDCs and clamored for by LDCs afraid of being left behind in the race for ever more sophisticated approaches to diagnosis and treatment.

Within the broad field of public health, as well, specialization has resulted in tremendous fissuring and, consequently, declining breadth of insight. Individuals have become specialized in such fields as environmental health, occupational health, tropical public health, international health, epidemiology, biostatistics, and toxicology. Specialization and sub-specialization have functioned as a double-edged sword—allowing very detailed understanding of particular areas of endeavor but raising barriers to appreciation of the interconnectedness of the various sub-specialties.

20TH-CENTURY ENVIRONMENTALISM AND PUBLIC HEALTH

Prior to the 1960s, progress and economic development were generally considered desirable ends in themselves—the negative impacts of industrial development on the environment and on human health and well-being were generally ignored or considered to be necessary evils. Rachel Carson's book, *Silent Spring*, written in the early 1960s, did much to galvanize action and to increase awareness of the damage that humankind's headlong rush for development was doing to the environment (and ultimately, to ourselves).

Activists and early environmentalists of the 1960s and 1970s tended to express themselves in uncompromising, extreme, and often fatalistic terms—which did very little to convert the unconverted but often had the opposite effect of raising mainstream resistance to their attitudes. They often pitted themselves against industrialists, government, and, sometimes, scientists, as they fought for causes such as the reduction and

---

respective institutions has come to be valued above all else. As a general rule, the more invasive and "high-tech" the approach, the more the physician is able to charge (and earn). Such interventions may be immensely beneficial in ensuring the well-being of individual patients but contribute little to the general health status and well-being of societies.

control of air and water pollution, the protection of habitats, prevention of food contamination by pesticides, animal rights and protection of species from extinction—often taking radical and non-negotiable positions. Rising social awareness and concern for environmental concerns today can, nevertheless, trace its historical roots to the diffusion of ideas from these early activists and environmentalists, and from the nature and health consciousness associated often with the "hippie" movement which began in the United States and spread to Europe. These initiatives later gave rise to strong environmental movements such as Greenpeace and the environmentally active political parties of Europe (Welsh & Butorin, 1990).

Nuclear accidents such as those that occurred at Windscale (United Kingdom), Three Mile Island (United States), and Chernobyl (Ukraine); highly publicized oiltanker spillages of polluting oil onto tourist beaches—which ruined the livelihood of fishermen and communities dependent on the tourist industry (Torrey Canyon and, later, the Exxon *Valdez*); growing concern regarding the disappearance of all forms of natural life from many rivers and lakes that had once been teeming with fish and other aquatic life—all these events have undoubtedly contributed to raising awareness and concern for the impact and implications of environmental degradation. A change in public opinion in Europe and the United States became discernible in the 1970s and 1980s, and the social and political base of environmentalism broadened and gained "respectability" as such thinking entered mainstream consciousness (Welsh & Butorin, 1990).

Along with problems within countries, ecologists and other scientists became increasingly concerned about environmental problems which crossed national boundaries and which affected the global "commons"—these included sea pollution, the impact of human industrial activity on the world's climate, and the likelihood that mindless overexploitation of nonrenewable resources such as oil and coal would soon lead to their exhaustion (concern for which was heightened as a result of the Organization of Petroleum Exporting Countries [OPEC]-initiated price hikes of the 1970s).

Such concerns led to the convening of the United Nations Conference on the Human Environment in Stockholm in 1972. This conference produced major advances in global public opinion on environmental issues and stimulated many countries, which did not previously have them, to establish environment ministries or agencies. The term "ecodevelopment" came to be the "buzzword"—it has since, in the late 1980s and early 1990s, come to be superseded by "sustainable development." The period following the Stockholm Conference saw significant advances in such fields as land-use planning, development planning, and rural development, as concern for ecosystem and wildlife preservation grew.

The scares and lessons of the 1960s and 1970s, unfortunately, failed to leave a lasting impression. Highly successful energy-conservation policies in reaction to the OPEC-initiated oil price hikes and a slump in industrial production led to a reduction in demand for oil and to a sinking of the price of oil. As soon as the price pressure was off, interest in energy conservation and the search for new and renewable energy sources waned. This, coupled with the arrival of pro-business governments in the United States and Europe, resulted in an international political climate unfavorable to environmentalism (Welsh & Butorin, 1990). This political change was reflected in the change in attitudes witnessed at the Nairobi conference convened by the United Nations Environment Programme in 1981 to assess progress on the Stockholm agenda (Morris Miller, personal communication). MDCs seemed disinterested in the proceedings and claimed that the major energy and environmental problems had already been solved. LDCs, on the other hand, had become increasingly aware of the growing deterioration of their environments and the resulting obstacles to the achievement of their development aspirations and loudly demanded help in dealing with the monumental tasks confronting them.

Seeking alternatives to nonrenewable energy sources, many developing countries embarked (often with encouragement and financing from international agencies such as the World Bank), in the 1970s and 1980s, on such programs as forests-for-fuels plantations, the use of more efficient cooking stoves, and efforts to harness hydroelectric power as a source of renewable energy. However, many such projects earned the wrath of environmentalists who were distressed, for example, that social forestry projects might be socially inequitable and ecologically unsound, or by the ecosystem destruction which often accompanied the construction of large dams for hydroelectric power.

A major step forward in the environmental movement came with its recognition that poor and indigenous people also had needs and rights. The 1982 World Conservation Strategy, for example, was an initiative of the International Union for the Conservation of Nature (IUCN) and the World Wildlife Fund for Nature (WWF) which focused on the need to preserve ecosystems for species protection but also recognized the need to ensure protection of the livelihood of rural and other less privileged sections of populations. Significantly, IUCN came to change its name to the International Union for the Conservation of Nature and Natural Resources (Welsh & Butorin, 1990).

Concern regarding the link between environmental deterioration and the prospects for future survival led to the appearance in 1987 of the World Commission on Environment and Development report "Our Common Future" (Bruntland, 1987). This was followed by the unprecedented preparatory process leading up to the United Nations "Earth Summit" in Rio de Janeiro in 1992. Agenda 21, the Earth Summit's enormous compendium of all the environment and development actions needed for the 21st century, contains a detailed chapter on each of 40 main problem areas which contribute to environmental damage and development failure (WHO Commission on Health & Environment, 1992). So pervasive are the links between improving environment, stimulating development, and maintaining human and ecological well-being that practically all of the problems addressed in Agenda 21 would be directly or indirectly influenced by innovative approaches to dealing with issues of environment, development and health and by efforts to achieve sustainable public health.

DISCUSSION

> The reasonable man adapts himself to the world: the unreasonable one persists in trying to adapt the world to himself. Therefore all progress depends on the unreasonable man.
>
> George Bernard Shaw, *Man and Superman*

We have, through the ages, experienced major shifts in the paradigms by which we have understood the links between the human animal and nature, the potential implications of our activities (including what we now call development) on the natural environment, and the interactions between environment, development and health: From accepting, in prehistoric times, that humankind's fate and well-being was completely dependent on nature and the environment; to developing holistic frameworks within which human well-being and the environment were seen to be in constant interaction—with health arising as a consequence of harmonious balance between the individual and his environment; to recognizing that humankind could alter our local environment to make it more conducive to human health and well-being; to pretending, over much of the last century, that humankind has absolute mastery over the environment and that it was essentially ours to use and abuse; to coming to terms, once again, with the realization that humankind's well-being is closely linked to the well-being of the environment. It is to be hoped that we have, in the process, learned many important lessons.

The social hygiene movement succeeded, without the benefit of the highly advanced body of scientific knowledge that is today at our disposal, in its efforts at cleaning up the environment and trying to create environments that were conducive to preventing disease and even promoting health. Its proponents did not embrace the specialization that characterizes today's approach to science and medicine wherein the focus is on deep, specific understanding in well-defined fields of study where specialists (or experts) are expected to know their field well but not necessarily to have a "big-picture" perspective. In contrast, the great innovators of the social hygiene movement had broad-based perspectives. They were physicians, economists, philosophers, physicists, sociologists, lawyers, engineers—individuals whose idea of knowledge was to have a reasonable understanding of how the parts fitted in with the whole.[13]

The specialization of the 20th century has created neat compartments for scientists working within their chosen field or specialty (or even subspecialty)—with no one taking any responsibility for issues across or at the boundary between disciplines. As a result, each has been concerned with advances and progress in her/his own field—the intellectual powers possessed by these gifted and intelligent individuals have tended effectively to be specifically rather than holistically applied. Everyone was too busy within her/his field and respected the expertise of others in other areas (and, perhaps, presumed too much of their social responsibility). With few people concentrating on the implications of our many endeavors on the "big picture," possibly assuming that someone else was so engaged, it took a considerable period of time before we began to recognize the damage we were causing to the environment and, ultimately, ourselves.

Knowledge has been prized above wisdom, technical competence over foresight, action over contemplation, and profit over social responsibility. The 20th century may be characterized as an age in which well-intentioned people have set about trying to solve the world's problems, relying on innovative and often high-technology solutions, with little insight or understanding of the potential implications of their activities. Consequently, new and previously unforeseen problems have often, almost invariably, arisen.

Only now are we realizing that our specialization-oriented and nonintegrative paradigms for development in the 19th and 20th century have led to the state the world is currently in—with massive environmental contamination, threatening overpopulation, large-scale loss of biodiversity, and substantial stress on global life support systems leading to accumulating carbon dioxide in the atmosphere and a hole in the ozone layer, among other signs.

---

[13] The environmental movement of today has many parallels with the social hygiene movement—it too is broad-based, is concerned with issues beyond any particular discipline, and has been able to attract the support of the general public, scientists, and politicians.

It has been said that the great challenges to humankind, such as absolute poverty, and dealing with global issues such as hunger or cross-border pollution, are the summits that need to be scaled if we are to truly progress as a species. Too often, these summits seem to be just too difficult to ascend—dealing with them requires a level of interdisciplinary or cross-disciplinary thinking that few today possess, and there is much controversy in trying to ascend them. Furthermore, attempting to do so would tend to be quite risky since individuals who seek to integrate broad-based perspectives are apt to be criticized by experts in specific areas, risk suffering major damage to their reputations, and, additionally, often have great difficulty publishing their findings. Investigators and practitioners who wish to pursue multidisciplinary or integrative approaches to problem-solving are often considered, in academic circles, to lack "focus" and to be spreading themselves too thin. Promotion up academic pathways tends to go to those who build a track record of publication in a particular area rather than those who publish in many different areas. Also, funding support for interdisciplinary work is often quite limited.

It has proven far easier and, from a career perspective, far wiser to identify an area in which to specialize, and to make a reputation as an authority in a clearly demarcated area as soon as possible. Only when one has built up a sizeable track record in publishing in a particular field of interest—and gets recognition from colleagues as an authority in the area—is it considered respectable to try to take on a more "big-picture" perspective. Dabbling in fields of endeavor outside one's area of specialty is often considered foolhardy (at least inadvisable) unless one has built up a storehouse of good will and credibility. There has tended, unfortunately, to be little place for the generalist.

We have, however, "hit the wall" with conventional scientific and technological paradigms—having gone as far as we could using in-depth knowledge and specialization as our principal means of raising the sum total of knowledge and understanding. In practically all our different disciplines and areas of focus we are seeing the need for greater insight and integration.

Issues that used to be nobody's interests but the experts and specialists have now become everybody's interests. Environmentalists were among the first to recognize that our "development" activities have direct and, often, dire consequences on the health and well-being of the other organisms that share this planet with us and that we are testing the homeostatic mechanisms that operate to maintain the global environment to the limit. The eyes of the environmentally conscious serve today to monitor the stresses that our developmental activities place on the environment and on human and ecological well-being. With their broad-based perspectives, and their use of multidisciplinary approaches to studying environmental and health impacts, they have begun to draw interactions and links that would otherwise have gone unrecognized.

A profusion of independent think tanks and nongovernmental organizations has started to challenge the status quo and to seek newer and better ways of dealing with the problems confronting humankind. Until these came into being, there were essentially only two options for those concerned about dealing with interdisciplinary concerns—taking on theoretical academic (often out of touch with reality) perspectives, or entering often highly bureaucratic and politically paralyzed government policy-making situations. Nongovernmental organizations (NGOs) have offered a viable third option. Within and across countries, NGOs have forced and accelerated developmental activities, they have taken up the challenge of helping to meet unmet needs, and they have shown by example the need for greater integration and transparency in international activities.

The challenges of achieving sustainable human development and sustainable public health will demand major changes in the way we educate and train future leaders in science, technology, and public policy for the 21st century—toward more insight, broader-based perspectives, and the use of interdisciplinary approaches and expertise to deal effectively with environment, development, and health concerns.[14]

REFERENCES

Arbuthnot, J. (1733). *An Essay Concerning the Effects of Air on Human Bodies.* London.

Boyle, R. (1666). General Heads for a Natural History of a Country, Great or Small. *Philosophical Transactions, 11,* 186–189.

Bruntland, G. (1987). *Our Common Future: Report of the World Commission on Environment and Development.* Oxford: Oxford University Press.

Chadwick, E. (1965). *Report on the Sanitary Conditions of the Labouring Population of Great Britain* [M.W, Flinn, editor]. Edinburgh: University Press.

Chen, C. C., & Bunge, F. M. (1989). *Medicine in Rural China—A Personal Account.* Berkeley: University of California Press.

Dubos, R. (1973). Environment. In Philip P. Wiener (Ed.), *Dictionary of the History of Ideas—Studies of Selected Pivotal Ideas. Volume II* (pp. 120–127). New York: Charles Scribner's Sons.

Hippocrates (1977). Airs, Waters, Places. In M. J. Adler & C. Van Doren (Eds.), *Great Treasury of Western Thought* (p. 1146). New York and London: R.R. Bowker and Company.

[14] The Leadership for Environment and Development (LEAD) program—initiated by the Rockefeller Foundation and now run independently through an NGO called LEAD International—seeks to promote just such innovation and change. Its work is discussed in chapter 28.

Leslie, C. (1988). Medicine. In Ainslie T. Embree (Ed.), *Encyclopedia of Asian History* (pp. 537–576). New York: McGraw-Hill.

McNeill, W. H. (1976). *Plagues and Peoples*. New York: Anchor Press.

Riley, J. C. (1987). *The Eighteenth-Century Campaign to Avoid Disease*. New York: St. Martin's Press.

Rosen, G. (1958). *A History of Public Health* (pp. 260–261). New York: MD Publications.

Shahi, G. S., & Lee, C. (1993) Population growth, demographic transition, and development: Lessons from the experience of newly individualizing countries. In 20th Annual NCIH Conference (Washington, DC, USA), Abstracts.

Snow, J. (1965). *Snow on Cholera*. New York and London: Hafner Publishing Company.

Weisbrod, B. A., Andreano, R. L., Baldwin, B. E., Epstein, E. H., Kelley, A. C., & Helminiak, T. W. (1973). *Disease and Economic Development: The Impact of Parasitic Diseases in St. Lucia*. Madison: University of Wisconsin Press.

Welsh, B. W. W., & Butorin, P. (1990). Environment and Development. In B. W. W. Welsh & P. Butorin (Eds.), *Dictionary of Development—Third World Economy, Environment, Society* (pp. 379–384). New York and London: Garland.

White, K. (1991). *Healing the Schism*. New York: Springer Verlag.

WHO Commission on Health and Environment (1992). *Our Planet, Our Health*. Geneva: World Health Organization.

Wilcocks, C. (1965). *Medical Advance, Public Health and Social Evolution* (p. 119). London: Pergamon.

Winslow, C. E. A. (1952). *The History of American Epidemiology*. St. Louis.

PART II
Conceptual Framework

3

Development, Health, and the Environmental Risk Transition

Kirk R. Smith

During the extensive study of the links between health and development that has been undertaken in recent decades, several conceptual frameworks have emerged that greatly assist in systematically organizing information and comparing the experience of different nations. Of most influence have been the Demographic and Epidemiologic Transitions, which focus on changes in fertility, mortality, and morbidity, all relatively easily quantifiable parameters. These transitions are key components in the overall Health Transition, which has been defined much more broadly to include cultural, social, and behavioral factors as well (Caldwell et al., 1990; Frenk et al., 1991). Absent until recently, however, was a way to systematically include environmental determinants of health (Bowonder, 1981; Kjellstrom et al., 1990; Hall, 1990).

Concurrently, but usually isolated from the health and development literature has been the birth and growth of environmental health risk analysis and assessment methods in the environmental and technology-assessment literatures (e.g., Carpenter et al., 1990; Edgerton et al., 1990; Kates et al., 1983; USNRC, 1983). The purpose here is to illustrate how these two strands of thought (health transition and environmental health risk assessment) can be melded together by the conceptual framework termed the "Risk Transition" (Smith, 1990).

DEMOGRAPHIC TRANSITION

This transition, first described before mid-century (Teitelbaum, 1975), involves a shift from Stage 1 (Traditional Equilibrium), in which population sizes are stable, due to high death rates as well as high birth rates; to Stage 2 (Population Explosion), when death rates decline more rapidly than birth rates; and eventually to Stage 3 (Modern Equilibrium), when birth rates decline and catch up with death rates (see Alshanksy & Ault, 1986). Although many countries have gone through such a transition, it is neither inevitable nor irreversible. Rather it is a pattern with many local variations and influenced by many factors.

The third stage, where low death rates are matched by low birth rates, is clearly the most desirable, but has been slow in coming for many developing countries. There is no need to let it occur at its own speed, however, for it can be accelerated by proper management; for example, death rates can be lowered more quickly by addressing specific risks by vaccinations and mosquito control, and birth rates can be lowered by enhancing the availability of birth control technologies and women's education.

EPIDEMIOLOGIC TRANSITION

As shown in Figure 3.1, the two components of the Demographic Transition are linked, one weakly (birth rates), one strongly (death rates), to the "Epidemiologic Transition," a concept first proposed in the late 1960s (Omran, 1971). It takes into account that the majority of developing countries are experiencing great reductions in some kinds of ill-health along with increases in others. The historically high "traditional" diseases associated with rural poverty trend downward during economic development although at different rates in different places and periods. Indeed, this overall downward trend in traditional disease is arguably the most important curve in human history (Caldwell et al., 1990).

The great reduction in traditional diseases that has generally accompanied development has usually led to a reduction in total ill health as can be seen in both national and international and both longitudinal and cross-sectional studies of trends in infant mortality, life expectancy, and other indicators of overall health.

At the same time as the traditional diseases decline, there tend to be an increasing a) fraction of deaths due to modern diseases, b) number of disease types, and c) morbidity. Modern diseases include the degenerative diseases, such as cancer, heart disease, and stroke, along with certain new types of accidents and occupational hazards. Industrialization, urbanization, and agricultural modernization bring attendant environmental pollution hazards that cause mainly "modern" diseases.

Since everyone must die of something, a more revealing index is life years lost to each class of risks. Overall life years lost has generally decreased with development. Historically losses due to modern diseases

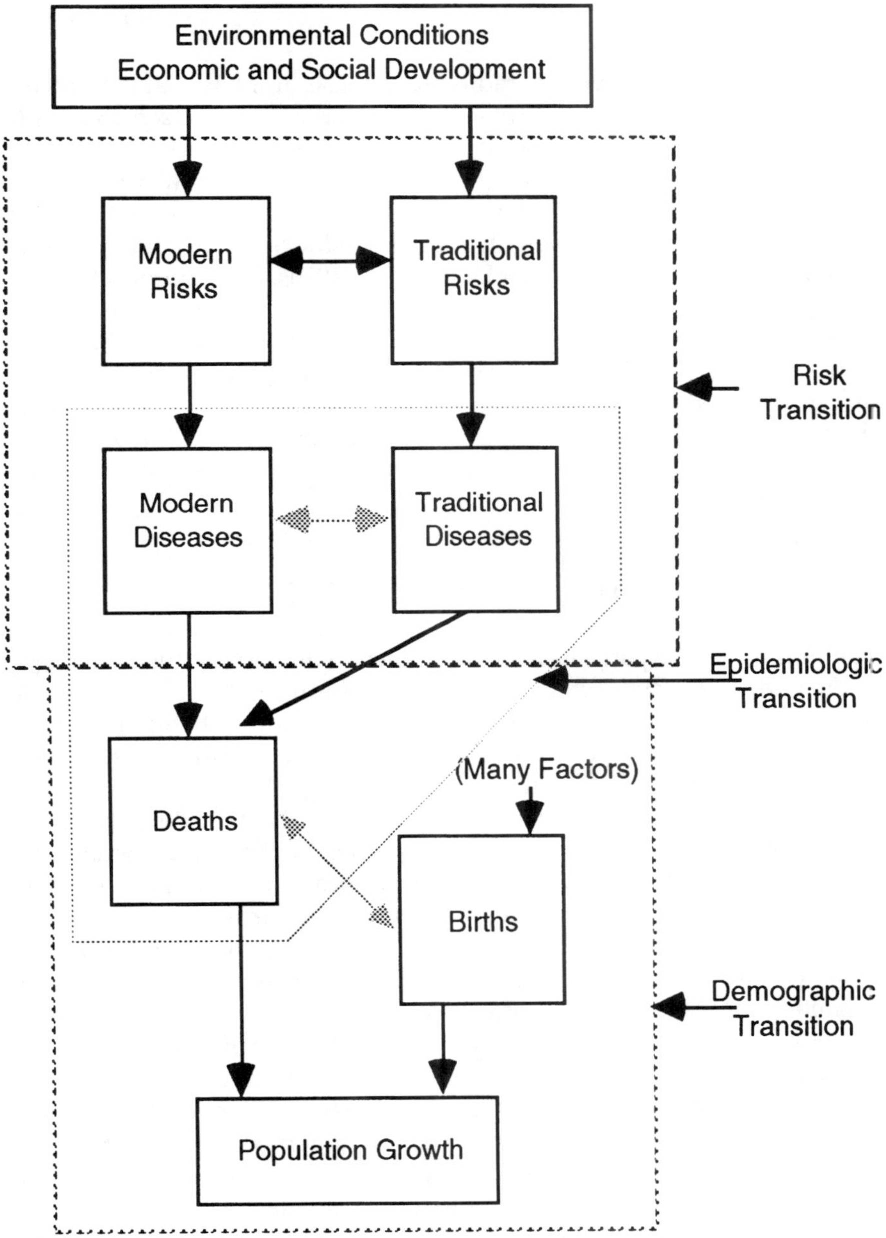

FIGURE 3.1 The three major parts of the Health Transition are shown in relation to one other. Note that the Epidemiologic Transition (shifts in the amount and fraction of traditional and modern diseases) is a response to the Risk Transition (shifts in the underlying risk factors), which may have occurred many years previously.

do not match those lost from traditional diseases until overall life expectancy reaches about 60 years. Total ill health has generally decreased with development because the reduction in traditional diseases more than counterweighs the rise of modern ones. In some cases, however, a stage may be reached where traditional diseases are all but squeezed out but modern diseases are still rising. There was evidence of this kind of upturn for infant mortality in the Soviet Union in the 1980s, for example. In recent years, the world has also witnessed too often the situation where large groups of people or even whole nations have moved back up the traditional disease curve because of setbacks in development caused, for example, by wars, natural disasters, or government mismanagement. Evidence of the latter is seen in Eastern Europe where, although most traditional diseases were declining, modern risks were apparently allowed to grow uncontrolled.

THE RISK TRANSITION

The shift of disease patterns from traditional to modern, is due to changes in the underlying risk factors for the various forms of ill health, as shown in Figure 3.1. Since one inevitably follows the other, it thus might be argued that there is no particular advantage in differentiating between the two, that is, between ill-health and risk. This might be so for some classes of disease, particularly those where there is a fairly short delay between changes in the risk factors and changes in ill health. For these, monitoring disease rates can be expected to be a fair indicator of what is happening and, thus, be a reasonably good guide for decision making.

For other classes of disease, however, present patterns of ill-health are quite poor indicators of actual risk. Consider the nearly archetypal case of cigarette smoking. Today's patterns of lung cancer reflect risk factors (smoking patterns) existing 10–40 years back. Because of this, it is possible to predict continued increases in ill health from smoking for U.S. women, who started smoking in large numbers some decades after men. Similarly, it is fair to say that Chinese men are today undertaking substantial risk due to their present smoking habits, even though, to date, there has been relatively little actual expression of that risk as ill health.

The distinction between risk and ill health is also important for another category of hazards, pollutants that make their way slowly through the environment, eventually reaching humans via food, air, or water. The release of the pollutant represents the creation of the risk (i.e., commitment to the health effect), even though there may be many years between the release and the disease, due to environmental and physiological latencies.

There are also situations in which risk is accrued, although not actually resulting in health damage. Although most nuclear power plants apparently operate without creating any significant ill-health, all do create risk, that is, even if a community nearby experiences no accidental radiation releases over the lifetime of the plant, it still has experienced risk and needs to take protective actions. Thus, an important difference between "ill health" and "risk" is the inclusion of, perhaps weighted, contribution from low-probability events in one, but not the other.

In a related way, modern risks also tend to differ from traditional risks in that many important outcomes do not have a unique cause. Unlike cholera, for example, which is caused by a single identifiable agent, a particular lung cancer cannot usually be confidently linked to a particular cause. It might have been air pollution (human or natural), asbestos, environmental tobacco smoke, a combination, or spontaneous. We can only make probability statements, at best.

This is true even when the impact is large. Consider again the archetypal case, smoking. The risk is huge—one third of smokers die young from their habit. This risk is much higher than most all major wars and plagues, but by being delayed and nonspecific, it is not perceivable by normal human senses. We require help from sophisticated scientific study and statistical interpretation to "see" it.

A more identifiably environmental example is lead pollution. It is now thought to have had disturbingly large impacts on children and adults throughout the world (Shy, 1990). Because its impacts are delayed and nonspecific (lowered intelligence and birthweight, stroke), even though large, they have been difficult to "see."

THE RISK OVERLAP AND RESULTING INTERACTIONS

There are significant differences within, as well as between, countries in the risk patterns of different population groups. Reporting average improvements, for example, masks the relatively greater progress made by women, children, and rural people when traditional risks decline (Greenberg, 1986).

The pace of the risk transition has changed such that traditional risks persist while modern risks start earlier in development. This results in a larger degree of "risk overlap," where some populations are exposed to a significant amount of both types, but in a rapidly changing pattern.

At the point marked A in Figure 3.2, modern risks have begun to rise, but traditional risks are still significant, although rapidly dropping. An example is where pesticide runoff starts to add to water pollution caused

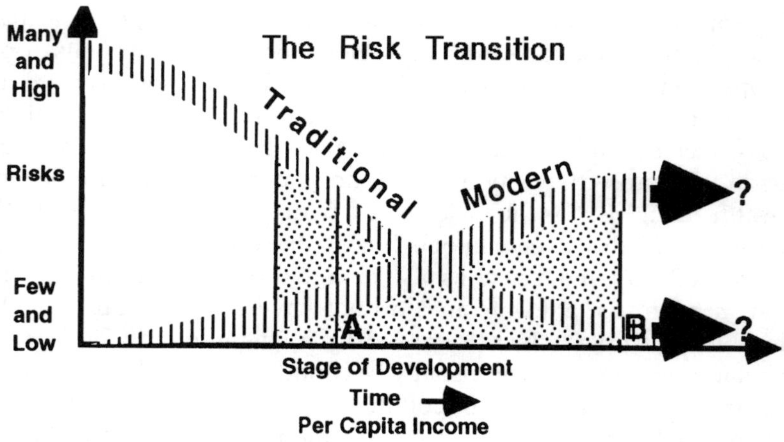

FIGURE 3.2 A conceptual illustration of the Risk Transition, showing the decline of traditional and the rise of modern risks. These curves precede the expression of the risk in damage, as portrayed in the Epidemiologic and Demographic Transitions. The shape of the two curves is not inevitable, but rather a combination of intrinsic environmental and social conditions, economic development, and risk-management efforts. Each country has the opportunity to guide its own transition. The fuzziness of the lines indicates the considerable uncertainty involved in validating risk indicators and monitoring their movements. The patterned area represents the *risk overlap*, where there may be important interactions between traditional and modern risks. The total risk (traditional plus modern) declines throughout the range, as it has for most parts of the world where economic development has continued (indicated, for example, as annual individual or population death rates).

by poor sanitation. Another example is offered by those places where urban air pollution from fossil-fuel combustion is rising while large village and urban air pollution exposures from household combustion of traditional biofuels still exist.

If these effects were merely additive, there might be no special need to consider interactions. Unfortunately, however, risk overlap can lead to interactions with important implications for risk assessment by leading to effects that magnify or mask the separate impacts of modern and traditional risks. Six kinds of interaction can be identified:

1. *Risk genesis*, where risk overlap may lead to creation of an entirely different sort of risks, e.g., mixing modern (motorized) and traditional (muscle-powered) vehicles, leads to new kinds of accident risks and risk-management needs.
2. *Risk synergism*, where exposure to one agent causes immunity or sensitivity to other agents, e.g., where traditional intestinal diseases

due to poor water quality increase sensitivity to waterborne and airborne modern pollutants.

3. *Risk mimicry*, where morbidity and mortality may be attributed to traditional sources of risk, but may be actually due to modern or synergistic risks, e.g., lung cancer being attributed to acute or chronic lung diseases.
4. *Risk competition*, where abnormally high or low risks of one disease may actually be an indication of the decrease or increase in the risks of an entirely different disease, e.g., where low lung-cancer rates may not necessarily mean that the risk of lung cancer is low, but just that people are dying of other diseases first and not living long enough to develop cancer.
5. *Risk layering*, where the movement of people or their activities concentrates risk in one region and dilutes risk in another, e.g., where rural–urban migrants are healthier than the average person left back in the villages.
6. *Risk transfer*, where efforts to control risk from traditional hazards may enhance modern risks (or vice versa), as when pesticides are used to control malaria (Whipple, 1985).

It may also be useful to distinguish two general types of risk overlap—local and global. Listed above were cases of *local* risk overlap involving the interaction of traditional and modern risks on a local scale, for example, scavengers at a municipal dump exposed also to industrial waste. These can be serious, but are amenable to various remedies. If hazardous materials are dumped elsewhere, overlap interactions are essentially eliminated (although not necessarily the individual traditional and modern risks).

Global risk overlaps, in contrast, will continue as long as there are great disparities anywhere on earth between the risk patterns (and other characteristics) of different groups. The most important global risks with these kinds of overlaps are ozone- and climate-threatening chemical releases.[1] Although mostly created by modern activities in countries well along in the Health Transition, these pollutants affect the whole world. Indeed, they will likely have their biggest impacts among peoples still burdened by traditional risks, including those with high vulnerability to environmental stress. Unlike local risk overlaps, the modern global versions cannot be avoided by releasing the pollution at another place. With these

[1] The most extreme global modern risk (non-specific, low-probability and high-consequence) is thermonuclear war, a never-yet-occurred but high-consequence hazard that has imposed substantial risk and need for protective actions, but little health effect to date (and perhaps never).

pollutants, for all practical purposes, emissions anywhere are emissions everywhere.[2]

NET RISK

Consider the different worldviews of the risk managers working in countries represented by points A and B in Figure 3.2. The risk manager at point B sees an increasing number and, in some cases, intensification of modern risks from development. The traditional risks have been mostly controlled and are of less concern. Thus, understandably, assessment efforts have been focused on quantifying and managing modern risks. At point A, however, important hazards of both traditional and modern sorts exist side by side, although trending in opposite directions. Introduction of technology and the resulting development (interpreted as a movement along the horizontal axis) that follows will, therefore, have a substantially different impact on overall risk in developing countries than in developed countries. On average a country at point A will experience a significant degree of *risk lowering* (movement down the traditional risk curve) from new technologies as well as *risk raising* (movement up the modern risk curve).

Although the overall result of development may be general risk lowering as shown in Figure 3.2, each technological project will have its own pattern, which may not be risk lowering in aggregate. To understand the overall or *net risk* from any particular project, regulation, or activity, therefore, will require evaluation of both classes of risk. The developing country risk manager will find that to adopt risk assessment methods from developed countries, which focus solely on modern risks, will be misleading.

In principle, assessments on both sides of the risk transition should incorporate consideration of risk-lowering as well as risk-raising aspects of development. Indeed, focusing only on the modern risk curve for each new project, as part of what might be called *microrisk* analysis, leads to the manifestly absurd *macrorisk* result that those communities with the most technology should be the least healthy, that Switzerland should be more unhealthy than Nepal.

Earlier this century, direct improvements in health care and public health seemed to be the principal causes of risk lowering. Recent analyses, however, seem to indicate weaker dependence after mid-century on factors other than income and education in enhancing life expectancy and

[2] AIDS can, perhaps, be considered a local disease made global by human activities. Given the worldwide movement of people and lifestyles, an AIDS case anywhere is beginning to be like an AIDS case everywhere.

decreasing childhood mortality. In general, health status seems now to be influenced by economic development more than previously in the developing countries of Asia and the Americas and to a lesser degree, Africa. This occurred mostly through diminution of the impact of the direct variables, rather than an increase in the effect of income.

These might be called "indirect" routes to risk lowering, to contrast them with "direct" routes such as health care. Indirect routes to risk raising include, for example, the impact of urban stress, as contrasted to such direct routes as chemical pollution. That they are indirect, however, need not mean that they are small, as in the well-known relationship between women's education and health (World Bank, 1993).[3]

In practice, little effort has gone into developing methods for assessing risk lowering. Whatever the resulting misrepresentation in developed countries, failing to conduct net risk analysis in developing countries will produce much larger distortions because of the more important role played by traditional risk. Many studies have been made of the overall relationship of economic development with health status, but few have conducted project-level analysis. It is at the project level, however, where decisions are made and policies are implemented. Such analysis requires understanding the changes due to a project on income, employment, training/education, housing, and other relevant factors as well as the impact of each of these on risk.[4]

An important component of developing country risk assessment, therefore, should be net risk analysis. This would acknowledge that the risk-lowering and the risk-raising aspects of projects need to be examined. To some readers, this may seem to be a thinly veiled rationalization for continued lax environmental and safety standards in developing countries. This is not the case. Rather, it is a call to judge technologies on a net risk basis so those that do not or only weakly reduce net risk can be rejected or modified to meet risk goals of the society. The criteria remain just the same as in past risk assessments focusing only on modern risk (i.e., those projects that are associated with much risk raising will be penalized). It seems appropriate in many circumstances, however, to also penalize those projects that bring little risk lowering (Shrader-Frechette, 1985). Risk is only one of the criteria by which projects are compared, but it is best done on a net risk basis.[5]

---

[3] Indeed, not only are the best environmental health investments likely to be indirect, e.g., women's education, but so may those aimed at ecosystem sustainability, i.e., local land use control.

[4] See, for example, Sagan (1987) for a provocative discussion of the role of family structure on health.

[5] See Smith & Lee (1993) for a discussion of urbanization and net risk analysis.

To be most useful, risk assessment in developing countries should be able to give guidance not only about individual actions, such as siting a particular facility or embarking on a new industry, but also on pathways of development that may incorporate trade-offs between economic growth and risk over many years. An example of this type of decision, apparently made without systematic quantification, however, is that of one Asian country in which government policy consciously chose cheaper but high-sulfur fuels for a defined period in order to quicken economic growth. Once a trigger level of income was achieved, however, cleaner fuels were phased into use.[6]

Another dynamic is the trend of some modern risks to become significant at earlier stages in the development process than in the past because of the impact of international and internal trade, communication, and foreign aid. Consequently, the period of risk overlap and need for net risk assessment may be increasing.

RISK MONITORING

A further rationale for focusing on risk rather than ill-health is suitability for management. Waiting to count who dies of what may be an adequate approach to understanding and controlling some traditional risks—dysentery for example—but is clearly inadequate for decoupled risks such as toxic metal poisoning and ozone depletion, for which the changes in risk factors greatly precede changes in ill-health. By the time there are actual changes in health, it is too late to do much.

For these hazards, we need to monitor further back along the causal chain. This runs, for example, from pollutant emissions, to environmental concentrations, exposures, doses, preclinical changes, and ill health, before leading to death (Smith, 1988). The best point along this chain to measure depends on a range of factors, including not only the time constants involved but also ease and cost of monitoring. Generally, points further back on the chain tend to be easier to monitor than those, like dose, relatively closer to effects. On the other hand, they are more removed in causation, introducing uncertainties because of gaps in knowledge about, for example, how emissions are translated into human exposures.[7]

[6] More persistent or long-range pollutants or those with irreversible effects would clearly complicate this type of assessment.

[7] The causal chain, and thus risk monitoring, can also be extended back even further, to the basic decision steps involved in embarking on this or any technology at all, as compared, for example, to exploring other ways to meet human needs and wants (Hohenemser et al., 1985).

CONCLUSION

There is not space here to discuss the Risk Transition over time, in which today's modern rising risks become tomorrow's traditional falling risks (Smith, 1990), nor how the complete lifecycle for some environmental risks fits the classical "Kuznets curve" of development, an inverted "U," in which things become worse before they become better (Panayotou, 1994). It is important to emphasize, however, that, like the Demographic Transition, the Risk Transition is not set in stone. Indeed, a major role for governments in the presently developing countries is to manage the Risk Transition in such a way that traditional risks continue to fall as rapidly as possible, while modern risks and risk overlaps are contained. The burden on risk assessment, however, is greater and significantly different than in developed countries where such techniques were first used.

REFERENCES

Bowonder, B. (1981). Environmental Risk Issues in the Third World. *Technological Forecasting and Social Change, 19*, 99.

Caldwell, J. C., Findley, L. S., Caldwell, P. et al. (Eds.) (1990). *What We Know About Health Transition*. Health Transition Series #2, vols. 1 & 2, Canberra: Australian National University.

Carpenter, R. A., Smith, K. R., Habbeger L., & Claudio, C. P. B. (1990). *Environmental Risk Assessment*. Manila: Asian Development Bank.

Edgerton, S. A., et al. (1990). Priorities for Study of Environmental Risk in Developing Countries. *Journal of Risk Analysis, 10(2)*, 273–283.

Frenk, J., Bobadilla, J. L., Stern, C., et al. (1991). Elements for a Theory of the Health Transition. *Health Transition Review, 1(1)*, 21–38.

Greenberg, M. R. (1986). Disease Competition as a Factor in Ecological Studies of Mortality: The Case of Urban Centers. *Social Science Medicine, 23(10)*, 929–934.

Hall, R. H. (1990). *Health and the Global Environment*. Cambridge: Polity Press.

Hohenemser, C., Kasperson, R. F., & Kates, R. W. (1985). Causal Structure. In R. W. Kates et al. (Eds.), *Perilous Progress*. Boulder, CO: Westview Press.

Kates, R. W., & Kasperson, J. X. (1983). Comparative Risk Analysis of Technological Hazards (A Review). *Proceedings from the National Academy of Sciences USA, 80*, 7027–7038.

Kjellstrom, T., & Rosenstock, L. (1990). The Role of Environmental and Occupational Hazards in the Adult Health Transition. *World Health Statistics Quarterly, 43(3)*, 188–196.

Olshansky, S. I., & Ault, A. B. (1986). The Fourth Stage of the Epidemiologic Transition: The Age of Delayed Degenerative Diseases. *Milbank Quarterly, 64(3)*: 355–391.

Omran, A. R. (1971). The Epidemiologic Transition: A Theory of the Epidemiology of Population Change. *Milbank Memorial Fund Quarterly, 49(4)*, 509–538.

Panayotou, T. (1994). Empirical tests and policy analysis of environmental degradation at different states of economic development. *Pacific and Asian Journal of Energy, 4(1)*, 23–42.

Sagan, L. A. (1987). *The Health of Nations*. New York: Basic Books.

Shrader-Frechette, K. S. (1985). *Risk Analysis and Scientific Method: Methodology and Ethical Problems with Evaluating Societal Hazards*. Dordrecht, Netherlands: D. Reidel.

Shy, C. (1990). Lead in Petrol—the Mistake of the XXth Century, *World Health Statistics Quarterly, 43(3)*, 168–176.

Smith, K. R. (1988). Total Exposure Assessment. *Environment, 30(8)*, 10–15; 33–38.

Smith, K. R. (1990). The Risk Transition. *International Environmental Affairs, 2(3)*, 227–251.

Smith, K. R., & Lee, Y. S. (1993). Urbanization and the Environmental Risk Transition. In J. D. Kasarda & A. M. Parnell (Eds.), *Third World Cities* (pp. 161–179). Newbury Park, Sage.

Teitelbaum, M. S. (1975). Relevance of demographic transition theory for developing countries. *Science, 188*, 420–425.

USNRC (U.S. National Research Council) (1983). *Risk Assessment in the Federal Government: Managing the Process*. Washington, DC: National Academy Press.

Whipple, C. (1985). Redistributing Risk. *Regulation, 9(3)*, 37–44.

World Bank (1993). *World Development Report 1993: Investing in Health*. New York: Oxford University Press.

4

The Interrelationships of Population Growth with Health and Human Habitat

Daniel Taylor-Ide, Carl E. Taylor, and Gurinder S. Shahi

The impact of health on population growth is clear, with improvements in health first helping reduce mortality and later affecting fertility. The intuitively expected impact of population growth on human habitat is not direct. Future growth will differ significantly because of aging of populations and accelerating urbanization. It is unclear whether the mitigating factors of social organization and technological amelioration can continue, as they have, to buffer the impact of population growth on human habitat and quality of life.

DYNAMICS OF POPULATION GROWTH

Transitions in mortality and fertility define the rate of natural increases in population (Brass, 1991). Although they interact in many ways, in this chapter mortality and fertility will be looked at separately, in order to balance causal influences.

The mortality transition: With improvements in health, death rates have tended to come down from about 40 per 1,000 in traditional societies to less than 10 per 1,000 in modern, developed societies. This decline in mortality (the mortality transition) has been associated with an increase in life expectancy and a marked change in causes of death. Pretransition mortality is largely in babies and children, who die from infections and malnutrition, health problems controllable by direct measures, although long-term prevention depends on basic behavioral change, such as better child-care practices and hygiene. Later in the mortality transition, deaths shift to older ages and the causes tend to be chronic and degenerative diseases, problems people often have to learn to live with. Prevention of these problems depends almost entirely on behavior change (Doll, 1992).

The fertility transition: Pretransition fertility is high, with a birth rate above 40 per 1,000. After the fertility transition, this comes down to about 15 per 1,000. Multiple proximate variables may lower fertility, including age at first pregnancy, birth spacing, family planning, and duration of cohabitation. How each of these operates varies greatly depending on underlying determinants such as: culture, marital patterns, education, role of women, and expectations for social and economic change.

The interval between these two transitions is known as the demographic gap, the period during which most population growth occurs (Blacker, 1993; Brass, 1991). The mortality transition almost always precedes the fertility transition. Some typical patterns are illustrated in Figure 4.1. In More Developed Countries (MDCs) the two seem to be coupled or linked (Shahi, 1994). In Europe and North America, the dual transitions took 100 to 200 years, as both mortality and fertility responded to general improvement in socioeconomic conditions (Cassen, 1993).

In Less Developed Countries (LDCs) the two transitions seem to be uncoupled, and population growth is rapid (Shahi, 1994). Efforts to reduce mortality accelerated at the beginning of this century, with greatly increased capacity to implement effective public health programs. There was little concern about population growth, since an expanding labor force was desired.

The experiences of the Newly Industrializing Economies (NIEs), in particular Hong Kong, Singapore, South Korea, and Taiwan, illustrate how fertility and mortality can be recoupled (Shahi, 1994). As a result of significant investment in economic and social development, these societies greatly shortened both transitions. (See dotted lines in Figure 4.1).

China, with 22 percent of the world's people, demonstrates that it is now possible for both transitions to be very rapid (Taylor, 1991). The mortality transition took 20 years, 1950 to 1970, but the fertility transition took only 10, 1970 to 1980. However, even in China, lowering fertility did not immediately stabilize population growth because of the biologically determined delay of about one generation during which increasing numbers of girls reach reproductive ages.

IMPLICATIONS OF POPULATION GROWTH

World population grew from 2 billion people in 1930 to five billion in 1990; and sixty years after that, by 2050, conservative estimates are that it will double again to 10 billion people (United Nations, 1992). To understand the impact of doubling the world population to ten billion people, it is important to look at who these people will be. During early stages of growth up to the present, high fertility and high death rates caused a pyramidal age distribution with fewer people in each cohort. High fertil-

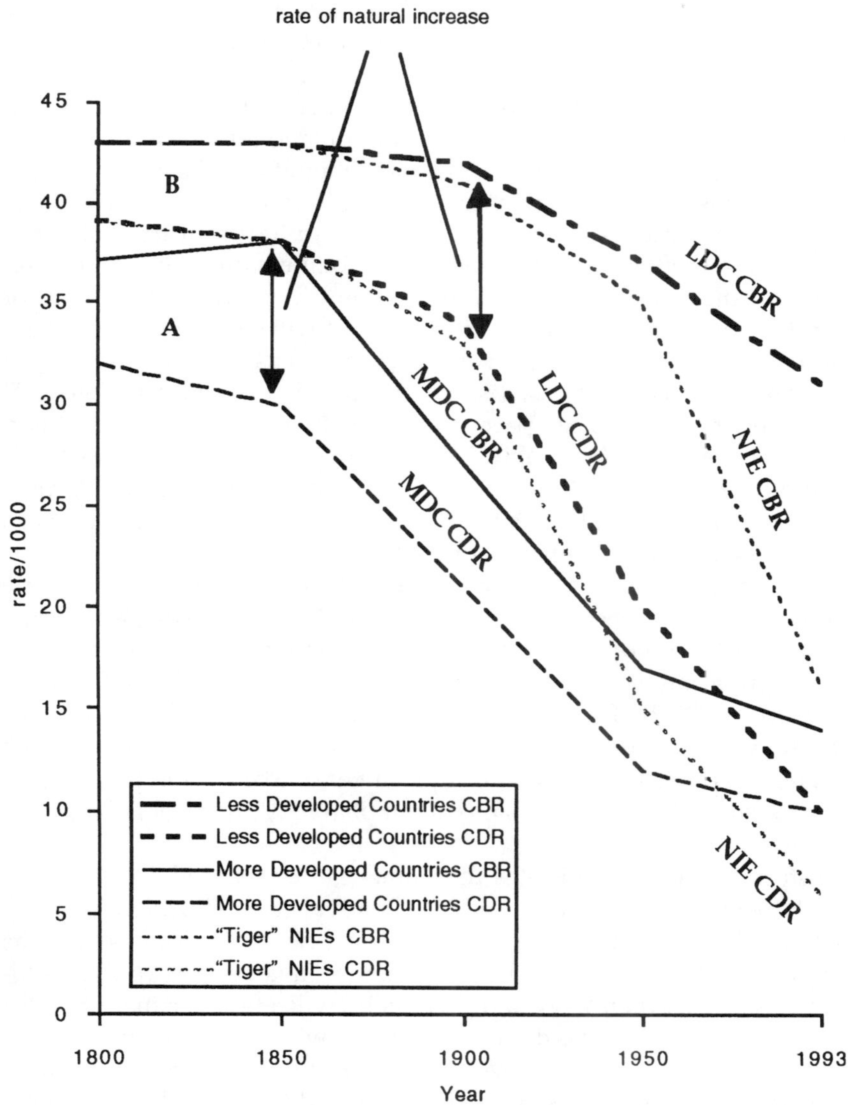

FIGURE 4.1 Changes in Crude Birth Rate (CBR) and Crude Death Rate (CDR) for East Asian "Tiger" NIEs, superimposed on experience of MDCs (A) and LDCs (B)—1800–1993.

ity was maintained as mortality decreased, especially child mortality, and this produced larger numbers in each surviving cohort. But, the basic distribution retained a pyramidal profile.

Over the next 60 years world population distribution will adopt the pattern already established in developed countries. The total number of births worldwide will roughly stay steady at 150 million per year, while deaths will show dramatic decreases in all age groups through 75. The population profile will shift from pyramidal to "bullet shaped" (United Nations, 1992). As the next five billion are added, these numbers will reflect adults who are now growing older, not new babies as was previously considered true when world population doubled.

A second major demographic dynamic is migration. The growing numbers of people will redistribute themselves directly because of a series of push and pull factors—some of which relate to health (warfare, famine, etc.) but more often relate to habitat (environmental impacts, food supplies, housing, and very importantly, economic opportunities). The major migratory dynamic worldwide has been, and will continue to be, urbanization. Of the five billion expected new people, most will live in cities, not rural areas (United Nations, 1989). Only in the wealthiest regions will cities likely be able to keep pace with needed local development. Otherwise urbanization will probably follow the haphazard, frequently chaotic growth of cities such as Calcutta, Lagos, Manila and Sao Paulo (Hardoy, 1992). By the year 2000 there will be more than 25 cities with populations exceeding 10 million (United Nations, 1989).

Significant effort has been devoted to mathematical modeling of future trends and convergences in the above dynamics, because of concern that an "overshoot"of population numbers and continuing levels of resource consumption might cause a collapse of modern civilization (Meadows, 1992; IIASA, 1992). These projects are still being debated and their assumptions examined. However, computer simulations make clear that the variables interrelate with great complexity and, while imperfect, tend to point toward sobering conclusions about planetary and regional carrying capacity.

Historical evidence indicates that limits can be reached for a civilization. Phoenicia, a remarkable and highly advanced civilization, with explorers who were able to sail around Africa 2000 years before the Portuguese, exhausted the cedars of Lebanon—a key source of shipbuilding and saw first their navy and then their civilization decline. The Irish Potato Famine of 1845 was directly associated with a population that grew from two million in 1700 to seven million people 150 years later. After a disastrous blight, Ireland's population dropped to four million, where it stabilized. The 7th century Mayan civilization may have become overly urbanized, so that it exceeded its food supply base. Easter Island in the

Pacific very likely expanded its numbers and flourished, to then exhaust its environmental resources, and collapse.

It is simplistic to make predictions about the future based on incomplete computer models or historical experience from a very different world. Population growth responds to many factors, and human health and habitat respond to even more. Furthermore, as the present world population expands, there are likely to be environmental and health impacts about which we know little. However, computer models, historical experience, and intuitive judgement provide the best evidence we have yet to work with.

POPULATION CHANGE AND THE ENVIRONMENT

Little evidence is available on direct associations between changes in human population numbers and environmental quality in defined local areas (Jolly & Torrey, 1993). For all animals other than people, increasing population size is directly linked with negative environmental consequences in food supply, habitat quality, altered intersocial dynamics, health status, and many other factors (Cassen, 1993). The biologically unique adaptability of *Homo sapiens* allows two variables to modulate and mediate the consequences of population growth and potential environmental change that result from larger numbers: technology and social organization (CIESIN, 1992).

Technology: Since the Stone Age, when our ancestors began to use tools, technology has grown in importance in altering the extent and efficiency of natural resource use and the resulting impact of population change on the environment (See Box 4.1.) Indeed, technological adaptation is one of the main expressions of socioeconomic development. A negative consequence is that through the expanded options provided by technology, consumption of natural resources has increased faster than population growth (Demeny, 1989). For example, use of technology as measured by U.S. energy consumption grew by 2.76 percent per year between 1960 and 1985, a period during which the U.S. population grew by only 1.33 percent per year. Furthermore, consumption of other resources that have finite limits, such as minerals and fossil fuels, also exceeded population growth (Meadows, 1992). Increasing consumption that results in the scarcity of a resource requires constant discovery of alternative resources, recycling, and efficiency. Up to the present, technological innovation has shown enormous adaptability. Doubling the population will test this capacity even more stringently.

Technologic innovation and capacity have not, however, been developed in equivalent efforts to reduce wastes generated by development (Brown, 1992). Pollutants and hazardous wastes mount with ever greater volume and toxic impact on health (Landrigan, 1992; Last, 1993). Delayed awareness of massive and cumulative chemical permeation of water tables and soil means that it will take many years to dissipate. A continuing problem will be to clean up wastes already generated. Poland is an example of a country where environmental consequences were ignored during a prolonged period of industrialization. It will cost $260 billion and take 30 years to adequately dispose of existing pollutants and hazardous waste, neither a sum nor a length of time the country can afford (World Resources Institute, 1992).

Social organization: Social organization is the second method populations use to modify their environment. This includes structure (urban/rural, extended/nuclear family, vocation/avocation, etc.) and societal aspirations (religion/social priorities, savings/spending, community/individual loyalty, concern for children, etc.). Although difficult to quantify, social structures and aspirations are shifting more rapidly worldwide than ever before. For example, population migration into the United States from Mexico is a primary force in the pressure for new economic trade structures in North America. New waves of social change sweep the world because of the power of modern communications such as television.

One demonstration of how social organization is accommodating population change is with the very important accommodation to increased aging in the United States. When there were few elderly people (and shorter life expectancy) and many younger people, care for the elderly was in the home. With increasing numbers of elderly, responsibility has

Box 4.1—Population Growth and Habitat—An Ancient Perspective

Herodotus, in the 5th century B.C., observed that population growth changed the land. "There once was a time," he reports, "when a man could walk the North African coast from Gibraltar to the Nile and always be in the shade of trees." No more. By the time of Herodotus, North Africa had changed, he goes on to say, "Man stalks across the landscape and deserts follow in his footprints." (As quoted in Hardin, 1993.)

shifted to societal mechanisms since the young do not have adequate resources, are more mobile, and less accessible. A previously successful Social Security system will need readjustment to accommodate this demographic shift. Social costs also rise as physical needs of the elderly increase for housing, health, and privacy (Doll, 1992). Social reorganization is also affected by increased political and economic power.

INTERRELATIONSHIP OF POPULATION CHANGE, HEALTH, AND ENVIRONMENTAL DEGRADATION

Ancient Chinese scholars and Ayurvedic Hindu sages stressed the influence of environmental factors on health. Hippocrates' classic work *On Airs, Waters and Places* gave detailed descriptions of geographical and historical determinants of disease as understood by the early Greeks. Modern science now tries to balance multicausal ecological analyses with continuing research on single causes and single interventions. The Rio Conference on the environment and its Agenda 21 stimulated renewed attention to understanding how changes in the environment influence long-term human and ecological well-being. In recent years, many reviews of environmental influences on health have appeared (McMichael, 1993; UNDP, 1990; UNFPA, 1990; UNICEF/UNEP, 1990; WHO, 1990). Five associations should be recognized here.

1. *Effect of Population Growth on Health.* Population growth influences human health both through general variables and by specific and direct effects. Most thoroughly documented is that high parity with short birth intervals greatly increases mortality and morbidity for mothers, infants, and children (Cochrane, 1993). The causes range from complications of pregnancy and nutritional problems, such as anemia, to the ways in which caring for large and young families make it difficult for parents to optimize care for the individual child. In addition, for several diseases, population density is associated with disease prevalence. Examples from developing countries include tuberculosis, a major cause of death in adults, and diarrhea and pneumonia, the two main causes of death in children (Mosley, 1993). The correlation of population density with such diseases is mostly because they are associated with poverty and poor hygiene.

2. *Effect of Health on Population Trends—The Child Survival Hypothesis.* Potential direct associations between mortality reduction and population growth have frequently been misinterpreted. The simplistic idea continues to be postulated that, since popula-

tions grow when mortality falls faster than fertility, then a logical solution would be to limit health services and concentrate on family planning. This causal assumption is false. Demographic analysis shows that, in almost all countries, fertility did not start to decline until after life expectancy had reached 55 years, largely as a result of greater child survival (Bongaarts, 1986; UNICEF 1992). It was observed early, that after babies died, there were shortened birth intervals before women became pregnant again. It became necessary to distinguish clearly that most of this effect was due to the biological effects of cessation of lactational amenorrhea, which is one of the main factors limiting the number of births worldwide.

Studies of the "child survival hypothesis" defined three factors that influenced the commonsense observation that parents tend not to limit the number of births until the survival of existing children is assured (Taylor, 1983).

a. "Replacement motivation" has a small but measurable effect that becomes apparent after birth rates have fallen and parents are limiting births to match deliberate decisions about family size. Studies in countries, such as France, where lactational amenorrhea is not a factor, show a shortened birth interval after the death of a child (Taylor, 1967).
b. Prospective field studies demonstrate that the most important factor producing synergism between health services and family planning is that integrated services are more effective and efficient than separate services for service providers and more acceptable to families. Family planning is more sustainable if integral to routine maternal and child care (Taylor, 1983). Unfortunately, international agencies have greatly complicated long-term and sustainable program development by promoting separate services for family planning. Many examples, such as Indira Gandhi's emergency family planning in India and the program in modern-day China, show that strong top-down family planning tends to produce public resistance.
c. When more children survive, parents realize they do not need to have extra children because of the expectation that some will die. Prospective field studies show that this "insurance motivation" is subconscious but that direct associations can be demonstrated (Taylor, 1983). The most important finding was that deliberate integration of services could use evidence of child survival as a means of promoting family-planning use. Family planning can be naturally and effectively introduced with comprehensive health services so that the poor, uneducated, and couples which had previously been most reluctant to use

family planning, increase their acceptance by 35 percent in high-caste families to 18 percent in low-caste families (Taylor, 1983).

3. *Impact of Aging on Health Status.* Aging has dramatic impact on health with much higher prevalence of chronic diseases as people age. Both the demand for and the expense of health care rapidly increase. This is in addition to the separate effect of greater affluence of older people, which results in rising expectations of service quality and technological sophistication. In the United States, where an aging population is already evident, 80 percent of all medical care costs pay for care in the last two years of life (Institute of Medicine, 1990).

4. *Urbanization.* As the primary response by which society accommodates expanding numbers, urbanization facilitates the delivery of health services because it concentrates people in urban areas thus increasing access to hospitals, health centers, health education, public health measures, and emergency care. However, large numbers can also overwhelm social services, transportation, and communication in inner cities and periurban slums, and thus reduce quality of health care, especially for the poor (Satterthwaite, 1993; Tabibzadeh, 1989). Despite these problems, most studies show that even in the worst slums access to services and the possibility of higher education results in mortality rates lower than in poor rural areas from which urban migrants come (Demeny, 1986).

   A further feature of urbanization is that it may increase the potential of food shortages because the proportion of people growing food is reduced. Poor, landless people are most likely to suffer silent hunger. A positive trend is that advances in urban agriculture make it possible for the urban poor to use modern technology to grow much of their food (Hardoy, et al., 1992).

5. *Famines and Chronic Food Shortages.* Since Malthus, famines have been considered a potential consequence of population growth with obvious health risk. Whereas famine may be a concern only in extreme conditions, hunger is not. Doubling the number of people requires more than doubling the amount of food needed because the quality of the diet for much of the world today needs to be greatly improved. The United Nations Food and Agriculture Organization (UNFAO) studied 115 developing countries and concluded that more than half will probably not be able to feed themselves by the year 2000 (UNFAO, 1984). Although dramatic food production increases have been achieved over the past decades, it may be that limits to further expansion of the Green Revolution are being

reached. Croplands are being degraded (loss of nutrients, chemical pollution, desertification, waterlogging, water and wind erosion, etc.) so that the usable land being brought into production currently equals the areas being lost (World Resources Institute, 1990). Irrigation is essential to continuing to expand food production, but countries in Africa, the Middle East, and Asia face increasing water shortages (FAO, 1986). Chemical fertilizers and pesticides are needed for high yields, but they can lead to toxicity hazards that may neutralize the benefits of increased food production. These and other constraints lead to projections that suggest there is a rising probability of global food shortages and resulting problems from malnutrition and silent hunger (Bread for the World, 1993).

THE EQUITY COMPONENT OF SUSTAINABLE DEVELOPMENT

Much of the above description of the impact of population growth on both environment and health might seem to suggest that there is little hope for humans, especially the poor. Rapidly rising numbers of people, excessive consumption of resources, and massive pollution appear to undermine sustainable development and the potential for improving human welfare (Erlich, 1990). Such concerns are becoming more frequent, even though earlier dire predictions have tended not to be fulfilled. Thus far, population growth has not brought an end to the good life.

We hold the more optimistic view that a focus on equity in distribution of services can facilitate a continuation of present positive trends. The pressure of increasing numbers can promote social awareness of the need to make difficult decisions. Decades of research have demonstrated practical means of action (Taylor, 1992). Humans are not like other animals which are limited by the carrying capacity of their environment. There are pragmatic and realistic alternatives (Jolly, 1993) to Maurice King's claim (1993) that, once a population enters a so-called "demographic trap," there is no way out, except to let babies deliberately die.

A basic principle of epidemiology is that to solve a health problem in a population, it is essential that control measures reach the people who are sick or at risk. This may seem self-evident, but it is a principle that has consistently been ignored in programming services for health, population, and development. Those providing services typically try to increase coverage rapidly, simply by making coverage available to people who are most accessible and among whom demand already exists. Trickle-down extension seldom works and the benefits almost always remain with the people who need them least. The main reason that programs such as childhood immunization work is that "surveillance and containment" specifically focus effort on the subgroups in a population where cases still occur. Surveillance for equity can focus action on families where health problems are concentrated.

A dramatic shift in orientation is needed to recognize the potential power of systematic means of making sure that benefits reach the unreached (World Bank, 1993). Equity becomes the common meeting ground for action, bringing together health, population, and development. Without specific provisions for equity, development is preferentially restricted to the affluent and powerful (even under socialized systems). The disenfranchised need the support of systems supporting equity set up from outside the community as a conditionality for funding.

Concern for equity has become almost axiomatic in international rhetoric, but action has not followed. In the UNCED global Agenda 21, the presumption is clearly stated—that nations possessing resources should assist those nations that do not have them. In the past 15 years, "Health for All by the Year 2000," or equity, has been the main slogan of the worldwide primary health care movement promoted by WHO and UNICEF. The vision of universal health care is now part of most national health policies worldwide—even the United States has, under President Clinton, joined in. The pressure for equity increases as more people are left out of basic benefits. Those with inadequate health care seem increasingly to demand that they be included. Those without education demand opportunities for their children. The poor seem to be more willing to use confrontation and social pressure to claim their rights. From Haiti, to Peru, to South Africa, a central component in worldwide movements toward democracy tends to be increasing pressure that resources be distributed more equitably. The countries of Eastern Europe and China, by contrast, are having difficulty maintaining earlier standards of equity during their current economic transitions.

What is promising is that standards and expectations for equitable development are rising. Technology and methods exist by which to make a great difference in the quality of life for the poor. One demonstration of this is that in the last 40 years improvements in child mortality have been greater than in all previous human history (UNICEF, 1993). A potential for equity exists.

Nonetheless, the disparity between rich and poor remains—and in many cases grows. The environmental consequences of this inequity are frightening. One-fourth of the global population consumes three-fourths of the world's natural resources and generates three-fourths of its solid waste. Less than 10 percent of the most affluent generate more than half of the heat-trapping greenhouse gases. The average U.S. resident produces 8.7 times more pollution than the average resident of China, and 14.3 times more than an Indian (World Resources Institute, 1992). What will happen to the global environment when the hundreds of millions of China and India start to assume their equitable share of economic wealth? The pursuit toward that equity will endanger the welfare of all.

CONCLUSION

The solution lies in finding ways to empower communities so that they can solve their own problems. Whereas a host of well-intentioned words have been spoken about "bottom-up" community development, the truth is that "top-down" leadership, technical assistance, monitoring, and resource allocation are also needed. How to create effective, self-reliant partnerships at the community level is no longer an unknown process. Neither is it impossible to expand from effective demonstrations at the community level to larger region-wide extensions at considerable levels of scale (Taylor-Ide, 1995).

Sometimes conditions have to get very bad before people spontaneously develop awareness and demand change. One unfortunate result is that environmental thresholds may be crossed, and permanent long-term damage may occur before consumption and behavioral patterns change. However, the pace of change, both negative and positive, seems to be accelerating. New approaches make it possible to get relevant scientific information from those who know to those who need to know. The key is to channel spontaneous currents for change and to use scientific surveillance to guide a shift to new paradigms for action. This approach can help people intervene at optimal and cost-effective points and minimize long-term damage to human environment. People can adapt technology and social organization to their local situations.

Community-based approaches can promote smooth transitions in health and demography. To facilitate effective care, mechanisms are needed to identify the groups with the greatest health problems in order to focus on meeting their needs. Surveillance for equity (Taylor, 1992) provides an analytical mechanism to combine an effective management tool with the moral imperative of reaching the unreached, and to help focus services for health, family planning, environment and socioeconomic development.

In the UNICEF *1992 State of the World's Children Report*, Jim Grant said that a new world ethic is needed (UNICEF, 1992). A recent article in *Science* (Stern, 1993) was even more radical, in suggesting that a new science, as well as a new ethic, are needed to understand human–

environment interactions. Equity should be a central concern of all societies as populations adjust to growth and redistribution.

Population growth resulting from delays in completing the health and demographic transitions has occurred in virtually every human community that survives. This growth interacts strongly with health and social systems. Two results of population growth are significantly greater demands from growing numbers of the elderly, and continued urbanization with increasing new health and environmental stresses. In the past it has been possible to limit environmental degradation by adapting technology and social organization. If progress in technology and social organization are not accelerated, health problems and food shortages will increase.

Effective ways of ameliorating the impact of population growth on human habitat and health now exist. The question remains whether we have the will to implement the necessary changes.

REFERENCES

Blacker, J. G. C. (1993). Trends in Demographic Change. *Transactions of the Royal Society of Tropical Medicine, 87, Supplement, S1,* 3–8.

Bongaarts, J. (1986). The Transition in Reproductive Behavior in the Third World. In J. Menkin (Ed.), *World Population and U.S. Policy*. New York: Norton.

Brass, W. (1991). Population Dynamics. In *Oxford Textbook of Public Health.*

Bread for the World (1993). *Hunger 1993—Uprooted People.* (Third Annual Report on the State of World Hunger). Washington, DC: Bread for the World Institute on Hunger and Development.

Brown, L., et al. (1992). *State of the World—1992.* New York: Norton.

Cassen, R. H. (1993). Economic Implications of Demographic Change. *Transactions of the Royal Society of Tropical Medicine, 87, Supplement, S1,* 13–18.

CIESIN (1992). *Pathways of Understanding, The Interactions of Humanity and Global Environmental Change.* University Center, MI: Consortium for International Earth Science Information Network.

Cochrane, S., & Sai, F. (1993). Excess Fertility. In D. T. Jamison et al. (Eds.), *Disease Control Priorities in Developing Countries.* New York: Oxford University Press.

Demeny, P. (1989). *Demography and the Limits to Growth.* (Population Council, Working Paper #2). New York: Population Council.

Doll, R. (1992). Health and the Environment in the 1990s. *American Journal of Public Health, 82,* 933–941.

Erlich, P. R., & Erlich, A. H. (1990). *The Population Explosion.* New York: Simon & Schuster.

Hardin, G. (1993). *Living Within Limits.* New York: Oxford University Press.

Hardoy, J. E., Mitlin, D., & Satterthwaite, D. (1992). *Environmental Problems in Third World Cities.* London: Earthscan Publications.

Institute of Medicine (1990). *Healthy People 2000: Citizens Chart the Course.* Washington, DC: National Academy Press.

IIASA (1992). *Population, Environment & Development.* Laxenburg, Austria: Author.

Jolley, C. L., & Torrey, B. B. (1993). *Population and Land Use in Developing Countries.* Washington, DC: National Academy Press.

King, M. (1993). Demographic Entrapment. *Transactions of the Royal Society of Tropical Medicine & Hygiene, 87, Supplement.*

Land, Food and People. United Nations Food and Agriculture Organization (UNFAO) (1984). Rome: UNFAO.

Landrigan, P. J. (1993). Commentary: Environmental Disease—A Preventable Epidemic. *American Journal of Public Health, 82,* 941–943.

Last, J. M. (1993). Global Change: Ozone Depletion, Greenhouse Warming, and Public Health. *Annual Reviews of Public Health, 14,* 115–136.

McMichael, A. J. (1993). Global Environment Change and Human Population Health: A Conceptual and Scientific Challenge for Epidemiology. *International Journal of Epidemiology, 22,* 1–8.

Meadows, D. H., Meadows, D. L., & Randers, J. (1992). *Beyond the Limits: Confronting Global Collapse, Envisioning a Sustainable Future.* Post Mills, VT: Chelsea Green Publishing.

Mosley, W. H., et al. (1993). The Health Transition. In D. T. Jamison et al. (Eds.), *Disease Control Priorities in Developing Countries.* New York: Oxford University Press.

Satterthwaite, D. (1993). The Impact on Health of Urban Environments. *Environment and Urbanization, 5(2),* 87–111.

Shahi, G. S. (1994). Implications of Population Dynamics and Natural Resource Use on Carrying Capacity and Sustainable Development. In *Proceedings of the First International Session of the LEAD Program.* New York: The Rockefeller Foundation.

Stern, P. C. (1993). A Second Environmental Science: Human–Environment Interactions. *Science, 260,* 25 June.

Tabibzadeh, I., Rossi-Espagnet, A., & Maxwell, R. (1989). *Spotlight on the Cities: Improving Urban Health in Developing Countries.* Geneva: World Health Organization.

Taylor, C. E., et al. (1983). *Child and Maternal Health Services in Rural India, Vol 2, Integrated Family Planning and Health Care.* (World Bank Research Publication). Baltimore: Johns Hopkins University Press.

Taylor, C. E., & Hall, M. F. (1967). Health, Population and Economic Development. *Science, 157,* 651–657.

Taylor, C. E., Parker, R., & Zeng, D. L. (1991). Public Health Policies and Strategies in China. In W. W. Holland et al. (Eds.) *Oxford Textbook of Public Health.* Oxford: Oxford University Press.

Taylor, C. E. (1992). Surveillance for Equity in Primary Health Care: Policy Implications from International Experience. *International Journal of Epidemiology, 21,* 1043–1049.

Taylor-Ide, D., & Taylor, C. E. (1995). *Community Based Sustainable Human Development: A Proposal for Going to Scale With Self-Reliant Social Development.* Primary

Environmental Care Discussion Papers No. 1. New York: UNICEF, Environment Section.

United Nations (1989). *Prospects of World Urbanization, 1998*. Population Studies #112: New York: United Nations.

United Nations (1992). *Long Range World Population Projects: Two Centuries of Population Growth: 1950–2150*. New York: United Nations.

UNICEF-UNEP (1990). *The State of the Environment—1990: Children and the Environment*. New York and Nairobi: United Nations Children's Fund and United Nations Environment Program.

UNICEF (1992). *The State of the World's Children Report*. New York: United Nations Children's Fund.

UNICEF (1993). *The State of the World's Children Report*. New York: United Nations Children's Fund.

UNDP (1990). *Human Development Report*. New York: Oxford University Press.

UNFA (1989). *The Water Crisis and Population*. Rome: United Nations Food and Agriculture Organization.

UNFPA (1993). *The State of the World Population Report—The Individual and the World: Population, Migration and Development in the 1990s*. New York: UNFPA.

World Bank (1993). *World Development Report 1993—Investing in Health*. New York: Oxford University Press.

WHO Commission on Health and the Environment (1992). *Our Planet, Our Health*. Geneva: World Health Organization.

World Resources Institute, & International Institute for Environment & Development, United Nations Environment Programme (1988). *World Resources 1988–1989*. New York: Basic Books.

World Resources Institute (1992). *World Resources, 1992–93, A Guide to the Global Environment*. New York: Oxford University Press.

5

Water and Environmental Sanitation—A Reflection on Capacity Building

Frank Hartvelt

What does water and environmental sanitation mean to the common man, woman and child?

- A girl carries a jug of water 4 hours a day: 2 hours going to the well, 2 hours coming back;
- A young child dies from dehydration caused by diarrhea;
- A mother tells her children to wash their hands after going to the latrine;
- A sanitary engineer designs a water and sanitation project;
- A technician repairs a water pipe;
- A garbage collector brings trash to a recycling site;
- A health worker gives oral rehydration therapy to a child;
- A doctor teaches hygiene practices to pregnant women;
- A community looks after its water supply.

Many more examples could be given to illustrate familiar scenes in the daily life of people and communities throughout the developing world.

In 1980, the General Assembly of the United Nations proclaimed the eighties to be the International Water Supply and Sanitation Decade (IDWSSD). Ten years later, statistics collected by the World Health Organization (WHO) stated that 1.3 billion people had gained access to potable water supplies and 700 million to sanitation. Impressive as these achievements might be, they could not hide the fact that they virtually matched the global population increase over that period.

The subject of water and sanitation is blessed with a rich literature. One finds scholarly works dealing with high technology, case studies ranging from one to fifty pages, thousands of project reports, declarations of international conferences, and many other types of documents and publications. The fascination with water and sanitation is described in ancient Egyptian texts and U.N. documents of the 1990s, spanning over four thousand years of recorded history. As stated by Mr. Daniel Okun, *in agua sanitas* led the ancient Romans to invest heavily in public water supply facilities, some of which are still in service. "Public water supplies in Western Europe and America resulted in the virtual disappearance of cholera and typhoid before immunizations and other medical measures were introduced."

Nowadays, bureaucrats require more complex justifications than the Romans when dealing with public investments, for example, sector-strategies formulation, effective demand, "willingness-to-pay" studies, pricing, cost recovery, community participation, and health impact.

The literature is rather sparse when it comes to describing the hopes and aspirations of people, whether women in a village or dwellers in cities. Recent years have witnessed a growing interest in studies on the impact of water supply and sanitation (Okun, 1988; Briscoe, 1993), empowerment of communities (Srinivasan, 1990), and health behavior (Boot & Cairncross, 1993).

One of the major lessons learned—and increasingly applied—from the IDWSSD, is that active participation by communities in the planning and implementation of water supply and sanitation projects is vital for the long-term functioning of these facilities, whether financed by small or large investments. For communities to make decisions they need access to information on technologies including improved wells, robust hand-pumps, piped systems and house taps, and techniques which help them to make the right choice such as the "willingness-to-pay" methodology and community management.

By placing the interests of communities and their component households at the forefront, local, national and international agencies will see, and are already seeing, their investments last much longer compared with the more traditional approach—now increasingly overtaken—of government project planning and implementation, where engineers and their crews go to a village, drill a bore hole, and install a pump—surrounded by onlookers who find it very interesting. (See Box 5.1.)

Experience shows that top-down approaches rarely work. "It is the government's pump and not our own," the villagers might comment. Therefore "it is the government's job to maintain it." However, the government is often ill-equipped to do the job. The opposite approach can be illustrated by the following anecdote, in which engineers had engaged in a dialogue with the villagers, especially the women, about the site selection and ownership of a new well. The women wanted the well close to

Box 5.1—Making Community Management Happen: Lessons from Experience*

Successful community management does not happen by accident. Projects and programs must actively and systematically pursue it as a goal, and create the right conditions in which a self-reliant, community-based approach can work. A study of 122 completed rural water supply projects from around the developing world revealed that the following factors positively contribute to raising the level of popular participation:

- The establishment of clear project goals and strategies, based on a consensus of agency and community views;
- A strong commitment by project managers to a participatory process and willingness to respond positively to community views;
- Willingness by managers and supervisors to listen to and respect the views of field-based staff;
- The development of flexible project strategies, with a high degree of decentralized control;
- A balance between community and agency decision-making powers, which favors the community;
- The extensive use of local knowledge and existing forms of local organization;
- Project approaches which fit comfortably into existing forms of local organization; and
- The existence of a broader social and political context which is conducive to popular participation and control.

* *Source*: *Community Management Today: The Role of Communities in the Management of Improved Water Supply Systems*. The Hague: IRC, June 1993.

their homes, next to trees, where they could not only fill their buckets with water but also chat in the shade of a tree. Furthermore, they wanted a pump they could easily maintain themselves, with a few tools and parts, an apron, wash-basins and water run-off to a fruit tree garden. The women said that they would collect monthly fees for maintenance, provided the community would own the pump. Thus everybody proceeded. After a year the village committee of three women responsible for pump maintenance and fee collection went to the local agricultural bank to deposit their money. Much to their surprise, the banker said he could not accept the money, since he could only accept money related to agriculture from people with some form of legal status. Since the women could fulfill neither requirement, they found themselves at an impasse. Fortunately, the local and foreign staff of the project intervened at the central government level with the ministries of agriculture, health, public works, and local government, resulting in the permission given to the agricultural bank to accept "nonagricultural" money from three women with community-group status. In addition, the women noticed that the fees collected far exceeded the cost of maintenance, whereupon the community decided to use the money to buy seeds for vegetable growing and some agricultural implements. Similar stories can be heard throughout the developing world, illustrating the natural link between environment, health, development, and community empowerment: no mud around the well, less diarrheal disease, extra income, and self-reliance (see Box 5.2).

Box 5.2—Three Key Hygiene Behaviors Could Lead to the Greatest Reduction in Diarrheal Morbidity*

- Safer disposal of feces, particularly feces of young children and babies and of people with diarrhea;
- Handwashing, after defecation, after handling babies' feces, before feeding and eating, and before handling food; and
- Maintaining drinking water free from fecal contamination, in the home and at the source.

* *Source*: *Improving Water and Sanitation Hygiene Behaviours: For the Reduction of Diarrhoeal Disease.* Geneva: WHO, June 1993.

Quantitative achievements of the IDWSSD show that the number of people with access to sanitation is half the number of people who gained access to safe water. While many reasons can be cited for this lag, as with water, the solution can be found in checking with the people as to their needs and aspirations. In recent years, a series of "willingness-to-pay" studies have been carried out for both water and sanitation. In brief, the method used in interviews with the local people is as follows: People are asked to consider different types and costs of technologies, ranging from low-cost, simple systems, to more expensive and sophisticated ones. For example, in the case of sanitation, they would consider an in-house latrine attractive, but would not be prepared to pay the higher price, as compared with a simple latrine in an outhouse in the yard. This method is more and more used in the preparation of loans and grants, whereby a part of the funds are covered by the people themselves, with the balance loaned and to be wholly or partially recovered from periodic collection of charges. Apart from monetary concerns, there are indications that local customs, convenience, privacy, and status play an important role in the decision-making process.

Whereas much experience has been gained with the improvement and expansion of water supply and sanitation in rural areas—with emphasis on low-cost community-based systems—much less is known on how best to deal with the people living between the rural areas and city centers—the urban fringe people.

People born in urban fringe areas, together with people from rural areas, who migrated to the cities, can be counted in the millions around many cities on all continents. Generally speaking, these people do not own the land on which they "squat" and have no or very limited access to municipal services (see Hardoy & Satterthwaite, 1989). For example, it is not uncommon to see water reservoirs on the outskirts of a city, with pipelines leading to the city center and areas where the better-off live, thus by-passing the unserved urban fringe populations. In spite of their poverty, these people in the so-called informal sector are resourceful in improving their lives. People in the *pueblos jovenes* of Lima, Peru, exemplify what can be done. Pooling resources, community representatives approached the city's water supply company and negotiated access to a huge water tank located in the hills outside the city. The company agreed to provide a limited quantity of water, and the community agreed to pay for the small-bore pipelines leading to a number of strategically located standposts where families could collect a minimum quantity of water daily. Their payments for this city water were much less than what they used to pay to mobile water vendors. Incidentally, community resourcefulness was also applied to create a transportation system to shuttle people to often far-away work places, to set up health clinics, organize basic education services in schools, and establish community centers.

Urban utilities in charge of water and sewerage conjure up images of big investments, big systems, and big deficits. Many utilities in developing countries are financially unviable, because the water tariffs are low and wastage and leakage are high (often exceeding 50 percent). Thus they need to depend on government subsidies to deal with operation, maintenance, and expansion. It is a paradox that the people who can afford to pay higher tariffs—the better-off in the cities—pay low rates, whereas the urban-fringe population—the poor and less well-off—pay a high price for water sold by private water vendors (up to ten times the price of city water). Fortunately, there is evidence that governments and municipalities are taking measures to make utilities more profitable and efficient to meet increasing demand and, in this process, they also increasingly rely

Box 5.3—Promoting Affordable Sanitation for the Urban Poor*

In Kumasi, Ghana's second-largest city, the UNDP/World Bank Water and Sanitation Programme has helped to improve both public and household latrines serving poor communities taking into account the results of a willingness-to-pay study. Small loans to tenant groups have supported construction of Ventilated Improved Pit (VIP) latrines in several neighborhoods. With advice and support from the Programme, management of public latrines has been taken over by private Ghanaian companies. The result is better services and savings for the city.

* *Source*: Improving Water and Sanitation Services for the Poor. (A UNDP-World Bank Water and Sanitation Programme document). World Bank, 1993.

on private-sector management or ownership. The key factor is to give utilities a large degree of financial and managerial autonomy. As in the case of rural and urban fringe populations, "enabling" the utility to run its business is the crux of the matter. (See Box 5.3.)

The foregoing sketches have been translated in more formal language found in the declarations of a number of international conferences which have taken place in recent years. A dominant feature found in these conferences, which are summarized below, was the realization that, if people, communities, and utilities are empowered to run their business—with the concomitant breaking-down of political, legal, and institutional barriers—they will take responsibility for their own development and will find the resources to do so, whether from within the community or with support from the outside—typically national and international agencies (multilateral, bilateral, and nongovernmental organizations) and the private sector.

It is now widely recognized that the best guardians of water resources and the environment are people working hand in hand with institutions. Institutions are found at all levels, with each of them playing its part and interacting within a larger whole: for example, women caretakers of wells, farmers' associations, community health centers, utilities, government ministries, and external support agencies. Indeed, better trained people and responsive institutions are essential to move ahead. In addition, people, both as providers and users of water for domestic purposes, agriculture, and industry, can no longer live in blissfull ignorance of each other. Consumers, technicians, engineers, economists, managers, and politicians have no other choice but to better understand each other and work together if social and economic needs are to be met in a balanced and equitable manner (Hartvelt & Okun, 1991). Clearly, safe water supply and sanitation, and availability of water for agriculture and industry, are the basic underpinnings of an environment for sustainable human development.

The international cooperation agenda for the nineties was shaped by six global meetings, each of which looked at the water and sanitation from a different perspective. A common theme in these meetings was the importance of capacity building. (See Box 5.4.)

Near the conclusion of the International Drinking Water Supply and Sanitation Decade, in September 1990, UNDP organized and the Government of India hosted the Global Consultation on Safe Water and Sanitation for the 1990s. The Consultation reviewed the progress during the Decade and made a number of recommendations for the future. These recommendations, endorsed by the U.N. General Assembly, formed the basis of actions which should be taken during the 1990s. During the Decade, the international community as a whole made the provision of improved water supply and sanitation facilities a top priority, and rallied to the support of Decade goals and objectives. Some 1.3 billion people in the developing world gained access to safe drinking water and 700 million to sanitation facilities for the first time in their lives. The New Delhi Statement, prepared at the Global Consultation, contained four guiding principles, two directly related to capacity building: "Strong institutions are essential for sustainable development," and "Capacity building is necessary to make community management effective . . ." Two others, environment and health, and financing and technology, depend for their implementation on strong sustainable institutions.

Box 5.4—Teamwork Makes Time for Capacity Building*

The development of a team approach based on close inter-ministerial collaboration has been found to be an important factor leading to success in the UNICEF-supported South West Integrated Programme (SWIP) in Uganda. The formation of teams, including community development and health workers, as well as technical staff, has helped to restrain the technicians desire to "get on with it" and ensure that the necessary time is taken to properly prepare communities for their future role as managers.

* *Source*: *Community Management Today: The Role of Communities in the Management of Improved Water Supply Systems.* The Hague: IRC, June 1993.

The concept of and prospects for capacity building were further elaborated during the UNDP Symposium, "A Strategy for Water Resources Capacity Building"—held in Delft, the Netherlands, in June 1991. A major issue addressed in the Delft Declaration is the daunting challenge "to satisfy the water needs of the exploding cities, given the equally increasing need for water for irrigated agriculture and the problems arising from urban and industrial pollution. In addition, to do this in a sustainable way, measures have to be taken to protect and conserve water as a major resource and unifying element of our environment. Experience shows that institutional weaknesses and malfunctions are a major cause of ineffective and unsustainable water services. This requires urgent attention to building institutional capacity at all levels. Pressure for improved local delivery of water services suggests that development of institutional capacity be more demand-responsive. Also, the need to better manage overall water resources coherently and facilitate allocation of water among all users suggests an expansion of national, integrated planning." The participants in the Delft Symposium, coming from developing countries, external support agencies, and institutions, recognized the importance of the capacity building process for sustainable development at national, subregional, and local levels. The capacity building concept was articulated as follows:

- Creation of an enabling environment with appropriate policy and legal frameworks;
- Institutional development, including community participation; and
- Human resources development and strengthening of managerial systems.

Subsequently, on the road to the Earth Summit in Rio (the United Nations Conference on Environment and Development—UNCED), a unique event took place in January 1992, in Dublin, Ireland: the International Conference on Water and the Environment. This Conference made recommendations for action at local, national, and international levels, based on four guiding principles: the finiteness and vulnerability of water resources; participatory approaches to water management involving users, planners, and policymakers; women playing a central part in the provision, management, and safeguarding of water; and the economic value of water. Again, capacity building was recognized as a principal element in the development, use, and management of water resources.

The United Nations Conference on the Environment and Development (UNCED, Rio de Janeiro, June 1992), elaborated the concept of sustainable development in its *Agenda 21*, which addresses water and environmental sanitation issues from different vantage points, for example, poverty, human settlements, agricultural and rural development, and integrated approaches to development, management, and use of water resources. Consistently, the vital role of people, communities, and institutions was emphasized.

Box 5.5*

"Community participation in decision-making cannot be put on tap, to be turned on and off when desired. Participatory methods must be consistent—and consistently used—throughout the cycle of planning, implementation and evaluation."

* *Source*: *Taking the Pulse: For Community Management in Water and Sanitation.* (UNDP, PROWWESS, September 1990).

Most recently, the Political Statement and Action Programme, adopted by the Ministerial Conference on Drinking Water and Environmental Sanitation—Implementing UNCED Agenda 21 (Noordwijk, The Netherlands, March 23–24 1994) singled out *capacity building* as the key concept for sustainable development of drinking water and environmental sanitation services. To quote, "We, the Ministers . . . stress that behavioural change, development of the knowledge base, education of experts, partnership of stakeholders, full commitment of all partners, and capacity building, are essential for success; seek to accelerate moves to develop enabling, supporting and regulatory frameworks which facilitate the maximum involvement of local agencies and individuals in programmes to improve the living environment; seek enhanced priority for institutional strengthening and human resource development programmes which will create organizational and management capacity for local delivery and upkeep of water and environmental sanitation services; advocate the application of sound economic principles to allocation and pricing of water, based on the principle that water is a social and economic good, while recognizing that it is a basic human need." The Noordwijk Political Statement and Action Programme—adopted by the United Nations Commission on Sustainable Development—provides a comprehensive and firm basis for action at the local, national, and international levels.

It is recalled that a strong commitment in favor of universal access to safe drinking water and sanitary means of excreta disposal emerged from the World Summit for Children in 1990 (New York), where world leaders agreed on goals for children and development in the 1990s including health, nutrition, water and sanitation, and basic education.

What is the response of the international community to the expectations raised and recommendations made by the Conferences in New York, New Delhi, Delft, Dublin, Rio, and Noordwijk? Virtually all international development agencies support water-related programs. International and regional development banks and many bilateral agencies have a substantial part of their grant or lending portfolios devoted to agricultural irrigation, water supply, and sanitation. Likewise, United Nations system agencies are very active in this area. By supporting the principles and recommendations of the above conferences, both developing countries and the external support agencies have committed themselves to adapt their water and environmental sanitation programs to the needs of the nineties and beyond.

The United Nations agencies are well placed to take a leading role in the response from the international community by providing policy, technical, and financial support to countries which are committed to reorienting their development cooperation programs in line with the aforementioned principles and recommendations, as applicable to the countries' conditions. In order to do so credibly, the United Nations agencies themselves need to reexamine and reorient their role in order to be up to the challenge.

The following interrelated approaches could be considered.

- Strong advocacy for water and sanitation as a critical factor impacting on health, economic, and environmental development. United Nations agencies should place water and sanitation squarely among other essential building blocks for sustainable human development.
- Explicit commitment to support the implementation of the principles and recommendations of the international conferences held in New York, New Delhi, Delft, Dublin, Rio, and Noordwijk.
- The functioning of the U.N. agencies as a "system," unencumbered by political and commercial strings attached to programs and projects. Agreement could be reached informally about "lead agencies" responsible for certain issues/areas related to water and sanitation, for example, water resources management, capacity building, environmental action plans, gender, urbanization, recycling, irrigation, and involvement of schools.
- Joint operations of U.N. agencies. Combining efforts at the country level, particularly drawing on the 400–500 engineers, social scientists, program and other officers working in the offices and projects of UNICEF, WHO, UNDDSMS (U.N. Water branch), UNDP, and the World Bank could potentially lead to a more effective and efficient support structure for sector development. This could include joint efforts to support preparation of sector strategies, testing and imple-

mentation of common approaches, multi-agency project funding and implementation, and so forth. Equally important, it would avoid overlapping.
- Linkages to U.N. deliberative and decision-making bodies, such as the General Assembly, ECOSOC, the Commission on Sustainable Development, and the assemblies and boards of U.N. agencies.
- Monitoring of global, regional, and country targets.

Recent years have witnessed a marked improvement in policy coordination among U.N. and bilateral agencies. Also, at the field level, one can observe increased interagency collaboration. Reality, however, suggests that economic and political forces impose limits, especially on the degree to which bilateral agencies are cooperating with others.

For its part, UNDP has adopted the following approach to "upstream" water sector development, translated into three interrelated global programs supported by UNDP and partner agencies.

1. *The UNDP/World Bank Water and Sanitation Program,* supported by ten bilateral agencies, which concentrates on low-cost, community-based water and sanitation, and increasingly on urban sanitation. The program is committed to a threefold strategy of working with partners to support sustainable investments, to build the capacity of governments and people to develop and maintain systems, and to exchange knowledge.
2. *The Utility Partnership: Capacity Building for Urban Water and Sanitation Utilities,* initiated by UNDP and the World Bank, which concentrates on improving the efficiency of utilities and water conservation/demand management.
3. *The Capacity Building Program for Sustainable Water Sector Development,* which emerged from the Delft Symposium. This program, which is currently being initiated and supported by UNDP, UNDDSMS (U.N. Water branch), the World Bank, and The Netherlands, places capacity building squarely among the financial, technical, social, and economic elements of water sector programs. To enhance the capacity building process in developing countries, water sector assessments are considered a necessary first step.

These three programs are prime factors in shaping "downstream" programs supported by UNDP and other external support agencies at the country level. Under the umbrella of capacity building, UNDP will devote increased attention to the following approaches. In terms of financing, greater efficiency should be combined with mobilization of additional resources. Second, new public–private partnerships are vital for sustaining water sector programs. Third, collaboration is stimulated among all

Box 5.6—Sustainable Human Development*

Sustainable human development is development that meets today's challenges of mass poverty and human deprivation, unprecedented inequalities and social disintegration, and chronic environmental decline. It is the kind of development that not only generates growth but also distributes it equitably. Rather than marginalizing people, it enhances their capabilities, empowers them to participate in the decisions affecting their lives, provides them with decent jobs, and lifts them out of poverty. It regenerates the environment, rather than destroying it.

Source: UNDP *Annual Report*, 1993.

participants in this effort, both nationally and internationally. Indeed, much money can be saved by avoiding duplicative efforts and applying proven solutions. Fourth, innovation is essential: fresh ideas, imaginative approaches, appropriate technologies, and new attitudes. In this connection, a wide array of technologies, techniques, and methodologies are available for testing, adaptation, and adoption. Finally, strengthening and adaptation of institutions, in tandem with human resources development, is a *conditio sine qua non* for the successful implementation of water and environmental sanitation programs in the long term.

In conclusion, the stage is set for a quantum leap by the developing countries themselves to serve the unserved with the help of the international community. The cause of sustainable human development will be well served.

REFERENCES

Alaerts, G. J., Blair, T. L., & Hartvelt, F. J. A. (Eds.) (1991). *A Strategy for Water Sector Capacity Building: Proceedings of the UNDP Symposium, Delft, the Netherlands, 3–5 June 1991.* (IHE Report Series 24).

Boot, M. T. M., & Cairncross, S. (1993). *Actions Speak. The Study of Hygiene Behaviour in Water and Sanitation Projects.* IRC International Water and Sanitation Centre and the London School of Hygiene and Tropical Medicine, IRC.

Briscoe, J. (1993). When the Cup Is Half Full. *Environment, 35(4).*

Hardoy, J., & Satterthwaite, D. (1989). *Squatter Citizen, Life in the Urban Third World.* London: Earthscan Publications.

Hartvelt, F., & Okun, D. (1991). Capacity Building for Water Resources Management. *Water International, 16(3).*

International Conference on Water and the Environment, Development Issues for the 21st Century, 26 January 1992, Dublin, Ireland; The Dublin Statement and Report of the Conference.

Ministerial Conference on Drinking Water and Environmental Sanitation: Implementing UNCED Agenda 21, Noordwijk, The Netherlands, 23–23 March 1994, Political Statement and Action Programme.

UNDP (1990). Some for All Rather than More for Some. *The New Delhi Statement, Report of the Global Consultation on Safe Water and Sanitation for the 1990s.* New Delhi, India: UNDP.

Okun, D. A. (1988). The Value of Water Supply and Sanitation in Developments: An Assessment. *American Journal of Public Health, 78(11).*

Srinivasan, L. (1990). *Tools for Community Participation: A Manual for Training Trainers in Participatory Techniques.* New York: PROWWESS/UNDP.

United Nations Conference on Environment and Development (UNCED), Rio de Janeiro, Brazil, 28–29 May 1992, Agenda 21.

UNDP (1993). *World Bank Water and Sanitation Program Annual Report, July 1992–June 1993.*

United Nations Development Programme (UNDP), *Annual Report 1993.*

United Nations, Water Resources: Progress in the Implementation of the Mar del Plata Action. Doc. E/C.7/199/8, New York, February 1991.

World Bank (1993). The Demand for Water in Rural Areas: Determinants and Policy Implications. *World Bank Research Observations 8, (1).*

6

Food Security—Its Implications on Health

Steven A. Esrey

INTRODUCTION

Historical Perspective

Food insecurity conjures up images of hunger and starvation. It is natural that people associate food security with the quantity of food, given the log of recorded famines throughout human history as well as the frequent periodic famines that have occurred in the world since 1945 (Foster, 1992). In 1798 Thomas Malthus of England predicted that population growth would outstrip the supply of food (Malthus, 1963). Although population has grown exponentially, as predicted, the world supply of food has kept pace with increases in population and there is currently enough food to ensure an adequate supply of protein and energy for all people. For example, over the past 25 years, per capita energy intake increased by 14%, from 9,974 kJ to 11,347 kJ, despite the addition of nearly 2 billion people during this time period (World Bank, 1992). However, millions of people do not have access to an adequate supply of food. Thus, Malthus' doomsday prediction has not yet occurred on a global level. The dire consequences of his prediction, hunger and starvation, however, exist today.

Systematic concerns with food security began with the declaration of food as a human right in 1948 (United Nations, 1948). During the next 30 years different institutions were established and conferences were held to deal with food, hunger, and cereal production. The World Food Crisis, which began in 1972, prompted the establishment of a Committee on World Food Security and a Global Information and Early Warning System by FAO. At this time interest in food security centered around large-scale food production initiatives. The famines of the mid-1980s produced national plans with economic incentives to alleviate the problem. Many of those efforts continue today.

Along the way, criticism of efforts to define food insecurity, and understand its causes, came from concerned groups and citizens (George, 1976; Lappé, 1979). They illustrated the myths about the perception of the problem and tried to redefine how to think about the issues. The recent explosion of information on food security has fostered a variety of views on the subject. Many disciplines address food security issues, and there are as many approaches and strategies as players, because the data are sparse, poorly defined, and imprecise, and a conceptual framework does not exist to rally people around a unifying approach. Furthermore, potential intervention strategies are numerous and poorly coordinated among the major institutions focusing on food security.

Definition of Food Security

Numerous attempts have been made to define food security, and more than 30 definitions were summarized recently (Maxwell & Frankenberger, 1993). All food security definitions incorporate multiple concepts. While definitions vary from source to source, in general, most adhere to the importance of access to an adequate supply of food (i.e., energy) for all people. Some definitions specify that food should be adequate for basic needs or for an active and/or healthy life. The following comprehensive, but succinct definition of food security is proposed: sustained access by all individuals to adequate and safe food for an active, healthy and productive life. This definition incorporates six key components, which are discussed below.

1. The term *sustained* connotes a time element to food security. People must be able to secure food at all times and not risk lapsing into even temporary periods of inadequate or unsafe food. In an ideal world, no one would be at risk of food insecurity. However, many of those at risk lapse into temporary food insecurity and, if the situation persists, wind up in a chronic food-insecure situation. Classification of food insecurity into transitory, seasonal, potential chronic, and chronic (Huddleston, 1990), masks the degrees of intensity or the severity of the situation (Maxwell, 1990). Both temporary and chronic food insecurity can be either severe or mild.
2. *Access to food* means the freedom to obtain food. It places equal emphasis on the production, distribution, and intake of food. Access to food also implies that the resources necessary to acquire food should be accessible to all individuals. Access further implies that the determinants (e.g., physical and economic assets) of food

security deserve higher priority than emergency measures to alleviate food insecurity. A distinction should be made between the term *intake* and the term *consumption*. Use of the term *consumption* could result in a different interpretation because economists understand it to mean acquisition to food, whereas nutritionists perceive it as ingestion (Jonsson & Toole, 1991).

3. The use of the term *individual*, instead of people, is intended to emphasize the importance of an individual, household or community level analysis, as opposed to a global or continental analysis. The world is not food insecure, but individuals are. The initial global approach was used, in part, because dietary adequacy was calculated by national food balance sheets, which included production and import data. More recently, the problem of food insecurity has been regarded as one of access to and intake of available food with a focus directed to individuals and households. A nation may have sufficient food for all those living within its borders, but pockets of food insecurity often exist in certain regions and many households have some individuals who are food insecure.
4. *Adequate food* has usually meant that people should consume sufficient energy. Adequate, however, is poorly defined, due, in part, to the changing recommended energy intakes over time (Payne, 1990) and variability in individual requirements, which are difficult to measure (ACC/SCN, 1993). The term has rarely included adequacy of protein or micronutrients such as iron, iodine, or Vitamin A (Kennedy et al., 1992). Monotonous diets may be deficient in one or more of these nutrients. Adequacy, therefore, should include other nutrients, as well as energy.
5. *A safe*[1] *supply* of food has implications for food that is free of contamination. Food contamination can be from any of the following sources: biological (e.g., Escherichia coli or Giardia lamblia), chemical (e.g., lead or mercury), pesticides (e.g., DDT and its metabolites), veterinary drugs (anabolic or antibacterial drugs), and toxins (myco-, marine, and plant). Contamination can occur in breast milk for infants, in weaning foods for young children, and in other food consumed by older children and adults. Safe food implies that these contaminants should exist below a level that does not threaten health and nutrition, or simply should not exist.

[1] Food safety is the official term used by the World Health Organization for all of the conditions and measures that are necessary mainly after harvesting, during storage, processing, distribution, and preparation of food to ensure that it is safe, sound, wholesome, and fit for human consumption.

6. Food security is necessary for *health* and to have an *active and productive life*. It has been well documented that inadequate or unsafe food can lead to lethargy, disease, learning disabilities, reproductive problems, and reduced worker productivity, among other health and non-health consequences (FAO/WHO, 1992b). Thus, ill health and lack of well-being are a direct consequence of being food insecure. Specifying the health-related consequences (i.e., outcomes) of being food insecure is necessary in order to: a) identify the indicator(s) for food security programs, b) estimate the magnitude of the problem, c) provide cut-off points for indicators that measure food security, d) understand mechanisms for intervening, e) identify target populations for intervention, and f) plan and evaluate interventions.

Indicators and Magnitude of the Problem

No single indicator measures all components of food security with any degree of precision. Furthermore, measurement nearly always focuses on proxy indicators related to food security, and the proxy depends, in part, on the conceptualization of the problem, and whether those at risk of, or those who are food insecure, are being sought. Global estimates do not identify problem regions nor do they identify the sociodemographic characteristics of those most vulnerable to food insecurity. This section, therefore, addresses three issues: the number of people who are food insecure, the composition of the population that is most food insecure, and the magnitude of the problem in different parts of the world.

Number of food insecure. The most commonly used indicators to measure food (in)adequacy are income, food intake (national food balance sheets), and anthropometry. Estimates of the number of food insecure for each of these indicators, by region of the world, are shown in Table 6.1. On the basis of these figures, about one-fifth to one-third of the developing world is food insecure.

Twenty percent of the population of the world do not consume even 80 percent of their caloric needs. A similar estimate is obtained if those considered to be severely poor, below 75 percent of the poverty line, are the criterion. An additional 10–20 percent could be considered at risk of becoming food insecure according to these definitions because many people consume between 80–100 percent of their caloric needs or are poor, but not severely poor. One-third of the population in developing countries are below the poverty line. This figure corresponds to the number of malnourished children—33 percent. As a point of comparison, levels of poverty in developed economies are generally low (3–7%). In the United States, 13 percent of all people and 20 percent of all children fall below 40

TABLE 6.1 Percent of Population and Number (in millions) Who Are Food Insecure Using Dietary, Anthropometric, and Income Data from Developing Countries

Country Group	Dietary Intake (<80% of Caloric needs) (FAO Food Balance Sheet, 1990)	Anthropometry (moderately or severely underweight; <–2 Standard deviations of the International Reference)	Income (Extreme poverty, < US$ 275/person/year)
Sub-Saharan Africa	37% (175)	30% (28)	30% (120)
Near East and North Africa	5% (12)	13% (5)	21% (40)
South Asia	24% (277)	60% (101)	29% (300)
Southeast Asia	17% (74)	31% (20)	9% (40)
China (includes countries in East Asia)	16% (189)	22% (24)	8% (80)
Middle America and Caribbean	20% (20)	15% (3)	12% (50) (Middle America and Caribbean and South America combined)
South America	38% (38)	8% (3)	
All developing countries	21% (785)	33% (184)	18% (630)

Sources: ACC/SCN, 1993; World Bank, 1990.

percent of adjusted median income (World Food Council, 1992). For anthropometry, by definition only 2–3 percent of children will be underweight in developed countries.

Other indicators have also been used to estimate food insecurity. For instance, a recent study in 14 African countries conducted by UNICEF estimated the number of food insecure by using a combination of two indicators, *physical and financial access* to food (Mwadime & Baldwin, 1993). The food insecure were defined as those whose food expenditures exceeded 60 percent of all expenditures and/or who travelled more than one hour to obtain food. The food insecure in these 14 countries ranged from 54 percent in Botswana to 98 percent in Mozambique, with a median of 78 percent.

Adult anthropometry can be measured by Body Mass Index (BMI), which is weight (kg)/height $(m)^2$, and values below 18.5 indicate chronic energy deficiency (James et al., 1988). Data provided during the 1980's from 11 Asian and ten African female samples indicate a mean BMI of 20.2 (Krasovic & Anderson, 1991). In Bangladesh the average BMI was less than 18.5, and in the Sudan it was 17.1.

Estimates of the food insecure using *micronutrients* have also been made (ACC/SCN, 1992). For instance, over one billion people (27%) in the world are anemic, and at least half of these are due to deficiencies in iron. Over one billion people are at risk of iodine deficiency, and over 200 million suffer from goiter, an enlargement of the thyroid gland, and cretinism. Nearly 200 million children live in countries where

Vitamin A deficiencies exist, and over 100 million suffer from Vitamin A deficiency.

Good estimates of *food contamination* are difficult to find. It was estimated recently that 15–70 percent of diarrhea episodes are due to food contamination (Esrey & Feachem, 1989). If nearly half of the 1,400 million episodes (Motarjemi et al., 1993) are due to food contamination, then most likely all pre-children suffer from contaminated food, assuming that all children experience episodes of diarrhea.

Difficulties interpreting estimates. When measuring the magnitude of the food insecurity problem, estimates should be interpreted with caution. First, any one component, or indicator, by definition, will underestimate the magnitude of the problem by excluding those who would be counted only by a different indicator that measures a different component. For instance, the number with energy-deficient diets and those exposed to contaminated food may be composed of overlapping and nonoverlapping individuals.

Second, a choice must be made for the cut-off level for any indicator, and such choices influence the magnitude of the problem (Brownie & Habicht, 1984). Depending on the cut-off level of the indicator, the number of food insecure could be doubled or cut in half. For instance, the poverty estimates in Table 6.1 are for the extremely poor, not all poor people. An additional 15 percent of the developing world live below the poverty line, but above the cut-off for extreme poverty (World Bank, 1990).

Third, the estimates from one indicator will identify some individuals as being food insecure, when in fact they are not. For example, anthropometric status of children is often used as an indicator of food insecurity. Some diseases, independent of inadequate or unsafe food, can lower anthropometric status of children.

Fourth, some indicators may identify those at risk and/or those who are actually food insecure. Because of the transitory, or seasonal, phase of food insecurity, errors will be associated with these estimates. For instance, in the Philippines, 60 percent of households that had been classified as having a diet that was greater than 80 percent of requirements, experienced a period below this level at least once during a 16-month study period (Haddad, Sullivan, & Kennedy, 1991). In a sample of Indian agricultural families over a nine-year period, 88 percent of households experienced poverty during this time, but only 19 percent remained poor during the entire period (World Bank, 1990).

Fifth, people adapt to conditions of food insecurity by reducing their intake and/or expenditure of energy. During periods of food insecurity, the weight or activity level of people may be reduced as a biological coping mechanism. Estimates of energy requirements for a reduced body size or a less active person will be lower than estimates for a person of more normal weight or activity, resulting in an underestimate of the number of food insecure.

Population characteristics: Poor populations, who spend a large proportion of their income on food, are either food insecure or at risk of becoming food insecure. The sociodemographic profile of the vulnerable was recently identified by looking at sources of income among malnourished rural poor in Africa, Asia, and Latin America (FAO/WHO, 1992a). In general, the food-insecure households are composed of large families with a high proportion of dependents, particularly young children. Those without land and smallholder farmers who depend on other risky sources of income were also likely to be food insecure. Traditionally, children under five years of age, pregnant and lactating women, and the elderly are the subpopulations among the poor who are most vulnerable to ill health.

Global distribution: All continents have food insecure (Table 6.1), but the two with the highest number and percent of the population, as well as attention by donors, are Asia and Africa (FAO/WHO, 1992a; World Bank, 1986). Of the two, Asia has the higher number due to the high number of food insecure in Bangladesh and India. The percent of food insecure in Asia and Africa have remained stable over time or only slightly increased, but the absolute numbers have increased due to increases in population (World Bank, 1986). Declines have occurred in East Asia and the Middle East, both in percent and absolute numbers.

One-fifth to one-third of the world is food insecure, depending on the indicator and cut-off point for food insecurity. An additional 10–20 percent could be considered at risk of becoming food insecure according to standard definitions. If the problems of food safety and micronutrients are considered, the number of food insecure will be larger. Large, landless families and children and women are at greatest risk, mostly in Asia and Africa, of being food insecure.

DETERMINANTS AND CONSEQUENCES OF FOOD SECURITY

UNICEF has developed a conceptual framework of the causes of malnutrition and death, and inadequate dietary intake and disease are the direct causes of malnutrition (UNICEF, 1990). Poverty, or lack of resources, is the root cause of malnutrition. Resources (environmental, economic and human) affect household food security, caring capacity of households (e.g., food-intake patterns) and environmental conditions (e.g., access to health-care services), all of which influence dietary intake and risk of disease.

Determinants of Food Insecurity

The major underlying problem of food insecurity is poverty. Poverty, which restricts access to resources with which to secure food, is linked to the proximal determinants of food insecurity, the economic, environmental, and sociodemographic situations of individuals. The problem of poverty is simply that poor people do not have sufficient resources to produce or purchase adequate and safe food for sustained food security.

Environmental determinants of food insecurity include land scarcity and degradation, dwindling fuel sources for cooking, pests, overuse of pesticides and fertilizers that reduce crop yield, water salinity due to overirrigation, climate, soil erosion due to overuse or lack of terracing, drought, political instability, war, insufficient access to water, and inadequate sanitation.

Economic determinants include under- and unemployment, low wages, sudden changes in income and prices of food stuffs, unfair terms of trade, exchange rates, and inadequate land ownership.

Demographic factors that are associated with food insecurity include place of residence (rural/urban), household size, lack of education, high numbers of dependent children, inappropriate feeding behaviors, long distance to markets, competing food demands from increasing population, displaced persons, and existing health status.

Each of the determinants affect the production, distribution, and intake of adequate and safe food. However, alleviation of one or more of the constraints listed above, or improvements in access to the resources to acquire food, does not guarantee an adequate and safe intake of food. Food that is acquired by production or trade must be prepared and fed to all individuals in sufficient quantity and quality to ensure food security. Thus, global production of food is less a problem than local distribution and intake of food.

Consequences of Food Insecurity

The consequences of food insecurity are many, but they can be categorized several ways. Health consequences include malnutrition and disease, which often interact in a synergistic fashion, sometimes ending in death. For instance, disease may lead to malnutrition, by causing a reduction in dietary intake, interfering with the absorption of nutrients, and increasing the demand for nutrients above normal levels to fight disease (Tomkins & Watson, 1989). Malnutrition often leads to an increase in the incidence and severity of disease by reducing the immune status of people. Furthermore, there is an increasing risk of death as children become more malnourished, even among children only mildly malnourished (Pelletier et al., 1993). In addition, food insecurity, depending on the duration, severity and timing in one's life can lead to cognitive deficits, reproductive problems, economic productivity losses, and changes in family structure (e.g., more female-headed households because males migrate for work), to mention a few. Each of these affect future health conditions of the food insecure.

Responses to Food Insecurity

Maxwell and Frankenberger (1993) developed a scheme to illustrate response strategies, by households and donors, to increasing risk of food shortages (Figure 6.1). In short, as people's resource base dwindles, their ability to respond to food shortages is weakened. Over time they become more vulnerable, increasing the risk of becoming chronically food insecure over time. There are three main parts to the Maxwell and Frankenberger scheme: household strategies, household vulnerabilities, and donor responses. The shape of the household strategies curve indicates that dwindling resources over time are associated with increased risk and severity (intensity) of food insecurity. Initial responses (Corbett, 1988) to inadequate food include efforts to minimize risk and manage losses of nonproductive assets (e.g., jewelry). During this time of behavioral change, people cope by making adjustments to the new situation. These include intake of fewer meals and altering dietary patterns (e.g., changing the staple cereal or switching to a tuber-based diet). Some biological changes result in a reduction in body size (e.g., weight loss) and expenditure of energy (e.g., reduced activity). Once coping strategies are no longer sufficient to deal with a dwindling resource base and the situation has not stabilized or returned to normal, certain adaptation strategies must be pursued. Adaptive responses result in the depletion of personal, family and community assets, including productive assets (e.g., land). Continued depletion of resources eventually results in permanent out-migration with increased morbidity, malnutrition, or death.

Initial coping strategies are more easily reversible than are adaptation strategies, and once productive assets are divested, it takes longer to recoup these assets when the situation has returned to normal. Donor responses, which range from developmental (preventive) to emergency relief (curative) efforts, will be discussed in more detail below.

RELATIONSHIP BETWEEN FOOD SECURITY AND HEALTH

Inadequate and unsafe food are two principal components of the state of being food insecure. Therefore, it is the health consequences of these

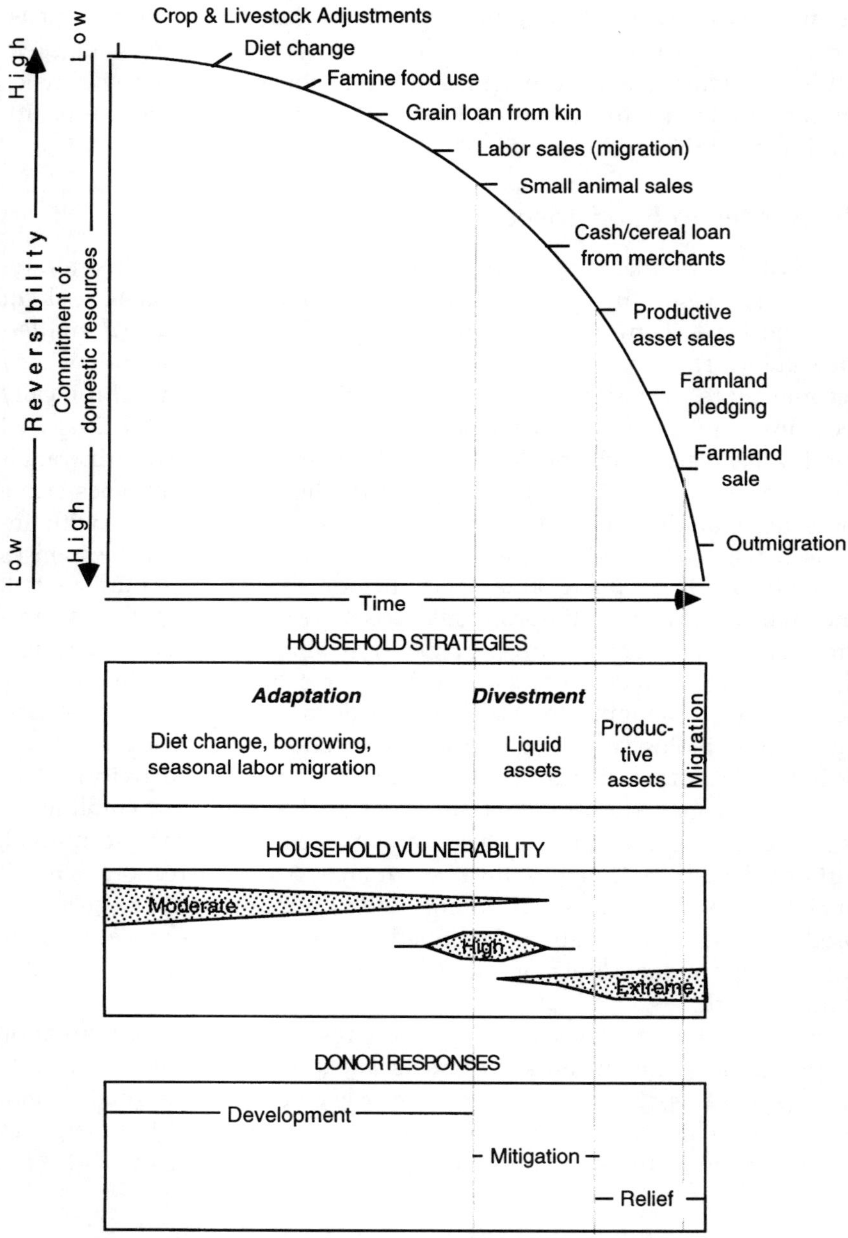

FIGURE 6.1 Responses to food insecurity by households and donors.

conditions that is important (Table 6.2). For the purposes of this section, inadequate food will be defined as deficient intakes of energy, protein and the major micronutrients (Vitamin A, iodine, and iron). For unsafe food the major types of contamination will be examined: biological and chemical. Biological agents that cause food-borne illness are mostly bacteria, viruses, and parasites. Many chemicals can be ingested in food (heavy metals, radioactive pollutants, chlorinated hydrocarbons, pesticide residues, veterinary drugs, mycotoxins, marine and plant toxins, and food additives). Contaminated food, if ingested in sufficient quantities, results in ill health among all segments of the population: infants, preschool and school-aged children, adults, and the elderly. The contaminants may enter the food chain at any point, from production to distribution and preparation prior to intake. Contaminants may be ingested with raw or cooked food. Table 6.2 summarizes the health effect of inadequate and unsafe food.

Food Quantity and Health

The health consequences of inadequate food, particulary energy, protein, and micronutrients, are numerous. Hunger and starvation are severe

TABLE 6.2 Examples of Types of Food Insecurity and Health Consequences

Type of Food Insecurity	*Health Consequences*
Inadequate intake of food	
Energy and protein	Marasmus (energy), kwashiorkor (protein), growth faltering, stunting, delayed age at menarche, increased susceptibility to diarrhea, increased severity and duration of disease, increased mortality, impaired mental development, low birth weight
Vitamin A	Eye damage, blindness, death
Iron	Anemia, reduced work capacity, susceptibility to infection, risk of maternal death at childbirth, impaired cognitive development
Iodine	Goiter/cretinism, reduced mental function and retardation, increased still births and abortions, infant death, delayed motor development, growth failure and stunting, speech and hearing defects.
Unsafe intake of food	
Biological	Diarrhea, growth failure, stunting, death, lethargy, nutritional deficiencies, abortions, fetal malformations, arthritis
Pesticides	Birth defects, low birth weight, cancer, depressed immunity, neurological problems

manifestations of food insecurity, and their physiology has been reviewed recently (Pellet, 1986). Many of the health problems of micronutrient deficiencies are well known, and have also been reviewed (ACC/SCN, 1992). This section briefly summarizes each.

Energy and protein deficits are common and often occur at the same time. They rarely occur in isolation of other nutritional deficiencies, and they share common health problems. Early stages of deficiency result in growth failure, and are readily measured by anthropometry. If severe growth failure occurs, this will lead to severe stunting, short stature relative to a healthy child of the same age, or wasting, which is thinness at a given height relative to a healthy child at the same height. Both stunting and wasting are associated with high mortality. Mental impairment also occurs among energy and protein deficient children. In children with low anthropometric values, decreased resistance to certain infections occurs and severity of diarrhea, such as longer episodes, is increased. Other ill-health conditions include delayed age at menarche, low birth weights, and decreased worker productivity.

The severe form of energy deficits result in marasmus, which is extreme wasting. In young children this can be due to early weaning. Low plasma insulin levels, loss of body fat, and muscle wasting occurs, and anemia, a condition in which the number of red blood cells is reduced, is common. Protein deficiencies, if severe, result in kwashiorkor, which is often a result of abrupt weaning in young children. Wasting is often masked because of edema. In protein deficiency, albumin levels and lipoprotein fractions are reduced. Infections usually precipitate both marasmus and kwashiorkor.

Vitamin A deficiency is caused mainly by low intakes of retinol and beta carotene, dietary sources of Vitamin A. Retinol commonly occurs in some animal products and beta carotene in fruits and vegetables, all of which tend to be consumed in low quantities among the poor. Deficiencies in Vitamin A are known to cause eye damage which, if left uncorrected, will lead to blindness. A review of recent studies indicates that Vitamin A deficiency accounts for a large number of preschool child deaths (Beaton et al., 1992). About 14 million preschool children had eye damage in 1991, and most of these resided in Asia. Up to 500,000 children go blind every year, most of whom die shortly after becoming blind. Eye damage can be reversed if the Vitamin A deficiency is diagnosed and treated early. If the detection is late, irreversible damage to the eye will occur.

Iron deficiency, the most common form of nutritional deficiency, affects mostly children and women in their reproductive years. Anemia, the common manifestation, occurs in over 500 million people as a result of iron deficiency, but it is possible to be deficient in iron without being anemic and anemic without being deficient in iron. Low intakes of iron, particularly heme iron found in animal products account for much of the iron deficiency in the world. Many health problems result from iron deficiency, including reduced work capacity, increased risk of maternal death at childbirth, diminished learning ability, and increased susceptibility to infection.

Iodine deficiency is a common disorder which afflicts over 200 million people in Latin America, Africa, and Asia. Low available iodine in the diet is the most common cause of iodine deficiency, but in some areas goitrogens in the diet, such as cabbage, turnips and rutabaga, can lead to iodine-deficiency disorders. The major overt health problem is goiter, sometimes with visible thyroid enlargement, but other consequences of iodine deficiency include mental retardation, and in pregnant women increased stillbirths, mischarge, and infant deaths. In infancy and childhood, iodine deficiency causes cretinism, growth failure, stunting, mental retardation, delayed motor development, neuromuscular disorders, speech impairment, and hearing defects.

Food Quality/Safety and Health

Biological contaminants cause the majority of food-borne illnesses (e.g., cholera, shigellosis, campylobacteriosis, and helminthiasis). The majority of foodborne cases from biological origins result in diarrhea, particularly in children under five years of age. Diarrhea can result in dehydration, electrolyte imbalance, growth failure, and death. Although most episodes are probably mild, death can occur in a small proportion of cases. However, given the large number of cases, it is possible that over 1,000,000 diarrhea deaths are caused by food-borne contamination (Esrey & Feachem, 1989). Even when death does not occur, nutritional status is usually compromised, at least temporarily, in part due to reduced food intake (Dickin et al., 1990). Other types of food-borne pathogens, such as *Toxoplasma* and *Listeria*, can cause abortions and fetal malformations (FAO/WHO, 1992b).

Other types of environmental pollution can also lead to food contamination. *Heavy metals* can cause serious problems, even death. These minerals often interact and disrupt the function of other essential nutrients. Sometimes the effects are reversible, but in other cases the effects may be permanent. For instance, lead poisoning, from the use of lead cans, which are still common in developing countries (UNEP/FAO/WHO, 1989), can lead to enzymatic and neurophysiological processes (Tarcher, 1992). Radiation pollution (e.g., Strontium-90) and chlorinated hydrocarbons (e.g., PCBs) can also enter food, and, if ingested in sufficient quantity, can lead to illness, sometimes of a chronic nature such as cancer.

Metals, such as lead and mercury, can accumulate in the body over an extended period of time. Although they can be consumed in food, they usually enter the food chain from non-agricultural sources. Mercury, in the form of methylmercury, accumulates up the aquatic food chain and becomes ingested with fish such as tuna and swordfish. Metals affect the nervous system and interfere in the metabolism of other nutrients (e.g., iron, zinc, and calcium) causing nutritional problems.

Exposure to *pesticides* in food occurs with breast milk (Jensen, 1983), and it is highest in fruits and vegetables consumed by most segments of the population (Rengam & Snyder, 1991). A high proportion (up to 70 percent) of imported and domestic fruits and vegetables in the United States have been found to have pesticide residues (Rengam & Snyder, 1991). This is likely an underestimate because testing cannot identify many residues (Gips, 1987). Imported food samples had a higher proportion of contamination than domestic samples, partly because use of certain pesticides banned in the West continues in many parts of the developing world (Gips, 1987). The health consequences of pesticide poisoning (i.e., occupational exposure) are well documented (Morgan, 1989). Teratogenicity, which is anything that adversely affects normal development of a fetus, has been documented for over 65 pesticides (Moses, 1989). Other health consequences include cancers, sterility, and neurologic problems (muscle weakness and paralysis, mental and psychological changes, and possibly Parkinson's disease (Moses, 1989, 1992). The effects of pesticide residues from ingested food are for the most part unknown. A recent study by a committee of the National Research Council in the USA (NRC, 1993) concluded that young children are exposed to higher levels of pesticide residues than adults and that they are more sensitive to these residues than adults. The committee recommended that pesticide use be determined more by health considerations than by agricultural practices.

Toxins occurring in other food sources can pose a health threat to humans. Aflatoxin can be found in cereals, nuts, legumes, and dried fruits with improper storage, and aflatoxin is associated with liver cancer. Ciguatera poisoning, the most common form of seafood poisoning, may lead to neurological problems. Plant toxicants, such as cyanide-containing roots and tubers (e.g., cassava) may pose a serious risk to nutritional status.

INTERVENTIONS TO IMPROVE FOOD SECURITY

Specifying and clarifying the six major components of the definition of food security is essential for identifying the steps required to design, implement, and evaluate strategies, policies, and interventions to reduce food insecurity. The first three (sustainability, access, and for all individuals) specify the approach and target population in developing a strategy. The first component, sustainability, implies that food-security approaches should move toward preventive (long-term development) and away from curative (short-term emergency relief) measures. Access implies the acquisition of a resource base, by redistributing or generating new assets, which allows for the procurement of food either by production or through purchases. The third component, for all individuals, offers a strategy choice of policies for either the general population or targeting the food insecure, the rural and urban poor, and the vulnerable, children, women in their reproductive years, and the elderly. The latter three components indicate the outcomes of a food-strategy policy. Adequate and safe food refer to the intake of energy, micronutrients and food free of contamination. The last component, health, requires the selection of an indicator with an appropriate cut-off point for evaluation of interventions.

To provide sustained access to food by people requires an integration of economic, environmental and sociodemographic solutions. The integration of these determinants is critical for production, distribution and intake of adequate and safe food. The joint consideration of production, distribution, and intake is critical, because access to adequate food does not guarantee equitable distribution which, in turn, does not guarantee intake.

Economic

The poor allocate the bulk of their resources to either the production or purchase of foods. Economic interventions, therefore, are designed to provide a more adequate resource base with which to procure food, whether by self-production or through purchases of marketed food. Economic schemes, though, are difficult to implement without adversely affecting other economic groups. For example, efforts to reduce the price of basic foodstuffs in urban settings to allow urban poor to obtain food may depress production in rural areas because of a lack of return on production. A brief summary of the major interventions follow.

Employment. Public employment schemes can increase the purchasing power of the landless poor. A program in Chile provided employment for 13 percent of the labor force, and in Peru 3.5 percent of the labor benefited from a public employment program (World Bank, 1990). In both countries, the poor and women were targeted.

Wages and Prices. Price policy is a double-edged sword. On the one hand, high prices for food can increase the return to producers. On the other hand, these high prices reduce the ability of the poor to purchase food. Ideally, high producer prices and low consumer prices are sought. In Zimbabwe, high maize prices, wage revisions (minimum set and increases restricted), and subsidized inputs to smallholder farmers has resulted in increased efficiency of production (ACC/SCN, 1993; Mumbengegwi, 1988). In Indonesia (Gillespie & Mason, 1991; Ellis, 1990; ACC/SCN, 1993), rice prices were stabilized and subsidized for consumers. To compensate producers, inputs were also subsidized. Such investments in Indonesia were made possible by oil revenues. This program has reduced poverty by more than 50 percent, increased food production, reduced food imports (21%) and food aid (95%), increased national energy intake (22%), and decreased the number of underweight children (10–15%).

Trade. Unfair trade practices can harm urban and rural poor. In the Dominican Republic, sugar production had been efficient, and it employed rural poor. A reduction in U.S. imports due to quotas, coupled with subsidized prices from the European Community, cut sugar production and employment in the Dominican Republic (World Bank, 1990). Fair trade should benefit countries with comparative advantages in the long term.

Land ownership. Land reform this century has occurred in many parts of the world as a result of colonialism, war, and social revolutions. The benefits of land reform on production have been variable, and success is dependent in part on the addition of other services or incentives. A successful attempt at land reform occurred throughout the Piaui Rural Development Project in Northeast Brazil (World Bank, 1990). Accompanying the distribution of 25 hectares per landowner was infrastructure, including roads, irrigation, and water supplies. Yields increased for dryland (10–40%) and irrigated farms, which increased the value of production (20–50%). However, land-tenure reform may require other inputs to be successful.

Transfer schemes. Transfer schemes can take the form of redistribution or insurance. Many countries have offered price subsidies on food products. They usually benefit the rich more than the poor but, in some cases, the food subsidy program has reached the poor. Because the poor spend so much on food, the benefit to them has been shown to be proportionally greater than the benefit to the rich in Egypt (Alderman & von Braun, 1984) and Sri Lanka (Edirisinghe, 1987).

Environmental

Environmental problems are becoming increasingly recognized as a threat to food security. Poverty contributes to environmental problems when the poor seek short-term exploitation of their environment to subsist on a day-to-day basis. Similarly, environmental problems contribute to poverty through soil erosion, salinization, and temperature changes, by causing lower yields and unemployment. Poor housing and inadequate services exacerbate diseases, which reduce worker productivity. The following interventions are designed to minimize the effect of the environment problems on food insecurity.

Infrastructure. In rural Bangladesh several villages obtained infrastructure, such as roads, electricity, markets, schools, and health centers (Ahmed & Hossain, 1988). Income from crops, wages, and livestock and fisheries increased by an average of 17 percent, compared with similar villages that did not receive infrastructure development. Providing domestic water supplies, another type of infrastructure, will allow women more time to produce and prepare food, and feed small children (Burger & Esrey, 1993).

Food quality. Improvements in food quality and safety are dependent on government, industry and consumers (FAO/WHO, 1992b). Industry includes the producer, transporter, storer, and the processor. Government must recognize the need for a safer food supply and create legislation that can be implemented. Many international codes have been established and could be implemented in developing countries. Consumers need to be educated on how to obtain, keep, prepare, and consume safe food.

Soil conservation. In the Loess Plateau in northwest China, a soil erosion control program consisted of reclamation of flatlands, terracing of hillsides, planting shrubs, fodder, and trees on hillsides, and better animal husbandry (Piazza & Doolette, 1990). This resulted in increased grain output, crop diversification, more animal products, and decreased soil erosion.

Protecting watersheds. Fresh water for irrigation, fishing, and drinking is being reduced and contaminated from human mismanagement. A glaring example is the Aral Sea area (World Bank, 1992). Overirrigation and heavy use of pesticides and fertilizers in the area has effectively destroyed the Aral Sea Basin. The fishing industry has all but disappeared, due to a drastic reduction in the water level, and agricultural production has been declining, in part due to the evaporation of the salts blown onto the land. Such disasters require that food-security efforts incorporate appropriate environmental practices.

Climate or disasters. Disasters, often due to climate changes, such as droughts and floods, necessitate the influx of food from external sources—either imports, or aid, or both. Sometimes it is difficult to move food through public channels, and delays can be critical to those most in need. In 1980 in Botswana, the government implemented a drought-relief program of food-supply management, employment generation, and agricultural assistance. After the drought of the mid-1980s, Botswana, despite lowered food production, witnessed a decline in the proportion of children who were underweight (Morgan, 1991). The public distribution of food occurred through public works and the use of a cash transfer to the public, giving them the resources to procure food from private traders.

Land scarcity. Land scarcity can be a result of overpopulation and low productivity of the land. This is a cause of deforestation in Nepal (Kumar & Hotchkiss, 1988). Deforestation has the effect of reducing output and income from agriculture, due to an increase in time to gather fuel and fodder. Lower income, less output, and less time for food preparation has resulted in decreased energy intake and lower nutritional status of children (Kumar, 1992). A forest-development project in Nepal increased land use values and prices for milk, and prevented soil erosion and flooding (Fargeix, 1992).

Socio-Demographic

The human element, socio-demography, forms the third basic cause of food insecurity. This aspect is related to both poverty and environmental problems. Overuse of marginal land leads to fragile soils, overgrazing, and flooding. Increased and misappropriate use of fertilizers, pesticides, and water pollutes the environment, thereby reducing yields. Under- and unemployment reduce purchasing power, and lack of education leads to poor environmental practices and failure to purchase safe and adequate food.

Education. Education is so often associated with better health and higher incomes that it is inconceivable to develop a food-security program without education. The higher the education, the higher the income generated, the lower the mortality rates (World Bank, 1990) and the greater the knowledge of preparing appropriate foods for young children (Guptill et al., 1992). Because women are critical to the preparation and feeding of food, female education should receive a high priority.

Timely warning. Food preparedness, through early warning and information systems, can be helpful to forecast when food shortages will occur, identify those most likely to suffer, and predict the magnitude of the projected need (Mason et al., 1984). Geographical mapping can be helpful in identifying those most likely to suffer in times of food shortages, as has been done in Bangladesh (World Food Program, 1992).

Breastfeeding promotion. Breastfeeding is the best way to feed young children. Thus, breastfeeding promotion is a useful food-security policy. Breastfeeding supplies important nutrients and protects against diseases like diarrhea, which exacerbates lack of adequate food. Breastfeeding is an enhancement to income, first by reducing the need to buy infant foods, and second by reducing the health-care expenditures by reducing diarrhea.

Provision of health-related services. Better health allows for greater production, better utilization of nutrients once ingested, and less expenditures for treatment of illnesses. Thus, provision of health services should be a priority in a food-security strategy. Major health services reported to be effective include immunization, water supplies, sanitation, and use of oral rehydration (World Bank, 1993).

Feeding programs. Supplementary feeding programs are a form of targeted subsidy. They have had mixed success wherever they have been tried. If the main problem is lack of intake, then supplementation can be highly effective (Beaton & Ghassemi, 1982). In addition, children have been reported to overcome the ill effects of diarrhea with adequate food (Lutter et al., 1989).

Food aid. Food aid remains an important donor response to food insecurity, in part as a measure to distribute surplus production. In emergency situations, such as famine and disaster relief, it is essential, but as much as possible, food aid should be linked to poverty reduction. Food distribution and food monetization have been successful in several countries (World Bank, 1990).

DISCUSSION

Summary

Indicators of food insecurity indicate that a large proportion (20–33%) of the world is food insecure. Many factors lead to food insecurity, but poverty is the underlying cause. Poverty, in turn, is associated with economic, environmental, and sociodemographic causes of food insecurity. Without the means to produce or trade for food, many people are vulnerable to severe food insecurity, whether measured by food intake, anthropometry, or income. The health consequences begin *in utero* and continue throughout the life cycle.

Future Directions

Interventions should move toward a development approach, and away from an emergency relief approach. Even when emergency relief is necessary, it should be compatible with a developmental approach. Developmental approaches to food security can increase the asset base of the poor, the group most vulnerable to food insecurity. Infrastructure development, such as roads, water supplies and sanitation, accompanied by land reform, transfer programs, education and provision of essential services, such as education and health care, are likely to have lasting effects. They allow for resource acquisition and the buffering of resources in times of transitory food insecurity.

The food insecure, who reside in both urban and rural areas, should be targeted. Use of nutritional surveillance, early warning systems, and mapping of vulnerable regions should be a high priority. This will require the use of a few key indicators that can be monitored over time.

Food insecurity will not disappear, but it is possible to improve the situation by stabilizing the resource base. Many different solutions have been tried in the past, some with great success. However, the problems are highly context specific. What has worked in one part of the world may not be appropriate for another, but the resolution of the issues discussed above should provide a common ground for agencies and donors.

REFERENCES

ACC/SCN (1992). *Second Report on the World Nutrition Situation. Volume I: Global and Regional Results.* Geneva: Administrative Committee on Coordination/Subcommittee on Nutrition.

ACC/SCN (1993). *Second Report on the World Nutrition Situation. Volume II: Country Trends, Methods and Statistics.* Geneva: Administrative Committee on Coordination/Subcommittee on Nutrition.

Ahmed, R., & Hossain, M. (1988). *Developmental Impact of Rural Infrastructure.* Bangladesh: International Food Policy Research Institute & Bangladesh Institute of Development Studies.

Alderman, H., & von Braun, J. (1984). *The Effects of the Egyptian Food Ration and Subsidy System on Income Distribution and Consumption.* (Research Report 45). Washington, DC: International Food Policy Research Institute.

Beaton, G. H., & Ghassemi, H. (1982). Supplementary feeding programs for young children in developing countries. *American Journal of Clinical Nutrition (Supplement), 35(4),* 864–916.

Beaton, G. H., Martorell, R., L'Abbé, Edmonston, B., McCabe, G., Ross, A. C., & Harvey, B. (1992). Effectiveness of Vitamin A Supplementation in the Control of Young Child Morbidity and Mortality in Developing Countries. (Report prepared for CIDA, Ottawa, Canada).

Brownie, C., & Habicht, J.-P. (1984). Selecting a Screening Cut-off or Diagnostic Criterion for Comparing Prevalences of Diseases. *Biometrics, 40,* 675–684.

Burger, S. E., & Esrey, S. A. (1993). Water and Sanitation: Health and Nutrition Benefits to Children. In P. Pinstrup-Andersen, D. Pelletier, & H. Alderman (Eds.). Beyond Child Survival. Ithaca, NY: Cornell University Press.

Corbett, J. E. M. (1988). Famine and household coping strategies. *World Development, 16(9),* 1099–1112.

Dickin, K. L., Brown, K. H., Fagbule, D., Adedoyin, M., Gittelsohn, J., Esrey, S. A., & Oni, G. A. (1990). Effect of Diarrhoea on Dietary Intake by Infants and

Young Children in Rural Villages of Kwara State, Nigeria. *European Journal of Clinical Nutrition, 44*, 307–317.

Edirisinghe, N. (1987). The Food Stamp Scheme in Sri Lanka: Costs, Benefits and Options for Modification. (Research Report #58). Washington, DC: International Food Policy Research Institute.

Ellis, F. (1990). The Rice Market and Its Management in Indonesia. *IDS Bulletin, 21(3)*, 44–51.

Esrey, S. A., & Feachem, R. G. (1989). Interventions for the Control of Diarrhoeal Diseases among Young Children: Promotion of Food Hygiene. *Control of Diarrhoeal Diseases*. Geneva: World Health Organization.

FAO/WHO (1992a). Improving Household Food Security. (Theme paper prepared for the International Conference on Nutrition, Rome, December.)

FAO/WHO (1992b). Protecting Consumers through Improved Food Quality and Safety. (Theme paper prepared for the International Conference on Nutrition, Rome, December.)

Fargeix, A. (1992). *Financing of Pollution Control Programs: Europe, Middle East and North Africa Region*. Washington DC: World Bank.

Foster, P. (1992). The World Food Problem: Tackling the Causes of Undernutrition in the Third World. Boulder, CO: Lynne Rienner.

George, S. (1976). *How the Other Half Dies: The Real Reasons for World Hunger*. New York: Penguin.

Gillespie, S., & Mason, J. (1991). Nutrition-Relevant Actions: Some Experiences from the Eighties and Lessons for the Nineties. (ACC/SCN, Nutrition Policy Discussion Paper, No. 10.)

Gips, T. (1987). Breaking the Pesticide Habit: Alternatives to 12 Hazardous Pesticides. (International Alliance for Sustained Agriculture, 1987–1, Minneapolis.)

Guptill, K. S., Esrey, S. A., Oni, G. A., & Brown, K. H. (1993). Evaluation of a Face-to-Face Weaning Food Intervention in Kwara State, Nigeria: Knowledge, Trial and Adoption of a Home-Prepared Weaning Food. *Social Science and Medicine, 36(5)*, 665–672.

Haddad, L. J., Sullivan, S., & Kennedy, E. (1991). *Identification and Evaluation of Alternative Indicators of Food and Nutrition Security: Some Conceptual Issues and an Analysis of Extant Data*. Washington, DC: International Food Policy and Research Institute.

Huddleston, B. (1990). FAO's Overall Approach and Methodology for Formulating National Food Security Programmes in Developing Countries. *IDS Bulletin, 21(3)*, 72–80.

James, W. P. T., Ferro-Luzzi, A., & Waterlow, J.C. (1988). Definition of Chronic Energy Deficiency in Adults: Report of a Working Party of the International Dietary Energy Consultative Group. *European Journal of Clinical Nutrition, 42*, 969–981.

Jensen, A. A. (1983). Chemical contaminants in human milk. *Residue Reviews, 89*, 1–128.

Jonsson, U., & Toole, D. (1991). Household Food Security and Nutrition: A Conceptual Analysis. (UNICEF, New York, mimeograph.)

Kennedy, E., & Haddad, L. (1992). Food Security and Nutrition, 1971–1991: Lessons Learned and Future Priorities. *Food Policy, February*, 2–6.

Krasovic, K., & Anderson, M. A. (1991). Maternal Nutrition and Pregnancy Outcomes: Anthropometric Assessment. (Pan American Health Organization, Scientific Publication No. 529, Washington, DC, pp. 208–209.

Kumar, S. K. (1992). *Women's Work Loads: A Key to the Dynamics of Low Agricultural Productivity and Environmental Degradation in Nepalese Hills.* Washington, DC: International Food Policy Research Institute.

Kumar, S. K., & Hotchkiss, D. (1988). *Consequences of Deforestation for Women's Time Allocation, Agricultural Production, and Nutrition in Hill Areas of Nepal.* Washington, DC: International Food Policy Research Institute.

Lappé, F. M., & Collins, J. (1979). Food First: Beyond the Myth of Scarcity. New York: Ballantine.

Lutter, C. K., Mora, J. O., Habicht, J.-P., Rasmussen, K. R., Robson, D. S., Sellers, S. G., Super, C. M., & Herrera, M. G. (1989). Nutritional Supplementation: Effects on Child Stunting Because of Diarrhea. *American Journal of Clinical Nutrition, 50,* 1–8.

Malthus, T. R. (1963). *An Essay on the Principle of Population or a View of Its Past and Present Effects on Human Happiness, with an Inquiry into Our Prospects Respecting the Future Removal or Mitigation of the Evils Which It Occasions.* Homewood, IL: RD Irwin.

Mason, J. B., Habicht, J.-P., Tabatabai, H., & Valverde, V. (1984). *Nutritional Surveillance.* Geneva: World Health Organization.

Maxwell, S. (1990). Food Security in Developing Countries: Issues and Options for the 1990s. *IDS Bulletin, 21(3),* 2–13.

Maxwell, S., & Frankenberger, T. R. (1993). *Household Food Security: Concepts, Indicators, Measurements: A Technical Review.* New York: UNICEF.

Morgan, D. P. (1989). *Recognition and Management of Pesticide Poisonings* (4th ed) (EPA—540/9-88-001). Washington, DC: United States Environmental Protection Agency.

Morgan, R. (1991). Social Welfare Programmes and the Reduction of Household Vulnerability in the SADCC States of Southern Africa. In: E. Ahmed et al. (Eds.), *Social Security in Developing Countries.* Oxford: Clarendon Press.

Moses, M. (1989). Pesticide-Related Health Problems and Farm Workers. *AAOHN Journal, 37(3),* 115–130.

Moses, M. (1992). Pesticides. In J. M. Last & R. B. Wallace (Eds.), *Public Health and Preventive Medicine* (13th Ed.). New York: Appleton and Lange.

Motarjemi, Y., Käferstein, F., Moy, G., & Quevedo (1993). Contaminated Weaning Food: A Major Risk Factor for Diarrhoea and Associated Malnutrition. *Bulletin of the World Health Organization, 71(1),* 79–92.

Mumbengegwi, C. (1988). The Political Economy of a Small-Farmer Agricultural Strategy in SADCC. In C. Bryant (Ed.), *Poverty, Policy, and Food Security in Southern Africa.* Boulder, CO: Lynne Rienner.

Mwadime, R., & Baldwin, S. (1993). *Household Food Security and Nutrition in Eastern and Southern Africa.* Nairobi: UNICEF.

National Research Council (1993). *Pesticides in the Diets of Infants and Children.* Washington, DC: National Academy Press.

Payne, P. P. (1990). Measuring Malnutrition. *IDS Bulletin, 21(3),* 14–30.

Pellet, P. L. (1986). The Physiology of Hunger and Malnutrition. In M. H. Forbes & L. J. Merrill (Eds.), *Global Hunger: A Look at the Problem and Potential Solutions*. Evansville, IN: University of Evansville Press.

Pelletier, D., Frongillo, E. A. Jr., & Habicht, J.-P. (1993). Epidemiologic Evidence for a Potentiating Effect of Malnutrition on Child Mortality. *American Journal of Public Health, 83(8)*, 1130–1133.

Piazza, A., & Doolette, J. (1990). The Impact of Combining Agricultural Techniques and Soil Conversation Measures in China's Loess Plateau. *Proceedings of the 1988 International Conference on Dryland Farming*. College Station, TX: Texas Agricultural Experiment Station, Texas A&M University.

Rengam, S., & Snyder, K. (1991). *The Pesticide Handbook: Profiles for Action*. Penang, Malaysia: International Organization of Consumers Union.

Tarcher, A. B. (Ed.) (1992). *Principles and Practice of Environmental Medicine*. New York: Plenum Medical Book Company.

Tomkins, A., & Watson, F. (1989). Malnutrition and Infection: a Review. (ACC/SCN, Nutrition Policy Discussion Paper # 5, Geneva.)

UNEP/FAO/WHO (1989). Assessment of Chemical Contaminants in Food. Report on the Results of the UNEP/FAO/WHO Programme on Health Related Environmental Monitoring. Global Environment Monitoring System (GEMS).

UNICEF (1990). Strategy for Improved Nutrition of Children and Women in Developing Countries. New York: UNICEF.

United Nations (1948). Universal Declaration of Human Rights. (General Assembly, Resolution 217A, 10 December.)

World Bank (1986). *Poverty and Hunger: Issues and Options for Food Security in Developing Countries*. Washington, DC: World Bank.

World Bank (1990). *Poverty, World Development Report, 1990*. New York: Oxford University Press.

World Bank (1992). *Development and the Environment, World Development Report, 1992*. New York: Oxford University Press.

World Bank (1993). *Investing in Health, World Development Report, 1993*. New York: Oxford University Press.

World Food Council (1992). The Global State of Hunger and Malnutrition: 1992 Report. (Presented at the Eighteenth Ministerial Session, Nairobi, Kenya, 23–26 June.)

World Food Programme (1992). *Food Aid Review, 1992, Geneva*.

7

Lifestyle and Cardiovascular Disease

Robert Beaglehole

INTRODUCTION

The phrase "lifestyle" has a variety of meanings. In this chapter it refers to the set of habits and customs that is influenced, modified, encouraged, or constrained by the lifelong process of socialization (Last, 1988). These habits and customs are often enduring and include use of substances such as alcohol, tobacco and other drugs; dietary habits; exercise patterns; and sexual activities. These habits have important implications for health and are directly responsible for at least 50% of the leading causes of death in developed countries, where noncommunicable diseases predominate, and an increasing proportion of deaths in developing countries where noncommunicable disease epidemics are emerging (Lopez, 1993).

The lifestyle theory of disease etiology stems from epidemiological studies which have identified the association of specific characteristics of individuals (risk factors) with a wide range of diseases. These individual lifestyle characteristics are determined to a large extent by environmental forces. The focus of this chapter is on major cardiovascular diseases (coronary heart disease, stroke, hypertension), but the lifestyle theory has been applied to all other preventable modern epidemics, from AIDS to self-inflicted injury.

Global Burden of Cardiovascular Diseases

It is estimated that 50 million deaths occur each year. The majority (39 million) occur in the developing world. Although it is difficult to accurately estimate the cause-specific number of deaths, globally about 10 million deaths are attributed to cardiovascular diseases. These cardiovascular disease deaths are equally distributed between developed and developing countries (WHO, 1995), although coronary heart disease predominates in the developed world, and stroke in developing countries. Hypertension is prevalent throughout the world, with prevalence rates, based on a single measurement of blood pressure, varying between 8 percent and 15 percent.

The cardiovascular disease epidemics are a 20th-century phenomenon. In most developed countries, coronary heart disease mortality rates are now declining, with the notable exception of Eastern European countries, which now have the highest rates in the world. The situation in developing countries is unclear because of the absence of reliable mortality data. In some developing countries, age-specific rates are declining, although the burden of cardiovascular disease will inevitable increase with the aging of populations.

The explanations for the recent trends in cardiovascular disease mortality rates are tentative, and are the subject of ongoing research (WHO MONICA Project, 1988). The favorable trends in cardiovascular disease mortality rates are associated with improvements in the level of risk factors in the community, and with changes in the management of established disease. It is likely that primary prevention is the major contribution to the decline in coronary heart disease mortality rates (Vartiainen et al., 1994).

The rapid change in cardiovascular disease mortality rates, together with variations in the occurrence of these diseases with migration, urbanization and other aspects of "modernization," provide clear evidence that these epidemics are preventable. Ultimately, the prevention of cardiovascular disease depends on the action of individuals, both sick and healthy. However, the choices available to individuals are externally conditioned by the strong environmental influence on cardiovascular disease risk factors and the limited options available for the management of disease.

CARDIOVASCULAR DISEASE: RISK FACTORS, LIFESTYLE, AND THE ENVIRONMENT

The causes of the modern cardiovascular disease epidemics are to be found in the environment; only environmental factors can account for rapid changes over time in the occurrence of cardiovascular diseases at the population level, and the major variations between countries. The underlying cause of the cardiovascular disease epidemic is nutritional imbalance. The major focus has been on the intake of fat and, particularly, saturated fat. The epidemiological evidence on the role of diet comes from both observational and experimental studies, and is supported by clinical, metabolic, and animal studies. However, the epidemiological studies have not all been congruent, and dissent is regularly expressed. The inconsistency can be attributed, at least in part, to the difficulty in precisely characterizing the long-term diet of individuals. Since the diet of a population tends to be homogeneous, individual variation may be greater than the variation between people. The epidemiological data, after adjustment for errors in the measurement of cholesterol, suggest that a one-percent reduction in mean population blood cholesterol is associated with a two- to three-percent reduction in coronary heart disease risk. It is now clear that the relationship between food, nutrition, and chronic disease in general is more complex than originally envisaged, and that an excessive intake of saturated fat is not the whole story. For example, recent research has emphasized the important potential protective role of essential fatty acids and antioxidants on the development of cardiovascular disease, particularly coronary heart disease (Wood & Oliver, 1992).

Hypertension, or high blood pressure is an important risk factor for both coronary heart disease and stroke. There is persuasive evidence that the average level of blood pressure in a population is environmentally determined, with nutrition playing a key role, particularly an excessive intake of salt, calories, and alcohol (Stamler, 1992).

Two other non-dietary risk factors act to increase the occurrence of cardiovascular diseases: tobacco use and physical inactivity. These risk factors have become widespread only in the 20th century, and both act upon the underlying vascular disease caused by inappropriate nutrition. The smoking of manufactured cigarettes became common in men after World War I and in women in many countries after World War II. The products of the tobacco industry are now responsible each year for approximately 3 million deaths worldwide, and this figure is projected to increase to about 10 million each year in the 2020s (WHO, 1993). Although the causal association of manufactured tobacco with lung cancer is stronger, more cardiovascular deaths are attributed to tobacco use because it is a much more common cause of death.

The use of tobacco shows marked variations within countries over time, and by gender, social class, and age group. In many developed countries smoking rates in socially advantaged and older people are falling. However, the increase of smoking is still common in young people, especially teenage girls. Women in societies in which gender equality is not a strong feature generally have low smoking rates. As the per capita consumption of tobacco has fallen in some developed countries in response to policy changes, the tobacco industry has looked to Eastern European and developing countries, particularly in Africa and Asia, to maintain its profitability.

The relationships between risk factors, lifestyle, and the environment is most obvious with regard to physical inactivity. A century ago, most people were physically active for subsistence, employment, and transportation. This situation is still widespread in the developing world. However, there have been major changes in physical activity patterns in the developed world, where it has become a leisure time activity indulged in by only a small, and usually economically advantaged, proportion of the population. Physical inactivity, in association with overnutrition, is responsible for increasing overweight as a serious health problem in much of the developed world.

An important conclusion from the epidemiological data is that the determinants of the overall health of a population must be distinguished from the determinants of disease in individuals. Rose (1985) used the phrase "sick individuals and sick populations" to emphasize this distinction. The underlying causes of major health problems such as the cardiovascular disease epidemics, are to be found in mass characteristics, which are, themselves, socially and economically determined.

THEORIES OF DISEASE

Three current theories of disease have some ability to explain the modern epidemics of cardiovascular disease: the lifestyle theory; the multifactorial theory; and the socio-structural theory (Tesh, 1988). These theories are, to an important degree, interrelated.

This lifestyle theory, with its focus on factors under the control of the individual, suggests that cardiovascular disease prevention is the responsibility of the individual. The supremacy of this theory can be attributed to its congruence with the dominant health ideology, which stresses the importance of individualism, and to its emphasis on personal responsibility for health as a (cheap) method to reduce the demand for medical care. The major practical objection to the lifestyle theory is that the prevention policies based on this theory are applicable only to a minority of the population. In particular, disadvantaged populations do not have the opportunities or resources to adopt effectively the prescribed changes to their personal behavior. In addition, the focus on individual behavior detracts attention from the powerful and overarching social, cultural, economic, and political determinants of this behavior. Furthermore, there is evidence that the lifestyle theory is not congruent with lay interpretations of the epidemiological data (Davison et al., 1992). It is not surprising, given the focus on individual responsibility for the prevention of heart disease, that the social class gradients in coronary heart disease death rates have increased in many developed countries (Marmot & McDowall, 1986).

The multi-factorial theory suggests that disease is caused by a large number of factors operating as part of a "web of causation." Each factor, in turn, is composed of many subfactors: unhealthy behavior, for example, is linked to poor education, poverty, unemployment, role models, and commercial pressures. This theory is not always differentiated from the lifestyle theory. Tesh (1988) identifies several practical weaknesses with the multi-factorial theory. First, it provides few clues about how to prevent disease because it does not identify key points of intervention. Furthermore, because it does not differentiate between the relative importance of factors, it assigns equal importance to different strategies which, in turn, means that educational strategies are usually preferred, even though they are often weak and inefficient. Finally, the theory encourages epidemiologists to search for more and more factors—rather than encouraging an understanding of the determinants of the most important factors and how they interact to produce disease.

The socio-structural theory, with its antecedents in the work of Virchow in the 19th century (Taylor & Rieger, 1985), has been suggested as an alternative to the multi-factorial maze. To be an improvement it would have to display a hierarchy of causality, lend itself to effective prevention programs and make room for nonempirical causes of disease (Tesh, 1988). The socio-structural theory has been handicapped by its simplistic identification with capitalism, and by the use of concepts which are difficult to investigate. The challenge for the socio-structural theory is to find the appropriate balance between the responsibilities of individuals and the need for social solutions. The prevailing ideology, which stresses economic and political individualism, enables governments to ignore their broader social responsibilities.

AN INTEGRATIVE CONCEPTUAL FRAMEWORK

There is a need for a conceptual framework for the epidemiology and prevention of cardiovascular disease which incorporates the multifactorial origin of these diseases, and integrates the roles of individuals and institutions. Campaigns focusing primarily on the behavior of individuals will continue to be successful among the socially and economically privileged members of society. However, other social groups, in which cardiovascular diseases are now concentrating, will not have the resources to respond to health-education campaigns. For the majority of the population, broadly based preventive interventions are necessary. Since the critical task now, after almost half a century of epidemiological research, is the primary prevention of cardiovascular disease, the framework should focus on the determinants of the incidence of cardiovascular disease. The determinants of case fatality are of less importance.

The importance of primary prevention suggests that a useful framework should have a strong health policy orientation. A useful framework must explicitly indicate that the powerful socio-economic determinants of cardiovascular disease can be favorably modified through health policy decisions. The lack of complete understanding of the mechanism involved should not preclude an increased emphasis on prevention. There is a strong precedent for effective prevention programs, despite only limited understanding of disease mechanisms.

Building on the work of Mosley and Chen (1984) and Evans and Stoddart (1990), an integrative framework for the prevention of cardiovascular disease has been proposed (Figure 7.1) (Beaglehole, 1995). Each component of the framework summarizes a complex set of activities, many of which require empirical investigation. The socioeconomic determinants operate along a variety of avenues. One pathway is directly through the modifiable risk factors and their impact on atherogenesis and thrombogenesis. Another pathway is mediated by health policy. A third important pathway operates through individual and community characteristics such as prosperity, relative deprivation, and social support (Wilkinson, 1989).

This type of conceptual framework is not favored by adherents of the free-market view of health care and public health. This school of thought, which dominates much of the health debate at both the international and national levels, would allow health to be largely determined by market forces, with minimal provision of public health services and primarily to prevent the spread of communicable diseases (Tollison & Wagner, 1993).

Implementation of the policy measures which stem from the proposed conceptual framework will not be easy, in part because public health worldwide is in disarray (White, 1991). The problem extends from the highest international level to the delivery of public health services at the community level. An advantage of this type of framework is that it highlights policy options and programs which have the potential to reduce social class differentials in the occurrence of disease. It also indicates the gap between our knowledge of the social and economic determinants of health, and the primary focus of health policy, which remains on the provision of medical care to individuals. This framework also emphasizes that the control and the prevention of the cardiovascular disease epidemics is possible. This conceptual framework encourages multidisciplinary research within a broad framework. It also acknowledges the complexity of the etiology of diseases and identifies the key areas for intervention.

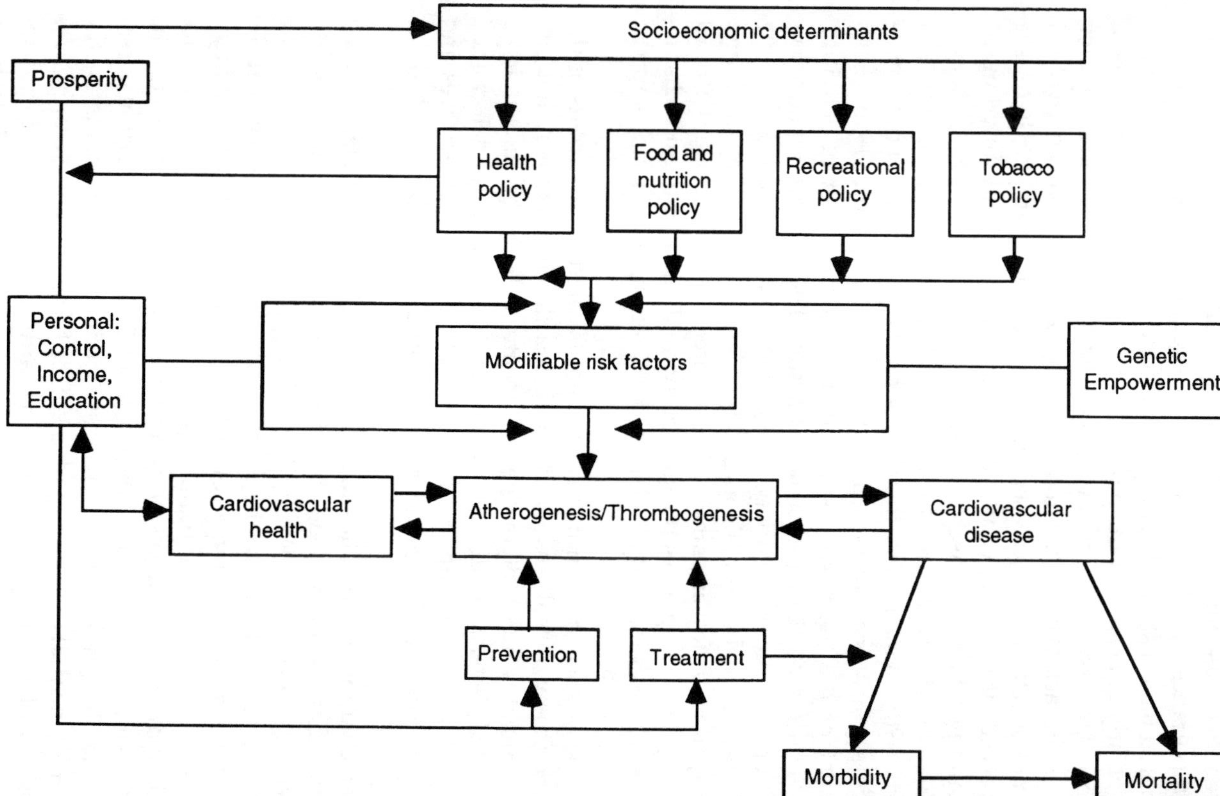

FIGURE 7.1 An integrative framework for the prevention of cardiovascular disease. (Robert Beaglehole, 1995). © 1995 Oxford University Press; used with permission.

Finally, this framework stresses the central role of environmental factors in causing the modern global cardiovascular disease epidemics.

REFERENCES

Beaglehole, R. (1995). Conceptual Frameworks for the Investigation of Mortality from Major Cardiovascular Disease. In A. Lopez, G. Caselli, & T. Valkonen, (Eds.), *Premature Adult Mortality in Developed Countries: From Description to Explanation*. Oxford: Oxford University Press.

Davison, C., Frankel, S., & Davey Smith, G. (1992). The Limits of Lifestyle: Reassessing "Fatalism" in the Popular Culture of Illness Prevention. *Social Science Medicine, 34*, 675–685.

Evans, R., & Stoddart, G. L. (1990). Producing Health, Consuming Health Care. *Social Science Medicine, 31*, 1347–1363.

Last, J. M. (1988). *Dictionary of Epidemiology. 2nd Edition*. Oxford: Oxford University Press.

Lopez, A. (1993). Assessing the Burden of Mortality from Cardiovascular Diseases. *World Health Statistics Quarterly, 46*, 91–96.

Marmot, M. G., & McDowall, M. E. (1986). Mortality Decline and Widening Social Inequalities. *Lancet, 2*, 274–276.

Mosley, W. H., & Chen, L. C. (1984). An Analytical Framework for the Study of Child Survival in Developing Countries. *Population and Development Review, 10 (Suppl.)*, 25–45.

Rose, G. (1985). Sick Individuals, Sick Populations. *International Journal of Epidemiology, 14*, 32–38.

Stamler, R. (1992). The Primary Prevention of Hypertension and the Population Blood Pressure Problem. In M. Marmot & P. Elliott (Eds.), *Coronary Heart Disease Epidemiology. From Aetiology to Public Health*. Oxford: Oxford University Press.

Taylor, R., & Rieger, A. (1985). Medicine as Social Science: Rudolf Virchow on the Typhus Epidemic in Upper Silesia. *International Journal of Health Service, 15*, 547–559.

Tesh, A. N. (1988). *Hidden Arguments: Political Ideology and Disease Prevention Policy*. New Brunswick, NJ: Rutgers University Press.

Tollison, R. D., & Wagner, R. E. (1993). Who benefits from WHO? *The Decline of the World Health Organization* (Research Report 18). London: The Social Affairs Unit.

Vartiainen, E., Puska, P., Pekkanen, J., Tuomilehto, J., & Jousilahti, P. (1994). Changes in Risk Factors Explain Changes in Mortality from Ischaemic Heart Disease in Finland. *BMJ, 309*, 23–27.

White, K. L. (1991). *Healing the Schism: Epidemiology, Medicine and the Public's Health*. New York: Springer-Verlag.

WHO MONICA Project Investigators (1988). The WHO MONICA Project (Monitoring Trends and Determinants in Cardiovascular Disease): A Major International Collaboration. *Journal of Clinical Epidemiology, 41*, 105–114.

WHO (1993). Tobacco-Attributable Mortality: Global Estimates and Projections. *Tobacco Alert*, January 1991 (revised October 1993).

WHO (1995). The World Health Report 1995. Bridging the Gaps. Geneva: WHO.

Wilkinson, R. G. (1989). Class Mortality Differentials, Income Distribution and Trends in Poverty 1921–1981. *Journal of Social Policy, 18*, 307–335.

Wood, D. A., & Oliver, M. F. (1992). Linoleic Acid, Antioxidant Vitamins and Coronary Heart Disease. In M. Marmot & M. Elliott (Eds.), *Coronary Heart Disease Epidemiology. From Aetiology to Public Health*. Oxford: Oxford University Press.

8

Health and Environment and the Urban Poor

Jorge E. Hardoy and David Satterthwaite

INTRODUCTION: THE URBAN CONTEXT

In recent decades, most Third World nations have experienced a rapid growth in their urban populations without the needed expansion in the availability of safe, adequate quality shelter, and in the provision of urban infrastructure and services which are essential to health in an urban environment. In most urban centers—from the large cities and metropolitan areas to regional centers and small market towns—much of the population lives in poor-quality shelters with inadequate or no provision for piped, treated water supply, provision for sanitation and drainage, paved roads, regular garbage collection, health care and emergency services, and provision for the needs of infants, children, and care-givers in terms of schools, social centers, and sites for play/recreation.

Between 1950 and 1990, the Third World's urban population grew from 286 million to more than 1.5 billion (United Nations, 1991). This urban population is now larger than the total population of Europe, North America, Japan, the former Soviet Union, and Australia combined. In these four decades, the urban population of Africa grew more than sevenfold, while that of Asia grew more than sixfold. The urban population in Latin America and the Caribbean grew less rapidly but, by 1990, more than 70 percent of this region's population lived in urban areas (United Nations, 1991).

For much of this urban population, housing conditions are very poor. In most cities, a large proportion of households live in one or two rooms in cramped, overcrowded dwellings in tenements, cheap boarding houses, or shelters built on illegally occupied or subdivided land. In many, there is a smaller proportion (which, in large cities may still number tens of thousands) who live and sleep in public or semi-public spaces, and who suffer the greatest difficulties in terms of access to water, sanitation, and security. In most cities, neither the government nor the formal private sector has contributed much to expanding the housing stock that is affordable to the low-income majority. During the last few decades, most new housing had been organized, planned, and built outside the law. Most urban inhabitants have no choice but to build, buy, or rent an illegal dwelling (or a legal dwelling illegally subdivided) because they cannot afford the cheapest "legal" house or apartment. It is now common for 30–60 percent of an entire city's population to live in homes and neighborhoods which have been developed illegally.

Water

Hundreds of millions of urban dwellers have no alternative but to use contaminated water—or at least water whose quality is not guaranteed. A small minority have water piped into their homes, while rather more have to collect water from a standpipe nearby. As one specialist commented, "those not served are obliged to use water from streams or other surface sources which, in urban areas, are often little more than open sewers, or to purchase water from insanitary vendors. It is little wonder that their children suffer frequently, often fatally, from diarrhoeal diseases" (Cairncross, 1990).

Sanitation

Around two thirds of the Third World's urban population have no hygienic means of disposing of excreta and an even greater number lack adequate means to dispose of waste waters (Sinnatamby, 1990). Most cities in Africa and many in Asia have no sewers at all. This is not only in the smaller cities; many major cities with a million or more inhabitants have no sewers. Rivers, streams, canals, gullies, and ditches are where most human excrement and waste water ends up, untreated. For those cities with sewers, rarely do they serve more than a small proportion of the population—typically the richer residential, government, and commercial areas. The majority of people in major cities such as Jakarta, Calcutta, Dar es Salaam, Accra, Khartoum, Kampala, and Manila live in housing lacking adequate sanitation. In India, defecating in the open is common practice, since one third of the urban population (over 50 million people) have no latrine of any kind, while another third rely on bucket latrines. A third may use latrines connected to sewers, but only 10 percent have sewage connections to their homes (Centre for Science and Environment, 1983).

Garbage services. An estimated 30–50 percent of solid wastes generated within urban centers remains uncollected (Cointreau, 1982). It is the poorer areas of the city which generally have the least adequate garbage collection service—or no service at all. Most poor households have very limited space (especially in tenements and high-density illegal settlements) which makes waste storage difficult—and few are able to transport garbage to a supervised dump site (Cointreau, 1982).

Health Care

There are too little data available to indicate the number of people lacking ready access to health care services in urban areas. Around 1.6 billion people in the Third World lack access to primary health care (WHO, 1991), and this would include several hundred million urban dwellers. These figures also underestimate the number of people lacking access to effective primary health care, since so many clinics are understaffed and lack essential drugs. A UNICEF report in 1990 noted that there has been a decline in health spending per person in more than three quarters of the countries in Africa and Latin America in recent years, and suggested that "hundreds of health clinics have been closed down and many which remain open are understaffed and lacking essential supplies" (UNICEF, 1990).

Overcrowding

The number of persons per room in most urban areas of the Third World is 3–5 times that in urban areas of the North. Many health problems affecting poorer groups are associated with overcrowding, including household accidents, acute respiratory infections, tuberculosis, and other airborne infections (WHO, 1992a). In the predominantly low-income residential areas in Third World cities, there is often an average of four or more persons per room and, in many instances, less than one square meter of floor space per person (for instance, see Aina, 1989, and Murphy, 1990). Diseases such as tuberculosis, influenza, and meningitis are easily transmitted from one person to another. Their spread is often aided by low resistance among the inhabitants due to malnutrition, and by frequent contact between infective and susceptible people.

ENVIRONMENTAL HAZARDS AND THEIR IMPACT ON HEALTH

Introduction

Box 8.1 lists seven kinds of health hazards that are common in urban environments. Four have a direct bearing on health: biological disease-

Box 8.1—Hazards to Health Within the Urban Environment

1. Biological pathogens or pollutants within the human environment that impair human health—including pathogenic agents and their vectors (and reservoirs)—for instance, the many pathogenic microorganisms in human excreta, airborne pathogens (for instance, those responsible for acute respiratory infections and tuberculosis) and disease vectors such as malaria-carrying (Anopheline) mosquitoes.
2. Chemical pollutants within the human environment—including those added to the environment by human activities (e.g., industrial wastes) and chemical agents present in the environment independent of human activities.
3. The availability, cost, and quality of natural resources on which human health depends—for instance, food, water, and fuel.
4. Physical hazards (e.g., high risks of flooding in houses and settlements built on flood-plains or of mud slides or landslides for houses on slopes).
5. Aspects of the built environment with negative consequences on physical or psychosocial health (e.g., overcrowding, inadequate protection against noise, inadequate provision of infrastructure, services, and common areas).
6. Natural resource degradation (e.g., of soil and water quality) caused by wastes from city-based producers or consumers which impacts on the health/livelihoods of some urban dwellers.
7. National/global environmental degradation with more indirect but long-term influences on human health:
   - the depletion of finite nonrenewable resource bases
   - wastes from human activities that contribute to possible threats to the functioning and stability of global cycles and systems and the increasing frequency of extreme climatic conditions (e.g., greenhouse gas emissions and gaseous emissions that contribute to the depletion of the stratospheric ozone layer).

Source: Satterthwaite, 1993.

causing agents (pathogens), chemical pollutants, a shortage of (or lack of access to) particular natural resources, and physical hazards. These are likely to be the four most pressing urban environmental problems in terms of their health impact in Africa and much of Asia and Latin America (especially for infants and children). Three others also influence health, although less directly: aspects of the built environment with negative consequences on people's health; natural resource degradation; and national/global environmental degradation (including a rising concentration of greenhouse gases in the atmosphere and the depletion of the stratospheric ozone layer).

Biological pathogens. Biological pathogens in the human environment—in water, food, air, or soil—represent the single most serious environmental problem in terms of their impact on human health (WHO, 1992a). Waterborne diseases are the single largest category of communicable diseases worldwide, and account for more than four million infant and child deaths per year (WHO, 1992a). In many Third World cities or city districts, waterborne diseases are among the major causes of infant and child death and a major cause of adult death. By contrast, very few fatal cases of waterborne diseases are now recorded in Europe or North America. Diarrheal diseases account for most infant and child deaths and a high proportion of illnesses. Risk factors include overcrowding, poor sanitation, contaminated water, and inadequate food hygiene (Rossi-Espagnet, Goldstein, & Tabibzadeh, 1991). Many studies of poor urban districts have shown diarrheal diseases to be a major cause of morbidity and mortality (see, for instance, Adedoyin & Watts, 1989; Misra, 1990; Songsore & McGranahan, 1993). Where water supplies and provision for sanitation are inadequate for high proportions of the entire population, they can remain one of the most serious health problems within citywide averages.

There are also various skin and eye infections, termed "water-washed infections," since they are related to poor hygiene and inadequate water supplies, but are not waterborne. They include scabies and fungal infections of the skin and trachoma (which may lead to blindness), all of which are very common in many hot climates (Cairncross & Feachem, 1993). Infections carried by lice such as relapsing fever and typhus, can also be much reduced by increased use of water for washing (Cairncross & Feachem, 1993). Among other water-related diseases, filariasis and intestinal worms (especially ascariasis/roundworm and trichuriasis/whipworm) stand out for the millions of urban people who are debilitated by them; only a small proportion of those with these diseases die of them, but they cause severe pain to hundreds of millions of people (WHO, 1992a). Various case studies have shown a high proportion of the population in particular low-income settlements or districts with large intestinal worm burdens—for instance in Manila (Auer, 1989), Kuala Lumpur (Bundey, Kan, & Rose, 1988) and Allahabad (Misra, 1990).

Many disease vectors live, breed, or feed within or around houses and settlements in urban areas. The diseases they cause or carry include some of the major causes of ill health and premature death in many cities—especially malaria (*Anopheles* mosquitoes) and diarrheal diseases (cockroaches, blowflies, and houseflies). There are severe problems with malaria in urban areas in large parts of Africa, Asia, and Latin America (Bradley et al., 1991; Rossi-Espagnet, Goldstein, & Tabibzadeh, 1991). There are also many other diseases caused or carried by insects, spiders, or mites including bancroftian filariasis (*Culex* mosquitoes), Chagas disease (*triatomine* bugs), dengue fever (*Aedes* mosquitoes), hepatitis A (houseflies, cockroaches), leishmaniasis (sandfly), plague (certain fleas), relapsing fever (body lice and soft ticks), scabies (scabies mites), trachoma (face flies), typhus (body lice and fleas), yaws (face flies), and yellow fever (*Aedes* mosquitoes) (Schofield et al., 1990). Many of these vectors thrive when there is poor drainage and inadequate provision for garbage collection, sanitation, and piped water supply water. *Anopheles* mosquitoes breed in standing water. The sandflies which transmit leishmaniasis can breed in piles of refuse or in pit latrines, while the *Culex quinquefasciatus* mosquitoes, which are one of the vectors for bancroftian leishmaniasis, can breed in open or cracked septic tanks, flooded pit latrines, and drains (Cairncross & Feachem, 1993). Leptospirosis outbreaks have been associated with flooding in São Paulo and Rio de Janeiro—the disease passing to humans through water contaminated with the urine of infected rats or certain domestic animals (Sapir, 1990).

Some diseases transmitted by insect vectors have long been urban problems; for instance, reports on malaria in Freetown (Sierra Leone) date from 1926 (Blacklock & Evans, 1926, quoted in Rossi-Espagnet, Goldstein, & Tabibzadeh, 1991) while colonial town planning regulations in Nigeria sought to protect the colonial populations from malaria by insisting on a building-free zone between European and non-European residential areas (Aradeon, Umo, & Aina, 1986). Other diseases remain concentrated in rural areas—especially those like schistosomiasis that are associated with water reservoirs and irrigation canals and ditches—although even schistosomiasis is widespread in many cities (Rossi-Espagnet, Goldstein, & Tabibzadeh, 1991). One reason is the number of infected rural inhabitants who move to urban areas. Another is that some disease vectors have adapted to urban environments or the expanding urban areas have produced changes in the local ecology that favor the emergence or multiplication of a particular disease vector; these help explain the rapid increase in lymphatic filariasis and malaria in urban populations (WHO, 1992a). The diseases spread by the *Aedes* group of mosquitoes (which include dengue, dengue haemorrhagic fever, and yellow fever) are serious health problems in many cities; pots and jars, small tanks, drums, and cisterns used for storing water in houses lacking regular piped supplies can provide breeding habitats for these mosquitoes (Rossi-Espagnet, Goldstein, & Tabibzadeh, 1991). So too can small pools of clean water within residential areas in, for instance, discarded tin cans and rubber tires (Cairncross & Feachem, 1993). Chagas disease, with an estimated 18 million people infected in Latin America, primarily affects poor rural households, as the insect vector rests and breeds in cracks in house walls. But it is increasingly an urban problem too, both through the migration of infected persons to urban areas (there is no effective treatment for the disease) and through the peri-urban informal settlements, where the insect vectors are evident (Briceno-Leon, 1990; Gomes Pereira, 1989).

Acute respiratory infections (especially pneumonia) are a major cause of infant and child death and ill health although their extent, their health impact, and the risk factors associated with them remain poorly understood (Bradley et al., 1991; Rossi-Espagnet, Goldstein, & Tabibzadeh, 1991). A fifth of all infant deaths in Porto Alegre (Brazil) were found to be due to pneumonia. Mortality rates from pneumonia were six times higher in illegal settlements than in other areas (and the main cause of infant death there) (Guimaraes & Fischmann, 1985). Respiratory infections are also among the most common sources of ill health among children and adults, as demonstrated in recent household surveys in Accra and Jakarta. In Accra, upper-respiratory tract infections were second only to malaria as the most common disease reported in outpatient facilities in Accra. In interviews with 956 women in Accra, 19.5 percent reported at least one respiratory problem symptom in the previous two weeks (Songsore & McGranahan, 1993). Interviews with women in 1,055 households in Jakarta found that 28.1 percent had suffered from one of five respiratory disease symptoms in the two weeks prior to the interview (Surjadi, 1993). Among these 1,055 households, there were 658 children aged six years or less, and 26.6 percent had suffered from respiratory disease in the two weeks preceding the interview, while 16.6 percent had suffered from fever (Surjadi, 1993).

The quality of the indoor environment has an important influence on the incidence and severity of respiratory infections—perhaps most especially through overcrowding, inadequate ventilation, dampness, and indoor air pollution from coal or biomass combustion for cooking and/or heating. A child who contracts bronchitis or pneumonia in the Third World is 50 times more likely to die than a child in Europe or North America (Pio, 1986). A recent WHO report summarized the problem:

> Acute respiratory infections tend to be endemic rather than epidemic, affect younger groups, and more prevalent in urban than in rural areas. The frequency of contact, the density of the population and the concentration and proximity of infective and susceptible people in an urban population promote the transmission of the infective organisms. Poorer groups . . . are much more at risk because of the greater proportion of younger age groups, limited health and financial resources, and overcrowded households in congested settlements with limited access to vaccines and antibacterial drugs. The constant influx of migrants susceptible to infection and possible carriers of new virulent strains of infective agents, together with the inevitable increase in household numbers fosters the transfer of nasopharyngeal microorganisms. (WHO 1992a, p. 204)

A lack of health care services which can implement effective immunization programs and overcrowded conditions helps ensure that the diseases spread by airborne infection or contact which are easily prevented by immunization such as diphtheria, measles, pertussis (whooping cough), and chicken pox remain major causes of ill health and infant and child death. Measles is a major cause of infant and child morbidity and mortality in poor urban areas (Foster, 1990). Tuberculosis, another vaccine-preventable disease, is the single largest cause of adult mortality worldwide, accounting for some three million deaths a year (WHO, 1992a). The incidence of tuberculosis is also linked to overcrowded conditions in urban areas. The highest incidence tends to be among populations living in the poorest areas, with high levels of overcrowding and high numbers of social contacts (WHO, 1992a). A combination of overcrowding and poor ventilation often means that TB infection is transmitted to more than half the family members (Cauthen, Pio, & ten Dam, 1988). Rheumatic fever and meningococcal meningitis are also among other diseases transmitted by biological pathogens, where overcrowded conditions increase the likelihood of transmission (Sapir 1990; WHO 1992a).

Crowded cramped conditions, inadequate water supplies, and inadequate facilities for preparing and storing food greatly exacerbate the risk of food contamination. McGranahan (1991) notes that:

> microbially contaminated food contributes to a high incidence of acute diarrhoea in Third World countries and foodborne diseases including cholera, botulism, typhoid fever and parasitism . . . microbial activity generally contributes to food spoilage while unsafe chemicals may deliberately be added to retard or disguise spoilage . . . food contamination is intimately linked to the sanitary conditions of food preparation, processing and even production. (p. 24)

In addition, "within the home, there are likely to be numerous interconnections and interactions among water, sanitation, flies, animal, personal hygiene, and food that are responsible for diarrhoea transmission" (Esrey & Feachem 1989).

Chemical pollutants in the urban environment: To date, most concern regarding health effects has centered on lead (in food, water, and air); indoor air pollutants from fuel combustion; toxic/hazardous wastes; and ambient air pollution. Lead is a particular concern, especially for children, because there is increasing evidence that relatively low concentrations of lead in the blood may greatly affect their mental development—and this is an effect that persists into adulthood (Needleman et al., 1991). Exposure to lead may also contribute significantly to higher risks of heart attacks and strokes in adults. The four major sources of lead are: exhausts from petrol-engined motor vehicles (except vehicles that use lead-free petrol); lead water piping (especially where water supplies are acidic); industrial emissions; and lead in paint. A study of blood lead levels in adult volunteers in ten cities between 1979 and 1981 found the highest lead concentration in Mexico City residents; lead blood levels were above the WHO guideline—and also 2–4 times higher than in cities where low-lead or lead-free gasoline was used (UNEP & WHO, 1988). In Mexico City and in Bangalore (one of India's major metropolitan centres), 10 percent of the sampled population had blood lead concentrations well above the WHO guideline, above which biochemical changes in the blood begin to occur (UNEP & WHO, 1987). A study in Mexico City in 1988 found that over a quarter of the newborn infants in Mexico City had lead levels in their blood high enough to impair neurological and motor-physical development (Rothenburg et al., 1989). A study in Bangkok that sought to rank urban environmental problems based on their health risks suggested that lead should be ranked with airborne particulates and biological pathogens (primarily acute diarrhea, dengue fever, dysentery, and intestinal worms) as the highest risk environmental problems (U.S. AID, 1990).

Regarding indoor air pollution, fumes from coal, wood, and other biomass fuels burned indoors are likely to be the main chemical hazard. Indoor air pollution from fuel combustion certainly affects more rural than urban dwellers, since many more rural households are regularly exposed to potentially harmful emissions from open fires or poorly designed stoves with inadequate attention to venting the flue gases. Estimates suggest hundreds of millions of rural inhabitants suffer from ill health from this; perhaps tens of millions of urban households are similarly affected. Certainly in many cities, coal and biomass fuels are widely used, especially among poorer households. The most serious health risks are from burns and smoke inhalation (WHO, 1992a). Chronic effects of smoke inhalation include inflammation of the respiratory tract caused by continued exposure to irritant gases and fumes which "reduces resistance to acute respiratory infections, and infection, in turn, enhances susceptibility to the inflammatory effects of smoke and fumes, establishing a vicious circle of pathological change. These processes may lead to emphysema and chronic obstructive pulmonary disease, which can progress to the stage where impaired lung function reduces the circulation of blood through the lungs, causing right-side heart failure (cor pulmonale) (Pandey, Basnayat, & Neupane 1989; WHO, 1992a). Cor pulmonale is a crippling killing disease, characterized by a prolonged period of distressing breathlessness preceding death. However, McGranahan (1991) notes that, while some studies have suggested that indoor air pollution has significant effects on health, others have been unable to show a clear link. "It is not clear whether this variation reflects methodological differences in discerning important real effects which do exist, spurious results in the few cases where significant health effects have been detected or underlying differences in the relative importance of indoor air pollution in different areas" (p. 23).

There are also the health impacts of air pollutants outdoors. In many Third World cities, the concentrations of air pollutants are already high enough to cause illness in more susceptible individuals and premature death among the elderly, especially those with respiratory problems (WHO, 1992a). Current levels of air pollution may also be impairing the health of far more people, but the links have not been proven. The (limited) data on air pollution in Third World cities also suggests that it is generally getting worse. An estimated 1.4 billion urban residents worldwide are exposed to annual averages for suspended particulate matter or sulphur dioxide (or both), which are higher than the minimum standards recommended by the World Health Organization (UNEP & WHO, 1988). The (limited) data available for Third World cities suggest the trend is toward increasing concentrations (UNEP, 1991). Comparable estimates are not possible for nitrogen oxides and carbon monoxide, although studies in particular cities or city districts suggest ambient air pollution levels that can impair health. There are also concerns about the health impacts of secondary pollutants formed as a result of reactions between primary pollutants and the air—for instance, acid sulphates and ozone (Waller, 1991).

In certain industrial centers, air pollution levels can be sufficiently high to show demonstrable health impairment. For instance, in Cubatao (Brazil), air pollution levels have been linked to reduced lung functions in children (Hofmaier, 1992). Links between health problems and air pollution levels have also been suggested by comparisons between the health of people in highly polluted areas within cities and those in less polluted areas; some of these have shown a strong association between the incidence of respiratory infections and pollution levels. In addition, in cities where acute episodes of high concentrations of air pollution occur at particular times (for instance, when high emissions coincide with particular weather conditions), an increased incidence of mortality among particularly vulnerable groups is common (WHO, 1992a). In Latin America, recent studies suggest that air pollution levels are sufficiently high in São Paulo, Rio de Janeiro, and Belo Horizonte, Bogotá, Santiago, Mexico City, Monterrey, and Guadalajara, Caracas, and Lima that a high priority should be given to their control (Romieu et al., 1990). One estimate suggests that over two million children suffer from chronic cough because of urban air pollution and that air pollution means an excess of 24,300 deaths a year in Latin America (Romieu et al., 1990). This same source estimated that some 65 million person days of workers' activities was lost to respiratory-related problems caused by air pollution. While the authors emphasize that these are rough estimates, they give an idea of the order of magnitude of the problem. Local topographical and climate conditions can exacerbate problems, as in Mexico City, where thermal inversions help trap pollutants within the valley in which the city is located.

There is also the health impact of chemical wastes dumped into water bodies or onto land sites. In most Third World cities, toxic/hazardous industrial and commercial wastes are disposed of in water bodies or land sites without special provision to treat them before disposal (to render them less damaging to human health and the local environment) or without measures to ensure that disposal itself isolates them from the environment. There is often little incentive for industry and commerce to reduce polluting emissions, since few are penalized and the penalties, when finally imposed, are so small as to be little deterrent. Reports from Third World cities of severe health problems arising from human contact with toxic or hazardous wastes are increasingly common (Hardoy, Mitlin, & Satterthwaite, 1992).

The health impacts of occupational exposures to chemical pollutants are also a significant source of ill health. Environmental hazards are evident in workplaces from large factories and commercial institutions down to small "backstreet" workshops and home-based work. They include dangerous concentrations of toxic chemicals and dust and inadequate ventilation, as well as other environmental hazards such as inadequate protection of workers from machinery and noise. Many case studies show a high proportion of the workers in particular industries or industrial plants whose health is affected by workplace exposures. For instance, a study of an Egyptian pesticide factory found that "about 40 percent of the workers had problems related to pesticide poisoning, ranging from asthma to enlarged livers" (Pepall, 1992, p. 15). In most countries, the scale of occupational injuries and diseases is almost certainly greatly underreported. For instance, the Mexican Social Security Institute reported an average of 2,000 to 3,000 cases of work-related illnesses across the country in 1988, but a study in just one large steel mill found 4,000–5,000 cases alone, with more than 80 percent of the workers exposed to extreme heat, loud noise, and toxic dust (Castonguay, 1992). A paper on Bangkok's environmental problems noted that a remarkable number of Thai workers are exposed to poor working environments, but that the number of workers suffering from occupational diseases is small. "This may be a reflection of the difficulties of linking disease to working conditions rather than revealing a satisfactory condition" (Phantumvanit & Liengcharernsit, 1989). Other studies have shown serious health impacts for workers from exposure to toxic chemicals—for instance, from benzene poisoning for leather workers in Turkey (Askoy et al., 1976) and lead poisoning for people working in lead-acid battery repair shops in Kingston, Jamaica (Matte et al., 1989).

Consideration must also be given to the large-scale accidents where chemicals had the central role in health impacts: the accidental release of methyl iso-cyanate at Bhopal (over 3,000 dead and perhaps 100,000 seriously injured) or the natural gas explosions in Mexico City in 1984 (over 1,000 dead). These and other large-scale accidents are often quoted as of major significance in terms of the health impact on urban populations. The attempts by European and North American industries to dispose of their toxic wastes in Third World nations have also received much publicity. The scale of the health impact arising from occupational exposures and from exposure to indoor and outdoor air pollution is likely to be larger and more widespread—but it remains largely undocumented. The next 20–30 years may show that the health impact of chemical pollutants in the Third World—in the air and water, and through direct exposure in the home or workplace—has been considerably underestimated.

Availability, Cost, and Quality of Natural Resources

The availability to any individual or household of such natural resources as food, fuel, and fresh water is obviously central to health. The environmental dimension is prominent, in that the ecosystem defines the limits for the availability of fresh water, soils, and forests but social, economic, and political factors are usually the dominant influences on who has access to them or to the land and water sources from which they can be drawn. While access to land and forests for fuel and food is normally considered a rural issue, there is increasing evidence that access to land on which food can be grown is important to poorer households in many cities, especially in poorer and less urbanized nations. For instance, a study by the Mazingira Institute pointed to the importance for most households in Nairobi (Kenya's capital and largest city) and other Kenyan urban centers of food they grow or produce themselves. Under such circumstances, access to land on which crops can be grown and some livestock raised becomes of great importance to most households (Lee-Smith et al., 1987).

Only rarely does a shortage of fresh water explain why so many urban households lack access to safe and sufficient supplies. It is much more common for these to be the result of the refusal by the government to allow them an adequate supply—for instance, because they live in illegal settlements and are considered to have no right to public services or because they live in a peripheral municipality within a large metropolitan center where local authorities lack the resources to provide water supplies. Although there are cities where overall shortages inhibit improved supplies, these are not the norm. In addition, it is not necessarily poorer households' lack of capacity to pay for water which explains inadequate provision. It is common for those in squatter settlements to pay private water vendors between four and 100 times as much per unit volume as the middle and upper income groups pay for publicly provided piped water (World Bank, 1988). Thus it is generally neither a lack of water nor a lack of willingness to pay which stops piped-water supplies reaching poorer areas (Cairncross, 1990).

Physical Hazards

The true extent of accidental injuries is often grossly underestimated. An analysis of accidents in children in ten Third World nations found that they were the main cause of death for 5–9-year-olds and 10–14-year-olds (Manciaux & Romer, 1986). Accordingly, for every accidental death, there are several hundred accidental injuries. One of the most common is road accidents—responsible worldwide for some 500,000 deaths each year and many times this number of serious accidents (WHO, 1992a). Many accidental injuries are linked to poor-quality, overcrowded housing. Burns, scalds, and accidental fires are more common in overcrowded shelters, especially when five or more persons often live in one room and there is little chance of providing occupants (especially children) with protection from open fires, stoves, or kerosene heaters. The risk of accidental fires is further increased in most urban dwellings because of the use of flammable materials (wood, cardboard, plastic, canvas, straw). Overcrowded dwellings also make it difficult to keep medicines and dangerous household chemicals (such as bleach) out of children's reach. Here, as in many environmental problems, the level of risk is usually compounded by social factors, such as a lack of adult supervision when most adults have to work. The health impact of accidents is also compounded by the lack of a health service that can rapidly provide emergency treatment, followed by longer-term treatment and care (Goldstein, 1990).

There are also the physical hazards for the land sites on which housing develops. In nearly all Third World cities there are large clusters of illegal housing on dangerous sites (for instance, steep hillsides, floodplains, or desert) or housing built on polluted sites (for instance, around solid-waste dumps, beside open drains and sewers, or in industrial areas with high levels of air pollution). Or housing develops in sites subject to high noise levels—for instance, close to major highways or airports. Most cities have large areas of unused and well-located land not subject to such hazards (Sarin, 1983). The problem is not a shortage of the resource (safe land sites) but the fact that poorer groups have no means to get access to these sites and governments do not intervene in their favor.

Aspects of the Built Environment with Negative Consequences on Health

Psychosocial health problems such as depression, drug and alcohol abuse, suicide, and interpersonal violence (including child and spouse mistreatment and abuse, and target violence such as teacher assault and rape) now represent among the most serious health problems in many cities in Europe and North America (WHO, 1992a). Many psychosocial disorders are associated with poor-quality housing and living environments. Many nonenvironmental factors are also important—for instance, the stress associated with inadequate income and insecure and strenuous livelihoods and insecure tenure for the shelter (for tenants or squatters), especially for those living with a constant threat of eviction.

Psychosocial health problems are becoming a major cause of death and morbidity among adolescents and young adults in many urban areas of the Third World or in particular districts within urban areas. For instance, psychosocial disorders are among the most important causes of death in cities as diverse as Shenyang and Rio de Janeiro (Bradley et al., 1991). Homicides were responsible for 5 percent of all deaths in São Paulo City in 1986 (Leitmann, 1991). Poor-quality and overcrowded housing and living environments contribute to the stress that underlies most psychosocial disorders, and these disorders may develop into particular diseases or impair the body's immune system.

Many physical characteristics of the housing and living environment can influence the incidence and severity of psychosocial disorders. These include noise, overcrowding, inappropriate design, and the stresses and difficulties caused in any house or residential area when there is inadequate or no provision for sanitation, garbage collection, and maintenance (Ekblad et al., 1991). Good-quality housing and living environments can greatly reduce stress and its health consequences—through sufficient space, location close to friends and family, easy access to desired services, and facilities for safe play for children and for recreation, minimum noise, and few personal hazards. Within the wider neighborhood in which the house is located, a sense of security, good-quality physical infrastructure (roads, pavements, drains, streetlights), and services (e.g., street cleaning), the availability of emergency services and easy access to educational, health, and social services, as well as cultural and other amenities, reduce stress and contribute to good mental health. In addition to the quality of the dwelling and its neighborhood, the subjective experience of the dwellers is also important for health—their level of satisfaction with the house and its neighborhood, and its location within the urban area.

The extent to which any individual or household has the possibility of modifying or changing their housing environment and working with others in the locality to effect change in the wider neighborhood is also an important influence on their health. Many critiques of public housing and of urban planning in Third World cities (especially "slum" and squatter clearance and redevelopment) have centered on the loss of individual, household, and community control (Turner, 1976). These often document the hardships caused to households and, on occasion, the negative health consequences, although they do not examine the social pathologies that might be associated with such changes. There is also a large and varied literature on the importance for the physical and mental health of individuals and "communities" of being able to command events which control their lives (Duhl, 1990). Medical doctors and psychiatrists are increasingly recognizing the importance of such a link (Duhl, 1990; WHO, 1992a).

There are also interacting variables that can promote or prevent the process that might lead to psychosocial disorder or disease (Ekblad, 1993). For instance, a social-support network may prevent stress from developing into stress-related disorders or diseases ". . . strong social networks and a sense of community organization in many rundown inner city districts . . . and squatter settlements . . . might help explain the remarkably low level of psychosocial problems" (WHO, 1992a, p. 215). The importance of such networks can also be seen in the increase in physical and mental ill health among populations relocated from inner-city tenements or illegal settlements to "better-quality" housing, partly because such networks became disrupted (Rossi-Espagnet, Goldstein, & Tabibzadeh, 1991; Turner, 1976). However, the precise linkages between different elements of the physical environment and each psychosocial disorder or disease are difficult to ascertain—and difficult to separate from other variables (Ekblad, 1993). In addition, care must be taken not to overstate the effects of environmental factors on psychosocial health when more fundamental social and economic factors, such as very low and unstable incomes and oppression or discrimination, underlie psychosocial disorders and very poor living environments.[1]

Local, Regional, National, and Global Natural Resource Degradation

Natural resource degradation caused by pollutants from city-based enterprises or households can influence the health of urban dwellers in a variety of ways. One example is through land or water used by urban households for urban horticulture being polluted by urban wastes. A second, more indirect route is damage to local food production outside the city from air or water pollution that then impacts on the health of poorer households through decreased food availability or higher prices—for instance, through local fisheries being damaged, or local fish and seafood being prohibited for human consumption because of their contamination by industrial wastes. An increasing number of reports document how city-generated wastes damage or pollute fish stocks in rivers, estuaries, and coastal waters, or damage vegetation through acid deposition derived from the emissions of urban-based vehicles, households, and industries (Hardoy, Mitlin, & Satterthwaite, 1992). Some urban populations suffer from water pollution caused by city-based activities degrading particular rivers or other water bodies "upstream."

The depletion of the stratospheric ozone layer and the increasing concentrations of what are termed "greenhouse gases" in the earth's atmosphere (and the possible, continued atmospheric warming) will have major health impacts for urban (and rural) populations. Some will be direct—for instance, increased heat stress from higher temperatures and a growing incidence of skin cancer from stratospheric ozone depletion. But the indirect health impacts are likely to be much greater—for instance, those arising from changes in agricultural production, sea-level rises (including flooding and damage to buildings, sewers and drains), disruption to cities' fresh water resources and the expansion in the areas where some of the most serious tropical disease vectors can survive and breed.

---

[1] See Cohen & Swift, 1993, for a discussion of this in Contra Costa County, California.

WHO BEARS THE HEALTH COSTS OF ENVIRONMENTAL PROBLEMS?

Factors Affecting Vulnerability

The presence of an environmental hazard (for instance, a pathogen, pollutant, physical hazard, or psychosocial stressor such as high noise level) does not necessarily mean that it will harm someone. This depends on characteristics of the individual, household, and social group exposed to the hazard. Certain individual or group characteristics can also influence the severity of the health impact.

Some characteristics influence whether ill health or injury from some environmental hazard can be avoided and/or the severity of the health impact:

- For biological pathogens, weak body defense (some a function of age and of nutritional status, some a function of acquired immunity);
- For physical hazards, people's physical limitations (e.g., children, disabled people, many older people with limitations to their mobility);
- For exposure to chemicals: age, activity (when exposed) and health status at the time of exposure. Certain groups are particularly susceptible to certain pollutants (for instance, asthmatics are more sensitive to certain common urban air pollutants). Genetic factors may influence sensitivity; and
- Social roles that increase duration and/or severity of exposure to environmental hazards.

There are also factors that influence how easily the individual, household, or social group can cope with environmentally induced illness or injury. These include:

- The extent of public, private, and community provision for health care and emergency response to accidental injuries or acute diseases;
- The individual's or household's ability to afford health care and emergency response, to purchase medicines, and take time off to recuperate when sick or injured;
- Individual, household, or community coping mechanisms once the hazard has caused sickness or injury; for instance, knowing what to do, whom to visit, and how to rearrange individual/household survival strategies.[2]

---

[2] This list draws from Corbett, 1989, and Pryer, 1989. In general, the literature on rural poverty seems to have developed a much more detailed understanding of what underpins vulnerability for poorer groups.

The people who are most vulnerable to environmental hazards are those least able to avoid them, who have the most serious health impact from them, and/or are least able to cope with the illness or injury they cause. Once one begins to examine what causes people's vulnerability to environmental hazards, the interaction between environmental hazards and social, economic, political, and demographic factors becomes clearer. "Health outcomes are not only influenced by environmental conditions but also by the inputs of health services, by the characteristics of the population and by the socio-economic conditions in which people live" (Stephens & Harpham, 1992). Virtually all environmental health problems in urban areas have a social, economic, or political underpinning in that it is social, economic, or political factors which determine who is most at risk and who cannot obtain the needed treatment and support when illness or injury occurs (Hardoy, Mitlin, & Satterthwaite, 1992). To give but one example, the high incidence of diseases associated with contaminated food and water in most poor urban communities is an environmental problem, in the sense that the disease-causing agents infect humans through ingesting water or food—but can also be judged to be a political problem, since nearly all governments and aid agencies have the capacity to greatly reduce current levels of morbidity and mortality by improved provision of water, sanitation, and drainage (Hardoy, Mitlin, & Satterthwaite, 1992). It can also be judged as a social or economic problem, in that it is lower income groups' limited means to pay for accommodation which usually underlies their poor housing conditions. This makes it difficult to isolate the impact of environmental factors on health as distinct from other factors.

Low-Income as a Risk Factor

The economic underpinning of environmental hazards becomes clear when comparing the hazards faced by poorer groups with those faced by richer groups. Most case studies on communicable diseases and morbidity and mortality show that the group most vulnerable are predominantly the poor—be they children, adults in crowded, unhygienic conditions, or workers in particular occupations (Bradley et al., 1991). Low-income groups are the least able to afford the homes that protect against environmental hazards, for instance, good-quality housing in neighborhoods with piped water, and adequate provision for sanitation, garbage collection, paved roads, and drains. In addition, higher income groups will generally have less dangerous jobs and work in occupations where occupational hazards are minimized.

Low-income households are also more vulnerable, because they lack the buffers to cope with illness or injury (Corbett, 1989). Low-income groups generally have the greatest difficulties in getting treatment for any injury or illness—for instance, emergency services in the case of a serious accident, and treatment from a health center or hospital (Goldstein, 1990). They have the least means to afford medicines and (generally) the least possibility of taking time off to allow recovery, because the loss of income from doing so would press heavily on their survival, and because they are unable to afford health insurance—or obtain the jobs for which health insurance is paid by the firm.

Low-income groups generally have the least access to fresh water—with all its implications for the ability to guard against water-related diseases. When water consumption per person in cities averages 20–40 liters per person per day (well below the minimum required for good health), most poorer groups' consumption is likely to be less than half the average (Hardoy, Mitlin, & Satterthwaite, 1992). In this sense, most Third World cities are comparable to cities in Europe and North America many decades ago, before it became the accepted responsibility of city or municipal governments to ensure that all citizens had access to piped water, sewers, drains, and garbage collection.

The Geography of Inequality

If there was sufficient information available to construct a map of a city, showing the level of risk from environmental hazards in each neighborhood, the areas with the highest risks would coincide with the areas with a predominance of low-income groups. In most Third World cities, the correlations between income levels and environmental hazards would be particularly strong in such aspects as the quality and quantity of water, the level of provision for sanitation, drainage, and solid waste collection, and the risk from floods, landslides, or other natural hazards. The reason is simply that poorer groups are priced out of safe, well-located, well-serviced housing and land sites. In many cities, there will be a strong correlation between indoor air quality and income, because poorer groups use more polluting fuels and more inefficient stoves (or open fires) which ensure a much worse air quality indoors. The fact that poorer groups also live in more overcrowded conditions exacerbates this and the transmission of infectious diseases. A high proportion of poor groups live in shacks made of flammable material, with higher risks of accidental fires. Poorer groups will generally have the least access to playgrounds, parks, and other open spaces managed for public use. The correlations between income level and level of air pollution may not be so precise. In certain "hot-spots," such as close to quarries, cement works, and industries with high levels of air pollution in their immediate surrounds, the correlation is likely to be strong. But the correlations are less clear when an entire city suffers from air pollution. In addition, particular "hot spots" for air pollution have often developed relatively recently, but if they persist and are well defined, they will eventually be reflected in housing and land prices (as richer groups move out and poorer groups move in).

Many studies on the differentials in health status or mortality rates between city districts (or boroughs or municipalities) show conditions in poorer areas to be much worse than the more wealthy areas or the city average (Bradley et al., 1991, Harpham, Vaughan, & Lusty, 1988). Infant mortality rates in poorer areas are often four or more times higher than in richer areas, with much larger differentials often apparent if the poorest district is compared to the richest district. Large differentials between rich and poor districts are also common in the incidence of many environment-related diseases—for instance, tuberculosis and typhoid. Differentials in the number of people dying from certain environment-related diseases are often very large—for instance, many more deaths in poorer communities are likely to come from diarrheal diseases and acute respiratory infections such as pneumonia and influenza. Maternal mortality rates are likely to be much higher than any city average in low-income districts where homes lack basic services, especially community-based health care with good prenatal services and emergency services. To date, the statistics showing differentials in maternal mortality have concentrated on those between rich and poor nations (where, among the poorest nations, maternal mortality rates can be 100 or more times that in the richer nations) (WHO, 1992a). There are also likely to be large differentials between most low- and high-income areas in the proportion of people who are disabled or chronically ill. Box 8.2 gives examples of differentials between different areas within a city in terms of pollution levels, access to public services, and health indicators.

To a large extent, capacity to pay for housing defines the scale of the environmental hazards present in the housing and living environment, including whether or not there is safe, sufficient water supplies, sanitation, garbage collection, and drainage. In most Third World cities, low-income individuals and households have very little chance of obtaining healthy legal accommodation within a neighborhood where environmental risks are minimized—that is, one with sufficient space, security of tenure, services, and facilities, and on a site not prone to flooding, water-logging, or landslides. Many low-income groups also have the constant fear of eviction; this is usually a permanent worry for most tenants, temporary boarders in cheap rooming houses, those in illegal settlements, and "land" renters.

The insecurity and environmental hazards arise from a combination of three factors: their low incomes; the refusal (or inability) of government to intervene to guarantee their access to shelters that are not so dangerous, or

Box 8.2—Intra-City Differentials in Environmental Hazards, Access to Public Services, and Health Indicators.

a. Differentials in environmental hazards

Mexico City. The highest concentrations of particulate matter in the air are found in the southeast and the northeast areas, which are predominantly low-income areas.

Bombay (India). A study in 1977 compared the health of residents in two districts with heavy concentrations of industries, with those in a district with very little industry. People in the industrialized districts suffered a much higher incidence of diseases such as bronchitis, tuberculosis, skin allergies, anemia, and eye irritation, and there was a notable rise in deaths from cancer in one of the industrialized districts.

Caracas (Venezuela). An estimated 574,000 people live in illegal settlements on slopes with a significant risk of landslides. Most of the areas continuously affected by slope failures have been low-income settlements.

b. Differentials in access to public services

Buenos Aires (Argentina). Of the 11 million or so inhabitants of the Buenos Aires metropolitan area, only 57 percent have running water and only 45 percent have connections to the sewer system. Virtually all of those in the Capital Federal (the center of the metropolitan area with some three million inhabitants) have piped water and connection to sewers. It is in the poorer, peripheral municipalities outside this central area but within the metropolitan area that a high proportion of the population lacks either running water or connection to sewers. For instance, in the municipalities of General Sarmiento, Merlo, and Moreno, less than five percent of the population have running water and less than four percent have connections to sewers. Three other municipalities have less than 12 percent of their population with running water, and less than ten percent with connections to sewers.

Accra (Ghana). In a survey covering 1,000 households, large differentials were found, according to income. In regard to water, 78 percent of the wealthiest quintile had in-house piped supplies, compared to six percent of the poorest quintile; only seven percent of the wealthiest quintile purchased water from vendors compared to 49 percent for the poorest quintile. For sanitation, 77 percent of the wealthiest quintile had flush toilets compared to seven percent for the poorest

Box 8.2—(*Continued*)

quintile; the poorest three quintiles depended mainly on pit latrines or pan latrines. Among the poorest quintile, 22 percent of households reported diarrhea among children under six in the two weeks prior to the interview compared with nine percent for the wealthiest quintile.

Surabaya (Indonesia). The wealthiest 20 percent of the population are reported to consume 80 percent of the public services, including those essential to a healthy environment.

Mexico City. Residents in the high-income Chapultepec consume on average some 450 liters of water per person per day; the average in Nezahualcoyotl is only 50 liters per day. Overall, nine percent of consumers account for 75 percent of the fresh water consumption, while two million people have very inadequate access to safe water supplies.

Santiago de Chile. In some of the richest districts, per capita water consumption per day is between 300 and 450 liters per day. In many of the poorer districts, it is 100 liters a day or less (for instance just 80 liters a day in La Pintana on the periphery).

c. Differentials in health indicators

Jakarta (Indonesia). Official estimates suggest an infant mortality rate for the whole city at 33 per 1000 live births, while estimates for some of the poorer areas suggest rates of four to five times the city average.

Karachi (Pakistan). In three low-income areas, between 95 and 152 infants per 1000 live births died before the age of one; in a middle class area, only 32 per 1000 died.

Manila (Philippines). In Tondo (one of the largest squatter settlements), the infant mortality rate was 210 per 1000 live births in the mid-1970s compared to 76 for nonsquatter areas in Manila. The proportion of people with tuberculosis in Tondo was nine times the average for nonsquatter areas; typhoid was also four times as common.

Port-au-Prince (Haiti). In the "slums," one in five infants die before their first birthday, while another one in ten die between their first and second birthdays. This is almost three times the mortality rates in rural areas and many times the rate in the richer areas of Port-au-Prince, where infant and child mortality rates were similar to those in urban areas of the United States.

Box 8.2—(*Continued*)

Pôrto Alegre (Brazil). Infant mortality rates among residents of "shanty towns" were three times as high as among the non-"shanty-town" residents. Neonatal mortality rates were twice as high, and post-neonatal mortality more than five times as high. Mortality from pneumonia and influenza was six times higher in "shanty towns" and from septicemia eight times higher.

Sao Paulo (Brazil). Infant mortality rates can vary by a factor of four, depending on the district. In the core area, it is 42 infants per 1000 live births, while in one of the predominantly poor periurban municipalities, the rate was 175 per 1000 live births. Infant death rates from enteritis, diarrhea, and pneumonia on the city's periphery were twice as high as in the core area.

Tianjin (China). A study of environment-related morbidity and mortality in the different subdistricts of the city found large variations. For instance, the average for subdistrict's infant mortality rate was 13, but it reached as high as 31 in one district. TB prevalence in the subdistricts averaged 172 per 100,000 people, with the highest subdistrict figure being 347 and the lowest just 54. There were also major differences in mortality rates for lung cancer and cervical cancer.

Sources: This is an updated and expanded version of a box first published in Hardoy, Mitlin, & Satterthwaite, 1992. It draws from the following studies: *Accra*: Songsore & McGranahan, 1993. *Bombay*: Centre for Science and Environment, 1983. *Buenos Aires*: Zorrilla & Guaresti, 1986. *Caracas*: Jimenez Diaz, 1992. *Jakarta*: Harpham, Garner, & Surjadi, 1990. *Karachi*: Aga Khan University students, 1986 (unpublished), quoted in Harpham, Lusty, & Vaughan. *Manila*: Basta, 1977. *Mexico City*: Schteingart, 1989. *Port-au-Prince*: Rohde, 1983. *Porto Alegre*: Guimaraes & Fischmann, 1985. *Santiago*: Espinoza, 1988. *São Paulo*: World Bank, 1984. *Surabaya*: Silas, Johan, quoted in Douglass, 1992. *Tianjin*: Bertraud & Young, 1990, quoted in Leitmann, 1991 (See Bibliography for full references.)

to the resources that allow them to build these themselves; and the refusal or inability of government to provide the community-based health care and emergency services which can do so much to prevent illness or injury and to limit its impact. If an individual or household finds "minimum standard" accommodation too costly, certain sacrifices must be made in the accommodation they choose in order to bring down the price. They usually make sacrifices in environmental quality. Although this means health risks and much inconvenience, these are less important for their survival than other items. For instance, expenditure on food or children's education or on (say) purchasing a second-hand sewing machine to allow a member of the family to earn additional income, are more important than "minimum standard" accommodation.

However, each low-income individual or household will have its own preferred trade-offs in terms of the size of accommodation, terms under which it is occupied, suitability of site, housing quality, location and access to infrastructure and services. For example, to bring down housing costs, a household of five persons might sacrifice space and live in one room, or sacrifice secure tenure and access to piped water and live in a self-constructed house on illegally occupied land. To understand the possibilities for improving the housing environment of such people, one must understand their very diverse needs and priorities. Complex questions have to be explored, including legality of site or house occupation, legality of the housing structure, and the terms under which the occupants live there (i.e., are they guests, legal tenants, illegal tenants, subtenants or owners?). Each person's or household's housing needs also change over time, so any government action seeking to improve shelter conditions must promote a range of housing solutions which match the diversity of needs of poorer groups.

Ironically, dangerous or polluted land sites often serve poorer groups well. For these are the only sites well located in regard to income-earning opportunities on which they have some possibility of living (illegally), because the environmental hazards make the sites unattractive for other potential users. It was the high concentration of low-income residents around the Union Carbide Factory in Bhopal, that resulted in several thousand deaths and over 50,000 serious injuries (Centre for Science and Environment, 1985). In Manila, some 20,000 people live around a garbage dump known as Smokey Mountain, where the decomposition of organic wastes produces a permanent haze and a powerful, rank smell affecting the whole area. Some of these people have lived there 40 years or more. Moving to a cleaner safer location is beyond their means, and many of them make a living scavenging on the dump, often sorting it with their bare hands (Jimenez & Velasquez, 1989).

Differentials Within Low-Income Groups

Among those with low incomes, there will be considerable differentiation in the scale and nature of environmental hazards to which they are exposed and in the severity of the illness or injury to which these contribute, because of their work, and because of the ineffectiveness of government provision to promote occupational health and safety. There are also particularly dangerous settlements and particular groups who face most difficulties getting access to water and washing and bathing facilities—such as pavement dwellers or those who sleep in open spaces, parks, and graveyards. Although Box 8.2 gives examples of inequalities between districts within a city, there will also be intra-household inequalities within low-income settlements and intra-person inequalities within households. For instance, when the infant mortality rate in the bustees of Delhi were found to be 221 per 1,000 live births, the infant mortality rate for the lowest castes in the bustees was more than twice this figure (Basta, 1977). A case study of a low-income settlement in the city of Khulna in Bangladesh found substantial intra-household differentials between the wealthier and poorer households in terms of the number of days lost by income earners to illness. The poorer households also lost a higher proportion of their total income from being ill (Pryer, 1993).

There is often a differentiation among low-income groups by level of education—both because illiteracy or low educational standards limit work opportunities, and because literacy and education can help people cope with problems. The health of any person is influenced by their knowledge, capacity, and motivation—or, in the case of dependents (especially infants and young children), by the knowledge and capacity of those who care for them. Various studies have shown an association between the level of education of the mother and the child mortality rate; the proportion of children who die young tends to be lower, the better educated the mother (the findings of such studies are summarized in Caldwell & Caldwell, 1985). The precise reason for this may be difficult to ascertain (Caldwell & Caldwell, 1985) but a mother's ability to read and to make use of health-education materials which advise on how to prevent child illnesses, and how to treat them, is obviously an advantage. The extent to which women have access to education is linked to the extent to which the society supports women's education, the level of priority given by the government to education, and the extent to which the national economy generates the resources to allow this to be funded.

There is also the differentiation within low-income groups caused by demographic and/or social characteristics, especially those related to age, and gender, and these are considered in more detail below.

Infants and Children

Infants and children are particularly vulnerable to certain environmental hazards. Environmental factors exert a strong influence on the fetus—for instance, through the mother's exposure to toxic chemicals in the workplace (UNICEF, 1992). The influence may be less direct as a result of environmental factors that influence the health and nutritional status of the mother—for instance, malaria contracted by pregnant mothers is often associated with low birth weights (which is also associated with higher rates of infant mortality).

Infants and young children are at greater risk of dying from many environment-related diseases than older children or adults—for instance, diarrheal diseases, malaria, pneumonia, or measles (UNICEF, 1992; WHO, 1992a). Infections and parasites arising from contaminated food or water can contribute much to undernutrition which, in turn, retards children's growth and lowers their immunity. Infants are also more at risk than adults from various chemical pollutants such as lead (in food, water and air) and high nitrate concentrations in water. The transfer of infants and young children from exclusive reliance on breast milk to formula milk and semi-solid and solid foods is often particularly hazardous for those living in housing which lacks safe water and the facilities needed for hygienic food preparation and storage. Infants and children are particularly at risk from various hazards commonly found in low-income areas—for instance, housing made of flammable materials, combined with overcrowding and widespread use of open fires or stoves or kerosene heaters/cookers means a high risk of burns, scalds, and accidental fires. Open sites used by children for play and sport are often contaminated with fecal matter and with household wastes (which also attract rats and other disease vectors). The increasing mobility of children as they learn to crawl and then to walk, and their natural curiosity and desire to explore, can also expose them to many environmental hazards, especially where space and facilities are lacking both outdoors and indoors. For instance, in poor and overcrowded dwellings, it is difficult to keep chemicals used in the home out of their reach. Where provision for safe play sites is deficient, children will play on roads, garbage heaps, and other hazardous places.

From the time that an infant first learns to crawl, through childhood and adolescence, the size and quality of the home and its surrounds will exert a powerful influence on the level of risk. This is illustrated in a survey of 599 slum children in Rio de Janeiro, which found that accidents accounted for 19 percent of all health problems. Most reported accidents were falls (66 percent), cuts (17 percent), and burns (10 percent) (Reichenheim & Harpham, 1989). The age of the child was an important determinant of accidents. Peaks in accidents were in the second and fifth year of life. The hazardous physical environment is only one variable in this. Another is the limited possibility for parental child care and supervision, when all adult members of a household work (Evans, 1988; Reichenheim & Harpham, 1989).

A poor physical environment can also inhibit or damage a child's physical and mental development (Myers, 1991). Children are especially vulnerable to deficiencies in provision for play and informal learning from their peers—with the particular needs also varying considerably at different ages. In most poor districts in cities, there is little formal provision of open space and facilities for such needs. Yet, the importance of safe and stimulating play is increasingly recognized in, for instance, the evolution of a child's motor skills and communication skills, problem-solving, logical thinking, emotional development, and social and socialized behavior (Hughes, 1990). Infants and children often suffer not only from a poor physical environment in the sense of overcrowded and hazardous housing and inadequate provision for play, but also from the parental stress and possible psychosocial disorders in caregivens which are promoted by deficiencies in the physical environment. Among the key psychological and social development needs of children are a need for interaction (to provide stimulation and reaction to the child), the need for consistency and predictability in their caregiving environment, and a need to explore and discover (Myers, 1991). It is easy to see how a poor physical environment makes these more difficult for parents to provide, although perhaps a more important factor is that in many low-income households, all adults work long hours in seeking to obtain sufficient income to survive. Ensuring child supervision, stimulation, and care is particularly problematic in such circumstances.

Certain occupations in which it is common for children or youths to work are associated with particular environmental risks—for instance, those who make a living from picking through garbage (Furedy, 1992). Many industries in Asia and Latin America make widespread use of child labor with such children exposed to high levels of risk from dangerous machinery, heat, toxic chemicals, and dust (Lee-Wright, 1990). Street children who have been abandoned by their families (or have run away from home) generally face a whole range of environmental hazards. The work they undertake may be particularly hazardous (for instance, dodging traffic on major highways, selling goods to passing motorists) and they often have no adult to whom to turn when sick or injured. They generally have very poor-quality accommodations (often sleeping in the open or in public places) and great difficulties in finding places to wash and defecate, and to obtain drinking water and health services (Patel, 1990). They are also exposed to child abuse—not least when child prostitution is one of the more dependable ways of ensuring sufficient income for survival. In addition, many children and youths imprisoned for crimes or vagrancy, or placed in corrective institutions may not only have to live in a very poor-quality environment, but also be deprived of the child–adult relationships and stimulation that are so important for child development (UNICEF, 1992). There are also other children in especially difficult circumstances who face particular environmental risks. For instance, a study by the Indian NGO SPARC in Bombay identified children of pavement dwellers and construction workers and "hotel boys" as particularly vulnerable, along with street children (Patel, 1990). The children of construction workers, who live on site, lack access to schools, day care, health facilities, water, and sanitation, and living on construction sites also poses particular hazards for children.

The total health burden imposed by the environment on children from low-income households is very poorly understood, because it is usually the result of the cumulative impact of a great number of environmental problems operating concurrently with many nonenvironmental problems. Manciaux (1988) points to the cumulative harmful effects of the ill events for children which, initiated before birth, remain with them throughout their lives. This may include undernutrition, to which environment-related diseases contribute, the illnesses and injuries which arise from environment-related diseases (whose health burden is much increased by inadequate or no health and emergency services), and the stress to which they are exposed by their environment and by the stress-related problems that their parents or carers face.

Differentiation by Sex and Gender Roles

Women are more vulnerable than men to many environmental hazards, some because of their sex (i.e., as a result of biological differences), some because of gender (i.e., as a result of the particular social and economic roles that women have, determined by social, economic, and political structures).[3] Pregnant mothers are particularly vulnerable to certain environmental hazards. As a recent WHO report noted, "the reproductive system is particularly sensitive to adverse environmental conditions. Every stage of the multi-step process of reproduction can be disrupted by external environmental agents and this may lead to increased risk of abortion, birth defects, fetal growth retardation and perinatal death" (WHO, 1992b). This particular vulnerability during pregnancy, childbirth, and the period just after childbirth is biologically determined, although the low priority given by governments and aid agencies to reducing this vulnerability is socially determined. Around half a million women die each year of causes related to pregnancy and childbirth, and this leaves around one million children without mothers (UNICEF, 1991).

There are other environmental hazards to which women are exposed more than men as a result of differentiation by gender role, as women take sole (or primary) responsibility for child rearing, household management, and subsistence production (Lee-Smith & Trujillo, 1992; Moser, 1987). The

[3] This section draws in particular on Moser, 1987, and Moser, 1993.

fact that women take most responsibility for child care means that they also have to cope with the illnesses and injuries to infants and children summarized above, to which environmental hazards contribute much. Caring for the sick, and laundering soiled clothes are particularly hazardous tasks when water supplies and sanitation and washing facilities are inadequate (Sapir, 1990). The people within a household who are responsible for water collection and its use for laundry, cooking, and domestic hygiene suffer most if supplies are contaminated and difficult to obtain—and these people are generally women. Poorer urban households more often use biomass fuels or coal for cooking and/or heating on open fires or poorly ventilated stoves. It is generally women (or girls), who take responsibility for tending the fire and cooking, who inhale larger concentrations of pollutants over longer periods (WHO, 1992a). It is usually women who take responsibility for firewood gathering and subsistence crop and livestock production in the millions of urban households where these are important components of households' livelihoods; rarely, if ever, do urban housing schemes make allowances for these activities, and urban land-use and zoning regulations usually discriminate against such tasks (Lee-Smith & Trujillo, 1992). Women and children are also most vulnerable to domestic violence, which may be much increased by poor-quality and overcrowded housing.

Women's vulnerability to all the environmental hazards linked to inadequate provision for water, sanitation, drainage, and garbage collection is much increased, because the practical needs of those responsible for child care and household management (overwhelmingly women) are rarely given the priority they should have in government-provided services or housing programs. Even when they are, women are rarely consulted about the most appropriate design and service provision (Moser, 1987; Oruwari, 1991). For instance, provision for health clinics (and provision for pre- and postnatal care) rarely receives the priority needed in terms of their cost-effectiveness in reducing health burdens. Health-care services rarely provide the needed focus on women's reproductive health (including advice and support for fertility control) which can do so much to reduce maternal mortality and severe health problems (Germain & Ordway, 1989). Where there is some public provision for health services, rarely are their locations and opening hours well suited to women's needs. The same is true for nurseries and child-care centers that can make it much easier for women to earn incomes (Moser, 1993). Public transport provision is often scheduled to serve primary income earners, but does not serve the needs of secondary income earners (often women), or those responsible for shopping, taking children to and from school, and visits to health centers (Moser, 1987, 1993). Regulations on residential zoning often prohibit the kinds of informal productive activities in which women commonly engage in their homes (Moser, 1987; Oruwari, 1992). Public provision for housing, housing finance, and skill training often implicitly or explicitly exclude women, including women who are household heads.

Among "low-income households," those headed by women usually face particular problems. In many low-income settlements 30 or more percent of households are headed by women, either because a male partner is temporarily absent, or because of separation or death (Moser, 1987). The woman is often the only income earner in the household and has to combine income-earning with child-rearing and household management—and thus faces all the problems noted above concerning the inadequacies in provision for infrastructure and services and the discrimination that prohibit the kinds of income-earning activities in which women commonly engage or deny them access to government programs. Housing or serviced site projects often allocate tenure of the unit to men, as household heads, although women are the primary users of housing and tenure rights "are a strategic gender need which ensures protection for themselves and their children in unstable or violent domestic situations" (Moser, 1993, p. 52). Women-headed households also have particular housing needs—for instance, their triple role greatly constrains their ability to take part in "self-help" housing schemes, yet rarely do government housing program make special allowance for them (Falu & Curutchet, 1991; Moser, 1993).

Migrants

Migrants or particular migrant groups may be more vulnerable to certain environmental hazards than long-term city residents. For instance, in-migrants may lack immunity to particular diseases that are common within the urban area to which they move, while those living there a long time have developed some immunity. The susceptibility of recent migrants to an endemic disease can set off a serious epidemic (Sapir, 1990). Migrants may be more at risk from diseases such as tuberculosis, leishmaniasis, and malaria, if these diseases are not common in their area of origin.

Migrants arriving in a city might also be particularly at risk from being unable to find accommodations and a source of income. However, assumptions that this will be the case have often proved to be incorrect. For instance, interviews with women in households in an inner-city bustee in Khulna (Bangladesh) found that 72 percent of the households with whom women had migrated received assistance from friends and relatives in finding accommodation, and 68 percent in finding employment (Pryer, 1992). Over half had stayed in the homes of friends and relatives when they arrived (Pryer, 1992). Discussions with women "slum" dwellers in Bangkok also found that nearly all those who migrated had a place to stay, where they could get help in the initial period while finding work and a place to live (Thorbeck, 1991). Except where natural disasters, wars, or other catastrophes force rural people to suddenly flee from their homes into urban areas, most migrants moving into a city have family, kin, or friends to whom they can turn for help when they first arrive. Many send one family member ahead to prepare the way for others and a strategy developed to minimize risk (for instance, retaining the right to use rural land while living in the urban area) (Hugo, 1993).

A certain proportion of migrants may be at greater risk than city-born or long-arrived inhabitants, because of particularly hazardous or poorly paid work—although this will tend to affect the poorer and less educated migrants. It is perhaps obvious that, all other things being equal, those who already live in a city will have advantages over newcomers in learning about new income-earning possibilities and in promotion within existing workplaces. Many migrants may be disadvantaged, in comparison with existing city-dwellers, in terms of the quality of accommodations they can find (or the quality relative to the cost). Immigrants are likely to be particularly vulnerable, especially if illegal, since they often face discrimination in housing and job markets, and may have no protection under law from exploitation by employers or landlords. Particular categories of migrants may be at particular risk. If women face discrimination in job and housing markets, access to education, and access to land, this will be reflected by gender differentiation in the form and scale of men's and women's population movements and in the incomes and the level of risk in jobs taken by men and women in urban areas (Chant, 1992). However, existing literature on vulnerable groups in urban areas may pay too much attention to migrants and too little attention to age, gender role, and income. In the literature about health problems in cities there appears to be a tendency to assume that most migrants to cities are very poor, ill-educated, ill-informed about conditions in cities, and unmotivated—which is highly inaccurate. It is also common to see assertions that migrants are at risk because they live in "slums" and illegal settlements, when it is low income, not length of time in the city, which is the main influence on who lives in such areas. Many illegal settlements have a predominance of city-born residents. Except for migrants, who suffer discrimination because of their migrant status, or who were forced into cities because of wars or other disasters, in most instances, the scale of environmental hazards confronting any city dweller is much more likely to be related to their income level than to their status as a recent migrant, well-established migrant, or city-born person.

SOME CONCLUSIONS

At least 600 million urban dwellers in Africa, Asia, and Latin America live in "life- and health-threatening homes and neighborhoods" because of the environmental hazards described in this chapter, especially hazardous sites and deficiencies in the size and quality of housing, and provision for safe and sufficient water supplies, sanitation, drainage, garbage disposal, and community facilities for children. The two most obvious reasons were inadequate incomes (because in most urban centers, an adequate home with basic infrastructure and services was too expensive for poor households) and a failure of government to address the most serious environmental problems. This can be seen in the failure of government in a number of tasks:

- Failure to ensure adequate provision for water supply, solid and liquid waste collection, and treatment systems, and safe landsites for new housing; and to ensure adequate provision of health care, which not only treats environment-related illnesses, but also implements preventive measures to limit their incidence and severity. This can only be undertaken cost-effectively, either by government or with its support. Part of this is due to the refusal of state or national government to permit city/municipal government the fund-raising powers it needs to achieve this effectively;
- Failure to implement pollution control; the problem is much more a failure to implement existing legislation than a lack of legislation;
- Failure to promote good practice in occupational health and safety standards; and
- Failure to support increased supplies of legal land site for housing—on a scale to have a downward pressure on land prices—within a planning framework which guarantees sufficient open space and minimizes infrastructure costs.

Governments have also failed to collect the taxes and user-charges from those who benefit from publicly funded infrastructure and services. The costs of these failures fall most heavily on poorer groups.

The extent of the health burden imposed by the environment on urban populations remains poorly understood. It is almost certainly underestimated, not only because of little data, but also because it is usually the result of the cumulative impact of a great number of environmental problems operating concurrently with many nonenvironmental problems. Michael Manciaux points to the cumulative harmful effects of the ill events for children that, initiated before birth, remain with them throughout their lives (Manciaux, 1988). This may include undernutrition, to which environment-related diseases contribute, the illnesses and injuries that arise from environment-related diseases (whose health burden is so much increased by inadequate or no health and emergency services), and the stress to which they are exposed by their environment and by the stress-related problems that their parents or carers face.

There is great variety in the range and relative importance of environmental hazards, both within and between cities, and in the nonenvironmental factors that underlie or interact with them. For instance, in most major cities, the environmental priorities for health improvement in an inner-city tenement will differ from those in an illegal housing development. In both, environmental hazards may be major causes of ill health, injury, and premature death. But the range of hazards and their relative importance will differ because of differences in (for instance) income level and its distribution, age structure, quality and kind of infrastructure and service provision, risk of flooding, access to health care and emergency services, and a host of other factors. What city populations need is a city-specific and neighborhood-specific understanding of the range of environmental hazards and their relative importance for health. This must be combined with an understanding of the groups most affected by them and the diverse mix of social, economic, political, and demographic factors that underlie the hazards. From this can come a city and neighborhood directed program to control environmental problems, reduce risks (especially for vulnerable groups), and ensure treatment is available where health impacts cannot be prevented. This emphasizes the need for national or international agencies to work with local groups—citizen groups and their community organizations, local doctors, and other professional medical or paramedical staff, NGOs, municipal organizations, workers' unions or associations—if accurate diagnoses are to be made and effective interventions undertaken.

Some caution is needed in predicting the likely impact on health of environmental improvements. An analysis of the causes of disease usually points to a wide range of factors (environmental, social, economic, political, genetic) and it is difficult to separate out the relative roles of one from the others. The contribution of diseases in which environmental factors have little or no influence to ill health and premature death in urban areas of the Third World has also been underestimated (Stephens, 1993). In addition, identifying causes is further complicated by the fact that environmental factors often operate concurrently and are interrelated, and many contribute by very indirect paths (Fox, Hall, & Elveback, 1970). While environmental modifications are often among the most effective ways to diminish the health impact of communicable diseases, other factors need to be addressed to reduce morbidity and mortality. For instance, malnutrition is among the most serious health problems among most poor urban populations. This is largely the result of inadequate incomes (that is, not an environmental hazard) although malnutrition may lower a person's immunity to communicable diseases such as diarrheal diseases (usually arising from contaminated food or water), which then exacerbates the malnutrition. In addition, it is not only environmental modification that can address environmental hazards. Some are much more easily addressed by boosting the human immune system (as in immunization for the vaccine-preventable diseases) or rapid treatment (for instance, early diagnosis and rapid treatment of pneumonia would save many infants' lives), or ensuring increased incomes that allow people to choose to spend more to obtain more healthy accommodations and better health services.

However, citizen-directed initiatives within poorer urban neighborhoods are much more likely to develop integrated responses to environmental and nonenvironmental problems, and to ensure that environmental action programs mesh with local needs and realities. It is much more the sectoral nature of specialist knowledge and government structure that deters such approaches. The challenge for governments and aid agencies is to develop the institutional means to provide a large and diverse group of community-based organizations with the resources to address those problems amenable to household and community action. This must be provided in ways that ensure that the needs and priorities of those most at risk are addressed. It must also be complemented by district and citywide health care services and programs to minimize environmental hazards and promote environmental health in all other areas. Where local authorities are weak and ineffective and provision for water supplies, sanitation, drainage, garbage collection, and health care inadequate, innovative solutions must be sought, perhaps through partnerships between municipal organizations, NGOs, and community organizations.

REFERENCES

Adedoyin, M., & Watts, S. (1989). Child Health and Child Care in Okele: An Indigenous Area of the City of Ilorin, Nigeria. *Social Science and Medicine, 29(12)*, 1333–1341.

Aga Khan University Students (1988). Unpublished paper, quoted in T. Harpham, T. Lusty, & P. Vaughan, *In the Shadow of the City: Community Health and the Urban Poor*. Oxford: Oxford University Press.

Aina, T. A. (1989). *Health, Habitat and Underdevelopment—with Special Reference to a Low-Income Settlement in Metropolitan Lagos*. London: IIED Technical Report.

Aradeon, D., Aina, T. A., & Umo, J. (1986). South West Nigeria. In J. E. Hardoy & D. Satterthwaite (Eds.), *Small and Intermediate Urban Centres: Their role in Regional and National Development in the Third World*. Hodder and Stoughton (UK) and Westview (USA).

Askoy, M., et al. (1976). Types of Leukaemia in a Chronic Benzene Poisoning. *Acta Haematologica, 55*, 67–72.

Auer, C. (1989). *Health Problems (especially intestinal parasitoses) of Children Living in Smokey Mountain, a Squatter Area of Manila, Philippines.* (MSc. Thesis, Swiss Tropical Institute, Department of Public Health and Epidemiology, Basel.)

Basta, S. S. (1977). Nutrition and Health in Low Income Urban Areas of the Third World. *Ecology of Food and Nutrition, 6*, 113–124.

Bertaud, A., & Young, M. (1990). *Geographical Pattern of Environmental Health in Tianjin*, China. (Research/Sector Paper, ASTIN, World Bank, Washington, DC.)

Blacklock, D. B., & Evans, A. M. (1926). Breeding Places of Anopheline Mosquitoes In and Around Freetown, Sierra Leone. *Annals of Tropical Medicine and Parasitology, 20*, 59–86.

Bradley, D., Stephens, C., Cairncross S., & Harpham, T. (1991). *A Review of Environmental Health Impacts in Developing Country Cities.* Urban Management Program Discussion Paper No. 6, The World Bank, UNDP and UNCHS (Habitat), Washington DC.)

Briceno-Leon, R. (1990). *La Casa Enferma: Sociologia de la Enfermedad de Chagas.* Caracas: Consorcio de Ediciones, Capriles C.A.

Bundey, D. A. P., Kan, S. O. P., & Rose, R. (1988). Age Related Prevalence, Intensity and Frequency Distribution of Gastrointestinal Helminth Infection in Urban Slum Childrem from Kuala Lumpur, Malaysia. *Transactions of the Royal Society of Tropical Medicine and Hygiene, 82*, 289–294.

Cairncross, S. (1990). Water Supply and the Urban Poor. In J. E. Hardoy, S. Cairncross, & D. Satterthwaite (Eds.), *The Poor Die Young: Housing and Health in Third World Cities.* London: Earthscan Publications.

Cairncross, S., & Feachem R. G. (1993). *Environmental Health Engineering in the Tropics: An Introductory Text* (second ed.) Chichester, England: John Wiley and Sons.

Caldwell, J. C., & Caldwell, P. (1985). Education and Literacy as Factors in Health. In S. B. Halstead, J. A. Walsh, & K. S. Warren (Eds.), *Good Health at Low Cost* (Conference Report) (pp. 181–185). New York: The Rockefeller Foundation.

Castonguay, G. (1992). Steeling Themselves with Knowledge: Report on the Work of Cristina Laurell. *IDRC Reports, 20(1)*, 10–12.

Cauthen, G. M., Pio, A., & ten Dam H. G. (1988). *Annual Risk of Tuberculosis Infection.* Geneva: World Health Organization.

Centre for Science and Environment (1983). *The State of India's Environment—A Citizen's Report.* Delhi.

Centre for Science and Environment (1985). *The State of India's Environment—A Second Citizens' Report.* Delhi.

Chant, S. (1992). Conclusion: Towards a Framework for the Analysis of Gender-Selective Migration. In S. Chant (Ed.), *Gender and Migration in Developing Countries* (pp. 197–206). London: Belhaven Press.

Cohen, L., & Swift, S. (1993). A Public Health Approach to the Violence Epidemic in the United States. *Environment and Urbanization, 5(2)*.

Cointreau, S. (1982). *Environmental Management of Urban Solid Waste in Developing Countries.* (Urban Development Technical Paper No. 5, World Bank, Washington, DC.)

Corbett, J. (1989). Poverty and Sickness: The High Costs of Ill-Health. *IDS Bulletin, 20(2),* 58–62.

Douglass, M. (1992). The Political Economy of Urban Poverty and Environmental Management in Asia: Access, Empowerment and Community-Based Alternatives. *Environment and Urbanization, 4(2).*

Duhl, L. J. (1990). *The Social Entrepreneurship of Change.* New York: Pace University Press.

Ekblad, S. (1993). Stressful Environments and Their Effects on Quality of Life in Third World Cities. *Environment and Urbanization, 5(2).*

Ekblad, S., et al. (1991). *Stressors, Chinese City Dwellings and Quality of Life.* (D12, Swedish Council for Building Research, Stockholm.)

Espinoza, V. (1988). *Para una Historia de los Pobres de la Ciudad.* Santiago: Ediciones SUR.

Esrey, S. A., & Feachem, R. G. (1989). *Interventions for the Control of Diarrhoeal Disease: Promotion of Food Hygiene.* Geneva: World Health Organization WHO/CDD/89.30.

Evans, J. L. (1988). Urban Slum and Squatter Settlements: Implications for Psychosocial Development and Well-being. In *Child Abuse and Urban Slum Environments.* (WHO/ISPCAN, Pre-Congress Workshop, WHO/MCH/86.15, Geneva, pp. 31–45.)

Falu, A., & Curutchet, M. (1991). Rehousing the Urban Poor: Looking at Women First. *Environment and Urbanization, 3(2),* 23–38.

Foster, S. O. (1990). Measles, the Ultimate Challenge in Urban Immunization. In *Universal Child Immunization—Reaching the Urban Poor.* (Urban Examples 16, UNICEF, New York.)

Fox, J. P., Hall, C. E., & Elveback, L. R. (1970). *Epidemiology, Man and Disease.* London: Macmillan.

Furedy, C. (1992). Garbage: Exploring Non-Conventional Options in Asian cities. *Environment and Urbanization, 4(2).*

Germain, A., & Ordway, J. (1989). *Population Control and Women's Health: Balancing the Scale.* New York: International Women's Health Coalition in cooperation with the Overseas Development Council.

Goldstein, G. (1990). Access to Life Saving Services in Urban Areas. In J. E. Hardoy, S. Cairncross, & D. Satterthwaite (Eds.), *The Poor Die Young; Housing and Health in Third World Cities.* London: Earthscan Publications.

Gomes, P. M. (1989). Characteristics of Urban Mortality from Chagas' Disease in Brazil's Federal District. *Bulletin of the Pan American Health Organization, 18(1).*

Guimaraes, J. J., & Fischmann, A. (1985). Inequalities in 1980 Infant Mortality among Shantytown Residents and Non-Shantytown Residents in the Municipality of Porto Alegre, Rio Grande do Sul, Brazil. *Bulletin of the Pan American Health Organization, 19,* 235–251.

Hardoy, J. E., Mitlin, D., & Satterthwaite, D. (1992). *Environmental Problems in Third World Cities.* London: Earthscan Publications.

Harpham, T., Garner, P., & Surjadi, C. (1990). Planning for Child Health in a Poor Urban Environment: The Case of Jakarta, Indonesia. *Environment and Urbanization, 2(2)*, 77–82.

Harpham, T., Vaughan, P., & Lusty, T. (1988). *In the Shadow of the City: Community Health and the Urban Poor*. Oxford: Oxford University Press.

Hughes, B. (1990). Children's Play—A Forgotten Right. *Environment and Urbanization, 2(2)*, 58–64.

Hugo, G. J. (1993). Migration as a Survival Strategy: The Family Dimension of Migration. Paper presented at the Expert Group Meeting on Population Distribution and Migration, Santa Cruz, Bolivia, 18–22 January. New York: U.N. Population Division and UNFPA.

Jimenez, R. D., & Velasquez, S. Aida (1989). Metropolitan Manila: A Framework for Its Sustained Development. *Environment and Urbanization, 1(1)*, 51–58.

Jimenez Diaz, V. (1992). Landslides in the Squatter Settlements of Caracas: Towards a Better Understanding of Causative Factors. *Environment and Urbanization, 4(2)*.

Lee-Wright, P. (1990). *Child Slaves*. London: Earthscan Publications.

Lee-Smith, D., Manundu, M., Lamba, D., & Gathuru, P. K. (1987). *Urban Food Production and the Cooking Fuel Situation in Urban Kenya—National Report: Results of a 1985 National Survey*. Nairobi, Kenya: Mazingira Institute.

Lee-Smith, D., & Trujillo, C. H. (1992). The Struggle to Legitimize Subsistence: Women and Sustainable Development. *Environment and Urbanization, 4(1)*.

Leitmann, J. (1991a). *Environmental Profile of São Paulo Urban Management and the Environment*. (Discussion Paper Series, UNDP/World Bank/UNCHS, Washington, DC.)

Leitmann, J. (1991b). *Tianjin Urban Environmental Profile, Urban Management and the Environment*: Discussion Paper Series, UNDP/World Bank/UNCHS, Washington, DC, April.)

Manciaux, M. (1988). Urban Slum and Squatter Settlements: Implications for Child Health. In *Child Abuse and Urban Slum Environments*. (WHO/ISPCAN, Pre-Congress Workshop, WHO/MCH/86.15, Geneva, pp. 20–30.)

Manciaux, M., & Romer, C. J. (1986). Accidents in Children, Adolescents and Young Adults: A Major Public Health Problem. *World Health Statistical Quarterly, 39(3)*, 227–231.

Matte, T. D., Figueroa, J. P., Ostrowski, S., Burr, G., et al. (1989). Lead Poisoning among Household Members Exposed to Lead-Acid Battery Repair Shops in Kingston, Jamaica (West Indies). *International Journal of Epidemiology, 18*, 874–881.

McGranahan, G. (1991). *Environmental Problems and the Urban Household in Third World Countries*. Stockholm: The Stockholm Environment Institute.

McGranahan, G. (1992). Household Environmental Problems. Paper presented at the International Workshop on Planning for Sustainable Urban Development, University of Wales College of Cardiff, July.

Misra, H. (1990). Housing and Health Problems in Three Squatter Settlements in Allahabad, India. In J. E. Hardoy, S. Cairncross, & D. Satterthwaite (Eds.), *The Poor Die Young: Housing and Health in Third World Cities*. London: Earthscan Publications.

Moser, C. O. N. (1987). Women, Human Settlements and Housing: A Conceptual Framework for Analysis and Policy-Making. In C. O. N. Moser & L. Peake (Eds.), *Women, Housing and Human Settlements*. London and New York: Tavistock Publications.

Moser, C. O. N. (1993). *Gender Planning and Development: Theory, Practice and Training*. London and New York: Routledge.

Murphy, D. (1990). *A Decent Place to Live—Urban Poor in Asia*. Bangkok: Asian Coalition for Housing Rights.

Myers, R. (1991). *The Twelve WHO Survive: Strengthening Programmes of Early Child Development in the Third World*. London and New York: Routledge.

Needleman, H. L., Schell, A., Bellinger, D., Leviton, A., & Allred, E. N. (1991). The Long-Term Effects of Exposure to Low Doses on Lead in Childhood: An Eleven Year Follow Up Report. *New England Jorunal of Medicine, 322(2)*, 83–88.

Omer, M. I. A. (1990). Child Health in the Spontaneous Settlements around Khartoum. *Environment and Urbanization, 2(2)*, 65–70.

Oruwari, Y. (1991). The Changing Role of Women in Families and Their Housing Needs: A Case Study of Port Harcourt, Nigeria. *Environment and Urbanization, 3(2)*, 6–12.

Pandey, M. R., Basnayat, B., & Neupane, R. P. (1989). Indoor Air Pollution in Developing Countries and Acute Respiratory Infection. *Lancet, 1*, 427–429.

Patel, S. (1990). Street Children, Hotel Boys and Children of Pavement Dwellers and Construction Workers in Bombay: How They Meet Their Daily Needs. *Environment and Urbanization, 2(2)*, 9–26.

Pepall, J. (1992). Occupational Poisoning: Reporting on the Work of Mohamad M. Amr. In *IDRC Reports, 20(1)*, Ottawa, 15.

Phantumvanit, D., & Liengcharernsit, W. (1989). Coming to Terms with Bangkok's Environmental Problems. *Environment and Urbanization, 1(1)*, 31–39.

Pio, A. (1986). Acute Respiratory Infections in Children in Developing Countries: An International Point of View. *Pediatric Infectious Disease Journal, 5(2)*, 179–183.

Pryer, J. (1992). Purdah, Patriarchy and Population Movement: Perspectives from Bangladesh. In S. Chant (Ed.), *Gender and Migration in Developing Countries*. London: Belhaven Press.

Pryer, J. (1993). The Impact of Ill-Health on Household Income and Nutrition in Khulna, Bangladesh. *Environment and Urbanization, 5(2)*.

Reichenheim, M., & Harpham, T. (1989). Child Accidents and Associated Risk Factors in a Brazilian Squatter Settlement. *Health Policy and Planning, 4(2)*, 162–167.

Rohde, J. E. (1983). Why the Other Half Dies: The Science and Politics of Child Mortality in the Third World. *Assignment Children, 61/62*.

Romieu, I., et al. (1990). Urban Air Pollution in Latin America and the Caribbean: Health Perspectives. *World Health Statistics Quarterly, 23(2)*, 153–167.

Rossi-Espagnet, A., Goldstein, G. B., & Tabibzadeh, I. (1991). Urbanization and Health in Developing Countries: A Challenge for Health for All. *World Health Statistical Quarterly, 44(4)*, 186–244.

Rothenburg, S. J., Schnaas-Arrieta, L., Perez-Guerrero, I. A., et al. (1989). Evaluacion del Riesgo Potencial de la Exposition Perinatal al Plombo en el Valle de Mexico. *Perinatologia y Reproduccion Humana, 3(1)*, 49–56.

Sapir, D. (1990). *Infectious Disease Epidemics and Urbanization: A Critical Review of the Issues*. Paper prepared for the WHO Commission on Health and Environment, Division of Environmental Health Geneva: WHO.

Sarin, M. (1983). The Rich, the Poor and the Land Question. In S. Angel, et al. (Eds.), *Land for Housing the Poor*. Singapore: Select Books, pp. 237–253.

Satterthwaite, D. (1993). The Health Impact of Urban Environments. *Environment and Urbanization, 5(2)*.

Schofield, C. J., et al. (1990). The Role of House Design in Limiting Vector-Borne Disease. In J. E. Hardoy, S. Cairncross, & D. Satterthwaite (Eds.), *The Poor Die Young: Housing and Health in Third World Cities*. London: Earthscan Publications.

Schteingart, M. (1989). The Environmental Problems Associated with Urban Development in Mexico City. *Environment and Urbanization, 1(1)*, 40–49.

Sinnatamby, G. (1990). Low Cost Sanitation. In J. E. Hardoy, S. Cairncross, & D. Satterthwaite (Eds.), *The Poor Die Young: Housing and Health in Third World Cities*. London: Earthscan Publications.

Songsore, J., & McGranahan, G. (1993). Environment, Wealth and Health: Towards an Analysis of Intra-Urban Differentials within Greater Accra Metropolitan Area, Ghana. *Environment and Urbanization, 5(2)*.

Stephens, C., & Harpham, T. (1992). The Measurement of Health in Household Environmental Studies in Urban Areas of Developing Countries: Factors to be Considered in the Design of Surveys. Urban Health Programme, London School of Hygiene and Tropical Medicine, February.

Surjadi, C. (1993). Respiratory Diseases of Mothers and Children and Environmental Factors among Households in Jakarta. *Environment and Urbanization, 5(2)*.

Thorbek, S. (1991). Gender in Two Slum Cultures. *Environment and Urbanization, 3(2)*, 71–81.

Turner, J. F. C. (1976). *Housing by People—Towards Autonomy in Building Environments*. London: Ideas in Progress, Marion Boyars.

UNEP (1991). *Environmental Data Report, 1991–2*, GEMS Monitoring and Assessment Research Centre, Blackwell, Oxford and Massachusetts.

UNEP and WHO (1987). *Global Pollution and Health—Results of Health-Related Environmental Monitoring*. Global Environment Monitoring System, United Nations Environment Programme and World Health Organization.

UNEP and WHO (1988). *Assessment of Urban Air Quality*. Global Environment Monitoring Service, United Nations Environment Programme and World Health Organization.

UNICEF (1990). *The State of the World's Children 1990*. Oxford: Oxford University Press.

UNICEF (1991). *The State of the World's Children 1991*. Oxford: Oxford University Press.

UNICEF (1992). *Environment, Development and the Child*, Environment Section, Programme Division, UNICEF, New York.

United Nations (1991). *World Urbanization Prospects 1990; Estimates and Projections of Urban and Rural Populations and of Urban Agglomerations*. United Nations, New York, ST/ESA/SER.A/121.

US AID (1990). *Ranking Environmental Health Risks in Bangkok*. Washington, DC: Office of Housing and Urban Programs.

Waller, R. (1991). Field Investigations of Air. In W. W. Holland, R. Detels, & G. Knox (Eds.), *Textbook of Public Health, Volume 2* (second ed.). Oxford and New York: Oxford University Press.

WHO (1990). *Global Estimates for Health Situation Assessments and Projections 1990*. Division of Epidemiological Surveillance and Health Situation and Trend Analysis, World Health Organization, Geneva, WHO/HST/90.2.

WHO (1991). *Health Trends and Emerging Issues in the 1990s and the Twenty-first Century*. Monitoring, Evaluation and Projection Methodology Unit, Division of Epidemiological Surveillance and Health Situations and Trend Assessment, World Health Organization, Geneva.

WHO (1992a). *Our Planet, Our Health*. Report of the Commission on Health and Environment, World Health Organization, Geneva.

WHO (1992b). *Reproductive Health: a Key to a Brighter Future*. WHO Special Programme of Research Development and Research Training in Human Reproduction, Geneva.

Wohl, A. S. (1983). *Endangered Lives: Public Health in Victorian Britain*. London: Methuen.

World Bank (1984). *Staff Appraisal Report: Brazil Second Health Project*. São Paulo Basic Health Care and National Health Policy Studies, Population, Health and Nutrition Department, Washington, DC.

World Bank (1988). *World Development Report 1988*. Oxford: Oxford University Press.

Zorrilla, S., & Guaresti, M. E. (1986). *Sector Agua Potables y Saneamiento: Lineamientos para una Estrategia Nacional*. Buenos Aires: U.N. Development Programme.

9

Global Economics, Environment, and Health

Faye Duchin

GLOBALIZATION

Health and well-being are governed by many factors, including changes in the status of the air, water, and land which can affect large numbers of people simultaneously. While the condition of the environment affects entire communities, the features of individual circumstances that determine physical well-being can vary widely even within a relatively small geographic region; these include nutrition, access to health-care services, and the characteristics of different kinds of work. Both the environmental and the individual factors are directly affected by economic growth, industrialization, and technological change. These phenomena can enhance the material conditions of life. The accompanying modernization of traditional institutional arrangements can also be desirable for individuals or groups (e.g., women). However, there are generally also unintended and undesirable social and environmental changes. These changes are taking place at all levels, from the local through the global.

Many of the environmental challenges posed by industrialization are local in nature and need to be resolved in terms of the specific details of the situation. At the same time, similar problems occur in many different locations, and the scope of the problems is increasingly extensive from a geographic point of view because of the growing scale of production. It is also true that the options for dealing with environmental degradation are highly interdependent, often in predictable ways; experience shows that the choice of a particular solution to one problem may generate other problems. For these reasons it is important to take a global perspective on environmental problems to provide guidance for actions at all levels.

Over the last few decades the globalization of the world's societies has become a physical reality and one that has relatively quickly become apparent to the general public. There have been two principal reasons for globalization, and both are attributable to technological advances. Through modern telecommunications, people in all but the most remote locations are exposed instantaneously to the world's crisis situations and familiarized with the day-to-day realities in far away places. Furthermore, modern transportation has made it possible to travel, and to trade and shift investments, among distant locations more quickly and more extensively than ever before.

The other major stimulus to global thinking was the ability to view the water planet from space and to measure and anticipate the possible effects of human activities not only on the water, the soil, and the minerals buried in it but especially on the atmosphere which is shared by the entire planet. The desire to "save the planet" reflects a concern that is not just environmental but quintessentially global.

The transfer of technology today is remarkably extensive and rapid compared to the past. One new characteristic of the technological professions is the explicit objective to design and implement technologies in ways that disrupt the biogeochemical systems of the planet as little as possible. With the globalization of ecological problems and concerns, the practice of industrial ecology, as it is called, will result in the reorientation of the field of engineering for the 21st century. This process has already begun.

Economists can provide a powerful conceptual framework for describing the world system in terms of human activities and decisions. And the economist's modeling framework can be used for the analysis and quantitative evaluation of alternative scenarios about the future based, in part, on the initiatives that originate in industrial ecology. However, the construction of such a modeling framework needs to be guided by broader economic theory and bolder policy options than those which are most familiar today. In particular, the scope of the theory needs to reflect the material structure, as well as the social structure, of the global economy; and it needs to be capable of analyzing the major potential structural changes, and the challenges related to them, that can be anticipated within a horizon of several decades. The overall structure has to be sufficiently integrated to capture the interdependencies that characterize this dynamically changing system. I have written in other places about an approach to the development and implementation of such a conceptual framework which I call structural economics (see Duchin, 1992, 1994, 1994b).

This chapter explores the conditions surrounding the future growth of the world economy (p. 165ff.), and the following section describes some of the major elements of transformation in its globalization over the next several decades. Projections about the likely future use of primary materials and associated air pollution provide some perspective on the nature of the challenges we face (see p. 169ff.). The last section takes up the alternatives surrounding the production, use, and disposal of a specific material, plastics, to demonstrate the need for an analysis of the trade-offs.

ECONOMIC GROWTH

According to the economic philosophy of the "liberal" state, the basic objective is to achieve increased prosperity through economic growth which in turn is pursued through improvements in efficiency, new technology, and free trade. This outlook has prevailed in the two centuries since the Industrial Revolution, a period that has experienced accelerated growth of both population and material well-being. With the fall of Communism, economic liberalization is virtually unopposed as a global political and economic philosophy, but there are very powerful reasons to believe that it will be significantly transformed in the course of the next century as competitive markets are subjected to a multilateral consensus expressed in new global agreements and institutions.

Economists distinguish three categories of factor inputs needed for the production of goods and services: capital, labor, and land, where "land" is interpreted as shorthand for all categories of inputs from the natural world. For an economy operating with a given set of technologies, growth in the delivery of goods and services to final users requires more factor inputs. Clearly, population growth can generate economic growth with the simple replication of existing methods by making use of the larger labor force as well as more land and other inputs. Of course, on a per capita basis, consumption would remain unchanged.

Malthus's concern about running out of land, and food, was at least temporarily put to rest by the enormous increases in yields resulting from new technology. The scientist who developed "artificial manure" was remarkably successful in his effort to obtain "big and ever increasing harvests lasting eternally" (Liebig, 1862; quoted in Krohn & Schafer, 1976, p. 31). The goal of unlimited increases in prosperity is unlikely to drive economists and engineers by the end of the 21st century, however; the objective will change because of far more modest population increases, environmental constraints, and different social values reflecting the new reality.

In the analysis of actual activities, economists in the 20th century have focused their investigation of growth almost exclusively on changing inputs of capital and labor both in theoretical discussion and in the "production functions" chosen for most empirical analysis. This emphasis is largely explained by the fact that the extraction of primary materials in agriculture and mining utilizes a very small portion of the labor force in the rich, industrialized economies which have been taken as the model for development, and air and water were considered free of charge. However, demographic and environmental pressures will shift the attention of economists to the third factor of production—natural resources. Its operational definition will require attention to the distinctions among the individual energy raw materials, which are neither renewable nor recyclable; the numerous mineral resources, which are potentially recyclable but not renewable; and water and soils of different qualities which are easily degraded. The different categories of pollution and environmental deterioration which are delivered back to the natural world also need to be accounted for as factors of production; they are "negative inputs" to production. While capital and labor obviously cannot be ignored, the primary materials which will increasingly occupy economists are also the inputs at the center of attention in industrial ecology.

A major reason that the developing countries are taking on a new importance in the world economy is that they will continue to be the locus for virtually all population growth over the next century and therefore offer the easiest opportunity for expanding production and consumption. Without population growth, an economy can still grow through employing higher quality factor inputs; the most practical avenue to exploit this option is through the upgrading of the skills and satisfaction of the labor force. New technologies can promote growth by enhancing the "productivity" of factor inputs; but they invariably involve not only a decrease in factor quantities per unit of output, but also a change in the quality or at least the mix of inputs. Some consequences include the generation of novel wastes, such as the chlorine-containing compounds that have appeared only in the past 50 years. However, the opportunities for actually implementing new technologies are limited when they are applied to the upgrading of capacity that is already in place rather than the construction of entirely new facilities to expand capacity. Individuals or firms may be able to generate more profit, if they are free to do so, by supplying the requirements of other countries with faster growing populations rather than investing in incremental improvements in production for the domestic market.

The size of the population has leveled off in the developed countries, and will probably also do so in the developing countries in the course of the next century. With less political pressure to continually "create jobs" for increasing numbers of labor force entrants, concerns about depleting resources or degrading the physical environment will lead to a shift in emphasis from growth to improvements in the quality of life. Until this happens, the asymmetry in population dynamics between the rich and poor countries will strongly influence the nature of their interactions.

TRANSFORMATION OF THE WORLD ECONOMY

Darwin's identification of competition as the mechanism for natural selection was influenced by the ideas of Malthus. The mutual reinforcement of the dominant role assigned to competition as the mechanism for change in both the biological and economic world views assured its fundamental role in Western thinking over the past century. It is significant that at the present time this view is being substantially moderated in our understanding of both the natural and the social spheres, and in our social practices, as these reinforcing changes in perspective will be more influential than either one could be alone. Increasing numbers of contemporary biologists are subscribing to Margulis's view that accommodation through symbiosis, involving the "merging of organisms into new collectives," is a major mechanism for evolutionary change. According to this view, life "did not take over the world by combat but by networking" (Margulis & Sagan, 1986, pp. 15, 18). The parallels are striking with the emergence of the global economy.

The global economy is emerging at a time of great transformation as the ideological confrontation of East and West is replaced by economic conflict and negotiation, largely over trade and aid, between North and South.[1] The countries in transition to a market economy can be expected to join the ranks of the developed economies over the next several decades as Europe—Central and Eastern, as well as Western—proceeds toward increasing unification in various dimensions. Regional economic blocs, based initially on trade and investment agreements, are also developing in America, in Asia, and among the Pacific Rim countries. The international competition associated with laissez-faire capitalism is, if anything, more fierce than ever. At the same time, it is undeniably operating within a context of long-term regional integration and emerging global institutional constraints. Environmental concerns will reinforce the pressures toward global dialogue and negotiation. They will also lead to agreements that assure the maintenance of an increasingly extensive global "commons" in reflection of the emerging view that threatened resources are

[1] According to conventional usage, the North includes the rich, industrialized countries; South is the developing countries; West is the market economies and East is the formerly socialist economies.

often better protected in this way than by either coercive power or as private property (Ostrom, 1990).

Only a small number of environmental disputes has so far been brought to court within the international trade community, but it is already clear that these conflicts raise questions far more complex than what conventional trade law can readily resolve. In anticipation of the avalanche of cases to come, the Secretariat of GATT (the General Agreement on Trade and Tariffs recently replaced by the new World Trade Organization) is calling for discussions leading to multilateral consensus about environmental objectives to hopefully bypass bilateral, case-by-case haggling in instances where new environmental concerns conflict with the older objective of removing barriers to trade to promote growth independently of any other considerations. The tuna and dolphin dispute between the United States and Mexico or the Danish bottle law and the reaction to it in Europe are but two early examples (see Lee, 1993, for a brief description of 22 such cases). In surprisingly explicit language, the GATT Secretariat has stated that it is "no longer possible for a country to create an appropriate environmental policy entirely on its own" (quoted in OTA, 1992, p. 24).

Environmental concerns (coupled with the attempt to protect domestic producers) are leading countries to erect barriers to trade, based on the production process and not just on the characteristics of the traded product. (This is true in the tuna and dolphin case, or in potential restrictions on imports of electronic components that were manufactured using CFCs that are being analyzed in connection with the Montreal Protocol.) By the middle of the next century, these pressures to provide a product **produced using a particular technology** will be a potent force for the globalization of technology. There is already a tendency to adopt modern technologies in new manufacturing sectors in developing countries, especially in foreign-owned factories. But the pressures for international sharing of techniques will spread far beyond manufacturing into areas that have until now been largely shielded from globalization by cultural differences. For example, trade-related requirements about the use of recycled materials will affect "lifestyle" since recycling, in any society, involves the establishment of procedures to be followed by individuals in their capacities as consumers and citizens. As another example, new legislation governing water pollution is bound to be similar in different societies as it will need to promote compliance with common process specifications.

Other pressures toward uniform social practices, which can already be observed, will also intensify. One example is the acceptance of a universal concept of human rights which is now considered a uniquely Western notion or at the least a luxury of rich countries. The other important example is the state's assumption of responsibility for social welfare which today absorbs roughly similar proportions of national income in the rich economies and in the formerly socialist economies (prior to the "transition") but is still extremely low in most developing countries.

Development has been understood in the post–World War II period to mean industrialization (combined with price-setting markets), and industrialization involves the processing of materials and the discharge of wastes. This is true even if industrial ecology succeeds in substantially reducing both the material input and the waste output. The environmental degradation takes the form of atmospheric pollution and the "mining" and toxification of water and soils. The faster the growth, the greater the challenge in keeping these inevitable by-products within socially acceptable limits.

The fruits of development can improve the diet and the overall level of physical comfort, and increased material wealth permits a society to invest resources in social services, like expanded public health and medical care and the provision of tap water and sanitation facilities. At the same time, the physical facts of industrial production inevitably and predictably expose individuals to new sorts of hazards. It is clear, for example, that the continued industrialization of the two Asian giants, China and India, will further elevate today's already high concentrations of atmospheric carbon and aggravate regional problems of acid rain with its attendant ill effects on health. The array of health problems that are familiar from the experience of the industrialized countries can be expected to accompany development just as surely as will improvements in the material standard of living.

ECONOMIC STRUCTURE, MATERIAL USE, AND POLLUTION

The last two sections have described the basic forces that are likely to govern growth and the transformation of the global economy over the next several decades. The specific paths actually followed, however, will have significant implications for economic and environmental outcomes and for the prospects for the more distant future. As a basis for evaluating some alternatives, the changing structure of the world economy is considered, with an emphasis on the use of primary materials.

The material structure of an economy can be described in terms of its natural endowments (of soil, water, primary materials, etc.), the accumulation of built capital (including roads, buildings, and machines), its pool of workers of different qualifications, and the characteristic ways in which these factors of production are used. The last, which is in the domain of industrial ecology, involves what gets produced or consumed, and how.

There is significant variation in the structures of different economies, compounded by the differences among cultures. Nonetheless, one can distinguish a few basic patterns. There are systematic differences in economic structure among the four groupings of regions that will be discussed below: the rich, industrialized economies; the economies of Eastern Europe and the former Soviet Union; the newly industrializing countries; and the rest of the developing countries. They differ with respect to their natural riches, the types of capital employed, the education and health of the work force, the amount of capital at the disposition of the average worker, the intake of protein and vitamins, and the per capita utilization of fuels and materials. Consequently, they also differ with respect to the technologies used in all sectors of the economy.

As globalization proceeds, all economies will tend to continue to move in the direction of today's industrialized economies in terms of their choices of technologies and the associated factor inputs. Over the past century, the economic motivation for mechanization and automation has been essentially to conserve on labor costs by the substitution of built capital for workers. Over the next several decades the selection pressures will also conserve resources and reduce pollution. New regulations and legislation will reinforce these choices by aiming to make them cost-effective.

A recent study about global air pollution examined the likely changes in the world economy over the period from 1980 to 2020 under alternative assumptions about future choices of technology in different regions (Duchin & Lange, 1994). The picture that emerges provides a detailed and concrete starting point for identifying where technological developments might have the most impact at averting the most problematic environmental changes.

The scenario incorporates optimistic assumptions about economic growth and about technological choices in the material-intensive and energy-intensive sectors in all parts of the world economy (a 16-region representation) over the next three decades. The scenario was intended to specify technical detail that could be consistent with the outlook expressed in the Brundtland Report (World Comission on Environment and Development, 1987), the publication that popularized the notion of sustainable development. It is optimistic in alleging that sharply improved material standards of living in the developing economies, further increases in per capita consumption in the rich economies, and the volume of population increases that are today being anticipated for the next century can be compatible with reduced pressures on the environment provided that we use sensible technologies such as extensive conservation of energy, recycling of metals, glass, and paper at rates approaching those achieved in only a few countries today, and the rapid adoption of the cleanest and most efficient technologies currently available or near commercialization. The scenario considered here departs from the Brundtland Report by also assuming that an increasing share of electricity, especially in Asia, will be generated by nuclear and hydroelectric power, an assumption that dampens the future demand for the fossil fuels and associated air pollution. Furthermore, the efficiency of energy used to generate electricity in China and India approaches that of Japan by 2020 under this scenario because the entire existing stock of capital is assumed to be modernized.

Economic results of this computation have been reported in other places; the discussion here is limited to material use and air pollution. For the four groupings of regions, Table 9.1 shows the growth in per capita material use between 1980 and 2020. The associated rates of growth of emissions of carbon, sulfur, and nitrogen are reported in Table 9.2.

Even under a scenario that is rather optimistic about conserving mineral resources, net consumption of all fuel and non-fuel resources increases over the 40-year period. On a per capita basis, however, net consumption of seven of the nine resources actually falls because of technological changes—by as much as 36 percent in the case of iron (see Table 9.1). This comparison strongly suggests that, over the next few decades, the impact of population growth on resource utilization will more than offset the economies that can be achieved by these technologies.

Population in the developing countries increases from 72 percent of the total in 1980 to 81 percent by 2020, and an even larger share can confidently be expected before world population stops growing. By 2020, per capita consumption of most materials is still highest in today's

TABLE 9.1 Projected Percentage Change in Per-Capita Use of Materials in the World Economy between 1980 and 2020 (by weight)

	RDE	NIE	ODE	ESU	WORLD[a]
Copper	–15%	58%	101%	15%	–18%
Bauxite	47	142	104	65	26
Nickel	–18	43	71	–10	–33
Zinc	11	44	121	2	–3
Lead	–40	38	141	10	–23
Iron	–26	6	10	–42	–36
Petroleum	–9	86	124	19	–2
Gas	–14	184	339	67	9
Coal	–30	176	57	–13	–17

Source: Duchin & Lange (1994).
Note:—The regions are Rich, Developed Economies (RDE), Newly Industrializing Economies (NIE), Other Developing Economies (ODE), and Eastern Europe and the former Soviet Union (ESU).
[a] The growth in per capita consumption for the world as a whole is in several cases lower than growth for all component regions. While the result may appear counter-intuitive, it reflects the rapid growth of population in the regions with the lowest per capita consumption.

TABLE 9.2 Emissions of Carbon Dioxide, Sulfur Oxides, and Nitrogen Oxides in the World Economy between 1980 and 2020

	1980	1990	2000	2010	2020
Carbon Dioxide (10^6 metric tons of carbon)					
Levels of Emissions					
Rich, Developed Economies	2,592	2,790	2,877	2,850	2,799
Newly-Industrializing Economies	249	339	573	738	997
Other Developing Economies	678	1,180	1,906	2,605	3,515
Eastern Europe and Former USSR	1,211	1,323	1,435	1,548	1,733
World	4,730	5,632	6,791	7,740	9,044
Regional Distribution					
Rich, Developed Economies	0.55	0.50	0.42	0.37	0.31
Newly-Industrializing Economies	0.05	0.06	0.08	0.10	0.11
Other Developing Economies	0.14	0.21	0.28	0.34	0.39
Eastern Europe and Former USSR	0.26	0.23	0.21	0.20	0.19
World	1.00	1.00	1.00	1.00	1.00
Per-Capita Emissions (kg/person)					
Rich, Developed Economies	3,067	3,070	2,978	2,671	3,073
Newly-Industrializing Economies	492	552	795	899	1,091
Other Developing Economies	250	352	463	532	624
Eastern Europe and Former USSR	3,210	3,269	3,351	3,433	3,681
World	1,066	1,067	1,089	1,078	1,122
Sulfur Oxides (10^6 metric tons of SO_2 equivalent)					
Levels of Emissions					
Rich, Developed Economies	51.3	45.4	42.0	37.6	34.6
Newly-Industrializing Economies	5.4	8.0	13.1	15.4	19.9
Other Developing Economies	18.9	28.8	40.7	49.8	59.2
Eastern Europe and Former USSR	49.5	45.0	41.3	37.4	33.6
World	125.0	127.2	137.1	140.2	147.3
Regional Distribution					
Rich, Developed Economies	0.41	0.36	0.31	0.27	0.24
Newly-Industrializing Economies	0.04	0.06	0.10	0.11	0.14
Other Developing Economies	0.15	0.23	0.30	0.36	0.40
Eastern Europe and Former USSR	0.40	0.35	0.30	0.27	0.23
World	1.00	1.00	1.00	1.00	1.00
Per-Capita Emissions (kg/person)					
Rich, Developed Economies	61	50	43	37	33
Newly-Industrializing Economies	11	13	18	19	22
Other Developing Economies	7	9	10	10	11
Eastern Europe and Former USSR	131	111	96	83	71
World	28	24	22	20	18
Nitrogen Oxides (10^6 metric tons of NO_2 equivalent)					
Levels of Emissions					
Rich, Developed Economies	35.2	34.8	35.4	34.4	31.8
Newly-Industrializing Economies	4.9	6.3	10.8	14.5	20.2
Other Developing Economies	9.6	16.5	25.6	35.1	48.9
Eastern Europe and Former USSR	19.3	20.6	22.3	24.2	26.5
World	69.0	78.2	94.1	108.2	127.4
Regional Distribution					
Rich, Developed Economies	0.51	0.45	0.38	0.32	0.25

TABLE 9.2 *(Continued)*

	1980	1990	2000	2010	2020
Newly-Industrializing Economies	0.07	0.08	0.12	0.13	0.16
Other Developing Economies	0.14	0.21	0.27	0.32	0.38
Eastern Europe and Former USSR	0.28	0.26	0.24	0.22	0.21
World	1.00	1.00	1.00	1.00	1.00
Per-Capita Emissions (kg/person)					
Rich, Developed Economies	42	38	37	34	30
Newly-Industrializing Economies	10	10	15	18	22
Other Developing Economies	4	5	6	7	9
Eastern Europe and Former USSR	51	51	52	54	56
World	16	15	15	15	16

Source: Duchin & Lange (1994).

rich economies, followed by the formerly socialist economies, the newly industrializing countries of Asia and Latin America, and then the other developing economies (see Table 9.1). However, there are some notable exceptions.

Not a single primary material among those in the tables is used by the two developing regions in proportion to their combined share of population in 1980, nor will it be in 2020. However, the disparity among regions is much lower for food (not shown in the table) than for fuel and non-fuel minerals. While plant-based foods will still dominate over animal products in the developing countries, the global harvesting of edible raw materials grows faster than that of minerals between 1980 and 2020. This growth reflects the steep rates of increased food consumption, especially of animal products, anticipated for the developing countries of Asia. A much closer look at the changing composition of the diet of different categories of households in all countries is clearly merited and amenable to this kind of approach, but it has not yet been carried out within this framework. A quantitative, structural analysis of household consumption, and of social welfare more generally, is far less developed than the multisectoral analysis of production.

Per-capita use of fossil fuels declines by 2020 in the rich economies due to a variety of measures including more fuel-efficient cars. Worldwide demand for gas actually doubles with very steep increases in the developing economies. According to these projections, Eastern Europe and the former Soviet Union remain very energy-intensive economies because of their industrial mix and a rather low starting point for energy-productivity. Despite massive increases in the use of energy in the developing economies, and the fact that fossil-fuel use is probably understated because of the large share assumed in this scenario for nuclear and hydroelectric power, their per capita use is still very low in 2020 by global standards.

Of the non-fuel minerals, only the use of bauxite increases worldwide on a per capita basis. Despite increased rates of recycling, total bauxite use more than doubles as aluminum increasingly substitutes for other materials in construction, in automobiles, and in other fabricated products. In the rich economies, demand for lead and iron actually falls and demand for nickel and copper is nearly flat. But the use of all of these metals, and of other materials not shown above like plastics and paper, will increase steeply in the developing economies even on a per capita basis.

The emissions reported in Table 9.2 for 2020 are substantially lower than what they would have been in the absence of technological change. But the problem is that these emissions still increase substantially between 1980 and 2020; in particular, carbon emissions nearly double. In addition, the locus of pollution decisively shifts from the rich countries, where historically most of it has originated, to the developing countries, where most future increase in population will take place. Material use and emissions are still much lower than in the rich countries on a per capita basis. However, substantial further increases are likely in the more distant future since people in developing regions can be expected to aspire to the material standards of those in the developed regions.

While the specific technical assumptions have not been spelled out here (but are documented in detail in the reference that has been cited), I believe this is an optimistic assessment of the consequences of doing things "smarter" but without major departures from today's technical practices. In terms of the use of all primary materials, such a scenario will put more, not less, pressure on the environment over the next several decades because the combined effects of population increase and improving the material standard of living in the developing countries will more than offset the savings in primary materials associated with the substitutions among materials, recycling, and other technological changes. To the extent that this analysis is credible, it provides the motivation for changes that go beyond industrial ecology.

INDUSTRIAL ECOLOGY AND THE USE OF MATERIALS

Much of the primary material that passes through the economic system, from automobiles to packaging or construction pipes, ends up sooner or later as solid waste. There are several emerging rules of thumb for solid waste management. One is to use less material in the first place ("source reduction"), to reuse or at least recycle products to the extent that is practical, and to dispose of remaining wastes in a manner that is environmentally benign. It is often necessary to reconceive product design and manufacturing to facilitate recycling, for example, by preferring a single material to composites. It is clear that practices in several countries, notably Germany (Fishbein, 1994), have already begun to move in these directions and will become widespread in the 21st century. But these prescriptions are far more complicated than they appear because there are many different ways of proceeding, all of which have different consequences that affect not only a single sector, but many parts of the structure of an economy as well. For the reasons which have been discussed in other parts of this chapter, we can expect a relatively rapid globalization of those solutions that appear to be successful. Then, for better or worse, there will tend to be a "lock-in" (Arthur, 1988), this time on a global scale, to these solutions which will make it hard to replace them even by superior ones for many decades to come. This prospect provides the motivation for taking a systematic approach to the in-depth evaluation of the different ways we might proceed. Potential solutions will involve both technological and social changes, and structural economic analysis can furnish a framework for evaluation.

One of the obstacles to the effective recycling of any material is the existence of a uniform waste stream of predictable volume. The investment in recycling facilities cannot be justified from a business or from a social point of view unless a steady, reliable source of inputs can be assured. This problem is faced for many materials, but none more so than plastics.

All parties today agree about the need to reduce polymer solid waste in landfills. This objective can be achieved by some combination of source reduction, degradability of the material, and recycling. The problems arise in achieving an appropriate and stable mix because the steps taken to satisfy one objective tend to thwart the other objectives.

One mechanism for source reduction is the substitution of other materials for plastics. However, the most celebrated comparisons, such as McDonald's former polystyrene foam "clamshell" package versus the replacement of bleached paper/polyethylene wrappers, or disposable versus cloth diapers, are inconclusive as to their environmental effects—in part because they have not yet been analyzed within a sufficiently integrated framework. Source reduction can also be achieved by changing the structure of consumption, or lowering overall consumption. After the initial economies, this option is likely to require significant changes in mainstream lifestyles. The prospects for what could be called the historic "consumption transition," based as in the "demographic transition" essentially on voluntary actions, are first beginning to be addressed. See Durning, 1992, for a discussion of the question, "How much is enough?"

The issue of degradability is similarly complicated. Petrochemical-based polymers are not intrinsically degradable, and truly degradable ones are still in early stages of commercialization. Of course, very little of the potential for degradation is actually realized in waste-disposal sites designed and managed as landfills rather than composting facilities. Furthermore, the shift in feedstock from hydrocarbons to biomass would have massive implications for the global economy.

A significant problem in the recycling of plastics is the expense of collection and the expense and difficulty of separation even among apparently homogeneous objects and polymers, not to mention objects of mixed composition and composite materials. The relative importance of different polymers, and the material composition of many objects, would need to change substantially if large-scale recycling of polymers were to be implemented. Further development would also be necessary for the separation of mixed plastics. Of course, in the unlikely event of a substitution away from plastics in many uses, and if those plastics in use will be largely biodegradable, there would be inadequate raw material to justify investing in a plastic recycling industry.

One current prospect is for the development of completely biodegradable polymers from biomass. Polymers derived from starches of annual crops such as corn and potatoes, fabricated using a "clean" production process according to the product description, are already in use in several applications like golf tees and pharmaceutical capsules. A significant program is also under way to commercialize polymers based on the jute crop of Bangladesh and India. It is hoped that this market can replace the traditional uses of jute which are lost as polypropylene replaces jute sacks for packaging grain, sugar, fertilizer, and cement (personal communication with I. Koons, UNDP).

Plastics are still displacing other primary materials and paper even in the rich economies, and their use is growing rapidly in developing countries. To the extent polymers are fabricated from biomass, the demand for the hydrocarbon feedstock is reduced. It could also reduce the solid waste that needs to be disposed of and precipitate the shift from landfills to composting facilities. But it puts pressure back on the land used to grow renewable crops.

The alternative roles that plastics might play in the global economy over the next fifty years may be a particularly fruitful case to study from both a technological and an economic point of view. While a shift to more easily recyclable or degradable materials may be desirable, it will also tend to compete for land with the production of food. What actually happens, by conscious decision or otherwise, may be only one small contributing factor to the global "big picture," but the vast differences that are sketched in the last few paragraphs suggest the importance of analyzing the alternative options.

CONCLUSIONS

Despite the difficulty of anticipating the technological practices of the future, it is clear that social priorities will require "internalizing the costs" of real and perceived environmental damage. Consequently, engineering design will economize on the use of mineral fuels and non-renewable materials and tend to favor fuels and materials of biological origin. The latter are attractive because they are renewable and degradable and sequester atmospheric carbon in their growing phase. As this transition ripples through the economy, it enhances the importance of new farming systems, new crops, and technologies for processing biological materials relative to mining activities and the processing of petrochemicals and metals.

The scope for computer-based automation will continue to increase in existing and new applications, including process control or the integration and coordination on a large scale of formerly separate activities of all types. People in their personal capacity will gain unprecedented access to public and private information and to on-line networking capabilities.

What has been called "eco-restructuring" will involve not only technological but also organizational changes. One of the most important has to do with transportation. A substantial shift away from the use of private automobiles to a combination of public transport and lowered mobility in the rich countries, and in the aspirations of the developing countries, would obviously result in substantial reductions in the demand for materials and fuels and the volume of atmospheric pollution. Given the powerful attraction of the private automobile, however, it will be necessary to demonstrate appealing "lifestyles" built around spatial organization and leisure activities that can be accommodated without cars. This challenge is as important, and as daunting, as any discussed in this chapter.

These kinds of changes could come about through intentional policy and design or, in the longer term, through the sheer physical impossibility for the world's expanding population to live as if resource exhaustion, environmental degradation, and social unrest were not happening. Hopefully, substantial change will be achieved through the former channels so that the involuntary adjustments will be less dramatic. Achieving this outcome will require, for starters, institutions that take a truly global approach to global problems, as opposed to one based on more narrow interests such as those of a particular country or industry. Such institutions are needed to build a support structure, a community or peer group, a constituency, and networks for those involved in all aspects of global thinking about local and global problems. Part of the work of this community is to bring together visionaries who can imagine possible solutions to seemingly intractable problems with analysts who can evaluate these ideas for their economic, social, and environmental implications without destroying their creative elements, and people of action who can facilitate or instigate the implementation of change at small and large scales in cases where such input is appropriate. This agenda represents an unprecedented challenge, but surely one whose time has come.

REFERENCES

Arthur, B. (1988). Competing Technologies: An Overview. In *Technology and Economic Theory*, edited by G. Dosi, C. Freeman, R. Nelson, and G. Silverberg. London: Pinter Publishers.

Duchin, F. (1992). Industrial Input-Output Analysis: Implications for Industrial Ecology. *Proceedings of the National Academy of Sciences*, Vol. 89, pp. 851–855, February.

Duchin, F. (1994). Input-Output Analysis and Industrial Ecology. In *The Greening of Industrial Ecosystems*, edited by Braden R. Allenby and Deanna J. Richards. Washington, DC: National Academy Press.

Duchin, F. (1994b). Structural Economics: Toward a Post-Normal Science of Ecological Economics. Paper presented at the Meeting of the International Society of Ecological Economics, San Jose, Costa Rica, October.

Duchin, F., & Lange, G. M. (1994). *The Future of the Environment: Ecological Economics and Technological Change*. New York: Oxford University Press.

Durning, A. T. (1992). *How Much Is Enough? The Consumer Society and the Future of the Earth*. New York: Norton.

Fishbein, B. (1994). *Germany, Garbage, and the Green Dot: Challenging the Throwaway Society*. New York: INFORM.

Krohn, W., & Schäfer, W. (1976). The Origins and Structure of Agricultural Chemistry. In *Perspectives on the Emergence of Scientific Disciplines*, edited by Gerald Lemaine, Roy Macleod, Michael Mulkay, and Peter Weingart. The Hague: Mouton Publishers.

Lee, J. R. (1993). Between Process and Product: Making the Link Between Trade and the Environment. Unpublished manuscript. School of International Service, the American University.

Margulis, L., & Sagan, D. (1986). *Microcosmos: Four Billion Years of Microbial Evolution*. New York: Summit Books.

Office of Technology Assessment, U.S. Congress (1992). *Trade and Environment: Conflicts and Opportunities*, OTA-BP-ITE-94. Washington, DC: GPO, May.

Ostrom, E. (1990). *Governing the Commons: The Evolution of Institutions for Collective Action*. New York: Cambridge University Press.

World Commission on Environment and Development (1987). *Our Common Future* (also known as the Brundtland Report). Oxford: Oxford University Press.

10

Gender, Environment, Development, and Health

T. O. Adekanye

INTRODUCTION

The objective of this chapter is to highlight gender issues in health, environment, and development. For this purpose, male–female differences in access to, and ownership of, resources as well as those in the control of output are indicated. Health-related factors, including life expectancy, mortality, and food and nutrition are considered. Attention is also paid to such environmental issues as resource depletion and degradation. These are then related to inter- and intra-generational fairness, as a core issue in sustainable development programming.

In the section below, a historical view of gender is taken, as a background for the rest of the chapter. Several random issues, some of which have made world headlines over the last 20 to 30 years, are considered. These have been selected in such a way as to give a global view of gender analysis in recent history, with particular reference to power, domination, and the process of empowerment. This immediately raises the central problem of differential access to power, wealth, and status and the control of their distribution. But the resolution of this is often based on biological or cultural factors. However, effective policy formulation for women in sustainable development centers primarily on such issues as education and acquired skills. Access to equal opportunities is therefore of crucial importance. This and other policy considerations are taken up later in this chapter.

HISTORICAL PERSPECTIVE

About 1970, the women's liberation movement gained prominence in the mass media in the West, particularly in the United States of America. The movement marked a watershed in gender aspects of socioeconomic relations, particularly the position of women in development. It called public attention to the condition of women, and helped to sensitize world opinion to the subjugation of women and unequal power-sharing between men and women. Underlying the women's liberation movement is partriarchy, descent on the male line, and possible universality of it. However, anthropological and historical evidence points to the evidence and tradition of matriarchy and gender equality. In ancient Egypt, Celtic Britain, and Japan, for instance, queens and empresses ruled, while men occupied subordinate roles. Also Spartan women owned two-thirds of the land. Arab women owned herds tended by their husbands. Egyptian women could charge their husbands interest on money lent to them. Babylonian women had exclusive rights over their dowries. Marriage contracts guaranteed equal rights for men and women. Women had right to divorce and alimony. These rights, guaranteed by social custom and legal codes, were recognized and exercised by women. However, the advent of monotheistic religions and the *interpretation* of tenets brought about a change (U.N., 1991).

The nature of agriculture can be used as an indicator of relative power-sharing between men and women. If it is arable, (cash) crop production, or livestock (particularly large animals), men appear to have more control. If horticultural, women tend to have greater control. For instance, the early food-gathering stage of human history and the horticultural history of Africa are said to have been fairly egalitarian and free of gender-bias, compared with the present agricultural system of the Western world (Blumberg, 1984).

An analysis of *power sharing*, however, goes beyond agriculture. It is, in particular, often related to biological and reproductive roles of women. Biological determinism is used as an explanation for regarding women as the *weaker sex*. Admittedly, pregnancy and lactation impose some constraints on women's productive capacity. Other than this, however, biological determinism really has no validity for ascribing a secondary role to women. In fact, medical evidence indicates that the young female child has biological advantage over the male (WHO, 1991).

Sociocultural factors are however used to reinforce the restrictive impact of the reproductive roles of women on their productive ones. When women are kept in seclusion for religious reasons, for instance, they are *literally* invisible (Pittin, 1990). Their productive base is thereby physically limited to virtually the confines of the family compounds. The issue here then is not that women are *naturally* less able to engage in productive activities but are, in this instance, *prevented* from doing so.

This raises the twin issues of the politics and the economics of power-sharing and the process of empowerment. The involvement of women in decision making is the exception rather than the rule in most countries of the world. The few exceptions include, for instance, the rather uncommon occurrence of a female prime minister, including Golda Meir in Israel, Bandaranaike in Ceylon, Indira Gandhi in India, and Margaret Thatcher in the United Kingdom. There have probably been less than twenty female heads of government (presidents and prime ministers) in the 20th century.

This leads to the issue of power, violence, and force. Men are more often involved in the use of force, whether in the more organized form of state power, the military, or even in the more basic form of animal hunting in pristine economies. This is perhaps an extension of the "babies" versus "brawn" issue. It is thus usually viewed with considerable surprise when women are involved in the use of violence.

However, the environment-related demonstrations by women in Europe in recent years and those over economic and political crises, as those in Nigeria, indicate that women can organize and use force, if necessary, to try to bring about needed change.[1]

The crucial question then, is, What does it all add up to? This question is answered here by taking a quick look at United Nations activities and other related issues. Starting from 1945, a deliberate attempt has been made by the U.N. to raise public and global awareness of gender issues in socioeconomic and political inequalities. Global agendas have also been drawn up from time to time to correct the inequalities. In 1946, for example, the United Nations Commission on the Rights of Women was formed for worldwide monitoring and promotion of women's rights. In 1952, the commission initiated the convention on the political rights of women. That was the first global mandate for equal political rights for men and women under the law. These were the rights to vote, hold public office, and undertake public functions. Equal rights for women in marriage and dissolution were taken up in the 1950s and 1960s. Then, 1975 was the International Women's Year and 1975–85 the U.N. women's decade, for equality, development and peace. In 1979, the U.N. General Assembly adopted the Convention on the elimination of all forms of discrimination against Women. The U.N. mid-decade conference on women took place in Copenhagen in 1980. The end of the U.N. decade for women conference took place in Nairobi in 1985 and forward-looking Strategies for the Advancement of Women were adopted (U.N., 1991a,

---

[1] But women are often victims of violence at home, in the workplace, and in society. In the United States of America, for instance, a woman is beaten every 18 minutes and 3 to 4 million are battered each year. In India, official statistics indicate that five women are burned in dowry-related disputes each day (U.N., 1991).

1991b). Also gender studies have blossomed all over the world and in most disciplines. This is due to the leadership given by the U.N. and the interest and work of feminist scholars, in the United States of America, Europe, and even here in Africa. The former Communist countries are also quickly catching up (Adekanye, 1993a, 1993b).[2] However, much still remains to be done.

The United Nations has, no doubt, sensitized government worldwide to the need to improve the condition of women. However, it is perhaps true in this sense to say that *there is a third world in every country*. Starting with the U.N. system itself, generally, less than ten percent of the top directorship posts were held by women in 1986 (Snyder, 1990). Furthermore, on a worldwide basis, including the United States of America and other developed countries, women receive about half to two thirds of men's income for comparable jobs. And, everywhere, women are usually the poorest of the poor, leading to the emergence of *female-centered families*. In the developing countries, admittedly, the problems of relatively lower incomes for women are exacerbated by other culture-related factors such as dowry-related deaths, and religious fundamentalism. Nonetheless, economic factors and not culture, or even biology, are perhaps the most important single determinant of women's secondary status worldwide. Although the importance of these other factors cannot be completely discounted, impeded access to resources and limited opportunities appear to be more responsible for gender inequalities conforming with the case of other types of inequalities—ethnic, class, or even racial.

CURRENT STATUS

In this section, the current situation of the differential position of men and women is considered. The discussion in the last section on relative access to opportunities, power, and control is developed further by examining the position of men and women in health, environment, and in the economy.

HEALTH

Relevant issues here for gender analysis of male–female differences in health include life expectancy, cause of death, maternal mortality, the health of girls, and acquired immune deficiency syndrome (AIDS) (U.N., 1991a, 1991b). Life expectancy has improved worldwide, and has increased for both men and women. Life expectancy is lower, worldwide,

---

[2] A conference took place, for instance, on Teaching Women's Studies in Lodz, Poland, in May, 1993. (See Adekanye, 1993b.)

for men than women, except in some developing countries such as Bangladesh and Nepal. Life expectancy has also increased more for women than men virtually everywhere. It is higher for both sexes in the developed than in the developing countries. However, the increase in the latter, averaging about 8 to 9 years, are higher than in the former, averaging about 4 years, between 1970 and 1990 (U.N., 1991a). Life expectancy for women is, on average, some 6.5 years higher than men's in the developed countries, compared with 5 years in Latin America and the Caribbean, 3.5 years in Africa, and 3 years in Asia and the Pacific. Further regional differences include an average life expectancy for women of 75 years or more for most developed countries, compared, for instance, with 54 years for Africa, and below 50 years for many countries of Asia and the Pacific. On a worldwide basis, the lowest life expectancies for women include those of Sierra Leone and Ethiopia in Africa, and Afghanistan and East Timor in Asia and the Pacific, at 42 or 43 years. Furthermore, because men tend to be older than women at marriage, women have an average widowhood period of 8 to 10 years worldwide.

Women still die, particularly in the developing countries, from childbirth and related causes, as well as from causes relating to their gender. These include infanticide, bride burning, and dowry deaths. Also, since women have now adopted lifestyles similar to men's, there is considerable increase in death relating to their personal behavior. For instance, while men's death from vehicle accidents remained virtually the same in 1980 as it was in 1950, women's rose by some 20 percent in the developed countries during this period, (U.N., 1991b). Maternal mortality rates (MMR) are still high in the developing countries, except in a few instances. MMR per 100,000 live births reaches a high of 600 deaths in Southern Asia, 600 deaths in Africa, 450 deaths in Southeast Asia, and 275 deaths in Latin America and the Caribbean. This compares very badly with an MMR of close to zero in most developed countries and 75 in Eastern Asia. The gap between the developed and developing countries is indicated by the fact that MMR is often less than 5 in the former, while it sometimes exceeds 1,000 in the latter. Furthermore, most causes of MMR are preventable. These include poor nutrition, abortion, anemia, poor handling of pregnancy complications, the use of untrained personnel, poor health facilities, and limited access to available facilities in remote rural areas of develoing countries.

Several factors affect the health of girls negatively, particularly in the developing countries. These include poor nutrition, early marriage, teenage pregnancy, the clear preference for male children and, in many countries of Africa and in the Middle East, female circumcision. These factors predispose girls to poor health, stunted growth, and pregnancy and delivery complications.

Other factors which are related to the health of women include the acquired immune deficiency syndrome (AIDS) and other sexually transmitted diseases, sexual assault, and rape. About a third of world AIDS sufferers (2 million) are women, an indication of the spread of AIDS among heterosexuals. Initially, it was assumed that AIDS affected only males in the West. However, it is having devastating effects on urban women, and is now regarded as the major killer of women aged 20 to 27 years in cities in Europe, the United States, and tropical Africa. However, there is often the feeling that sexually transmitted diseases (STDs) and sexual assault take place more commonly in the developed countries where there is greater sexual permissiveness compared with the developing countries.

ENVIRONMENT

Relevant gender-related issues considered in the discussion of the environment undertaken here include urbanization and migration, water and sanitation, fuel and electricity, and resource depletion, degradation, and pollution. Urbanization and migration appear, on balance, to have more negative impact on women, whether they move to the cities or get left behind in the rural areas. When women get left behind in the rural areas, they are *de facto* heads of family. They are more affected by overwork, overcrowding, and the poor living conditions in the cities, when they migrate. Also, they tend to have relatively poorer skills than men, and therefore have lower chances of employment. Very often, too, they join the pool of the unemployed or partially employed in the informal sectors. Available migration indices indicate that the proportion of women in urban population has increased by approximately 70 percent, compared with just about 23 percent for rural areas, in 1970–1990. Furthermore it is mainly in Africa, Asia, and the Pacific that the rural female population is growing. Some 85 percent of world rural female population live in these three regions. Other environment-related gender issues include the problems of international migration and those of refugee women.

Water and sanitation problems unknown to women in developed countries are encountered by women in the developing countries. Available estimates indicate that up to 17 hours per week are spent by women in fetching water for household use in developing countries.[3] Access to

---

[3] It has been estimated that in Kenya, with a population of 23 million in 1988, women spent a collective 9 million hours a day on fetching water (Snyder, 1990).

good sanitation facilities is even worse. This is so for both urban and rural areas. For instance close to 80 percent of the population in the rural areas, and about 50 percent in the urban areas of Africa lack adequate sanitation facilities. Furthermore, women are generally responsible for household waste disposal and sanitation in the developing countries.

The major responsibility for fetching fuel for cooking, heating, and lighting in developing countries is essentially women's. Apart from the time spent, there are the health hazards associated with the use of fuel wood, charcoal, dung, or crop residues in the developing countries. Estimates for India indicate, for instance, that, while cooking, women inhale as much carcinogen as if they had smoked 20 packs of cigarettes per day. Indoor gas and electricity cooking facilities, which have less direct deleterious impact on the health of women, are not much used in the developing, compared with the developed, countries.

Resources depletion, degradation, and pollution of the environment appear to be caused, both in the developed and developing countries, more by the activities of men. Men have the economic and political power, and decisions are made very often without consulting or considering women. In agriculture, for instance, such environmental problems as erosion, forest depletion, and overexploitation of land resources are more associated with the activities of men. Men are, more often than not, the saw millers involved in felling trees.[4] Also, with the *Green Revolution*, the use of such agro-chemicals as fertilizers and pesticides, the construction of huge dams, and the emergence of new pests due to non-cropping have had negative impact on the environment. Men are very often the main recipients of the innovations entailed in the Green Revolution in different parts of the developing world.[5]

---

[4] The supply of fuel wood is disappearing fast, at a rate estimated to be about 16 million hectares of tropical forests per annum (Snyder, 1990).

[5] The *Green Revolution* denotes the change in traditional agricultural systems, marked by considerable increase in productivity. Starting with maize in Mexico and rice in the Phillippines, *miracle* varieties of these crops have been developed through research in association with the Rockefeller and Ford foundations. Several countries have now had the *Green Revolution experience*, involving the use of improved seed and other complementary factor inputs, particularly fertilizer and irrigation. However, development literature is now going *beyond* the Green Revolution to *sustainable* agriculture, in order to counter the negative impact of the Green Revolution on the environment and the poorer segments of the society. (See, for instance, the FAO, 1993, Conway & Babier, 1990, Pearce et al., 1990, and ILEIA, 1993.)

WORK AND THE ECONOMY

Food and agricultural production, the informal sector, the formal sector, the impact of education and the overall invisibility of women are discussed in this section. The example of Africa is perhaps most relevant here. Africa is *the* region of female farming, compared with other regions of the world. This had been confirmed by Boserup (1970), the Economic Commission for Africa (ECA/FAO 1976), and several other independent researchers work (Adekanye, 1981). Women provide some 60–80 percent of the labor input in agriculture, particularly for food production, processing, and the trade in food.[6] But they have limited control of resources and output. Also, women predominate in the informal sectors, thereby being the poorest of the poor. In African economies, for instance, they are the small food vendors. They work at construction sites as water carriers. They provide much of the labor in cottage industries. The unregulated nature of the informal sector means than the women are often subject to abuse, exploitation, and low incomes.

Women's education is generally lower than men's.[7] Furthermore, men tend, in general, to acquire the more technical and the more productivity- and income-enhancing skills. As against this, women tend to go into the "softer" professions—nursing and secretarial positions, for instance. Consequently, their incomes are generally lower than men's, by about one third to one half, even in the developed countries. Men generally occupy the top positions in most professions and the top decision-making organizations.

Women's invisibility can be categorized as statistical, sociocultural, economic, infrastructural, and environmental (Adekanye, 1993a). The *statistical invisibility* of women derives from incomplete recording of women's work. For instance, when women are in full seclusion for religious reasons, that are kept away from meeting male visitors. Yet, men are more often the enumerators for censuses and surveys. There is also the issue of methodological procedures. Very often, when women's work is recorded, it is often regarded as a proportion of men's. There is also the free, unrecorded, and therefore *unvalued* women's household work which generally does not enter into national statistics.

Sociocultural invisibility of women is due to such factors as seclusion for religious reasons, as well as patriarchy, with descent along the male

---

[6] The proportion of women's share in family food production has actually been estimated at 80 percent for Africa, 60 percent for Asia and the Pacific, and 40 percent for Latin America. (See Snyder, 1990.)

[7] Approximately two-thirds of all world illiterates are women, while 65 percent of adult females are literate, compared with 79 percent for men (Snyder, 1990).

line. *Economic invisibility* of women is due to low incomes associated, for instance, with underrecording, undervaluing of their work, and the unpaid nature of household work indicated above. *Infrastructural invisibility* is due to poor and traditional women's technology, relative to men's in many developing countries. For instance, men are often the first and sometimes the only recipients of innovations and planned changes, including extension services, cooperative development, the introduction of cash crops, and so forth. *Environmental invisibility* of women includes such instances where women can only use marginal farm land.[8]

NIGERIA

A Nigerian overview is provided below to give an empirical content to the discussion.[9] Salient aspects of the health of women in Nigeria include a high fertility rate, which is about five children born alive. The MMR is also one of the highest in the world, at about 600 per 100,000 live births. There is still considerable reliance on traditional birth attendants, and delivery at home. Very often the problem is not just that of *accessibility* to health facilities because of problems with transport. There is also the problem of *acceptability*—many health facilities provided in remote areas remain unused.[10] Other health problems of women include teenage marriage, and pregnancy complications because of the practice of female circumcision. (Some public enlightenment campaigns against the practice of female circumcision are now being mounted.) Food consumption and nutritional problems predispose women to anemia and other pregnancy complications. Men generally eat the choicest portions of food. In polygamous households, husbands tend to "circulate" between the cooking pots of the different wives. Although social beliefs and taboos are disappearing, where they do exist, they tend to limit women's nutritional intakes. For instance, pregnant women sometimes do not eat eggs, which are involved

---

[8] It has been said for Malawi, for instance, that "the most apparent relationship between women and the environment arises through the link between women, poverty, and land degradation. The poverty profile of Malawi shows that across all households, female-headed households make up a large percentage of the poor and core poor households. . . . It is mostly the poorer households that are marginalized into the smaller plots (<0.5 ha), steeper slopes (>12%) and less fertile soils, when the pressure on the land increases or the existing quality of land declines (Buchner, 1991, p. 2a).

[9] This section is based essentially on empirical surveys of women undertaken in Nigeria. (See Adekanye, 1985, 1988a and 1988b, 1991.)

[10] For example, during the field work for the UNICEF Project, some well-equipped rural health clinics were underutilized in Bauchi State of Northern Nigeria. (See Adekanye, 1988b.)

in the reproductive cycle of chickens. Morbidity and mortality are still unbearably high for women and are, in most cases, due to preventable causes, such as bad handling and inadequate facilities. The primary health care programme of government has tried to bring health care to the women. Achievement is, however, still very small compared with requirement.[11]

Very little attention has been paid to environmental conservation in Nigeria, until recently. The activating incident was the dumping of toxic waste in Southeastern Nigeria by a foreign firm. Also, Federal and State Governments in Nigeria have annual "tree planting" ceremonies on a day set aside for this purpose. However, little attention is paid to the environment during the rest of the year. The gender issues relating to the environment in Nigeria include overexploitation of natural resources, and problems of water supply, waste disposal, and energy supply and utilization. Agricultural resources have been subjected to such abuses as indiscriminate application of chemical fertilizers, overgrazing in the North, leading to desert conditions, and overcropping leading to serious gully erosion in parts of the Southwest, and the Southeast of Nigeria. Women, more often than not, are left with such marginal lands. Furthermore, they are more directly involved in urban and rural households' waste management and disposal. Facilities are rudimentary. Electricity and potable water reach less than 20 percent of all households. Women and children therefore spend hours fetching water and fuel wood. The Federal Environmental Protection Agency (FEPA) has Federal and State offices. Its impact has, however, not really been felt, particularly at the grassroots level.

Relevant aspects of the Nigerian socioeconomic situation include low education for women, the use of traditional technologies, and the ensuing low productivity, preponderant involvement of women in food and agricultural production and low incomes.[12,13] Nigeria is still essentially agri-

---

[11] In general, women are less healthy than men. The incidence of anemia is high, for instance, about 2.1 percent of female patients at the General Hospital in Offa, Kwara State, were treated for anemia in 1987. The proportion of all women (rural and urban) suffering from anemia in Nigeria is, in all probability, higher than this, so that at least 10 percent of all women suffer from anemia.

[12] For example, there were more girls than boys in Oyun Local Government Area of Kwara State in 1987/88, with a male/female ratio of 0.93 to 1.00. There were, however, slightly more boys than girls in the secondary schools, with a male/female ratio of 1.02 to 1.00. For tertiary education, there were more than two boys for every girl, giving a male/female drop-out ratio of 0.3 to 1.00 for the secondary schools, so that for every boy that dropped out, more than three girls dropped out.

[13] The 1987 survey (Adekanye, 1988) revealed, for instance that average income

cultural, despite the economic importance of petroleum production and export. Although agriculture contributes only about 30 percent of the Gross Domestic Product (GDP), it employs about 70 percent of the people. Productivity is low, due to the use of traditional methods and implements. Nigeria, along with other African countries, has the problem of burgeoning debt. Available indications from countrywide studies are that, for instance, the Structural Adjustment Programme (SAP), introduced in Nigeria in 1986, has had limited, if any, positive effects on productivity, output, and income. Income increases in agriculture have therefore been nominal, particularly because of severalfold increases in input costs.

Women, who are the rural food producers, and are in charge of family food, health, and nutrition, have been doubly hit. Nigeria's spiraling inflation has been cost push–demand pull, structural, and imported. Survival is therefore a daily worry. The Better Life for the Rural Women Programme was initiated by the wife of the former president, Babangida, in 1987. However, other than calling attention to the conditions of women (which, in any case, the U.N. has been doing globally) it seems to have achieved little, particularly when the huge costs involved (much of which are unaccounted for) are considered. Up-to-date and reliable data are unavailable. But the general indication is that, not only is there increasing feminization of poverty, but there is also a negative correlation between work and returns for the women.

THE NEW GLOBAL AGENDA

In the new global agenda for the 1990s and beyond, for gender aspects of health, environment, and development, there is a consensus and convergence of opinions and action plans by several international organizations, including the United Nations Development Programme (UNDP), the United Nations Development Fund for Women (UNIFEW), the International Labour Organization (ILO), and the World Health Organization (WHO). The basic issue is that the productive and reproductive roles of women, worldwide but more so in developing countries, are such that concerted action needs to be taken. This is to call attention to the condition of women, as has been done by the U.N. since 1946. But, more importantly, it goes beyond this—by specifying and monitoring progress on action plans targeted at improving women's condition. Of paramount importance is the holistic approach and inter-program relationships. The relevant programs center principally on sustainability, that is, meeting

---

per women was 952 Naira (the Nigerian currency) per annum, compared with 1,349 Naira per man, indicating a 30-percent edge for the men in Kwara State of Nigeria.

women's current needs without endangering the chances of future generations meeting their own. Aspects of this include the need to reduce disparities between men and women, urban and rural, rich and poor, as well as Health for All by the Year 2000, including the problem of an aging population and the well-being of adolescents. Identified monitoring indicators for women's health include maternal mortality, family planning, access to health facilities, and female proportion of infants with low birth weights. Also, the education of women is regarded as being of primary importance, as a basis for improving women's health and socioeconomic status.

Environmental problems of central focus include increasing urban slums, rural isolation, and the nonavailability of basic facilities. Also, the provision of credit to facilitate access to appropriate technologies for women, and changes in laws to facilitate equal access for men and women to employment opportunities and development institutions, should receive attention. Furthermore, the United Nations Children Fund (UNICEF) and WHO are specifically working together on selected aspects of women's and children's health, including female children's food and nutrition and that of lactating mothers, access to information to prevent too-early, too-late, too-many, or too-closely-spaced pregnancies, and to prenatal care for pregnant women.

The United Nations (1991) has also indicated challenges to the year 2000 for women covering legal, health, education, economic, and peace-related issues. These problems and solutions are generally known. What is perhaps lacking is the will for action. Very often therefore, *de jure* is different from *de facto* equality, so that, at the threshold of the 21st century, there is equality in theory but inequality in practice, for the vast majority of the world's women.

SUMMARY

This chapter has focused attention on gender-related inequalities in health, environmental, and socioeconomic issues. A historical review indicates that, although patriarchy and ascribing a secondary role to women appear to be universal, it was not always so. Current assessment of the role and status of women indicate that, particularly in the developing countries, women are less healthy than men. Maternal mortality rates are still unbearably high, sometimes reaching 1,000 per 100,000 live births, due, in many cases, to preventable causes. Women constitute half of the world's population. They perform two-thirds of the world's work. They, however, receive only 40 percent of the world's income, and own less than one-hundredth of the world's property. Women are more easily affected by environmental and other hazards. They are, for instance, more readily consigned to the use of marginal lands in agriculture. The ongoing structural adjustment in many developing countries has led to a cutback in health and other social services that affect women. However, the United Nations has led a spirited global campaign, particularly since 1975, the International Women's Year, and has indicated challenges to the year 2000, for gender equality.

CONCLUSION

The major conclusion that emerges from the analysis and discussion of gender issues in this chapter is that, on a worldwide basis, but more so in developing countries, women have not been properly brought into mainstream development programming. A "trickle-down" approach has generally been adopted. In any case, power is not usually given but it is very often wrestled. This is not advocating a war of the sexes. It is merely to call attention to the fact that there is need for more women-centered projects.

POLICIES

Sustainable development entails not just growth in income but also the distribution of this and concern for the weak, the deprived, the environment, and for future generations. At least two policy instruments are necessary for promoting sustainable development for the world's women. These are *developmental education* and *appropriate technology*. Developmental education is education that is economically useful. Appropriate (and environmentally friendly) technology is that body of knowledge and implements that are relevant to women's needs and suitable to the environment. These two policy instruments, taken together, are necessary for the empowerment of women—equipping them for better employment, better health management, and decision-making roles.

REFERENCES

1. Adekanye, T. O. *Women and Agriculture in Nigeria,* United Nations Economic Commission for Africa (ECA), ATPCIN/B1/11, Addis Ababa, 1981.
2. Adekanye, T. O. "Women in Agriculture in Oyo, Ogun, Kwara States of Nigeria" in J. P. Mulligan, *Nigeria: Farm Family Enterprise Development,* Pre-Identification Survey Report, International Fund for Agricultural Development (IFAD), June 1985.
3. Adekanye, T. O. "Women and the Development of Agricultural Cooperatives in Nigeria", Report of a survey commissioned by UNDP/ILO/FDAC Project NIR/83/041, April, 1988 (a).

4. Adekanye, T. O. "A Situational Analysis of Women in Nigeria", Report of a study commissioned by the United Nations Children's Education Fund (UNICEF) Lagos, 1988 (b).
5. Adekanye, T. O. "Technology and Training for Rural Women", Report of a Ford Foundation Assisted Project in selected villages of South Western Nigeria, December, 1991.
6. Adekanye, T. O. "Gender Bias in African Agriculture and Sustainable Development": The Case of Nigeria", paper presented at the Conference "Out of the Margin, Feminist Perspectives on Economic Theory", Amsterdam, the Netherlands, June 1993.
7. Adekanye, T. O. "Women at Work in the Rural Economies of Africa: The Case of Nigeria", paper presented at the Conference on Teaching Women's Studies, University of Lodz, Poland, May 1993b.
8. Barbier, E. D. *Sustainable Agriculture and the Resource Poor: Policy Issues and Options, HED/UCC* London Environmental Economic Centre LEEC paper 88-02.
9. Blumberg, R. L. "A General Theory of Gender Stratification", in R. Collins, *Sociological Theory*, Jossey-Bass, London, 1984.
10. Boserep, E. *Women's Role in Economic Development*, George Allen & Unwih, London, 1970.
11. Buchner, G., et al. "Gender, Environmental Degradation and Development: The Extent of the Problem", London Environmental Economics Centre, paper 91-04.
12. Conway, G. R. and Barbier, E. S. *After the Green Revolution: Sustainable Agriculture for Development*, Earthscan Publications Ltd., London, 1990.
13. ECA/FAO, "Women, Population and Rural Developments in Africa", Women's Programme Unit, FAO, Rome MT/HO440/E/1/3850, 1976.
14. FAO, *Ceres* No. (vol. 25 no. 5) September–October 1993.
15. *ILELIA Newsletter* for Low External Input and Sustainable Agriculture, Vol. 9, No. 2, July 1993.
16. Pearce, D., et al. *Sustainable Development: Economics and Environment in the Third World*, Earthscan Publications, London, 1990.
17. Snyder, M. "Women: The Key to Ending Hunger", *The Hunger Project Papers*, No. 8, August 1990.
18. United Nations. *Women-Challenges to the Year 2000*, New York, 1991.
19. United Nations. *World's Women: The Trends and Statistics 1970–1990*. New York, 1991.
20. World Health Organisation. *Women, Health and Development*. Progress Report by the Director-General WHO/FHE/WHD/95.5.
21. WHO. "Women's Perspectives and Participation in Reproductive Health", Report of a Pre-Congress Workshop organised by the Joint WHO/Task Force, Singapore, 11–12 September 1991.

11

Tropical Environments, Man, and Vector-Borne Diseases

Norman G. Gratz

INTRODUCTION

Much has been written in the last two to three decades about how the major environmental changes which have occurred in the urban and rural areas of the tropical world have affected the health of their inhabitants. In rural areas, the changes in the environment have been caused, for the most part, by large-scale water development projects such as dams and the extensive irrigation works, and the consequent expansion in agriculture. Widespread deforestation has also resulted in important environmental changes. The environmental changes in the urban areas of the tropical, developing countries have been largely due to the rapid, unplanned urbanization from an influx into the cities of migrants from rural areas, seeking what they believe will be better opportunities for jobs and economic improvement. The extent of the urbanization which has occurred has far exceeded the ability of most tropical municipalities to provide adequate supplies of safe drinking water, safely dispose of solid and liquid wastes, or provide minimal satisfactory housing for their populations (Gratz, 1973; Rossi-Espagnet, et al., 1991).

In both rural and urban areas the environmental changes have caused major changes in the vector and rodent populations, often greatly increasing areas in which they breed and, consequently, increasing the transmission of the diseases they carry. The natural environments in most of the tropical countries, prior to intensified irrigation and agricultural development and urbanization were, in any event, favorable to the proliferation of arthropod vectors and rodent reservoirs and to the diseases they transmit. Before the advent of modern insecticides and chemotherapeutic agents, malaria, plague, yellow fever, sleeping sickness and many other diseases transmitted by mosquitoes, fleas, lice, tsetse flies and other vectors were perennially the cause of an enormous number of cases of disease often associated with heavy mortality. In those rural areas of the tropics where no development projects have been undertaken, little has changed as regards the environmental predisposition which favors development of sylvatic vectors and disease transmission.

There are tropical countries in which the incidence of some of the vector-borne diseases has been reduced either as a result of control programs against a particular disease or its vectors or, often, as a result of overall economic and social development in the country accompanied by improvements in environmental conditions and improved health services. In countries where such improvements have not taken place, vector-borne disease transmission continues much as before. The appearance of vector resistance to pesticides used for their control, the development of parasite resistance to drugs or, unfortunately, socioeconomic unrest which disrupts the normal fabric of society, may result in epidemic outbreaks of disease as the underlying conditions favoring transmission have not changed. The health of the human population has a profound impact upon the economic and social condition of a nation, just as the economic state of a country determines to what level of health service it can aspire. In most of the tropics, the vector-borne diseases continue to threaten the ability of people to improve their quality of life (Wijeyaratne et al., 1994). Thus any environmental changes which worsen the health situation will be likely to hamper development.

Currently we stand at a watershed in respect to the incidence and prevalence of this group of infections. Until recently, the favorable process of development, improved tools for disease control, and the greater availability of health services, have reduced the prevalence of such diseases as malaria, plague, louse-borne typhus, louse-borne relapsing fever, and filariasis. Despite concern about the recrudescence of malaria, and the spread of dengue and certain other infections in most countries, the incidence of some of the worst of this group of diseases have not returned to the levels they were at the early part of this century. While it seems unlikely that bubonic plague will again cause tens or hundreds of thousands of deaths every year in India or China, or that sleeping sickness will virtually depopulate entire regions of Africa, in many parts of the world and particularly so in the tropics, the ecological and environmental conditions would still permit the rapid recrudescence of many of the diseases. The outbreak of plague in India in September 1994, is a case in point. In recent years there have indeed been recrudescences and epidemics of several of the vector-borne diseases; these will be described below and show the threat of what might occur where there are further environmental changes favoring vector development and disease transmission. Global warming is already a topic of concern, as even a small increase in the mean temperature could favor expanded distribution of important disease vectors such as the tsetse fly in Africa and the endemic areas in which disease transmission takes place (Cook, 1992).

The following will review the nature of the environmental changes which have already resulted in increased vector and rodent populations, and increased disease transmission in urban and rural areas of the tropical world. Examples will also be given of instances in which purposeful alterations to the environment have succeeded in reducing vector population densities and controlling disease transmission, and how these favorable changes could be further extended. The effects of environmental changes in urban and rural areas will be considered separately.

URBAN ENVIRONMENTAL CHANGES AND THEIR EFFECT ON VECTOR-BORNE DISEASES

Most of the environmental changes in urban areas of the tropics are due to the great expansions of their populations. In 1981, the World Health Organization stated that "... if the present trend towards urbanization continues, by the year 2000 half the world's population will be urban. Eight out of ten people in the industrial countries will be urban residents, while the corresponding figures for the developing world will be four out of ten. It is estimated that by the year 2000, out of the 15 largest metropolitan areas, 12 will be in the developing countries" (WHO, 1981).

Urbanization has been taking place over a long part of man's history but is now rapidly accelerating in the developing countries, especially of Asia and Latin America, where urban industrial development has led to an increasing demand for laborers in the cities. Growing numbers of people leave the land and their farms to migrate to the cities. The large numbers of people migrating to metropolitan areas seeking casual labor often bring malaria with them for they have a significantly higher rate of malaria infections than persons native to the city (Sethi et al., 1990). The urbanization process which began more recently in the less developed countries, is now occurring with a rapidity that far exceeds the ability of the governments, national and municipal, to cope with the greatly increased urban populations especially in the provision of adequate water, sanitation and health services. Migrants into the cities are generally among the poorest portion of the population, often including a large proportion of illiterates, poorly prepared to obtain other than the lowest levels of employment. Their levels of income do not enable them to pay for even rudimentary, let alone, adequate medical attention where such services are not provided

TABLE 11.1 Percent of Population in Urban Areas of Selected Countries of Asia and Percent of Population with Access to Safe Water[@]

	1970*	1985*	1990#	1995#	@urban/rural
Bangladesh	7.6	—	16.4	19.5	29/43
China	—	22	33.4	40.8	81/40
India	22	25	27	29.4	80/47
Indonesia	17.1	25	30.5	35	40/32
Korea, Rep.	41.1	64	72	77.4	86/61
Malaysia	27	38	43	47.2	90/49
Myanmar	22.8	24	24.8	26.2	38/15
Pakistan	24.9	29	32	34.7	84/28
Philippines	31.8	40	42.6	45.6	65/43
Thailand	13.2	18	22.6	25.9	—
Vietnam	—	—	21.9	24.1	90/30

*Source: Asian Development Bank, 1989.
#WHO, 1990.
@in 1985 ADB, 1989.

free by the government or municipality. This lack of services can result in a proliferation of the vector-borne diseases. Table 11.1 shows the rate of urbanization in some countries of Asia since 1970 and the projection for the increases to 1995, along with data on the availability of safe drinking water supplies.

Access to a "safe water supply" in many instances means only access to a neighborhood standpipe on the street. In many countries these communal water taps have water only intermittently, perhaps no more than several hours a day. When the water runs, it is stored by householders to lessen dependence on the unreliable supply. This storage of water in household containers, in most of the tropics, is the most important source of breeding of the mosquito vectors of dengue. In 1985, the WHO estimated that one-quarter of the Third World's population did not have access to an adequate, safe water supply (nor even access to supplies not necessarily safe for health). (WHO, 1988).

HEALTH CONSEQUENCES OF URBANIZATION IN THE TROPICAL WORLD

Where urbanization has been rapid and unplanned and adequate sewage disposal systems do not exist, liquid wastes, including human wastes, are disposed into open sewage ditches which usually lead to the nearest water course. Not only is this the major cause of gastrointestinal diseases such as infant diarrheas and other intestinal infections, but these polluted water streams and pit latrines are the main breeding sites of the mosquito vectors of filariasis in large areas of Asia, East Africa, parts of the Caribbean, and South America (WHO, 1992). The lack of adequate solid waste disposal systems and the consequent accumulations of solid organic wastes provides food for rats and breeding sites for house and filth flies.

While the large cities of the developed countries have not been entirely successful in providing a desirable level of health services for their expanding populations, the developing countries have great difficulties in providing adequate health services for their existing populations, let alone for the flood of new migrants from rural areas. In the developed countries, urban and overall population growth has now slowed to low rates and the major impacts of urbanization on health result from technological and psychosocial problems (WHO, 1991a), while those in the tropical, developing world are still mostly caused by communicable diseases.

Often the true statistics of health among the squatter populations of cities simply do not appear as they are not "official" residents of the city (Basta, 1977). The migrant from rural areas to the cities, searching for a better quality of life, may find that he and his family have replaced one set of diseases for another. While there is often a decline in mortality and to some extent, morbidity rates among the migrants, this is primarily due to more ready access to at least some type of health services in the cities; in the rural areas of much of the developing world, health services are often neither readily available nor easily accessible. In fact, the migrant to urban areas will be exposed to environmental conditions in the cities absent in the rural areas which include large, crowded, poorly built and maintained housing structures, with few or no facilities for the sanitary disposal of wastes or refuse and an unsafe, and often irregular water supply (Gratz, 1973).

Africa has been particularly vulnerable to the ill effects of rapid, unplanned urbanization. There is a continuing migration to the cities but only poor housing and inadequate sanitation facilities exist to serve the rapidly growing urban population.

The following reviews the magnitude of the most important vector-borne diseases in the urban areas of the tropical disease endemic countries, i.e., dengue, malaria and filariasis. The extensive literature on the subject reflects the seriousness of the problem; only a few affected cities will be considered to illustrate the general situation. Along with the vector borne diseases, there are several rodent-borne diseases that are particularly prevalent in urban areas including murine typhus and, increasingly, haemorrhagic fever with renal syndrome (HFRS). These will not be dealt with in the following review as their extent and epidemiological importance warrants separate consideration. It need only be mentioned that the poor sanitary conditions in many cities of the tropical developing world encourage multiplication of rodent populations, and of human diseases including bubonic plague, of which they serve as reservoirs.

Arboviruses

There are more than five hundred arboviruses, or arthropod-borne viruses of man. Not all of these are known to cause disease in man, but the incidence of several which do is greatly increasing as a direct consequence of environmental changes favorable for the breeding of their vectors.

Dengue and Dengue Haemorrhagic Fever

Dengue has been recognized as a distinct, mainly urban, disease entity for almost two centuries. Great pandemics of dengue in which hundreds of thousands of cases occurred have been recorded in southern Europe, the Mediterranean, and the Americas. Epidemics were recorded in China, Southeast Asia, South America and the southern gulf states of the United States of America and seasonally as far north as Philadelphia in the 19th century. In the 20th century, more than 600,000 cases occurred in Texas in 1922, in Australia more than half a million cases were recorded in an epidemic in Queensland-New South Wales in 1926, and more than a estimated million cases occurred in 1927–1928 in Athens, Greece. Dengue remains one of the most common and widespread urban diseases of the tropics and is spreading to rural areas and new geographical regions. In 1906 the first evidence was published that the mosquito *Aedes aegypti* was the vector of the disease.

In 1954, pediatricians in Manila, Philippines, published the first reports of a newly recognized disease syndrome which has been named dengue haemorrhagic fever (DHF) or dengue shock syndrome (DSS). Unlike classical dengue which has a very low mortality and attacks all age groups, the DHF syndrome is particularly prevalent among children; without intensive hospital care, mortality of up to 5 percent or more may occur. Following its recognition in the Philippines, the disease syndrome has now spread to most of the cities of Southeast Asia and many of the islands in the South Pacific. In 1981 it spread to the Americas, with the first recognized outbreak of DHF during a large epidemic of dengue and DHF in Cuba. Since then DHF has occurred in several other countries in the Americas including Mexico, Brazil, Jamaica, Honduras, Nicaragua, Colombia, Puerto Rico, and Venezuela. During a dengue epidemic which took place in Venezuela from late 1989 to early 1990, 3,108 cases of DHF and 73 deaths were reported. Dengue is widespread in Africa, but no cases of DHF have been reported from the continent. Dengue is now the arboviral disease with the greatest public health impact on man and the present pandemic will probably continue to spread to all areas in which its mosquito vector occurs, and where the threat of the development of DHF occurring is always present. DHF is among the ten leading causes of pediatric hospitalization and death in the urban areas of at least eight tropical Asian countries in which at least 1.5 million hospitalizations and 33,000 deaths have occurred between the mid-and late-1950s and 1988. Although DHF is increasing in villages and small towns, it remains most serious in urban areas.

In the Americas, the failure of the attempt to eradicate *Ae. aegypti* from the hemisphere, resulted in the reinfestation of most countries in South and Central America by the species; dengue reappeared soon after the return of its vector. The number of cases has been steadily mounting along with the spread in the geographical distribution of *Ae. aegypti* and massive epidemics of dengue have occurred in many urban areas (Hayes & Gubler, 1992). DHF outbreaks can be very serious. During the course of a very large epidemic outbreak of dengue-2 in Cuba in 1981 (Khouri et al., 1986), there were 344,203 reported cases of dengue: 116,000 patients required hospitalization, 1,109 of these cases were serious, and there were 159 deaths (Guzman et al., 1984). Despite its dense populations of vectors, the United States had had only a few indigenous cases of dengue in Texas in the last decade, but large epidemics of the disease occurred in cities of the southern United States in the past. As recently as 1945, the virus was reintroduced into Louisiana by veterans returning from the Pacific (Hayes et al., 1971). At least 80 to 100 known cases of dengue are introduced into the United States every year; potential vector populations of *Ae. aegypti* and *Ae. albopictus* (a species introduced into the United States) are common throughout the southern United States and these cases could well be the sources of new outbreaks.

The extent of the global increase of dengue haemorrhagic fever is evident from Table 11.2. The spread of dengue and its sometimes fatal DHF/DSS syndromes are almost entirely the result of humans carrying the virus

TABLE 11.2 Global Reports of Dengue Haemorrhagic Fever, 1956–1990

Time interval	No. years	No. cases	Mean no. cases/yr
1956–1980	25	1,070,207	42,808
1981–1985	5	1,002,048	200,410
1986–1990	5	1,210,135	242,027

infection from one country to another country; a person may be bitten by an infected *Aedes* in one country and, before any clinical symptoms appear, board an aircraft for a destination far from where he or she was infected. If the destination is infested by *Aedes* species that can transmit the virus, a single viremic individual will suffice to introduce the disease to a new region.

Though considerable progress is being made in the development of a vaccine, for the time being, none is available to prevent infection by the virus nor is there a specific cure for the disease. Control of transmission must, therefore, be by control of the vector mosquito or by the prevention of its breeding. Although sequential adulticiding by ultra-low volume (ULV) insecticide applications can provide rapid and sustained control, their cost is high (Gratz, 1991); the best manner of ensuring that vector densities remain at levels which do not permit a high level of disease transmission, is to alter the environment so as to make it unsuitable for vector proliferation. In Asia and the Americas this would require that as many as possible of the containers providing larval habitats for *Ae. aegypti* must be removed or made unsuitable for breeding.

Much effort has been made in Asia and Latin America to reduce breeding of the vector through enlisting the participation of the community in eliminating the containers in which *Ae. aegypti* breeds. Lloyd and colleagues (1994) undertook an education program in Merida, Yucatan, Mexico, to make the community aware of the breeding sites of *Ae. aegypti*; they considered that the education program was successful but because of the difficulty of disposal of the trash from the community and the multiplicity of breeding sites of the vector, reductions in vector density were not substantial. Only 54 percent of all the containers in which larvae bred were considered disposable by the community.

Yellow Fever

Yellow Fever has caused major urban outbreaks of disease with high mortality in the Americas and Africa. There have been no outbreaks of urban yellow fever in the Americas for almost 50 years but urban yellow fever still occurs in Africa, particularly in Nigeria (WHO, 1987; Nasidi et al., 1989); because of the high densities of *Ae. aegypti* in most cities of Africa south of the Sahara and in Latin America, the risk of urban epidemics remains high. Despite the safe, effective and long-lasting vaccine which is available, the extent of population coverage by vaccination is rarely satisfactory (Cordellier, 1988). Because large numbers of cases of yellow fever have recently occurred, especially in Nigeria, the vaccine will become part of the Expanded Programme of Immunization in West Africa (Monath & Nasidi, 1993).

Yellow fever transmission persists in natural foci in Africa and in South America, in sylvatic cycles involving monkey reservoirs and mosquito vector species found in forests or jungles. In Latin America, man is occasionally involved in the wild cycle when working in the jungle and is bitten by a mosquito that has previously fed upon an infected monkey. In Africa and in Latin America, both cycles may occur when an individual, infected by yellow fever in a sylvatic area returns to his or her village and falls ill. A man–mosquito–vector–man cycle may begin if a domestic or peridomestic species of *Aedes* is present in or immediately around the village. For reasons not understood, yellow fever has never entered Asia. Should this occur, and transmission begins in urban areas, the results could be quite disastrous in light of the favorable environment for the disease which includes dense human populations and very high vector densities throughout the region.

Control of an urban outbreak of yellow fever must involve the simultaneous and rapid implementation of mass vaccination and the application of adulticides to effect a rapid reduction of the adult mosquito population carrying the virus. In urban areas that may be subject to the introduction of yellow fever virus, environmental control of the potential larval habitats of *Ae. aegypti* is obviously the method of choice. Unfortunately, environmental control acts too slowly for emergency control and adulticides must be rapidly applied as ULV sprays.

There are other arboviruses transmitted in urban areas such as chikungunya virus, also transmitted by *Ae. aegypti,* which occasionally appear as epidemic outbreaks.

Malaria in Urban Areas

There are about 100 million new cases of malaria every year with about one million deaths, mainly infants (WHO, 1991b); 80 percent of the cases of malaria and a large proportion of the deaths occur in Africa. Along with populations at risk in the other tropical areas of the world, 40 percent of the world's population lives in areas where malaria transmission occurs.

Urban transmission is growing more severe as rural migrants bring malaria infections to the cities (Kumar et al., 1991; Marques, 1986; Sethi et al., 1990). Certain vector species have particularly adapted to urban environment, usually those which breed in containers such as water tanks, wells, and cisterns.

Urban Malaria in Africa

Malaria in African cities is transmitted by the same species of vector as in rural areas, i.e., members of the *Anopheles gambiae* complex. Vectors breed in the outskirts of the cities and frequently within them. The rapid rate of urbanization in Africa has caused a change in distribution of mosquito populations and species. Malaria has become rather less important in the centers of the cities where construction has reduced the areas available for breeding of anophelines. Manmade pollution reduces the suitability of surface water collections for *Anopheles* though *Culex quinquefasciatus* has adapted very well to such pollution.

Because urban inhabitants have a low level of immunity to malaria, the risk of epidemics is considerable wherever *Anopheles* vector densities are high. Transmission rates in urban areas can be quite high. Greenberg and colleagues (1989) reported that 38 percent of the hospital admissions of children in Kinshasa, Zaire, were for malaria and there was a 21 percent mortality rate among them. Over 70 percent of the malaria cases among children and 80 percent of the deaths were less than 5 years of age. Mulumba and colleagues (1990) found that in six districts of Kinshasa, the prevalence index of malaria was 50 percent and the annual incidence of fever attacks, probably from malaria, was 50 percent. The parasite index was particularly high from the age of two years to ten. The district where the child lived was important with more transmission in the outskirts and less in the built-up center.

A study was made in Ougadougou, the capital of Burkina Faso, to determine the part played by malaria in the etiology of febrile illnesses observed in three community clinics in the city (Coulibaly et al., 1991). The prime cause of fever attacks, among children coming to the clinics, was malaria. In the 5–14-year age group, malaria was responsible for more than half of the febrile illnesses during the rainy season and beginning of the dry season. When six different areas of the same city and three nearby villages were compared (Sabatinelli et al., 1986), the parasite index in the city was 16 percent of the population and indices were 51 percent to 88 percent in the villages. The highest parasite rates in the cities were associated with focal breeding of *An. gambiae*. Nenasseni and colleagues (1988) found that there was a considerable difference between malaria in the city of Bobo Dioulasso, Burkina Faso, and the nearby villages. In the center of Bobo the number of infected bites per year is less than five, while 130 infected bites could be expected in the villages. Nevertheless, during the rainy season, malaria was the cause of 50 percent of the fever cases in the city. The authors concluded that urbanization in Africa is generally unfavorable to *Anopheles*, but very favorable to polluted water breeding *Culex quinquefasciatus*; a city inhabitant will receive some 25,000 bites per year from this latter species.

Trape and Zoulani (1987a) studied the impact of urbanization on malaria in Brazzaville, Congo Republic. They observed that urbanization reduces malaria at first by filling up empty spaces and later by the pollution of surface waters. They also found (Trape & Zoulani, 1987b) that inhabitants of Brazzaville receive an average of 22.5 malaria infective bites per year from *Anopheles* and, in some districts of the city, as many as 100. Often, it is the poorest and most poorly housed inhabitants who suffer the most from the disease.

Because of the need for ever greater amounts of food for the expanding cities, rice cultivation has greatly increased throughout Africa. Urban marshes and periurban market garden areas are being converted to ricefields; *An. gambiae* represents 92.3 percent of the mosquitoes breeding in these fields. In Bouake, where urban and periurban ricefields have greatly increased, anopheline biting rates of 300 bites/man/night have been recorded (Dossou-yovo et al., 1994).

Urban Malaria in Asia

In many tropical and semitropical Asian cities, including Bangkok, Dacca, Hong Kong, Jakarta, Rangoon, Singapore, and Kuala Lumpur, environmental conditions no longer favor breeding of *Anopheles* species, and malaria transmission has ceased altogether or is at an extremely low level. On the other hand, malaria remains a serious problem in most cities of India and Pakistan.

Urban Malaria in Southeast Asia

Throughout India and Pakistan, the main urban vector of malaria is *An. stephensi* which breeds in wells, containers, and in water tanks on the roofs. In construction sites in Delhi large numbers of 200 liter (55 gallon) drums hold water for construction work, and many are positive for *An. stephensi* (Pattanayak et al., 1977). In parts of Delhi the main vector of malaria is also the main vector in most rural areas of India, i.e., *An. culicifacies*. The built-up area of Delhi has expanded and is surrounded by a number of riverine areas; the pools in the riverbeds are particularly suitable for the breeding of this species and cause much malaria transmission in the city. In India, Sethi and colleagues (1990) reported that 12.84 percent of the migrants into Delhi had malaria as compared to 6.9 percent of the native population. The migrants frequently visit their home villages where malaria rates are high and serve as important reservoirs for maintaining transmission when they return infected with malaria from their visits to the villages.

In all, about 11 percent to 12 percent of the malaria transmission in India occurs in urban areas. The proportion of cases caused by *Plasmodium falciparum* is growing. To control malaria, 125 urban control programs covering a population of 43 million people have been formed (Pattanayak et al., 1981). The reasons for the increased urban transmission includes a slackening of malaria control measures, rapid urban growth, and poor environmental sanitation. Improved environmental measures within the city would control malaria transmission by reducing vector breeding sites but it seems unlikely that such improvements will come about very soon.

Urban Malaria in Latin America

Urban malaria transmission is not an important problem in any of the major cities in South or Central America with the exception of some cities in Brazil where the risk of malaria transmission is growing. Malaria transmission in the Amazon region has greatly increased due to a constant movement of workers to and from the Amazon who return to the cities with malaria. When they settle in the outskirts of the cities, close to the breeding of anopheline vectors, they may start local transmission (Souza et al., 1986).

Urban Filariasis

Filariasis is a disease of considerable public health importance in many cities of the tropical, developing world, especially in Southeast Asia, parts of China, the coastal areas of East Africa and some cities of the Americas. It has been estimated by the WHO (1992) that 72.8 million people are infected with *W. bancrofti*. Bancroftian filariasis is caused by the helminth *Wuchereria bancrofti*. The adult worm lives in the human lymph system and in its most advanced clinical form may give rise to elephantiasis as a result of the worm parasites blocking the flow of lymph to and from the limbs. The eggs laid by the female worm hatch and circulate in the bloodstream as microfilariae (mf); if this stage is ingested by a suitable species of mosquito when it takes a blood meal, the parasite develops into an infective stage in the mosquito's body and can be transmitted to another person at a later blood meal. Although lymphatic filariasis is not life threatening, it can lead to chronic suffering and the lifelong disability known as elephantiasis.

Of the three species of human lymphatic filariasis only *Wuchereria bancrofti* is important in urban areas. In cities of Asia, East Africa, and the

Americas where bancroftian filariasis is present, the vector is *Culex quinquefasciatus* which breeds in the polluted water in sewage ditches, pit latrines, septic tanks or any surface water with organic pollution. In Africa, filariasis is transmitted by *Anopheles gambiae* or *An. funestus* (also the vectors of malaria) and, only in East Africa, by *Cx. quinquefasciatus* as well.

Cx. quinquefasciatus densities are closely related to adverse changes that man has produced in the environment by allowing accumulations of polluted water. Densities of larvae and emerging adults can reach extremely high levels and, as noted above, an inhabitant of Bobo Dioulasso in Burkina Faso, West Africa, may receive 25,000 bites a year; in Kinshasa, Zaire the number of bites per night by this species was 400 (Karch et al., 1993). Fortunately, *Cx. quinquefasciatus* is not a vector of filariasis in West African cities. The species feeds at night, readily biting man both indoors and outdoors, and can be an intolerable nuisance in most large cities of the developing world where environmental conditions favor its breeding.

Urban Filariasis in Asia

In Southeast Asia and the Western Pacific regions some 43.8 million people are infected by *W. bancrofti*. Filariasis is particularly a problem in India, parts of Indonesia, Myanmar (Burma), and parts of Bangladesh, Nepal and Sri Lanka and to a lesser extent in the Philippines and some of the Pacific islands. It was a problem in China but control programs have greatly reduced the incidence of the disease in that country.

India currently reports an estimated 374 million persons living in filariasis endemic areas and about 45 million infected persons (WHO, 1992). In Calcutta, 20 percent of the persons examined at the School of Tropical Medicine were filariasis carriers and 30 percent of them showed clinical symptoms. The overall prevalence of filariasis in the city is about 20 percent. *Cx. quinquefasciatus* constitutes 95 percent of the mosquito populations in the city. Hati and colleagues (1989) estimated that a person exposed to mosquito biting in Calcutta would receive 55,028 bites/year and at least 177 infective bites would transmit 319 infective larvae. High biting rates, similar to those mentioned, have been reported from many cities of India, all related to the poor sanitation conditions allowing dense mosquito breeding in polluted water. Even the capitol of India, Delhi, has not been spared. Raina et al. (1992) studied some 5,000 slum dwellers in three areas in Delhi over a three-year period. They remarked that due to the rapid urbanization and influx of persons from rural areas, the slums have "appalling sanitary conditions" without any amenities provided by the municipality. At least 2.2 percent to 6.3 percent of the inhabitants examined were carrying microfilaria and the densities of the vector, *Cx. quinquefasciatus* breeding in the open sewage, were very high.

Filariasis transmission is also high in Yangon, Myanmar, mainly because the sewage disposal system is in a poor state of repair and *Cx. quinquefasciatus* breeding is intense. Sporadic application of larvicides has had little impact on the vector population or transmission and, so far, there is no funding to renovate and repair the sewage system.

Because of its extensive primary health care system, China had been largely successful in the control of urban filariasis transmission. Millions of persons have been examined to detect the infection and well over two hundred million were treated between 1956 and 1991. Infection rates are now very low and, in most places, transmission has been interrupted though the infection remains endemic in a number of foci (Sun & Chen, 1992).

Urban Filariasis in Latin America

There are foci of bancroftian filariasis in the Americas in Brazil, Dominican Republic, Costa Rica, Guyana, Haiti, Trinidad, and Suriname. The prevalence of infection in Greater Recife, Brazil, is between 2 percent to 15 percent among communities of low socioeconomic status. In Santo Domingo in the Dominican Republic rates are 7 percent to 26 percent and Georgetown, Guyana, about 6.4 percent. In north coastal Trinidad, Nathan (1981) showed that 15 percent of the inhabitants in the village studied were circulating mf in their blood; it was estimated that there were 17,948 bites per year by *Cx. quinquefasciatus* but the rate of infection in the mosquito was low, as the low survival rate of the mosquito generally did not let it live long enough to transmit the infective stage of the parasite. The disease is an important public health problem in Haiti due to the high densities of *Cx. quinquefasciatus*, a result of the poor level of sanitation. Around the city of Logane, Haiti, 33 percent of the population were positive for filariasis transmitted by *Cx. quinquefasciatus* breeding in the effluent of rum distilleries (Raccurt et al., 1988).

Chemical control of the vector *Cx. quinquefasciatus*, if efficiently carried out and maintained over a long period of time, could reduce the population densities of the vector but is costly to sustain. Only environmental improvements leading to permanent reductions in the larval habitats of the vector are likely to have a major impact on transmission of the disease. The installation of underground sewage systems is often hampered by their cost but open-ended mosquito control programs, the continued transmission of the infection, and the maintenance of pest mosquito control programs are also costly to the endemic countries.

ENVIRONMENTAL CHANGES IN RURAL AREAS AND THEIR EFFECT ON VECTOR-BORNE DISEASES

The environmental changes in the rural areas of the tropical developing countries in the last few decades have been profound, covering large geographical areas. Most of the major alterations in the environment are associated with water development projects including dams and irrigation projects. Virtually all of the changes have occurred in countries already endemic for vector-borne diseases and where this group of diseases are among the major public health problems.

Man's attempts to increase food and energy supplies have led to extensive dam construction to provide power and water for the irrigation of crops. The overall effect of dam construction on vector and snail-borne diseases, particularly schistosomiasis, has been reviewed in much detail by Hunter and colleagues (1982). The great areas covered by irrigation from water development projects provides extensive areas in which breeding of mosquito vectors occurs and heightens transmission of the diseases they carry. The water development project in the Mahweli development area in Sri Lanka has involved dam construction and irrigation which have increased mosquito vector densities and changed the composition of the mosquito population favoring those which happen to be vectors (Ramasamy & Ramasamy, 1993; Amerasinghe & Indrajith, 1994). In Thailand, Bunnag et al. (1979) studied the effect of the construction of a dam on the Quae Yai river basin on malaria vector density and malaria incidence. Downstream of the dam vector density was high and active transmission of malaria had begun as a result of deforestation, resettlement and irrigation.

One of the largest epidemics of malaria associated with dam construction and irrigation was that which occurred in the Cukurova plain of Turkey following the completion of a dam and associated major irrigation system (Hunter et al., 1993). An earlier malaria eradication program in the country had been extremely successful; by 1968 only 137 imported cases of *P. vivax* were reported from Turkey. However, between 1970 and 1974 a steady increase of malaria cases was noted in a focus in the Cukurova plain near Adana, though construction of the irrigation project in the area had begun after malaria had disappeared. The provision of cheap and abundant water for irrigation throughout all parts of the plain allowed intensive agricultural development and created a need for large numbers of agricultural workers. Some 400,000 temporary workers were employed annually during the harvest season, many of whom came from neighboring countries and carried malaria parasites. Malaria recrudescence on the Cukurova plain was so rapid that the malaria control service was unable to cope with it or procure an adequate supply of insecticides. At the same time the main vector in the area, *An. sacharovi*, had become resistant not only to DDT but, by 1974, to most other insecticides available for residual applications. This was probably caused by exposure of mosquito larvae to the agricultural insecticides being used. By 1978 there were 87,867 cases of malaria reported in the area. The number of cases has since remained high. To assure adequate production of food for expanding human populations, the crop lands covered by irrigation has expanded from 10.98 percent of the croplands in 1965 to 15.5 percent in 1988 and continues to increase (FAO, 1989).

Irrigated agriculture contributes significantly to the world's food supply, but it also contributes to the world's health problems. In most of those countries where over 30 percent of the arable land is under irrigation, e.g., Cuba, Egypt, Guyana, Iran, Iraq, Pakistan, Peru, Saudi Arabia, Suriname, and Yemen, there are major parasitic disease problems including malaria, filariasis, Japanese encephalitis, and schistosomiasis.

Irrigated Rice and Vector-Borne Diseases

The irrigated crop most closely associated with vector-borne disease problems is rice; almost everywhere the crop is grown, mosquito vectors of disease are found breeding in the rice fields. Rice grows best in areas of high temperatures, high humidity, prolonged sunshine and an assured water supply and these are the very climatic conditions that are conducive to the breeding of sunloving species of mosquito (Bang, 1988). Rice is the main food of 60 percent of the world's population and is grown on 35 percent of the irrigated land (Coosemans & Mouchet, 1990). The growing importance of rice as food is evident in the expansion of rice farming and by 1985 rice was grown on over 146 million hectares worldwide. About 77 million ha (53 percent of the world's rice area) are irrigated.

The two diseases most commonly associated with mosquito breeding in ricefields are Japanese encephalitis in Asia and malaria in Asia, Africa and to a lesser extent in Latin America (Gratz, 1988). Rice growing today is not necessarily associated with the most serious malaria problem areas of the world though irrigated ricefields produce the highest densities of anopheline mosquitoes. Aside from tropical Africa, the most serious malaria problems are in areas where the creation of new malaria foci has occurred as result of new agricultural or mining developments. Such areas attract migrant populations whose mobility poses difficult problems for control and who have little immunity to malaria (Najera, 1988). Numerous studies have shown that rice cultivation, at least in Africa, has greatly increased the density of vector anophelines, e.g., Faye et al., 1993 in Senegal; Khaitbu, 1991 in Zanzibar; Maiga, 1992 in Niger; Robert et al.,

1992 in Cameroon, etc.). A similar association between the introduction of rice cultivation and increased anopheline breeding has also been seen in Brazil (Forattini et al., 1993). Although increased vector populations have not always resulted in increased malaria transmission, there are many instances where increased transmission and the new ricefields are closely associated (Goonasekere & Amerasinghe, 1988).

Rice cultivation also favors the development of culicine mosquito vectors of arbovirus diseases. The most important arbovirus causing human disease associated with ricefields is Japanese encephalitis (JE) whose distribution ranges from far eastern Russia, Korea, Japan, and through southeast Asia, including Malaysia, Thailand, Myanmar (Burma), Sri Lanka, and the countries of the Indian subcontinent, including India, Pakistan, Nepal, and Bangladesh. Although it is subsiding in China, Japan and the Republic of Korea, the infection is spreading geographically and its transmission is intensifying in parts of Bangladesh, Myanmar, India, Nepal, Thailand, and Vietnam (Umenai, 1985).

Japanese encephalitis is the leading cause of viral encephalitis in Asia and approximately 50,000 sporadic cases are estimated to occur every year in China, Korea, Southeast Asia, and parts of Oceania. Virus transmission occurs over a greater area than is recognized by epidemiological surveillance. Infection may lead to death but also to overt encephalitis in a small proportion of cases and to residual neuropsychiatric sequelae in at least 30 percent of the infections. The disease occurs mainly in children younger than ten years of age. Activated and inactivated vaccines are available and can provide protection for at least three years (WHO, 1994). In some countries, the rate of vaccination is high enough to reduce the incidence of the disease but in others its incidence continues to increase and remains a grave public health problem because of the high incidence of serious sequellae that necessitate long-term medical attention.

There are many potential mosquito vectors of JE but only a limited number are thought to play an important role during human outbreaks. These include *Culex tritaneiorhynchus, Cx. vishnui, Cx. gelidus* and *Cx. fuscocephala* (Pant, 1979). All of these species have one thing in common: they breed primarily in or immediately around ricefields in tropical zones and even temperate zones such as in China and Korea. Population densities of these vector species expand as land is placed under rice cultivation.

The control of mosquitoes breeding in ricefields is difficult; because of the vast areas involved, use of larvicides to control larvae breeding in the fields is excluded by the cost of attempting adequate coverage and by the necessity of repeated treatments due to the short persistence of pesticides in fields with a constant flow and change of water. Despite this, attempts have been made to control mosquito larvae breeding in ricefields with chemical pesticides with little but temporary success. In field trials in Thailand, an insect growth regulator, pyriproxyfen, substantially reduced larval densities in the rice fields for a period of six weeks but adult mosquitoes migrating from neighboring, untreated fields (Thongrungiat & Kanda, 1991) soon increased adult densities again. The intensive use of fertilizers and fungicides on rice crops has had the desirable side effect of reducing the breeding of the vector populations but the pesticides used to control rice pests also lead to the development of insecticide resistance in mosquito populations.

Some success has been met with using residual space sprays applied to pigsties and cattle sheds where several of the ricefield breeding vectors of JE rest. Wada (1989) considered that the use of insecticide impregnated bednets to control adult mosquitoes seeking a blood meal would be more economical and at least as effective as residual spraying of pig pens. Insecticide sprays, particularly ultra-low-volume applications, can achieve temporary reductions in vector populations when applied from the ground (Shim et al., 1977), or from the air (Self et al., 1973). Igarashi (1992) concluded that JE vector control was not cost-effective and that immunization, with one of the two effective vaccines, was the only effective method of control. Unfortunately, immunization rates in some of the poorest endemic countries are too low to adequately protect the population.

It is possible to obtain high rice yields without multiplying vector populations. Various water management methods have been used to achieve this including intermittent irrigation which seems to be the most suitable method for the prevention of malaria and arbovirus vector breeding. This system requires the periodic drainage of the irrigation water to dry the soil surface for the period that would be necessary for larval mosquito development. Where water cost is high, this system also has the economic value of saving water and even seems to increase grain and straw yields. Probably, the only economically feasible way of preventing or reducing the densities of mosquitoes breeding in ricefields would be by manipulation of irrigation water.

Much interest has been shown in the use of biological control agents for mosquito vector control in ricefields as it is commonly believed that these agents will have the least impact on nontarget organisms in the environment. Larvivorous fish have been used for the control of mosquitoes since about the turn of the century. In the last few decades, a growing number of studies have been carried out to determine what exactly is the impact and best manner of use of the larvivarous fish. In 1971 Hoy and colleagues evaluated the fish *Gambusia affinis* for the control of mosquitoes breeding in ricefields in California; they found that the degree of control was directly related to the rate at which the rice fields were stocked with fish. Control of ricefield mosquito populations with fish has also been reported from India, Russia, China and Indonesia. The presence of extensive surface vegetation in the ricefield impedes the control of the larvae (Shumkov, 1985) and some authors have found that the use of fish failed to control mosquito larvae in ricefields mainly because the fish consumed the natural predators of mosquito larvae (Bence, 1988; Blaustein, 1992).

Fish ponds are, in fact, often associated with increased breeding of anopheline vectors of malaria. The fish raised are not necessarily effective predators on mosquitoes and the frequent presence of surface algae prevent fish reaching the mosquito larvae. The breeding of *Anopheles sundaicus*, an important vector of malaria in the coastal areas of Indonesia, was virtually eliminated on the north coast of Java by the early 1960s through habitat reduction in lagoons, the careful management of fishponds, and use of insecticides. Unfortunately, the species persists on the coast due to a high degree of insecticide resistance and environmental conditions that greatly favor prolific breeding of the species in inadequately tended fishponds and lagoons. The elimination of the natural mangrove swamps and the introduction of marine fishponds have created ideal conditions for the species which prefers to breed in brackish water. Because of strong tides, wave action and sand bar formation, brackish water lagoons are formed during the dry season that are ideal for the breeding of the vector. Eliminating the lagoons is difficult and may not be desirable and biological control measures being considered (Soeroto Atmosoedjono et al., 1992) may not be cost effective.

Many field trials have been carried out with the bacterial control agents *Bacillus thuringiensis* H-14 (var *israelensis*) and *B. sphaericus* in ricefields and the results have been encouraging; however, as with chemical larvicides, labor for repeated treatments is necessary (Yu Ziniu & Yu Longsheng, 1990) and may make their use too costly.

ENVIRONMENTAL CHANGES BY DEFORESTATION AND VECTOR-BORNE DISEASES

Deforestation in Africa, Southeast Asia, and Latin America has been the cause of extreme alterations to the environment. Aside from the undesirable ecological changes produced by the loss of the forests and the consequent loss of animal and plant species, there are many changes which more immediately affect human populations such as the construction of roads, the migration of populations into the cleared lands, the development of agriculture on land of marginal quality and, finally, exposure of human populations to disease (Walsh et al., 1993). The felling of forests to plant crops such as rubber, cocoa and coffee and the building of roads, attracts migrant labor into the new agricultural areas. The workers usually arrive with little or no immunity to the endemic infections such as malaria, leishmaniasis, onchocerciasis and arboviruses, often leading to epidemic outbreaks of vector-borne and other diseases among the new settlers. In many parts of West Africa deforestation has resulted in the replacement of a relatively innocuous forest onchocerciasis strain by a savanna form of the parasite much more likely to cause blindness.

In the last 20 years there has been an increase of over 75 percent in the transmission of malaria in Brazil which is almost entirely the result of the colonization of the Amazon region of the country and the destruction of its forests. Some 200,000 migrants a year reach the State of Rondonia in northwest Brazil in search of work and in search of land for farming (Sawyer, 1986). New roads have been constructed into the Amazon forest and barrow pits along the sides of the roads, mining sites with many small and large pools left from the excavation for gems have all resulted in an increase of breeding of the vector, *An. darlingi*, and, thereafter, a steady increase in the incidence of malaria (Marques, 1987). The migrants into the area are poorly housed, have little information about malaria and how they might prevent infections from it and are particularly exposed to the disease. The situation has been aggravated by the widespread development of resistance to the antimalarial drugs in *Plasmodium falciparum* strains and by the recent appearance of *P. vivax* resistance to chloroquine originating in the Amazon area (Garavelli & Corti, 1992).

An epidemic of malaria in provinces of southern Thailand was associated with deforestation. In 1986, the price of coffee increased by almost 100 percent. This prompted the clearance of substantial tracts of forest in the southern part of the country near the Malaysian border where coffee was already being grown. The ecological changes resulting from the felling of the forest were favorable to a vector of malaria, *An. minimus*, whose populations increased in the cleared areas. The persons involved in clearing the forests and working in the newly cultivated tracts began to contract malaria in 1986 and this increased to peak levels in 1987 among the large numbers of non-immune individuals who had come to the region to work (Saravudh Suvannadabba, 1991).

Forest malaria is a also a problem in most of Southeast Asia mainly associated with the existing environment of the forests. It is characterized by transmission of malaria by vector-species who feed and rest almost entirely outdoors making it impossible to control the vectors by indoor residual spraying of houses. However, the ecology in the forest region is being rapidly changed by deforestation. As human populations increase, pressure steadily mounts for land and increasing numbers of persons in the region seek employment in the forests in tree clearing and later in the cash-crop agriculture that follows the forest clearing. In this region, deep forest surrounded by forest fringe areas represent the core area of the malaria ecosystem; the vast areas cleared of forest are then used for plantations of rubber, coffee and tea or cleared even further and used for growing rice, sugar cane and tapioca. The ecological changes resulting from the destruction of the forests alters malaria transmission either through changes in the species of vectors or by increasing man-vector contact or both (Sharma, 1991).

Deforestation may also be causing an increase in tsutsugamushi disease or scrub typhus, a rickettsial disease endemic in the Western Pacific and Southeast Asia. The reservoirs of this infection are rats of the genus *Rattus* and the vectors are parasitic mites. Both flourish in scrub areas where forest has been cut down and scrub-type vegetation has replaced tree growth. Increased incidence has been reported from several countries and may be due to an increase in the ecological areas that favor the rat reservoir and mite vector.

In another set of circumstances, deforestation and resettlement combined have changed the environment to the detriment of tsetse fly vectors of animal African trypanosomiasis and human sleeping sickness. Certain regions of the Gambella area of Ethiopia were heavily infested with tsetse flies; agricultural development programs and resettlement has been implemented in the area. A resurvey in 1989–1990 showed that 155,000 ha of land previously infested with tsetse is now free from the fly. The natural vegetation is being replaced by farmland with villages and the wildlife in the area which were the usual blood sources for the flies, is being hunted out. Nigatu and colleagues (1992) who studied the changes believe that there is a danger of the tsetse fly species changing their feeding habits to domestic animal and human hosts and again increase in density becoming vectors of animal trypanosomiasis and human sleeping sickness.

In Latin America, several studies have shown that deforestation, colonization schemes, resettlement and cultivation of new lands are associated with widespread human infection from the sandfly transmitted disease, leishmaniasis (Wijeyaratne et al., 1994). Parenthetically, immigration of persons from rural areas with a high level of leishmaniasis can also create serious foci in cities. One of the most serious endemic areas of leishmaniasis in the world can be found in Khartoum Province in Sudan where an epidemic in 1985–1986 involved some 10,000 human cases and was probably produced by a massive immigration of people from a drought-stricken and war-torn area of the country who settled in squatter fringes of the city starting indigenous transmission (Safi, 1988).

CONCLUSIONS

The environmental changes which most affect vector-borne disease transmission in rural areas are dams and the associated increase in irrigation networks, but virtually any major change in the rural environment of the vector-borne disease endemic countries may have profound effects on the vector populations or small mammal reservoirs of diseases. Occasionally, these changes may be favorable from the human viewpoint, reducing vector densities as a result of ecological alterations that hamper vector development. More often, the environmental changes in the disease endemic areas are related to the provision of more irrigation water which results in increased mosquito vector densities and, consequently, increased transmission of disease. In some instances the environmental changes have been unfavorable to the main vector species in an area but they may be replaced by secondary vectors which increase transmission.

The increased human population densities in the cities of the tropical, developing countries have usually been accompanied by environmental changes favoring vector proliferation and increased disease transmission. The incidence of dengue, dengue haemorrhagic fever, chikungunya and other arboviruses, malaria and bancroftian filariasis has greatly increased in many tropical cities as a result of changes in the environment. Under the existing socioeconomic conditions of many large cities in Asia and Latin America and most large cities of Africa, transmission will probably remain intense as long as there are no fundamental environmental improvements making it less suitable for vector multiplication. Urban improvements may require major funding from municipal and national governments for such large-scale undertaking as the provision of piped water supplies to all urban areas and to individual houses, the installation of underground sewage disposal systems and organization of satisfactory solid waste disposal. In most large tropical urban centers, particularly in the least-developed countries, funding is almost always inadequate to provide these major sanitation facilities to avert or correct the disease encouraging environmental changes.

There is a close relationship between economic development and improvements in the environment to reduce the extent of vector breeding and the incidence of disease transmission. Improved economic conditions can also result in improved health services, including better diagnostic and treatment services. However, development projects do not always have favorable outcomes for man's health. Many of the environmental changes which have adverse effects on human health, result from irrigation projects intended to improve agricultural production. Many have been planned without adequate assessment of the health risks involved.

Only recently has there been a greater awareness of the effect that water resource development projects may have on the environment. This has led to the realization that increased attention must be given to risk assessments of factors likely to be associated with water development projects. If such assessments are carried out while projects are still in the planning stages, the information can be incorporated into the planning and construction of the projects and adverse environmental changes averted.

REFERENCES

Amerasinghe, F. P., & Indrajith, N. G. (1994). Post irrigation breeding patterns of surface water mosquitoes in the Mahaweli Project, Sri Lanka, and comparisons with preceding developmental phases. *J. Med. Entomol. 31(4)*, 516–523.

Basta, S. S. (1977). Nutrition and health in low income areas of the third world. *Ecology of Food and Nutrition, 6*, 113–124.

Bang, Y. H. (1988). Vector-borne diseases associated with rice cultivation and their control in Southeast Asia. In *Vector-borne disease control in humans through rice agroecosystem management*. International Rice Research Institute, pp. 93–100.

Bence, J. R. (1988). Indirect effects and biological control of mosquitoes by mosquito fish. *J. Appli. Ecol., 25*, 505–521.

Blaustein, L. (1992). Larvivorous fish fail to control mosquitoes in experimental rice plots. *Hydrobiologia, 232*, 219–232.

Bunnag, T., Sornmai, S., Pinithponngse, S., & Haranisuta, C. (1979). Surveillance of waterborne parasitic infections and studies on the impact of ecological changes on vector mosquitoes of malaria after dam construction. *Southeast Asian J. Trop. Med. Pub. Hlth, 10(4)*, 656–660.

Cook, G. C. (1992). The effect of global warming on the distribution of parasitic and other infectious diseases. *J. Roy. Soc. Trop. Med., 85(11)*, 688–690.

Coosemans, M., & Mouchet, J. (1990). Consequences of rural development on vectors and their control. *Ann. Soc. Belge Med. Trop, 70*, 5–23.

Coulibaly, C. O., Guiguemde, T. R., Lamizana, L., Ouedraogo, J. B., & Dabiret, E. (1991). La part du paludisme dans le affections febriles en milieu urbain de Ouagadougou (Burkina Faso, Afrique de l'Ouest). *Ann. Soc. Belge Med. Trop., 71*, 5–10.

Dossou-yovo, J., Doannio, J., Riviere, F., & Duval, J. (1994). Rice cultivation and malaria transmission in Bouake City, (Côte d'Ivoire). *Acta Tropica, 57*, 91–94.

FAO (1989). The state of food and agriculture. Rome, Food and Agriculture Organization of the United Nations.

Faye, O., Fountenille, D., Herve, J. P., Diack, P. A., Diallo, S., & Mouchet, J. (1993). La paludisme en zone sahelinne du Senegal, 1. données entomologiques sur la transmission. *Ann. Soc. Belge Med. Trop., 73*, 21–30.

Forattini, O. P., Kakitani, I., Massad, E., & Marcucci, D. (1993). Studies on mosquitoes and anthropic environment. 2-Immature stages, research at a rice irrigation system location in southeastern Brazil. *Rev. Saude Pub. Sao Paulo, 27(4)*, 227–236.

Garavelli, P. L., & Corti, E. (1992). Chloroquine resistance in *Plasmodium vivax*: the first case in Brazil. *Trans. Roy. Soc. Trop. Med. Hyg., 86*, 128.

Goonasekere, K. G. A., & Amerasinghe, F. P. (1988). Planning, design and operation of rice irrigation schemes—their impact on mosquito-borne diseases. In *Vector-borne disease control in humans through rice agroecosystem management*. International Rice Research Institute, pp. 41–50.

Gratz, N. G. (1973). Mosquito-borne disease problems in the urbanization of tropical countries. *Crit. Rev. Environment. Control, 3(4)*, 455–495.

Gratz, N. G. (1988). The impact of rice production on vector-borne disease problems in developing countries. In *Vector-borne disease control in humans through rice agroecosystem management*. International Rice Research Institute, pp. 7–12.

Gratz, N. G. (1991). Emergency control of *Aedes aegypti* as a disease vector in urban areas. *J. Am. Mosq. Control Assoc., 7(3)*, 353–365.

Greenberg, A. E., Ntumbanzondo, M., Ntula, N., Mawa, L., Howell, J., & Davachi, F. (1989). Hospital-based surveillance of malaria related paediatric morbidity and mortality in Kinshasa, Zaire. *Bull. Wld Hlth Org., 67(2)*, 189–196.

Guzman, M. G., Kouri, G., Morier, L., Soler, M., & Fernadez, A. (1984). A study of fatal hemorrhagic dengue cases in Cuba, 1981. *PAHO Bull., 18(3)*, 213–220.

Hati, A. K., Chandra, G., Bhattacharyya, A., Biswas, D., Chatterjee, K. K., & Dwibedi, H. N. (1989). Annual transmission potential of bancroftian filariasis in an urban and a rural area of West Bengal, India. *Am. J. Trop. Med. Hyg., 40(4)*, 365–367.

Hayes, E. B., & Gubler, D. J. (1992). Dengue and dengue hemorrhagic fever. *Pediatric Infect. Dis., 11(4)*, 311–317.

Hayes, G. R. Jr., Scheppf, P. P., & Johnson, E. B. (1971). An historical review of the last continental U.S. epidemic of dengue. *Mosq. News., 31(3)*, 422–427.

Hoy, J. B., O'Berg, A. G., & Kauffman, E. E. (1971). The mosquitofish as a biological control agent against *Culex tarsalis* and *Anopheles freeborni* in Sacramento Valley rice fields. *Mosq. News., 31(2)*, 146–152.

Hunter, J. M., Rey, L., & Scott, D. (1982). Man-made lakes and man-made diseases. *Soc. Sci. Med., 16*, 1127–1145.

Hunter, J. M., Rey, L., Chu, K. Y., Adekolu John, E. O., & Mott, K. E. (1993). Parasitic diseases in water resources development. Geneva: World Health Organization.

Igarashi, A. (1992). Epidemiology and control of Japanese encephalitis. *Wld Hlth Stat. Quart., 45*, 299–305.

Karch, S., Asidi, N., Manzambi, Z. M., & Salaun, J. J. (1993). La faune culicidienne et son nuisance a Kinshasa (Zaire). *Bull. Soc. Path. Exot., 86*, 68–75.

Khaitbu, A. I. (1991). Irrigation development and malaria incidence in Zanzibar. *Amer. Assoc. Advanc. Sci.*, 121–126.

Khouri, G., Guzman, M. G., & Bravo, J. (1986). Hemorrhagic dengue in Cuba: history of an epidemic. *PAHO Bull., 20(1)*, 24–30.

Kumar, A., Sharma, V. P., & Thavaselvam, D. (1991). Malaria related to constructions in Goa. *Indian J. Malariol., 28(4)*, 219–225.

Lloyd, L. S., Winch, P., Ortega-Canto, J., & Kendall, C. (1994). The design of a community-based health education intervention for the control of *Aedes aegypti*. *Am. J. Trop. Med. Hyg., 50(4)*, 401–411.

Maiga, M. A., Sanogo, N., & Kone, N. (1992). Paludisme dans le villages colons a Kolongotomo, office du Niger-enquete demographique, epidemiologique et socio-economique. *Med. AFr. Noire, 38(7)*, 474–479.

Marques, A. C. (1986). Migration and the desemination of malaria in Brazil. *Mem. Inst. Oswaldo Cruz., 81* (supplement II), 17–30.

Marques, A. C. (1987). Human migration and the spread of malaria in Brazil. *Parasitology Today, 3(6)*, 166–170.

Monath, T. P., & Nasidi, A. (1993). Should yellow fever vaccine be included in the expanded program of immunization in Africa? A cost-effectiveness analysis for Nigeria. *Am. J. Trop. Med. Hyg., 48(2)*, 274–299.

Mulumba, M. P., Wery, M., Ngimbi, N. N., Paluku, K., Van der Stuyft, P., & De Muynck, A. (1990). Le paludisme de l'enfant a Kinshasa (Zaire) influence des saisons de l'age, de l'environment et du standing familial. *Med. Trop., 50(1)*, 53–63.

Najera, J. A. (1988). Malaria and rice: strategies for control. In *Vector-borne disease control in humans through rice agroecosystem management*. International Rice Research Institute, pp. 123–132.

Nathan, M. B. (1981). Bancroftian filariasis in coastal north Trinidad, West Indies: intensity of transmission by *Culex quinquefasciatus*. *Trans. Roy. Soc. Trop. Med. Hyg., 75(5)*, 721–730.

Nasidi, A., Monath, T. P., DeCock, K., Tomori, O., Cordellier, R., Olaleye, O. D., Hatty, O., Adeniyi, A., Sorungbe, A. O., Ajose-Coker, A. O., Van der Laan, G., & Oyediran, A. B. O. (1989). Urban yellow fever epidemic in western Nigeria, 1987. *Trans. Roy. Soc. Trop. Med. Hyg., 83*, 401–406.

Nenasseni, R., Gazin, P., Carnevale, P., & Boudon, D. (1988). Paludisme urbain a Bobo Dioulasso, Cah. ORSTOM ser. *Ent med. Parsitol., 25(3/4)*, 165–170.

Nigatu, W., Abebe, H., Hadis, M., & Lulu, M. (1992). The effect of resettlement and agricultural activities on tsetse populations in Gambella, south-western Ethiopia. *Insect Sci. Application, 13(6)*, 763–770.

Pant, C. P. (1979). Vectors of Japanese encephalitis and their bionomics. (WHO unpublished document, VBC.79.7342.)

Pattanayak, S., Rahman, S. J., Samnotra, K. G., & Kalra, N. L. (1977). Changing patterns of malaria transmission in urban Delhi. *J. Com. Dis., 9(4)*, 150–158.

Pattanayak, S., Roy, R. G., Samnotra, K. G., & Bendley, M. S. (1981). Urban malaria scheme of the National Malaria Eradication Programme of India. *Indian J. Malariol., 18*, 21–27.

Raccurt, C. P., Lowrie, R. C., Katz, S. P., & Duverseau, Y. T. (1988). Epidemiology of *Wuchereria bancrofti* in Loegane, Haiti. *Trans. Roy. Soc. Trop. Med. Hyg., 82*, 721–725.

Raina, V. K., Tripathi, V. C., Ram, R., Kuma, A., & Verghese, T. (1992). Status of lymphatic filariasis in some select slum clusters of Delhi. *J. Com. Dis., 24(2)*, 92–96.

Rajasekariah, G. B., Parab, P. B., Chandrashekar, R., Deshpande, L., & Subrahmanyam, D. (1991). Pattern of *Wuchereria bancrofti* microfilaremia in young and adolescent school children in Bassein, India, an endemic area for lymphatic filariasis. *Ann. Trop. Med. Parasitol., 85(6)*, 663–665.

Ramasamy, R., & Ramasamy, M. S. (1993). Changes in malaria vector prevalence in Sri Lanka: the need for local surveillance. *Ceylon Med. J., 38*, 43.

Robert, V., Van den Bock, A., Stevens, P., Slootweg, R., Petraaca, V., Coluzzi, M., Le Goff, G., Di Deco, M. A., & Carnavale, P. (1992). Mosquitoes and malaria transmission in irrigated ricefields, in the Benoue valley of northern Cameroon. *Acta Tropica, 52*, 201–204.

Rossi-Espagnet, A., Glodstein, G. B., & Tabibzadeh, I. (1991). Urbanization and health in developing countries: A challenge for health for all. *Wld Hlth Stat. Quart., 44(4)*, 185–232.

Sabatinelli, G., Bosman, G., Lamizana, L., & Rossi, P. (1986). Prevalence of paludisme a Ougadougou et dans le milieu rurale limitrophe en periode de transmision maximale. *Parassitologia, 28*, 17–31.

Safi, S. H. E. (1988). Current situation with regard to leishmaniasis in Sudan, with particular reference to the recent outbreak of cutaneous leishmaniasis in Khartoum. In *Research on control strategies for the leishmaniasis: Proceedings of an international workshop held in Ottawa, Canada, 1–4 June, 1987.* (IDRC Manuscript Report 184e.)

Sarvudh Suvannadabba (1991). Deforestation for agriculture and its impact on malaria in southern Thailand. In *Forest Malaria in Southeast Asia* (pp. 221–226), Eds. Sharma, V. P. and Kondrashin, A. V., New Delhi.

Sawyer, D. R. (1986). Malaria on the Amazon frontier: economic and social aspects of tranmission and control. *Southeast Asian J. Trop. Med. Pub. Hlth, 17(3)*, 342–345.

Self, L. S., Ree, H. I., Lofgren, C. S., Shim, J. C., Chow, C. Y., Shin, H. K., & Kim, K. H. (1973). Aerial applications of ultra-low-volume insecticides to control the vectors of Japanese encephalitis in Korea. *Bull. Wld Hlth Org., 49*, 353–357.

Sethi, N. K., Choudhri, Y., & Chuttani, C. S. (1990). Role of migratory population in keeping up endemicity of malaria in metropolitan cities in India. *J. Com. Dis., 22(2)*, 86–91.

Sharma, V. P., Chusak Pratsittisuk, & Kondrashin, A. V. (1991). Magnitude of forest-related malaria in the WHO Southeast Asia Region. In *Forest Malaria in Southeast Asia*, Sharma, V. P. and Krondrashin, A. V. Eds, New Delhi.

Shim, J .C., Ree, H. I., Mathis, H. L., & Self, L. S. (1977). Ground aerosols of ultra-low-volume premium sumathion for the control of *Culex tritaeniorhynchus* in Pusan, Korea. *Korean J. Entomol., 8(2)*, 31–38.

Shumkov, M. A. (1985). The influence of vegetation on the intensity of the consumption of mosquito larvae and pupae by the fry of mosquitofish. *Med. Parazitol., 5*, 71–74.

Soeroto Atmosoedjono, Bangs, M. J., & Arbani, P. R. (1992). The use of species sanitation and insecticides for malaria control in coastal areas of Java. *Bull. Hlth Stud., 20(3)*, 1–15.

Souza, S. L. de, Dourado, M. I. C., & Noronhs, C. V. (1986). Migracoes internas e malaria urbana-Bahia, Brazil. *Rev. Saude Publ, Sao Paulo, 20(5)*, 346–351.

Sun De-jian, & Chen Pu-lin (1992). Filariasis survelliance at the post control stage in China. *Southeast Asian J. Trop. Med. Pub. Hlth., 23(3)*, 369–376.

Thongrungiat, S., & Kanda, T. (1991). Efficacy of pyriproxyfen for the control of *Culex triateniorhynchus* in an open rice field in Bang Len, Nakhon Pathom Province, Thailand. *Trop. Biomedicine, 8*, 113–116.

Trape, J. F., & Zoulani, A. (1987a). Malaria and urbanization in Central Africa: The example of Brazzaville. I. Results of entomological surveys and epidemiological surveys. *Trans. Roy. Soc. Trop. Med. Hyg., 81 (Suppl. 2)*, 10–18.

Trape, J. F., & Zoulani, A. (1987b). Malaria and urbanization in Central Africa: the example of Brazzaville. II: relationships between urbanization and the intensity of malaria transmission. *Trans. Roy. Soc. Trop. Med. Hyg., 81 (Suppl. 2)*, 19–25.

Umenai, T., Krysko, Bektimirov, T. A., & Assaad, F. A. (1985). Japanese encephalitis, current worldwide status. *Bull. Wld Hlth Org., 63(4)*, 625–631.

Wada, Y. (1989). Control of Japanese encephalitis. *Southeast Asian J. Trop. Med. Pub. Hlth, 20(4)*, 623–626.

Walsh, J. F., Molyneux, D. H., & Birley, M. H. (1993). Deforestation: Effects on vector-borne diseases. *Parasitology, 106 (Suppl:S55–S75).*

WHO (1981). *Global Strategy for Health for all by the Year 2000.* World Health Organization, Geneva.

WHO (1987). Yellow fever epidemic-Nigeria. *Wkly. Epidem. Rec., 62*, 155.

WHO (1988). Review of progress of the International Drinking Water Supply and sanitation Decade, 1981–1990: eight years of implementation. (Report by the Director-General (Document EB83/3, 1988).)

WHO (1991a). Urbanization and the urban environment. *Wld Hlth Statis. Quart., 44*, 198–203.

WHO (1991b). World malaria situation in 1989. *Wkly Epidem. Rec., 22*, 157–163; and *23*, 167–170.

WHO (1992). Lymphatic filariasis: The disease and its control. (*Tech. Rpt Ser. no. 821*, Geneva.)

WHO (1994). Inactivated Japanese encephalitis virus vaccine. *Wkly Epidem. Rec., 69(16)*, 113–118.

Wijeyaratne, P. M., Jonmes Arsenault, L. K., & Murphy, C. J. (1994). Endemic disease and development: the leishmaniases. *Acta Tropica, 56*, 349–364.

Yu Ziniu, & Yu Longsheng (1990). Large scale evaluation of larvicidal preparation of *Bacillus thuringiensis* H-14 for mosquito control in town and rural environment in China. *Bull. Soc. Vector Ecol., 15(2)*, 189–195.

12

Species Extinction, Biodiversity Loss, and Human Health

Eric Chivian

"The loss of diversity is the most important process of environmental change . . . because it is the only process that is wholly irreversible."—E. O. Wilson[1]

". . . one species [Homo sapiens] has become so efficient at reproducing itself and dominating all other forms of life that it is in the act of endangering all species, including itself."—D. E. Koshland[2]

"Learn from the beasts the physic of the fields."—A. Pope

INTRODUCTION

Human activity is causing the extinction of animal, plant, and microbial species at rates that are thousands of times greater than those which would have occurred naturally,[3] approximating the largest extinctions in geological history. When Homo sapiens evolved, some 100,000 years ago, the number of species that existed was the largest ever to inhabit the earth.[1] Current rates of species loss are reducing these levels to the lowest since the end of the Age of Dinosaurs, 65 million years ago, with estimates that one quarter of all species will become extinct in the next 50 years.[4]

This chapter is adapted with permission from "Species Extinction and Biodiversity Loss: The Implications for Human Health," by Eric Chivian, in *Critical Condition: Human Health and the Environment*. (E. Chivian, M. McCally, H. Hu, A. Haines, Eds., Cambridge, MA: MIT Press, 1993.)

With thanks to E. O. Wilson, Richard Schultes, Stephen Morse, Andrew Spielman, Paul Epstein, David Potter, Nan Vance, Rodney Fujita, Michael Balick, Suzan Strobel, and Edson Albuquerque.

In addition to the ethical issues involved—that we have no right to kill off countless other organisms, many of which came into being tens of millions of years prior to our arrival—this behavior is ultimately self-destructive, upsetting the delicate ecological balance on which all life depends, including our own, and destroying the biological diversity that makes soils fertile, creates the air we breathe, and provides food and other life-sustaining natural products, most of which remain to be discovered.

The exponential growth in human population, coupled with an even greater rise in the consumption of resources and in the production of wastes, is the main factor endangering the survival of other species. Global warming, acid rain, the depletion of stratospheric ozone, and the discharge of toxic chemicals into the air, soil, and fresh and salt water ecosystems—all these ultimately lead to a loss of biodiversity. But it is habitat destruction by human activities, particularly deforestation, that is the greatest destroyer.

This is especially the case for tropical rainforests. Less than 50 percent of the area originally covered by prehistoric tropical rain-forests remains,[3] but they are still being cut and burned at a rate of approximately 142,000 square kilometers each year, equal in area to the countries of Switzerland and the Netherlands combined. This is a loss of forest cover each second the size of a football field.[3] It is this destruction which is primarily responsible for the mass extinction of the world's species.

The diversity of life in these forests is extraordinary. For example, one investigator found an average of 300 distinct tree species in a series of one-hectare plots in Peru;[5] the total native species of trees in all of North America is 700! E. O. Wilson discovered 43 species of ants (from 26 genera) on a single tree in these same Peruvian forests,[6] about the same number of ant species for the entire British Isles. This enormous biological diversity has led many to conclude that while tropical rainforests comprise only 6 percent of the world's land mass, they contain perhaps 50 percent of the total species on Earth.

Estimates of the total number of species vary widely. Approximately 1.5 million species have been recorded and given scientific names;[7] two thirds of these are in temperate regions, and most are insects. But given the enormous diversity of life in tropical rainforests, and based on figures extrapolated from species counts of canopy-dwelling beetles in Panama (dropped by an insecticidal fog), Erwin[8] and others[4,9] have estimated that there are somewhere between 10 and 100 million different species on Earth.

Even if a conservative estimate of 20 million total world species is used, then ten million species would be found in tropical rainforests, and at current rates of tropical deforestation, this would mean 27,000 species would be lost in tropical rainforests alone each year, or more than seventy-four per day, three each hour.[3]

This chapter will examine the human health implications resulting from this widespread loss of biological diversity. It is the author's belief that if people fully comprehended the effect these massive species extinctions will have—in foreclosing the possibility of understanding and treating many incurable diseases, and ultimately, perhaps, in threatening human survival—then they would recognize that the current loss of biological diversity represents nothing less than a medical emergency and would demand that efforts to preserve species and ecosystems be given the highest priority.

THE LOSS OF MEDICAL MODELS

Three groups of endangered animals, far apart in the animal kingdom—dart-poison frogs, bears, and sharks—offer striking examples of how important models for biomedical science are in danger of being squandered by man.

Dart-Poison Frogs

The entire family of dart-poison frogs, the Dendrobatidae, found in the American tropics, is threatened by destruction of its habitats—the lowland tropical rainforests of Central and South America.[10] These brightly colored frogs, which include more than 100 species are particularly sensitive to deforestation, as they often live only in very specific areas of the forest and cannot live naturally anywhere else. Through the work of Drs. Charles Myers, John Daly and Edson Albuquerque,[10–12] who are rushing to collect and study these unique animals before they disappear, scientists have come to understand that the toxins they produce, used for centuries to poison arrows and blowgun darts by Central and South American Indians, are among the deadliest natural substances known. They are also enormously useful to medicine. The active ingredients of the toxins are alkaloids, nitrogen-containing ring compounds almost exclusively found in plants (morphine, caffeine, nicotine and cocaine are examples). The alkaloids bind selectively to specific ion channels and pumps in nerve and muscle membranes. Without them, knowledge of these basic units of membrane function, found throughout the animal kingdom, would be very incomplete.

Batrachotoxin, for example, one of the most potent of all the toxins produced by dart-poison frogs, binds to a specific site in sodium channels;[12] it has been critically important in defining the action of this fundamental molecular structure.

In addition to their value in basic neurophysiological research, dart-poison frogs also offer valuable biochemical clues for the production of new and potent analgesics that have a mechanism of action different from that of morphine, of new medicines for cardiac arrhythmias, and of new treatments for the alleviation of some neurological diseases such as Alzheimer's disease, myasthenia gravis, and amyotrophic lateral sclerosis.[10] If rain forest destruction continues at its present rate in Central and South America, these extremely valuable frogs will be lost.

Bears

The growing black market trade in Asia for bear parts, with bear gallbladders being sold for their reputed medicinal value (worth 18 times their weight in gold), and paws for gourmet food,[13] coupled with continued hunting and the destruction of habitats, has imperiled bear populations in many parts of the world. If some species of bears become extinct, we will all be the poorer, not only because they are beautiful, fascinating creatures that fill important ecological niches, but also because some species possess several unique physiological processes that may provide important clues for treating various human disorders.

"Hibernating" (or more accurately "denning")* black bears, for example, are immobile for up to five months in the winter, yet do not lose bone mass.[14] In contrast to humans, who would lose almost one fourth of their bone mass during a similar period of immobility (or lack of weight bearing), bears continue to lay down new bone, making use of circulating calcium in their blood.[15] Understanding the mechanisms of how they accomplish this feat may lead to effective ways of preventing and treating osteoporosis in the elderly (an enormous problem leading to fractures, pain and disability), in those confined to bedrest for long periods, and in astronauts subject to prolonged states of weightlessness.

In addition, "hibernating" bears do not urinate for months. Humans who cannot excrete their waste products in urine for several days build up high levels of urea in their blood and die from its toxicity. Somehow bears recycle their urea to make new proteins, including those in muscle.[16] If we could determine the mechanism of this process, it might lead to successful, long-term treatments for those with kidney failure, who must now rely on regular detoxification by kidney dialysis machines, or on transplantation.

---

* True hibernators, like the marmot, woodchuck, and ground squirrel, show a marked lowering of body temperature during hibernation and are not easily aroused. Black bears, by contrast, "hibernate" at near normal body temperatures and can be fully responsive to defend themselves instantly.

Sharks

Like bears, many species of sharks are being decimated because of the demand for shark meat, especially in Asia where shark fins for soup command prices as high as $100 a pound.[17] Because sharks produce few offspring, grow slowly, and take years to mature, they are highly vulnerable to overfishing.

Sharks have been around for almost 400 million years and have evolved highly specialized organs and physiological functions that have protected them against virtually all threats, except slaughter by man. The wiping out of populations and extinction of some of the 350 species is likely to be a major disaster for human beings.

For one, as the "apex" predator of the oceans, sharks are critical to the maintenance of healthy marine ecosystems by culling out sick and weak prey, and their absence could trigger severe disruptions in the balance among other populations, with potentially marked effects on marine food supplies. In addition, sharks may have the most advanced sensory systems of all the vertebrates,[17] with highly sophisticated and sensitive auditory, visual, vibratory, "smell," and electric field receptors, and a large and complex brain. Understanding these unique sensory physiologies may provide insights into our own relatively "primitive" systems and suggest ways for assisting those with sensory impairments.

The immune systems of sharks (and of their relatives, skates and rays) seem to have evolved so that the animals are almost invulnerable to developing cancers and infections. While tumors are often seen in other fish and molluscs,[18] they are rare in sharks. Preliminary investigations have supported this finding. It has proved impossible, for example, to produce tumor growth in Nurse sharks with repeated injections of known potent carcinogenic substances.[17] And researchers at the Massachusetts Institute of Technology have isolated a substance, present in large amounts, from Basking shark cartilage[19] that strongly inhibits the growth of new blood vessels toward solid tumors, and thereby prevents tumor growth.

Sharks may also provide valuable models for developing new types of medications to treat infections. A unique compound, squalamine, recently isolated from the tissues of the dogfish shark, has demonstrated potent activity in laboratory tests against a variety of bacteria, fungi and parasites through mechanisms not yet understood. A steroid, chemically similar to cholesterol but different from all other known classes of antibiotics, squalamine may lead to new antibiotics for infectious organisms that have become resistant to standard drugs.[20]

Other Models

Other toxins and chemical compounds found in a wide variety of animals, some of which are endangered, have also shown great promise in providing research models for understanding human physiology and disease. A few will be mentioned here:

1. *Conus Toxins* are small peptides produced by predatory cone snails (a large genus of venomous snails numbering approximately 500 species and found in tropical reef communities), each of which may produce a different type or assortment of venoms.[21] These toxins are so numerous that they rival in diversity the alkaloids of plants and the secondary metabolites of microorganisms (which supply us with many of our most important antibiotics). Conus toxins interact with a wide variety of channels and receptors in neuromuscular systems,[21] most of which have yet to be characterized. Several conus toxins are now standard tools in neurophysiological research, and some are used in clinical medicine, for example, as a diagnostic test for myasthenia gravis.
2. *Pseudopterosins* are highly active substances from the Caribbean sea whip, another reef creature, which have potent anti-inflammatory and analgesic activity through mechanisms not previously defined.[22] More potent than currently available nonsteroidal anti-inflammatory agents such as indomethacin, these substances may prove invaluable in understanding and treating cellular responses that produce pain and inflammation.

   Coral reefs, the "rainforests of the seas," and their resident organisms such as cone snails and sea whips are increasingly threatened with destruction worldwide,[23] by overfishing, by increased seawater temperature, and by the discharge of pollutants from agriculture, industry, and sewage.
3. *Bradykinin potentiating factors.* In the 1960s, it was found that the venom from pit vipers contained compounds that enhanced the response to bradykinin, a potent vasodilating agent, by blocking its destruction. Subsequent work led to a greater understanding of the role of the renin-angiotensin system in the maintenance of blood pressure and to the development of an entirely new class of extremely effective and safe medications to treat essential hypertension, the angiotensin converting enzyme, or ACE, inhibitors.[24] Examples are captopril and lisinopril.

Countless other examples could be mentioned of known unique plants, animals, and microorganisms (and there are likely to be millions more still unknown), holding the secrets of billions of evolutionary experiments, that are increasingly threatened by human activity and in danger of being lost forever to medical science.

THE LOSS OF NEW MEDICINES

Plant, animal, and microbial species are themselves the sources for some of today's most important medicines and make up a significant proportion of the total pharmacopoeia. Farnsworth, for example, has found that 25 percent of all prescriptions dispensed from community pharmacies in the United States from 1959–1980 contained active ingredients extracted from higher plants.[25] A much higher percentage is found in the developing world. As many as 80 percent of all people living in developing countries, or roughly two thirds of the world's population, rely almost exclusively on traditional medicine using natural substances, mostly derived from plants.

The knowledge held by traditional healers, often passed down orally over centuries, has led to the discovery of many medicines that are widely used today—quinine, physostigmine, d-tubocurarine, pilocarpine, and ephedrine to name a few.[26] But that knowledge is fast disappearing, particularly in the Amazon,[27,28] as native healers die out and are replaced by more modern medical practitioners. Botanists and pharmacologists are racing to learn these ancient practices, which, like the forest plants they employ, are also endangered species.[25,27,28]

Quinine and Quinidine

Quinine was one of the most important finds in the New World by Europeans. Extracted from the bark of cinchona trees by South American Indians who used it to treat fevers, it was shown to be highly effective in curing malaria, still one of the most widespread and deadly diseases of the tropics. Quinine has been replaced largely by synthetic analogues, but is making a comeback as drug resistance has begun to develop to the more widely used synthetic drugs.[29]

It was noted that some patients who also had atrial fibrillation while being treated for malaria with cinchona extracts converted to normal sinus rhythm.[30] Subsequent investigations established that it was the d-isomer of quinine, quinidine, that was most effective in this process. Today quinidine is one of the most widely used drugs in the treatment of cardiac arrhymias, both atrial and ventricular.

D-Tubocurarine

Curare is a generic term for a group of chemicals derived from South American vines of the genus chondrodendron that are used by South American Indians as arrow poisons. After the paralyzing properties of the curares become known to explorers, the curares became the object of intensive research, leading in 1932 to their being used as treatments for tetanus muscle spasms and for other spastic disorders, and in 1942 as muscle relaxants during general surgery.[31] The most active agent in the chondrodendron extract was d-tubocurarine, and it is this compound, and its various synthetic derivatives, that have become some of today's most important drugs. Almost all general surgery relies on these neuromuscular blocking agents to achieve deep muscle relaxation (especially important during abdominal and orthopedic operations), without requiring high doses of general anesthetics.

Vinblastine and Vincristine

While exploring claims by practitioners that the tropical periwinkle plant (vinca rosea) could be used to treat diabetes mellitus, Noble observed that his treated laboratory rats had granulocytopenia and bone marrow suppression.[32] Subsequent studies with a variety of tumors in test animals established that periwinkle extracts were highly effective in preventing replication in tumor cells, and led to the purification of two vinca alkaloids that showed significant anti-tumor activity—vinblastine and vincristine. Vinblastine is effective against testicular tumors, Kaposi's sarcoma (seen in AIDS), neuroblastoma, and cancer of the breast in women, but is particularly effective against Hodgkin's disease, achieving marked improvement in 50–90 percent of cases.[32] Vincristine has been shown to be the most effective agent known against acute childhood leukemias, increasing the remission rate from 20 percent to 90 percent.[32] Massive deforestation in Madagascar has threatened the rosy periwinkle, leading to its cultivation in large plantations.

Streptomycin

The above pharmaceuticals are all derived from tropical forest higher plants, but microorganisms from tropical soils are also fertile resources for medicines, and are also lost through deforestation. Stimulated by the discovery of penicillin from bread mold, Waksman and his co-workers made a systematic search of fungi from tropical soils during the period 1939–1943.[33] Their search led to powerful antibiotics from fungi of the

Streptomyces genus, most importantly streptomycin, which was shown to inhibit growth of the tubercle bacillus and which became a major treatment for tuberculosis and for other infectious diseases, including streptococcal bacterial endocarditis and plague. These discoveries subsequently led to a generation of broad spectrum antibiotics and antifungal agents from other tropical soil fungi—neomycin, amphotericin, chloramphenicol and erythromycin, to name a few.

All of the above are derived from tropical organisms, and it is in the tropics, particularly in the rain forests, that the greatest diversity of life can be found. But temperate regions are also vast storehouses of medicines, about which extremely little is known. A few of the most important will be mentioned below.

Aspirin

Hippocrates noted that the ancient Greeks used a brew of willow leaves as an analgesic in childbirth,[34] but it was not until the mid-18th century that a British clergyman, Edmund Stone, discovered that the bark of the willow tree (Salix alba) could lower fevers.[35] The active ingredient, salicin, was isolated during the 19th century and made more palatable as acetylsalicylic acid (now synthesized in the laboratory) by Felix Hoffman at the German pharmaceutical firm Bayer as the century came to a close. Americans consume 16,000 tons of aspirin per year for a variety of problems—for pain relief (particularly in muscles and joints and for headaches), for fevers, for use as anti-inflammatory agents (especially for rheumatoid arthritis), and more recently as a preventive against thrombotic myocardial infarctions and strokes. The exact mechanisms by which aspirin achieves all these wonders has remained obscure, but in the last 20 years, research has shown that aspirin's main effect is the blocking of prostaglandin synthesis.[35]

Digitalis

Digitalis from the foxglove plant (digitalis purpurea), an herb popular in gardens for its beautiful flowers, was used by Welsh physicians in the 13th century, but its effectiveness in treating peripheral edema ("dropsy") and in stimulating the heart was not described until the 18th century.[36] Today digitalis as digoxin and digitoxin is very widely used for increasing the contractility of cardiac muscle in heart failure, and in treating atrial flutter and fibrillation, as well as paroxysmal atrial and AV nodal tachycardia.

Taxol

The drug Taxol, derived from the bark of the Pacific yew tree (taxus brevifolia) in old growth forests of the Pacific Northwest is one of the success stories of the National Cancer Institute's screening program that has been looking for plants, animals, and microbes with anticancer activity. Discovered in 1962,[37] Taxol has been shown to be highly effective in unresponsive cases of advanced ovarian cancer,[38] with 30 percent of patients having significant remissions. Taxol is currently the most effective treatment available for this disease, and has been called "the most promising cancer-fighting discovery in 15 years".[39] It has also been found to be effective in acute leukemias[40] and in other malignancies.[41]

Great concern has been expressed, as it is estimated that four mature yew trees (it takes 100 years to reach full maturity) are needed to produce enough Taxol to treat a single case of ovarian cancer. However, clear-cut forestry practices in the Pacific Northwest have squandered the yew supply,[42] and synthesis of the extremely complicated Taxol molecule may not be commercially feasible.[37] There are indications, however, that there may be other sources of supply—other yew species also contain Taxol, and a fungus, Taxomyces andreanae, which grows on the inner bark of the Pacific yew, has been shown to synthesize Taxol independently.[43]

Ricin

Ricin, a compound from the seeds of the castor bean plant (Ricinus communis) has been of interest for centuries to those contemplating homicide, because of its extreme toxicity to man in quantities difficult to detect.[44] In recent years, this highly potent cytotoxic agent (only one, or at most a few, molecules are needed to kill most cells),[44] has been a key factor in the development of immunotoxins, antibody-toxin compounds that are extremely useful in bone marrow transplants and in treating autoimmune diseases, but are particularly important in the treatment of cancers.[45]

Immunotoxins are the present day equivalent of Paul Ehrlich's "magic bullet," an idea he developed almost 100 years ago based on his studies of antigens and antibodies.[46] The principle is that a molecule that specifically recognizes and binds to a target cell is joined to another that is highly toxic to that cell, resulting, in the ideal case, in the selective destruction of the target cells. Ricin is currently being joined to monoclonal antibodies that are developed from and bind to specific tumor cells.

It is widely believed that immunotoxins using ricin, and other cytotoxic agents derived from plants, fungi and bacteria, will lead to significant new advances in cancer chemotherapy.[47]

Cytarabine

The oceans, despite being filled with countless highly evolved organisms containing bioactive compounds likely to yield useful medicines, have produced only one drug in current use, cytarabine, also known as ara-C or cytosine arabinoside (the Upjohn trade name is Cytosar-U).

It had been noted that sponges (along with sharks and tunicates) rarely contain tumors,[18] perhaps as a consequence of their synthesis of substances that inhibit carcinogenesis and/or tumor growth. The discovery of large amounts of arabinosyl nucleosides, compounds with marked antimetabolite activity, in the Caribbean sponge (Tethya crypta)[48] seemed to offer an explanation for the absence of tumors in this sponge species, and led to the synthesis of cytarabine, based on the structure of these nucleosides. Arabinosyl nucleosides are pyrimidine analogs, compounds that inhibit DNA synthesis or RNA function.[32]

Cytarabine is the single most effective drug for inducing remission in acute myelocytic leukemia in children and adults[32] and is also, in combination with other cancer chemotherapeutic agents, useful in the treatment of non-Hodgkin's lymphomas and acute lymphocytic leukemias.

POTENTIAL NEW MEDICINES

The search for new pharmaceuticals is actively under way, with the National Cancer Institute, and several of the major pharmaceutical houses (Merck, Bristol-Meyers Squibb and others) leading the field, and new companies and researchers entering the market with strategies that employ ethnobotanical knowledge.

Other highly promising medicines from plants and animals include: potent new anticoagulants from vampire bats,[49] and from leeches, black flies and ticks;[50] antiviral compounds from fireflies;[51] and unique antitumor medicines from mosses,[52] marine tunicates,[53] and bryozoans.[18]

Scientists have analyzed the chemistry of less than 1 percent of known rainforest plants for biologically active substances[54] (and of a similar proportion of temperate plants),[55] and of even smaller percentages of known animals, fungi, and microbes. But there may be tens of millions of species in the forests, in soils, and in lakes and oceans as yet undiscovered. With the massive extinctions currently in progress, we may be destroying in the process new cures for incurable cancers, for AIDS, for arteriosclerotic heart disease and for other illnesses that cause enormous human suffering.

DISTURBING ECOSYSTEM EQUILIBRIA

Finally, the loss of species and the destruction of habitats may upset delicate equilibria among ecosystems on which all life depends, including our own.

Food Supplies

Food supplies, for one, may be seriously threatened. Deforestation, for example, can result in significantly reduced rainfall in adjacent agricultural areas and even in regions at some distance,[56,57] compromising crop productivity. The loss of topsoil from erosion, another consequence of deforestation, can have an irreversible negative impact on crops in forested regions, particularly in areas of hilly terrain, such as in regions of Nepal, Madagascar, and the Philippines.

Bats and birds are among the major predators of insects that infest crops or eat them. Both are being lost in record numbers,[58,59] with untold consequences for agriculture. "Disappearing at a faster rate than any other group of vertebrates," 40 percent of all bat species, the total of which accounts for one quarter of all known mammalian species, are endangered or threatened.[58] Bats are also major pollinators and dispersers of the seeds of rainforest trees and shrubs, including bananas, avocados, dates, peaches, figs and cashews. A single short-tailed fruit bat in a single night can disperse up to 60,000 seeds.

Overfishing; aquatic and marine pollution; the destruction of coastal wetlands, mangrove swamps and coral reefs (all of which are the nurseries for many species of food fish); and the blocking of fresh water spawning runs have together reduced fish stocks to dangerously low levels, endangering a major portion of the world's population which relies almost exclusively on fish protein for its dietary needs.

Finally, we use only a small number of plants for the production of food, having barely tapped the enormous potential of other tubers, greens and fruits. As species extinction among plants rapidly proceeds (for the first time in geologic history),[3] valuable new food crops, some of which may thrive in the altered climates of future decades or under conditions of increased UV light, may be lost. Major efforts to preserve plants for future agricultural use have been under way in recent years by the storage of seeds in "seed banks."

Infectious Diseases

Infectious diseases may increase substantially or become epidemic, as the equilibria between hosts and parasites and predators and prey are disturbed by habitat destruction or by a loss of biodiversity. The complexities of these interactions have only just begun to be understood. Six examples will be mentioned here.

1. The cutting down of tropical rainforests and the introduction of villages displaces forest rodents, depriving sandflies, which carry protozoa of the genus Leishmania, of their usual reservoir hosts, and causing them to turn temporarily to biting humans instead.[60] The resulting disease, leishmaniasis, affects over 12 million people worldwide,[61] and can be found in several forms, from painful and often disfiguring ulcerations of the skin and mucous membranes (seen, for example, in the so-called "chicleros ear" among rubber tappers in the Amazon), to severe systemic illnesses involving the liver, spleen, kidneys, or the gastro-intestinal tract that carry a mortality of 75–95 percent in untreated cases.

   In a similar manner, ticks, tsetse flies (which carry African sleeping sickness), sylvan mosquitoes, and kissing bugs (which carry Chagas' disease, an endemic disease in many areas of Central and South America that affects 15–20 million people and is the leading cause of heart disease in these zones)[62] can, in the short term, infect people who destroy their forest habitats and drive out their usual hosts.
2. When natural landscapes are greatly altered and their ecosystems damaged by human activity, foreign insect species, usually introduced by accident, seem to thrive in preference to native species.[63] Consider the Asian tiger mosquito, Aedes albopictus, which came to the United States in water-filled used tires and is now multiplying rapidly, being better adapted than native mosquitoes, in damaged environments in 21 states. A. albopictus has been demonstrated to carry eastern equine encephalitis (EEE), a viral encephalitis with a mortality of 30 percent, in Polk County, Florida,[64] and there is concern that the mosquito could precipitate epidemics of EEE in areas where the virus is already endemic. Aedes albopictus is also a competent vector for dengue fever and yellow fever, and, although its opportunistic feeding habits make it less of a danger to man than its cousin Aedes aegypti, the prime dengue and yellow fever vector which feeds almost exclusively on human hosts, it could still pose a major public health threat to the United States, especially if increases in precipitation and tempera-

ture from global warming enlarge its range (along with that of Aedes aegypti) to more northerly latitudes.[65]

3. The proliferation of vectors can also result in outbreaks of infectious diseases. The massive losses in bat[58] and in bird[59] populations worldwide, for one, may have enormous consequences for the spread of insect-borne diseases.

   Other conditions can support increases in vector populations as well. The cutting of oak or maple forests, for example, with the practice of leaving stumps (seen in clear-cutting) results in the formation of sprout-encircled water basins that provide ideal breeding grounds for the mosquito Aedes triseriatus, which carries La Crosse encephalitis.[66] This widespread viral illness, which accounted for 5–6 percent of all acute central nervous system disease in the midwestern region of the United States from 1966–1986[67] (and is also found in the northeastern United States), is chiefly seen in boys between the ages of five and ten. Although it carries a relatively low mortality, 2 percent, it can result in much higher percentages of residual seizures and behavioral problems.[67]

4. When reservoir hosts multiply, one can see a spread of infectious diseases. For example, the unprecedented increases in deer populations in North America, in part an outgrowth of the destruction of deer predators, as well as, more importantly, from reforestation, has led to a burgeoning of the deer-feeding tick population and to outbreaks of Lyme disease in exposed populations.[60] Lyme disease, an illness caused by the bacterial spirochete Borrelia burgdorferi, can present as a mild, short-lived flu-like syndrome with a characteristic rash, or in untreated conditions, as a chronic illness with arthritic and neurologic complications.[68]

5. The history of malaria offers important lessons about the effects of human activity on the spread of vector-borne diseases. It has been hypothesized that malaria initially became a major public health problem several thousand years ago in western Africa when early "slash and burn" agriculture began to encroach upon the rainforests.[69] The newly cleared areas favored the breeding of the malaria-carrying mosquito Anopheles gambiae, which fed mostly on human beings, over the more omnivorous mosquito species that were less able to adapt to the new environments.

   More recently, in Brazil, malaria has reached epidemic proportions as a consequence of massive settlement and environmental disruption of the Amazon basin. Largely under control in Brazil during the 1960s, malaria has exploded 20 years later, with 560,000 cases reported in 1988 (500,000 in Amazonia alone).[70] In large part, this epidemic was a consequence of the influx of huge numbers of people who had little to no immunity to malaria, who lived in makeshift shelters, and wore little protective clothing. But it was also an outgrowth of their disturbing the environment of the rainforest, creating in their wake stagnant pools of water everywhere—from road construction, from silt runoff secondary to land clearing, and from open mining—pools where Anopheles darlingi, the most important malaria vector in the area, could multiply unchecked.[70]

6. Finally, the story of "emerging" viral illnesses may hold valuable clues for understanding the effects of habitat destruction on human beings. Argentine hemorrhagic fever, for example, a painful hemorrhagic viral disease having a mortality of between 3 and 15 percent[71] has occurred in epidemic proportions since 1958 as a result of the widespread clearing of the pampas of central Argentina and the planting of corn.[70] The virus is carried by the native mouse Calomys musculinus, which has adapted to and flourished in the corn fields. As the original biologically diverse grasslands have been increasingly replaced by corn monoculture, Argentine hemorrhagic fever has spread dramatically, from an area covering 6,000 square miles in 1955 to one of 40,000 square miles in 1990.[70]

   Another viral infection with hemorrhagic manifestations that has recently "emerged" is Kyasanur Forest disease, a sometimes prolonged systemic illness with a mortality of about 5 percent that is carried by Haemaphysalis spinigera ticks in the tropical forests of Mysore in southern India.[67] The spread of this disease is thought to result from deforestation and the introduction of sheep grazing into the cleared areas, favoring a proliferation of the tick vectors.[72]

In both these cases, the mechanisms seem clear—the disease vectors, whose numbers were held in check by various natural ecosystem balances, proliferated in the new environments to which they were better adapted than their competitors, and spread their viruses to man.

But the "emerging" viral illness which has had the greatest impact on human health, and which may be a harbinger of future viral outbreaks is AIDS, caused by the human immunodeficiency virus—types 1 (HIV-1) and 2 (HIV-2). There is general agreement that the current AIDS epidemic originated from non-human primates in Africa, which have acted as natural, asymptomatic hosts and reservoirs for a family of immunodeficiency viruses.[73] Good genetic evidence exists for the links of HIV-1 to a simian immunodeficiency virus in African chimpanzees[74] and of HIV-2 to another simian virus in African sooty mangabeys.[75,76] Are these cross-species viral transmissions between non-human primates and man the result of human encroachment into degraded forest environments? If this is the case, we may be witnessing with AIDS the beginning of a series of viral epidemics originating from tropical rainforests[77] (where there may be tens of thousands of viruses that could infect humans), some of which may be as lethal as AIDS (approaching 100%) but spread more easily, for instance, by airborne droplets. These potential viral diseases could become the most serious public health consequence from environmental disruption of the rainforests.

Other Effects

But it may be the disruption of other interrelationships among organisms, ecosystems and the global environment, about which almost nothing is known, that may prove the most catastrophic of all for human beings. What will happen to global climate and to the concentration of atmospheric gases, for example, when some critical threshold of deforestation has been reached? Forests play crucial roles in the maintenance of global precipitation patterns and in the stability of atmospheric gases.

What will be the effects on marine life if increased ultraviolet radiation causes massive ocean phytoplankton kills, particularly in the rich seas beneath the antarctic ozone "hole?" These organisms, which are at the base of the entire marine food chain and which produce a significant portion of the world's oxygen and consume a significant portion of its carbon dioxide, are highly vulnerable to ultraviolet damage.[78–80]

What will be the consequences for plant growth if acid rain and toxic chemicals poison soil fungi and bacteria essential for soil fertility? There has already been a 40–50 percent loss in species of fungi in Western Europe during the past 60 years, including many symbiotic mycorhizal fungi,[3] crucial to the absorption of nutrients by plants. No one understands what the effects of this loss will be.

Scientists do not know the answers to these and other critically important questions. But there are worrisome biological signals which suggest that major damage to global ecosystems has already occurred. The rapid simultaneous disappearance of many species of frogs worldwide, even in pristine environments far from people, indicates that they may be dying as a consequence of airborne pollutants or from some global environmental change, such as increased ultraviolet radiation.[81] The immediate cause of death, in many of the cases, seems to be from opportunistic infections (the amphibian equivalents of the kinds of infections seen in AIDS patients), secondary to a collapse of their immune systems.[82]

Closer to humans, marine mammals such as striped dolphins in the Mediterranean, European harbor seals off the coast of Scandinavia and of northern Ireland, and beluga whales in the Saint Lawrence River are also dying in record numbers. In the case of the dolphins and the seals, some of the deaths seem to be due to infections by morbilli viruses (canine distemper virus) causing pneumonias and encephalitides,[83,84] perhaps also the consequence of compromised immune systems. In the case of the whales, chemical pollutants such as DDT, the insecticide Mirex, PCBs, lead, and mercury seem to be involved, suppressing the belugas' fertility and causing their deaths ultimately by a variety of tumors and pneumonias.[85] The beluga carcasses were often so filled with these pollutants that they could be classified as hazardous waste.

Are these "indicator species," like canaries that die in coal mines containing poisonous gasses, warning us that we are upsetting fragile ecosystem balances that support all life, including our own? The 50 percent drop in sperm counts in healthy men worldwide during the period 1938–1990,[86] the marked increases in the rate of congenital malformations of the external genitalia in males in England and Wales from 1964–1983,[87] the dramatic rise in some cancer incidence rates for white children in the United States from 1973–1988,[88] and the steady growth in the mortality rates for several cancers worldwide for the last 3 to 4 decades,[89–92] all suggest that environmental degradation may be starting to compromise not only the survival of frogs, marine mammals, and other animal, plant, and microbial species, but that of the human species as well.

SUMMARY

Human activity is causing the extinction of animal, plant and microbial organisms at rates that may well eliminate a quarter of all species on earth within the next 50 years. There are incalculable human health consequences from this destruction:

1. The loss of medical models to understand human physiology and disease
2. The loss of new medicines that may successfully treat incurable cancers, AIDS, arteriosclerosis, and other diseases that cause great human suffering
3. the upsetting of equilibria among ecosystems on which all life, including human life, depends.

Major efforts to protect natural habitats and preserve animal, plant, and microbial species are required to prevent these medical catastrophes from occurring.

REFERENCES

1. Wilson, E. O. (1989). Threats to Biodiversity. *Scientific American, September, 261,* 108–116.
2. Koshland, D. E. (1991). Preserving Biodiversity. *Science, 253(5021),* 717.
3. Wilson, E. O. (1992). The Diversity of Life. Cambridge, MA: Harvard University Press. 1992.
4. Ehrlich, P. R., & Wilson, E. O. (1991). Biodiversity Studies: Science and Policy. *Science 253(5021),* 758–762.
5. Gentry, A. H. (1988). Tree Species Richness of Upper Amazonian Forests. *Proceedings of the National Academy of Science USA, 85,* 156–159.
6. Wilson, E. O. (1987). Biotropica, *19,* 245.
7. May, R. M. (1988). How Many Species are There on Earth? *Science, 241,* 1441–1449.
8. Erwin, T. L. (1983). *Bulletin Entomological Society America, 30,* 14.
9. Stork, N. E. (1988). *Biological Journal of the Linnaean Society, 35,* 321.
10. Brody, J. E. (1990). Using the Toxin from Tiny Frogs, Researchers Seek Clues to Disease. *New York Times,* Jan. 23.
11. Albuquerque, E. X., Daly, J. W., & Withlop, B. (1971). Batrachotoxin: Chemistry and Pharmacology. *Science, 172,* 995–1002.
12. Myers, C. W., & Daly, J. W. (1983). Dart-Poison Frogs. *Scientific American 248(2),* 120–133.
13. Montgomery, S. (1992). Grisly Trade Imperils World's Bears. *Boston Globe,* March 2, 23–24.
14. Rosenthal, E. (1992). Hibernating Bears Emerge with Hints about Human Ills. *New York Times,* April 21, C1 and C9.
15. Floyd, T., Nelson, R. A., & Wynne, G. F. (1990). Calcium and Bone Metabolic Homeostasis in Active and Denning Black Bears. *Clinical Orthopaedics and Related Research, 255,* 301–309.
16. Nelson, R. A. (1973). Winter Sleep in the Black Bear. *Mayo Clinic Proceedings, 48,* 733–737.
17. Stevens, W. K. (1992). Terror of the Deep Faces Harsher Predator. *New York Times,* Dec. 8, C1 and C12.
18. Tucker, J. B. (1985). Drugs from the Sea Spark Renewed Interest. *BioScience, 35(9),* 541–545.
19. Lee, A., & Langer, R. (1983). Shark Cartilage Contains Inhibitors of Tumor Angiogenesis. *Science, 221,* 1185–1187.
20. Altma, L. K. (1993). Sharks Yield Possible Weapon Against Infection. *New York Times,* Feb. 15, A8.
21. Olivera, B. M., Rivier, J., et al. (1990). Diversity of Conus Neuropeptides. Science, *249,* 257–263.

22. Look, S. A., Fenical, W., et al. (1986). The Pseudopterosins: Anti-inflammatry and Analgesic Natural Products from the Sea Whip *Pseudopterogorgia elisbethae. Proceedings of the National Academy of Science, 83*, 6238–6240.
23. Williams, E., & Bunkley-Williams, L. (1990). The World-wide Coral Reef Bleaching Cycle and Related Sources of Coral Mortality. *Atoll Research Bulletin, 335*, 1–71.
24. Garrison, J. C., & Peach, M. J. (1990). Renin and Angiotensin (Chapter 31). In Goodman and Gilman's *The Pharmacological Basis of Therapeutics*. (8th edition). New York: Pergamon Press.
25. Farnsworth, N. R. (1990). The Role of Ethnopharmacology in Drug Development. In *Bioactive Compounds from Plants*. (Ciba Foundation Symposium *154*, 2–21).
26. Farnsworth, N. R., Akerele, O., et al. (1985). Medicinal Plants in Therapy. *Bulletin of the World Health Organization, 63(6)*, 965–981.
27. Schultes, R. E. (1991). Dwindling Forest Medicinal Plants of the Amazon. *Harvard Medical Alumni Bulletin, Summer*, 32–36.
28. Balick, M. J. (1990). Ethnobotany and the Identification of Therapeutic Agents from the Rainforest. In *Bioactive Compounds from Plants*. (Ciba Foundation Symposium, *154*, 22–39.)
29. Webster, L. T. (1990). Drugs Used in the Chemotherapy of Protozoal Infections: Malaria (Chapter 41). In Goodman and Gilman's *The Pharmacologic Basis of Therapeutics* (8th Edition), 978–998.
30. Bigger, J. T., & Hoffman, B. F. (1990). Antiarrhymic Drugs (Chapter 35). In Goodman and Gilman's *The Pharmacologic Basis of Therapeutics* (8th Edition), 840–873.
31. Taylor, P. (1990). Agents Acting at the Neuromuscular Junction and Autonomic Ganglia (Chapter 9). In Goodman and Gilman's *The Pharmacologic Basis of Therapeutics* (8th Edition), 166–186.
32. Calabresi, B. A., & Chabner, B. A. (1990). Antineoplastic Agents (Chapter 52). In Goodman and Gilman's *The Pharmacologic Basis of Therapeutics* (8th Edition), 1209–1263.
33. Sande, M. A., & Mandell, G. L. (1990). Antimicrobial Agents: The Aminoglycosides (Chapter 47) In Goodman and Gilman's *The Pharmacologic Basis of Therapeutics* (8th Edition), 1098–1116.
34. Saltus, R. (1991). New Uses for Aspirin, Give it Star Billing. *Boston Globe*, Dec. *30*, 21–22.
35. Weissmann, G. (1991). Aspirin. *Scientific American, January*, 84–90.
36. Hoffman, B. F., & Bigger, J. T. (1990). Digitalis and Allied Cardiac Glycosides (Chapter 34). In Goodman and Gilman's *The Pharmacologic Basis of Therapeutics* (8th Edition), 814–839.
37. Daly, D. (1992). Tree of Life. *Audubon, March/April*, 76–85.
38. McGuire, W. P., Rowinsky, E. K., et al. (1989). Taxol: A Unique Antineoplastic Agent with Significant Activity in Advanced Ovarian Epithelial Neoplasms. *Annals of Internal Medicine, 111(4)*, 273–279.
39. FDA Panel Backs Taxol as Cancer Drug. (1992). *New York Times*, Nov. 17, C13.
40. Rowinsky, E. K., Burke, A. J., et al. (1989). Phase I and Pharmacodynamic Study of Taxol in Refractory Acute Leukemias. *Cancer Research, 49*, 4640–4647.

41. Donehower, R. C., et al. (1987). Phase I trial of taxol in patients with advanced malignancies. *Cancer Treatment Reports, 71*, 1171–1177.
42. Egan, T. (1992). Trees That Yield a Drug for Cancer are Wasted. *New York Times*, Jan. 29, A1 and A12.
43. Stierle, A., Strobel, G., & Stierle, D. (1993). Taxol and Taxane Production by Taxomyces andreanae, an Endophytic Fungus of Pacific Yew. *Science, 260*, 214–216.
44. Houston, L. L. (1988). Introduction. In *Immunotoxins* (*Cancer Treatment and Research*) (ed.) Frankel AE. Boston: Kluwer Academic Publishers.
45. Vallera, D. A., & Myers, D. E. (1988). Immunotoxins Containing Ricin (Chapter 10). In *Immunotoxins* (*Cancer Treatment and Research*) (Ed.) Frankel, A.E. Boston: Kluwer Academic Publishers.
46. Ehrlich, P. (1956). The Relationship Existing Between Chemical Constitution, Distribution and Pharmacological Action. In *The Collected Papers of Paul Ehrlich, Vol. I.* (Eds.) Himmelweite, F., Marquandt, M., and Dale, H. London and New York: Pergamon Press.
47. Lambert, J. M., Goldmacher, V. S., et al. (1991). An Immunotoxin Prepared with Blocked Ricin: A Natural Plant Toxin Adapted for Therapeutic Use. *Cancer Research, 51*, 6236–6242.
48. Ruggieri, G. D. (1976) Drugs from the Sea. *Science, 194*, 491–497.
49. Gardell, S. J., Ramijit, D. R., et al. (1991). Effective Thrombolysis Without Marked Plasminemia after Bolus Intravenous Administration of Vampire Bat Salivary Plasminogen Activator in Rabbits. *Circulation, 84(1)*, 244–253.
50. Bank, N. U. (1991). Leeches, Snakes, Ticks and Vampire Bats in Today's Cardiovascular Drug Development. *Circulation, 84(1)*, 436–437.
51. Rinehart, K. L., Holt, T. G. et al. (1990). Bioactive Compounds from Aquatic and Terrestrial Sources. *Journal of Natural Products, 53(4)*, 771–792.
52. Cassady, J. M., Gaird, W. M., & Chang, C. (1990). Natural Products as a Source of Potential Cancer Chemotherapeutic and Chemopreventive Agents. *Journal of Natural Products, 53(1)*, 23–41.
53. Rinehart, K. L., Shal, P. D., et al. (1981). Marine Natural Products as Sources of Antiviral, Antimicrobial, and Antineoplastic Agents. *Pure and Applied Chemistry, 53*, 795–817.
54. Gottlieb, O. R., & Mors, W. B. (1980). *Journal of Agricultural Food Chemistry, 28*, 196.
55. Schultes, R. E. (1992). Personal Communication. Jan. 24.
56. Wilson, E. O. (1988). The Current State of Biological Diversity. In *Biodiversity* (Ed. Wilson, E.O.) Washingon, DC: National Academy Press.
57. Shulka, J., Nobre, C., & Sellers, P. (1990). Amazon Deforestation and Climate Change. *Science, 247*, 1325.
58. Brody, J. E. (1991). Far from Fearsome, Bats Lose Ground to Ignorance and Greed. *New York Times*, October 29, C1 and C10.
59. Terborgh, J. (1990). *Where Have All the Birds Gone?* Princeton, NJ: Princeton University Press.
60. Spielman, A., & Kimsey, R. B. (1991). Zoonosis. In *Encyclopedia of Human Biology*, Vol 7. (ed.) Dulbecco R. San Diego: Academic Press.

61. Locksley, R. M. (1991). Leishmaniasis (Chapter 160). In Harrison's *Principles of Internal Medicine* (12th Edition) (Eds.) Wilson, J.D., et al. New York: McGraw-Hill Book Co.
62. Kirchhoff, L. V. (1991). Trypanosomiasis (Chapter 161). In Harrison's *Principles of Internal Medicine* (12th Edition), 791–795.
63. Berenbaum, M. (1992). Invaded by Insects. *New York Times*, June 11, 19.
64. Mitchell, C. J., Niebylski, M. L., et al. (1992). Isolation of Eastern Equine Encephalitis Virus from Aedes albopictus in Florida. *Science, 257*, 526–527.
65. Shope, R. (1991). Global Climate Change and Infectious Diseases. *Environmental Health Perspectives, 96*, 171–174.
66. Telford, S. R., Pollack, R. J., & Spielman, A. (1991). Emerging Vector-Borne Infections. *Infectious Diseases of North America, 5(1)*, 7–17.
67. Sanford, J. P. (1991). Arbovirus Infections (Chapter 148). In Harrison's *Principles of Internal Medicine* (12th Edition), 725–739.
68. Steere, A. C. (1991). Lyme Borreliosis (Chapter 132). In Harrison's *Principles of Internal Medicine* (12th Edition), 667–669.
69. Morse, S. S. (1990). Stirring Up Trouble: Environmental Disruption Can Divert Animal Viruses into People. The Sciences. *New York Academy of Sciences, September/October*, 16–21.
70. Kingman, S. (1989). Malaria Runs Riot on Brazil's Wild Frontier. *New Scientist, 123*, 24–25.
71. Sanford, J. P. (1991). Arenavirus Infections (Chapter 149). In Harrison's *Principles of Internal Medicine* (12th Edition), 739–741.
72. Morse, S. S. (1991). The origins of "New" Viral Diseases. *Environmental Carcinogens and Ecotoxicity, C9(2)*, 207–228.
73. Allan, J. S. (1992). Viral Evolution and AIDS. *Journal of the National Institute of Health Research, 4*, 51–54.
74. Huet, T., Cheynier, A., et al. (1990). Genetic Organization of a Chimpanzee Lentivirus Related to HIV-1. *Nature, 345*, 356.
75. Hirsch, V. M., Olmsted, M., et al. (1989). An African Primate Lentivirus (SIVsm) Closely Related to HIV-s. *Nature, 339*, 389.
76. Gao, F., Yue, L., et al. (1992). Human Infection by Genetically Diverse SIVsm-related HIV-2 in West Africa. *Nature, 358*, 495.
77. Preston, R. (1992). Crisis in the Hot Zone. *New Yorker, October 26*, 58–81.
78. Schneider, K. (1991). Ozone Depletion Harming Sea Life. *New York Times*, Nov. 16, 6.
79. Roberts, L. (1989). Does the Ozone Hole Threaten Antarctic Life? *Science, 244*, 288–289.
80. Bridigare, R. R. (1989). Potential Effects of UVB on Marine Organisms of the Southern Ocean: Distribution of Phytoplankton and Krill during Austral Spring. *Photochemistry Photobiology, 50*, 469–478.
81. Blakeslee, S. (1990). Scientists Confront an Alarming Mystery: The Vanishing Frog. *New York Times*, Feb. 20, B7.
82. Yoffe, E. (1992). Silence of the Frogs. *New York Times*, Dec. 13, Section 6: 36–39, 64–66, 76.
83. Domingo, M., Ferrer, L., et al. (1990). Morbillivirus in Dolphins. *Nature, 348*, 21.

84. Kennedy, S., Smyth, J. A., et al. (1988). Confirmation of Cause of Recent Seal Deaths, *Nature*, *335*, 404.
85. Dold, C. (1992). Toxic Agents Found to be Killing Off Whales. *New York Times*, June 16, C4.
86. Carlsen, E., Gimercman, A., et al. (1992). Evidence for Decreasing Quality of Semen During the Past 50 Years. *British Medical Journal*, *305*, 609–613.
87. Matlai, P., & Beral, V. (1985). Trends in Congenital Malformations of External Genitalia. *Lancet*, Jan. 12, *1*, 108.
88. Angier, N. (1991). Study Finds Mysterious Rise in Childhood Cancer Rate. *New York Times*, June 26, D22.
89. Kurihara, M., Aoki, K., & Tominaga, S. (Eds.) (1984). *Cancer Mortality Statistics in the World*, Nagoya, Japan: University of Nagoya Press.
90. Davis, D. L., Hoel, D., et al. (1990). International Trends in Cancer Mortality in France, West Germany, Italy, Japan, England and Wales, and the USA, *Lancet*, August 25, *336*, 474–481.
91. Davis, D. L., & Hoel, D. (Eds.) (1990) Trends in Cancer Mortality in Industrialized Countries, *Annals of the New York Academy of Sciences*, 609.
92. Hoel, D. G., et al. (1992). Trends in Cancer Mortality in 15 Industrialized Countries, 1969–1986. *Journal of the National Cancer Institute*, *84(5)*, 313–320.

13

Global Climate Change and Public Health

Jonathan A. Patz

INTRODUCTION

The public health challenges presented by global climate change clearly demand an international perspective, as the potential health effects will be diffusely spread across large populations in multiple regions. Such widespread hazardous exposures which may occur from climate change present a new level of risk, with which the public health community is unfamiliar. First, most health problems have been addressed on a regional, if not a local level. Even the worldwide smallpox epidemic was eradicated by strategic targeting of localized outbreaks. Second, the identification of single etiologic agents, including microorganisms, chemical toxins, and specific human behaviors has led to major gains in public health; the health effects expected from climate change, however, may involve exposure factors (or processes) which are non-specific, indirect-acting, and not well understood.

Development is also central to policy directed toward climate change. Development accounts for the creation of anthropogenic greenhouse gases (causing the initial problem), and defines the extent to which nations remain vulnerable to the consequences of climate change (e.g., poorer countries without infrastructural capacity to adapt to changes will suffer most). Future development scenarios are essential for predicting the level of greenhouse gas emissions, which serve as the foundation upon which health assessments are attempted.

In presenting the potential health effects of climate change, it must be understood that an enormous degree of uncertainty accompanies each element of the assessment. Human health risks will emerge from the last step within a complex causal chain of events, with inherent uncertainties at each level (McMichael, 1993). First, scenarios of carbon cycles (particularly CO_2 as the predominant greenhouse gas) must be established based on assumptions and estimates of population growth, extent of industrial development, land use practices, and status of technological advances.

Next, based on estimated predictions of future greenhouse gas concentrations in the atmosphere, the effect on climate must be determined by either mathematical modeling or historical analogue analysis. These methods carry their own set of assumptions which apply to climate dynamics. For the indirect health consequences (which, in fact, may prove to be the most significant), another level of uncertainty is introduced at the level of "ecological responses" to climate shifts (for example, distribution of diseases carried by insect vectors may be determined by alterations in vegetative land cover or by microclimate changes).

The Intergovernmental Panel on Climate Change (IPCC) issued its first assessment report in 1990, with supplements in 1992, 1994, and 1995. From its first assessment, the IPCC concluded that emissions, primarily from industry and destruction of greenhouse gas "sinks" (via poor landuse management, especially deforestation) have substantially increased the concentrations of greenhouse gases beyond natural processes. Without major policy shifts, preindustrial carbon dioxide levels are expected to double by the middle of the next century, yielding a 1.5–4.5°C rise in average global temperature (Intergovernmental Panel on Climate Change, 1990a).

This chapter makes no assertions as to whether or not climate change will occur; this is for the IPCC and climatology community to attempt to determine. The following health related issues, therefore, rely on the IPCC conclusions based on their greenhouse gas scenarios and climate modeling analysis. Even when assuming specific IPCC figures, however, quantification of the health effects still remains difficult at this stage of understanding.

BACKGROUND

The major greenhouse gases (GHGs) consist of carbon dioxide, methane, nitrous oxide, and chlorofluorocarbons (CFCs). These gases allow sunlight to penetrate to the earth's surface, yet trap infrared radiant heat from escaping. Anthropogenic greenhouse gases have steadily increased since the beginning of the industrial revolution resulting in the current atmospheric CO_2 concentration approximating 350 ppm, which is more than 25 percent above pre-industrial levels. Furthermore, the annual rate of CO_2 rise has increased threefold over the past 35 years (Intergovernmental Panel on Climate Change, 1990b).

Stratospheric ozone depletion also contributes to climate change. Ozone destruction is occurring primarily from reactions with halogen-free radicals from chlorofluorocarbons (CFCs), along with other halocarbons and methyl bromide (Molina & Rowland, 1974). These effects were recognized as early as the 1970s, and the United States EPA banned these inert propellants in aerosols in 1978. It was not until 1985 that widespread international concern swelled when an antarctic-based British team discovered the "hole" in the ozone layer (Farman, 1985). Subsequent passage of the Montreal Protocol in 1987, with amendments in 1990 and 1992, has already mandated sharp cuts in CFC production. Yet, with half-lives of 70–110 years, CFCs' continued erosion of stratospheric ozone is anticipated through the next century (Schneider, 1990).

Ozone specifically blocks the penetration of ultraviolet-B radiation (UV-B), which contains the most biologically destructive wavelengths of 290–320 nanometers. UV-B levels are predicted to increase particularly in temperate and arctic zones, since an association has been established between higher latitudes and the extent of ozone thinning (Stolarski, 1992). In 1993, researchers using a sensitive new spectroradiometer in Toronto, Canada, discovered that current ozone depletion has caused local increases in ambient ultraviolet-B radiation of 35 percent in winter and 7 percent in summer, relative to 1989 levels (Kerr & McElroy, 1993). Average ozone loss has been estimated at 2.7 percent per decade during the period from 1979–1991, correcting for solar cycle and other factors (Gleason, 1993).

CURRENT STATE OF KNOWLEDGE

Humans have a great capacity to adapt to aversive environmental conditions. There are, however, limits to physiologic accommodation. Heat-stress, for example, is a recognized direct consequence of extreme temperature and humidity. Mortality from cardiovascular and respiratory disorders in the elderly population has been documented to occur more commonly during times of elevated environmental temperatures (Kilbourne, 1989).

Climate conditions also geographically define many insect-carried diseases. Infectious agents which cycle through a cold-blooded species (invertebrates) to complete their development, are most susceptible to subtle climate variations (Dobson & Carper, 1993). Diseases whose pathogens, vectors, or hosts are affected by climate change include: malaria, schistosomiasis, filariasis, leishmaniasis, onchocerciasis (river blindness), trypanosomiasis (Chagas and African sleeping sickness), dengue, yellow fever, and arboviral encephalitis. Endemic malaria, for example, is generally limited to regions with average annual temperatures above 16°C (Maskell, 1993).

The health effects of climate change present a relatively new public health concern which has emerged since the recognition of the potential for global warming and can be grouped under the principal processes through which physical changes are anticipated to occur, namely: (1) temperature elevation with concomitant precipitation changes; and (2) thermoexpansion of oceans causing sea-level to rise. These changes may lead to an increased frequency of heat waves and hazardous air pollution episodes, reduced soil moisture, higher incidence of extreme weather events, and coastal flooding (Intergovernmental Panel on Climate Change, 1992a). Subsequent health effects may include an increase in: (1) heat-related mortality and morbidity; (2) infectious diseases, particularly those that are arthropod-borne; (3) malnutrition from threatened food supply; and (4) general public health infrastructural damage from weather disasters and sea-level rise (aggravated by subsequent climate-related human migration).

Increased ambient UV radiation from stratospheric ozone thinning can be regarded as a third component of climate change. The direct health impacts from increases in UV-B include: (1) skin cancer; (2) ocular diseases; and (3) immunosuppression. Indirect effects to health may occur primarily from crop damage by ultraviolet radiation. These outcomes relate to several of the health outcomes from greenhouse warming. UV-induced immunosuppression, for instance, can affect the course of infectious diseases, and crop damage by UV can compound adverse climate effects on food supply (see Figure 13.1).

Health Effects of Altered Temperature and Rainfall

Heat-Related Morbidity and Mortality

Weather conditions exceeding threshold temperatures and persisting for several consecutive days can cause increased mortality in the population. In large urban areas, poor housing combined with the urban "heat island" effect further worsens conditions. Elevated night-time temperature readings are the most significant meteorological variable contributing to heat-related mortality; the greenhouse effect is predicted to especially affect these minimum temperatures (Kalkstein & Smoyer, 1993). Temperate and polar regions are expected to warm disproportionately more than tropical and subtropical zones (Intergovernmental Panel on Climate Change, 1990a). The National Aeronautics and Space Administration (NASA) predicts that average summer temperatures in New York and St. Louis, for

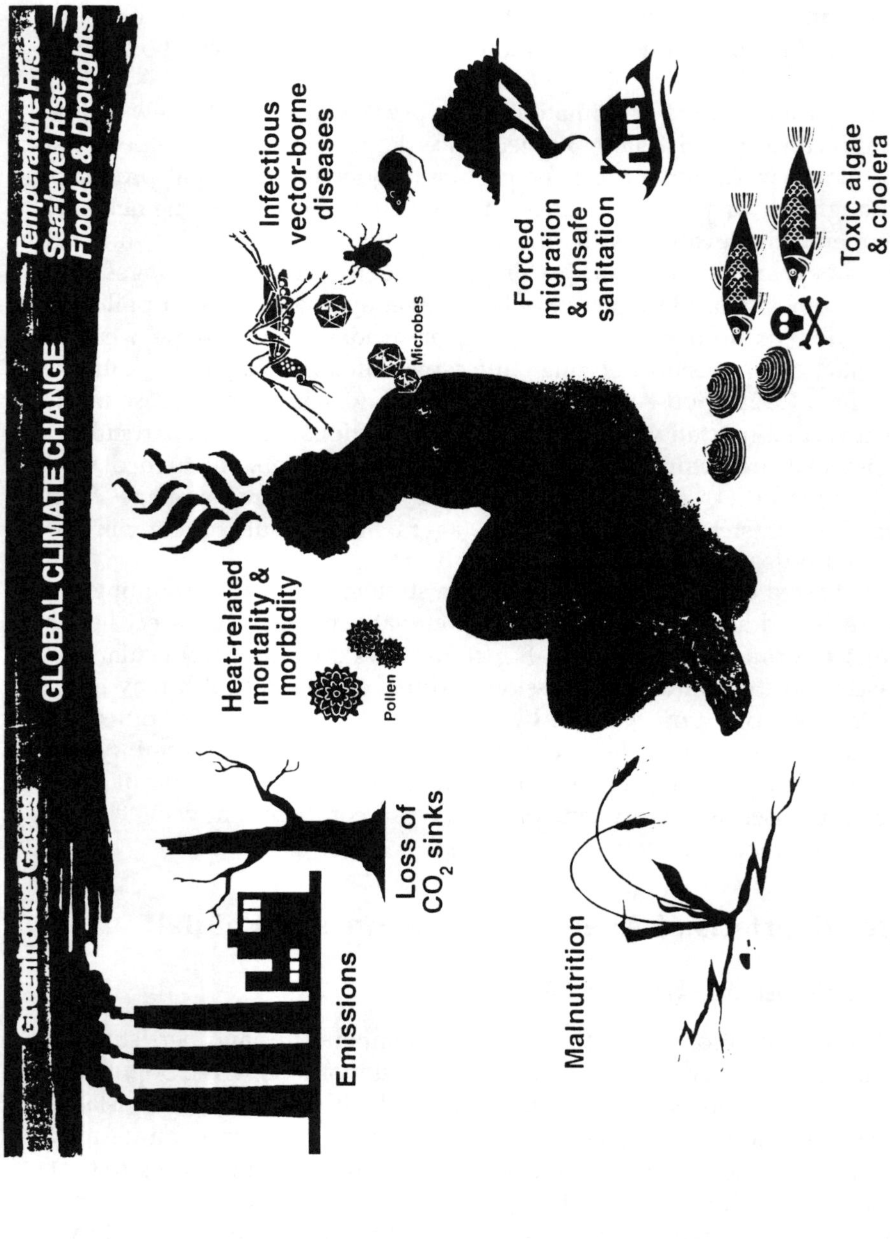

FIGURE 13.1 Public health effects of climate change.

example, would rise by 3.1° and 3.9°C, respectively, if ambient CO_2 doubles. Even with adjustment for physiologic acclimatization, annual summer mortality in temperate cities such as these (where populations are less adapted to oppressive weather) could rise over fourfold (Kalkstein & Smoyer, 1993).

The combination of warmer temperatures and increased ambient UV radiation could worsen air pollution, especially over urban areas. UV-photodecomposition of NO_2 in the presence of volatile organic compounds results in the production of tropospheric (ground-level) ozone, part of photochemical smog. Tropospheric ozone is a potent pulmonary irritant. Of course, fossil fuel emissions, accounting for much of greenhouse warming, also increase the incidence of respiratory illness, such as asthma and bronchitis, which can be exacerbated by higher temperatures that accelerate atmospheric chemical formation of caustic acid aerosols (Grant, 1990).

A steadily increasing proportion of the world's population lives in urban centers. Compared to 1900, when 15 percent of the populace inhabited cities, in the year 2000, half of all humans will live in large cities (McMichael, 1993). Under the conditions of global warming, the hazards to human health (i.e., heat island effect and harmful air pollution) may become significant public health problems given current trends in urbanization.

Infectious Diseases

Climate models used by the IPCC (1992) indicate that high latitudes in the northern hemisphere will experience the largest temperature elevation. Minimum winter temperatures are expected to change most, potentially allowing for certain viruses and parasites to extend into regions previously uninhabitable. In addition to direct climate effects on vectors, transformation of environments could have marked implications for diseases whereby the geographic range or life cycle of vector and/or reservoir host species is defined by environmental conditions.

Temperature determines vector infectivity by affecting pathogen replication, maturation, and the period of infectivity (Longstreth & Wiseman, 1989). Elevated temperature and humidity also intensify the biting behavior of most insects and are associated with increased human host vulnerability through removal of protective clothing. Extreme heat, on the other hand, can shorten insect survival time or disrupt pathogen development.

Malaria. Malaria is the most prevalent vector-borne disease globally, and causes 1 to 2 million deaths annually. The malaria parasite does not develop at temperatures below 16°C (Gilles, 1993). Malaria extending to higher altitudes (as a surrogate for latitude) has been documented in Rwanda in 1987, coinciding with atypically hot, wet weather (Loevinsohn, 1994).

Arboviruses. Arboviruses, which are also mosquito-borne, represent another climate-sensitive infectious disease. These include: encephalitis, dengue, and yellow fever. For example, epidemics of St. Louis encephalitis (SLE), the most common arboviral encephalitis in the United States, generally occur south of the 22°C June isotherm, but northerly outbreaks have occurred during unseasonably warm years. Human outbreaks are highly correlated with several-day periods when temperature exceeds 27°C (Shope, 1990).

In California, field studies on SLE indicate that a 1°C increase in temperature significantly shortens the elapsed time between a mosquito blood-meal and viral replication to the point of infectivity within the vector (the extrinsic incubation period). Adjusting for reduced adult mosquito survival at elevated temperatures, a 3–5°C temperature increase is predicted to cause a significant northern shift of SLE outbreaks (Reeves, 1994).

Dengue. Dengue is widespread in Asia, Africa, the Caribbean, tropical America, Oceania, and Australia. Thus far, the range of the primary mosquito vector, *Aedes aegypti,* has been limited to 35° latitude because freezing temperatures kill both larvae and adults. Warming trends, therefore, may shift vector and disease distribution to higher latitudes and altitudes.

Prevalence of dengue appears to be sensitive to climate factors. In Mexico in 1986, the most important predictor of dengue transmission was found to be the median temperature during the rainy season, with an adjusted fourfold risk observed between 17°C and 30°C; also, in locales averaging temperatures less than 19.3°C during the rainy season, no seropositive persons were identified (Koopman et al., 1991). Lab studies support this field data. *In vitro,* the extrinsic incubation period for dengue type-2 virus was 12 days at 30°C and only seven days at 32–35°C (Watts et al., 1987). This temperature effect of shortening the incubation period by five days alone translates to a potentially threefold higher transmission rate of disease (Koopman et al., 1991).

Other Emerging Diseases. Hantavirus, recently found to be the cause of human fatalities primarily in the southwest United States, has long been established in rodents and the new outbreak was felt to be related to climate/ecological conditions (Wenzel, 1994). Six years of drought, followed by extremely heavy precipitation in the spring of 1993, resulted in a 10-fold increase in the number of deer mice, which carry hantavirus. Similarly, Ebola outbreaks in African monkeys have coincided with the end of the rainy season (Morell, 1995).

Marine Effects

Increases in phytoplankton (or algae) globally have been a consequence of poor erosion control management, liberal agricultural application of fertilizers, and coastal sewage release all resulting in effluents rich in nutrients which promote algae growth. Such conditions that favor this growth could be augmented by warmer sea surface temperatures expected with global warming. Overharvesting of fish and shellfish (algae consumers), coupled with widespread pesticide use toxic to fish, further contributes to plankton overgrowth (Epstein et al., 1993).

Harmful marine phytoplankton blooms include red tides causing diarrheal and paralytic diseases and amnesic shellfish poisoning. *Vibrio cholera* has been found to be harbored by marine phytoplankton, thus blooms could represent an expanded reservoir from which cholera epidemics may initiate (Huq et al., 1990).

Again, it is apparent that the health outcomes of climate change cannot be assessed in isolation from other human activities affecting the environment. In the case of marine effects, oceanic warming may simply augment inimical changes resulting from poorly planned coastal and agricultural development.

Food Supply

Climate change could adversely affect agriculture both by long-term changes, such as reducing soil moisture through evapotranspiration, and, more immediately, by extreme weather events such as droughts, flooding (and erosion), and tropical storms. "CO_2 fertilization" that can enhance photosynthesis may initially benefit plants (Intergovernmental Panel on Climate Change, 1990a). Accounting for this, nonetheless, agriculture in developing countries may suffer most; it is estimated that in these nations, 40–300 million additional people will be at risk from hunger due to climate change (Parry & Rosenzweig, 1993).

A substantial number of coastal settlements depend on fish as their main food staple. Rapid sea-level rise from global warming (see next section) could damage both coral reefs and estuaries that support much of today's fisheries which are already threatened by overfishing (Intergovernmental Panel on Climate Change, 1990a).

Disruptive Weather and Sea Level Rise

Sea level may rise at a relatively rapid rate of two to four centimeters per decade due to thermal expansion of oceans, and increased thermal energy in the atmosphere is expected to produce more severe storms. For example, with double atmospheric CO_2 levels, hurricane strength could increase by as much as 40 percent (Intergovernmental Panel on Climate Change, 1990a). Such events could destroy dwellings and public health infrastructures, such as sanitation systems and stormwater drainage (Intergovernmental Panel on Climate Change, 1992a). Vulnerable populations in low-lying coastal areas and small islands would be forced to migrate to safer locations. Among these environmental refugees, the spread of infectious diseases could be amplified due to overcrowding and poor sanitation, and native populations would be at risk from potential influxes of infected individuals (WHO, 1990). Psychological impacts must also be considered from post-traumatic stress syndrome following major storms.

Saline intrusion of coastal aquifers would diminish fresh water supply and coastal farmland in addition to causing frank inundation. For example, a sea-level rise of one meter would destroy 15 percent and 20 percent of agriculture in Egypt and Bangladesh, respectively (Intergovernmental Panel on Climate Change, 1990a).

Forced migration from any event can pose serious public health consequences. The Rwandan refugees, who in 1994 were crowded into border camps during their mass exodus from military upheaval, suffered a cholera epidemic that ravaged the camps killing tens of thousands. A recent outbreak of pneumonic plague struck Surat, India, in September, 1994. Among several possible explanations given for the epidemic was exceptional flooding from heavy monsoons which left many drowned cattle across the land, or an abundant food supply for multiplying rats (carrying infected fleas). The IPCC's general circulation models suggest exacerbation of monsoons in regions where they already occur (Intergovernmental Panel on Climate Change, 1992b).

The example of pneumonic plague in India not only illustrates vulnerabilities by geographical location, but also by the present status of human living conditions. The health of impoverished populations living in overcrowded, unsanitary conditions is already threatened by infectious disease; the additional effects of climate change must be viewed in this context of a public health crisis already existing in much of the developing world.

Stratospheric Ozone Depletion

Direct Health Effects of Ultraviolet-B Radiation

Ultraviolet-B radiation contains the most biologically destructive wavelengths of 290–320 nanometers, and is specifically blocked from reaching the earth by the ozone layer. UV-B induces the formation of pyrimidine dimers within DNA molecules, which if unrepaired can evolve to cancer (IARC, 1992). Non-melanoma skin cancer (squamous and basal cell carcinoma) and superficial spreading melanoma are correlated with sunlight exposure.

Melanoma incidence has increased by 20–50 percent every 5 years over the past two decades in Western populations (Coleman et al., 1993). While there is no direct relationship between cumulative ultraviolet exposure and melanoma, excessive UV exposure during childhood is associated with incidence. For a sustained 10 percent decline in the stratospheric ozone layer, non-melanoma skin cancer cases could rise by 26 percent, or 300,000 globally per year; melanoma could increase by 20 percent, or 4,500 more cases annually (UNEP, 1991).

Half of all blindness results from ocular cataract formation, which has been associated with UV-B radiation (Taylor, 1990). Amino acids and membrane transport systems in the lens of the eye are especially prone to photo oxidation by oxygen radicals generated by UV-B irradiation (IARC, 1992). A doubling of UV-B exposure could cause a 60 percent increase in cortical cataracts over current levels, according to one large prospective study which utilized personal dosimeters (Taylor, West, Rosenthal, et al., 1988). UNEP estimates that a 10 percent sustained loss of stratospheric ozone would result in nearly 1.75 million extra cataracts annually (UNEP, 1991). Other ocular effects of UV-B exposure include photokeratitis, photokerato-conjunctivitis, pinguecula, and pterygium (or overgrowth of the conjunctival epithelium), and climatic droplet keratopathy (IARC, 1992).

UV-B in animal studies can alter the ability of the immune system to function effectively both on the "local" level of antigen processing and presentation to T-cells, and on the "systemic" level whereby lymphokine (biochemical messenger) production and resultant T-helper/T-suppresser cell ratios are affected. Consequently, the course of infectious skin diseases, such as onchocerciasis, leishmaniasis, and dermatophytosis can be exacerbated, and immunosurveillance of transformed, precancerous epidermal cells may be rendered less effective. Preliminary studies further show an influence in vaccine efficacy (Kripke & Morison, 1986; IARC, 1992).

Indirect Effects of UV-B

UV-B radiation inhibits photosynthesis (UNEP, 1991), and historically, the formation of the shielding ozone layer was what allowed terrestrial plants to become established. Weakening of food crops susceptible to UV-B damage could further extend the impacts on agriculture due to climate changes and sea-level rise. UV damage to algae in polar regions where ozone thinning is more pronounced could both be detrimental to the marine food chain and exacerbate the greenhouse effect.

DISCUSSION

Health research has thus far been quite successful in identifying single etiologic agents, including microorganisms, chemical toxins, and specific human behaviors. Yet, with the possible exceptions of heat waves and increases in weather disasters, direct (single agent) hazards to health will be few. Many threats will be mediated through complex environmental feedbacks, underscoring the relationship between ecosystem dynamics and long-term human health. It is this newly appreciated link between the condition of natural ecosystems and the long-term health of human populations that must be incorporated to address questions about the sustainability of development and of global human health.

The time scale over which health consequences may occur presents another major hurdle to health risk assessment. Many health-related sequelae will occur gradually, making them difficult to decipher from normal background variation. Establishing strategic long-term surveillance and monitoring represents one important step to take.

New Monitoring Initiatives

A geographic method of organizing and storing data will be essential, since much of the health risk analysis will require the superimposition of data on disease incidence, vector populations, demographics, and climate with linkage to specific geographic locations (see Chapter 23). Remote sensing (or remote satellite imaging) can be useful in the analysis of diseases when their distribution or epidemiology depends on climate and landscape features which determine habitats. Vector-borne diseases are particularly influenced by spatial and temporal fluctuations in vector populations. In combination, geographical information systems (GIS) and remote sensing technology may serve as a useful analytical tool and potentially as an early warning technology to prepare local health professionals for local shifts in disease patterns.

An attempt is currently under way to monitor the earth system in its entirety. For more comprehensive climate monitoring, the Global Climate Observing System (GCOS) is merging the World Meteorological Organization's (WMO) World Weather Watch and Global Atmosphere Watch with existing programs of other international organizations. The World Weather Watch comprises the largest current observation system in the world, and includes satellites, telecommunications, and data processing facilities (WMO, 1992).

The Global Ocean Observing System (GOOS) is a new endeavor sponsored by the Intergovernmental Oceanographic Commission of the UN Educational, Scientific and Cultural Organization (UNESCO), WMO, and the International Council of Scientific Unions (ICSU). Satellite and underwater instruments will be utilized to monitor changes in the oceans. The Global Terrestrial Observing System (GTOS) is being created by UNEP, UNESCO, WMO, ICSU, and the Food and Agricultural Organization (FAO), and will monitor land-based alterations in the environment (ICSU, 1993; WMO, 1992).

Preventive Measures

Adaptive Options. Since some amount of climate change may be inevitable, adaptive options to reduce unavoidable health consequences must be considered. Examples include: urban planning to reduce the heat island effect and improve housing; disaster preparedness programs and weather watch/warning systems; land-use planning to minimize erosion, flash-flooding, and unnecessary deforestation (e.g., halting the creation of rangeland for meat exportation); genetically engineered, climate-resistant crops; and vector-control, disease surveillance, and expanded vaccination efforts.

When considered in total, these adaptive measures will offer varying amounts of protection to human health, however, and may only be temporizing measures. Adaptive control measures may also have unintended costs which must be considered. For example, over-dependence on agricultural pesticides not only leads to insect resistance but also eliminates natural, beneficial, predatory organisms. The adverse effect on public health and the environment due to current pesticide use is estimated to be between \$100–\$200 billion annually (Pimental, 1990).

Population Policy. Population growth is one of the driving forces behind both increased CO_2 emissions and deforestation. In 1990, approximately 300 million women indicating a desire for family planning had no access to such services (Haines & Parry, 1993). Family planning remains a priority health strategy for most immediate health needs, as well as for reducing population pressure leading to global climate change.

Regarding abatement of climate change, there may be as much rationale for international assistance directed toward curbing population growth as toward curbing deforestation. Yet, industrialized nations must first show a commitment to constrain their current consumption patterns or shift to alternative energy sources before considering population dynamics in the carbon balance (in fact, population growth more likely degrades other environmental resources more immediately related to public health).

As for regional vulnerabilities to climate change sequelae, population growth alone puts more people at risk than does a one meter rise in sea level over 100 years, due to overcrowding in coastal areas most at risk of flooding (WHO, in press). With population growth rates highest in these coastal areas most vulnerable to sea-level rise (e.g., India, Bangladesh, West Africa, and island nations in the Indian Ocean), further need for stabilizing population is reinforced.

Precautionary Measures. In spite of new monitoring and research enterprises, it may not be possible to collect sufficient empirical evidence to guide policy within an appropriate time frame. Given the complexities of the analysis of health effects of climate change, precautionary measures ought to be considered along with new research efforts.

Precautionary measures aimed at reducing greenhouse warming will also have inherently beneficial "side effects" for public health. Reducing air pollution and population growth, for example, have obvious short-term positive impacts on health. In a sense, these short-term gains weigh favorably in the policy debate which must consider potentially irrevocable and widespread health consequences together with vast uncertainties.

Reductions in greenhouse gases may be accomplished through industrial emission control, energy conservation measures, land-use policies to maximize the extent of CO_2 "sinks," and population policies to achieve both reduced demand for energy and destruction of these vegetative CO_2 sinks. Full cooperation between nations, including expanded technology transfer and economic reimbursement for preservation of natural resources in impoverished countries, and equity in the expected responses from developed and developing countries will be critical to successful implementation of these recommendations.

North/South Cooperation. UNCED demonstrated the political impossibility of separating the issues of environment from those of development (Williams, 1993). Likewise, with new appreciation for ecosystem/human health linkages, it is also difficult to separate human health concerns from those of both development and the environment.

As densely populated poorer nations begin to develop, their contribution of GHG emissions is expected to far surpass that of the present industrialized community, especially if conventional technology is utilized (World Bank, 1992). Efforts to transfer improved technology are, thus, a high priority. Without such arrangements, sovereign nations have no reason to refrain from financially benefiting through the use of energy-inefficient technology or the harvesting of their natural resources.

Industrialized and developing countries will need to fully cooperate for meaningful steps in abating global warming. Developing countries can influence the course of global warming by their choices of land use policy and technologies as their development inevitably accelerates. Affordable technology will need to be transferred to these countries in a timely fashion before current inefficient energy policies of many industrialized nations are adopted. As the inherent value of tropical rain forests and other greenhouse sinks is realized, full accounting of their value on the "global common market" may show more sustained profitability and health benefit when left intact.

CONCLUSION

Risks that are distributed widely across populations (as will be the case for climate change) will necessitate preventive measures on a population rather than individual level (Rose, 1992). Many diseases are climate dependent and are on the rise (and regarding vector-borne diseases, treatment and pest control measures are failing). Anticipatory prevention of these diseases in the event of climate change cannot be ignored.

Developing countries will suffer disproportionately more from the consequences of climate change, though industrialized nations are presently more responsible for GHGs in the atmosphere. In the future, poorer countries will influence the course of global warming significantly more, both through the technologies they choose to adopt as their development accelerates, and by land-use practices. Developed nations will need to embrace more environmentally sound energy policies and promptly transfer new (and affordable) technology to the developing world.

With the shortcomings of adaptive measures, more emphasis should be placed on monitoring and interdisciplinary research to guide policy makers in decisions around the logic of pursuing more "upstream" preventive options of GHG mitigation. At the same time, we must appreciate the enormous challenges inherent in these complex new research requirements and the delay in which results will likely emerge. Therefore, in addition to research, prompt precautionary measures and cooperation between rich and poor nations to abate the process of climate change must not be postponed to a point when intervention becomes ineffective.

REFERENCES

Coleman, M., Esteve, J., & Damiecki, P. (1993). *Trends in cancer incidence and mortality*. Lyon: International Agency for Research on Cancer.

Dobson, A., & Carper, R. (1993). Biodiversity. *Lancet, 342* (October), 1096–1099.

Epstein, P. R., Ford, T. E., & Colwell, R. R. (1993). Marine ecosystems. *Lancet, 342* (Nov), 1216–1219.

Farman, J. C., Gardiner, H., & Shanklin, J. D. (1985). Large losses of total ozone in Antarctica reveal seasonal ClOx/NOx interaction. *Nature, 315*, 207–211.

Gilles, H. M. (1993). Epidemiology of Malaria. In H. M. Gilles & D. A. Warrell (Eds.), *Bruce-Chwatt's essential malariology*. London: Edward Arnold Div. of Hodder & Stoughton.

Gleason, J. F., Bhartia, P. K., Herman, J. R., et al. (1993). Record low global ozone in 1992. *Science, 260*, 523–526.

Grant, L. D. (1990). Respiratory effects associated with global climate change. In J. C. White (Ed.), *Global atmospheric change and public health*. New York: Elsevier.

Haines, A., & Parry, M. (1993). Potential effects on health of global warming. *World Resource Review, 5(4)*, 430–448.

Huq, A., Colwell, R. R., Rahman, R., et al. (1990). Detection of Vibrio cholerae 01 in the aquatic environment by fluorescent-monoclonal antibody and culture methods. *Appl Environ Microbial, 56*, 2370–2373.

IARC (1992). *IARC monographs on the evaluation of carcinogenic risks to humans: solar and ultraviolet radiation*. Lyon: International Agency for Research on Cancer.

ICSU (1993). *Understanding our own planet: an overview of major international scientific activities*. Paris: International Council of Scientific Unions.

Intergovernmental Panel on Climate Change (1990a). *Climate change: the IPCC impacts assessment*. Canberra: Australian Government Publishing Service.

Intergovernmental Panel on Climate Change (1990b). *Climate change: the IPCC scientific assessment*. Cambridge: Cambridge University Press.

Intergovernmental Panel on Climate Change (1992a). *Climate change 1992: the supplementary report to the IPCC impacts assessment*. Canberra: Australian Government Publishing Service.

Intergovernmental Panel on Climate Change (1992b). *Climate change 1992: the supplementary report to the IPCC scientific assessment*. Cambridge: Cambridge University Press.

Kalkstein, L. S., & Smoyer, K. E. (1993). The impact of climate change on human health: some international implications. *Experiencia, 49*, 469–479.

Kerr, J. B., & McElroy (1993). Evidence for large upward trends of ultraviolet-B radiation linked to ozone depletion. *Science, 262* (Nov), 1032–1034.

Kilbourne, E. M. (1989). Heat waves. In M. B. Gregg (Ed.), *The public health consequences of disasters 1989* (pp. 51–61). Atlanta: US Department of Health and Human Services, Public Health Service, Centers of Disease Control.

Koopman, J. S., Prevots, D. R., Marin, M. A. V., Dantes, H. G., Aqino, M. L. Z., Longini, I. M. J., & Amor, J. S. (1991). Determinants and predictors of dengue infection in Mexico. *American Journal of Epidemiology, 133*, 1168–1178.

Kripke, M. L., & Morison, W. L. (1986). Studies on the mechanism of systemic suppression of contact hypersensitivity by UVB radiation, II. Differences in the suppression of delayed and contact hypersensitivity in mice. *J Invest Dermatol, 86*, 543–549.

Loevinsohn, M. (1994). Climatic warming and increased malaria incidence in Rwanda. *Lancet, 343* (March), 714–718.

Longstreth, J., & Wiseman, J. (1989). The potential impact of climate change on patterns of infectious disease in the United States. In J. B. Smith & D. A. Tirpak (Eds.), *The potential effects of global climate change in the United States*. Washington, DC: US Environmental Protection Agency.

Maskell, K., Mintzer, I. M., & Callander, B. (1993). Basic science of climate change. *Lancet, 342*, 1027–1031.

McMichael, A. J. (1993). *Planetary overload: global environmental change and the health of the human species*. Cambridge: Cambridge University Press.

Molina, M. J., & Rowland, F. S. (1974). Stratospheric sink for chloro-fluoromethanes: chlorine atom-catalyzed destruction of ozone. *Nature, 249*, 810–814.

Morell, V. (1995). Chimpanzee outbreak heats up search for Ebola origin. *Science, 268*, 974–975.

Parry, M. L., & Rosenzweig, C. (1993). Food supply and the risk of hunger. *Lancet, 342*, 1345–1347.

Pimental, D. (1990). Estimated annual worldwide pesticide use. In *Facts and Figures: International Agricultural Research*. New York: The Rockefeller Foundation.

Reeves, W. C., Hardy, J. L., Reisen, W. K., & Milby, M. M. (1994). The potential effect of global warming on mosquito-borne arboviruses. *J Medical Entomology, 31(3)*, 323–332.

Rose, G. (1992). *The strategy of preventive medicine*. Oxford: Oxford University Press.

Schneider, S. H. (1990). *Global warming: are we entering the greenhouse century?* New York: Vintage Books.

Shope, R. E. (1990). Infectious diseases and atmospheric change. In J. C. White (Ed.), *Global atmospheric change and public health. Proceedings of the Center for Environmental Information*. New York: Elsevier.

Stolarski, R., Bojkov, R., Bishop, L., Zerefos, C., Staehelin, J., & Zawodny, J. (1992). Measured trends in stratospheric ozone. *Science, 256* (Apr), 342–349.

Taylor, H. R., West, S. K., Rosenthal, F. S., et al. (1988). Effects of ultraviolet radiation on cataract formation. *N Engl J Med, 319*, 1429–1433.

Taylor, H. R. (1990). Cataracts and ultraviolet light. In J. C. White (Ed.), *Global atmospheric change and public health: proceedings of the Center for Environmental Information*. New York: Elsevier.

UNEP (1991). *Environmental Effects of Ozone Depletion: 1991 Update*. Nairobi: UN Environment Programme.

Watts, D. M., Burke, D. S., Harrison, B. A., et al. (1987). Effect of temperature on the vector efficiency of Aedes aegypti for dengue 2 virus. *Am J Trop Med Hyg, 36*, 143–152.

Wenzel, R. P. (1994). A new hantavirus infection in North America. *N Engl J Med, 330(14)*, 1004–1005.

WHO (1990). *Potential health effects of climatic change*. No. WHO/PEP/90.10. World Health Organization.

WHO (in press). *Climate and health in a changing world*. Geneva: World Health Organization.

Williams, M. (1993). Re-articulating the third world coalition: the role of the environmental agenda. *Third World Quarterly, 14(1)*, 7–29.

WMO (1992). *GCOS: responding to the need for climate observations* No. 777. World Meteorological Organization.
World Bank (1992). *World development report 1992: development and the environment*. Oxford: Oxford University Press.

14

The Importance of Coastal Management to Human Health

*Philomène A. Verlaan**

INTRODUCTION

Why devote an entire chapter to coasts, a geographical region that represents only about 8 percent of the surface of the planet? Why do not other chapters address the importance to human health of other physical regions such as uplands, river valleys, forests and plains? The answer is that the role of these other regions in the global loop of human health, environment and development is less important, and less instructive, than that of the coast, for four reasons: demographic pressure, cumulative environmental burden, intensive development and absence of boundaries.

Demographic Pressure

The coastal 8 percent of the planet is the home of 75 percent of the world's current population of 5.5 billion and includes the poorest people of the planet (FAO, 1991a). Most of the projected doubling of the world's population by 2050 is expected to be concentrated in coastal cities (FAO, 1991a).

Cumulative Environmental Burden

The coastal population bears the cumulative burden of environmental stress. It suffers not only from the consequences of activities and over-

* The author is writing purely in her personel capacity and the views expressed are in no way to be construed as reflecting the position of UNEP on any of these matters.

crowding along the coast itself but also from the consequences of upstream and inland development. The latter include pollution, deforestation, damming of rivers, inadequate management and use of soil, water, pesticides and fertilizers (FAO, 1991a). The concentration of cumulative, multi-source environmental degradation in a small, confined and overcrowded area is a major contributor to poor human health and is a characteristic of most coastal zones.

Intensive Development

Much of the increase in economic development either physically occurs on the coast, or depends on features best offered by the coast. The result is more and usually incompatible—hence conflicting—demands on this small area for food, shelter, energy, employment, waste disposal, transport, shipping, tourism and recreation (FAO, 1991a).

The coastal zone is not a biological desert. On the contrary, in their coral reef ecosystems alone, coasts host biodiversity riches that are at least equal to those of tropical rain forests. Together with mangroves, seagrass beds and wetlands (including salt marshes, estuaries, deltas and mudflats), these ecosystems offer a treasure trove of resources to their human neighbors. Coastal ecosystems are among the most biologically productive on earth: annual gross production is almost three times that of most forests, grasslands and croplands (Odum, 1971); they are vital for protection of the land from the sea, as filters for pollutants, and as the source of food, shelter, breeding areas and nursery grounds for a wide variety of organisms, including 95 percent of humankind's marine-based food (FAO, 1991b). Populations of developing countries of the tropical and subtropical regions derive between 40–100 percent of their animal protein from the sea (FAO, 1991b). In Asia alone over 1 billion people, including especially the poorest, who can afford no substitutes, depend almost totally on fish for their animal protein (FAO, 1991b). Seafood is an essential nutritional supplement to the mostly carbohydrate diet of the poor in Asia and Africa, and, as a protein source, is essential for children (FAO, 1991b).

Absence of Boundaries

The sea implacably reflects the effects of coastal activities and disregards all political boundaries. Health, environment and development on coasts must be considered simultaneously in their local, regional and international context.

THE PRINCIPAL ANTHROPOGENIC THREATS TO HUMAN HEALTH ALONG THE COASTS

Because the focus of this book is on human health, a deliberately anthropocentric view of the benefits to human health of environmentally sound management of coastal regions is taken throughout this chapter. A truly anthropocentric approach, as long as it is also equitable, may well be the best way to preserve the rest of the environment and investments in development as well.

The World Health Organization (WHO) defines health as including the absence of disease, protection from life- and health-threatening pathogens, pollutants and physical hazards; it is also a function of the ability to obtain adequate food, water and shelter (WHO, 1991). Coastal populations face increasing levels of the former and suffer commensurately declining abilities to provide themselves with the latter.

The principal anthropogenic sources of disease, in their current order of importance, are: sewage, chemicals, heavy metals and radionucleides.

Sewage

Most disease is caused by untreated or poorly treated domestic sewage in the coastal zone (GESAMP, 1991). Bathing in and consuming seafood from water contaminated by sewage transfers a remarkable variety of diseases to the coastal population. These include ear, eye and skin infections, infectious hepatitis, poliomyelitis (Linden, 1990), salmonella, shigella, campylobacteriosis, cholera, typhoid, meningitis, and pneumonia (Laws, 1993). Children under five are at particular risk (GESAMP, 1991).

Seasonal influxes of visitors to the already crowded coasts result in even more sewage-related disease. Coastal populations of tropical and subtropical developing countries are most vulnerable, but those from industrialized countries are not exempt. In the United States, for example, it was estimated that between 1946 and 1980 over 1,300 outbreaks of waterborne diseases occurred, causing about 350,000 cases of illness (Laws, 1993). The steady rise in sewage-related disease is directly related to the growing population along the shores of all developed and developing countries at all latitudes (Bryceson et al., 1990; GESAMP, 1991; Fan & Côté, 1991; Laws, 1993; Linden, 1990).

Algal blooms are stimulated by sewage discharges enriched in nutrients such as nitrogen and phosphorus. This phenomenon is often, and erroneously, referred to as eutrophication, leading to the further erroneous conclusion that eutrophication is a harmful event. In fact, eutrophication is a continuous (not episodic), complex and natural process in nearly all bodies of water. It is a function of accumulating levels of biomass and nutrients together with increased productivity and decreasing depth of the body of water concerned from sedimentation. Nothing is intrinsically harmful to human health about eutrophication. "Cultural" eutrophication is simply the anthropogenic acceleration of eutrophication . . . brought about by discharges of organic wastes and/or nutrients" (Laws, 1993). Algal blooms are not synonymous with eutrophication, "cultural" or "natural."

Certain algae, especially the dinoflagellates that appear in "red tides," are harmful to human health. They produce neurotoxins that cause paralytic shellfish poisoning (PSP) in humans who eat shefllfish that have consumed these algae and concentrated the toxins (GESAMP, 1991). PSP causes respiratory paralysis and death by asphyxia. Other dinoflagellates produce diarrheic toxins that cause severe gastrointestinal disorders known as diarrheic shellfish poisoning (DSP), when shellfish contaminated by these organisms are eaten. No fatalities have been reported so far for DSP (GESAMP, 1991). Yet other dinoflagellates produce ciguatoxins that cause ciguatera in humans eating contaminated herbivorous fish and their predators in the tropics and subtropics. Ciguatera has long-term debilitating effects on neurological, cardiovascular and gastrointestinal functions. Fatality rates range from 0.1–4.5% (GESAMP, 1991).

Other marine flagellates, such as diatoms, are being linked to diseases: memory loss, other neurological disorders and fatalities can result from a neurotoxin-causing amnesic shellfish poisoning (ASP) when humans eat contaminated shellfish (GESAMP, 1991). The types and number of these algal toxins in the marine environment is unknown. The possibility of disease outbreaks related to new ones must not be ignored (GESAMP, 1991). Toxic algal blooms are certainly increasing dramatically worldwide (Cherfas, 1990; WRI, 1992–93).

Chemicals and Heavy Metals

This source of disease is caused by runoff of pesticides and herbicides, and by industrial effluent containing chemicals and heavy metals. Marine-related disease—as opposed to the effect on human health of drinking contaminated fresh water—is primarily caused by eating contaminated seafood. The most notorious, but by no means unique, example of disease and death from this source is found in Minamata Bay, Japan, caused by the coastal population eating mercury-tainted seafood which was linked to the discharge of mercury-laden effluent (GESAMP, 1991; Laws, 1993).

Some 80,000–100,000 chemicals are on the market today (Laws, 1993), and 500–1,000 new chemicals enter the market every year; their role in the environment and their effect on human health are usually unknown (GESAMP, 1991). Those already known to be dangerous to human health include various synthetic organic compounds, such as polychlorinated biphenyls (PCBs) and halogenated hydrocarbons, petroleum hydrocarbons, pesticides such as DDT (dichloro-diphenyl-trichloro-ethane) (GESAMP, 1991; Davies, 1991; WRI, 1992–93), antifoulants (e.g., tributyl tin) (Farrington, 1991) and the heavy metals cadmium, lead, arsenic and mercury (GESAMP, 1991), selenium, tin, copper (WRI, 1992–93).

Most dangerous are those chemicals which persist in the marine environment and are concentrated by bio-accumulation up the food chain. The assessment of the level of contamination of a coastal area is inadequate if it relies only on concentrations of chemicals and metals found dissolved in the water column because the concentration in sediments and biota may be far higher (Laws, 1993).

Exposure to chemicals and heavy metals in seafood affects human health in several ways, depending on what and how much is consumed (GESAMP, 1991; Laws, 1993). Their presence is increasing in the coastal marine environment. The few toxicological studies have addressed only short-term, fatal consequences of pollutants, not effects of long-term, low-level exposure (Olsen et al., 1989), particularly when pollutants are acting in combination (Stumm, 1987). Far more attention must be given to the direct contact between humans and water, and to other mechanisms transferring toxic compounds to humans (Laws, 1993). Contamination of coastal groundwater for drinking must not be neglected, as it may be exacerbated by intrusions of polluted seawater.

Oil pollution receives massive media coverage when it occurs, especially if a tanker accident is involved. Yet most oil pollution results not from accidents but from normal operations. Oil in the marine environment presents no significant risk to human health. Contamination is transferred by eating oil-polluted seafood. This has such an unpleasant taste at such low concentrations of oil that its consumption is unlikely (Laws, 1993). However, the poor may have no alternative to oil-tainted seafood. Ship-based oil pollution is the most widely regulated source of pollution of the marine environment, which now constitutes at most 10% of that pollution (Cormack, 1992). Oil pollution from land-based sources is of more immediate concern, and it is virtually unregulated.

Radionucleides

This human health hazard is caused by discharges of nuclear reactors and reprocessing plants, industrial, scientific and medical use, dumping of radioactive waste and testing of nuclear devices (Laws, 1993). Of particular concern are the many radionucleides incorporated into living organisms. These can behave in the body like their stable counterparts, or mimic essential elements like calcium and potassium, or be inhaled and concentrated in the lungs (Laws, 1993). The effects on human health of radiation include various cancers and leukemia, genetic defects, fetal and infant mortality and reduced longevity generally (Laws, 1993). Young children and fetuses are more vulnerable than adults; those parts of the body with rapidly dividing cells are most susceptible to radiation damage (Laws, 1993).

Marine organisms appear to be similarly sensitive to radiation. Some are capable of concentrating radionucleides to a level far higher than that of the surrounding water. The main risk to human health is the transfer of concentrated radionucleides to humans by consumption of seafood (Laws, 1993). As with chemicals and heavy metals, all possible pathways for transfer must be considered in determining the level of radionucleide contamination in coastal waters, including coastal groundwater (Laws, 1993). The level of radionucleide contamination in coastal waters is not yet as severe a threat to human health as are the other hazards (GESAMP, 1991). Radioactive waste disposal is a growing problem. Although more attention has been given to the international regulation of such disposal than any other potentially polluting substances (see, e.g., Cormack, 1992), the existing international legal mechanisms of control rely on national enforcement. While the disposal issue remains unresolved, this hazard to human health will increase.

Malnutrition

Pollutants and activities that destroy coastal habitats and ecosystems contribute to the decline of the marine fauna on which the coastal populations rely for food. These activities include overfishing, destruction of inshore breeding areas, nurseries, habitats and migration paths, sedimentation from erosion caused by logging and clearing of forests, reduction in nutrients by upstream dams and changes in salinity from dams and irrigation schemes (Olsen et al., 1989; Cherfas, 1990; UNGA, 1991). The much-vaunted alternative of aquaculture must be treated with caution; considerable evidence exists that aquaculture causes more problems than it solves (UNGA, 1991). Coastal resources are rapidly being degraded and lost throughout the world (see, e.g., WRI 1992–93; GESAMP, 1991; Linden, 1990, and references therein). A healthy coastal habitat for marine organisms must be maintained because 95 percent of the world's fish catch reproduces inshore and feeds on organisms that must spend part of their developmental cycle in coastal waters. Breaking the marine food chain reduces a vital source of protein for coastal populations and undermines their nutritional base. The poor and especially their children are most severely disadvantaged; for them seafood is not a luxury, but an essential part of their diet.

Physical Hazards

Coastal populations risk physical hazards from the consequences of inappropriate construction on or alterations to the coastline. Clearing and building on barrier islands and mangrove swamps, dredging, mining of beach sand, gravel and coral reefs and generally living and building too close to the sea renders the coastal population vulnerable to storms, flooding and their associated ills. Upstream activity such as logging and damming also changes coastal topography and can cause or exacerbate dangerous floods and landslides (Olsen et al., 1989; FAO, 1991a). The poorer members of the coastal population are once again most at risk. (Olsen et al., 1989; FAO, 1991b).

COASTAL DEVELOPMENT AND HUMAN HEALTH

Two fundamental misconceptions persist in the thinking about the management of the marine environment. The first is that unlimited anthropogenic wastes can be absorbed harmlessly by the marine environment. The second is that the health of the coastal regions is so dependent on international cooperation that no one country can achieve any significant improvement in its own jurisdiction by itself. The effect of these two misconceptions is to condone the absence of efforts to reduce or eliminate environmentally harmful activity.

The physical limitation of the ocean's capacity for waste absorption was formally and explicitly acknowledged in 1985 by the foremost, and most conservative international marine scientific body, the Joint Group of Experts on the Scientific Aspects of Marine Pollution (GESAMP, 1986). Only four years later GESAMP concluded that current levels of use of the marine environment as a sink for wastes could not continue:

"Man's fingerprint is found everywhere in the oceans. Chemical contamination and litter can now be observed from the poles to the tropics and from beaches to abyssal depths" (GESAMP, 1991). The open ocean is described as only "relatively clean," while in coastal waters the contaminant level has built up to "significant levels, particularly in poorly flushed areas." "Poorly flushed areas" are those whose topography is such that connections with other marine waters and the open ocean are physically limited, so that contaminants remain and build up close to the shores of their source and are not carried away by tides and currents to become some other country's problem. Poorly flushed areas include estuaries, deltas, lagoons, bays, enclosed and semi-enclosed seas (GESAMP, 1991).

Note the emphasis on the deteriorating state of poorly flushed areas. A country that intends to improve the coastal marine environment for public health reasons should not permit discussion of how much more waste that environment can absorb.

In response to the functional helplessness claimed by national management authorities, it must be argued that physical and political realities in fact place the protection of the public health of the coastal population within the clear and sole responsibility of those same authorities of the country asserting sovereignty over those coasts.

The most important, and most frequently ignored, physical reality is that over 80 percent of sources of marine pollution are land-based. Most pollutants originate locally and stay inshore. Because of the second physical reality that these areas are poorly flushed, their concentration is not substantially increased by imports from other marine environments (i.e., other countries). This is why the open ocean is still "relatively clean."

The political reality is that coastal states have all the rights they need to provide for the public health aspects of the waters not only off their coasts but as far seaward as 200 nautical miles. The coastal pollution most harmful to public health is generated in a country's own backyard and most of it stays well within its twelve nautical-mile territorial sea. The ability of a country to safeguard the health of its coastal population from the hazards enumerated above is in no way hampered by either the action or inaction of the international community or its neighboring countries.

From both the human health and the national development perspectives, it is reasonable to expend time, money and effort on understanding and managing coastal zones wisely. This region is one of the most benign and hospitable to humans on the planet. Its primary importance to the prosperity of both developed and developing countries has been described. Prosperity is necessary to maintain human health.

CURRENT COASTAL MANAGEMENT PROGRAMS

No programs to manage the coasts include human health in calculating costs and benefits associated with the development and use of coastal and marine resources. The cost to a government of the death, disease and debilitation of its citizens associated with inappropriate development and management of coastal resources remains unquantified.

The absence of human health as a variable to be considered in the management of the coastal zone is characteristic of a general inability of countries throughout the world to implement a coherent and integrated system for the management of the heavily populated coastal zones. This inability is manifested on all scales, from the local to the international, with all forms of government, regardless of the level of national prosperity or foreign aid, and it results neither from ignorance nor from lack of national income. The knowledge required for coastal management is easily available and inexpensive to apply, even for the least developed countries. Developing countries such as Sri Lanka have been able to design and adopt—although not implement—a nationwide coastal management plan. Developed countries such as the United States have not yet achieved a truly national, integrated and implemented coastal management plan. Even in those countries with plans on their books, examples of their successful implementation are yet to be found.

The discharge of wastes to the marine environment is an activity directly related to human health and is addressed by an extensive array of international and regional treaties. These treaties consider the marine environment to be a global concern, which "states have the obligation to protect and preserve." (Article 192 of the 1982 United Nations Convention on the Law of the Sea (LOS Convention). The LOS Convention enteredinto force on November 16, 1994. As of July 1995, 75 countries had ratified it, and 159 signed it during the period when it was open for signature. The LOS Convention is the overarching, global, and widely supported treaty establishing a comprehensive legal order for the oceans, including measures "to prevent, reduce and control pollution of the marine environment from any source" (Article 194). It reinforces the earlier 1972 Convention on the Prevention of Marine Pollution by Dumping of Wastes and Other Matter (London Convention) and the 1973 International Convention for the Prevention of Pollution from Ships, as modified by its 1978 Protocol (MARPOL 73/78) which control waste disposal from ships in the sea. Between them, these two Conventions cover oil, chemicals, packaged goods, plastics, sewage and garbage; the incineration of wastes at sea and dumping industrial and radioactive wastes from ships are prohibited. (Other conventions also deal with oil, specifically.) The sea is defined under the London Convention as "all marine waters other than the internal waters of States." Under the LOS Convention the entire marine environment is protected, including internal waters. "From any source" means the LOS Convention covers pollution from land-based sources, even if these originate far inside the terrestrial jurisdiction of the coastal state (for a detailed discussion of this point, see Boyle, 1992). Twelve regional marine environmental conventions, which between them cover most of the coastal zones of the world, have similar requirements.

A plethora of formal and informal intergovernmental regional and subregional discussions on pollution of the marine environment are always in progress in various fora throughout the world. The most recent and ambitious international effort to deal with, *inter alia,* land-based sources of wastes in the marine environment is the draft Global Program of Action for the Protection of the Marine Environment against Pollution from Land-Based Sources (UNEP (OCA)/LBA/IG.2.3). It has been developed under the auspices of the United Nations Environment Program, and it was adopted at an intergovernmental meeting held in Washington, D.C. in November, 1995. The Programme of Action is not a legally binding treaty. It is to assist states in taking joint and individual action to deal with this problem in light of the overarching obligation imposed by the LOS Convention within a coherent and internationally agreed framework.

Despite this impressive array of regulatory activity, effective control of waste disposal in the marine environment is likely to continue to be elusive. This may be in part because human health has played no role in the design of these regulations. The same deficiency exists in regulations for the management of other aspects of the coastal zone. An important but generally ignored indicator of the practical inadequacy of coastal zone management efforts is the steady deterioration of living conditions there, as measured by the increasing number and severity of human health hazards. The final section addresses the policy implications of this conclusion.

COASTAL MANAGEMENT FOR PUBLIC HEALTH

The principal reasons why integrated coastal zone management has not been achieved so far are common to developed and developing countries, and are as follows:

a. multiple uses, each with its own sectoral management
b. no communication between sectors or between their regulators in government
c. disregard of links between upland activities and their downstream consequences
d. no cross-cutting political constituency
e. lack of political will
f. primacy of neoclassical economic development objectives and short-term financial gains (see e.g., Olsen et al., 1989; GESAMP, 1991; Juda & Burroughs, 1990; Cormack, 1992).

The result is a long-standing, familiar regulatory impasse, for which remedies have been sought in the identification of new organizing principles, mostly centered around an "ecosystem management" approach. This approach has several problems. The physical or administrative boundaries of an ecosystem unit are widely disputed. The United States, for example, has a national Coastal Zone Management Act in which the coastal zone remains undefined. Even where the boundaries have been agreed, the institutions in the ecosystem representing its various uses (e.g., fisheries, ports and harbors, transport, forestry, tourism, mining, offshore oil and gas, waste disposal, defense, etc.) retain their own sectoral and political constituency and remain unchanged. Intersectoral meetings may occur, but no overarching standard or set of scales is available against which to evaluate the competing costs and benefits of proposed individual sectoral courses of action within the ecosystem unit, or to assess the net result for the country as a whole.

In the interest of protecting the environment and encouraging sound development, it is counterproductive to use the environment as the overarching standard against which to assess development plans, or vice-versa, for several reasons. First, the approach is flawed: that which is itself being measured cannot also serve as a standard of measurement.

Second, both standards are vulnerable because of uncertainty as to human cause and its developmental and environmental effects and because of the inadequate quantification of environmental and developmental costs and benefits, which makes it difficult to compare alternative uses of a resource. The application of such concepts as the precautionary principle and the increasing sophistication of "green" accounting methods are making inroads into these vulnerabilities but the work is too far from complete to provide useful guidance to decision makers.

Third, society will not accept any standard which does not assign the overarching value to people. It is immaterial whether or not this societal position is correct; it is the reality within which workable solutions to the environment-development impasse must be found.

This reality is reflected in the familiar argument that "the people" will be disadvantaged if a certain "development" is delayed, altered or halted in the interests of the environment, or that "the people" will be disadvantaged if that same environment is damaged in the interests of development. Curiously, the symmetry of the two arguments stops short of the people themselves. The people being disadvantaged are always different depending on the side taken in the argument.

Policymakers have tended to consider "the people's advantage" and "development" as more positively related than "the people's advantage" and "environment." The preceding sections have shown that this tendency is unjustified where human health and development in the coastal zone is concerned. Here health cannot be considered as an advantage for the people to be associated with development. More generally, i.e., beyond the coastal zone, it is a justifiable conclusion that the environment is indeed an inappropriate organizing principle for assessing the merits of a development plan, and both environment and development considerations are inappropriate to assess the advantages of any plan to the people.

Human health itself is proposed here as an alternative organizing principle against which to assess claims that proposed activities are good or bad for the environment and for development.

Human health is an objectively identifiable and overarching human interest shared by all the citizens of a country. The health of some people of a country may be improving as a result of development. But when that same development is also causing the deterioration in health of other people in that country, a serious issue of social equity arises. What level of death, disease and general deterioration of quality of life of its citizens will be officially supported by a country as the price of its development? What proportion of its citizens will pay what part of this price? Will they be asked whether they want to pay? Can they refuse to pay? The equal right to the protection of this overarching interest of all the people in their health cannot, in good conscience, be denied by a country's policymakers to all, or any group, of their citizens by asserting that either environmental or developmental considerations should override health considerations. Furthermore, both the environment and development are likely to benefit from a human health standard.

With regard to the environment, if human health as defined by WHO is well and universally protected, it is most likely that the environment will also be well served. For example, seawater that is clean enough for small children will be clean enough for marine life. With regard to development, careful attention to designing activities so as not to cause the deterioration of human health will ensure that the people are not enfeebled, because the cost of their ill health also burdens a country's economy and impedes its development.

CONCLUSION

The problems with managing environment and development in the coastal zone are not unique to the coasts. The inability to agree on an organizing principle underlies the functional paralysis that has so far resulted from attempts to address these issues in any context. The public health approach suggested here is not limited in its application to the coastal region either. This area would, however, be suitable to test this idea. Successful management of the coasts will provide all the examples, techniques and institutional mechanisms necessary for their extrapolation and application further inland. Problems of human health along coasts are remarkably similar for both "developed" and "developing" countries. Lastly, if the environment-development issue cannot be solved on the coast, it will be even more intractable inland.

REFERENCES

Boyle, A. E. (1992). Land-based sources of marine pollution: current legal regime. *Marine Policy* 16/1:20–35.

Bryceson, I., De Souza, F., Jehangeer, I., Ngoile, M. A. K., & Wynter, P. (1990). State of the marine environment in the East African region. UNEP Regional Seas Reports and Studies No. 113. UNEP, Nairobi, Kenya.

Cherfas, J. (1990). The fringe of the ocean—under siege from land. *Science, 248*:163–165.

Cormack, D. (1992). Land-based sources of marine pollution: scientific and technical background. *Marine Policy 16/1*:5–19.

Davies, T. (1991). Human health implications of pollution of the coastal ocean, in: *Proceedings of the National Forum on Ocean Conservation* (p. 78). The Smithsonian Institution, Washington, DC.

Fan, Z., & Côté, R. P. (1991). Population, development and marine pollution in China. *Marine Policy 15/3*:210–219.

Farrington, J. W. (1991). Sources of marine pollution, in: *Proceedings of the National Forum on Ocean Conservation*. (pp. 68–69). The Smithsonian Institution, Washington, DC.

Food and Agriculture Organization of the United Nations (FAO) (1991a). Development of Coastal Areas and Enclosed Seas, Research Paper No. 4. UN, Rome, Italy.

Food and Agriculture Organization of the United Nations (FAO) (1991b). Living Marine Resources, Research Paper No. 5. UN, Rome, Italy.

Juda, L., & Burroughs, R. H. (1990). The prospects for comprehensive ocean management. *Marine Policy 14/1*:23–35.

United Nations Joint Group of Experts on the Scientific Aspects of Marine Pollution (GESAMP) (1986). Environmental capacity: an approach to marine pollution prevention. UNEP Regional Seas Reports and Studies No. 80. UNEP, Nairobi, Kenya.

United Nations Joint Group of Experts on the Scientific Aspects of Marine Pollution (GESAMP) (1991). The State of the Marine Environment. UNEP Regional Seas Reports and Studies No. 115. UNEP, Nairobi, Kenya.

Laws, E. A., (1993). Aquatic Pollution, 2d ed. John Wiley & Sons, New York, NY.

Linden, O. (1990). Human impact on tropical coastal zones. *Nature & Resources 26*, 4:3–11.

Odum, E. P. (1971). *Fundamentals of Ecology*, 3rd ed. W.B. Saunders, Philadelphia, PA.

Olsen, S., Hale, L., DuBois, R., Robadue, D., & Foer G. (1989). Integrated resources management for coastal environments in the Asia-Near East region. The University of Rhode Island, Narragansett, RI.

Stumm, W. (1987). Impact of resource use on the hydrosphere and aquatic ecosystems, in: Dahlem Workshop on Resources and World Development. D. J. McLaren & B. J. Skinner (Ed.). Wiley Interscience, New York, N.Y.

United Nations General Assembly, Preparatory Committee for the United Nations Conference on Environment and Development (UNGA) (1991). Protection of Oceans, All Kinds of Seas Including Enclosed and Semi-enclosed Seas, Coastal Areas and the Protection, Rational Use and Development of Their Living Resources. Doc. A/CONF.151/PC/69, UN, New York, NY.

World Health Organization of the United Nations (WHO)(1991). *Our Planet, Our Health*. WHO, Geneva, Switzerland.

World Resources Institute (WRI)(1992–93). Oceans and Coasts, in: *World Resources 1992–93*. Basic Books, New York, NY.

15

The International Debt Crisis and Its Likely Impact on Health, Environment, and Development: The African Perspective

Adeniyi Osuntogun and Olu Oluwasola

INTRODUCTION

The issue of the world debt crisis has received considerable international attention in recent times and with the current drive toward sustainable development, the discussion is expected to remain with us for some time to come.

Little attention has hitherto been paid to the implication of the debt burden on health and health delivery among debtor nations. Still the interconnection between debt, economic development, health and environment have not been explored. Hence, this chapter attempts to fill this gap.

BACKGROUND TO THE DEBT CRISES IN SUB-SAHARAN AFRICAN COUNTRIES

Before the 1970s, the external debt situation of Third World countries, particularly the newly independent Sub-Saharan African nations, was relatively small. The loans were obtained from official sources with the majority of creditors being foreign governments and international finance institutions like the International Monetary Fund (IMF), the World Bank and Regional Development Banks (Todaro, 1989). Most of the loans were of the concessionary interest rate nature, that is, they were meant to expand the export base of the recipient nation. The private international commercial banks did not consider the newly independent African states creditworthy to be advanced loans. In any case, there were clients in the buoyant manufacturing industries and economies of Europe, North America and Japan, and Africa was given the least consideration by these commercial banks.

However, with the recycling of massive Arab petro-dollar surpluses in the early to middle 1970s, especially in the private capital market rather than the International Monetary Fund or The World Bank, private commercial banks began to play major roles in international lending. The extension of the credit to the Third World nations (particularly Sub-Saharan countries) was facilitated by two factors. In the first place, economic depression in the industrially developed countries following the 1973 oil shock made it possible for the private commercial banks to seek for clients outside the developed world.

Second, the larger lodgements of the petro-dollar fund provided larger funds that the depressed economy of the industrialized countries could not fully utilize (Todaro, 1989).

With huge capital reserves, the international credit agencies began to make imprudent lending to the Third World countries of Sub-Saharan Africa. In fact, they invited Sub-Saharan African governments to take loans even when the loans were unnecessary (as in the U.S.$1 billion and U.S.$1.145 billion jumbo loans advanced Nigeria in 1978 and 1979, respectively). Even where the loans were meant for unviable projects and/or contracted by "unviable" governments, the private commercial lending agents went ahead imprudently to advance loans. This has been the genesis of the Third World debt problems.

Sharp rises in interest rates from the concessionary rates of 2 percent to between 11 percent and 20 percent, the reduction of the average moratorium from 7.1 years to 2 years and the decline of average maturity period from 24.4 years to 7.1 years (World Bank, 1984–1985) followed the sourcing of funds from private international commercial banks. The changes in the size, structure and terms of external borrowing have had serious implications for developing countries, especially in Africa. In addition to the changing nature of external loans, the dollar experienced a sharp rise in value in the 1980s which exacerbated the debt situation.

Developed countries did not help the situation much. The development of protectionist measures in the industrialized countries and the highly volatile prices for primary commodities resulted in substantial loss in revenue to developing African countries. It must be pointed out that primary commodity prices were fixed at the world market, with little emphasis, if any, on the economic interest of developing countries.

Beside the external factors responsible for the debt problem in Sub-Saharan African countries, there are a number of internal factors that aided and sustained the debt issue.

Sub-Saharan African countries do not have the economic and administrative capacities as well as the necessary capital and infrastructural base required for the prudent and profitable utilization of loans. This factor, coupled with the burden of corrupt and inept leadership, has created a situation where most of the benefits from foreign loans (and in some cases the actual loan) have accrued mainly to the foreign creditors and the few local ruling elites in the debtor nation who have had a hand in the sourcing and execution of such loans.

The debtor nations often invest borrowed funds in projects that cannot earn substantial returns to defray the loan under the agreed terms. In fact in most cases, political considerations determine what, how and where such funds are invested. In the long run they ended up as "abandoned projects" or they become "white elephant projects" that produce nothing to show for the colossal amount of money wasted on them.

As a result of the absence of an indigenous capital base, most of the countries indulge in high levels of conspicuous consumption in relation to the country's resources. In fact, they live on the borrowed funds to satisfy their consumption needs instead of investing them to build the capital base. When it was evident for most of these indebted Sub-Saharan African countries that their fragile economy could not sustain their consumption pattern, most chose the alternative of borrowing rather than adapting their policies to meet the exigencies of unfavorable world market price fluctuation on their primary commodities. Finally, the value of the currencies of these countries could not be justified by their economic fortunes. Coupled with insular commercial policies domestic prices have been grossly distorted. This has resulted in economic imbalances, cheaper import goods with growing budget and current account deficits.

Currently, most Sub-Saharan African nations are grappling with heavy indebtedness with Nigeria and Cote D'Ivoire classified as belonging to the seventeen middle-income highly indebted countries whose probability of debt default is very high. There are twenty-six severely indebted low income countries of which twenty-four are in Sub-Saharan Africa (World Bank Report, 1990).

DIMENSIONS OF THE EXTERNAL DEBT CRISES

From 1970 to 1989, a period of 20 years, the total external indebtedness of developing nations increased from U.S.$68.4 billion to U.S.$1,262.8 billion (Todaro, 1989). This represents an increase of 1,846%. At least 10 percent of the total debt during the period under discussion was owed by Sub-Saharan African countries. By 1990, the total debt for Africa was U.S.$161 billion (United Nations Report, 1991).

Debt service payment among less developed countries increased from U.S.$11 billion to U.S.$158.8 billion. Interest payments and payments on principal seem to run neck-to-neck. In fact, in the years 1983 and 1984, interest payments exceeded principal payments. Sub-Saharan African debt service payments have been low. The highest debt service payments have resulted mainly from the inability of Sub-Saharan African nations to honor their debt obligation. Such overdue debts are rescheduled and capitalized which further increases the debt stock and thus the debt burden on these countries.

The debt service ratio as a percentage of export elucidates the stress of external debt on Africa. While the ratio for all less developed countries reached 19.1% in 1987, the Sub-Saharan African countries recorded up to 28.85% in 1985 and 25.5% in 1987. Analysis further shows that the debt export ratio of less developed countries increased from 99.4% in 1970 to 167.8% in 1986 and 139% in 1989. For Africa, the situation has been worse, reaching up to 239.7% in 1987 and 232% in 1989.

IMPLICATIONS OF THE CRISES ON DEVELOPMENT IN SUB-SAHARAN AFRICA

The debt problem has had a profound although deleterious effect on the Third World economies. It has effectively stunted economic development with attendant negative effects on economic growth; provision of social services and infrastructural facilities; the polity and general well-being of the people. In fact, it has condemned 80% of the world populace to an unprecedented poverty-stricken existence without a hope of getting out of the woods.

In Sub-Saharan Africa, the extent of these debt-related problems has reached a catastrophic level. As the United Nations Report (1991) emphasized, Africa's debt problem is a unique burden. About 60% of Africa's debt is owed to official creditors (both bilateral and multilateral). The remaining 40% is owed to private creditors and are on a short-term basis. The debt owed the private creditors amounts to $100 billion and servicing this debt costs Africa $14 billion annually.

Implications on the Environment

With 72% of the population of the Sub-Saharan African countries below the poverty line; with most governments not performing and even repressive; with increasing debt burden and decreasing revenue, environmental considerations are unaffordable luxuries. Thus the debt crises have had serious implications for the environment. Osuntogun (1992) pointed out that the debt crises have both eroded the capacity of the Third World countries to care for the environment, and led some developing countries to discountenance, continuing damage to the environment.

The World Watch Institute summed it up that "lack of capital has made it nearly impossible for developing countries to invest adequately in forest protection, soil conservation, irrigation improvement, more energy efficient technologies, or pollution control devices." Even worse, growing debts have compelled them to sell off natural resources, often their only source of foreign currency. Like a consumer forced to hock the family heirlooms to pay credit card bills, developing countries are plundering forests, decimating fisheries, and depleting water supplies—regardless of the long-term consequences.

Myers (1993) pointed out that many deep and pervasive environmental problems are associated with trade and the debt crisis. The need for foreign exchange to service debts and fund efforts to expand exports add to other pressures on natural resources. As people are pushed into poverty, in part by government measures to deal with debt, and as prices rise faster than incomes, the daily struggle for survival forces the poorest to exploit the ecologically fragile environments.

With the fall of primary commodity prices in the world market and thus dwindling revenue from these primary commodities, it is doubtful if Sub-Saharan African countries will be able to export their way out of the debt and poverty problems. As these countries increase their exploitation of their natural resources for dwindling foreign exchange to pay their debt, their environment will be worse for it while the debt obligation will not be met.

There will be a severe constraint on the demand side in the light of the difficulty in obtaining the necessary capital to build new power plants or expand existing ones. With most of the Sub-Saharan African countries at a phase of intensive capital development and at the same time under intensive pressure to service their foreign debts, it becomes difficult to divert scarce capital to achieve an environmental objective that at best will pay off only in the longer term. The International Monetary Fund enjoins countries adopting Structural Adjustment Programmes to remove subsidies on domestic and petroleum energy products. This has increasingly driven the poor masses who constitute the bulk of the populace (72%) to desecrate the forest in their bid to source alternative cheaper fuel woods.

The debt problem has increased the level of poverty in Africa which has led to serious degradation of both the rural and urban environment. In the

Sahel and Sudan regions of Sub-Saharan Africa, harvesting of fuel wood, shifting agriculture and animal husbandry have caused the extension of the desert into former grasslands. In the forest regions, poor agricultural practices and soil management has led to degradation, especially in the areas with young sedimentary rocks. Forest and animal species are adversely affected through lumbering, bush burning and shifting agriculture—all of which have roots in poverty and the inavailability of required capital to invest in the modern production methods that are environmentally friendly. Today, soils in Sub-Saharan countries are so desecrated that many of them have experienced severe food shortages and famine.

Implications on the Economy

The economies of most countries in Sub-Saharan Africa (excluding South Africa) have always been very fragile because they have been based on the export of single (or a few) primary commodities whose prices are determined at the international market. With a fall in the prices of these commodities, revenues accruing from the export trade to Sub-Saharan African countries have been substantially reduced.

In addition to dwindling export revenue, there has been a sharp decline in capital inflows in the form of new loans by banks. Debt service payments to private and official creditors resulted in a negative net outflow of nearly U.S.$30 billion between 1983 and 1990 (United Nations Report, 1991). Thus with dwindling resources, the ability to service the external debt and at the same time sustain domestic economic growth is severely constrained. The Swedish International Development Authority (1992) pointed out that indebtedness increases budget deficits in African countries which has not helped their already overburdened economies.

International financial institutions, notably the International Monetary Fund, have imposed a package of austerity measures debtor nations. In the main, the package requires the debtor nations to liberalize trade, adopt competitive exchange rates through the devaluation of their national currencies, cut public expenditure, freeze/cut wages, remove subsidies, privatize and commercialize and unale an across-the-board deregulation of the economy. This package, known as the Structural Adjustment Programme, has been adapted by several Sub-Saharan African countries including Nigeria, Ghana and Kenya.

The structural adjustment program has fuelled inflation through currency devaluation. High inflation rates lead to high interest rates which negatively affect investment and consequently lead to unemployment. While inflation has stifled industrial investment in Africa, the high cost component of imported raw materials and spare parts resulting from devaluation has forced many industries to close down and, consequently, employees retrench.

The debt burden has further aggravated deteriorating aggregate performance of the productive sectors of the economy, a chronic balance of payment deficit, a wide gap between government earnings and expenditure, the collapse of social services and infrastructure, a drastic decline in living standards and external assets. Economic problems and heavy indebtedness have led to political unrest in most parts of the region as governments (mostly military dictatorships) become repressive and high-handed to cover up their inability to satisfy the yearnings of the people. Political instability, chaotic interest rates and high inflation rates further discourage foreign investment and thus deprive the region of much needed capital inflows.

The growing external indebtedness and dwindling government earnings have intensified urban squalor and massive rural poverty. Expenditure in social programs like education, health, housing, welfare and social security has declined in nominal as well as real values. The transport sector has not been spared either. The debt problems and dwindling earnings have also led to heavy internal indebtedness as governments are forced to source for funds in the domestic capital market or fail to honor domestic debt obligations.

The poor countries lack the capacity to repay their debt, which makes it more difficult to obtain necessary funds to finance trade and development projects. It reduces their capacity to import goods and services required to lubricate the countries' industries, thus stifling export growth and capacity utilization. This combination of problems often forces the countries to fail to honor debt obligations which further reduces their creditworthiness in the international capital market. The Swedish International Development Authority (1992) observed that poor countries have to pay between 20% and 40% higher prices for imported goods compared to wealthier, more creditworthy countries as the former increasingly find it difficult to raise new loans and are precluded from dwindling short-term and commercial credit.

The debt problem consequently has attacked the Sub-Saharan African countries' economies on all fronts. Today the economic problems resulting from the debt problem have metamorphosed into political unrest that have plagued countries in West, East, Central and South Africa. In fact most of these countries have for some time now been dependent on foreign assistance to survive.

Implications on Health

The consequences of the debt problem on environment also has serious implications on health in Sub-Saharan African countries. The consequences have adversely affected the effective delivery of health services. Until the escalation of the debt crises, significant progress had been made. Infant mortality had fallen by 37% while life expectancy increased from 40 to 42 years. With the debt problem, revenue accruing to most govenments has diminished and resulted in a decrease in government expenditure on social services including health. At the same time, population growth has been rising by 3.2% a year while the gross national product per capita has been falling by an average of 2.8% a year from 1980 (UNDP Report, 1991).

Deforestation resulting from the desire of debtor nations to export timber or farm produce for foreign exchange has various impacts on the environment—which, in turn, directly or indirectly affect the health of people (particularly the rural and urban-poor). Important medicinal herbs are also not spared during lumbering or bush burning. This seriously affects the people below the poverty line who cannot afford the very high cost of modern health care. Deforestation also changes the ecosystem making the availability of edible bush-animals very scarce. This affects the protein intake of poor people who cannot afford the very high cost of beef or fish.

Deforestation has also adversely affected the ground water, level which is the main source of potable water for the people in the drier part of the Sudan. As desertification encroaches, even the few surface water available dries. This affects farm crops and cattle as well as the availability of portable water which in turn leads to many water-borne diseases. In fact people in Mali, Niger, and Chad have been forced by water shortage and other related problems to migrate into more humid countries like Nigeria where they ended up as destitutes and beggars.

Lack of investment capital for pollution control has caused many water sourses supplying the rural folks with drinking water downstream to be polluted and, as a result, many health hazards like cholera become prevalent in most rural areas.

The degradation of land affects the productive capacity of the soil which in turn affects the food crop production since modern farm inputs are not easily available. The result is that there are severe food shortages, famines, diseases and deaths in many parts of Sub-Saharan Africa.

SOLVING SUB-SAHARAN AFRICAN COUNTRIES DEBT PROBLEMS

The world is in agreement that the only way to salvage the economies of the Sub-Saharan African countries is to find a solution to their over U.S.$160 billion foreign debt and over U.S.$25 billion annual debt service payments. Africa's total debt is virtually equal to her entire annual economic output. This has had its effect on the social, political and economic cohesion and development of Africa. In fact, many development-oriented aid and multilateral assistance packages have failed as a result of the socio-political and economic problems engendered by foreign as well as domestic indebtedness.

The initial attempts at solving Africa's debt problem were initiated by the Western capitalist countries and a number of proposals were put forward. These included the Baker plan; the Bradley proposal; the Herrhausen proposal; and the Lawson plan. These plans and proposals were ostensibly made to avoid payment default by the Third World nations. They all involved long-term rescheduling of Third World debts (with the capitalization of interest which further increases the quantum of debt), accessing more loans to debtor nations (the economies of these countries cannot sustain new loans) and the adoption of the International Monetary Fund brand of the Structural Adjustment Program.

Structural Adjustment Programmes involve control of credits and public expenditure; reduction (removal) of subsidies on food and petroleum products; lowering of real wages, cutbacks in public services, export promotion, devaluation of currency and liberalization of trade. All these have had a negative effect on the economies and environments of Sub-Saharan African countries.

Poverty, poor standards of public health and inadequate education as well as structural weakness (Swedish International Development Agency, 1992) in the economies of the Sub-Saharan African countries seriously hinder structural adjustment. In fact available evidence in Nigeria has shown that it has increased the level of poverty to an unprecedented level with serious negative implications on all the sectors (except the speculative financial sector) of the economy. Thus, structural adjustment has not succeeded in "bailing" out poor countries from their debt problem. In fact, the burden of debt itself hinders economic reforms while increasing poverty makes it impossible for people in such countries to bear the pains of the International Monetary Fund-touted adjustment program.

However, the industrial world since the Toronto Summit of 1988 had written off or reduced certain categories of African debts. Up to 1990, the cancellations totalled about U.S.$7.6 billion (United Nations, 1991). However, the benefits of such initiatives have been limited because of small numbers of beneficiary countries and the magnitude of their debt burden.

Under the Trinidad terms the stock of eligible debt is to be reduced by two-thirds with repayment on the remaining debt spread over twenty-five years.

To solve the debt problem effectively, the creditor nations must reduce substantially the stock of debt by the cancellation of all official bilateral debts as well as semi-official debts. There should also be a substantial reduction in the commercial debts while interest rates should be lowered.

Second, there is the need for global pressure on the indebted Sub-Saharan African countries to democratize. Inept, corrupt and military dictatorship should give way to democractic reforms.

It is important to check capital flight, the adoption of unsustainable economic policies and the increasing repression of the people who need to be reassured by their country's leadership to be able to adjust to the pains of the economic reforms.

Finally, the Sub-Saharan African countries should adjust their economies, making ways for the reforms that will promote domestic production and consumption of goods and services, development of indigenous skills and technology and the alleviation of poverty. In calling for economic reform, it does not necessarily mean a religious adherence to the International Monetary Fund-touted conditionalities. Each debtor nation must identify its own priorities and adjust its economy accordingly.

REFERENCES

Myers Norman (Ed.) (1993). *GAIA: An Atlas of Planet Management*. Anchor Books.

Osuntogun, A. (1992). Energy, Trade, Debt and the Environment. Paper submitted for the Meeting of National Programme Directors of the LEAD Programme : New York. October 26–28, 1992.

SIDA (1992). *A Way Out of the Debt Trap: Proposal to Relieve the Debt of the Poorest and Most Indebted Countries.* Swedish International Development Authority (SIDA) (June 1992) Publication.

Todaro, M. P. (1989). *Economic Development in the Third World,* (4th edition). Longman.

United Nations Report (1991). *African Debt: The Case for Debt Relief.* Produced by the Africa Recovery Unit/CPMD Department of Public Information. U.N.O., New York.

World Bank (1991). *World Debt Tables: 1990–1991 Edition*. (World Bank, Washington, DC).

16

The Impact of Military Activities on Development, Environment, and Health

Victor W. Sidel and Gurinder S. Shahi

INTRODUCTION

Wars among nations or within nations (the latter often called "civil disturbances," "civil wars" or, more recently, "low-intensity wars") interfere with development by directly damaging people, land, and infrastructure, by disrupting social organization, by displacing people and by diverting human and financial resources that might have been employed for development. Wars pollute the environment, of the nation in which the war is being fought as well as that of nearby nations or even the global environment. In addition to their indirect effects on health through delayed economic and social development, damaged environment, and diversion of resources that might have been used for medical care services and for public health, wars, of course, lead directly to the killing and maiming of both combatants and civilian populations (Levy & Sidel, 1996).

Even when wars are not actively being fought, military preparation and the supporting economic, social and political climate may slow or reverse development, cause environmental damage, and harm health by diversion of needed resources and by psychological trauma. In this analysis the term "military activities" will therefore be used to include (1) the active use of weapons in war, civil disturbances, civil war and low-intensity war (which we will summarize as "war"); (2) weapons development, production, testing, storage, transport and disassembly and disposal, and military training ("military preparation"); and (3) the prevalence of military-oriented attitudes and practices within a nation or in the world ("militarism").

Many societies that appear to be at peace are in fact preoccupied with the possibility of war and with preparations for war. This was the case, for example, in the United States and the Soviet Union between the end of World War II and the fall of communism in Eastern Europe and the former Soviet Union. Although there was no official war, the era was marked by the greatest arms race that the world has ever known, with the United States spending approximately 7% and the U.S.S.R. approximately 12 percent of their respective GDPs in attempting to ensure parity or superiority in conventional weapons and weapons of mass destruction and in supplying arms to the other nations. In the United States, the period led to the build-up of over 12,000 nuclear warheads with an explosive equivalent to more than 6 billion tons of TNT, one thousand times more than the explosive power of all the weapons used during World War II. The Soviet Union built nuclear weapons in similar numbers and similar explosive power. In both countries production and testing of nuclear weapons, and of chemical weapons as well, caused severe environmental pollution. Furthermore the investment in these and other weapons came at the cost of economic and social development. The consequences in the U.S.S.R. were worse than in the U.S. with people living with constant shortages of basic necessities as resources were funneled to keeping military production and military operations functioning (Sivard, 1993).

Even in the wealthiest countries, investment in arms diverts resources that could have been used for investments in health, education or socioeconomic infrastructure instead of the economically unproductive effort of developing ever more powerful weapons of terror and destruction. Japan and West Germany in contrast were constrained from military spending for any purpose other than defense after World War II; their constitutions forbade the development of any offensive capability, a requirement imposed on these countries by the victorious Allied nations for their roles in initiating and continuing the war. West Germany and Japan spent less than 2 percent of their respective GDPs on the military and used resources that would otherwise have been diverted to military activities to build the second and third largest economies in the world and impressive social infrastructures.

The situation in the United States and U.S.S.R. described as the "Cold War" was not unique to these countries. Recent history is full of examples of countries that lived in states of heightened tension with each other without actually going to war. Israel and the Arab states fought three short but intense wars in the last three decades, but spent much of the rest of the time building up military capability (often supported by the U.S. or the U.S.S.R.). Similarly, Pakistan and India have seen similar rivalries build up, with flare-ups having occurred at least four times.

Sometimes the threat of war comes not from outside the country but from within. This problem tends to arise in situations where there is intense rivalry for power by conflicting political parties, ethnic groups or egos, or where countries are irregular patchworks artificially kept as one (often a legacy of colonial history) but in fact consist of sharply different social, cultural, religious and ethnic groups that may feel little or no sense of common destiny. Africa, the Middle East and South Asia, for example, include many such artificially carved-up entities. Colonialists divided the land according to their self-interest and signed treaties reshaping "their" territories with scant regard to the fact that some peoples had their homelands divided while in other cases different peoples were being forced to live together in one country in a manner previously unknown to them. The Kurds, for example, now find themselves and their land split to form parts of Iraq, Turkey, and Iran. Eritreans find themselves living in Ethiopia. Nigeria is a land with over 40 tribal groups, with three major tribes, working hard to maintain unity as part of a legacy left them by the British. India, a hodge-podge of hundreds of kingdoms and principalities is today styled "the world's largest democracy," but ethnic and racial tensions flare up from time to time as they have during the last decade in Punjab, Assam and Kashmir.

The republics of the former Soviet Union, which were a product of colonial domination of many racial and ethnic groups by Russians, now find themselves trying to sort out the impact of years of suppression of cultural identities and political self-determination. "Ethnic cleansing," which has devastated the former Yugoslavia and threatens to do the same in several Central Asian republics, is the most extreme and destructive manifestation of attempts to express cultural, social, and religious self-determination.

THE IMPACT OF MILITARY ACTIVITIES ON DEVELOPMENT

In addition to the extensively reported direct impact of the weapons used in war, other military activities divert people, financial resources and national will from development, environmental protection, and the promotion and protection of health. Indeed in many ways the most devastating impact of military activities is the diversion to military purposes of resources that might have been used to improve the quality of life, the social and physical environment and the health of the people of the world (see Box 16.1). Between 1945 and 1992, over 20 trillion dollars (valued in 1992 dollars) were spent on the world's military forces. Military expenditures worldwide during the 1980s climbed to almost one trillion dollars

Box 16.1—The Opportunity Costs of Diversion of Resources to Military Activities

Small reallocations of the funds being spent on arms to spending on health could produce enormous benefits. The annual total of $1 trillion is equivalent to $2.5 billion each day, over $100 million each hour, almost $2 million each minute, and $30,000 each second (Sidel, 1985).

- The cost of one hour's world spending on arms is equivalent to the entire cost of the successful 20-year effort to eradicate smallpox from the earth.
- The cost of three hours of world arms spending would pay for all of the World Health Organization's annual budget.
- The cost of one half-day of world arms spending annually could pay for the full immunization of all the children in the world against the common infectious diseases.
- The cost of four days of world military spending would pay for a five-year program to control malaria, probably the world's greatest cause of death due to illness.
- The cost of three weeks of world arms spending would pay for primary health care for every child in the poor countries of the world, including safe water supplies and full immunizations.

Source: Sidel, 1985.

annually, an amount in constant dollars close to three times the level of 1960. These resources, had they been devoted to human welfare, would have permitted an enormous increase in economic development, in improvement in the quality of life and therefore in the preservation of world peace and security (Sivard, 1993).

Annual military spending in the United States rose steadily during the 1980s from $140 billion to almost $300 billion annually in current dollars. After correction for inflation and population growth, this translates to a growth in spending on the military for each U.S. resident from approximately $800 to $1,200 annually during the decade. The $2 trillion spent on the military during the decade contributed significantly to a ballooning of the federal budget deficit, resulting in the U.S. national debt expanding from less than 1 trillion dollars in 1980 to nearly 4 trillion dollars today (Sivard, 1993). The diversion of resources to finance the enormous military expenditures and the resulting debt have severely curtailed expansion of governmental appropriations for environmental protection and for health and human services. During the decade of the 1980s, as U.S. military spending (corrected for inflation) rose 46 percent, spending for human welfare fell precipitously: federal appropriations for housing fell 77 percent, for education 70 percent, for employment and training 48 percent, for mass transportation 33 percent, and for child nutrition 19 percent.

The U.S. economy provides one of the world's highest standards of living, but beneath this veneer of wealth lies the reality of America's being destitute. The gulf between the rich and poor has widened. Some 29 million people lived below the poverty line in 1980; by 1992 that number had grown to 36.9 million, 14.5 percent of the population (U.S. Bureau of the Census, 1993). The median income of all families with children and parents under 30 years old fell 32 percent from 1973 to 1990. One-quarter of children under 6 and one-fifth of those under 18 lived in poverty; nearly 50 percent of black children under 18 were poor (Sidel, 1992; The State of America's Children, 1992).

Research and development is vital to improving public health and the quality of life. In the U.S., governmental funding for research on health and human services pales in comparison to funding for military research. Just as a growing proportion of the federal budget has been devoted to the military, so too has the bulk of research and development funding. Of course, along with the diversion of revenue from support for needed research, arms spending diverts highly trained people from working to improve health and the quality of life to working on military projects—in the 1980s, as many as 30 percent of U.S. scientists and engineers worked on such military projects (Sidel, 1988).

An even greater impact was felt in the Soviet Union during this period because although its arms spending was comparable to that of the U.S., its GDP was far lower. The proportionately greater diversion of funds to military purposes did proportionately greater damage to its economy and was one of the major factors in its economic collapse (Gorbachev, 1987).

Globally, the almost $1 trillion spent on arms annually in the 1980s by the world's nations was equivalent to the annual incomes of 2.6 billion people in the 44 poorest nations, one-half the world's population (Sivard, 1991; Grant, 1992). World expenditures on weapons *research* alone exceed the combined spending on developing new energy technologies, improving human health, raising agriculture productivity, and controlling pollutants (Brown, 1986).

UNICEF called the 1980s "The Decade of Despair." For the world's poorest people, average incomes dropped by 10 percent to 25 percent. In the 37 poorest countries, spending on health was reduced by 50 percent and on education by 25 percent. In over 50 nations, primary school enrollment fell (Grant, 1992). It has been estimated that close to one billion people (nearly one in every five living persons) live in absolute poverty, 780 million people are undernourished, 850 million are illiterate, 1.5 billion have no access to medical facilities, an equally large number are unemployed, and one billion people are inadequately housed (Report of the International Conference on the Relationship Between Disarmament and Development, 1987).

THE IMPACT OF MILITARY ACTIVITIES ON THE ENVIRONMENT

Impact on the Physical Environment

The United States military establishment is the world's largest "industry." In 1986 the DOD estimated that the military produced about 400,000 tons of hazardous waste annually (Hazardous Waste, 1989). Since the DOD does not comply with the Environmental Protection Agency's Toxics Release Inventory, there is no way accurately to evaluate the total amounts released. Some authorities place the figure as high as 500,000 tons—more than the top five U.S. civilian chemical companies combined. In the U.S., an estimated two-thirds of chlorofluorocarbon-113 emissions, depleters of the ozone layer, are contributed by the military (Defending the Environment, 1989; Ruff, 1992; Siegel, 1991; 1992; Shulman, 1992). Among the DOD and DOE installations that contain identified toxic waste sites hazardous to public health and the environment, approximately 100 are listed as Superfund National Priority List sites—the most dangerous hazardous waste sites—and few such sites have been designated "cleaned up" (Military Installations, 1992).

Military bases generate large quantities of a wide variety of toxic substances, including fuels, pesticides, solvents, polychlorinated biphenyls, and phenols. Tanks and airplanes are washed with caustic cleaning compounds and solvents that are drained onto the ground or into ditches. Electroplating shops that repair metal parts for military equipment generate cyanides, acids, and heavy metals. Chemical propellant bags used to fire artillery shells at firing ranges are regularly burned at military bases (Defending the Environment, 1989; Siegel, 1991; Shulman, 1992).

Although the full details are still not known, military bases in the territories of the former U.S.S.R. and its Warsaw Pact allies were no less destructive to their surroundings. There is evidence that controls on environmental despoilment were even weaker than in the United States and that the pollution caused by military activities may have been even greater.

The examples above refer largely to the environmental impact of "peacetime" military activities. At times of war, the environment can be devastated by the impact of explosives, incendiaries, and defoliants which can destroy animals and crops, crater the land, and denude vegetation. In addition, war prevents sound environmental management. The displacement of massive numbers of people may cause additional ecologic damage (Ruff, 1992; Westing, 1984a).

In Vietnam an estimated 2.2 billion hectares of forest and farmland were denuded as a direct result of bombing, mechanized land clearing, napalming and defoliation by the United States and South Vietnam. Some 72 million liters of herbicides were used to destroy food crops and to deny forest cover to Vietcong forces; one of them, Agent Orange, was sprayed over 35 percent of southern Vietnam between 1961 and 1971. Dioxin contained in the spray persists, with elevated levels still found in soil, food, wildlife, human breast milk, and adipose tissue. An estimated 20 million square meters of commercial timber, 135,000 hectares of rubber plantations, and 124,000 hectares of mangroves were destroyed. Restoration and regeneration from this massive environmental damage is still at an early stage (Ruff, 1992; Westing, 1984a,b).

The United States used about 14 million tons of high explosives in Vietnam, creating approximately 25 million bomb craters, covering about 200,000 hectares. Transport, agriculture, and forestry were disrupted; many craters filled with stagnant water, forming breeding sites for malaria-carrying mosquitoes (Ruff, 1992).

Vietnamese hospitals continue to report new victims, many of them children, from left-over munitions and mines (Ruff, 1992). Death and injury from land mines in Cambodia also continue to occur (Land Mines, 1991). Land mines left over from the 1988–1991 civil war have caused similar casualties in Northern Somalia (Hidden Enemies, 1992). The problem affects a wide range of countries including Afghanistan, Angola, Cambodia, El Salvador, Ethiopia, Iraq, Mozambique, Nicaragua, Northern Somalia, Vietnam, and former Yugoslavia. It is estimated that at least 85 million and possibly more than 100 million unexploded land mines currently lie scattered through at least 62 countries (Arms Project, 1993).

In the Persian Gulf, ecologic damage was caused by bombing and by oil-related pollution. The air war in the Gulf lasted for a month and a half; the ground war was over in 100 hours. Still, in this short time more weapons were reportedly used than in the protracted Vietnam war. In what may have been the most intense air war in history, it has been estimated that some 250,000 individual weapons were dropped by aircraft—or roughly 6,000 weapons a day—including some 60,000–80,000 cluster bombs, scattering 12–16 billion "bomblets." In February 1991, Iraq ignited 752 oilwell fires in Kuwait; these were extinguished more rapidly than had been expected, but the health and environmental impact of the smoke produced is still largely unknown. In addition, huge pools of oil caused by leakage from sabotaged wells that did not ignite still cover large parts of Kuwait; the oil penetrates the soil and kills plants, birds, and insects (Ibrahim, 1992; Arkin, 1991).

Impact on the Social Environment

Huge military budgets and the military's access to control of a nation's weaponry have increased military participation in social and governmental activities in many countries, aided in many cases, at least indirectly, by professional training and equipment provided by the major powers. In an analysis of 112 developing countries, the number under some form of military rule has shown a rise from 26 in 1960 to 52 in 1982 to 61 in 1992 (Sivard, 1993).

Military rule tends to be associated with militarization of the economy and with repression and human rights violations, with concomitant increases in the danger of war and also of domestic repression. Countries under military control tend to have many more people under arms than other countries and have, on average, experienced six times as many years of war than have other less-developed countries (LDCs) (Sivard, 1993).

Militarized governments appear to survive through the use of tactics of fear and repression to "subdue the opposition, bottle up change, and ensure the control of resources that nourish power." In fully 58 of the 61 countries under military control in 1992, the most extreme forms of repression, including torture, brutality, disappearances, and political killings were used by the authorities against their own citizens. While other LDCs cannot claim to have unblemished human rights records, at least such practices are not "institutionalized" and abuses tend to occur much less frequently in countries not under military control (Sivard, 1993).

Impact on Social Infrastructure and Carrying Capacity

The ability of a country to provide adequately for its people requires conditions of peace and the development of necessary infrastructure (Shahi, 1994). People in developing countries are much more likely to find their lives disrupted by natural disasters, civil strife and war than are people in industrialized countries.

As explained in Box 16.2, such events can also reduce the carrying capacity of affected countries and territories, lead to increased migration

Box 16.2—Carrying Capacity and Refugees

The carrying capacity of a region or territory refers to the maximum population of a given species (for our purpose, humans) that it will hold sustainably at any given level of technological, social and health care input. In traditional human societies, carrying capacity tended to be low because of the occurrence (from time to time) of famines, epidemics and wars which tended to keep population levels down (Shahi, 1994). These societies tended to be characterized by high rates of mortality and of fertility. With increasing knowledge and technological competence (through the application of improved understanding of public health needs, agricultural innovation, better housing and nutrition, etc.) modern society has been relatively successful at removing the barriers to carrying capacity—hence causing carrying capacity to rise—the result being expressed as a rapid fall in mortality and an unprecedented rise in human populations (Shahi, 1994).

With development, improvements in quality of life, rising affluence, and associated changes in social and cultural values and norms, populations undergo a "demographic transition" characterized by low mortality and low fertility and population levels tend to stabilize as they have done in the moderately developed countries (MDCs) (Shahi, 1994).

The high carrying capacity of modern agricultural lands depend largely on farmers having good soil, access to high quality seeds, fertilizers to supplement fertility of the soil, etc. A substantial part of agricultural produce—the excess carrying capacity—is "exported" to urban areas where large numbers of people are concentrated in relatively small areas (Shahi, 1994).

Urban centers are fairly recent innovations in anthropological terms—becoming commonplace only within the last 5,000 or so years and depending on excess capacity in agriculture to help sustain the urban residents. It is important to note that these urban areas have little or no "intrinsic" carrying capacity—it being generally impossible to produce much food in cities (Shahi, 1994). They depend, therefore, almost completely on living through the import of food and other necessities (either from rural hinterlands or from outside the region or country). At times of peace, it is difficult enough to provide for the needs of people—this is especially so in developing countries with their rapidly growing populations and much lower levels of affluence (and, hence, their lower "reserve" capacity to deal with emergency situations).

Box 16.2—(*Continued*)

From time to time, the occurrence of natural disasters such as droughts or earthquakes can severely disrupt the lines of supply of food and other necessities—resulting in major outbreaks of disease, starvation, etc. Man-generated emergencies—largely through the impact of militarism and social disruption—can have similarly difficult consequences.

In effect, these disasters temporarily reduce the total carrying capacity of the land—severely restricting access to food and water supply, disrupting the means of livelihood of the affected people through which they acquire the resources to purchase food and water, and increasing the likelihood of outbreaks of epidemics of infectious disease, all of which tend to lead, if not quickly resolved, to massive suffering, starvation and death, and serve as important push factors for the creation of refugees.

from these trouble spots, and the creation of large number of refugees. Migrating from one's home is never easy. It means disrupting oneself from one's social and cultural roots and placing oneself in totally alien and even frightening environments. The push of poverty and the pull of opportunity already draw millions of people from rural areas to urban areas within countries. Migrating across national borders can be even more difficult. But devastation of home, breakdown of social infrastructure associated with military activities, and inability to provide for one's basic needs are too often the forces that push individuals over the brink.

War can be devastating to a country, with thousands of soldiers ransacking the farms and taking away the produce of farmers, their primary source of livelihood. Laying of mines, curfews and destruction of roads, bridges, infrastructure often mean that farmers have no way to get what is left of their produce to market, often resulting in its spoilage. Lack of access to fertilizers and seed often means that farmers tend to overburden the soil and lead to depletion of its nutrients. With crop yields declining and few opportunities to earn a decent living, rural families often have little choice but to migrate from their fields in search of alternative means of livelihood. When they get to the cities, breakdown of infrastructure (such as lack of communications, social welfare systems and roads, lack of access to safe drinking water supplies, and lack of food in the city due to problems in bringing it from the countryside and failure of foreign ships or planes to bring it in) means that the urban population often starves. The haves can take their possessions and wealth and escape to a country that will take them. The have-nots end up as starving refugees, such as those we have seen coming out of Somalia and Ethiopia, where civil war combined with natural drought to devastate the lives of those affected.

THE IMPACT OF MILITARY ACTIVITIES ON HEALTH

The physical trauma caused by the use on human beings of weapons of war is obvious. Sivard has identified 149 wars, defined as armed conflicts involving one or more governments and causing the deaths of 1,000 or more people per year, from 1945 to 1992. She estimates there were 23 million deaths due to these wars, 7,500,000 deaths among military personnel and 14,500,000 deaths among civilians (Sivard, 1993).

Some of the other direct medical effects of use of weaponry are less clear. For example, a startling rise in childhood cancer cases, leukemia being the most prevalent, in post-war Iraq has been reported by Dr. Eric Hoskins and a Harvard study team. The team suggests this increase may be attributed to an armor-piercing shell, commonly used during the Gulf War, made from depleted uranium. Literally thousands of these "penetrators" are reported to be scattered throughout the Iraqi landscape. Made from the depleted by-product of enriched uranium used in nuclear reactor rods and warheads, the weapon is used because of its extreme density and its ability to burst into flames on impact. Researchers have noted that the potential danger lies in the after-effects when the depleted uranium shell is left to oxidize in the open air. Uranium particles may easily enter the body causing cell damage which can lead to cancer.

Among all the factors that interact to cause illness, which include genetic, infectious, degenerative, and traumatic factors, it is widely accepted that social, economic, and other environmental causes are the most important (McKeown, 1988). These factors, of course, include poverty, homelessness, hunger, lack of education, and lack of family and community support. Similarly, among all the factors that lead to failure to obtain needed health and human services, the most important are social, economic, and environmental. These barriers include geographic maldistribution of services, and racial, sexual and economic discrimination. Studies in developing countries demonstrate, for example, that the most important determinants of infant mortality include household income and literacy of the mother. The health effects arising from the diversion of human and financial resources from health and human services to preparation for war, while less obvious, may thus be even greater than the direct physical impact of war.

Similar consequences have been seen in industrialized countries in which resources have been diverted to preparation for war. In the United States, for example, the gap in health indices between haves and have-nots have been increasing (Sidel, 1991b). Since poor children are less likely to be immunized at an early age or, are less likely to have adequate nutrition or housing, or to use primary medical care in a timely fashion, their rates of morbidity and mortality are higher than for well-off children. Even before they are born, their mothers are less likely to have adequate nutrition or timely prenatal care. As a result, the rates of premature birth, of low-birth weight, of infant mortality, of infectious disease morbidity and mortality are higher for poor children (The State of America's Children, 1992). Studies in the United States of the impact of the Women's, Infants', and Children's Supplemental Feeding Program (WIC) demonstrate that measures to overcome social and economic deprivation among pregnant women, mothers, and their infants can make an enormous difference in the outcome of pregnancy and the growth and development of children (Rush, 1988), yet fewer than fifty percent of those who are eligible for these programs are receiving benefits. Resources that might have been used for these programs were instead diverted to military activities.

Along with the impact of military activities on physical health, there is substantial evidence of their impact on psychological health. Since 1980 the American Psychiatric Association has recognized post-traumatic stress disorder (PTSD) as a specific defined diagnostic category. This diagnosis officially recognizes the psychic reactions long noted among concentration camp survivors and other victims of war on violence, replacing less precise diagnoses such as "combat neurosis" and "shell-shock." During World War I the British Army reported that 7 to 10 percent of the officers and 3 to 4 percent of the other ranks suffered "mental breakdown." The psychological impact of war or even threat of war on civilian populations, particularly on children, may be even more devastating (UNICEF, 1985; Gersons, 1992).

V. THE IMPACT OF SPECIFIC TYPES OF WARS OR WEAPONS SYSTEMS

A. "Low-Intensity" War

Armed conflicts within a country, which were usually called "civil wars" or "civil disturbances" in the past, have since World War II taken on a new intensity in many countries as a result of the military support of one side or the other in the conflict by one of the major world powers. Such wars, which include those in Vietnam, in Nicaragua and in Afghanistan, have been called "low-intensity conflicts" or "low-intensity wars" (Klare, 1988; Morelli, 1984). Such wars can be as destructive or even more destructive to the economic and social fabric of a nation as overt war between nations (Sociedad Nicaragüense, 1993).

"Conventional" Weapons

The extensive destructiveness, either intended or "collateral," of the use of what are now called "conventional weapons" (in contrast to "weapons of mass destruction") harms the environment and delays or reverses development (through the destruction of infrastructure) in addition to inflicting direct injury to humans. Conventional weapons include explosives, incendiaries and projectiles. In addition, new weapons such as fuel–air explosives (FAE), are included in this category. Since herbicides and defoliants are not usually considered chemical weapons within the meaning of arms control agreements, they must (perversely) be classified as "conventional" as well. The problems posed by landmines, discussed in an earlier section, must be considered part of conventional war as well.

Nuclear Weapons

Use

The short-term effects of use of nuclear weapons on human populations are well-known from studies of the effects of the nuclear-fission-based bombs used to destroy Hiroshima and Nagasaki in 1945. There has fortunately been no experience with the use of nuclear fusion-based bombs in war but there are extensive estimates, based on nuclear tests in the atmosphere and underground, of the impact of the use of these much more powerful weapons that can generate an explosive power one thousand times or more as great as those used over Japan.

The effects of nuclear weapons are caused by:

1. *Blast*—exposure to the mechanical force of the explosion, traveling at the speed of sound;
2. *Heat*—exposure to intense heat, traveling at the speed of light, and to the effects of massive fires (conflagrations and fire storms); and
3. *Radiation*—immediate exposure to gamma ray and neutron flux generated by the initial nuclear explosion and long-term exposure to the radionuclides produced by the explosion.

Factors determining the extent of the medical effects produced by a nuclear explosion include the size and type of weapons used, the distance of the explosion above the hypocenter on the earth's surface, the distance of human beings from the hypocenter, the weather conditions and the nature of the terrain. In the case of nuclear explosions near human populations, the number of casualties will be immense and barriers to effective medical care enormous. The most important of the barriers to care are the sheer numbers of casualties and the fact that the explosion itself will have destroyed hospitals and other medical facilities and killed or injured large numbers of medical personnel (Leaf, 1986; Solomon, 1986; Sidel, 1962; World Health Organization, 1987).

The potential climatic and environmental consequences of use of nuclear weapons include the cooling of the earth's surface due to atmospheric soot and dust (often called "nuclear winter") (Turco, 1990), depletion of stratospheric ozone, radioactive fallout, and chemical pollution. Climatic effects may persist for years, and ecological effects may last decades or more. These consequences will place major stress on organized agriculture and aquatic and terrestrial plant and animal life.

The amount and type of climatic and environmental effects, of course, depends on the number, type and pattern of use of nuclear weapons, the season at the time of the use of weapons, the amount and character of the materials ignited or injected into the atmosphere and other uncertainties. Mechanisms of prompt and delayed scavenging and removal of pollutants from the atmosphere are also important.

With regard to the long-term impact on health, much has been written about psychological damage suffered by survivors of the bombing of Hiroshima and Nagasaki. In addition immunosuppression may be caused by increased levels of ionizing radiation, enhanced UV-B due to ozone depletion, burns and trauma, malnutrition, and psychological effects of bereavement and depression. Epidemic and endemic disease may also be increased by sanitation deficiencies, proliferation of vectors of disease, and effects of malnutrition and immunosuppression (Lifton, 1986; Schell, 1982; Solomon, 1986).

Production

Environmental risks and damage related to the nuclear weapons production cycle include those associated with uranium mining and processing, production of weapons-grade plutonium, assembly and transportation of nuclear weapons, nuclear testing in the atmosphere and underground, storage of nuclear weapons, and disassembly of nuclear weapons with the required disposal of uranium, plutonium, tritium and the chemical triggers.

In the United States, the Department of Energy (DOE) administers directly or through private contracts a complex of over 280 facilities in 20 sites located in 13 states. The land mass of the complex comprises 3,350 square miles, more than the areas of the states of Delaware and Rhode Island combined (Geiger, 1992).

Construction of nuclear weapons has caused vast environmental damage and hazards to health. The production of a single pound of plutonium creates 150 gallons of high-level radioactive waste together with hazardous chemicals, more than 25,000 gallons of low- to intermediate-level waste, and more than 1.1 million gallons of contaminated cooling water (Renner, 1991). A recent report by a special commission of International Physicians for the Prevention of Nuclear War and the Institute for Energy and Environmental Research documents the ways in which the production of plutonium for nuclear warheads has left the U.S. and the U.S.S.R., and to a lesser extent the other nuclear powers, burdened with millions of tons of radioactive waste products (Hu, 1992). Enormous environmental problems have been identified at U.S. nuclear weapons production facilities (Defending the Environment, 1989; Complex Cleanup, 1991).

Similar problems of radioactive and other toxic pollution from nuclear weapons production are known to have occurred in the territory of the former Soviet Union. In October 1992, the Russian affiliate of the International Physicians for the Prevention of Nuclear War (IPPNW) released *The Atom Declassified* (Yemelyanenkov, 1992) documenting publicly for the first time all the major sites in the former U.S.S.R. affected by nuclear weapons production. IPPNW, in 1995, sponsored the publication of *Nuclear Wastelands*, an extensive documentation of pollution from nuclear weapons production in the U.S., Russia, and other countries (Makhijani et al., 1995).

A recent report by the Physicians Task Force on the Health Risks of Nuclear Weapons Production, organized by Physicians for Social Responsibility, analyzed the deficiencies in studies conducted by the DOE of disease and death in the nuclear work force. The report demonstrates that the DOE studies offer no firm basis for the DOE's official position that the health of workers and the public has been adequately protected (Geiger, 1992).

3. *Testing*

Approximately 1,900 nuclear test explosions have been conducted since 1945 by six nations (the United States, Soviet Union, Great Britain, France, China and India) at some 35 sites around the world. Until 1963 the tests were conducted on sites open to the atmosphere, with production of radionuclides that were carried by prevailing winds all over the world.

reaching the ground as radioactive "fallout." Collection of children's deciduous teeth showed them to contain radioactive strontium-90, which could only have come from the tests. Iodine-131, with a short half-life that permitted the timing of its deposition, was detected in the food chain leading to the milk supply. The clear danger to humans, particularly to children, led to a worldwide protest against atmospheric nuclear test explosions.

In 1963 the Limited Nuclear Test Ban Treaty, which banned nuclear weapons test explosions open to the atmosphere, in space and under water, was signed by over 100 countries. The U.S., U.S.S.R., and Great Britain, signatories to the treaty, moved their tests underground. France and China did not sign the treaty; France continued nuclear test explosions open to the atmosphere until 1974 and China until 1980. Underground tests, of which there have already been 1400, vent radiation into the atmosphere and deposit underground large amounts of long-lived radionuclides such as strontium-90, cesium-137 and plutonium-239. Some of these deposits will undoubtedly eventually make their way into the biosphere by leaching into groundwater or through other leakage (Robbins, 1991).

Disassembly

Not only production, testing, storage and use but even the process of destruction of weapons can lead to environmental and consequent health damage. In 1989 the U.S. Senate expressed concern that the Department of Defense has devoted too little money and effort to finding ways to comply with nuclear arms reductions in "an environmentally benign manner." Pursuant to the Intermediate-Range Nuclear Forces (INF) Treaty, hundreds of Pershing missiles were burned in the open air or exploded on a test stand at the Pueblo Army Depot in Colorado. These procedures can release clouds of toxic hydrochloric acid when the missiles' solid fuel combines with moisture. The implementation of deeper arms cuts would mean destroying hundreds of additional nuclear missiles (Defending the Environment, 1989). Disassembly of nuclear weapons at the Pantex plant in Texas leads to the storage of plutonium from the weapons in "igloos" at the plant and the transport of other components for storage at distant sites.

Chemical Weapons

Use

Chemical weapons, which have been known since antiquity, are designed to produce direct chemical injury to their targets, in contrast to explosive or incendiary weapons which produce their effect through blast or heat. Although the use of chemical weapons was outlawed by the 1899 Hague Declaration, during World War I these weapons (including, in order of use, tear gas, chlorine, phosgene, and mustard) were employed first by the Germans and then by the British and the other Allies. Overall, 125,000 tons of chemical weapons were used during World War I, resulting in 1.3 million casualties. By the time the United States entered the war, these weapons were being used so widely that one-quarter of all casualties in the U.S. expeditionary force in France were caused by them (Sidel, 1989; United Nations; World Health Organization).

Abhorrence of chemical weapons was so great that, in 1925, 28 nations negotiated the Geneva Protocol for the "prohibition of the use in war of asphyxiating poisonous or other gases and of all analogous liquids, materials or devices and of bacteriological methods of warfare." The Protocol prohibited the use, but not the development, production, testing or stockpiling of these weapons. Furthermore many of the nations ratifying the Protocol reserved the right to use such weapons in retaliation and the Protocol became in effect a "no first use" treaty. The United States was one of the initial signers, but the U.S. Senate did not ratify the treaty until 1975 (Sidel, 1989; Wright, 1990, pp. 368–369).

Despite the Protocol, use of chemical weapons continued. Italy used mustard gas during its invasion of Abyssinia (Ethiopia) and Japan used mustard and tear gases in its invasion of China. Germany, with its sophisticated dye and pesticide industries, developed cholinesterase inhibitors known as nerve gases and the United States and Britain also stockpiled chemical weapons during World War II; transportation and storage accidents caused casualties but there was no direct military use. Following World War II, chemical weapons were used by Egypt in Yemen; mustard and nerve gas were used in the Iran–Iraq war; and Iraq used chemical weapons against Kurdish villages in its own territory. Chemical weapons stockpiles and production facilities in Iraq were ordered destroyed by the United Nations following the 1991 Persian Gulf War, but the United States, the Soviet Union, and Iran are known to retain chemical weapons stockpiles and a number of other countries either have stockpiles or facilities for rapid chemical weapons production (Sidel, 1989).

Troops can, to a large extent, be protected against these weapons by the use of gas masks and impenetrable garments. Civilian populations, on the other hand, clearly cannot be adequately protected. Israel, for example, is said to have a gas mask and a self-injectable atropine syringe available for every civilian in the country, but this limited protection against chemical weapons entering the lungs and even more limited protection against nerve agents will not protect against weapons such as mustard that attack the skin. Furthermore, poorly trained civilians are more likely to injure themselves with equipment like self-injectable syringes, which caused injuries to 228 children in Israel during the Persian Gulf War even though nerve agents were never used (Amitai, 1992).

Production and Testing

In addition to the dangers associated with their actual use, there are health and environmental risks involved in other chemical weapons activities. Tests of mustard gas, nerve agents and psychochemicals, including LSD, during World War II involved thousands of military personnel, many of whom subsequently claimed disabilities from the exposure; records of participation and of effects are so poor that only a small fraction of those who participated could even be identified. Production of chemical weapons has been associated with serious accidents to workers and to high levels of pollution of both the production sites and nearby communities. Environmental risks and damage related to the chemical weapons production cycle include risks of development and production, testing, transportation, storage of aging weapons, and even weapons "demilitarization," since toxic ash is produced by their incineration (Sidel, 1993).

Partly as the result of concerns about the effects of chemical weapons tests on the environment, President Richard Nixon in 1969 declared a moratorium on U.S. chemical weapons production. During the Reagan presidency, however, the United States began producing new chemical weapons and increased annual spending on "defensive" biological warfare research by more than 500%. There are approximately 150 public and private U.S. chemical and biological warfare (CBW) laboratories in more than 30 states and 15 foreign countries that are of questionable safety and that may be vulnerable to theft or sabotage and may pose environmental risks (Defending the Environment, 1989; Wright, 1990; Sidel, 1991; U.S. Congress, 1988).

In May 1988 the Subcommittee on Oversight of Government Management of the Senate Governmental Affairs Committee issued a report on its 18-month investigation of CBW safety practices. The report detailed "serious deficiencies" and lapses in the management of safety issues and "completely inadequate" attention paid to potential safety problems. There have been laboratory fires, missing containers of viruses, lost or leaking shipments, assorted spills, infected workers, and even worker deaths. Workers and surrounding communities have not been adequately protected from the possible accidental release of deadly diseases and chemicals, and there is no system for reporting accidents (Defending the Environment, 1989; U.S. Congress, 1988).

Storage

The mean age of the "old" weapons (produced before 1969) in U.S. chemical weapons stockpiles is about 25 years. In 1988 Army officials told a congressional subcommittee that the stockpile includes "more than one thousand" leaking weapons and that the problem is likely to worsen in future years (Defending the Environment, 1989; U.S. Congress, 1988). In 1993, the General Accounting Office of the U.S. Congress issued a report stating that "communities near the nation's eight chemical munitions storage sites (Pine Bluff, AR; Anniston, AL; Pueblo, CO; Newport, IN; Lexington, KY; Aberdeen, MD; Umatilla, OR; and Tooele, UT) are unprepared to deal with the accidental release of lethal chemicals" (Warren, 1993).

"Demilitarization"

In 1985 Congress ordered the Army to destroy 90% of its old chemical weapons by 1994, later extended to 1997. Tens of thousands of tons of chemical agents in bulk containers and in filled munitions are to be destroyed by incineration at nine storage sites (eight in the United States and one at Johnston Atoll in the Pacific Ocean). One method of incineration being tested requires the risky disassembly of chemical agents and munitions before burning. A second method, cryofracture, eliminates disassembly but not risk. Cryofracture deep-freezes munitions with their chemical contents before they are crushed in a huge press and incinerated. Both methods produce hazardous ash and scrubber wastes. An additional risk of cryofracture is dispersal of deadly chemicals by explosion of a munition in the furnace. The Army acknowledged that emergency response planning is inadequate. Disposing of chemical weapons is perhaps second only to radioactive waste disposal among serious threats to the environment from military programs (Defending the Environment, 1989).

Similar problems exist in the former Soviet Union. With a stockpile measuring at least 50,000 metric tons of chemical agents, the former Soviet Union must also find a safe method for incinerating the weapons. Local opposition forced the Soviet government to close a facility at Chapayevsk on the Volga River designed to destroy chemical weapons, and local opposition is blocking demolition at other sites (Defending the Environment, 1989).

Biological Weapons

Use

Biological weapons depend upon their ability to infect and multiply in the attacked organism. In this they differ from toxins, which are biological products but when used as weapons may be classified as chemical weapons. Biological weapons are extremely hard to defend against and are not as controllable or predictable in their use as are chemical weapons (Geisler; Sidel, 1989; United Nations; World Health Organization).

According to testimony at the Nuremberg trials, prisoners at German concentration camps were infected in tests of biological weapons. Britain and the United States, fearing that the Germans would use biological weapons in World War II, developed their own biological weapons. The British tested anthrax spores on Gruinard Island off the coast of Scotland; the island remained uninhabitable for decades. The United States developed anthrax and brucellosis as biological weapons but did not use them (Sidel, 1989). Japanese troops in the 1930s dropped rice and wheat mixed with fleas carrying plague from planes, resulting in plague in areas of China that were previously free of it. Extensive experiments were conducted during World War II in Japanese laboratories on the effects of a wide variety of organisms being tested for possible use as biological weapons on prisoners of war from a number of different countries; anthrax, plague, gas gangrene, encephalitis, typhus, typhoid, hemorrhagic fever, cholera, smallpox, and tularemia were tested (Wright, 1990, pp. 352–361). The U.S. acquired this information after the end of the war but, unlike the 1949 Soviet prosecution of twelve of those involved in work, the U.S. never tried any of the participants. Instead, U.S. researchers met with Japanese biological warfare experts in Tokyo and urged that the experts be "spared embarrassment" so the U.S could benefit from their knowledge (Powell, 1981; Williams, 1989).

After World War II development of biological weapons continued in a number of countries. There have been numerous allegations of military use of such weapons but every one of the reports remains unsubstantiated.

Production and Testing

Environmental risks and damage related to the biological weapons production cycle include risks of development and production, and storage. In the United States, for example, it was revealed in 1969 that in the 1950s and 1960s the University of Utah had under contract conducted secret experiments at the U.S. Army Dugway Proving Ground involving large-scale field testing of biological weapons, including tularemia, Rocky

Mountain spotted fever, plague and Q fever. A large infrastructure of laboratories, test facilities and production plants related to biological weapons was constructed; by the end of the 1960s the U.S. had stockpiles of at least ten different biological and toxin weapons (Cole). An outbreak of pulmonary anthrax in the U.S.S.R. in 1957 may have been caused by accidental release from a Soviet biological weapons factory; Soviet authorities at the time attributed the outbreak to contaminated meat, but doubt has been cast on this explanation.

In 1969 the Nixon Administration with the concurrence of the Defense Department, which declared that "biological weapons lacked military usefulness," unconditionally renounced U.S. development, production, stockpiling and use of biological weapons and announced that the U.S. would unilaterally dismantle its biological weapons program. In 1972 the U.S.S.R. ended its opposition to a separate biological weapons treaty (it had urged a more comprehensive treaty) and the Convention on the Prohibition of the Development, Prevention and Stockpiling of Bacteriological (Biological) and Toxin Weapons and on Their Destruction was negotiated. The U.S., the U.S.S.R. and 100 other nations signed the Biological Weapons Convention (BWC), which prohibits (except for "prophylactic, protective and other peaceful purposes") the development or acquisition of biological agents or toxins, as well as weapons carrying them and means of their production, stockpiling, transfer or delivery. It was ratified by the U.S. Senate in 1975, the same year in which the Senate belatedly ratified the 1925 Geneva Protocol. As of 1987, 110 nations had ratified the BWC and an additional 25 nations had signed but not yet ratified it. Until the 1988 Intermediate Nuclear Force (INF) Treaty, it was the only treaty in modern times to prohibit possession as well as use of weapons. Many ethically related problems of interpretation, inspection, verification and enforcement remain (Wright, 1990, pp. 26–68; 370–376; 379–383).

"Defensive" Research

U.S. biological weapons production is said to have stopped and all stockpiles are said to have been destroyed, but "defensive" research on biological weapons continues in the U.S. and other countries, is seen by many as "ambiguous and provocative" and continues to pose a health threat (Sidel, 1991a). Furthermore, the use of biological engineering techniques offer the "promise" of development of genetically-altered organisms not known in nature and "perfection" of others as effective weapons. It is possible to tailor-make organisms for use as biological weapons that would be stable so that they will travel long distances and still be infectious, would rapidly infiltrate the population, would cause debilitating effects very quickly, and would be resistant to antibiotic treatment (Piller, 1988). Use of biological weapons, particularly of new agents produced or modified by genetic engineering, could cause widespread disease among humans, other animals, or plants, disease that may not be treatable by any known methods (Wright, 1990).

DISCUSSION

Despite the problems and possible devastation that military activities can cause, realities in the world as it has existed have required the vast majority of people to believe that in the event of threat they must be willing to fight to protect themselves, their families and their communities. We might idealistically look forward to the day when there will be no more nation states and the associated dangers of nationalism, when we all can live in peace with each other, when no person takes up arms against another. Perhaps one day humankind will truly reach the stage when military establishments can be removed and we can start enjoying the fruits of the "peace dividend" in the form of greater social and infrastructural investment, when each individual can achieve her or his maximum potential without fear of being taken hostage by international terrorists, some of whom masquerade as national governments. Unfortunately, that day is not yet here.

Is there, then, a need for some form of military activity? The answer most people would give today is almost certainly "yes." As we increase the role of the United Nations in the aftermath of the Cold War and give increased prominence to working through the rule of international law to settle disputes and to seek justice for perceived grievances, perhaps individuals and peoples and nations will find less and less reason to take up arms against each other. This will necessarily require increasing the role of international peacemakers and peacekeepers, as well as increased prominence and action on the part of international entities such as the United Nations General Assembly and Security Council and the International Court of Justice (World Court). For the countries which have not been given a fair opportunity to be heard, which have found their legitimate problems and grievances suppressed by the intellectual blindspots wrought by the Cold War and its distorting influence, great changes from current "business as usual" will be required. For the countries that have strong offensive capability and have long cowed the rest of the world, such a situation would be difficult to accept. Whether we can move from a world where "might is right" to one where justice prevails depends on whether those currently in power are willing to relinquish some of their might. The UN Security Council, for example, for too long has experienced overrepresentation from the former colonial powers and insufficient representation from the developing world. The structure has been maintained despite considerable changes in the dynamics of international relations and the relative importance of these once-great powers. How long can this be allowed to continue?

The reduced suppression of long-held ethnic and nationalistic sentiments in the new nations in Yugoslavia and other new states has led to "ethnic cleansing" and the very real threat of socio-political disintegration. While it is not surprising that such events are happening, they do not seem necessary. In parts of the former Soviet Union and Eastern Europe, the concept of "ethnic diversity" has come into vogue. However, instead of using it to refer to many ethnic groups living in peace and harmony with each other while respecting, celebrating and productively using their similarities and differences (much as the term "biodiversity" is used in ecology), it has come to be associated in these areas with the right of ethnic groups for self-determination, with the elimination of potentially "polluting" influences of other racial or ethnic groups. This way of thinking has been used to justify the perversion of "ethnic cleansing." Until we exhaust ourselves with killing and maiming each other or have the courage to reach across age-old ethnic divides to live peacefully with each other, it seems a sad but true fact that we will need some sort of self-defense capability to cope with threats that may arise.

Maintenance of peace can be viewed as a public or a "common" good in that it provides that everyone can share in its benefits and one person's enjoyment of peace does not occur at the expense of other people's enjoyment and benefiting from it. However, as with any common resource, there is a tendency for it to be abused as individuals try to subvert it to serve their own purposes. Society needs vigilance in maintaining peace. The body maintains its health through adequate nutrition and exercise, physical protection such as adequate clothing and housing, and risk avoidance; if these fail, the body protects itself through a strong immune system. Analogously, there is a need for some minimal level of defense capability to help society preserve the benefits of peace if other measures to prevent war fail. Just as excessive activity of the immune system can be detrimental to health (resulting in conditions such as auto-immune diseases) or an immune system operating without checks and balances can destroy the body (as in leukemia), so can lack of effectiveness of the immune system (as in AIDS). There is therefore a need for balance.

Similarly, there is need for balance between "appropriate" military activities and peace. But what constitutes "appropriate" activities? Obviously the maintenance of sufficient weapons that could destroy the world several times over is inappropriate and excessive. Some societies may need sufficient capability to defend themselves from possible threats, internal and external. Others require stronger, possibly offensive capability, in the event that they are required to play a protective role as the world's "policemen."

If, however, declaration of war is declared illegal, if countries are required to follow due process in appealing to the UN General Assembly in getting their concerns adjudged by the "World Court," and if countries agree to abide by the decisions of the Court and General Assembly, this would obviate the need for much armed conflict. We need to strengthen international jurisprudence and a recognition by all countries of an international code of ethics and appropriate behavior. No country should be allowed to take action on any other without first having exhausted all possibilities. This would, however, require that the international system takes on a stronger and more "activist" approach to dealing with the threat of such actions.

Activities in any member state or between member states that clearly fall outside the spirit of the UN charter should be taken to task. Countries that break the rules should realize they cannot get away with it. World leaders, including dictators and rulers who today discriminate against minorities with impunity, must be made answerable to a higher authority. Other countries, or citizens of their own country, should be able to bring charges against them in the World Court. Criminal and irresponsible behavior cannot go unpunished. World leaders who choose to infringe upon the rights of their people should, in turn, have their rights restricted, and be ostracized. During the days of superpower rivalry, any effort to increase accountability would have been checked by political maneuvering of one or the other of the superpowers. The window of opportunity we now have can and must be used.

In listing the range of actions needed to reduce military activities and their consequences, an analogy may be made with the widely accepted definition of the levels of prevention of disease: (1) Primary prevention consists of averting the occurrence of a disease or injury; (2) secondary prevention consists of reducing the consequences of a disease or injury; and (3) tertiary prevention (more commonly called rehabilitation) consists of repair of the disability produced by a disease or injury.

Primary prevention as applied to military activities requires cessation of as many of these activities as possible, eliminating those with the greatest potential dangers first. In the current world context, this means complete abolition of weapons of mass destruction and reductions in conventional arms. But ridding the world of weapons of mass destruction will itself require a series of steps. For nuclear weapons the steps include: (1) total cessation of nuclear test explosions, a ban which is now verifiable by seismographic methods; (2) strengthening of the Nuclear Nonproliferation Treaty at its renegotiation in 1995; and (3) rapid reductions in the stockpiles of nuclear weapons in all nations with a goal of eventual abolition. There are grounds for confidence that these steps are under way. A moratorium on nuclear explosive testing among four of the five major nuclear powers and action by the United States Congress to mandate a moratorium on testing based on specific conditions is further cause for optimism, although there is much to be done to achieve the conditions. The nuclear test explosions conducted by China and France, since 1993 need not start a general resumption of testing if there is general agreement to maintain the moratorium. Progress is also being made in the Committee on Disarmament in Geneva toward a verifiable Comprehensive Test Ban Treaty. Nuclear arms reduction under START1 and START2 also show signs of progressing.

For chemical weapons, what is required is full implementation of the 1993 Chemical Weapons Convention banning development, production, stockpiling, testing, transfer, or use of chemical weapons. The Chemical Weapons Convention (CWC), which prohibits the development, production, storage and transfer of these weapons and calls for their demilitarization, was approved by the United Nations General Assembly in 1992 and signed by 136 nations in Paris in 1993. Additional nations are becoming signatories and ratification of the CWC and adoption of implementing legislation is now proceeding in the signatory nations, but many ethically related problems with the sites and methods for demilitarization of the weapons, with challenge inspection and other forms of verification and with penalties for non-compliance remain to be solved (Smithson, 1993).

For biological weapons the major task is strengthening of the 1972 Biological Weapons Convention by plugging the loopholes that permit so-called "defensive" research and instituting verification measures. Similar curbs on conventional weapons are needed, such as the "Convention on the Manufacturing and Reduction of Arms Stockpiling, Production and Transfers," which is being prepared by a number of non-governmental organizations.

Secondary prevention of the consequences of military activities requires their reduction to a "sustainable" level. Here, too, there is evidence of some progress. The republics of the former U.S.S.R., driven by economic necessity, have begun sharply to curtail arms expenditures. Among the smaller nations, Costa Rica has consistently over the past three decades spent little on arms and has used the freed resources to spend on improvement in its health and social conditions. In the U.S., although there has been some reduction in arms expenditures, the reduction has been small and arms expenditures in 1994 are projected to remain at a level of $277 billion annually. Projections of reduced global arms expenditures suggest that the U.S., which in the 1980s spent 23 percent of the world's arms expenditures, will be spending 45 percent of the world's arms expenditures by 1997.

Making the military "sustainable" would imply ensuring that the military does not consume excessive resources and does not bring about changes to society and the environment at the expense of future options. Such a military should be well integrated into the lives of members of the community in which it operates and fully accountable for its actions and its impacts on society and the environment. It should also seek to contribute meaningfully to the national well-being and to socioeconomic development. How can this be achieved? One way is to have a largely volunteer military or conscription, with professional soldiers kept to a minimum and the bulk of members of the military members of society who contribute their time and energy to helping maintain and achieve social justice.

Military establishments tend to be very well organized and to function relatively efficiently for the purposes for which they have been established. However, because they generally tend not to be organized for contribution to social and economic development, they are generally not very effective at generating useful inputs to GDP. Making military establishments more directly socially and economically relevant is a challenge well worth pursuing.

The nations of the world must also act to repair the environmental damage caused by the production, use or dismantling of weapons, which we may think of as tertiary prevention. Again such efforts have begun, as we have noted, in a number of countries.

CONCLUSION

While military activities clearly have had major repercussions for health, the environment and development, historic social and political changes around the world give much ground to hope that reform is already under way. The end of the Cold War, the collapse of communism, the rise of global consciousness of the need to protect the environment and to deal with issues such as abject poverty and the abuse of human rights all point to a window of opportunity that needs to be taken advantage of for global benefit. It seems likely that the future will bring a review of the role of the military in many countries and that this will be accompanied by more rational allocation of resources to promote social and economic development. The International Conference on the Relationship Between Disarmament and Development has summarized the choices:

> The world can either continue to pursue the arms race with characteristic vigour or move consciously and with deliberate speed towards a more stable and balanced social and economic development within a more sustainable international economic and political order; it cannot do both. (Report of the International Conference on the Relationship Between Disarmament and Development, 1987)

Presidents and prime ministers from 71 nations agreed at the United Nations World Summit for Children on a series of affordable and achievable goals for the year 2000. Among these goals: the elimination of polio, neonatal tetanus, and guinea worm disease; a 90% reduction in measles; an 85% immunization rate among one-year-olds; a 50% cut in childhood diarrheal deaths and in malnutrition of 5-year-olds; and a 33% reduction in child deaths from respiratory infection. Reaching these goals, UNICEF estimates, would require an additional $20 billion per year. These as yet unattainable goals represent, for example, the reallocation of just 10 percent of military expenditures in the developing world and 1 percent in the industrialized world (Grant, 1992).

As the nations of the world learn to work cooperatively toward achieving common goals in international trade and environmental protection, it is to be hoped that their unity of purpose in dealing with adversity will also be strengthened. We are at a major crossroads in the history of humankind on this planet. We must strive to leave a safe, sustainable and peaceful world to our posterity.

REFERENCES

Amitai, Y., Almog, S., Singer, R., et al. Atropine poisoning in children during the Persian Gulf crisis. *JAMA*, 1992; 268: 630–632.

Arkin, W. M., Durrant, D., Cherni, M. *On the impact of modern warfare on the environment: a case study of the Gulf War*. Washington: Greenpeace, 1991.

Arms Project of Human Rights Watch and Physicians for Human Rights. *Landmines: A Deadly Legacy*. New York: Human Rights Watch, 1993.

Brown, L. R. Redefining national security. In: Brown LR, ed. *State of the world 1986*. New York: W.W. Norton, 1986.

Cole, L. A. *Clouds of secrecy: the army's germ warfare tests over populated areas*. Totowa, NJ: Rowman and Littlefield, 1988.

Complex cleanup: the environmental legacy of nuclear weapons production (Doc.#OTA-0-484). U.S. Congress Office of Technology Assessment, Washington: U.S. Government Printing Office, 1991.

Defending the environment? The record of the U.S. military. *The Defense Monitor* (Washington: Center for Defense Information) 1989:18(6):1–8.

Geiger, H. J., Rush, D. *Dead reckoning: a critical review of the Department of Energy's epidemiologic research*. Washington, DC: Physicians for Social Responsibility, 1992.

Geisler, E., Ed. *Biological and Toxin Weapons Today*. London: SIPRI/Oxford University Press, 1986.

Gersons, B. P. R., & Carlier, I. V. E. Post-Traumatic Stress Disorder: The History of a Recent Concept. *British Journal of Psychiatry (1992)*, 161, 742–748.

Gorbachev, M. *Perestroika: New Thinking for our Country and the World*. New York: Harper and Row, 1987.

Grant, J. P. *The state of the world's children 1992*. Oxford: UNICEF/Oxford University Press, 1992.

Hazardous waste: DOD efforts to reduce waste. (Doc#GAO/NSIAD 89-35) Washington: General Accounting Office, 1989.

Hidden enemies: land mines in northern Somalia. Boston: Physicians for Human Rights, 1992.

Hu, H., Makhijani, A., & Yih, K. *Plutonium: deadly gold of the nuclear age*. Cambridge, MA: International Physicians Press, 1992.

Ibrahim, Y. M. Kuwait battling huge pools of oil. *New York Times*, April 21, 1992, A1.

Klare, M. T., & Kornbloth, P., Eds. *Low Intensity Warfare: Counterintelligence, Proinsurgency and Anti-Terrorism in the Eighties*. New York: Pantheon Books, 1988.

Land mines in Cambodia: the coward's war. Boston: Physicians for Human Rights, 1991.

Leaf, A. New perspectives on the medical consequences of nuclear war. *New England Journal of Medicine* 1986; 315:905–912.

Levy, B.S., Sidel, V.W. (Eds.). *War and Public Health*. New York: Oxford University Press, in press, 1996.

Lifton, R. J. *Death in Life: Survivors of Hiroshima*. New York: Random House, 1968.

McKeown, T. *The Origins of Human Disease*. Oxford: Basil Blackwell Ltd., 1988.

Makhijani, A., Hu, H., Yih, K. (Eds.). *Nuclear Wasteland*. Cambridge, MA: MIT Press, 1995.

Military installations with toxic waste sites. Washington: Physicians for Social Responsibility, 1992.

Morelli, D. R., & Ferguson, M. M. Low-intensity conflict: an operational perspective. *Military Review* 1984; 64(11): 15.

Piller, C., & Yamamoto, K. R. *Gene Wars: Military Control Over the New Genetic Technologies*. New York: Morrow, 1988.

Powell, J. W. A hidden chapter in history. *Bulletin of the Atomic Scientists*, 1981; 37(8):45–49.

Renner, M. Assessing the military's war on the environment. In: Brown, L.R., Flavin, C., Postel, S., et al., Eds. *State of the world 1991. A Worldwatch Institute report on progress towards a sustainable society*. New York: W.W. Norton, 1991:132–152.

Report of the International Conference on the Relationship Between Disarmament and Development. New York: United Nations, 1987. United Nations publication A/CONF.130/39.

Robbins, A., Makhijani, A., & Yih, K. *Radioactive heaven and earth: the health and environmental effects of nuclear weapons testing in, on and above the earth*. New York: Apex Press, 1991.

Ruff, T. A. The environmental effects of military activities. *Global Security* (Medical Action for Global Security, United Kingdom affiliate IPPNW), Summer 1992, pp. 9–12.

Rush, D. The national WIC evaluation. *Am J Clin Nutr* 1988; 48:389–519.

Schell, J. *The Fate of the Earth*. New York: Knopf, 1982.

Shahi, G. S. Implications of population dynamics and natural resource use on carrying capacity and sustainable development. In: Binger, A., & Shahi, G.S., Eds. *Proceedings of the 1st International Session of the LEAD* (Leadership for Environment and Development) Program. New York: The Rockefeller Foundation, 1994.

Shulman, S. *The threat at home: confronting the toxic legacy of the U.S. military*. Boston: Beacon Press, 1992.

Sidel, R. *Women and children last: the plight of poor women in affluent America*. Revised ed. New York: Penguin Books, 1992.

Sidel, V. W., Geiger, H. J., & Lown, B. The medical consequences of thermonuclear war II. The physician's role in the post attack period. *New England Journal of Medicine* 1962; 266:1137–1145.

Sidel, V. W. Destruction before detonation. *Lancet* 1985; 2:1287–1289.

Sidel, V. W. The arms race as a threat to health. *Lancet* 1988; 2:442–444.

Sidel, V. W. Weapons of Mass Destruction: The Greatest Threat to Public Health. *JAMA* 262:680–82, 1989.

Sidel, V. W. Biological weapons research and physicians: historical and ethical analysis. *PSR Quarterly* 1991A; 1:31–42.

Sidel, V. W. The health of poor and minority people in the inner city. *NY State J Med* 1991B; 91:180–182.

Sidel, V. W. Farewell to arms: The impact of the arms race on the human condition. *PSR Quarterly* 1993; 3:18–26.

Sidel, V.W. The international arms trade and its impact on health. *British Medical Journal*, 1995; 311:1677–1680.

Siegel, L. *Operation Ozone Shield: The Pentagon's War on the Stratosphere*. Boston: National Toxics Campaign Fund, 1992.

Siegel, L., Cohen, G., Goldman, B. *The U.S. military's toxic legacy*. Boston: National Toxic Campaign Fund, 1991.

Sivard, R. L. World military and social expenditures 1993. Washington: World Priorities, 1991.

Sivard, R. L. World military and social expenditures 1993. Washington: World Priorities, 1993.

Smithson, A. E. *The Chemical Convention Handbook*. Washington, DC: Henry L. Stimson Center, 1993.

Sociedad Nicaragüense de Médicos por la Paz y La Defensa de la Vida. *La Guerra de Nicaragua—Conflicto de Baja Intensidad: Effectos y Consecuencias en un Pais Subdesarrollado*. (*Nicaraguan Society* of Doctors for Peace and the Defense of Life. *The War in Nicaragua: The Effects of Low Intensity Conflict on an Underdeveloped Country*) (Available in English and Spanish) Cambridge, MA: International Physicians for the Prevention of Nuclear War, 1993.

Solomon, F., Marston, R., eds. *The Medical Implications of Nuclear War. Washington,*

DC: Institute of Medicine of the National Academy of Sciences, National Academy Press, 1986.

The state of America's children 1992. Washington: Children's Defense Fund, 1992.

Turco, R. P., Toon, O. B., Ackerman, T. P., Pollack, J. B., & Sagan, C. Climate and smoke: an appraisal of nuclear winter. *Science* 1990; 247:166–176.

UNICEF. *Children in Situations of Armed Conflict*. New York: UNICEF, 1985.

U.S. Bureau of the Census. Current Population Reports. Poverty in the United States, 1992. Washington, DC: U.S. Government Printing Office, 1993.

U.S. Congress. Senate. Report of the majority staff of the Senate Subcommittee on Oversight of Government Management on DOD's safety programs for chemical and biological warfare research. Washington: U.S. Senate, 1988.

Warren, D. R. Chemical Weapons Storage: Communities are Not Prepared to Respond to Emergencies. (GAO/T-NSIAD-93-18). Washington, DC: U.S. General Accounting Office, 1993.

Westing, A. H., Ed. *Environmental warfare: technical, legal and policy appraisal*. (Stockholm International Peace Research Institute/ United Nations Environmental Program Series.) London: Taylor & Francis, 1984A.

Westing, A. H. (ed). *Herbicides in war: the long term ecological and human consequences*. (Stockholm International Peace Research Institute/United Nations Environmental Program Series.) London: Taylor & Francis, 1984B.

Williams, P., & Wallace, D. *Unit 731: The Japanese army's secret of secrets*. London: Hodder and Stoughton, 1989.

World Health Organization. *Health Aspects of Chemical and Biological Weapons: Report of a WHO Group of Consultants*. Geneva: World Health Organization, 1970.

World Health Organization. *Effects of Nuclear War on Health and Health Services*. Second Edition. Geneva: World Health Organization, 1987.

Wright, S., Ed. *Preventing a Biological Arms Race*. Cambridge, MA: MIT Press, 1990.

Yemelyanenkov, A., Popov, V. *The atom declassified: points of view*. Berlin: H & P Druck (Offsetdruckerei: Körtestrasse 10, Berlin 61), 1992.

17

Global Migration of Hazardous Industries

Joseph LaDou

INDUSTRIAL EXPANSION IN THE DEVELOPING WORLD

Two-thirds of all industrial investment in developing countries over the past decade can be attributed to foreign companies and foreign investors. During the 1980s, a global financial market began to emerge. In a span of ten years, international bank lending by the major developed countries rose from 4 percent of gross domestic product to 44 percent. Between 1986 and 1990, foreign investment by the United States, Japan, West Germany, France, and Britain grew at an annual rate of 27 percent. Global cross-border investment is now estimated to be $1.7 trillion (Castleman, 1995). For many nations such investment is the primary source of new jobs.

There are about 35,000 multinational corporations, with 147,000 foreign affiliates. Much of the investment in the developing world comes from these corporations. The total annual sales of the 350 biggest multinational corporations are equal to one-third of the combined gross domestic products of the industrial world, and exceed by far that of the developing world. In addition, there is a significant and growing investment in developing countries that is provided by foreign investors through international mutual funds, investment syndicates, or a variety of other investment options; and by residents and institutions of the developing countries, usually in association with foreign investment. The majority of industrial activity in the developing world is sponsored by these usually nameless sources whose record of attention to workplace health and safety and to the environment is far less acceptable than that of the multinationals.

Most investment in developing countries goes to Asia. Between 1986 and 1990, East and Southeast Asia received $14 billion, Latin America $9 billion, and Africa $3 billion. Central Europe is now openly competing for a share of global investment. India, Vietnam, Egypt, Nicaragua, and Uzbekistan have recently liberalized their ownership rules to increase their attractiveness to investors.

Japanese companies and investments are found in almost every country in the world. With limited land and great population density, Japan has a pressing need to export its waste-producing industries. A survey of Japanese multinationals found that 80 percent of their investments in Asia had become profitable within two years, compared with 20 percent of those in America. Both Japan and the United States have significantly realigned their investment strategies toward Asia in recent years. Western European nations have exported hazardous and environmentally outmoded industries to Africa and the Middle East, and are now beginning to export them to Central Europe. Western European corporations are the largest investors in Bangladesh, India, Pakistan, Singapore, and Sri Lanka (LaDou, 1991).

China and India, with the world's largest populations, have had dramatic policy reversals in recent years, and as a result have welcomed industries from many countries. United States corporations are dominant in China, Hong Kong, Indonesia, the Philippines, Taiwan, and Thailand.

REASONS FOR THE MIGRATION OF INDUSTRY TO THE DEVELOPING WORLD

The migration of industry from developed to developing countries is usually explained by the lower cost of labor. Labor costs are a small fraction in developing countries of what they are in the developed countries. A World Bank study by Low and Yeats suggests that labor intensity is not so important a factor in explaining the migration of industry as is commonly accepted. Only 15 percent of the products of environmentally "dirty" industries are manufactured by labor-intensive production processes. Environmentally dirty industries were defined as those incurring the highest level of pollution abatement and control expenditures in the United States. Of these, none is 10 percent more labor-intensive than the U.S. average for all manufacturing activity (Low & Yeats, 1992).

Companies also establish operations abroad to reduce transportation costs by producing within foreign markets, to overcome trade barriers, and to avoid fluctuations in currency markets. Many companies attempt to explain their exported manufacture as an inevitable result of global trade. Some companies, however, migrate to developing nations to escape occupational and environmental regulations and enforcement at home. But it is unlikely any company would ever admit to such a motivation.

In the developed countries, industry provides jobs, pays taxes that support community services, and is subject to environmental and occupational health laws. As industrialized nations enact laws to limit the environmental hazards associated with many industrial operations, production costs rise and undermine competitive advantages. To offset this problem, manufacturers move many of their hazardous operations to the newly industrialized countries. They are welcomed because the creation of an infrastructure in many developing nations relies on industrial expansion by foreigners. When industry migrates to developing nations, companies not only take advantage of lower wages, but also benefit from the low tax rates in communities that are not spending much on such things as sewage systems, water treatment plants, schools, and public transportation. When companies establish plants in developing countries, their tax burden is a small fraction of what it would be in most developed countries.

Developing countries seldom have enforceable occupational and environmental regulations. They are concerned with overwhelming problems of unemployment, malnutrition, and infectious diseases, often to the exclusion of environmental hazards. Newly industrialized countries are eager for the financial benefits that foreign companies and foreign investors bring them. However, these benefits bring profound social and ecological problems.

The positive economic and social results of industrial activity in Third World nations are accompanied by serious environmental degradation. The major cities of developing nations are now reeling with the impact of air pollution, the absence of sewage treatment and water purification, and the growing quantities of hazardous waste buried in or left on the soil or dumped into rivers or the oceans. In many of the world's countries, there are no environmental regulations, or if they exist at all, there is little or no enforcement.

According to a World Bank report, the amount of sulfur dioxide, nitrogen dioxide, and total suspended particulates in the air—three of the most dangerous industrial pollutants—increased by a factor of ten in Thailand, eight in the Philippines, and five in Indonesia between 1975 and 1988. Five of the seven cities in the world with the worst air pollution are in Asia. With energy demand doubling in Asia every 12 years, Asian countries in the next ten years will produce more sulfur dioxide than Europe and America combined.

The work force of developing nations is accustomed to working in small industry settings. Generally, the smaller the industry, the higher the rate of workplace injury and illness. These workplaces are characterized by unsafe buildings and other structures; old machinery; poor ventilation; noise; and with workers of limited education, skill, and training; and employers with limited financial resources. Protective clothing, respirators, gloves, hearing protectors, and safety glasses are seldom available. The companies are often inaccessible to inspection by government health and safety enforcement agencies. In many instances, they operate as an "underground industry" of companies not even registered with the government for tax purposes. Many investors in foreign plants allow no spending on occupational health and safety training and equipment and virtually no attention to the environment until the investment returns a profit. For most new companies, this takes years.

In a study of the migration of environmentally "dirty" industries, Low and Yeats investigated the trade statistics for 109 countries. In 1988, developed countries accounted for three quarters of all shipments of these products, with almost 40 percent of world exports coming from the European Economic Comunity (EEC). During the period 1968–1988, there was a drop of over 6 percent in shipments of dirty products originating in North America (from 20.5 to 14 percent of world trade) and a more than doubling (from 3.4 to 8.4 percent) of the share originating in Southeast Asia. If one looks at the share of dirty goods in total exports from each region, Eastern Europe, followed by Latin America with the Caribbean, are the two regions with the highest concentration of dirty products. In these vast regions of developing countries, dirty products account for over one-fifth of total exports (28 percent in the case of Eastern Europe). The study demonstrates a relative decline in the importance of these exports in developed countries, while Eastern Europe, Latin America, and West Asia show an increasing and alarming reliance on the export value of dirty products (Low & Yeats, 1992).

PROBLEMS AND ABUSES IN INDUSTRY IN THE DEVELOPING WORLD

Mexico provides a dramatic example of the impact of rapid industrial growth in a newly industrialized country. Mexico appears to be willing to tolerate a number of negative environmental consequences to take advantage of the jobs and income provided by foreign-owned industries. Cooperative agreements between Mexico and other countries have created the establishment of foreign manufacturing facilities in northern Mexico, known as "maquiladoras."

Labor costs in Mexico are far below those in Korea, Taiwan, Hong Kong, and other countries that have been used for offshore manufacturing. Furthermore, the distance and cost of transporting materials from the United States to northern Mexico are less. Thus, nearly 2,000 companies have established plants along the U.S. border to assemble their products using low-cost labor, and return the finished products to the parent companies.

Under the Border Industrialization Program (BIP) instituted by the Mexican government in 1965, manufacturers are allowed to send raw materials and equipment to Mexico. If they agree to take back the finished products, the entire exchange is accomplished without the payment of export or import taxes. At present, maquiladoras employ about 500,000 workers. Virtually all the new jobs created in Mexico in the past decade resulted from the rapid growth of the maquiladoras. The poor and the jobless from all over Mexico headed northward in hope of employment in the maquiladoras. Mexico was not prepared for the major population shift the lure of jobs along the U.S. border would create. The cities they arrived at were ill prepared to receive them. There was no housing, and tens of thousands of the workers are still subsisting in cardboard huts in squatters' camps that have no sanitation, water, heat, or electricity.

The sheer numbers of workers and their families would daunt the most prosperous cities. For example, the population of Nogales has increased fourfold to 250,000 since 1970, and that of Juarez risen from 250,000 to 1.5 million. Because of the population shift, unemployment and underemployment are at levels close to the experience in Mexico when the BIP was instituted. Unemployment is at least 25 percent, probably much higher.

The dumping of hazardous wastes is fostered by international greed and lax Mexican surveillance of industrial practices. Under Mexican laws, materials brought in by plants for processing are to be returned to the country of origin or recycled in Mexico after obtaining a special permit. But only about 60 percent of these materials leave Mexico; the remainder is believed to be disposed of illegally in sewers, drainage systems, and landfills. Water and air pollution are the most obvious results of the rapid industrialization of this region. Mexico has some of the most severe environmental problems in the world, many of which could have been avoided if industries had been properly regulated.

Many critics of the Border Industrialization Program consider it to be little more than an attempt to keep Mexicans from crossing the border to obtain jobs in the United States. If that was the intent of the agreement with Mexico, it has not worked. Mexican immigration is an increasingly difficult political problem on both sides of the border.

EXPLOITATION OF WORKERS

The common public perception of offshore industries is that of the major transnationals. Far more common than these industrial giants are the many thousands of small companies owned by foreign interests and operated or supervised by local managers. The ability of most of the foreign governments to regulate industry or even to monitor the passage of goods and materials is extremely limited. Migrating industries, including virtually all the multinationals, conform to the inadequate environmental and occupational health and safety standards of the host country. Consequently, worker fatality rates are much higher in newly industrialized countries than in the developed nations, and workplace injuries occur with rates common to the developed nations during the early years of the Industrial Revolution. In this regard, the Industrial Revolution is taking place all over again, but with much larger populations of workers and in many more countries.

There is no worldwide effort to maintain occupational safety records. The International Labour Office (ILO) estimates that 180,000 worker fatalities and 110 million workplace injuries occur each year. If the developing countries continue their current rate of industrial growth, these figures will double by the year 2025.

Virtually all of the world's population growth is occurring in the Third World. At present, the labor force in developing countries totals around 1.76 billion, but it will rise to more than 3.1 billion in 2025—implying a need for 38–40 million new jobs every year (Kennedy, 1993). This being the case, worker demands for better working conditions are not likely to occur.

Women Workers

Both absolute and relative rates of labor force participation among women in the manufacturing sector have increased substantially. The overall participation rate for women in the industrial labor force increased significantly in those nations where development strategies focused on export processing. The availability of low-wage women workers is a major ingredient in the success of such places as Taiwan.

The University of California, the Johns Hopkins School of Public Health and Hygiene, and the University of Massachusetts have all studied the health of American semiconductor workers. The studies collectively demonstrate that women have a major increase in the risk of miscarriage when they work in semiconductor cleanrooms where a broad array of chemicals is necessary to the manufacture of integrated circuits. Neither the semiconductor industry nor the U.S. Government has responded with the funding of further studies. The cause of the reproductive hazard is not known at this time. The semiconductor industry has been rapidly migrating to the developing nations of Southeast Asia. Some researchers participating in these studies observed that the companies are laying off workers and shutting down the plants so rapidly that these studies will probably be the last of sufficient size to be conducted with U.S. workers to give reliability to the findings.

The migration of American and Japanese semiconductor companies to Southeast Asia is dramatically demonstrated in the newly industrialized country of Malaysia. Over the past 20 years Malaysia became the world's third largest semiconductor manufacturer, and the world's largest exporter of semiconductors. It is very unlikely that foreign companies will continue to fund research on occupational and environmental health in a distant country with foreign workers. The savings realized by foreign manufacture of semiconductors will be enhanced by the ability of these companies to neglect health and safety as do many of their international rivals. The miscarriage rate of semiconductor workers will be ignored by governments and by industry in newly industrialized countries. Workers, for the most part, will not recognize the association between work and miscarriage.

Child Labor

Children account for up to 11 percent of the workforce in some countries in Asia, up to 17 percent in Africa, and up to a quarter in Latin America. The condition of child workers has worsened dramatically in recent years (ILO, 1992). Children are the most easily exploited of all workers, and in the developing world, their numbers are ever increasing. Few countries have developed comprehensive plans to deal with child labor.

Levi Strauss produces 50 percent of its jeans and shirts overseas. Its 400 foreign contractors are being assessed by the company itself which finds that 25 percent treat their workers badly. Its contractor in Bangladesh routinely used child labor. Levi Strauss now requires contractors to improve health and safety standards and pay no less than prevailing local wages. The new policy is considered so important an achievement, it is reported in a U.S. business magazine. The recommendation that exporting countries observe their company's health and safety standards wherever they operate is hardly a new idea. It has been emphasized by governments of developed countries for over half a century.

Occupational Diseases

The incidence of occupational diseases has never been greater than it is today. The United Nations estimates that 6 million occupational disease cases occur each year worldwide. Occupational diseases occur with greater frequency in the developing countries, and they occur with greater severity. Among miners, construction workers, and asbestos workers in some developing countries, asbestos is the major cause of disability and ill health, and by some counts, the major cause of death. The occupational and environmental hazards posed by asbestos products do not discourage the asbestos industry from promoting asbestos in the Third World where demand for low-cost building materials outweighs health concerns.

Silicosis

One-third of the urban Chinese population reports a history of occupational dust exposure. This is reflected by the fact that more than one million Chinese have silicosis. Silicosis is rare in developed countries, but is the most common occupational disease in China, the most populated country in the world. In Malaysia, silicosis occurs in one-quarter of the quarry workers and one-third of tombstone makers. Yet, silicosis is entirely preventable.

Lead Poisoning

Lead smelting and refining are migrating from developed countries to developing countries. Recycling of lead products also passes from developed countries to poorer nations that are often ill prepared to deal with the occupational and environmental hazards created by lead. Developed nations have few lead smelters today, this industrial activity having passed to the newly industrialized countries. Many lead-smelting activities in the developing world operate with technologies that are unchanged from a century ago. The air of most large Third World cities contains sufficient lead to affect the health of children. Many developing countries still rely on lead pipes to convey drinking water. Lead is also a problem in unlabeled cosmetics and other consumer goods, and some traditional medicines contain high levels of lead.

When developed countries boast of accomplishments in the area of lead recycling, almost invariably the lead is recycled in developing countries and returned to the developed countries as finished products. This is the comfortable arrangement the United States enjoys with Mexico, Taiwan, and a number of other poorer countries.

In developing countries, governments and industries accept the transfer of hazardous materials knowing that reasonable exposure levels will not likely be legislated or enforced. Many products containing lead, such as gasoline, batteries, paints, inks and dyes are produced in developing countries by companies that are foreign-owned and the products are then sold internationally by the controlling interests.

Pesticide Poisoning

In developing countries, where the majority of workers are in agriculture, pesticides are often applied by hand, or without proper protection of workers who use spray equipment. Three million pesticide poisonings occur each year in Southeast Asia alone. Most pesticide manufacture in developing countries is done by foreign-owned companies or local companies with capital invested by foreigners. The use of pesticides in the developing countries is growing rapidly as they learn the advantages that such chemicals offer to the agricultural industry and as they gain the capability to produce the pesticides in their own countries.

Pesticides such as DDT and DBCP, which are banned in most developed nations, are widely sold and used without restrictions in the Third World. When health hazards cause removal of a pesticide from a developed country's market, the pesticide often finds its way to the unregulated markets in developing countries. It is entirely legal for a U.S. company to manufacture and distribute a chemical that is banned for use in the United States, so long as the sale and distribution are in another country whose laws are not violated by the transfer. For example, the insecticides chlordane and heptachlor were banned for agricultural uses in the United States in the 1970s. Yet between 1987 and 1989, the U.S. manufacturer of these chemicals produced and exported nearly 5 million pounds of the insecticides to some 25 countries (Jamall & Davis, 1991).

Chemical Exposure

The chemical industry is one of the most rapidly growing industrial sectors in the emerging global economy. The chemical companies of the developed countries are found throughout the world. Many smaller chemical companies migrate to the developing countries making the chemical industry a major contributor to environmental contamination. As population growth and industrialization continue throughout the poorer regions of the world, demand for pesticides, chemical fertilizers, and industrial chemicals grows as well. To compound this problem, chemicals that are banned in developed countries are often manufactured in increased quantities in the newly industrialized countries. DDT is a compelling example. Its worldwide production is at record levels, yet it has been illegal to produce or use DDT in most developed countries since the 1970s.

SOME SOLUTIONS TO THE PROBLEMS OF INDUSTRIAL EXPANSION IN THE DEVELOPING WORLD

The experience of industrialized countries with the costs of occupational health and safety and environmental programs is that a very substantial financial burden is being shifted to newly industrialized nations. The World Bank estimates that ill health caused by pollution costs as much as $3 billion a year in lost productivity in Bangkok alone. The cost of pollution in the big cities of Asia is nearing 10 percent of urban GDP. The cost of clean-up is perhaps 1–2 percent of GDP. Postponing the investment will raise costs later. The cost of future accidents such as Bhopal, mitigation of environmental damage, and effects on the public health are not often discussed with candor in the Third World. The consequences of global industry may produce widespread international conflicts when the long-term economic realities of industrial migration become more apparent.

International organizations must take a stronger lead in approving and coordinating technology transfer. The shameful practice of exporting obsolete and hazardous technologies to developing countries when these processes can no longer satisfy the environmental standards of the developed countries must be stopped. International agreements must replace the perverse incentives that threaten the world's environment.

There have been many efforts to control the behavior of industry. The OECD Guidelines for Multinational Enterprises, the UN Code of Conduct on Transnational Corporations, and the ILO Tripartite Declaration of Principles Concerning Multinational Enterprises and Social Policy attempt to provide a framework of ethical behavior. The Basel Convention on the Control of Transboundary Movements of Hazardous Wastes and Their Disposal became international law on May 5, 1992. Although it halts most hazardous wastes from crossing borders, it also serves to institutionalize a trade in wastes that reflects the need for political compromise.

Developing nations seldom support the adoption of the environmental standards of the developed world. In some instances, opponents argue that it is a matter of national sovereignty that allows each nation to develop its own standards. In other cases, there is long-standing resentment of any foreign influence, especially from the nations that have already increased their standards of living from the industrial activities that are now being regulated. Developing nations take the position that after they have the standard of living of the developed nations, they will then adopt stricter regulatory policies. When developed nations are asked to provide developing nations with industries whose technology is environmentally benign, interest in industrial migration lessens dramatically.

Some international lending institutions are now producing environmental impact assessments (EIAs) when the host country is unable to perform this task. The local impact potential of at least certain hazardous industry sitings ought to be mandatory, and occupational health and safety standards could be added to plant-siting assessments.

Many developed nations have established recommended exposure levels for workers that cannot be exceeded without regulatory or legal action. In developing countries, exposure standards are often non-existent, not enforced, or too lax to be of use. International standards can and should be developed. Developing countries, and particularly the foreign companies that manufacture there, can be given a reasonable period of time to comply with the standards that are enforced throughout most of the developed world. If this is not done, some workers in these countries will pay an inordinate part of the cost of industrialization.

The American labor movement is pressing for unilateral action to be taken by the developed nations to influence the practices of countries that choose either not to regulate or not to regulate in harmony with other countries. One proposal is that, through the General Agreement on Tariffs and Trade (GATT), the United States and other signatories could require observance of Minimum International Labor Standards (MILS) for health and safety practices and child labor. Labor exerted much of the political influence leading to the passage of the Occupational Safety and Health Act in the United States. This influence is vital in the international arena.

The most logical international standard of occupational health and safety is the development of an international workers' compensation insurance system. Workers in all countries are entitled to the basic benefits of workers' compensation law. Workers' compensation insurance provides economic incentives for employers to provide a safe and healthful work environment. Workers in all countries, regardless of the ownership of the company, should receive this benefit. At present, only 16 percent of workers in Africa, 43 percent in Latin America, and 23 percent in Asia enjoy protection from social security schemes (Rantanen, 1992).

There must be an international legal system to deal with the environment, and there must be an enforcement capability strong enough to discourage even the most criminal of polluters. Industries must be required to internalize environmental costs and reflect them in the prices of products. Strict liability provision in the laws of all countries could be developed for both property and third-party damage. Thus, the waste generator would be responsible for waste management from production to disposal through an international system of strict liability (Casto, 1995).

Developing countries do not have large, well-funded environmental groups such as exist in developed countries. Enforcement will require the training of personnel and the support of governments that, until recently, placed so much emphasis on industrial expansion that the issue of environmental protection was not even a consideration.

REFERENCES

Castleman, B. I.: The Migration of Industrial Hazards. *Int J Occup Environ Health, 1(2)*, 85–96, 1995.

Casto, K.: The Environmental Audit. *Int J Occup Environ Health, 1(2)*, 124–196, 1995.

International Labour Office: World Labor Report 1992. International Labour Organization, Geneva, 1992.

Jamall, I. S., & Davis, B.: Chemicals and Environmentally Caused Diseases in Developing Countries. *Infectious Disease Clinics of North America, 5(2)*, 365, 1991.

Kennedy, P.: *Preparing for the Twenty-First Century*. Random House, New York, 1993.

LaDou, J.: Deadly Migration. Hazardous Industries' Flight to the Third World, *Technol Rev., 94(5)*, 47–53, 1991.

Low, P., & Yeats, A.: Do "Dirty" Industries Migrate? Chapter 6, in *International Trade and the Environment*, Patrick Low (Ed.), World Bank, Washington, D.C., 1992.

Rantanen, J.: Development of an Occupational Health and Safety Program in Third World Countries. Chapter 2, in *Protecting Workers' Health in the Third World*. R. R Reich & T. Okubo (Editors), Auburn House, New York, 1992, p. 17.

18

Environmental Chemical Disasters

Gamal H. El Samra and M.M. El Batanouny

INTRODUCTION

Environmental chemical disasters can be defined as environmental deterioration due to extensive contamination with chemicals.

After the second World War, there was rapid growth and expansion of the chemical industry. This has led to the occurrence of hundreds of chemical accidents. The Major Hazard Incident Data Service (MHIDS), one of the most comprehensive data banks, contains over 3,000 records concerning chemical accidents which have occurred in the last 25 years with an off-site impact in some 95 countries (Bertazzi, 1989).

In the Middle East, especially in the Arab world, as well as in Egypt, there is no definite body concerned with recording of major incidents or environmental disasters, inspite of the occurrence of hundreds of them. The Middle East area has experienced several major wars in the last 50 years, the last being the Gulf War, beside the emergence of oil as a major economic activity, with its risks of spill, explosion and environmental pollution.

Industrial chemical disasters do not only strike workers, but also the general population and the surrounding environment, i.e., air, soil, water, vegetations, seas and even buildings. The United Nations Environment Program (UNEP), in 1980, estimated that 60,000 chemicals are in use worldwide, with the addition of about 1,000 chemicals every year (Holdgate et al., 1982).

Types of Environmental Chemical Disasters

Environmental chemical disasters can be divided, from the prevention point of view, into:

1. Those due to sudden, unexpected release of unusual quantities of toxic chemicals during a short period of time, resulting from fires,

explosions, chemical reactions, mechanical failure or otherwise, resulting in acute effects. The number of new cases decreases and they become less severe as time goes by. Chronic and delayed effects may occur. This also includes accidental consumption of large doses of toxic chemicals in food or water. The most common chemicals which caused such disasters are chlorine, gasoline, ammonia, sulfuric and hydrochloric acids. More than 50 percent of those events occurred during transportation. Acute chemical releases and major accidents happen every year all over the world, but chemical disasters which cause death and injuries on a large scale, are fortunately not very common. The worst of this kind of disaster happened in Bhopal, India, in 1984, and caused the death of thousands and injured about 250,000 people. In the days after the incident, it is estimated that nearly 100,000 people sought medical care for health problems caused by the exposure.

2. Those due to gradual release of a toxic substance that reaches man directly or indirectly. Accumulation leads to health effects that may be subacute or chronic. Cases increase in number and severity with time, unless there is intervention to stop the release. Deaths or delayed effects (genetic, carcinogenic, etc.) may be observed. An example of this type happened in Finland, in a county named "Karkola." In the population center, there was an industrial facility including a sawmill, located over an important ground water area. From 1930, the mill used 7–10 tons per year of fungicides (tri-, tetra- and pentachlorophenol). In 1987, it was noted that the ground water and local water plant were contaminated with chlorophenol. The population of the community were exposed to chlorophenol by drinking water and by eating fish which was caught from a nearby contaminated lake. This was a probable cause of the higher incidence of non-Hodgkin's lymphoma among men in "Karkola." Another example is the toxic oil syndrome, which happened in Spain in 1981, where 314 patients died and over 20,000 persons were affected in a period of about 13 months. An epidemiological study revealed the association of this disease with the consumption of an inexpensive denatured rape seed oil, sold in unlabeled plastic containers by street vendors. The Minamata disease is also a famous example of this type. A similar episode happened in Iraq, due to the use of seed grains treated with mercury fungicide.

3. Those due to air pollution from industrial, domestic, transport, or other activities which are acceptable under normal weather conditions; but under certain topographic and climatic conditions (such as temperature inversions, anti-cyclonic weather, or fog, etc.),

concentrations of pollutants (for example, particulates, sulphur dioxide, and fog) increase to dangerous levels causing acute or subacute health effects. In general, when we refer to acute episodes of air pollution, we have in mind three classic incidents: the Meuse Valley in Belgium (1930), Donora, Pennsylvania (1948), and London fog (1948). In these incidents, there were temperature inversions continuously for 3 or 4 days, during which time the concentration of pollutants (mainly smoke and sulfur dioxide) rose well above the normal levels for these heavily polluted areas.

Table 18.1 shows the famous environmental chemical disasters which occurred in many countries, worldwide. The table gives some important data; place of the incident, the chemical involved, the source of the chemical, the incident outcome in terms of death, injuries, or number of people being evacuated. It does not give the environmental impact. While there are examples from many parts of the world, developing countries are poorly covered, obviously because of lack of systematic collection and publication of relevant data from these countries.

HEALTH EFFECTS OF ENVIRONMENTAL CHEMICAL DISASTERS

Environmental chemical disasters may result in acute exposure to hazardous chemicals. Symptoms may be immediate or delayed for one or several hours. In some cases, however, symptoms may appear days, weeks, months, or even years after the acute exposure. Symptoms may be local (eyes, skin, respiratory tract, gastrointestinal tract), systemic or both. Most common acute systemic symptoms are those related to the central nervous system (excitation, depression), circulatory system (arrhythmia, cardiac depression), gastrointestinal tract (vomiting, diarrhea) and blood (methaemoglobinaemia, hemolysis). Delayed symptoms can be seen from any organ system, but most commonly from the respiratory tract (delayed pulmonary edema), kidney, liver or blood-forming organs.

The most common route of exposure in major accidents is inhalation of gases that are stored under pressure. Those will spread rapidly, and over a wide area. Another likely route of exposure is the skin. Ingestion of the toxin is less likely to occur unless drinking water or food have been contaminated either by accident or sabotage.

Post-Disaster Stress

Increasing attention is being paid to psychosocial stress disorders. The term Post Traumatic Stress Disorder (PTSD) was introduced to the

TABLE 18.1 Examples of Famous Chemical Disasters

Agent	Source	Location	Year(s)	No. of Exposed Population	No. of ill Population	No. of Deaths	Health Effects
Sulphur compounds and others (acid fog and smog)	Air pollution with anticyclonic weather + temperature inversion	Meuse valley, Belgium	1970	Unknown	Many elderly people with cardiorespiratory illness	60	Aggravation of Chronic Obstructive Pulmonary Disease (COPD), respiratory failure + increased risk of acute & chronic respiratory illness
		Donora, Pensylvania, USA	1948	Unknown	6,000	20	Same as above
		Poza Rica, Mexico	1950	Unknown	320	22	Same as above
		London, UK	1952	Unknown	too many	4,000	Same as above
		London, UK	1962	Unknown	too many	750	Same as above
		New York, USA	1953	Unknown	too many	200	Same as above
			1962	Unknown	too many	405	Same as above
			1963	Unknown	too many	168	Same as above
			1960	Unknown	too many		Same as above
Aniline (possibly)	Contaminated cooking oil	Spain	1981	Unknown	20,000	340	Acute phase: fever, skin rash, nausea, vomiting, diarrhea, pulmonary edema. Chronic phase:

							peripheral neuropathy, muscular wasting, pulmonary hypertension, scleroderma, liver dysfunction.
Hexachlorobenzene (HCB)	Ingestion of wheat seed treated with a fungicide	Turkey	1955–60	Unknown	5,000	500	Porphyria Cutanea Tarda; weakness, weight loss, blistering, photosensitivity of skin, skin infections, hepatomegaly, dark urine. In infants: growth retardation, and seizures.
Polychlorinated biphenyls	Contaminated rice oil	Japan	1968–73	Unknown	1,200	22	Yusho Disease; Hypersecretion of eyes, acneform eruptions, skin hyperkeratosis and dark pigmention of skin, nails & mucous membranes, severe headache, nausea, numbness of extremities.

TABLE 18.1 (*Continued*)

Agent	Source	Location	Year(s)	No. of Exposed Population	No. of ill Population	No. of Deaths	Health Effects
Methyl Mercury	Ingestion of seed grain treated with mercurial fungicide	Iraq	1959–60 1971–72	Unknown Unknown	7,000	500	Severe malaise, paresthesia of extremities, slurred speech, ataxia, constricted visual field, severe brain damage in infants of exposed mothers, chorea, loss of vision, hearing and speech.
	Discharge of mercury from industry in Minamata bay, resulting in biomagnification in fish leading to human poisoning (Minamata disease).	Minamata Bay, Japan	1953–61	Unknown	111 with neurological disease, 40 with congenital malformations	41	
Cadmium	Contaminated rice and water with cadmium from a nearby mine discharging waste water into a local river from which people drink and irrigate rice.	Japan	1939–54	Unknown	200	—	Ita-Itai "Ouch Ouch" disease; severe pain in bones, waddling gait, aminoaciduria, glycosuria, severe osteoporosis with multiple fractures.

Chlorine	Cargo train accident with tanks containing liquified chlorine.	Missouga, Canada	1979	250,000	—	—	Acute respiratory distress with cough, dyspnea, chest pain, hemoptysis. Acute pulmonary edema and chronic pneumonitis.
Dioxin	Release of polychlorinated dibenzo-p-dioxins (PCDDs) from an industrial plant.	Seveso, Italy	1976	27,000	—	—	Chloracne, polyneuropathy, optic neuropathy with diminution of vision, nystagmus. Hepatomegaly with elevated serum enzymes.
Methyl Isocyanate	Release of large amounts of methyl isocyanate from a pesticide factory due to explosion of storage tank.	Bhopal, India	1984	Population at Bhopal	250,000	2,500	Wheezing, chest tightness, cough, suffocation and pulmonary edema. Immediate: skin and respiratory irritation, causing pulmonary edema. Later: COPD and bronchial hyper-reactivity.

standard psychiatric nomenclature in 1980 on the basis of the great amount of work done on the consequences of stressful experiences of survivors of catastrophies, both man-made and others. Bertazzi (1989) mentioned five major components of the stressful experience of the disaster:

1. Uncertainty with fear of the presence of unknown health damage from the disaster with a strong feeling of lack of protection.
2. Housing and job insecurity with evacuation of area inhabitants, the fear of contamination of homes and premises.
3. Social rejection; people in the contaminated area may suffer from discrimination for sometime as if they carry some mysterious and noxious contagion.
4. Media siege; for months and years, professionals in the media come to the area from everywhere. This may have possible negative effects on people in the area.
5. Cultural pressure; people of the area become the target of many other conflicting public pressures on how to behave or, perhaps, what to expect.

ENVIRONMENTAL AND ECOLOGICAL IMPACTS OF DISASTERS

Disasters can produce profound environmental changes. After a disaster occurs, the rapidly changing environment can produce a disruption of patterns of life. In some cases, basic public services such as water supply, waste water disposal and solid waste removal can be seriously affected. In others, quality of air and water can be seriously impaired. In some disasters, the population may be forced to live temporarily in crowded unsanitary conditions which can lead to severe stress to individuals and increase in morbidity and mortality. The socioeconomic conditions change sometimes drastically with deterioration of the environmental conditions and consequently there may be an imminent danger of epidemics, especially of enteric diseases due to:

- Enhanced transmission of pathogens;
- Deterioration of sanitary conditions through overcrowding and overloading of the facilities; and
- Disruption of local control programs due to diversion of resources.

PREVENTION

Chemical Accidents With Sudden Release of Chemicals

Chemical accidents have a significant potential to threaten life and to damage human health and the environment. To cope with acute chemical accidents it is necessary to plan long before chemical accidents, to respond to chemical emergencies, and to rehabilitate people and areas affected. This is only possible if accident hazards imposed on the community have been properly identified and evaluated. Pre-planning should identify the specific sites that contain hazardous materials. In addition, emergency personnel should be alert to the locations in their communities that utilize hazardous materials (African Workshop on Technological Disasters, 1990).

Awareness and Preparedness for Emergencies at Local Level (APELL)

In late 1986, following various industrial accidents that occurred in both highly industrialized and developing countries, resulting in adverse impacts on the environment, the United Nations Environment Program (UNEP) suggested a series of measures to help governments, particularly in developing countries, minimize the occurrence and harmful effects of chemical accidents and emergencies (UNEP, 1988). In this context, the UNEP, Industry and Environment Office (IEO) has developed, in cooperation with industry, a handbook on Awareness and Preparedness for Emergencies at Local Level (APELL), designed to assist decision makers and technical personnel in improving community awareness of hazardous installations, and in preparing response plans should unexpected events at these installations endanger life, property or the environment. APELL has two main goals:

1. Create and/or increase community awareness of possible hazards within the community.
2. Based on this awareness, develop a cooperative plan to respond to any emergency that these hazards might present.

The APELL handbook provides the basic concepts for the development of local action plans, which can be adapted to the local conditions. Its specific objectives are:

- Provide information to the concerned members of the community on the hazards involved in industrial operations in their neighborhood, and the measures taken to reduce these risks.

- Review, update or establish emergency response plans in the local area.
- Increase local industry involvement in community awareness and emergency response planning.
- Integrate industrial emergency plans with local emergency response plans for the community to handle all types of emergencies.
- Involve members of the local community in the development of the overall emergency response plan.

The Objectives of an Emergency Plan

- Accident prevention;
- Containment of the accident within the smallest area if it happens;
- Proper handling of the situation in case of accident to minimize the damage; and
- Rehabilitation of victims, environment, and industrial plant or other sites of accidents.

The emergency plan should be based on careful study of sources of danger, should be flexible, and the official responsible for implementation of the plan should be very clearly identified.

The following are the basic requirements for an emergency plan for chemical disasters:

1. Proper and accurate definition of all substances used in industry whether raw materials, intermediates, end-products or by-products, and characterization of their physical and chemical properties and degree of toxicity.
2. Defining—for each industry—sites of potential accidents and sources of such accidents which may be:
   - industrial processes;
   - storage areas;
   - transport;
   - cleaning and maintenance operations;
   - waste disposal; or
   - agricultural activities.
3. Making use of available information on similar situations, e.g., accidents, after careful analysis of causes and effects.
4. Estimation of amount of toxic chemicals liable to be released in the environment, factors affecting dispersion, approximate expected environmental levels, extent of area affected, and the speed of dispersion.
5. Defining properties and characteristics of area at risk, relation to other parts of industrial plant, neighboring plants or residential

areas, density of pollution, topography, climatic and weather conditions as they affect the dispersion, wind speed and direction and possibility of contamination of surrounding areas in the case of accidents.

6. Study of health effects on man and other biota and effects on environment in general; degradation, biomagnification and transport through the food chain.
7. Gather information on control measures in cases of handling of toxic chemicals and how they are confined in such a way as to minimize their effects, and methods of dealing with these effects.
8. Assigning the responsibility of implementation of the plan at all levels: centrally and at different locations where there are risks, and defining precisely the role of every person involved at all levels. Easy communication between all levels should be guaranteed 24 hours a day.
9. Procedures for dealing with emergencies should be clearly defined at the site of risk, at plant level, at community level and at state level.
10. Guarantee coordination between personnel responsible for the implementation of the plan and emergency services available in the community and the state like police, civil defense, fire brigade, transport system, emergency medical services, hospitals, armed forces, and social relief agencies, locally, nationally and internationally.
11. Resources: trained manpower, and medical and social relief equipment. Up-to-date information on available resources as far as experience, materials and personnel are concerned.
12. A system for data collection, including all above-mentioned information, information on similar situations and accidents; analysis of data and their use in control and prevention. This system should be the only source for public information and dissemination of facts about accidents or dangerous situations.
13. Organization of community participation.
14. Sound physical planning requires the allocation of special areas for dangerous industries far away from residential areas. Ensure that housing complexes do not expand in the direction of dangerous industries.

Prevention of Chemical Disasters Due to Gradual Release of Toxins

Pollution usually occurs due to industrial activity and discharge of toxic substances in waterways and water bodies. Gradual release of toxic materials may lead to accumulation of these materials in water bodies and aquatic ecosystems and toxic pollutants may undergo chemical transformation and biomagnification in these systems. Consumption of polluted water or food, especially sea foods, may lead to health effects. Prevention requires previous identification of the possible sources of water pollution. Local legislations should set standards for disposal in the waterways or water bodies; regular monitoring and enforcing the standards are essential. Injecting liquid waste into underground reservoirs should not be permitted and care should be taken that solid waste does not contaminate waterways or water bodies.

Prevention of Chemical Disasters Resulting from Air Pollution Episodes

The strategy for preventing this type of chemical disasters depends on eliminating or reducing emissions which could, in case of unfavorable weather conditions, accumulate and produce levels of air pollution that may threaten the health and well-being of the population. Zoning and city planning should take into consideration weather conditions, topography and the direction of prevailing winds. Industry should consider the use of no-waste and low-waste technologies and recycling of materials. The use of electric power is the least polluting but if petroleum fuels are used efficient combustion technologies will reduce smoke, hydrocarbons and carbon monoxide and low sulphur fuels reduce SO_2 emissions. Engineering control measures and air cleaning devices are useful but the discharge of emissions through stacks should be avoided as much as possible. Legislative measures include reasonable standards and environmental monitoring and efficient law-enforcing machinery. Special attention should be given to prohibit uncontrolled garbage incineration, control of emissions from power stations and reduction of pollution by automobile exhaust.

On an international level, the United Nations General Assembly issued its resolution 42/169 on 11 December 1987, in which it decided to designate the 1990s as the "International Decade for Natural Disaster Reduction." The objective would be to reduce, through concerted international actions, loss of life, property damage and social and economic disruption caused by natural disasters, particularly in developing countries. As a product of the activities based on this resolution an experts group adopted in 1989 the "Tokyo Declaration" on the International Decade for Natural Disaster Reduction. The group of experts called on: (1) *The people* of the world, as well as their governments, to work toward greater security against natural disaster; (2) *The governments* of all countries to participate actively in the decade by educating and training their citizens to increase awareness, by enhancing social preparedness, by integrating disaster consciousness into their development programs, and by making available the power of science and technology to reduce disaster loss. (3) *The United Nations,* scientific and technological institutions, nongovernmental organizations and the private sector to support international and regional cooperation on disaster-related activities and to contribute to the transfer of disaster-reduction technology, particularly in disaster-prone developing countries. A number of the United Nations agencies have actively participated in the implementation of the Tokyo Declaration. The WHO had several activities on global as well as on regional levels. The WHO regional activities in support of country level action may include: (a) Promotion and technical support to vulnerability analysis of the existing essential health-related services as well as hazardous industries or deposits in disaster-prone areas. (b) Adoption of disaster-resistant design in the planning of essential health services in areas prone to natural disasters. (c) Inclusion of basic concepts of disaster prevention and preparedness into the academic curriculum of the medical, nursing, sanitary engineering and other health-related schools or faculties. (d) Education/information to the general public on issues related to disaster prevention and preparedness by all possible means. (e) Prevention and preparedness at the com-munity level. Regional programs for emergency preparedness have also been implemented by the WHO regional offices. Various efforts have also been made by the International Program on Chemical Safety (IPCS) which issued, in 1981, a special publication on "Emergency response to chemical accidents."

REFERENCES

1. Pier, A., Bertazzi: Industrial disasters and epidemiology. *Scandinavian Journal of Work, Environment and Health, 15*: 85–100, 1989.
2. Martin Holdgate, Mohamed, A., Kassas, Gilbert White: The World Environment, 1972–1982. UNEP Report, 1982, pp. 408–428.
3. African Workshop on Technological Disasters, Proceeding, 26–30 November, 1990, Addis Ababa, Ethiopia.
4. UNEP Industry and Development: Awareness and Preparedness for Emergencies at Local Level, April–June, 1988.

PART III
Approaches and Methodologies

19

The Role of Epidemiology, Controlled Clinical Studies, and Toxicology in Defining Environmental Risks

Shabbir M. Moochhala, Gurinder S. Shahi, and Ila L. Cote

INTRODUCTION

The widespread production of chemicals on an industrial scale is, in human historical terms, a relatively recent development. We face, today, massive environmental problems resulting from production, transport, storage, use, handling and disposal of chemicals—problems that never seemed to trouble societies in previous centuries, when use of, and exposure to, such substances was largely confined to traditional crafts and trades. Along with the exponential increase in general use and availability of potentially hazardous chemicals, has come vastly increased risks to workers, the population at large, and the environment.

There are, at present, over 80,000 man-made chemical substances in commercial use throughout the world, of which some 4,000, accounting for 99.9 percent of the total volume, are in common use in many countries. There are, for example, as many as 600 generic pesticides available commercially.[1] Sufficient data to evaluate the potential health effects of the majority of these chemicals is lacking.[2] Additionally, a great variety of naturally occurring chemicals are in general use—many of which are mined or extracted in developing countries. While use of potentially hazardous chemical substances seems intertwined with the process of economic and social development, a sustainable development process would require that human health and the environment are protected from harmful side effects.[3–5]

The tragic impact of accidental exposure to some of these hazards, and associated urgent calls for action by the public to public health authorities and other national and international regulatory bodies with responsibilities for health, were important determinants in the evolution of modern toxicology. The development of the field has occurred along two broad fronts, one being characterized by increased public awareness of the possible dangers of chemicals and resulting in efforts by responsible authorities to devise effective control measures; the second by the enormous progress being made in understanding the molecular mechanisms of chemical interaction with cellular functions and genetics (for example, in carcinogenesis or teratogenesis).

At the public health level, there have been clear indications of the need for some regulatory measures to ensure safety in the use of dangerous chemicals since the earliest days of the modern chemical industry. Unfortunately, it often took the occurrence of distressing health consequences or catastrophic events before effective control and protective measures were instituted. Epidemiological investigation was often critical in demonstrating the link between particular exposures and the occurrence of these problems.[6–7]

Regulatory agencies tend generally to use three major categories of scientific information for evaluating toxic chemicals in defining environmental risks.[8–10] These include: (a) epidemiology,[11–14] (b) controlled clinical exposure,[15–18] and (c) toxicology.[19–23] These three disciplines provide qualitatively different information—each with unique advantages and limitations. Additionally, *in vitro* studies and evaluation of structure–activity relationships are often used to support the interpretation of information from these main categories.[24–28]

EPIDEMIOLOGY, CONTROLLED CLINICAL STUDIES, AND TOXICOLOGY AS MULTIDISCIPLINARY APPROACHES IN DEFINING HEALTH RISK—ADVANTAGES AND LIMITATIONS

Epidemiology

Environmental epidemiological studies, which attempt to associate disease or other adverse outcomes with environmental exposures, have the advantage of measuring an effect in humans at exposure conditions that are, by definition, realistic.[29–30] The first demonstration that benzene was a carcinogen came from epidemiological studies of rubber workers.[31] It was not until several years after these studies that benzene was shown to cause cancer in animal studies.[32,33] Studies of the London smog pollution episode in 1952 demonstrated that the high levels of pollution from coal combustion could cause mortality, particularly in the very young, the elderly, and those with existing cardiopulmonary disease.[34] Evaluation of similar effects in animal studies would be difficult, given the complexity of the exposure in London and the lack of good animal models for certain susceptible populations, for example, the asthmatics.[35–36]

In general, epidemiology has been helpful in the evaluation of working environments or other environments where exposure concentrations are relatively high or exposed populations are very large.[37–39] Additionally, the application of new techniques, such as meta-analysis—for analyzing large or many data sets relevant to the same chemical(s)—is beginning to increase the potential of epidemiological studies to provide further insight into environmental risks and hazards.[40–42]

Several factors limit the use of epidemiological studies by regulatory agencies to help define risk from environmental exposures. One is the frequent lack of good exposure information, regarding both chemical species to which exposure occurs and also actual concentrations of exposure.[43–46] For example, the lack of good exposure information limits the ability to quantify the effects of ambient air pollution. The Harvard University 'Six City' Study has shown that ambient outdoor nitrogen dioxide (NO_2) monitoring devices are inadequate in accurately assessing exposure to NO_2, because of the importance of indoor exposure to the gas which these devices cannot monitor.[47–48]

Another limitation is that epidemiological studies of worker populations may be unsuitable for predicting health effects in the general population. The general population is more heterogenous than the worker population and for some pollutants, may exhibit a greater range in susceptibility.[49] Thus, studies of lead workers would greatly underestimate the toxicity of this pollutant in the population of concern for ambient exposures, namely, children under the age of 5 years.[50–51]

Further, epidemiological studies are frequently limited by the need for a relatively large increase in disease incidence (twofold or more), given the sample sizes generally available for such investigations. For example, a study by Enterline notes that it would require a large population, about 1,000 people, to detect a 50 percent excess in deaths from lung cancer at an asbestos exposure level of $2\,f/cm^3$.[52]

Last, epidemiological investigations can show a correlation between an exposure and an effect in the population only after the harm has been incurred. In some cases the lag time between exposures and observed effects can be decades. From a public health perspective, this is disadvantageous, since such studies would not prevent the occurrence of toxicity. Recent efforts to utilize biological markers of exposure or effect of exposure, such as DNA adducts and urinary mutagens,[53–54] as part of epidemi-

TABLE 19.1 Advantages and Limitations of Epidemiological Studies

Advantages	Limitations
(1) Effects measured in humans	(1) Effects measured often relatively crude (morbidity, mortality)
(2) Exposure conditions realistic	(2) Difficulty in defining exposure, problems with confounding exposures
(3) Full range in human susceptibility frequently expressed	(3) Costly and time consuming
(4) Occurrence of interactive effects among individual chemicals	(4) *Post facto*, not protective of health
	(5) Increase in risk must be at least 2× to be detected

ology studies, may result in preventive actions before the occurrence of toxicity. Table 19.1 summarizes the advantages and limitations of epidemiological studies.

Controlled Clinical Studies

Controlled clinical studies of humans exposed to pollutants address some of the difficulties of epidemiology studies. The exposures can be controlled and quantified, the effects are observed in humans, and the exposed population can be chosen to consist of susceptible individuals, such as asthmatics or exercising individuals. Thus, changes in airway resistance in asthmatics exposed to ozone and SO_2 during exercise have been important in the U.S. Environmental Protection Agency's evaluation of the U.S. National Ambient Air Quality Standards (NAAQS) for these pollutants.[55–58] Given the subtlety of these changes (nonsymptomatic bronchioconstriction), and the fact that they occur only in a selected subset of the general population (asthmatics constitute about 4 percent of the total general population), these effects would not likely be detectable using epidemiological approaches in the general population.

One advantage of clinical exposure studies is that they are controlled experiments performed with humans—but this is also their major limitation. Since these studies must be limited to short-term effects that are easily reversible, they cannot be used directly to evaluate the potential of a chemical to cause chronic toxicity. Furthermore, because of the relative subtlety of the changes observed in these studies, their clinical significance and potential public health implications are often debatable. Also, although some susceptible populations, such as mild asthmatics, can be tested, individuals with a greater degree of impairment, such as asthmatics who require continual medication, are usually not considered to be appropriate subjects for these studies because of the greater potential for

TABLE 19.2 Advantages and Limitations of Controlled Clinical Studies

Advantages	Limitations
(1) Effects measured in humans	(1) Relatively low-exposure concentrations and short-term exposure
(2) Well-defined, controlled exposure conditions	(2) Limited to relatively small groups (usually <50 individuals)
(3) Ability to measure relatively subtle effects	(3) Limited to short-term, reversible effects
(4) Potential to study subpopulation (e.g. asthmatics)	(4) Costly
	(5) Some susceptible subpopulations not appropriate for study

harm during exposure. Table 19.2 summarizes the advantages and limitations of controlled clinical studies.

Toxicology

Toxicological studies constitute the third major source of information for assessing the risk associated with chemical exposure [59–62]. Toxicology is a science of experimentation in which one uses experimental animals or, broadly speaking, controlled cell systems, microbes, cell cultures, and the like, under highly controlled circumstances that may permit deliberate exposure of the experimental life forms. These studies allow the investigator the greatest degree of control over exposure conditions, the population exposed, and the effects measured. One can readily evaluate the very subtle effects of acute and chronic exposure. For example, one could demonstrate morphological and numerical changes in the pulmonary type I and type II cell populations in rats exposed to 0.12 ppm ozone or 0.5 ppm nitrogen dioxide.[57,63–64] It would have been difficult to describe this effect using other approaches, and yet the effect is clearly of concern for humans who can be exposed to comparable concentrations in the ambient environment.

The ability to manipulate experimental conditions permits evaluation of the effect of many variables on the response to toxic chemicals. Thus, Elsayed and Mustafa were able to demonstrate the protective effect of vitamin E on the acute toxicity of NO_2 in mice.[65] The role of metabolism in determining susceptibility to polycyclic aromatic hydrocarbon-induced carcinogenesis has been evaluated in studies of genetic variants in mice.[66] In their studies, Shahi and colleagues have shown that 1-methyl-4-phenyl-1,2,3,6-tetrahydropyridine (MPTP)-induced neurotoxicity in mice, manifested by depletion of brain dopamine levels, could partially be protected by an aromatic hydrocarbon hydroxylase inducer (beta-naphthoflavone) pretreatment or by cigarette smoke exposure.[67] Such studies can be important in predicting modifiers of toxicity in humans and predicting susceptible populations.

Last, animal toxicology studies are uniquely suited to the study of pollutants for which epidemiology studies are premature and for which clinical exposure studies would be unethical, due to uncertainties about potential health effects. Using an animal bioassay, it could, for example, be demonstrated that emissions from residual coal burning stoves are highly toxic and that emissions from wood-burning stoves are moderately toxic to the lung as compared with the potent pneumotoxin, alpha quartz.[68] Similarly, the toxicity of phosgene, an extremely toxic gas which can be formed photochemically in urban air, can be evaluated.

The limitations of toxicological studies fall into two broad categories: (a) difficulties in extrapolating from animals to humans; and (b) difficulties in extrapolating from the high exposures commonly used in animal studies to the lower exposures typically experienced by humans. Interspecies extrapolation is complicated by the greater homogeneity of laboratory animals compared with humans, controlled conditions of housing and diet, innate genetic factors, and other variables.[69–70] The relevance of trichlorethylene (TCE)-induced hepatocarcinogenesis in the mouse to humans, for example, has been questioned on the basis of differences in peroxisomal proliferation in the liver in the two species.[71–72] Similarly, it is possible that effects may be observed at the high concentrations typically used in animal studies that are not relevant to effects which would occur at ambient exposure concentrations, where detoxication pathways are not saturated. Large collections of macrophages with unusual appearance are observed, for example, in rats in the presence of high concentrations of diesel particulates, under conditions where particle clearance mechanisms from the lung are probably overwhelmed.[73] Such macrophages are not observed at lower exposure concentrations and their significance to humans, who are exposed to diesel particulates at levels which are orders of magnitude lower than those employed in the animal studies, is questionable. Table 19.3 summarizes the advantages and limitations of animal toxicology studies.

The evolution of toxicology discussed above relates primarily to humans. The basic toxicological knowledge generated because of concerns about human health has relevance to all living organisms—even though non-human life forms has tended to come well down on our priority list for action. The discovery of widespread environmental and ecological contamination with DDT and PCBs, for example, have raised awareness of the potential harm that human-generated chemicals (often released with little forethought) can have on the environment and on the many ecosystems that share life on this planet. Such concerns have, in recent

TABLE 19.3 Advantages and Limitations of Animal Toxicology Studies

Advantages	Limitations
(1) Ability to measure many types of responses, using all types of techniques	(1) Uncertainties in extrapolation of animal response to human response
(2) Readily manipulated exposure conditions	(2) Housing, diet, genetic variability etc., of questionable relevance to humans
(3) Ability to assess effect of host characteristics (e.g., sex, age) and other modifiers (e.g., diet) of response	(3) Exposure concentrations and time frames often very different from those experienced by humans
(4) Easier to assess factors underlying toxicity	

years, generated considerable developments in fields such as environmental toxicology and ecotoxicology and led to a greater understanding of the close link between human and ecological health.[74–75]

CONCLUSION

It can be concluded from the preceding discussion that there is no single "best" approach to defining risks arising from environmental exposure to natural and synthetic chemicals. The rational approach, in such circumstances, is to take all sources of information into account.

Despite their limitations, epidemiological studies and controlled clinical studies are most applicable to directly examining the effects of hazards in the environment on humans. Effects such as elevation of absolute and relative rates of mortality or morbidity; increased incidence or prevalence of signs, symptoms, or disease; or shortened time-to-event may all be evidence of a toxic hazard or other risk factor. When the effects of exposure are large, epidemiological or controlled clinical studies will yield firm evidence of causality. However, when the effects of exposure to potentially toxic chemicals are small, or become apparent only after a long interval, or where there is little or no previous data or experience relating to human exposure to a particular chemical (natural or synthetic), epidemiologic evidence must be supplemented by toxicological and other data (such as structure–activity relationship studies) to convincingly demonstrate causality.

Knowledge of the basic concepts of toxicology is also necessary to understand health effects secondary to, for example, exposure to hazardous or toxic substances. In most occupational and environmental exposure situations, the dose of exposure is not known. In addition, there may be simultaneous exposure to many potentially hazardous compounds. Thus, great difficulty may arise in predicting and attributing health effects. An understanding of the nature of such exposures in terms of the mechanism of toxicity of the chemical(s) or material(s) in question, and of the principles of exposure assessment and dose–response assessment are critical in evaluating and determining causation, predicting possible consequences and instituting appropriate interventions.

Hence, epidemiology, clinical studies, and toxicology can usefully and practically complement each other to define environmental risks and to further our understanding of the links between environment, development, and human and ecological health.

REFERENCES

1. World Health Organization Regional Office for Europe and the Center for Environmental Management and Planning (1992). In: *Environmental and Health Impact Assessment of Development Projects*, Turnbull, R. G. H. ed., Elsevier Applied Science.
2. Cote, I. L., & Vandenberg, J. J. (1994). Overview of health effects and risk assessment issues. In: *The Vulnerable Brain and Environmental Risks*, Vol 3: Toxins in Air and Water, Isaacson, R. L., & Jenson, K. F. (Eds.), Plenum Press, New York.
3. Wasserman, O. (1991). The epidemiology of toxic stews. *Acta Oncol., 30:* 15–25.
4. Jeyaratnam, J. (1993). Occupational health issues in developing countries. *Environ. Res., 60(2)*: 207–212.
5. Vainio, H., Matos E., Boffetta, P., Kogevinas, M., & Wilbourn, J. (1993). Occupational cancer in developing and newly industrialized countries. *Ann. Acad. Med. Singapore, 22(2)*: 170–181.
6. Goldsmith, J. R. (1990). The usefulness of epidemiology in environmental health protection. *Public Health Rev., 18(3)*: 183–236.
7. Wegman, D. H. (1992). The potential impact of epidemiology on the prevention of occupational disease. *Am. J. Public Health, 82(7)*: 944–954.
8. U.S. Environmental Protection Agency (1986). The risk assessment guidelines of 1986. *Fed. Regist., 51:* 33,992–34,054.
9. Henschler, D. (1992). Evaluation of adverse effects in the standard-setting process. *Toxicol Lett.*, 64–65: 53–57.
10. Vainio, H., & Cardis, E. (1992). Estimating the human cancer risk from the results of animal experiments: relationships between mechanisms and dose-rate and dose. *Am. J. Ind. Med., 21(1)*: 5–14.
11. Krewski, D., Wigle, D., Clayson, D. B., & Howe, G. R. (1990). Role of epidemiology in health risk assessment. Recent Results. *Cancer Res., 120*: 1–24.
12. Burke, T. A. (1992). Understanding environmental risk: the role of the laboratory in epidemiology, evaluation, and policy setting. *Clin. Chem., 38(2)*: 1519–1522.
13. Lemasters, G. K. (1993). Epidemiology methods to assess occupational exposures and pregnancy outcomes. *Semin. Perinatol., 17(1)*: 18–27.

14. McDonnell, W. F., Zenick, H., & Hayes, C. G. (1993). U.S. EPA's ozone research program: a strategy for assessing the effects of ambient ozone exposures on morbidity in exposed populations. *J. AWMA, 43(7)*: 950–954.
15. Hackney, J. D., & Linn, W. S. (1983). Controlled clinical studies of air pollutant exposure: Evaluating scientific information in relation to air quality standards. *Environ. Health Perspect., 52*: 187–191.
16. Folinsbee, L. J. (1993). Human health effects of air pollution. *Environ. Health Perspect., 100*: 45–56.
17. Gerrity, T. R., Bennett, W. D., Kehrl, H. R., & Dewitt, P. (1993). Mucociliary clearance in inhaled particles measures at two hours after ozone exposure in humans. *J. Appl. Physiol., 74(6)*: 2984–2989.
18. Koren, H. S., Graham, D. E., & Devlin, R. B. (1992). Exposures of humans to a volatile organic mixture: inflammatory response. *Arch. Environ. Health, 47(1)*: 39–44.
19. Greim, H. (1991). General introduction into the toxicology of environmental chemicals. *Prog. Histochem. Cytochem., 23*: 20–26.
20. Scialli, A. R. (1992). Advances in reproductive toxicology. *Curr. Opin. Obstet. Gynecol., 4(3)*: 359–364.
21. Ryan, L. (1992). The use of generalized estimating equations for risk assessment in developmental toxicity. *Risk Anal., 12(3)*: 439–447.
22. Meijers, J. M., Swaen, G. M., Schreiber, G. H., & Sturmans, F. (1992). Occupational epidemiological studies in risk assessment and their relation to animal experimental data. *Regul. Toxicol. Pharmacol., 16(3)*: 215–222.
23. Schlesinger, R. B., & Graham, J. (1992). Health effects of atmospheric acid aerosols: a model problem in inhalation toxicology and air pollution risk assessment. *Fundam. Appl. Toxicol., 18(1)*: 17–24.
24. Augsten, K., & Guttner, J. (1991). New microtechniques in toxicopathology. *Arch. Toxicol. Suppl., 14*: 50–54.
25. Shields, P. G., & Harris, C. C. (1991). Molecular epidemiology and the genetics of environmental cancer. *JAMA, 266(5)*: 681–687.
26. Hanke, J., & Indulski, J. A. (1992). The role of biological markers in toxicology. *Pol. J. Occup. Med. Environ. Health, 5(2)*: 119–128.
27. Albertini, R. J., Nicklas, J. A., Fuscoe, J. C., Skopek, T. R. Branda R. F., & O'Neill, J. P. (1993). *In vivo* mutations in human blood cells: biomarkers for molecular epidemiology. *Environ. Health Perspect., 99*: 135–141.
28. Aust, S. D., Chignell, C. F., Bray, T. M., Kalyanaraman, B., & Mason, R. P. (1993). Free radicals in toxicology. *Toxicol Appl. Pharmacol., 120(2)*: 168–178.
29. Becklake, M. R. (1990). Epidemiology and surveillance. *Chest, 98(5)*: 165S–172S.
30. Griffith, J. D., & Garry, V. F. (1994). *Neurologic disease in molecular epidemiology: principles and practice.* Schulte, P., & Perera, F. (Eds.), Academic Press.
31. Infante, P. F., & White, M. C. (1983). Benzene: epidemiologic observations of leukemic cell type and adverse health effects associated with low level exposures. *Environ. Health Perspect., 52*: 75–82.
32. Maltoni, C., Conti, B., & Cotti, G. (1983). Benzene: a multipotential carcinogen. Results of a long-term bioassay performed at the Bologna Institute of Oncology. *Am. J. Ind. Med., 4*: 589–630.

33. Snyder R., Witz, G., & Goldstein, B. D. (1993). The toxicology of benzene. *Environ. Health Perspect., 100*: 293–306.
34. Lipfert, F. W. (1980). Sulphur oxides, particulates and human mortality: Synopsis of statistical correlation. *J. Air Pollut. Control Assoc., 30*: 366–371.
35. Frampton, M. W. (1991). Environmental factors and atmospheric pollutants. *Semin. Respir. Infect., 6(4)*: 185–193.
36. McDonnell, W. F., Muller, K. E., Bromberg, P. A., & Shy, C. M. (1993). Predictors of individual differences in acute response to ozone exposures. *Am. Rev. Resp. Dis., 147(4)*: 818–825.
37. Abbey, D. E., Mills, P. K., Floyd, F. P., & Beason W. L. (1991). Long-term ambient concentrations of total suspended particulates and oxidants as related to incidence of chronic disease in California Seventh-day Adventists. *Env. Health Perspect., 94*: 43–50.
38. Hall, N. E., & Rosenman, K. D. (1991). Cancer by industry: analysis of a population-based cancer registry with an emphasis on blue-collar workers. *Am. J. Ind. Med., 19(2)*: 145–159.
39. Dockery, D. W., Pope, C. A., Xiping, X., Spengler, B. G., & Speizer, F. E. (1993). An association between air pollution and mortality in six U.S. cities. *N. Engl. J. Med., 329*, in press.
40. Hasselblad, V., Eddy, D. M., & Kotchmar, D. J. (1992). Synthesis of environmental evidence: nitrogen dioxide epidemiology studies. *J. Air Waste Manage. Assoc., 42(5)*: 662–671.
41. Schwartz, J., & Dockery, D. W. (1992). Particulate air pollution an daily mortality in Stubenville, Ohio. *Am. J. Epidemiol., 135*: 12–19.
42. Benignus, V. A. (1994). Behavioral effects of carbon monoxide: meta analysis and extrapolations. *J. Applied Physiol.*, in press.
43. Smith, T. J. (1991). Pharmacokinetic models in the development of exposure indicators in epidemiology. *Ann. Occup. Hyg., 35(5)*: 543–560.
44. Sim, M. R., & McNeil, J. J., (1992). Monitoring chemical exposures using breast milk: a methodological review. *Am. J. Epidemiol., 136(1)*: 1–11.
45. Ulfavarson, U. (1992). Validation of exposure information in occupational epidemiology. *Am. J. Ind. Med., 32(1)*: 125–132.
46. Thomas, D., Stram, D., & Dwyer, J. (1993). Exposure measurement error: influence on exposure-disease. Relationships and methods of correction. *Annu. Rev. Public Health, 14*: 69–93.
47. Quakenbush, J. J., Kanarek, M. S., Spengler, J. D., & Letz, R. (1982). Personal monitoring of nitrogen dioxide exposure: Methodological considerations for a community study. *Environ. Int., 8*: 249–258.
48. Neas, L. M., Dockery, D. W., Ware, J. H., Spengler, J. D., Speizer, F. E., & Ferris, B. G., Jr. (1990). Association of indoor nitrogen dioxide with respiratory symptoms and pulmonary function in children. *Am. J. Epidemiology, 134*: 204–219.
49. Jarvholm, B. (1992). Dose-response in epidemiology-age and time aspects. *Am. J. Ind. Med., 21*: 101–106.
50. U.S. Environmental Protection Agency (1990). Air quality criteria for lead: supplement to the 1986 addendum. EPA-600/8-89/049F. Washington, D.C.

51. Mushak, P. (1992). Defining lead as the premiere environmental health issue for children in America: criteria and their quantitative application. *Environ. Res., 59(2)*: 281–309.
52. Enterline, P. E. (1983). Epidemiologic basis for the asbestos standard. *Environ. Health Perspect., 52*: 93–97.
53. National Research Council. (1989). *Biologic Markers in Pulmonary Toxicology*. National Academy Press, Washington, D.C.
54. National Research Council. (1992). *Biologic Markers in Immunotoxicology*. National Academy Press, Washington, D.C.
55. Horstman, D. (1993). Comparative risks of prolonged exposure to low-level ozone with emphasis on respiratory disease. *Proceedings U.S./Dutch International Symposium on Comparative Risk Analysis and Priority Setting for Air Pollutant Issues*. Keystone, CO., June 7–11.
56. U.S. Environmental Protection Agency (1994). Air quality criteria for ozone. EPA-600/8-94/xxx. Washington D.C., in press.
57. U.S. Environmental Protection Agency (1994). Air quality criteria for sulfur dioxide. EPA-600/8-94/xxx. Washington D.C., in press.
58. McDonnell, W. F. (1994). Prediction of Acute Ozone Response as a Function of Exposure Rate and Total Inhaled Dose. *J. Applied Physiol.*, in press.
59. Lewtas, J. (1993). Complex mixtures of air pollutants: characterizing the cancer risk of polycyclic organic matter. *Env. Health Perspect., 100*: 211–218.
60. Luster, M. I., Selgrade, M. J. K., Germolac, D. R., Burleson, F. G., Kayama, F., Comment, C. E., & Wilmer, J. L. (1994). Experimental studies in immunosuppression:approaches and assessment. In: *Immunotoxicology and Immunopharmacology*, 2nd edition. Dean, J. et al., (Eds.), Raven Press, New York.
61. MacPhail, R. C. (1994). Behavioral analysis in neurotoxicology. In: *Toxicological Interpretation of Neurobehavioral Data*. Weiss, B., & O'Donoghue, J. (Eds.), Raven Press, New York.
62. Johnson, B. L. (1993). Neurobehavioral toxicology in the 21st century: a future or a failure? *Environ. Res., 62(1)*: 114–124.
63. Crapo, J. D., Barry, B. E., Chang, L. Y., & Mercer, R. R. (1984). Alteration in lung structure caused by inhalation of oxidants. *J. Toxicol. Environ. Health., 13*: 301–321.
64. Mercer, R. R., Russell, M. L., & Crapo, J. D. (1994). Cell number and distribution in human and rat airways. *Am. J. Resp. Cell and Molec. Bio.*, in press.
65. Elsayed, N. M., & Mustafa, M. G. (1982). Dietary antioxidants and biochemical response to oxidant inhalation. I. Influence of dietary vitamin E on the biochemical effects of nitrogen dioxide exposure in the rat lung. *Toxicol. Appl. Pharmacol., 66*: 319–328.
66. Kouri, R. E., & Nebert, D. W. (1977). Genetic regulation of susceptibility to polycyclic hydrocarbon induced tumors in the mouse. In: Hiatt, H. H., Watson, J. D., & Winstyen, J. A. (Eds.), *Origins of Human Cancer*, Cold Spring Harbor Laboratory, New York.
67. Shahi, G. S., Das, N. P., & Moochhala, S. M. (1991). MPTP induced neurotoxicity: partial protection against striato-nigral dopamine depletion by cigarette smoke exposure and by beta-naphthoflavone pretreatment. *Neuroscience Lett., 127*: 247–250.

68. Beck, B. D., & Brain, J. D. (1982). Prediction of the pulmonary toxicity of respirable combustion products from residual wood and coal stoves. In: *Residential Wood and Coal Combustion*. Air Pollution Control Association. Pittsburgh, Pennsylvania.
69. Grandjean, P. (1992). Individual susceptibility to toxicity. *Toxicol Lett., 64–65*: 43–51.
70. Tepper, J. S., Costa, D. L., & Lehmann, J. R. (1994) Extrapolation of animal data to humans: homology of pulmonary physiological responses with ozone exposure. In: *Toxicology of the Lung*, 2nd edition, Gardner, D. E. et al., (Eds.), Raven Press, New York, 217–251.
71. Elcombe, C. R., Rose, M. S., & Pratt, I. S. (1985). Biochemical, histological and ultrastructural changes in the rat and mouse liver following the administration of trichloroethylene: possible relevance to species differences in hepatocarcinogenicity. *Toxicol. Appl. Pharmacol., 79*: 365–376.
72. Allen, K. L., Green, C. E., & Tyson, C. A. (1987). Comparative studies of peroxisomal enzyme induction in hepatocytes from rat, cynomologus monkey and human by hypolipidemic drugs. *Toxicologist, 7*: 63–64.
73. White, H. J., & Grag, B. D. (1981). Early pulmonary response of the lung to inhalation of high concentration of diesel particles. *J. Appl. Toxicol., 1*: 104–110.
74. Malins, D. C., & Osterand, G. K. (1991). Perspectives in aquatic toxicology. *Annu. Rev. Pharmacol. Toxicol., 31*: 371–399.
75. Pritchard, J. B. (1993). Aquatic toxicology: past, present, and prospects. *Environ. Health Perspect., 100*: 249–257.

20

The Place of Occupational Health and Epidemiology Within the Context of Environmental Health

J. Jeyaratnam

INTRODUCTION TO OCCUPATIONAL HEALTH

The discipline of occupational health is a relatively recent development in modern medicine. Hippocrates, the pioneer of modern medicine, urged physicians of his day, 2,500 years ago, to routinely enquire of all their patients their family name, location of their abode, and age on the basis that these had an influence on health and disease. But it was Ramazzini just 300 years ago who urged physicians to add one more question to those proposed by Hippocrates and ask their patients "What is your occupation?" This delay is indicative of a lack of understanding of the relationship between work and health, till relatively recent times.

The World Health Organization defines occupational health as the promotion and maintenance of the highest degree of physical, mental, and social well-being of workers in all occupations. This means that occupational health is the concern about the *total health of all persons at work.* So defined, occupational diseases constitute only one aspect of the health concerns of the working population. An occupational disease may be defined as a disease where factors in the work environment are essential and predominant in its causation; it usually affects exposed workers exclusively. Implicit in this definition of an occupational disease is that such diseases are eminently preventable.[1]

Today's concern about environmental health is the concern about human activity and its impact on the environment which in turn is likely to damage human health—a concern which is largely consequent to the following developments:

1. *Global industralization.* Nations which were agricultural are rapidly industrializing.
2. *Modernization of agriculture.* Today agriculture is using a large number of chemicals which have the capacity to cause environmental damage.
3. *Mass disasters,* e.g., Chernobyl, Bhopal, Seveso
4. *Climatic changes and ozone depletion.*
5. *Recognition of diseases* whose causation is attributed or linked to environmental damage, e.g., cancers.

OCCUPATIONAL AND ENVIRONMENTAL HEALTH

The recent rapid growth in interest in environmental health has created a dilemma as to its identity as a speciality in the field of health. The public interest in environmental health was not matched by a well-developed speciality in the health field which could respond to its needs and concerns. This resulted in occupational health/medicine being identified as the established speciality most suited to take on responsibility for the needs of environmental health/medicine. There are several areas of common ground between occupational and environmental health to justify such a position. A comparison of the factors in the work environment influencing the health of the working population (occupational health) and that of the general environment affecting the health of the community (environmental health) is shown in Table 20.1. It would be evident that there exist several areas of similarity between the work environment and the general environment affecting health. An important distinction between the two is that the exposure in the work environment is limited in time, that is, duration of exposure, and to healthy adults, whereas general

TABLE 20.1 Comparison of Occupational Health (OCH), & Environmental Health (EVH)

OCH	EVH
Hazards in workplace environment	Hazards in community environment
Hazards largely in air	Hazards in air, soil, water and food
Hazards are physical, chemical, biological and psychosocial	Hazards are physical, chemical, biological, and psychosocial
Route of exposure: inhalation, dermal	Ingestion, inhalation, and dermal
Exposure period: 8 hrs/day, 40 hrs/week for working life	Exposure lifelong
Exposed population—adults, usually healthy persons	Vulnerable population—children, adults, old people, and sick people

environmental exposure could be lifelong and the full spectrum of the population is exposed.

Often the distinction between the work environment and the home environment may not be clearly defined. This is particularly seen in agriculture and small-scale industries. The interrelationship between work practices and environmental contamination is demonstrated in a recent study in Taiwan.[2] It was shown that kindergarten school children had an elevated blood lead level as a consequence of contaminated air and soil from a nearby lead recycling smelter. It was also observed that the average IQ of these children was significantly lower than that of a comparable group of children.

The disciplines of environmental health and occupational health have a similar approach to containing the problem. Grandjean[3] states that the preventive strategies used in environmental and occupational health are clearly similar. The emphasis is on primary prevention. The pollution must be stopped at the origin. Dangerous products or procedures must be substituted by those that are safer. If emissions are unavoidable the release must be minimized or confined.

Ducatman and colleagues[4] state that environmental health like occupational health combines clinical, epidemiologic and toxicologic approaches to the diagnosis, prevention, and treatment of detectable human disease or other adverse effects from exposure to external physical, clinical, or biologic factors. It uniquely seeks to understand external causation and then to adopt policy, engineering, or human factor interventions to prevent or mitigate the caused outcomes.

Given this background, this chapter deals specifically with the epidemiological issues of commonality and interrelationship between occupational health and environmental health.

EPIDEMIOLOGY IN OCCUPATIONAL AND ENVIRONMENTAL HEALTH

Environmental epidemiology has been described as the part of Environmental Health Science and Management that specifically deals with the occurrence of health impacts of the environment (description), the links between exposure and health effects (analysis of causation), and the links between interventions and reduced or avoided effects (evaluation of prevention).[5]

Occupational epidemiology has been stated[6] to deal with occurrence relation between work-related diseases and the factors determining their outbreak and course. "Occurrence relation" is a term that Miettinen has used particularly for describing the study of the relation of an outcome parameter to its determinants.

Epidemiological studies among working populations provide an assessment of the work environment as to its potential to harm human health. The factors in the work environment which may cause damage to human health could be: (1) chemical and physical agents, (2) biological agents, (3) factors linked to accidents, and (4) psychosocial factors. One of the uses of epidemiological studies, particularly occupational, is in establishing safe levels of exposure to the working population. Needless to state, all of the other uses of epidemiology such as etiology of disease, natural history, description of health status, and evaluation of services and intervention are relevant to both occupational and environmental epidemiology. But this chapter will focus attention on the interrelationship between occupational and environmental epidemiology in terms of setting standards in the work environment and the general environment. Such an approach is in reality a process of risk management whereby an attempt is made to ensure that the population at risk is limited in exposure to an acceptable level of risk. A component part of determining an acceptable risk is an attempt at quantitative assessment of risk; in which epidemiological data play an important part. At this point it is pertinent to define risk as a compound measure of the probability and magnitude of an adverse effect, whereas a hazard is defined as the inherent property of a system or agent that could cause injury or damage. In the process of risk management the step of hazard identification and risk estimation involves epidemiology and epidemiologists. Arising from such information is the setting of safety standards, such as permissible exposure limits, in occupational settings. These standards in the work environment as set out by the American Congress of Governmental Industrial Hygienists are known as Threshold Limit Values (TLVs) and are based on 8 hours exposure per day for a 5-day work week for an exposed population of healthy adults. It has been proposed[7] that these safety standards for toxic agents could be modified as safety standards for the general community. For instance, to allow for the 24-hour exposure of the general community to an environmental pollutant, the TLV should be reduced by a factor of 3. Further to allow for the situation where the general community consists of the young, the aged and the sick the TLV should be further reduced by a factor of 10. Finally it is suggested that TLVs in the work environment for chemical agents be made more stringent by a factor of 30 and adopted as a safety standards for the community.

The International Agency for Research on Cancer (IARC) uses epidemiological data in categorizing the carcinogenicity of an agent. Often these epidemiological data utilized for the evaluation of carcinogenicity are obtained from occupational epidemiological studies, particularly the cohort and case-control studies. This again is an example of the use of occupational epidemiological data in assessing carcinogenicity of an agent in relation to human exposure through the general environment.

A further use of occupational epidemiological data for environmental exposure is the use of safety factors in deciding on safe levels of exposure. For instance in the case of non-carcinogenic compounds, the Acceptable Daily Intake (ADI) is defined for man by dividing the No Observed Effect Level (NOEL) by a safety factor which may range from 1–5,000, depending on criteria which include the availability of human data usually based on occupational epidemiological data.

Ducatman[9] in a recent review on occupational and environmental medicine stated that the high dose exposures of the employed population provides information on issues pertaining to the general community.

Ducatman[9] cites important and interesting examples to demonstrate the interrelationship between occupational and the wider environmental aspects of public health practice, stating that relatively higher dose exposures to discrete populations at work provide data for decisions pertaining to the general population. The following examples are referred to by Ducatman.

Asbestos

There is a great deal of expenditure in the United States for asbestos control in public schools under the Environmental Protection Agency's Asbestos Hazard Emergency Response Act. The controversy is as to whether such expenditure is necessary and justified. But Ducatman in his paper examines the evidence from occupational exposure data and concludes that it is not possible to categorically state that no deaths would occur from the removal of environmental controls over building asbestos.

Dioxin

Dioxin was studied among environmentally exposed populations in the Vietnam War with equivocal results. This was largely due to difficulties in characterizing the extent of exposure among exposed and non-exposed persons. But studies among occupational populations have more accurate indicators of exposure levels and the general consensus from such data is that dioxin-contaminated herbicides are carcinogens. Thus again demonstrating that better understanding of environmental outcomes will result from studies that address the exposed working populations. There is evidence from such studies that dioxin-contaminated herbicides are carcinogens.

Epidemiological data derived from occupational cohort studies can be used for general environmental risk assessment. The data from occupational epidemiological studies will need to be fitted into various mathematical models for extrapolation to low exposure situations. These mathematical models are usually variants of the multiplicative or the additive model or a combination of both. Further, for such an exercise it is necessary to have baseline information, which is usually available for vital statistics, nonexposed subjects in the study cohort or an internal control group.[10]

Diesal Exhaust Fumes

The usage of the multiplicative model in assessing the risk of lung cancer in the general population exposed to diesel exhaust fumes, based on occupational epidemiological studies, is shown in a paper by McClellan.[11] The baseline data are that of U.S. population 230 million persons with a life span of 70 years with 10,000 annual deaths due to lung cancer. The occupational epidemiological studies by Harris[12] on London transport workers exposed to diesel exhaust provide two estimates for proportional risk due to exposure to diesel engine exhaust. In the first instance Harris calculated an upper 95 percent confidence limit of 5×10^4 proportional increase /$\mu g/m^3$ per one year of exposure. Based on this, the estimate for proportional risk due to exposure to diesel engine exhaust is as shown below:

$$5 \times 10^4 \frac{\text{increased lifetime risk}}{\mu g/m^3 \text{ per year}} \times 70\text{yr} \times 1 \times 10^5 \text{ cancers/yr}$$
$$= 3{,}500 \text{ lung cancers/year.}$$

McClellan also made a second estimate based on the Harris[13] study with a maximum likelihood estimate of a 1.23×10^4 proportional increase in lung cancer/$\mu g/m^3$ exposure for one year. On this basis the estimate for proportional risk due to exposure to diesel engine exhaust is as shown below:

$$1.23 \times 10^4 \frac{\text{increased lifetime risk}}{\mu g/m^3/\text{yr}} \times 70\text{yr} \times 1 \times 10^5 \text{ cancers/yr}$$
$$= 860 \text{ lung cancers/year.}$$

McClellan also refers to another approach utilizing epidemiological data together with results of *in vitro* potency of diesel exhaust, a method pioneered by Harris, Albert and colleagues and called the comparison potency method.

Harris[13] states the final step in a risk assessment process is risk characterization, which is the estimation of the incidence of health effect for a given population under various conditions of human exposure. To illus-

TABLE 20.2 Risk Characterization for Diesel Exhaust Exposures If 20 percent of the Light-Duty Vehicles Are Diesel-Powered

Diesel Exhaust Exposed Population	Diesel Exhaust Particle Exposure (ug/m³)	Added Annual Lung Cancer Risk (cancers/ 10^5 people)	Total Lung Cancer Risk
Typical urban resident	0.5	0.05	~200
Urban residents near freeway	6.0	0.6	
Workers on urban freeway	35.0	3.5	
Workers in urban street canyon	30.0	3.0	
		Annual Lung Cancer Risk	
Comparison population			
smokers		80	~100,000
nonsmokers		7	~10,000

From McClellan (1986).

trate the risk characterization step, one may use the lung cancer risk estimate in combination with the exposure assessment data. Results of this aggregation are shown in Table 20.2 (Cuddily et al.).[14] They estimated that use of 20 percent diesel vehicles in the light duty fleet would be expected to cause less than 200 lung cancers/year in the United States. This figure must be considered in the perspective of the present incidence of lung cancer in the United States. Currently it is estimated that approximately 100,000 lung cancers per year occur in smokers and an additional 10,000 lung cancers per year in nonsmokers.

It would be evident from these examples that information from occupational epidemiology has found extensive usage in making decisions regarding outcomes in the general population as a consequence of exposure to hazards in the environment. This situation demonstrates the interrelation between occupational health and environmental health, suggesting that the discipline of occupational health probably has the greatest potential to contribute to and address the issues of the newly emerging discipline of environmental health.

REFERENCES

1. WHO. *Our Planet, Our Health.* WHO, 1992, Geneva.
2. Jung-Der Wang, Chang-Sheng Jong, Yaw-Huei Huang, & Zueng-Sang Chin. Lead Contamination Around a Kindergarten Near a Battery Recycling Plant. *Bull. Environ. Contam. Toxicol. 1992; 49*: 23–30.
3. Grandjean, P. Occupational and Environmental Health—Common Goals. *European Bulletin on Environment and Health. 1992; 1(3)*: 3–5.
4. Ducatman, M. A., et al. What is Environmental Medicine? *Journal of Occupational Medicine. 1990; 32(11)*: 1130–1131.

5. WHO. Global Networks to Strengthen Education, Training and Research in Environmental Health. PEP/GEENET/93.13. 1993, Geneva.
6. Hernberg, S. *Introduction to Occupational Epidemiology*. 1992. Lewis Publishers, Michigan.
7. WHO. Health and Safety Component of Environmental Impact Assessment. Environmental Health Series 15. WHO. 1987. Copenhagen.
8. WHO. Lead. Environmental Health Criteria, No. 3. 1977. Geneva.
9. Ducatman, M. A. Occupational Physicians and Environmental Medicine. *Journal of Occupational Medicine. 1993; 35(3)*: 251–259.
10. Layard, M. W., & Silvers, A. Epidemiology in Environmental Risk Assessment. In *The Risk Assessment of Environmental Hazards*. Ed. Dennis J Panstenbach 1989. John Wiley & Sons, New York.
11. McClellan, R. O. Health Effects of Diesel Exhaust: A Case Study in Risk Assessment. *American Industrial Hygiene Association Journal. 1986; 47(1)*: 1–13.
12. Harris, J. E. *Potential Risk of Lung Cancer from Diesel Engine Emissions*. 1981; National Academy Press, Washington, DC.
13. Harris, J. E., Diesel Emissions, & Lung Cancer. *Risk Analysis. 1983; 3(2)*: 83–100.
14. Cuddily, R. G., Griffith, W. C., McClellan, R. O. Health Risks for Light Duty Diesel Vehicles. *Environmental Science & Technology, 1984; 18*: 14A–21A.

21

Assessing Health Impacts of Environmental Exposures

C. J. Hong

HISTORICAL PERSPECTIVE

Assessing health impact from environmental exposures evolved from making clinical diagnoses of cases of individual patients suffering from diseases which were directly or indirectly associated with environmental exposures such as cholera from water contaminated by *Vibrio cholerae* and pulmonary tuberculosis from close contact between tuberculosis patients and their family members or friends, the latter situation being aggravated by overcrowding.

There are basically two types of environmentally related hazards: "traditional" health hazards—infectious and parasitic diseases which remain the most pressing health issues in many developing countries, and "modern" health hazards—chronic non-infectious diseases such as cardiovascular or cardiocerebral diseases and cancer which are more prevalent in developed countries. Nevertheless, some developing countries are confronted with both the traditional and modern health hazards during the course of their development. Modern technology has brought a dramatic increase in the production and consumption of man-made chemicals. A major proportion of these chemicals enters the environment as industrial wastes or finds use as components in consumer products, posing health risks as well as benefits. Pesticides, herbicides and fertilizers enter the environment as a result of direct application; sulfur oxides, nitrogen oxides and polycyclic aromatic hydrocarbons enters the environment as a result of the fossil-fuel combustion process. Industrial waste materials are discharged into the environment through complex and interrelated pathways, the toxicity of many of these chemicals has not been thoroughly studied. All these make health impact assessment a most challenging task, though it has never been easy to quantify the health risks involved in an environmental health impact assessment, from subjective grading to sophisticated modelling.

Goals and Objectives

Development is a two-edged sword in terms of its effects on health. In general, the economic and technological improvement brought about by development will decisively help raise living standards and health of the people concerned, but neglect of potential environmental factors or negligence in development planning and inadequately controlled or unthought-of side effects may have a profound impact on the health and well-being of the community.

People of all nations, industrialized or otherwise, need development to improve their living standards and to meet their future needs, but its adverse health effects should be avoided by all means. The goal of assessing health impacts is to ensure the health of the people concerned in a systematic way by which changes in their environment are studied and weighed carefully so that the health condition of the people would not be endangered by such changes and would even be improved during the course of the development. In order to cope with this situation and to make up for inadequacies in forecasting health effects of development projects and to provide a scientific basis for the setting of standards pertaining to the environment, it is crucial to be able to make a valid assessment of health impacts. For this purpose, people need to have better knowledge of how to assess health effects from various environmental exposures, which, in turn, can lead to a better understanding of the environment and its interaction with human health, as well as the preservation or creation of an environment that would both promote health and is suitable for future sustainable development.

The question of how to define an adverse health effect is of critical importance for assessing health impacts from environmental exposure. Considerable controversy exists concerning what constitutes an adverse health effect. According to one view, any evidence of biological or functional change is considered to be an adverse health effect. According to others, evidence is required of both an irreversible decrement in the ability of the body to maintain homeostasis or normal function, and an enhanced susceptibility to the deleterious effects of other environmental factors. In this latter view, differentiation between "adverse" and "non-adverse" effects requires considerable knowledge of what are reversible changes and what are not, as well as "acceptable" subtle deviation or departure from "normal" physiological, biochemical or behavioral changes in question. Some of the difficulties in assessing health impacts are associated with the wide variations which might occur but are generally considered to be still within "normal" ranges.

The objectives of a health impact assessment are:

1. Evaluation of existing health conditions of the people concerned;
2. Analysis of the contribution of various environmental factors to different health indicators or disease end-points;
3. Studying the incidence and prevalence of diseases to see whether they are related to environmental exposures when such an association is suspected;
4. Prediction or projection of probable health effects of a proposed development project;
5. Raising the awareness of communities, making them aware of their health problems and their environmental determinants, be it air pollution, water pollution, unsanitary waste disposal practices, overcrowding, construction of a new plant, change of water course, deforestation, or other factors with potential health consequences.

Approach and Strategy

Health impact assessment is based on the health status of the population concerned and the expected or projected environmental pollution levels. In general, a health impact assessment is composed of two steps in its approach: (1) a qualitative assessment of relevant biomedical and toxicological data to determine whether a certain environmental exposure may pose, directly or indirectly, any risks upon health of the population concerned; and (2) if this aid exposure is capable of causing adverse health effects, a quantitative assessment or projection of the dose-effect relationship in the population concerned to provide the basis for deciding on the advisability of a development project from the health perspective, or for recommending safe exposure levels or other relevant measures to be taken to ensure health and well-being of the people.

Selection and Development of Sensitive and Specific Health Impact Assessment Methods

Early assessment of the health status of the population was limited to the use of mortality data because these were the only data available in most countries and thus could provide a basis for comparison. However, mortality data do not always accurately reflect the underlying morbidity and are particularly inappropriate in the case of certain diseases for which the fatality rate is low, yet which are nevertheless important causes of morbidity, such as chronic respiratory diseases which plague tens of millions of people but the mortality of which is relatively low. Data on causes of death are also less reliable for the elderly because of the multiple pathological conditions often present among the elderly at the time of death. Unfortunately, comprehensive and comparable population-based morbidity data are generally not readily available, or are difficult to obtain.

Since many of the environmental exposures encountered in health impact assessments are related to chemicals, and diseases caused by chemicals have been observed in most organs after high levels of exposure in occupational settings, industrial or occupational medical data are among the most important data sources for health impact assessments. Diseases encountered in occupational settings include various chronic pulmonary diseases (pneumoconiosis, silicosis, asbestosis, byssionosis), acute lung diseases (acute alveolitis, etc.), allergic reactions of the respiratory tract and of the skin, diseases affecting the central and peripheral nervous system (mercury or manganese poisoning, lead poisoning), the cardiovascular system, the hematological system (lead poisoning, benzene and other solvent exposures), liver and bile system, renal system, reproductive system (embryotoxic and genetic effects) as well as malignant tumors of all sites (due to asbestos, arsenic, nickel, benzene, carbon tetrachloride, aromatic amines, and other exposures). Extrapolations from occupational exposures have led to the identification of health risks to the general public. For instance, information of health-damaging effects of occupational exposure to lead and asbestos have been instrumental in identifying lead and asbestos as health threats to the general public and led to their phasing out in the domestic environment. Identification of a serious health problem among workers in a particular industry often serves as a warning or sentinel that the general population might be exposed to similar agents which are detrimental to health.

However, since the general population is exposed to concentration levels much lower than those found in occupational settings, and might be exposed to a number of harmful agents simultaneously, this makes assessment of health impacts from environmental exposures more challenging. What is more, because most manifestations of diseases associated with environmental exposures are non-specific, it is usually difficult to determine the extent to which exposure to environmental agents contribute to the onset of the said disease or to the deterioration of health or exacerbation of existing diseases. The etiology of most diseases is multifactorial and the contribution of any single environmental agent to the total disease incidence is often difficult to differentiate from other etiologic factors of the exposed population. There is also increasing evidence that some environmental factors may interfere with or lower the resistance of the body, thereby increasing the body's susceptibility to diseases.

With the limited data sources and availability of health indicators on the one hand, and the complexity and variability of the problems on the other, selection and development of sensitive and specific health impact assessment methods enjoy high priority in the strategy for assessing health impacts.

Standardization of Methods to Ensure Validity and Comparability

Health impact assessment methods need to be uniform or standardized to ensure validity and accuracy of findings as well as comparability of results. In view of the limited availability of data pertaining to environmental exposures and their health impacts, it is in the interest of all parties concerned to make full use of all the relevant health impact assessment data available so that these data could be pooled together and shared among professionals working in this field, with environmental exposures beginning from very mild exposures to heavy exposures and health effects from mild body burden to emergence of symptoms and incidence of diseases to elevated mortality.

In view of the limited resources at our disposal, the need for and advantage of more uniformity in health impact assessment methods, uniform terminology and diagnostic procedures, agreement on the range of sub-clinical or biological changes which could be considered as "normal" (taking into consideration the differences between various ethnic, racial or national groups) and closer international cooperation is obvious. Promoting the use of standardized methods would ensure validity and comparability of the assessment, but care should also be taken to modify the methods according to local conditions and needs. Physicians in North America may not be familiar with liver cancer and its early symptoms because it is not common there, and may have difficulty in diagnosing the disease at an early stage, while doctors in temperate climate countries may not have much experience in dealing with tropical diseases and their early symptoms and variations as well. Therefore local participation in health impact assessments is an essential component of the endeavor, because physicians stationed there are the people who know the local situation and its intrinsic relations and complications best.

Study of Sensitive or Vulnerable Sub-Groups

People in the community are exposed to environmental pollutants generally at concentrations much lower than those encountered in occupational settings. This calls for the improvement of the sensitivity of methods used in health impact assessments in order to detect the often small increases in morbidity or deviations in organ functions which are attributable tc environmental exposures in the general population. Because the exposed populations include persons representing a spectrum of sensitivities to the agent under study, one way to improve the sensitivity of the health impact assessment method is to focus on the more sensitive or vulnerable sub-groups in the exposed general population. Many adverse health impacts of environmental agents have been ascertained in susceptible subpopulations.

Susceptibility or vulnerability is the state of being readily affected. In hypersusceptible persons, expected health effects occur at a lower exposure level than in the majority of the population. In hyperreactive persons, the health effects of an agent are qualitatively those expected but quantitatively increased.

Sensitive or vulnerable sub-groups include: infants, young children, women of childbearing age, pregnant women, the elderly, and people with disease or genetic predispositions.

Infants and Young Children. Infants and young children are particularly vulnerable to environmental exposures because of their structural and functional characteristics. These may affect their vulnerability when exposed to environmental insults due to their:

- Larger body surface area in relation to weight: A newborn infant weighing 3.5 kg is one-twentieth of the weight of a 70 kg man, but the surface area of the infant is one-eighth as great. Therefore the area of skin that could be exposed to an environmental pollutant is 2.5 times as great per unit body weight in a naked child as in a naked adult. This is particularly important when assessing health impact from exposure to gaseous or liquid chemicals;
- Higher metabolic rate and oxygen consumption: Because of higher metabolic rate, the volume of air passing through the lungs of a resting infant is twice that of a resting adult per unit body weight, hence twice as much of any chemical in the air will reach infant lungs as will teach the lungs of an adult per unit body weight;
- Functional immaturity of organs and systems of the body: Most organs and systems of an infant have not reached structural or functional maturity at birth. Development of the nervous system continues in postnatal life, much of the myelination of the brain takes place after birth and continues until adolescence. The full number of neurons is not reached until about 2 years of age. The structural development of the lung also continues postnatally with increase in alveolar surface area. The lymphocytes responsible for producing antibodies, the gastrointestinal, endocrine, and reproductive systems as well as renal function are all immature at birth. The activity

of many liver enzyme systems which metabolize endogenous and exogenous substances may also be low in the newborn infant.

Exposure of infants to chemicals can give rise not only to immediate health effects, but also to disturbed maturation of organ systems as well as their altered response to other environmental factors at a later stage.

Women of Childbearing Age and Pregnant Women. Many changes which occur during pregnancy can have significant impacts on the toxicodynamics of a particular chemical. The changes in body weight, total body water, plasma proteins, body fat, and cardiac output will alter the distribution of many xenobiotic compounds.[2]

Women who might be exposed to such exposures are at particular risk and therefore should not only be evaluated for their own health, but also for their pregnancy outcomes. Special attention should be paid to pregnant women who have been or might be exposed accidentally or over an extended period of time to chemicals such as mercury, ethylene oxide, for example, during their pregnancy, even when they appear to be in good health.[3,4] However, health effects on the progeny due to environmental exposure of their fathers also needs to be considered.

The Elderly. The United Nations has defined people of 60 years and over as the aged.[5] Nevertheless, many countries are using 65 years and over as the definition of the elderly. The corresponding number for this age group will be 423 million by the year 2000, of whom 230 million will be in developing countries.[6]

The health conditions of the elderly are quite different from those in the early or middle age of human life. Many chronic diseases which begin at an early age may extend into advanced age. Some asymptomatic pathological conditions occurring in middle age may become symptomatic in later years. The elderly have been subjected to long-term exposure to environmental agents. The source may have been polluted air, water, food, or products made of inorganic or organic chemicals with which people frequently come into contact in their daily life or during their occupational activities. In general, the elderly are more susceptible to adverse effects of environmental exposures. This is partly because of the declining and deteriorating physiological functions brought about by the long process of aging which leads to impaired immune functions, declining pulmonary, cardiovascular and renal functions; and partly because the elderly, having lived long in an environment containing various harmful agents, may suffer from their cumulative effects even when the exposure levels have been relatively low. Some age-specific diseases may lead to increased susceptibility to adverse environmental exposures. This vulnerability might be the result of intrinsic biological aging, high prevalence of various age-related diseases, or a combination of all of these factors.

Current Status

Assessment of Exposure

Though assessment of exposure is not a part of health impact assessments *per se*, the validity of the former is a prerequisite and crucial in the proper implementation of the latter. Oftentimes insufficient or incorrect exposure data are found to be the underlying cause which mars an otherwise carefully planned health impact assessment.

In general, environmental exposure levels can be assessed either by (1) assessing the external exposure, or by (2) assessing the internal exposure which approximates the actual dose at target organs and thus provides a better estimate of exposure than that obtained by assessing the external exposure. However, past internal exposure data are rarely available and current data difficult to obtain.

It is essential to obtain exposure data which are representative of the actual exposure of the population at risk. Due to constraints in resources, many health impact assessment studies are based on estimated exposure from data obtained at air or water monitoring sites. A single site may be assumed to be representative of a large area (which is hardly the case, especially in a big city) and the number of monitoring sites are often limited because of resource constraints. Under such circumstances, modelling techniques are useful only if there are a reasonable number of monitoring sites in a city and even so they are only a partial answer to assessment of the actual exposure.

Since environmental monitoring has drawbacks in providing true and representative exposure data for health impact assessment, personal sampling has been introduced in recent years. First used in occupational settings, this approach has gradually found application, though still very gradually, in the field of health effect studies of the general population. However, there are considerable difficulties in using the personal sampling technique in health impact assessment in a community because of the large number of subjects involved and the difficulty in soliciting cooperation from each of them, not to mention the difficulty encountered in using personal sampling devices on young children and the elderly as well as the cost involved. Nevertheless, since environmental exposure is a function of concentration, duration and frequency of intake, personal monitoring has the prospect of being used in community studies with limited numbers of subjects if sensitive and specific devices which are convenient to carry, inexpensive, and do not require the use of a suction pump are available.

Another approach of assessing exposure is through biological monitoring. Parameters of internal exposure or uptake are measured as the result of external exposure through ambient air, water or food. Biological monitoring is a measurement of total exposure, irrespective of the source of pollution or route of entry, while in environmental monitoring, it would be necessary to measure all sources of external exposure as well as the duration for the assessment of total exposure. Internal exposure is the result of external exposure and of the life style or characteristics of the subjects exposed. For example, in the case of exposure through the respiratory tract, we need to know not only the pollutant's concentrations in the air, but also the physical activity pattern and respiratory volume of the subject. Thus the actual exposure is much better assessed by biological monitoring, because the impact of personal behavior, age, sex, disease status, and differences in uptake, absorption and metabolism is taken into account. Furthermore, biological monitoring is able to pinpoint the groups or individuals actually at risk, and may therefore be used on a larger number of subjects than would be the case with personal monitoring.

The report of a study on the assessment of human exposures to cadmium and lead by means of biological monitoring stresses the importance of quality assurance procedures in the study.[7] With these established, it was possible to make valid comparisons of the blood levels of lead and cadmium among residents in a number of cities around the world.

However, biological monitoring has its own limitations, such as inconvenience to the subjects, a certain degree of health risk if invasive procedures are used in collecting samples, as well as other ethical issues. Moreover, biological monitoring is possible only in the case of chemicals which can be measured in biological samples. It can not be used in the case of pollutants which exert their effects primarily at the point of absorption, e.g., sulfur oxides, nitrogen oxides, ozone, or photochemical oxidants.

The pitfalls to avoid in assessing exposure are exemplified by a review of studies on the relationship between organic chemicals in drinking water and incidence of cancer.[8] These pitfalls include: the chosen indicator agent or agents may not necessarily represent the potential agent which would have the health impact under study, uneven distribution of pollutants in place and time, no data available on past exposure levels, existing records are inadequate for yielding exposure data, classification of individuals on the basis of residence may be inaccurate with respect to total exposure, individual variation in water consumption, and differences between administrative districts and water distribution areas.

In assessing exposure over long periods of time, special attention should be paid to possible changes in sampling schemes and analytical methods which may invalidate the consistency, accuracy, and comparability of data.

Assessment of Health Impacts

Spectrum of Health Effects. In assessing health impacts, a broad spectrum of health effects is involved, including changes in body burden, subclinical immunological or functional changes which may or may not be associated with incidence of diseases (or perhaps just because of a matter of time?), change in spontaneous abortion rate, change in the pattern of aging, early signs and symptoms of diseases, incidence and prevalence of well-defined diseases (both acute and chronic), disability, and mortality.

This spectrum of health effects can be viewed as a pyramid, with elevated body burden at the bottom and mortality at the top. Mortality under normal conditions involves a relatively small proportion of the population concerned, and the sensitivity of mortality changes is, in general, less than that of functional changes. On the other hand, changes in body burden and subclinical immunological or pulmonary functions are manifested in relatively large proportions of the population and are generally more sensitive to environmental exposures.

Specific and Non-Specific Health Effects. Specific health effects from environmental exposures include physiological, biochemical, pathological and clinical effects such as decrease in cholinesterase activity when exposed to organophosphorus pesticides, ataxia and concentric constriction of visual fields from methylmercury exposure as a result of damage to the cortex, skin pigmentation from exposure to arsenic, and dental or skeletal fluorosis as a result of long-term exposure to fluoride.

However, if most of the health effects associated with environmental exposures were specific, the assessment of health impacts from environmental exposures would have been much easier, more clear-cut and well defined than it is today. Unfortunately, a great number of health effects from environmental exposures are nonspecific, which make the assessment of health impacts from such exposures more difficult and challenging.

Nonspecific health effects include: (1) increase in the host's susceptibility or sensitivity to biological pathogens, resulting in elevated incidence of infectious diseases; (2) decrease in the host's immune function, as demonstrated by the lowering of various immune function parameters; (3) effects on reproductive functions, as reflected in elevated rates of spontaneous abortion, preterm delivery, and congenital malformations; (4) increase in incidence of malignant tumors; (5) developmental deficiency or retardation in children (both physiological and mental development retardation); (6) decrease in various organ functions and alteration in the activity of numerous enzymes; and finally, (7) shortening of life span as a result of one or more effects mentioned above.

However, many of the health effects induced by environmental exposure may be diagnostically vague. They may, excepting those having specific effects, lack a specific feature, and because of their multifactorial or heterogeneous etiologic characteristics, be manifested in similar effects though resulting from different causes. Although symptoms can be elicited by questionnaires, the underlying causes of which still need to be differentiated or elucidated by excluding or controlling for confounders through well-designed questionnaires.

Degree and Intensity of Health Effects. Degree of health effects begins from the most mild effects down to the most serious ones, namely:

1. No change in any physiological functions aside from slight increase in body burden (e.g., slight increase in blood level of lead, a reflection of the amount of lead absorbed by the body, but which does not imply that there is imminent risk of lead poisoning);
2. Physiological changes without any known pathological or pathophysiological changes;
3. Pathophysiological changes which are precursors of manifestation of diseases (e.g., further increase in blood level of lead and increase in δ-ALA in urine, which generally imply an increase in the risk of lead poisoning; or decrease in the cleaning function of ciliary movement in the upper respiratory tract, but with no respiratory symptoms or diseases observed at this stage);
4. Manifestation of well-defined diseases, e.g., attack of asthma, onset of acute respiratory infections, detection of malignant tumors, etc.;
5. Exacerbation of existing diseases which may lead ultimately to terminal stage of the disease or death.

The intensity of the health effects of an individual from environmental exposures depends both on the level of environmental exposures and on the susceptibility or responsiveness of the subject.

Acute and Chronic Effect. In general, people exposed to high levels of environmental pollution, even for a relatively short period of time, are liable to develop signs and symptoms of an acute nature, while people exposed to low levels of pollution for an extended period of time are potentially liable to develop chronic pathological changes. However, there are exceptions. Clinically acute effects may also result following long-term low-level exposure, e.g., epileptic convulsion after long-term exposure to dieldrin. On the other hand, short-term exposure to certain chemicals such as nitrogen dioxide at relatively high concentrations may bring about chronic after-effects. Therefore, care should be exercised to avoid hasty conclusions pertaining to the acute or chronic nature of a health impact.

Direct and Indirect Measurement of Health Impact. In health impact assessment, one of the first things people have on their agenda is to evaluate the status quo of the health conditions of the people involved, or a baseline study upon which later estimation or projection of health outcome can be superimposed. To meet this objective, direct measurement or investigation of the health conditions of the participants is to be preferred, no matter whether it is in the form of a questionnaire by which subjective response is sought, or some kind of objective examination (e.g., radiographic examination, functional tests, hemato-morphological examinations, etc.) performed. However, indirect measures such as absenteeism from school or workplace and hospital admissions can also provide valuable information as to the extent of the problem and therefore should not be overlooked.[9–11]

Some Methodological Issues

Validity, Accuracy, and Reliability. Before embarking on any health impact assessment, people need to be sure that the methods and measurements to be used are valid and accurate. The validity of a measurement is determined by the extent to which it relates to the effect that it is intended to measure. Validity often depends on the criteria of what is a true characteristic of the health effect under study. It also depends on what is used as the standard. The validity of a test method can often be checked by applying it to a well-defined population, and comparing the results with the results obtained from another well-established method used on the same population.

Accuracy is the difference between the measured value and the true value. The smaller the difference, the better the accuracy. However, it is always difficult to arrive at the true value unless a number of objective, independent methods for measuring the same effect can be utilized and the results are found to be identical. Occasionally, "dummy" questions which are etiologically unrelated to the suspected cause may be used to test the accuracy of a survey, such as incidence of injury in a respiratory disease study. If it is found that incidence of injury is "associated" with air pollution level or cough, people have reason to doubt the accuracy of such a questionnaire or the quality of the interview.

Reliability is the measure of consistency or reproducibility and is dependent on accuracy. In general, the reliability of a measuring device can be determined by frequent tests in which everything is identical except the time. This approach can also be used in testing out questionnaires where identical questions are used in different parts of the questionnaire to see if the responses are the same.

Some physical conditions or physiological functions display distinct diurnal or cyclical variations. These should be taken into account when making such measurements. Particular care should be taken in dealing with such variations when comparing findings at the international level to ensure comparability.

Sensitivity and Specificity. Sensitivity of a measurement or test is determined by the proportion of all persons with a particular health-related characteristic such as a disease or change in certain body function that can be detected by the measurement or test, while specificity is determined by the proportion of all persons involved lacking a particular health characteristic who are correctly identified as not having the characteristic by the measurement or test. In general, an increase in sensitivity will mean a decrease in specificity. Sensitivity and specificity of a measurement or test are determined by what is expected from a health impact assessment. A method with very high sensitivity but poor specificity would be meaningless from the preventive medicine perspective. On the other hand, a method with high specificity but poor sensitivity would miss a sizable proportion of people who are inflicted with the disease through environmental exposure or are at high risk.

Judicious Use of Toxicological Data. Assessment of health impact is based on the current health condition of the people involved and an assessment or projection of the health status of the same people who would be exposed to certain environmental exposures or exposures to be either because of a development project or an expected major change in the environment. Though epidemiologic studies on the health effects of similar projects would be most helpful and revealing, such data are rather limited and difficult to obtain. Therefore people have to rely heavily on relevant toxicological data pertaining to the agent of interest. However, since many toxicological data are based on different species of laboratory animals, and the exposure concentrations or dosages are usually several folds higher than those to be expected in a development project, particular care should be exercised in the extrapolation of such data to human beings. The most difficult problem in the extrapolation of animal toxicological data to human beings is the conversion from one species to another. For most chemicals, the pathogenesis of poisoning is the same in humans and in other mammals, and the signs of intoxication are also similar or analogous. Man may be more sensitive to an environmental agent than certain laboratory animals, but there are also many cases where some animal species are more sensitive than man. When extrapolating from animal data to human beings, a species conversion factor determined on the basis of biological considerations and the information on the test species is usually applied. Because of the uncertainties involved with regard to the biological as well as the mathematical reliability of methods for extrapolating from one species to another and from high doses to low doses, dependence on somewhat arbitrary uncertainty factors is still being used. In general, the size of the uncertainty factor depends on the nature of the toxic effects, the quality of toxicological data and the type and size of the population to be protected. In some cases, the uncertainty factor may be a value that has been used with reasonable success and is therefore perpetuated.[12–14] Of course, if human toxicological data, including data obtained from epidemiological studies of people exposed to a toxic chemical under normal conditions of use, occupational accidental poisoning data, and the data from observations in volunteers are available, the validity of the extrapolation would be appreciably enhanced.

Moreover, toxicological experiments are usually conducted using purified chemicals, while in a real life setting of a health impact assessment, people would be exposed to a multitude of chemicals or agents with possible impurities. 2,4-Dichlorophenoxyacetic acid (2,4-D) with tetracholorodibenzo-p-dioxins as impurities or contaminants is just one of the numerous examples encountered in real life.

As current methods of extrapolation from lab animal data to human beings usually deal with exposure to a single substance whereas the actual human environment contains a large number of hazardous chemicals or agents that can interact and considerably modify their health effects, and data on the combined toxicity of several chemicals are rather limited, make the assessment of health impact is more challenging, and poses urgent demands on the development of better methods.

Even in dealing with environmental epidemiological data, because of differences in susceptibility of populations and other factors (national, racial, ethical, regional), exposure–effect relationships derived from one group of people should only be used with reservation for other groups.

Design and Administration of Questionnaires. In the study of health effects, the effects under study or the definition of a case should be clearly defined. A case definition is a set of criteria for deciding whether an individual should be classified as having the condition of interest. This is essential, though not always easy, since many of the health effects from environmental exposures are nonspecific and the signs and symptoms may not be so typical. The use of well constructed and tested questionnaires is a method frequently used in eliciting such information.

In the construction of symptom questionnaires, it is essential to pose precise questions in order to reduce variations which may result when different investigators ask people about their symptoms. Identical, or at least very similar questions about the respondents' conditions should be asked to ensure comparability of results. To ensure the validity of questionnaires, the disease or relevant symptoms being assessed should be defined accurately. In comparing the incidence or prevalence of diseases, it is essential that the levels of sensitivity and specificity of the method used should be similar and consistent both for the population of interest and for the control population so that comparison can be made and health impacts from the environmental exposures assessed. The British Medical Research Council's Committee of Aetiology of Chronic Bronchitis developed a respiratory symptoms questionnaire, on the basis of which the American Thoracic Society and the Division of Lung Diseases of the National Heart and Lung Institute of the United States developed the ATS-DLD standardized questionnaire for use in respiratory diseases study.[15] The London School of Hygiene developed a standardized Cardiovascular Questionnaire. These questionnaires have been translated into different languages and used in a number of countries with success.[16–18]

Self-completed versions of the symptoms questionnaires have been developed to avoid observed variation, with various degree of success. However, self-completed questionnaires tend to be incomplete and the return rate may not be satisfactory. They have not found wide use in health impact assessment, though they have been used in the form of diaries in epidemiologic studies.[19]

In addition, the method of administering questionnaires should also be standardized and the interviewers comparably trained to reduce systematic errors.

The problem of determining the exact number of false positives and false negatives for questionnaires is difficult because of lack of a suitable reference. Validation should therefore be based on correlations with some kind of objective measurements closely related to the health effect or disease under investigation, such as pulmonary function tests, radiographic examinations or electrocardiograms. The use of questionnaires in combination with objective measurements or tests is an important tool and a major approach in assessing health impacts.

Subclinical Functional Tests and Lab Measurements. Before manifestation or onset of disease, a number of preclinical or subclinical functional tests can be utilized to determine if the body is functioning normally when subject to environmental exposures. These tests include assessment of body burden, pulmonary function tests, immunological indices, x-rays, and other related tests.

Body Burden. Body burden is a measurement of the amount of environmental pollutants accumulated in the body and can be detected in biological specimens, e.g., mercury, cadmium, arsenic, fluoride, etc. Hair, nail, urine, and blood are biological specimens which are used extensively. The measurement of hair, nail and urine is generally acceptable in most countries since it is noninvasive during the collection of specimens, though in certain remote mountainous areas the cutting of hair or nails may pose some problem because of superstition. The amount of mercury and cadmium in hair have been found to be closely related to symptoms among people exposed to mercury and cadmium for an extended period of time.[20]

Urine is a suitable indicator medium for the assessment of exposure to inorganic arsenic, since the elimination of arsenic takes place mainly via the kidneys. However, the use of arsenic level in hair as a body burden indicator is limited, because no reliable method is available for distinguishing between arsenic from external contamination and arsenic which has been absorbed and metabolized in the body. The same also applies when measuring mercury and cadmium levels in human hair. The hair should be repeatedly and thoroughly washed before subject to measurement.

Pulmonary Function Tests. Pulmonary function tests include those that assess lung function during an expiratory maneuver, and those that measure airway resistance, particularly small airway function. The test procedures have been standardized (NIOSH), and generally comprise parameters such as FVC, FEV_1, FVC/FEV_1, FEF_{25}, FEF_{50}, FEF_{75}, MMEF, etc. However, these tests are function tests. They can not be used to determine a specific disease, though are most valuable in determining whether the pulmonary function has been affected by environmental exposures. Nevertheless, the big problem is in deciding to what extent the test is able to distinguish abnormal functions from normal functions. Though there are normal ranges of values which take into account the height and weight of the subject, they are based on white males in the prime of their life designed for the recruitment of physically fit workers, therefore not readily applicable to children or women, not to mention people of a different race with smaller statue or other anthropologic characteristics.

Immunological Function Tests. Human beings are exposed to a wide range of chemicals and agents which might interact with the immune system. The interaction of toxic chemicals with humans is dependent on the chemical structures, duration of exposure, concentration in the environment, and age of the people involved, since people are particularly susceptible during neonatal period and old age.

The health implications of decreased immune function are increased risk of infectious diseases, exacerbation of existing diseases, allergies, as well as development of neoplasia. The uniqueness of the immune system is its extreme complexity and the widespread dispersion of its cellular constituents. As the cellular elements of the immune system interact with foreign elements, they are theoretically always in the front line of defense as far as exposure to environmental chemicals and agents is concerned. A toxic chemical may compromise a certain fraction of the reserve and the clinical significance of such damage is related to the size of the reserve and the time interval between reduction of function and the necessity for an effective physiological response. When it comes to an assessment of altered function in the immune system, consideration has to be given to the various subsets of effector and regulatory cells which may exhibit different sensitivities to toxic agents, and, as a result, the activity of the immune system may be modified both as to the kind of response as well as its magnitude.

Immunotoxicology studies in lab animals on the effect of common air pollutants such as SO_2 and NO_x have shown that these agents could increase susceptibility to respiratory infections. Interference with humoral and cell-mediated immunity in the lung are dependent on the concentration of the agent as well as the duration of exposure. However, the conditions of such studies still fall far short of those that are found in actual exposure situations.

By and large, decrease in certain immune function indices may mean a decrease in the human defense capacity against the insult of environmental agents, and therefore may serve as an early warning sentinel for potential adverse health effects or diseases. However, a seemingly toxic effect of an agent on a particular immune response may not necessarily lead to a detectable clinical manifestation of disease. This may be due to the fact that the immune system has a capacity to recover from insult by a rapid regeneration of that particular cell population. More studies are needed in utilizing immune indices in assessing health impacts.

Radiographic Examinations. Aside from providing a means for the systematic recording and ranking in a reproducible way of radiographic changes in the chest produced by dust, radiographic examinations can also be used in the study of particulate air pollution for finding changes in lung markings as a result of chronic cough or bronchitis, as well as for early detection of lung cancer and skeletal fluorosis from environmental exposures. The advantage of this measurement is that the findings are recorded and can be used in comparison with later radiographs. The disadvantage of the method is that except for occupational diseases such as silicosis and pneumoconiosis, the radiographic signs of obstructive lung diseases and other lung changes have not yet been standardized, which limits it application in health impact assessment.

Hematological Examinations. Blood cells are one of the most accessible human tissues. Their accessibility makes it possible to be used in health effect assessment. The information obtained through hematological examinations is pertinent both to disorders of the hematological system and to diseases primarily affecting other organs in which blood cell changes occur as secondary manifestations. However, there is a wide range of "normal" values for most blood elements. The counts or measurements cited as "abnormal" also differ in different countries. For instance, the amount of hemoglobin considered to be normal in an East Asian population may not be considered normal in a European population. In general, routine blood counts are not very sensitive for detecting small differences in health status between populations due to differences in environmental exposures. Nevertheless, accurate differential white blood cell counts, in conjunction with a total leucocyte count, may be of value in certain health impact assessments. Modern instrumentation has been helpful in making hematological measurements feasible in field studies. For instance, in the study of lead absorption, a single drop of blood placed on a filter paper automatically inserted into a fixed fluorometer can provide an immediate digital reading of zinc protoporphyrin, free erythrocyte protoporphyrin, and erythrocyte protoporphyrin levels. These species of protoporphyrin are increased following lead absorption and are useful in assessing the health effect of inorganic lead exposure.

Reproductive Outcomes. Because of the complex integrated nature of reproduction, abnormal reproductive performance provides a sensitive indicator of certain environmental exposure. Measurements of reproductive performance include: spontaneous abortion, stillbirth and neonatal death, birth weight, and congential malformations.

Spontaneous abortion: "Spontaneous" or induced impairment in development often results in embryonic death during early pregnancy. However, in spontaneous abortions occurring in the first trimester, about 60% exhibit chromosomal aberrations. This high background of spontaneous abnormalities makes it difficult to detect a small increase in the overall incidence that might be caused by a single environmental agent.

Stillbirth and neonatal death: Though stillbirths and neonatal deaths are well recorded in some countries, their low frequencies make them weak indicators of adverse health effects of environmental exposures.

Birth weight: Subtle effects of environmental exposure may be detected by differences in the mean and variance of birth weight, which might otherwise go unnoticed if the frequency of birth weight under a specific or fixed value is measured. However, before low birth weight can be associated with environmental exposures, alternative explanations such as differences between cases and controls in age of mother, pregnancy weight, social-economic status, diet, and ethnicity must be excluded.

Congenital malformations: In an area where chemical contamination has occurred or is anticipated, surveillance for congenital malformations may be of value. A full description of the malformations observed should be recorded. When exposure to a potential teratogen is suspected, exposed persons should be compared with a similar group of people who are not exposed. If the circumstances do not permit the selection or study of such a cohort group, internal comparison such as high exposure versus low exposure may be an alternative choice. Another approach is to study all the children of exposed mothers in an effort to identify clustering of specific types of malformation. If a cluster is found, knowing the nature of the exposure may suggest a relationship to a particular environmental exposure. The malformations observed should be recorded with other etiological factors such as heredity or infection of mother during pregnancy.

Neurotoxicity Tests. The nervous system is protected from external influences by a number of barriers. The blood-brain barrier has an important function in preserving the chemical constitution of the nervous system, but some substances, particularly those lipid soluble ones, may still cross the blood-brain barrier.

Interest in this area has been growing in recent years, not only because of increased public concern over the impact of environmental agents on human health, but also because the nervous system has been shown to be particularly vulnerable to chemical insult. Therefore there has been an increased demand for improved methods for the detection of neurotoxic effects and the assessment of health impact in this area.

As behavior is the final product of nervous system activity, toxicant induced changes in the nervous system may be reflected by behavior changes. Thus behavior analysis serves as a useful tool in this respect.

Regardless of whether the site of action is the nervous system itself or some other organ system, changes in performance, sensorimotor function or cognitive function are parameters likely to be adversely affected by environmental exposures.

DISCUSSION

Some Misconceptions Pertaining to Development and Health

People tend to think that health will improve with development, but it is not necessarily so. In reality, health of the population may even deteriorate with the advance in development, if the development is not sustainable and appropriate measures are not taken to offset the adverse effects, both to human health and to the environment. There are numerous examples of unanticipated deterioration in environment and health because of development projects, e.g., the building of big dams which led to formation of small creeks upstream providing breeding ground for vectors of schistosomiasis. If proper health impact assessment had been conducted and the issue of the creation of breeding place of disease vectors taken into account, appropriate preventive measures could have been taken to address such health risk. Development will bring with it health only if people work conscientiously for it in assessing all the health impacts involved in development projects and take all the necessary measures in safeguarding health.

The Quest for a Single Health Index in Assessing Health Impacts

Since environmental exposure is often multifactorial and environmental agents may have multiple routes of entry, e.g., chronic respiratory diseases aggravated by suspended particulate and sulphur dioxide in ambient air, or dental and skeletal fluorosis from uptake of fluoride through ingestion of water containing high concentrations of fluoride or inhalation of air polluted with fluoride from high fluoride-containing fossil fuels, there have been attempts to try to find a single composite pollution index encompassing all facets of environmental exposure,[21] and there have also been attempts in trying to use a single health-effect index for a multitude of health impacts. Though the former got some application particularly among environmental scientists in different parts of the world, the latter did not find much application in public health sectors worldwide, because it is difficult, if not impossible, to find a single expression which can encompass such a broad range of health effects as is the case in health impact assessments.

Development of Internationally Acceptable and Standardized Methods for Assessing Health Impacts

Methods should be judged on the basis of (1) accuracy and reliability of the results obtained, (2) availability of qualified personnel and equipment in the area where assessment of health impact is to be performed, and (3) acceptability by the population involved.

Because of the reasons outlined in "Approach and Strategy," standardized methods which are internationally acceptable would be of tremendous help in this respect.

Avoidance of Unnecessary Duplication of Efforts in Health Impact Assessment

Low a level unnecessary duplication of efforts in a health impact assessment is both meaningless and wasteful, if data and conclusions from other similar situations are available and can be adapted to local conditions. Promotion of sharing of relevant information in health impact assessments is in the interest of all parties concerned. This would mean tremendous savings in manpower and cost where such resources are scarce. And it is in this area that international cooperation can play an important role and render useful and most sought-of service to all countries. Care should be exercised, however, in not repeating mistakes made elsewhere, and all necessary changes be made to adapt to the local situation.

FUTURE DIRECTIONS

Further Improvement in Methodology

Though there has been marked progress in environmental toxicology and environmental epidemiology in recent years, the methods used in assessing health impacts from environmental exposures still fall far short of the demand. Development of all stages in various parts of the world with various climatic conditions and racial groups calls for more specific, more cost-effective and less time-consuming methods for health impact assessments. International cooperation and standardization of methods would provide the necessary launchpad toward achieving this end.

Development of Methods in Assessing Health Impact of Global Environmental Problems

Continued population growth, irrational use of natural resources, and increasing generation of wastes have created unsustainable demands on the environment. There are limits to the exploitation of nonrenewable resources in the world and to the capacity of our planetary system to support population growth and to absorb wastes. Only recently have these limits become apparent. Health impacts associated with rapid population growth, industrial development, rapid urbanization, hazardous waste disposal, transboundary movement of hazardous wastes, long distance transport of air pollutants, acid rain, ocean pollution, ozone depletion and global warming are areas which people have little or limited experience in coping with.

Rapid Urban Growth

Many countries have failed, either because of financial constraints or lack of awareness of environmental consequences, to ensure that rapid urban growth should be accompanied by appropriate investment needed in providing the necessary and indispensable infrastructure and services in conformity with their degree of development. Methods for assessing health impacts from environmental exposures arising from rapid urban growth have not been systematically developed and therefore merit our attention.

Industrial Development as a Result of Outdated Technology Transfer

It is not uncommon for hazardous industries or unsuitable outdated technologies and machines to be transferred to developing countries, since it is cheaper to transfer production there than to meet the increasingly stringent environmental and health regulations of developed countries. This will bring about tragic repetition of disasters encountered in developed countries in previous decades. Given the lack of resources in coping with such environmental hazards in developing countries, the situation might even be worse. The toxic gases and liquid wastes will in turn affect the whole world, since there is only one planet which all of us inhabit—the earth.

Hazardous Waste Disposal

The disposal of hazardous wastes poses special problems in many countries. Most industrial wastes are either disposed of as liquid wastes which run untreated into streams, creeks, rivers, or other nearby water bodies; or are disposed of on land sites with few safeguarding measures to prevent those living nearby or neighboring water sources, both surface and underground, from contamination. Health impact assessment from exposure to hazardous wastes is an area in which more research is needed.

Transboundary Movement of Hazardous Wastes

The transfer of toxic or hazardous wastes from developed to developing countries is an issue of increasing concern. Since the cost of transporting hazardous wastes to rudimentary or make-shift storage or dumping sites in developing countries is only a mere fraction of the cost of complying with the regulations for safe storage or disposal and subsequent cleaning up of those sites in developed countries, transboundary transportation of hazardous wastes is becoming a global health problem. Because of the very limited resources for dealing with such exposures in most of the developing countries, the health impact from such practice might be more damaging than in developed countries. This is an area about which very little is known.

Long-Distance Transport of Air Pollutants

Sulphur and nitrogen oxides in ambient air, aside from having local health effects, can be transported by atmospheric circulation over long distances when emitted from high stacks. Large modern fossil-fuelled power stations generally have high stacks (180–200 m and over) for dispersing flues. Though this lowers the exposure of local populations to suspended particulate and sulphur oxides, it gives rise to long-distance transport of atmospheric pollutants. Sulphur and nitrogen oxides are converted to sulphuric and nitric acids which in turn lead to acidic precipitation far away from the emission point.

Though the adverse effects of acid precipitation on ecosystems have been studied in detail, not much is known about its health impact on human beings. Acidification of soil as a result of acid precipitation can mobilize metals it contains, making them more readily available to enter fresh water and the food chain, with the possibility that they may affect people through ingestion of food.

On the other hand, acidic waters may corrode piping and plumbing and thus give rise to elevated levels of metals in drinking water, which poses a potential risk of impairment in neurophysiological development in children.[22]

Metal of concern is aluminum. Concentrations of aluminium in natural waters are dependent on the pH value of the water. High concentrations of aluminium have been detected in water from shallow wells in areas having acidic precipitation. Statistical association between concentration of aluminium in drinking water and the occurrence of Alzheimer's disease in the general population has been reported,[23] though no causal relationship has been established.

Hence it is possible that human exposure to metals is increased by mobilization of metals in the environment as a result of acidification. If increased exposure occurs in the population where some health effect caused by metals has already occurred, an increased occurrence of adverse health effects is to be expected because of the superimposition. Methods for assessing the adverse health impacts arising from acidification need to be developed.

Ozone Depletion

Ozone is continuously produced and destroyed in the stratosphere through complex photochemical reactions under sunlight. The balance between production and destruction results in a constant amount of stratosphere ozone around the globe, which plays an extremely important role in absorbing part of the biologically damaging fraction of the ultraviolet rays coming from the sun, shielding the earth and the life on it from a major portion of ultraviolet radiation. Depletion of the stratospheric ozone layer has implications both for health and agricultural production. Ozone depletion may be linked to the increase in prevalence of cataract and skin cancer. The potential health impact of changes in agricultural production due to ozone depletion is unknown. All these call for development of methods for assessing such health impacts.

Global Warming

Carbon dioxide, nitrogen oxides, chlorofluorocarbons (CFCs) and methane are gases having the property of absorbing the energy re-emitted by the earth's surface while letting the incoming solar radiation pass through. Thus they act as an energy trap and preserve the heat in the atmosphere. Studies on atmospheric carbon dioxide concentrations in the past decades have shown that the currently increasing concentrations of carbon dioxide and the release and accumulation of other "green-house effect" gases are higher than those in the past, and if this trend continues, may lead to a substantial warming up of the atmosphere. Even partial melting of the ice in the Arctic Circle and in Antarctica as a result of global warming would mean elevation of sea levels throughout the world and submergence of many important coastal cities and harbors which in turn would lead to massive migration of population creating numerous health problems. This is an area in which little has been studied.

Ocean Pollution

All wastes eventually reach the ocean through either atmospheric deposition or land runoff and outfall discharges. The resulting pollution of sea water is widespread though the degree of pollution varies from place to place. The contamination of seafood and beach water by bacteria, viruses or fungi is now almost a matter of universal concern. Chemical contamination of sea food is also a source of concern around industrial outfall and shallow waste-dumping sites. Because of the flow of water current in the sea and the complexity of food chain in oceans, little is known about their health impacts.

CONCLUSIONS

Assessing health impacts of environmental exposures deals with exposures from a single environmental agent to a multitude of environmental agents; from past exposure, current exposure, to exposures expected from development projects; from the relatively simple and straightforward ones such as the construction and operation of a factory or a mine with its potential emission of harmful gases and discharge of toxic effluents polluting the neighboring environment, to the more complex ones as is the case in the construction of big dams which may have wide-ranging repercussions.

Knowledge of almost all branches of medical sciences, from physiology, biochemistry, pathology, to clinical medicine are made use of in assessing health impacts from environmental exposures, but the mainstay of the methods used is based on a combination of environmental toxicology and environmental epidemiology. The validity and accuracy of a health impact assessment relies on the quality of the assessment, and the quality of the assessment depends on the methods used in the assessment process. Methods used should be sensitive, specific, consistent and comparable. The need for more standardized methods and procedures is self evident. Promoting the use of internationally standardized methods would ensure both validity and comparability, but, of course, due care should be taken to adapt the methods to local conditions and needs, and should be locally acceptable. In short, top quality, international comparability and acceptability, adaptation to local situation and participation of local staff, as well as cooperation and timely feedback from the community are crucial to the success of a health impact assessment.

Because of the limited availability of data pertaining to environmental exposures and their health impacts, it is in the interest of all parties concerned to make full use of all the relevent health impact assessment data so that these data could be pooled together and shared among professionals working in this field, which, in turn, will reduce duplication of efforts and contribute to a more sustainable environment and a healthier population.

REFERENCES

1. *Our planet, our health,* Report of the WHO Commission on Health and the Environment, 1992:21, World Health Organization Geneva.
2. Mattison, D. R. et al, 1991. Symposium: Phamacokinetics in Developmental Toxicology. Physiological Alterations During Pregnancy: Impact on Toxicokinetics. *Fundamental and Applied Toxicology, 16*:215–218.
3. EHC 118: Inorganic Mercury, 1991:104–107, World Health Organization, Geneva.
4. EHC 55, 1985. Ethylene Oxide:55–56, World Health Organization, Geneva.
5. World Health Statistics Annual, 1987. World Health Organization, Geneva.
6. WHO Division of Epidemiological Surveillance and Health Situation and Trend Assessment, 1990: Global Estimates for Health Situation Assessment and Projections,:3, World Health Organization, Geneva.
7. Vahter, M., ed. 1982: Assessment of Human Exposure to Cadmium and Lead Through Biological Monitoring, Stockholm, Karolinska Institute, 136, Prepared for the United Nations Environment Programme and World Health Organization by National Swedish Institute of Environmental Medicine and Department of Environmental Hygiene, Karolinska Institute, Stockholm.
8. Wilkins, J. R. et al., 1979: Organic chemical contaminants in drinking water and cancer, *American Journal of Epidemiology, 110*:421–448.
9. Ransom, M. R. et al., 1992: Elementary school absences and PM10 in Utah Valley, *Environmental Research 58*:204–219.
10. Romieu, I. et al., 1992: Air pollution and school absenteeism among children in Mexico City, *American Journal of Epidemiology, 136(12)*:1524–1531.
11. Cody, R. P. et al., 1992: The effect of ozone associated with summertime photochemical smog on the frequency of asthma visits to hospital emergency departments, *Environmental Research, 58*:184–192.
12. EHC 6: Principles and Methods for Evaluating the Toxicity of Chemicals, Part 1. 1978:38, World Health Organization, Geneva.
13. Hoel, D. G. et al., 1975: Estimation of risks of irreversible toxicity, *Journal of Toxicity and Environmental Health, (1)*:133–151.
14. National Research Council, Committee on Pesticides in the Diets of Infants and Children, 1993:323–363, National Academy Press, Washington, D. C..
15. Ferris, B. G., 1978: Epidemiology standardization project, *American Review of Respiratory Disease, 118(6)*:1–120.
16. Rose, G. A. et al., 1982: Cardiovascular survey methods, 2nd ed., WHO Monograph Series No. 56, World Health Organization, Geneva.
17. Osterman, J. W. et al., 1990: Evaluation of the ATS Respiratory Disease Questionnaire among French-speaking Silicon Carbide Workers, *Canadian J. of Public Health, 81*:66–72.

18. Tao, X. G. et al., 1992: Priority among air pollution factors for preventing chronic obstructive pulmonary diseases in Shanghai, *The Science of the Total Environment, 127*:57–67.
19. Hammer, D. I. et al., 1974: Los Angeles Student Nurse Studies, *Archives of Environmental Health, 28*:255–260.
20. Friberg, L. et al. (Ed.), 1985. Cadmium and Health: A Toxicological and Epidemiological Appraisal, v.1.CRC Press, Inc., Boca Raton.
21. Walsh, P. J. et al., 1978: Composite hazard index for assessing limiting exposures to environmental pollutants: formulation and derivation, *Environmental Science and Technology, 12*:799–802.
22. Needleman, H. L. et al., 1991: The long-term effects of exposure to low doses of lead in childhood, *New England Journal of Medicine, 322*:83–88.
23. Martyn, C. N. et al., 1989: Geographical relation between Alzheimer's disease and aluminum in drinking water, *Lancet, 1*:59–62.

22

Comparative Health Risk Assessment: A Method for Setting Priorities in Environmental Health

Eugene Brantly, Robert Hetes, Barry Levy, Clydette Powell, Linda Whiteford, and May Yacoob

INTRODUCTION

Developing countries throughout the world are experiencing rapid urban population growth and gradual industrialization. These trends greatly influence the public health problems that developing countries confront. The "pre-transition" infectious diseases associated with inadequate sanitation, contaminated water supplies, poor housing, and overcrowded living conditions continue to compromise the health of millions of people, especially in peri-urban settlements. At the same time, increases in industrial employment, use of hazardous materials, traffic congestion, air pollution, and cigarette smoking, among other changes, are increasing the occurrence of "post-transition" diseases, such as work-related and traffic-related injuries, respiratory disease, heart disease, and cancer (Jamison, 1991).

Because of these trends, local and national governments in developing countries face an increasingly complex set of environmental health problems. To use public funds wisely, public health and environmental officials need tools that will help them set priorities among a range of

---

Preparation of this chapter was sponsored by the Office of Health and Nutrition, U.S. Agency for International Development (USAID) through the Water and Sanitation for Health (WASH) Project. The paper is based upon work performed under tasks at WASH and another USAID contract, the Technologies for Primary Health Care Project (PRITECH).

problems and make sound policy decisions about which problems deserve their attention.

In the United States, the federal Environmental Protection Agency (USEPA) is gradually adopting health risk assessment as the common approach for evaluating the potential public health impacts of environmental pollutants and conditions regulated by its various programs. The USEPA and several states have also begun to use comparative risk assessment as a means for comparing environmental problems and setting priorities among them.

The U.S. Agency for International Development (USAID) and the USEPA have sponsored several studies in developing countries and in Central and Eastern Europe in which comparative health risk assessment methods have been applied. Each study estimated the potential public health impacts of a range of problems and then ranked the problems according to the predicted magnitude of the impacts. This paper provides a brief introduction to comparative risk assessment, discusses the principal problems encountered in using risk assessment in developing countries, and describes the methodology used in a USAID-sponsored study in Quito, Ecuador.

RISK ASSESSMENT METHODS AND RESULTS

Health Risk Assessment

Health risk assessment methods are relatively well developed and have been described elsewhere. The analysis involves four components. An example of results from an assessment are shown in Box 22.1.

Hazard Identification is a qualitative determination of whether human exposure to an agent has the potential to produce adverse effects. It involves an evaluation of all available toxicological and epidemiological data and other relevant biological and chemical information for the agent under consideration.

Exposure Assessment involves determining the nature and site of populations exposed to a toxic agent, and estimating or characterizing the intensity and duration of their exposure. Under ideal conditions, exposure assessment includes determining environmental concentrations by monitoring or modeling; estimating the magnitude, duration, and frequency of human exposure for relevant subpopulations; estimating the dose received by those subpopulations; and characterizing the exposed populations and subpopulations, especially those at a potentially higher risk. The geographic distribution and other characteristics of the exposed population, such as age distribution, gender proportions, occupation, socioeconomic status, activities and activity levels should be determined.

Box 22.1 Example of Results From Risk Assessment

Health Risk Assessment in Quito, Ecuador:
Population: 1.1 million

Average daily intake per person of
Pesticides in food:
 44.3 μg/day heptachlor
 11.0 μg/day aldrin
Cancer Potency:
 4.50 $(mg/kg/day)^{-1}$ for heptachlor
 17.00 $(mg/kg/day)^{-1}$ for aldrin
Health Effects:
 0.3 to 9.1×10^{-3} individual lifetime cancer risk
 up to 150 excess cancer cases/year in Quito

Dose–Response Assessment defines the quantitative relationship between the administered or received dose of a substance and the prevalence of an adverse health effect in an exposed population. This relationship, described by a mathematical dose-response model, is used to estimate the probability of occurrence of the effect given an estimate of human exposure to the substance. Because the mechanisms of action of many toxic substances and chemical mixtures are not well understood, statistical models are used that best represent the available data. If available, dose-response estimates based on human exposure (i.e., epidemiological data) are preferable to those derived from animal data. For most toxins, however, the only available data are from controlled laboratory experiments involving test animals.

Risk Characterization means estimating the future incidence of an adverse health effect in a population attributable to its exposure to a particular substance, based on an estimate of the population's exposure to the substance and the dose-response model for the substance. When sufficient data are available, risk characterization should include estimates of individual risk (the probability of an adverse effect occurring in the average individual in a population) and population risk (the number of cases of the adverse effect that are likely to occur in the exposed population).

Hazard identification and dose-response assessment are processes which generally occur independent of a particular risk assessment study. The principal undertaking in a site-specific risk assessment is to identify the substances to which the subject population is exposed and to estimate the magnitudes of their exposure to each substance. The exposure assessment is usually based on measurements of the substances in various media (air, water, soil, food) or on fate-and-transport modeling using estimates of emissions from known sources. Once the exposure assessment has been completed, the appropriate dose-response model is used (or developed, if necessary) to calculate the risk estimate. Methods for estimating the impacts of carcinogens are most well developed, while methods for characterizing noncarcinogenic health effects have been developed more thoroughly in recent years.

Comparative Risk Assessment

Comparative Risk Assessment is a relatively new methodology that builds on health risk assessment, plus other analytical methods used to estimate the potential ecological and economic impacts of environmental problems. Comparative risk assessment was developed explicitly as a means for ranking a diverse set of environmental problems in terms of the severity of their impacts on public health, ecological integrity, and economic welfare, to determine which of the problems should have high priority for public action. The USEPA and several states have conducted comparative risk assessment studies. USEPA has recently published guidelines for conducting comparative risk assessments (USEPA, 1993), and a recent review describes various critiques of the approach (Finkel & Golding, 1994). An example of results from a comparative risk assessment by USEPA for the southeastern U.S. is shown in Box 22.2.

The value of comparative risk assessment is demonstrated in the contrasting cases of radon and hazardous wastes. Beginning with the U.S. public's concern over Love Canal and other abandoned hazardous waste sites, the Superfund program for identifying and cleaning such sites has been one of the USEPA's largest and most expensive programs. In retrospective analyses, the USEPA has determined that such sites actually pose a fairly small health risk to the public at large, although there may be relatively large risks to small groups of people living close to such sites. In the wake of these findings, funding for the Superfund program has been reduced. In contrast, funding has been greatly increased for research and

Box 22.2 Example of Results from Comparative Risk Assessment, U.S. Environmental Protection Agency, Region 4 (Southeastern U.S.)

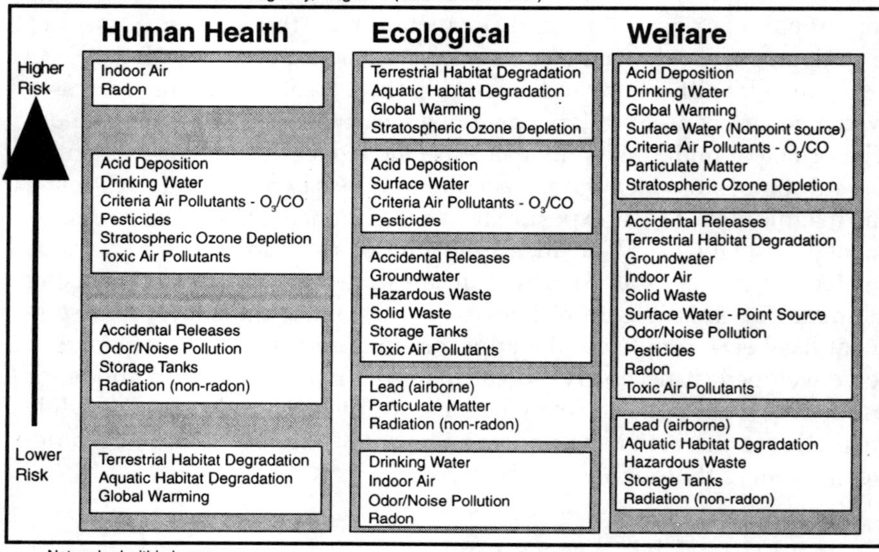

Not ranked within boxes

public education concerning radon, since it was determined that high indoor concentrations of radon pose a very high health risk to large segments of the U.S. population.

Comparative Health Risk Assessment in Developing Countries

Comparative health risk assessment differs from the "comparative risk assessment" described by USEPA in that it evaluates a range of environmental problems only on the basis of their human health impacts, without considering ecological or economic impacts. To avoid confusion, the author(s) have referred to comparative health risk assessment elsewhere as "environmental health assessment"; the former phrase, however, is more descriptive.

USEPA and USAID have sponsored several comparative health risk assessments outside of the U.S., including assessments in Bangkok, Quito, the Czech Republic, Romania, Russia, Cairo, and India. Results from the studies in Bangkok and Quito are shown in Box 22.3 to illustrate the conclusions that such studies generate—a prioritized list of environmental health problems grouped into high-, medium-, and low-risk categories, for the population of the city as a whole, in some cases, for defined subgroups.

Box 22.3 Results from Two International Risk Assessments

RISK CATEGORY	ENVIRONMENTAL HEALTH PROBLEMS		
	BANGKOK	QUITO	
		Full Urban Area	Poor Urban Districts
High Risk	√ *Particulates in Air* √ *Microbiological Diseases (water & sanitation)* √ *Lead*	√ *Particulates in Air* √ *Microbiological Disease (food)* √ *Pesticides (food)*	√ *Particulates in Air* √ *Microbiological Disease (food, water, excreta)* √ *Pesticides (food)* √ *Occupational Disease & Injury* √ *Indoor Air Quality*
Moderate Risk	√ *CO* √ *Metals Other Than Lead*	√ *Traffic Injuries* √ *Indoor Air Quality* √ *Occupational Disease & Injury* √ *Microbiological Disease (excreta)*	√ *Traffic Injuries* √ *Solid & Hazardous Waste Disposal*
Low Risk	√ *Toxic Air Pollution* √ SO_2, NO_2, O_3 √ *Surface Water* √ *Ground Water* √ *Food Contam. (pesticides & metals)* √ *Solid & Hazardous Water Disposal*	√ *Solid & Hazardous Waste Disposal* √ *Lead (air, blood)* √ *Microbiological Disease (water)*	√ *Lead (air, blood)*

CHALLENGES FOR USING COMPARATIVE HEALTH RISK ASSESSMENT IN DEVELOPING COUNTRIES

Obviously, health risk assessment methods have been developed to deal with the environmental health problems of advanced industrial societies. They cannot be applied in a less developed country without substantial modification. There are four principal challenges to using health risk assessment methods in developing countries. These are discussed below and are summarized in Box 22.4.

Range of Environmental Health Problems to be Addressed

> An assessment of environmental health risks in developing countries must include "pretransition" diseases, for which there are no models describing the probabilistic relationship between dose or causal factors and response.

The three principal causes of illness and death in developing countries (at least in infants and children) are diarrhea, acute respiratory infections, and vector-borne diseases. These conditions are in large part associated with a lack of basic environmental infrastructure and public services that citizens of advanced industrial societies take for granted: safe supplies of

Box 22.4 Risk Assessment Methodology

Special challenges of conducting risk assessment in developing countries

ISSUE	RESPONSE
Scope of assessment includes problems not addressed in U.S. studies, such as infectious diseases, for which there are no dose-response models.	Use clinical data and ethnographic data collection methods to estimate disease rates.
Limited data on environmental sources and exposures, and on health outcomes.	Combine risk assessment, epidemiological methods, and ethnographic methods
Some standard U.S. assumptions used for determining exposure are inappropriate to other cultures	Adjust assumptions; conduct special studies as required.
Ranking risk involves subjective judgment and values that differ from those held by U.S. Consultants	Assist host country counterparts to develop framework within which they rank the risks

water and food that are protected from microbial contamination; adequate sanitation and surface drainage for handling sewage, sullage, and rain; frequent collection and removal of household wastes; and adequate ventilation for indoor combustion sources used for cooking and heating, as well as for other airborne contaminants such as tobacco smoke and microbes.

Predictive models are not yet available that would allow us to measure the physical environmental conditions or exposures related to these diseases and predict their future impacts on health. The best way to determine their relative significance in a particular setting, therefore, is to collect current information on mortality and morbidity rates from public sources (e.g., clinics and health ministries), recent surveys, or interviews.

Data Availability

> Data on environmental conditions are less available, less representative, and less reliable in developing countries than in advanced industrial countries.

Data on environmental conditions (e.g., air quality, water quality, contamination of food) provide the starting point for most health risk assessments in industrialized countries. Information on the concentrations of pollutants in the environment is combined with information on activity and consumption patterns to estimate exposure to a particular substance, from which researchers estimate dose and then use dose-response models to estimate health risks.

Data on environmental conditions are frequently unavailable in developing countries and, where they are available, they are often from one-time studies rather than routine monitoring. They apply, therefore, to particular times, locations, and populations which usually do not represent the conditions under study. There is no good answer to this problem in the short term, since it is financially impossible to generate new environmental data for a comparative heatlh risk assessment. The only realistic strategy is to use whatever data are available from various sources—for example, environmental quality statistics from environmental agencies and public service providers, such as the water and solid waste services; information on the types and locations of emission sources from ministries of industry, energy, mining, agriculture, and others; and special studies prepared by academic institutions and international development agencies.

Conclusions derived from analysis of these data must then be subjected to a "reality check" by comparing them with information derived from public health statistics and interviews with knowledgable officials as well as with community and nongovernmental organizations. One must use all of these sources, recognizing that their quality and representativeness affect the reliability of the study's conclusions in a way that is unquantifiable. Even in industrialized countries, some people criticize comparative risk assessment for not being purely scientific and quantitative. Using the methodology in developing countries requires even more judgment and produces conclusions that are more qualitative than quantitative. Over the long term, these problems will be addressed by gradual improvements in routine environmental monitoring programs. One of the most important outcomes of a comparative risk assessment study in a developing country is to identify environmental problems which are likely to have significant health impacts but which cannot be fully characterized at the present because of a lack of sufficient data.

Exposure Assumptions

> Typical assumptions used to determine exposure rates and patterns may be inappropriate due to cultural differences.

Risk assessors use standard assumptions (e.g., volumes of air and water consumed per day, average body weight), information on consumption (e.g, typical diet), and information on time and activity patterns (e.g., time spent indoors vs. outdoors and at various degrees of exertion) to estimate a population's exposure to toxic contaminants present in the environment. Some of these factors are obviously subject to great variation across cultures. Such information may not be available for a study in a developing country. Reasonable assumptions can be developed, however, using a combination of locally available information (e.g., average body weights, life spans), standard assumptions (respiration and water consumption), and original data generated through ethnographic investigations (diet composition, time/activity patterns).

Subjective Values Implicit in Risk Ranking

> Ranking the risks of various diseases that may affect different age, gender, and social groups involves subjective judgments that should reflect the values of the culture in which they occur.

Comparing and ranking the risks of different diseases to different groups necessarily involves subjective choices based on social values. An outside expert adviser cannot hope to anticipate or fully discover the full range of values that should be reflected in ranking risks from different diseases (e.g., diarrhea, guinea worm, tuberculosis, malaria, and various cancers) or to different groups (e.g., children vs. working adults vs. older adults). Different cultures each attach their own unique set of values to losses in lifespan or various bodily functions, and also to the illness or death of different group members defined by age, gender, and ethnicity.

Comparative risk studies in the U.S. have been criticized for being elitist and undemocratic when rankings are developed by "experts" rather than by a panel that truly represents the affected groups. This is even more true when the advisers come from a totally different culture than that for which risks are being characterized and ranked.

In comparative risk assessment studies conducted in developing countries, it is imperative that the rankings be developed by a representative panel of local officials, experts, and citizens, rather than by the outside advisers. Although most of the studies conducted to date by USAID and USEPA have used local consultants, none of them have relied on local people to develop the risk rankings. This is an area in which much additional effort is needed.

METHODOLOGY

Components of the Comparative Health Risk Assessment

This section describes the methods used in a comparative health risk assessment performed in Quito, Ecuador in June, 1992 (Arcia et al., 1993).

For the reasons given above, the study in Quito differed in four principal ways from analogous studies in the U.S.:

- The Quito study relied more heavily on public health data (i.e., morbidity and mortality rates by cause and location) to identify potential environmental health problems;
- The assessment team collected original ethnographic data to aid in identifying environmental health problems and understanding the relevance and meaning of information on environmental and health conditions obtained from other sources;
- The assessment was performed by a multidisciplinary team including a physician, epidemiologist, and medical anthropologist, in addition to persons with expertise in the more typical disciplines of environmental science (monitoring) and toxicology; and
- The assessment relied almost totally on qualitative characterizations of risk rather than quantitative estimates and, therefore, the method used for ranking risks was quite simple.

The Quito study integrated three approaches to investigating public health problems: typical health risk assessment, as described by USEPA (USEPA, 1987, 1993); health effects (outcome) assessment, as developed and practiced by epidemiologists (ATSDR, 1992); and ethnographic investigation of health related behavior, as developed and practiced by medical anthropologists (Scrimshaw & Hurtado, 1987). The health risk assessment and health effects assessments used existing (secondary) data on environmental quality and the occurrence of environmentally related diseases. The ethnographic investigation generated original (primary) data. The health risk assessment methodology has been described and illustrated above (Box 22.1). The following subsections will describe the methods used in the health effects assessment, ethnographic investigations, and risk ranking.

Health Effects (Outcome) Assessment

The health effects assessment uses traditional epidemiological methods and concepts. Its objective, however, is not to identify previously undescribed cause-and-effect relationships between environmental exposures and health effects. Rather, its purpose is to use information on known cause-and-effect relationships to determine which types of illness and causes of death in the subject population—and, therefore, what portion of current morbidity and mortality rates—are potentially attributable to environmental causes.

Ideally, the health risk assessment and the health effects assessment complement each other. The risk assessment uses information on environmental conditions to predict health impacts; the impacts it predicts should be manifest in the public health data, except for diseases such as cancer which have a long latency period. The health effects assessment uses information on public health conditions to identify environmental health problems that might otherwise be missed, because data on the causal conditions are not available. With one type of information in hand, the researcher knows to look for the other. When the environmental condition and its associated health outcomes are both manifest in available data, the assessment team can reliably conclude that the environmental health problem exists. When a potential problem appears only in the environmental data (cause) or only in the public health data (effect), the team can still conclude that the problem exists, but is less confident in doing so.

An investigator can use several sources for data on health outcomes. Morbidity and mortality data are usually available through public sources, such as a ministry of health, local health department, or clinics and hospitals. Individuals within private institutions, such as universities and public research institutes, as well as international development agencies, may also have valuable data if they conduct research germane to the subject. Such data will frequently cover a population that is defined differently than the subject population in the risk assessment; when possible, manual or computer manipulation should be used to isolate information that pertains to the subject population (i.e., to obtain the correct "denominator").

When an investigator examines secondary data, it is important to know how the data have been gathered. The following five issues should be considered:

- Have data been generated through an active or passive surveillance system? A passive surveillance system receives incoming data and, therefore, generally suffers from substantial underreporting of cases.
- Does the investigator have some sense of the timeliness of the data? For example, are there lags in reporting such that the data do not reflect recent trends?
- Do differential reporting rates exist? Do some areas, districts, or provinces report more completely than others? Are there any factors, such as cost, staffing, or vested interests, which cause such circumstances to exist?
- Are clear definitions used consistently among all reporting units?
- What means of case confirmation exists for those reported cases? Are some cases misclassified as non-cases, or vice versa?

When using hospital- and clinic-based data, the investigator must consider the estimated proportion of the population afflicted with an illness or adverse outcome that may never seek health care or that has limited access to health care facilities. In addition, some environmental exposures lead to minor illnesses, which may not require medical attention. There could be a large number of such minor illnesses without creating a clinical record of the health impact on the population. Other forms of bias also affect the quality of health outcome data: reporting bias results from health care providers reporting diseases differently (e.g., tuberculosis and pneumonia both being reported as acute respiratory infections); diagnostic bias results from some providers reporting cases more reliably because they have better reporting systems or more interest in the condition; misclassification bias results from one disease being mistakenly reported as another (e.g., byssinosis as chronic bronchitis or asthma); and detection bias results from failure to detect certain diseases because adequate methods or equipment for detecting a disease are not available (e.g., missing pesticide poisonings due to a lack of equipment for measuring cholinesterase activity). Finally, the completeness of reporting systems and the speed and reliability with which data are entered into the health information system will also affect the outcome assessment.

Even when particular environmental conditions and the health outcomes typically associated with such conditions are both manifest in available data, it may be incorrect to conclude that a cause-and-effect relationship exists in this instance. Assessment teams will rarely be able to avoid this error, but certain problems should be kept in mind. Cause-and-effect relationships in environmental health are often multidimensional on both ends. One type of exposure may lead to several outcomes. For example, exposure to lead may cause a variety of neurologic, hematologic, and renal disorders. Exposure to one substance may cause various outcomes depending on the route of entry, magnitude and duration of exposure, the chemical form of the agent, or the age of the person exposed. On the other hand, a particular health outcome may have several discretely different etiologies. For example, acute respiratory illness may be caused by infectious agents, irritating chemicals, particulates such as cotton dust, or allergens. Moreover, environmental exposures may exacerbate an underlying disorder attributable to other causes, such as chronic bronchitis or asthma.

Missing data should be addressed in any investigation. Identifying the reasons for the lack of data is a good protection against making unfounded conclusions about health outcomes. It is important for the investigator to state his or her assumptions about the missing data and potential impact on the analysis.

Ethnographic Investigations

As stated earlier, environmental data and health outcome data complement each other in the ideal case. More typically, one or the other is missing. Data from ethnographic investigations can provide the missing link. Through interviews, focus groups, and observations, the assessment team can obtain information on what people know about the environmental conditions in which they live and the illnesses from which they suffer. Moreover, original data are often needed in order to estimate or characterize people's behavior and activity patterns (e.g., their water sources, uses, and consumption rates) and, thereby, their exposure to environmental contaminants.

Collecting original data through ethnographic investigations is particularly important for characterizing the environmental health risks of poor and marginalized populations. Environmental conditions in slums and peri-urban areas are rarely captured in official environmental statistics. Similarly, these areas are rarely served by public health facilities and, thus, the health conditions of their residents are not reflected in clinic-based health data. Going to peri-urban neighborhoods and interviewing their residents is the best way of filling in the gaps in official data and discovering the environmental health problems that have the greatest impact on these population groups.

Ethnography is the field study of culturally specific behaviors, values, and social patterns. It provides a mechanism to study what people do, how they explain their actions, and what they perceive as meaningful constraints on their behavior. Ethnography combines the use of qualitative and quantitative data, as well as primary and secondary data.

The use of ethnographic techniques in health risk assessment relies heavily on the collection of primary data that tends to be qualitative. While a review of pertinent secondary literature is necessary, the most critical techniques are focus group research, in-depth key informant interviews, and semistructured observations.

Focus Group Research is a technique used to gather data in a limited timeframe. A focus group can be defined as a carefully planned discussion designed to obtain information on a specific set of topics (Krueger, 1988; Aubel & Mansour, 1989; Eng, Naimoli, & Naimoli, 1991). Such groups are usually composed of seven to ten people who are carefully selected according to specific criteria. The group should be relatively homogenous to facilitate rapid cross-identification and communication.

Multiple focus groups work best when used to build on the results of previous groups (Debus, 1989). Participants should be selected for their knowledge relative to the research. For example, for health risk assessment, community members with experience in health education or occupational health problems might be brought together to obtain relevant information.

In order for focus group research to be effective, the investigator must carefully select participants, use locally known and respected assistants, design appropriate research questions and "probe" questions, choose a neutral location for the groups, and use a trained facilitator (Kumar, 1987; Scrimshaw & Hurtado, 1987).

Analysis of focus group data can take several forms; regardless of the level of detail required, however, the focus groups should be tape recorded and the tapes analyzed for linguistic themes, behavioral categories, perceptions of risks, descriptions of health symptoms, and frequency. Ensuring the careful exchange of information between the facilitator (who may be from outside the culture being studied) and the community-based assistants is central to the analysis.

In-Depth Key Informant Interviews are used to obtain information that may be too complex to acquire during a focus group. Key informants are individuals the researcher knows and values for their opinions and insights. They should be living in the community being studied and have knowledge relevant to the issue being researched. Often key informants have provided detailed insight on issues raised through other research techniques.

In-depth interviews may take several hours and may require multiple visits. The information is carefully noted and cross-indexed with related topics. Researchers also can conduct in-depth interviews of community decision makers, although they do not serve the same function as interviews with key informants. Key informants help cross-validate other types of information; such interviews can only work effectively when the researcher has established a history of trust and respect with the key informant. In-depth interviews with decision makers, on the other hand, are mainly to gather opinions or to access secondary or quantitative data controlled by the decision-maker's office, such as census data.

Semi-Structured Observations are first-hand, on-site observations by the researcher. They provide a necessary reliability check on information gathered through other techniques. When people in focus groups describe their behaviors related to garbage disposal, for instance, the researcher should note their descriptions and check if direct observations validate the information provided. Research focusing on environmental health risks should include observations of garbage dumps, household refuse removal systems, the use and condition of sanitation facilities, access to drinking water or other household patterns for water retrieval and storage. Food handling practices, such as food purchasing, preparation, and storage, and family and household hygiene practices, such as handwashing and waste removal, should also be observed. Observations might also focus on informal sector occupations, such as home-based shoe repairers, ambulant vendors, and woodworkers, or formal sector occupations, such as textile and metal workers.

Integration of Ethnographic Data. Throughout the project, ethnographic data generated through the focus groups, key informant interviews, and semi-structured observations are integrated into the overall analyses through a variety of techniques. These techniques include discussing information in meetings of the assessment team, performing written analyses, ranking focus group topics, involving other members of the team in conducting on-site observations, and cross-editing work with other members of the team.

The focus group research should be conducted during the initial phases of the field project, and the information generated should be provided to the other members of the team early in the field study. This will enable other members of the team to seek environmental and health data that confirm or extend the information obtained through the ethnographic investigation. Data from the focus groups and other methods should be recorded according to categories being used by other members of the team (e.g., wastewater, occupational health, air pollution). Information provided by the focus groups will help other team members identify appropriate field sites for direct observations, such as homes, workplaces, and garbage dumps. This will give all members of the research team actual on-site experience and will facilitate integration of the ethnographic data.

In the final stages of the risk assessment study, focus groups can be used to rank the various environmental health risks that have been identified. This information can be used directly or it can be incorporated into the team's evaluation of data and the development of an overall ranking to which other groups also contribute. The result of the focus group ranking should be shared with key informant members of the communities for their feedback and comments. The information is then integrated into the final formal ranking of environmental health risks.

Although ethnographic data can be rich in information, there are some limitations. Selection of the communities from which to draw the focus group participants, the selection criteria used, the scope and phrasing of the questions, the choice of meeting site, the identities of community-based assistants, and the skill of the facilitator all influence the quality of the information gathered. A careful researcher recognizes the methodological constraints and attempts to control them.

Organizing an Ethnographic Investigation. The following summarizes the activities that should be performed before, during, and after the in-field portion of an assessment in order for the ethnographic investigation to be productive.

Pre-Field Activities:

- Decide on criteria for selection of focus group participants
- Select focus group locations
- Find neutral meeting sites
- Arrange for local community members to assist focus group facilitator
- Develop realistic timeframe and budget for focus groups
- Develop appropriate topic-specific questions and associated probes with other team members
- Design analysis structure for results

In-Field Activities:

- Meet, select, and train candidates for community-based assistants
- Check conditions at meeting sites
- Review selection constraints for participants
- Pretest linguistic appropriateness of questions and probes
- Pretest for sequencing of focus group questions
- Conduct focus groups
- Conduct key informant interviews
- Select criteria for recording on-site observations
- Perform on-site observations
- Analyze results from focus groups, key informant interviews, and on-site observations
- Integrate ethnographic data into team data base
- Obtain problem rankings from focus groups and share results with key informants for their feedback
- Complete the analysis of all data and draft preliminary report
- Cross-edit written draft with other team members
- Write and present field report

Post-Field Activities:

- Meet with project directors and other team members to review conceptual issues and data limitations
- Discuss findings and agree on final conclusions
- Incorporate new information and revise report as necessary

Integrating and Ranking Environmental Health Risks

Ranking risks requires comparing a wide variety of health effects that differ in occurrence and severity. Health endpoints may range from an acute disease or illness that is not life threatening to one that causes death. In addition, there may be a wide range of data available for each environmental concern. Where health outcome data are not available, exposure data may have to be used; and where exposure data are not available, surrogates for exposure, such as information on use of a hazardous substance, may have to be used. As a result, the confidence and type of risk estimates may also vary greatly, with some risks being characterized in quantitative terms, while others may be limited to qualitative descriptions. How to compare "apples and oranges" is often a difficult task. As a result, comparative risk assessment is often subjective and relies on professional experience and judgment. This applies to assessing the validity of data and assessing the certainty of conclusions drawn from various studies and data sets as well. Data must be analyzed and integrated before ratings can be prepared.

Traditional risk assessment methods use a qualitative matrix for classifying risk levels, depending on (1) the probability of occurrence and (2) the relative severity of an adverse health effect. In general, such methods use three risk levels (low, medium, and high) (Pierson, 1991). The Quito study used a rating system employing five scoring levels in an attempt to obtain more resolution in levels of severity and probability. These rankings were ultimately combined into a three-tiered summary ranking.

The score for probability of effect (Table 22.1) is based on the percent of the total population that is likely to be exposed to a hazard and either a qualitative or quantitative estimate of those experiencing an adverse effect. For example, for every 100 people in the city, 75 (75 percent) may be exposed to air pollution. However, only 50 of these 75 people may actually experience an effect (i.e., 66.7 percent of those exposed). Hence, the *probability* of effect is 75% × 66.7% = 50% (probability of effect score = 1). When only qualitative descriptions are available, the descriptive terms "very low" to "very high" can be used.

The score for severity of effect (Table 22.2) reflects the severity of health effects that, in the investigator's judgment, are most likely to occur, based on prior laboratory, clinical, or epidemiological studies. For example, it is known that exposure to certain types of air pollution may lead to serious

TABLE 22.1 Scoring for Probability of Effect

Probability of Effect (probability of exposure × probability of effect among those exposed)	Score
0–.10 (Very Low)	5
0.11–0.20 (Low)	4
0.21–0.30 (Medium)	3
0.31–0.40 (High)	2
0.41–1.00 (Very High)	1

TABLE 22.2 Scoring for Severity of Effect

Severity of Effect (seriousness of impairment × duration)	Score
Very mild	5
Mild	4
Moderate	3
Serious	2
Death	1

acute respiratory disorders. These acute disorders may range in severity from reduced ability to exercise to increased incidence of bronchitis. Air pollution may also result in respiratory dysfunction, wherein a person's respiratory capacity may be significantly and permanently reduced, or even more serious and permanent diseases, such as lung cancer. Hence, the severity score is 2.

Using numerical scores may imply a greater degree of accuracy and certainty than is actually present in the ratings. Subjective elements are inevitably involved in assigning a score for probability of effect and severity of effect. The experienced investigator uses information drawn from experience in other countries, the uncertainty associated with dose-response coefficients for a particular variable, and subjective judgment regarding the percentage of people expected to be exposed. In some cases, the score may be based on the upper limit percent of people likely to be exposed (e.g., ≤75 percent), while in other cases, it may be based on a lower limit (e.g., ≥50 percent). In some cases, the quantitative estimates are used as a guide and adjustments may be needed when a comparison is made between environmental health problems. For example, when two environmental health concerns are evaluated separately, similar scores may be assigned initially. However, when the two are compared, adjustment may be made to one or the other if professional judgment indicates that the two risks may differ either in severity or probability of effect.

The total score assigned to the environmental risk is the sum of the scores for likelihood of effect and severity of effect as shown in Figure 22.1. Items with high severity and high probability of effect will be grouped on the upper left-hand corner of the matrix. These are the items posing the highest environmental health risk to the population.

After risk ratings have been assigned to all of the problems being evaluated, the ratings should be grouped into low-, medium-, and high-risk categories. The ratings will often cluster naturally into groups and the break-points will be more or less obvious. In the Quito study, risk ratings clustered into three groups and risk categories were defined as follows:

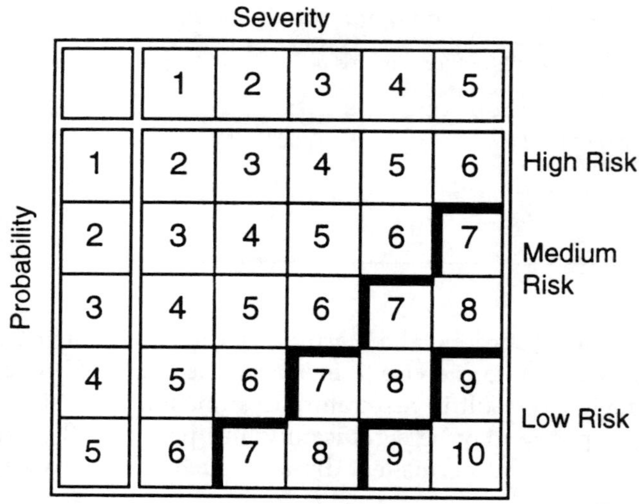

FIGURE 22.1 Matrix illustrating sum of scores of severity of effect and probability of effect.

Low Risk	9 to 10
Moderate Risk	7 to 8
High Risk	1 to 6

For example, an environmental condition presenting a high probability of effect (i.e., 1) to a toxicant that causes serious permanent damage to an organ system (severity score of 2) would have a total risk score of 3 and be considered a high-risk problem.

Conversely, situations ascribing a low probability of effect to toxicants that cause minor health effects would be grouped on the lower right-hand corner of the matrix and would be deemed low-risk problems. Scores along any diagonal, lower left to upper right, would be considered equivalent. High-severity, low-probability effects are assumed to be equivalent in overall importance to low-severity, high-probability effects, and the scoring system reflects this.

Limitations in Interpreting Results

The investigator must be cautious in interpreting results from this methodology because it often relies on limited data and best estimates. As better data become available, the methodology should be applied again and rankings redone. Nevertheless, this methodology can provide useful information, especially on the relative priority of environmental health problems.

Investigators should recognize that this methodology has a number of limitations, including the following:

- Some data may be out of date;
- Some data may be for a larger or smaller geographic area than the one targeted;
- Some data may have been collected using varying definitions of illness, injury, or disability; and
- Sample data may not be representative of the whole target population.

In addition, this rankings are based solely on the predicted health impacts of certain environmental conditions, and do not take into consideration the cost of steps needed to mitigate those conditions, the resources available for mitigation, or the relative cost-effectiveness of alternative approaches to mitigation.

CONCLUSIONS

Health risk assessment techniques were originally developed to predict the long-term public health impact of environmental health problems with long latency periods, such as cancer. Predictive methods are needed because the impact of exposure to carcinogens cannot be measured directly. Over time, environmental regulatory institutions in the United State have moved beyond the initial use of risk assessment for setting individual standards and are now using comparative risk assessment as an important tool for establishing priorities and setting public policy. More and more, public officials, private advocates, and academicians are urging that risk assessment be adopted as a basic framework for setting environmental health policy.

USAID is exploring the potential for using comparative risk assessment techniques to help developing country governments set priorities in their environmental health programs. USAID has sponsored two risk assessment studies to date: the first in Bangkok, Thailand, conducted in 1990 and sponsored by the Office of Housing, in collaboration with the U.S. Environmental Protection Agency; the second in Quito, Ecuador, conducted in 1992 by the Office of Health.

Using risk assessment techniques in developing countries presents several challenges that have not been confronted to the same degree in applications in the United States. The most important of these are summarized in Box 22.4. USAID's risk assessment studies in Bangkok and Quito have involved first attempts to deal with some of these challenges. This report has described the approaches used in the EHA in Quito to evaluate infectious diseases and injuries, as well as cancer; to use interviews, focus groups, and observations as a critical source of information for augmenting the minimal quantitative data available on environmental quality and exposure; and to deal with the limitations in data accessibility. Other challenges will be addressed in future efforts, particularly the need to transfer risk assessment skills to host country institutions, as well as to involve community groups and nongovernmental organizations in the conduct, interpretation, and use of risk assessments. These challenges define the context for USAID's continuing effort to develop risk assessment methods that are appropriate for use in developing countries.

The authors of this chapter believe that the EHA methodology holds much promise. It has been developed with the specific intent of adapting the rationale and approach of health risk assessment to developing countries. It has been tested in an urban and a rural setting, where it proved helpful in identifying and prioritizing environmental health problems (Arcia et al., 1993). It should now be applied in other developing countries to assist those countries in assessing and prioritizing their environmental health problems.

REFERENCES

Agency for Toxic Substances and Disease Registry. (1992). *Public Health Assessment Guidance Manual.* Atlanta: ATSDR.

Arcia, G., Brantly, E., Hetes, R., Levy, B. S., Powell, C., Suárez, J., & Whiteford, L. (1993). *Environmental health assessment: A case study in the city of Quito and the county of Pedro Moncayo, Pichincha Province, Ecuador.* WASH Field Report No. 401. Arlington, VA: WASH Project.

Aubel, J., & Mansour, M. (1989). Qualitative community health research: A Tunisian example. *Health policy and planning 4(3)*:244–251.

Debus, M. (1989). *Methodological review: A handbook for excellence in focus group research.* Washington, DC: Academy for Educational Development.

Eng, E., Naimoli, J., & Naimoli, G. (1991). Acceptability of childhood immunization to Togolese mothers: A sociobiological perspective. *Health Education Quarterly 18(1)*:97–110.

Finkel, A. M., & Golding, D. Eds. (1994). *Worst things first: The debate over risk-based national environmental priorities.* Washington, DC, and Baltimore, MD: Resources for the Future and Johns Hopkins University Press.

Jamison, D. T., & Mosely, W. H. (1991). Disease Control Priorities in Developing Countries. *American Journal of Public Health 81(1)*:15.

Krueger, R. (1988). *Focus Groups: A Practical Guide to Applied Research.* Sage Publications.

Kumar, K. (1987). *Conducting Group Interviews in Developing Countries.* U.S. Agency for International Development: Program Design and Evaluation Methodology Report No. 8.

Pierson, T. K. (1991). *The Role and Methodology of Environmental Risk Assessment: A Framework for Developing Countries*. Staff Working Paper, Center for International Development, Research Triangle Institute. Research Triangle Park, NC.

Scrimshaw, S., & Hurtado, E. (1987). *Rapid Assessment Procedures for Nutrition and Primary Health Care*. Los Angeles: UCLA Latin American Center for Publications.

U.S. Agency for International Development. (1990). *Ranking Environmental Risks in Bangkok, Thailand*. Office of Housing and Urban Programs Working Paper.

U.S. Environmental Protection Agency. (1987). *Risk Assessment Guidelines of 1986*. Office of Health and Environmental Assessment. EPA 600-8-87/045.

U.S. Environmental Protection Agency. (September, 1993). *A Guidebook to Comparing Risks and Setting Environmental Priorities*. EPA 230-B-93-003.

23

Using Geographical Information Systems (GIS) for Understanding Environment and Health in the Developing World

Kenneth M. Green

INTRODUCTION

During the last several decades, the relationship between health and the environment has been acknowledged to be of great concern. In particular, tropical diseases such as yellow fever, river blindness, malaria, and as was recently experienced in India, plague, have been intensely studied by true multidisciplinary teams of specialists. For example, extensive ecological, biological, medical and sociological studies were carried out in Latin America to understand the course of malaria. Disease management and health planning can not be effectively undertaken unless there is a clear understanding of numerous sector pieces of information (e.g., vector biology, meteorology, land use analysis, occupational history, resource extraction, pesticide use, etc.).

In addition, many development planning activities have been associated with extensive modification of natural resources and the environment. Many of these activities are known now to have direct health effects. It is generally recognized today that the past practices of heavy use of pesticides to increase agricultural productivity have serious detrimental impacts on both the environment and human health. These impacts are considered in this paper under the realm of risk assessment, and consider both human health and ecological risk assessment in parallel. Development agencies have recognized that in the last decade these past uncontrolled settlement and development measures had high environmental, economic and social cost and that "sustainable development" practices should become institutionally integrated into the framework of development planning.

The cadre of professionals who believe that development and improved human health are linked to the environment is growing. Furthermore, there is common recognition that these goals can be accomplished only through an integrated or multidisciplinary approach. This approach recognizes that traditional sector planning, although still important, does not properly have a *holistic vision of planning*. Consequently, decision makers responsible for development planning need meaningful and timely thematic information associated with physical, biotic and socioeconomic aspects. The overall objective of this endeavor is to provide a framework for integrated planning that takes into consideration all sector needs. The goal is to examine the trade-offs and *ecological, economical and sociological costs* associated with strategies linked to health care services. Today's technical world offers a useful tool to assist in this process.

Modern data management and analysis practices now rely on a wide variety of computer hardware, software, and telecommunications equipment. This chapter focuses on a specialized set of data management and analysis tools, called Geographic Information Systems (GIS), which have the potential to enhance this integrated human health and ecological risk assessment process. GISs are decision-support systems that can use spatial data to support interdisciplinary studies and facilitate analysis with unique data integration and display functions. The purpose of this chapter is to serve as a guideline both for managers who want to determine whether a GIS may be appropriate for their program needs, as well as for managers who are "sold" on GIS technology and wish to develop a specific GIS application.

INTEGRATED ENVIRONMENTAL AND HEALTH PLANNING

Integrated environmental and health planning will illuminate the relationships between the biophysical, socioeconomic and health layers of information through the integrative strengths of the GIS database. First, data concerning vegetation, geology, geomorphology, water resources, and climate and soils need to be integrated to develop an appropriate biophysical classification system.

Socioeconomic layers of information will include: land use and occupation; demographic dynamics; living standards; economic dynamics; and the infrastructure of the regional territory. Existing agricultural zones, industrial zones, residential zones, urban centers, recreation areas, and other units will be portrayed. Additional information should include the location and service area of schools, health centers, agricultural extension, and native cultures. Corridors of commerce inclusive of primary roads, secondary roads, feeder roads, and waterways will be included. The end result will be a comprehensive set of maps and an interactive digital database. The integrative product will be a map that portrays all aspects related to the population and infrastructure of the state.

Health-related information includes incidence and distribution of disease, location and profile of sources of pollution, and measures of environmental quality, (e.g. water quality, air quality, etc.). In addition, health care service facilities can be identified and located according to numerous factors such as location and size of population served, distribution of road networks, and health profiles for any household or geographic subdivision.

In a strategic planning process, these layers of information will be synthesized in a collaborative effort among multidisciplinary staff. Discussions are required to clearly define the purpose of such an effort, and understand how this information can be used for future development planning efforts.

Sector experts will have a strong inclination toward their own program needs, and this process will require consideration of all factors to achieve equal understanding. A common classification scheme will need to be developed so that the interests and concerns of all the sector specialists remain apparent. Such a process will require iterative attempts before a final scheme is finalized.

Any proposal for an integrated environmental and health development plan will require a projection of the expected benefits, "basic human needs," (improved income stream, increases in production, generation of employment, better solid waste collection and disposal, human and animal waste collection and disposal, improved health care delivery, better nutrition, etc.) and costs (construction, operation and maintenance, depletion of resources, pollution effects, etc.). All development schemes consist of specific project components that require valuative criteria, such as net present value, internal rates of return, cost-benefit ratio, and repayment possibilities.

This integrated approach will be expected to:

- determine the levels of technology, credit, knowledge, information, marketing, etc. that are needed to support the target users, and ensure that the development planning projects are formulated on these levels;
- examine the human activities that could contribute to environmental impacts, natural hazards and the social and cultural factors that could influence project vulnerability during and after implementation;

- prepare area-specific human health and ecological risk assessments and appropriate risk reduction measures for all proposals;
- offer mitigation opportunities based on several development options so that choices can be available for each development proposal;
- examine the compatibility of all proposals from the perspective of local (municipal) and regional changes as projected in the GIS database;
- define the specific instruments of policy and management required for the implementation of the overall strategy and include monitoring components.

When all of the above considerations (and more) are defined and understood, the Development Team will then be able to design a "masterplan." When using a GIS, this is really a modification of the existing GIS data at many thematic and subsequent integrative layers.

OVERVIEW OF GEOGRAPHIC INFORMATION SYSTEMS

Geographic Information Systems provide data input, storage, manipulation, analysis and display capabilities for geographic, cultural, political, environmental and statistical data in a common spatial framework. The data analyzed are a collection of spatial information (represented by points, lines and areas) and their associated attributes (characteristics of the features which the points, lines, and polygons represent). Examples of point data may include drinking water wells, dams, monitoring stations, and mountain peaks. Lines are commonly used to represent rivers, roads, or contours. Soil classes, crop types, political jurisdictions, and drainage basins are represented as area or polygon data. Some sources of data for GISs include maps, aerial photographs, censuses, field notes, satellite photos and meteorological records.

The advent of sophisticated computers with mass digital data storage devices has facilitated the integration of spatial data analysis, statistics, and computer graphics into comprehensive "turnkey" geographic information systems. GIS technology bridges the disciplines of computer science (e.g., image processing and pattern recognition), information management, cartography, and environmental management. The geographic information system is distinguished from other forms of information systems by its ability to perform spatial analysis.

There are many kinds of GIS turnkey systems. Some overlap exists in terms of their capabilities. Since technology and software are constantly changing, it is probable that vendors will be able to add extra capabilities without adding substantially to prices in the near future. One significant technology change during the last several years has been the availability of microcomputer-based GISs. These systems have virtually replaced the more expensive mini and mainframe systems used only a few years ago. Selection of an appropriate GIS software "toolbox" must be linked to clearly defining data analysis needs.

Spatial Data Features

The geographic location of each data item (or "attribute") is a key identifier used to describe and organize data in a GIS. Maintaining the integrity of this spatial descriptor as part of the data base record permits normal data base management system operations and adds the capability to manipulate and analyze data geographically. The concept of data analysis in relation to geographic position is commonly encountered in epidemiological studies.

One frequently used analytical approach is to assign colors or patterns to multiple map themes and overlay them with colored transparencies to reveal spatial relationships. This process of overlaying maps is a major function of a GIS. GISs also provide other analyses, including cross tabulations of data, attribute selections, Boolean combinations, modeling and customized displays.

Geographic data can be represented using either of two formats—raster/grid or vector/polygon data structures. Raster/grid data refers to attribute values and spatial references tied to specific x, y intersections or grids in space (e.g., latitude/longitude). Fine grid spacing allows high resolution, and good definition of spatial characteristics. Scale is also important in grid spacing since large scale (small area) studies require higher levels of accuracy and finer grid spacing. In contrast, small scale (larger area) studies do not require rasters or grids in such fine detail. Vector/polygon data structures, on the other hand, describe unique lines or forms of geographic features. A lake, for example, can be described by the coordinates which comprise the circumference of the outer lake boundary and can be captured and stored in the GIS as a "tracing" of these features. The geographic attributes of the lake may remain constant even as the resolution of the lake boundary coordinates changes.

Data Input

The data entered into a GIS often include spatial data from maps, remote sensors (aerial photography and satellite imagery), and environmental monitoring. GISs require entry of two distinct types of data: geographic references and attributes. Geographic reference data are the coordinates which describe the location of spatial information. This type of data entry usually occurs via a process known as digitization. A special peripheral device—a digitizer—is used to convert a drawing or map into a digital format. Most GIS projects require a large digitization data input process consuming many man-hours of effort. Attribute data entry (e.g., water quality parametric values) often occurs via key entry at a terminal, reading a magnetic tape, or downloading from a separate computer system.

Since data which form the GIS data base often come from different sources, and since digitization may be done by staff with varying levels of skill, most GIS data base development efforts involve extensive levels of data validation and quality assurance. An initial and ongoing commitment to data quality is generally rewarded by confidence in the graphical and analytical results of the GIS.

Data Base Management and Data Storage

The characteristic which distinguishes a GIS from other data base management systems and manual map overlay procedures is the way a GIS stores the spatial data and makes it available for user access and analysis. Derived maps and data sets may become part of the GIS data base in a feedback process that permits future retrieval and display without rerunning the analysis procedure. These map and data layers can be superimposed during analysis to produce various map products with the GIS information display functions. This data generation process requires special spatial analysis and tabulation capabilities provided through the data base management system. Since the analysis and processing limits of each GIS vary from vendor to vendor, the anticipated analytical methods and data base management requirements should be well understood before selecting a particular system.

Efficient data storage organizes the spatial data in a format which permits rapid and accurate updates and corrections to the data base. Data storage refers to how the data formats and structures are supported during data operations. Frequently a data dictionary is used to organize a data base and record information about the geographic and attribute information in the system. Some of the information stored about data bases includes data structures, formats, and access methods. Data dictionaries can be very helpful and important tools, especially for managing active and growing geographic information systems.

Data Manipulation and Analysis

The GIS data base management system provides the ability to query, manipulate, and extract both geographic reference and attribute data. One of the major functions of a GIS is the analysis of multiple layers of data in a selected geographic area. With a GIS, standard statistical manipulations of attribute data are possible, as are Boolean queries of attribute data files, generation of mean and standard deviation for numerical data ranges, and classification of data into mappable units. Other GIS data manipulation and analysis capabilities include querying unique spatial distributions of data and asking questions about data to display the unique spatial arrangements which meet a specific criterion.

Information Display

Information display includes the representation both of raw data and of the results of data manipulation and analysis. Outputs fall into several categories: maps, charts, graphs, surface models, listings, and hybrid representations. The form in which outputs are presented (medium of presentation) also varies, and includes: CRT images (monochrome or color), color slides (from virtual images or directly from graphic bit planes), film plots (print-ready masters), video disk images (requiring digital to analog image conversion), floppy disks of digital image data, microfilm (or "fiche") copies of graphic images, or printed hard copy graphics.

It is important to realize that outputs (as previously described) are distinct from spatial analysis. Geographic/spatial analysis of data usually precedes data display, although initial display of "raw" data can serve as a useful hypothesis tester for attribute and/or spatial data analysis. A comprehensive geographic information system supports various computer mapping/graphics peripherals that provide most of the types of outputs described.

USING GIS TO INTEGRATE INFORMATION

Data loaded into the GIS may come from a multitude of sources. These data may have been newly collected or acquired from existing data bases. In either case, decisions will have to be made concerning quality assurance of the data before incorporation into the GIS.

The spatial data used in the GIS will contain attributes such as raw data values, test scores, or indices that must meet GIS data input formats. In addition, the spatial data itself may be in the form of published maps, printed tables, digital map attributes or digital tabular files. Incorporation of data attributes such as source, scale, projection, geographic location, year of acquisition, and reliability must be defined and standardized prior to data loading.

Creating the Database

The method of data input can include downloading, digitizing, scanning and keyboard entry. The selection of a data input process should be tailored to the volume of data requiring input, the peripherals supported by the GIS, and manpower and time constraints. Digitizing requires many man-hours of tedious work and establishment of input protocols to maintain acceptable data quality standards. Loading data into the GIS from other data bases is often complicated by a need to reformat the data to comply with the host computer or GIS data record format. Graphic data is commonly the most difficult data to reformat. Anticipation of format conversion needs is required for realistic GIS data input planning since format conversion represents substantial levels of effort by programming and technical staff. When data are acquired from manual files of historic or newly collected spatial data, and then automated in-house, the data input process is generally less complicated because data formats are well understood.

Using GIS for Analysis

Data access and manipulation functions permit retrieval of specific data by any attribute or combination of attributes. Well-designed DBMS software generally provides these capabilities by using existing structured queries. However, customer queries are often needed and require DBMS software modification.

A map library should provide rapid indexing to all digital maps within the data base. This library can be maintained as an on-line index and provide the user the capability to query by project identification, geographic area, or place name. The need for a map library increases as the size and complexity of a GIS data base grows.

Use of a data dictionary will assist in maintaining an inventory of map and other spatial data sources used in the GIS. A description of data attributes for each map, photo, or image used in the GIS data base can be catalogued and described in text form. Additionally, quality assurance standards can be included in the data dictionary. Experience shows that insufficient documentation may handicap GIS operation.

Data manipulation can also include tabular and graphic display of the GIS data. Tables and listings may be displayed and printed on CRTs, printers or plotters. Data display is an important step for data base verification and subsequent data analysis.

GIS data analysis requires extensive computer processing for calculating areas, distances, buffers, volumes, overlays, frequency occurrences and Boolean combinations. The power and flexibility of the GIS become readily apparent during these analysis processes. Proper data base design will fulfill user expectations and avoid disillusionment.

Modeling of spatial data is often an important program analytical need. The GIS may contain modeling algorithms, or modeling may be conducted in an independent external computer environment. When using a separate system for modeling, results can be incorporated into the GIS through the input methods discussed above and retained as part of the GIS data base for other analysis objectives.

Data Validation and Quality Assurance

Data validation ensures that acquired data meet acceptable data quality standards and quality assurance (QA) maintains data integrity throughout GIS data processing. The spatial data incorporated into the GIS must be verified to ensure proper formatting. Using reformatted data increases the risk of data conversion errors. Program management and GIS staff must determine what level of QA is needed for acceptable data quality. This determination dictates what data validation processes are required in the GIS. Data quality standards must be maintained throughout data retrieval, display, analysis and modeling functions. During data retrieval and display, mechanisms for detecting errors in base data can ensure improved data quality. Additionally, QA algorithms can be used to check erroneous data ranges and values. It is also necessary that data maintenance activities employ QA standards (e.g., scheduled backups). General guidelines for GIS acquisition are provided in Appendices 1 and 2.

USING GIS TO INTEGRATE AND PORTRAY HUMAN HEALTH AND ECOLOGICAL RISK ASSESSMENT

The compilation process will result in a set of maps that reflect several types of information. In the risk assessment overview scheme presented (see Figure 23.1), four broad categories: source characterization, scope of influence, exposure assessment and risk assessment or determination are used. Figure 23.2 illustrates how the GIS database supports this integrated analysis.

This information is designed to clearly identify:

- potential threats to human health and the environment (including the location and characterization of these threats);
- the bio-physical factors associated with these threats;
- the concentration and exposure of these threats;
- human and ecological susceptibility;

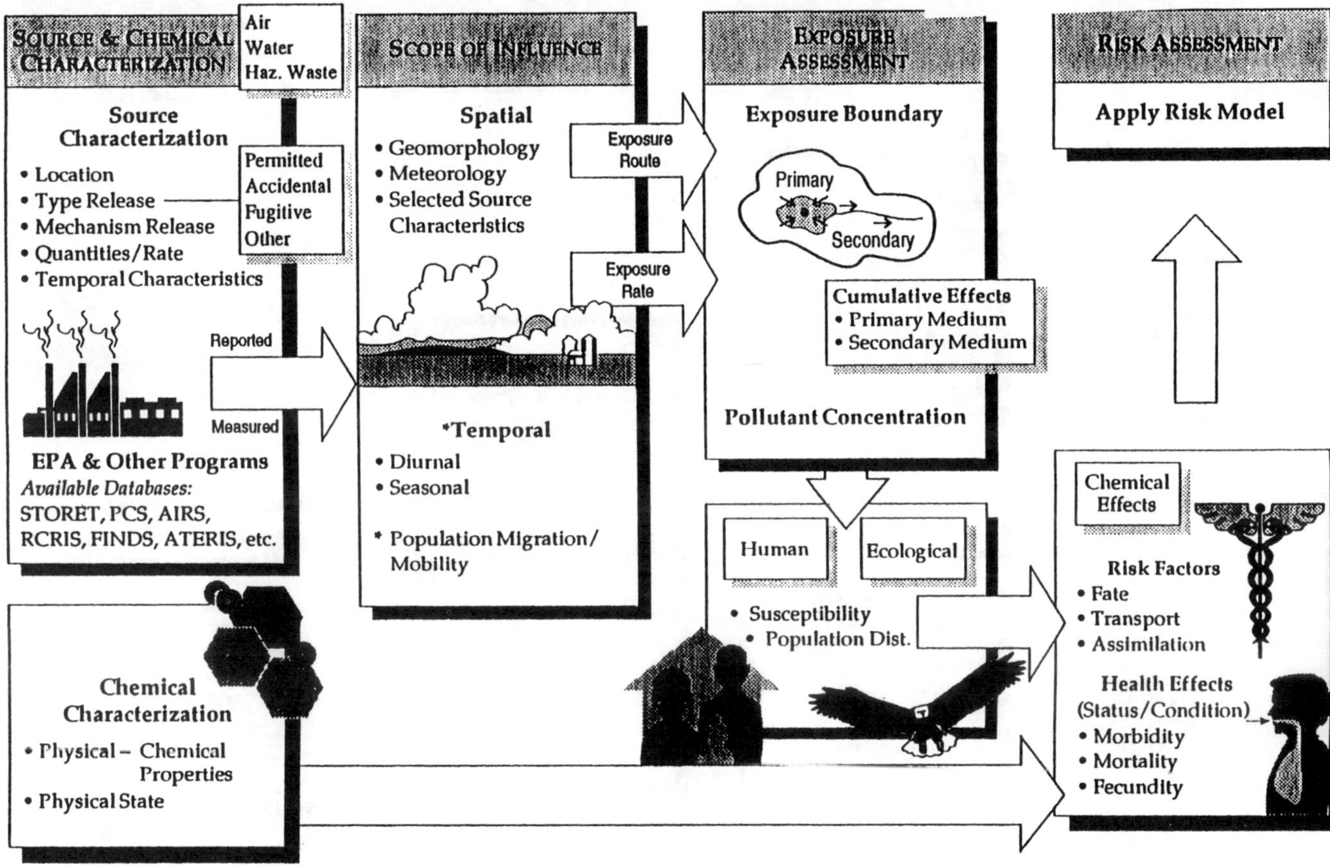

FIGURE 23.1 Risk assessment overview.

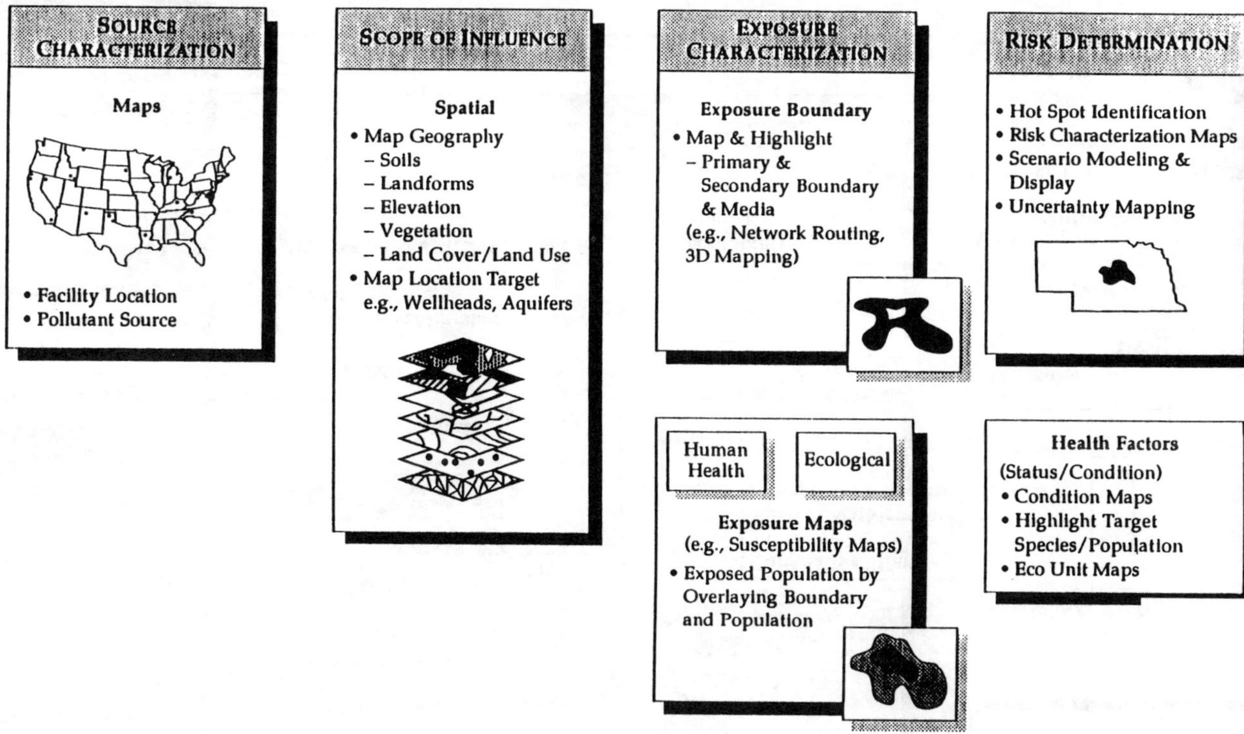

FIGURE 23.2 Role of GIS in Risk Assessment.

- health and chemical effects; and
- risk determination models.

The human health risk assessment component can be based on any number of analytical techniques. In general, several exposure and effects models are commonly available and can be incorporated into the GIS process. These models take into account pollutant influences. This GIS database can also be used for epidemiological analysis, focusing on disease data and associated disease factors (e.g., location of susceptible populations, location of sources of disease vectors, etc.).

All atmospheric, hydrologic, geologic and wildfire phenomena, because of their location, severity and frequency, have the potential to affect humans, their structures and activities adversely. This "human health" concern can also be analyzed with the GIS database.

Although humans can do little to change the incidence of most natural hazards, they influence the outcome of these phenomena in terms of disasters. As observed throughout history, human intervention can increase the frequency and severity of natural hazards. For example, when intensive settlement is undertaken in an area of poor soil stability, low nutrient value and high erodibility, there exists a greater "risk" that this land will become more unstable after human intervention with forest clearing, and large-scale agriculture production. An extreme case of such destructive human intervention is the eventual "desertification" of once highly vegetated areas, that once cleared of their natural cover, can never recover.

The ecological concerns represent issues such as areas of endemic species, biologically important zones, areas with threatened or endangered species, existing reserve, research and park areas, and native tribal lands. Data input from the thematic efforts including vegetation and fauna mapping will provide the basis of these "natural" units. The "risk" component generally includes a methodology for scaling the degree of instability of these units. For example, an area with several endangered vertebrate and plant species might be ranked high for "conservation" concern, but have a low risk value because there is little likelihood of any threat occurring to this area in the near and distant future, based on all the information available. Contrast this situation with another area that has the same conservation value, but is likely to be impacted by current chemical impacts unless risk reduction and/or mitigation factors are introduced. The risk of this latter area is far greater than the former.

Integrated Risk Assessment: St. Lucia Case Study

This study provides a framework for determining trends of pesticide use in St. Lucia based on a preliminary analysis in the Roseau watershed. The concern about agro-chemical inputs to the environment in St. Lucia and the Eastern Caribbean Region has been expressed in numerous forums during the past several years. Impacts associated with both human health and environmental risk are to date still unknown. The existing positive economic gains of the estimated 10,000 banana farmers in St. Lucia have contributed to an attitude that favors transforming more fragile lands into banana and increasing productivity. This trend is associated then with greater demands for chemical inputs such as fertilizers and pesticides which in turn leads to increased environmental pesticide contamination. This contamination can be measured by monitoring the amounts of pesticides used as measured at the farmer level and subsequently determining the chemical fate and transport of these chemicals. Such research is required to provide a realistic picture of the state of affairs of pesticide contamination to the island's farmlands, aquatic ecosystems, and humans.

St. Lucia is an independent Caribbean island of volcanic origin in the Windward chain at altitude 14° North. The island forms two physical regions: the south and central regions are geologically young and consists of mountain peaks of which the highest is Mt. Gimie at 950 m (3,100 feet) and steep walled valleys; the northern half of the island is older and erosion has reduced it to ridges and wide flat valleys. The topography of the island is rugged with the main drainage systems radiating from the mountain peaks. The river channels in the upper catchment areas are deeply incised into the volcanic terrain (Figure 23.3).

The island is 616 km^2 (238 square miles) in size, 43.4 km (27 miles) long and 23.5 km (14 miles) wide. The climate is tropical with a dry season typically from January to June and a wet season from July to December. However, the seasons are not always distinct. Annual rainfall ranges from 1,300 mm (50 in.) on the coast to 4,500 mm (180 in.) in the mountains. The 1986 island population was 140,000 with the major population concentration in the City of Castries with 33,600 people.

Agriculture Systems in St. Lucia

As in most of the Eastern Caribbean islands, St. Lucia's economy is based on agriculture export, although its importance has declined over the last years in comparison to the growing tourism sector and light manufacturing. Only in 1980 was agriculture export below 50 percent of the total domestic export, primarily as a result of hurricane damage.

The prevailing export crop is bananas, which represent half of all domestic exports. This situation is comparable to that of the other Windward islands, such as Dominica (citrus), Grenada (nutmeg), and St. Vincent (bananas).

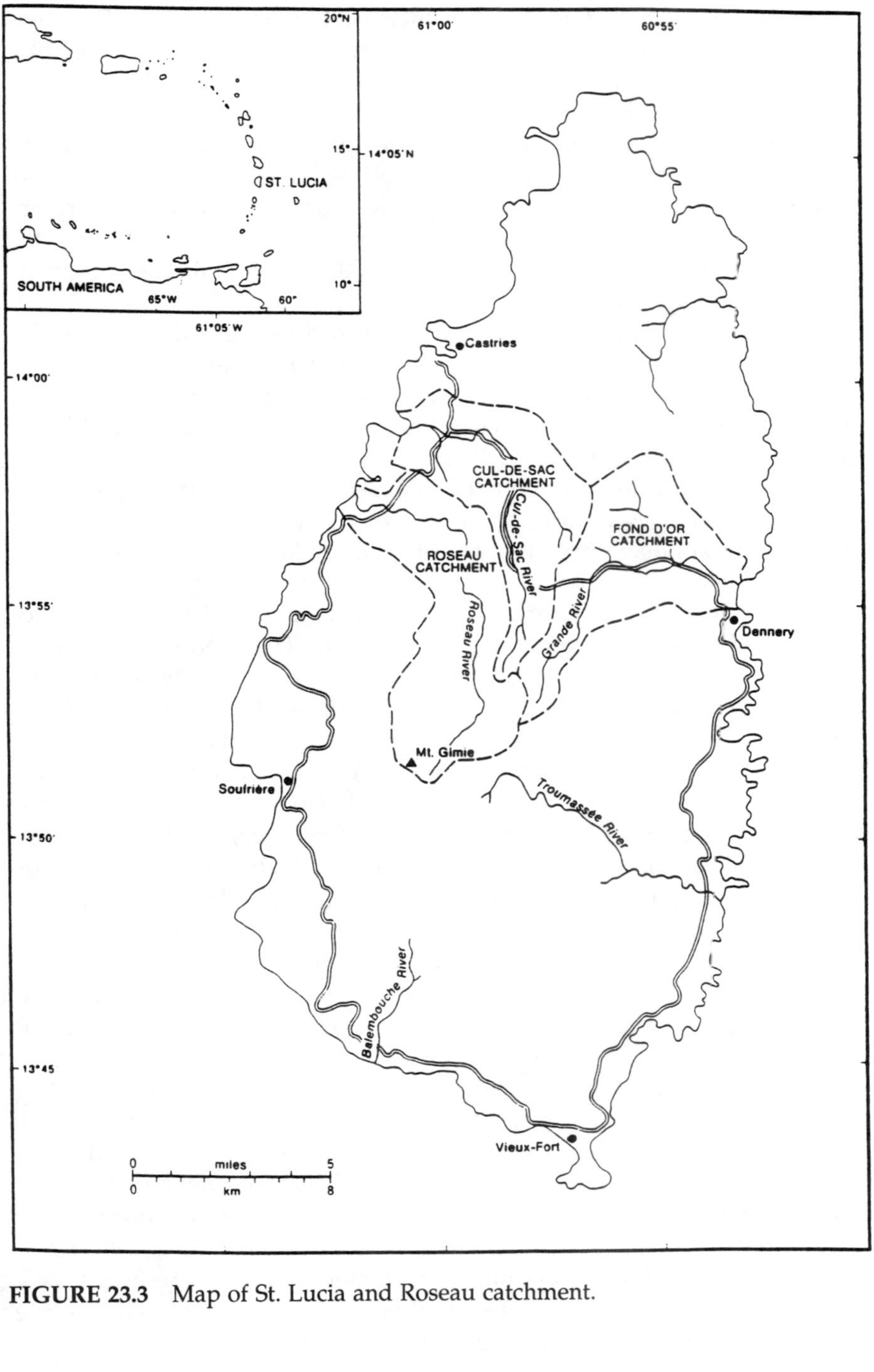

FIGURE 23.3 Map of St. Lucia and Roseau catchment.

The banana export figures have increased steadily from 1952 when GEEST entered the St. Lucian market to purchase the "green gold." Unlike sugar cane, banana crops can be harvested without seasonal interruptions and the agriculture technology is not limited to large-scale economies. These advantages reinforced the trend toward bananas, both for estates and small holders in the 1950s and 1960s, so that the whole island economy has become extremely dependent on one cash crop. Furthermore, the number of registered banana farmers (i.e., members of the St. Lucia Banana Growers Association) is 10,000, but the number of actual growers is thought to be closer to 7,000.

Although slight differences in farming practices occur throughout the island between individual farmers, several common patterns exist:

Land clearing: Grass and shrubs of fallow land have to be burnt off at the end of the dry season. If virgin land has to be cleared, the farmer cuts down the large trunks with an axe or cutlass before burning the vegetation. Application of the herbicide paraquat (Gramaxone), a defoliant, is regularly used to clear vegetation from virgin or fallow land. Banana farmers may apply paraquat to their fields up to eight times per year.

Planting and nursery operations: Bananas are planted 8 ft. × 8 ft., as recommended by the Banana Growers Association. The lateral shoots, called "suckers," or pieces of the trunk with a bud are planted in holes about 40 cm deep, sometimes filled with some fertilizer. Plants such as citrus, pear, cashew, mango, etc., are intercropped with banana.

Weeding: Weeding is done manually or chemically. Farmers use "Gramaxone," which is supplied by the Banana Growers Association. However, it is also used for the destruction of grass vegetation in dasheen and other root crop stands as late as three months before harvest. A less polluting method is cutlassing or hoeing the weeds. However, this method is rather time-consuming, and the farmers prefer spraying.

Fertilizing and pesticide use: Nearly all the farmers use the "ordinary" NPK fertilizer (ration of 12:8:24) of the Banana Growers Association for bananas and intercropped trees, dasheen, other rootcrops, and even for vegetables, though they normally only receive fertilizer for banana fields. Most of the farmers fertilize at the official rates, 113 g, 226 g, and 340 g during the first three months, respectively, and then they continue with 340g per plant every three months. Furidan pellets for root spoilage of bananas is put into the holes while planting the young suckers. Premicid, which is available at the shops in Castries, is sprayed for nematodes every three months.

Drainage and irrigation: On hillsides, farmers dig drainage furrows ca. 30–50 ca. wide to a depth of about 30 cm, to avoid waterlogging of the crop. Irrigation occurs on some of the largest valley banana stands.

Mounding and staking: Rootcrops (e.g., yams) and vegetables, which prefer sandy soils are grown on individual mounds or rows about 30 cm high. Some varieties of tomatoes and some legumes are staked so that they can climb higher.

Fastening, deflowering, and sleeving: To prevent banana pseudostems from falling down in heavy winds, farmers tie the stems with synthetic nylon rope. Nearly ripe banana bunches are deflowered and later sleeved in blue plastic bags to keep bats, birds, and other pests from consuming the fruit.

Harvesting: Bananas are harvested when still green. The farmer cuts down the bunch and carries it on his head to the banana boxing plant, and then transports the boxes via pickup truck to the GEEST boat.

It is estimated that about 16,000 acres, or about 11 percent of the total land area of St. Lucia, is under banana cultivation. These bananas are grown under two major cropping patterns:

Large-scale agriculture: Areas devoted primarily to commercial agriculture organized in medium-sized and large estates. Most of these lands are in the alluvium valleys or gently sloping hillsides, often with a monoculture stand of bananas.

Intensive small farming: Areas where plots of land, one to five acres in size, contain banana interspersed with coconut, fruit trees, root crops, and cocoa. Often these farm plots are on moderate to steep slopes.

Agrochemical Inputs

Recent statistics (1988) indicate the following consumption of major pesticides in St. Lucia: Herbicides: Gramaxone, Reglone, Roundup, Dalaphone, Maloran; Insecticides/Nematocides: Furadan, Namacur, Mocap; Fungacides: Calixin, Benlate, Tilt, Punch.

The potential human and ecological hazards of a pesticide depend on its toxicity and the amount taken up by a person or component of the ecosystem. The World Health Organization (WHO) has classified pesticide products into four categories of toxicity, from extremely hazardous to slightly hazardous. The pesticides and associated hazards are summarized in Table 23.1.

The Roseau Watershed

The Roseau River basin is the largest in St. Lucia, at some 40 km^2 (9880 ac.) in area. The headwaters rise on the eastern and northern slopes of Mt. Gimie (950 m, 3,117 ft.), with the river reaching the sea at Roseau Bay, approximately 20 km downstream (Figure 23.4). The basin is mostly natural forest in the upper and middle reaches, but this gradually gives way to

TABLE 23.1 Summary of Pesticides Used in St. Lucia and Associated Toxicity and Ecological Hazards

Pesticide Name	WHO Category	Ecological Risk
Benlate	III	toxic to fish
Calixin	II moderate	
Captan	III	
Chloradane	II moderate	highly persistent
Furadan	Ib high	toxic to fish, birds and other wildlife
Gramaxone	II moderate	hazardous to terrestrial wildlife and aquatic ecosystems
Heptachlor	Ib high	highly persistent
Mencozeb	III	
Mocap	II moderate	hazardous to birds
Primicid	Ib high	

WHO Classification: Ia—extremely hazardous
Ib—highly hazardous
II—moderately hazardous
III—slightly hazardous

agriculture and rural communities in the lower reaches. The river valley is deep, steep-sided and vee-shaped in the upper two-thirds of the basin, but eventually opens into a narrow flat alluvial valley, dominated by banana production. The two largest tributaries are the Millet River, 8.5 km^2 (2100 ac.) in area, and the Ravine Cendre de Feu, 3 km^2 (740 ac.).

Average rainfall over the basin ranges from more than 3,550 mm (140 in.) in the headwaters to less than 1,780 mm (17 in.) at the coast. Hydrometric records of run-off from late 1982 to mid-1986 at WASA's Cableway gauging station in the middle reaches show the minimum recorded mean daily flow to be 0.17 m^3/s (3.23 lmgd), with dry season mean daily flows often as low as 0.22 m^3/s (4.18 lmgd). The river is flashy, and has a recorded maximum mean daily flow of 6.73 m^3/s (127.9 lmgd) in the two and a half years of record. Hillside land accounts for 88 percent of the watershed, with only 12 percent containing slopes less than 3 percent.

The Pilot Study Project—Model Farms

As early as 1975, GEEST Industries (W.I.) Limited offered to dispose of 1932 acres of the 5,880 acres it held in two large estates—Cul de Sac and Roseau. The withdrawal of GEEST in Roseau was augmented with the creation of St. Lucia Model Farms, a partnership of GEEST, the St. Lucia Government, the European Development Fund, and the Commonwealth Development Corporation (CDC). There are now 115 valley farms of 5 acres each for pure stand banana production and 60 hillside farms with 12 acres apiece for banana and fruit production. Model Farms has redevel-

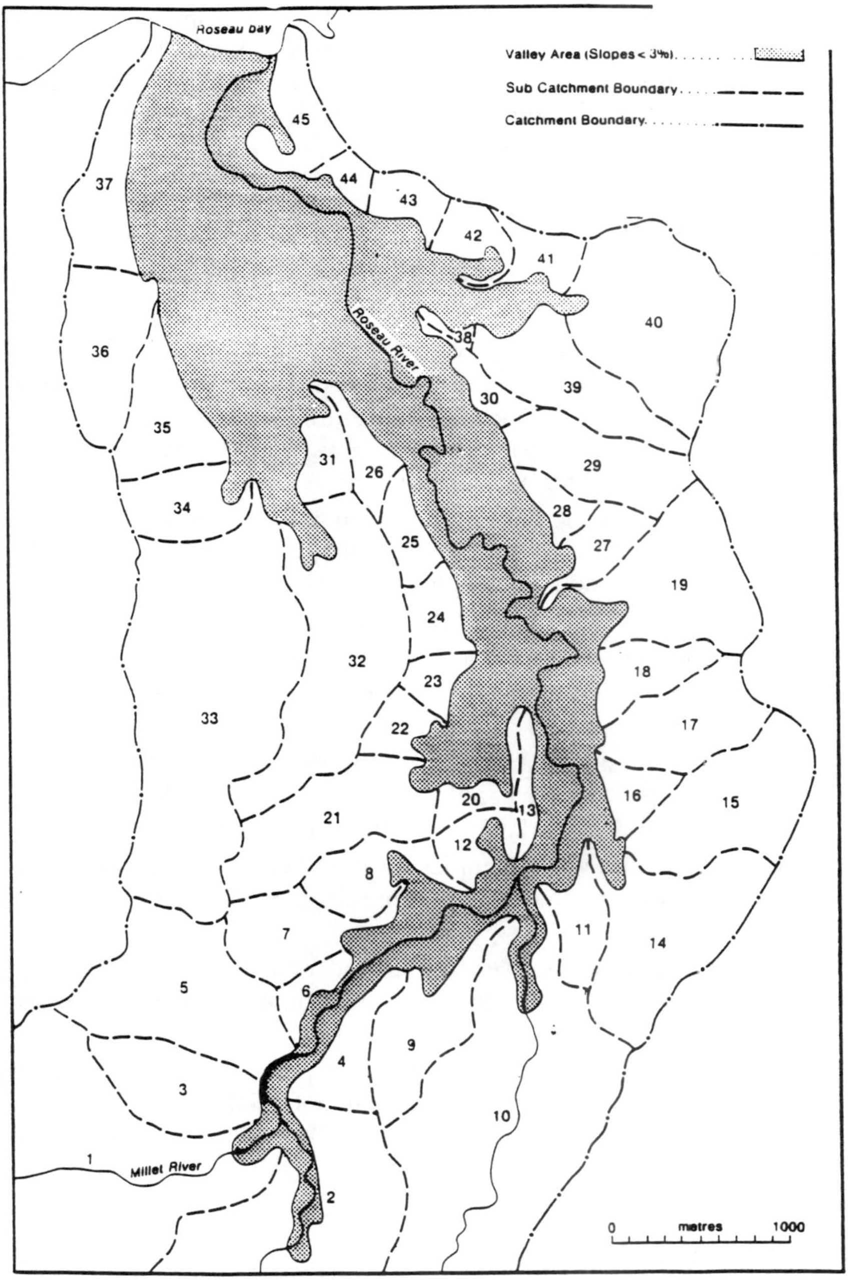

FIGURE 23.4 Existing drainage of the Roseau catchment.

oped valley lands (levelling, drainage, roads, irrigation), and provided access to and necessary terracing on hillside farms. Model Farms has also provided and maintained the basic infrastructure (boxing plants, transport, etc.) necessary to guarantee efficient marketing, and provided technical support to the farmer.

Assimilating Data

The following information is needed to develop the appropriate GIS database:

1. Collect information on present land use in the Roseau Valley at a scale of 1:2,500 based on 1979 aerial photography, OAS land use maps, Stanley & Associates maps (for the CIDA Roseau Dam Study), CIDA forestry maps for the area from May 1989, and Model Farms maps and farmer information;
2. Develop a land use classification system based on the OAS system with at minimum the following categories: agriculture- banana, mixed banana, non-banana: forest; rural settlements;
3. Provide equivalent detail at the same scale for slope categorization;
4. Collect rainfall data for one year data period for the area;
5. Develop run-off estimates by month per land use/slope type for the Model Farms area;
6. Assimilate pesticide and fertilizer application rates by month for the 1988–1989 period based on Model Farm data for farmer and farm plots (see Table 23.1 for pesticide use summary);
7. Collect soil and water samples for the upper and lower watershed and test for agrochemical concentration during the dry and wet seasons;
8. Collect biological samples from the near coastal zone in the mouth of the Roseau River and in the confluence of the Millet and Roseau Rivers; and
9. Detail the chemical name, chemical properties, amount applied by land use type per time of year and potential concern to human health and environmental risk in the valley of each major agrochemical.

GIS Analysis

Preliminary GIS work was undertaken in 1989 in the Ministry of Planning. Pilot exercises included field survey work to conduct soil surveys and measure topography with the Ministry of Agriculture technical staff.

Agrochemical input data was collected from the Model Farms Project and a filed protocol established to collect the remaining chemical fate and transport information.

The GIS database, once complete, can then be used to develop a preliminary model on agrochemical inputs and fate and transport for at least two major pesticides. The final analysis would include an assessment of impacts and risks to human health and the environment following the guidelines discussed earlier.

CONCLUSION

This chapter discusses an integrated approach to improving the understanding between bioresources, environment and health. This approach is not new and has many practitioners throughout the international development community. The use of GIS to integrate this information is demonstrated through the application of a risk assessment framework.

The author has worked for several decades in the arena of international development and human health and ecological risk assessment. The ability to understand the multitude of factors associated with these activities continuously remains a challenge, and GIS provides a tool to portray these pieces of the puzzle. The steps required to establish a useful GIS database are also important in an integrated planning exercise because it requires a multidisciplinary approach to data acquisition and analysis. Another important goal of GIS applications, is the ability to portray data and information in a fashion that leads to improved decision making.

APPENDIX 1. MANAGEMENT CONSIDERATIONS

Organizational management planning a GIS implementation need to: define applications and objectives; determine the scope of the GIS applications; identify existing data sources; determine staffing requirements; establish data validation measures, estimate life cycle/staffing costs; and establish GIS standards.

Define Applications and Objectives

Initially, a thorough evaluation of GIS needs is required before attempting to acquire a system. Identification of how program activities and decision making will be improved with GIS tools is mandatory. A thorough analysis of needs requires answers to the following questions:

- What agency activities will be supported by the proposed GIS activity?

- How will these program activities be supported?
- What are the anticipated benefits of these GIS activities (timeliness, workload, and enhanced management)?
- How can these GIS applications also provide cross-program assistance?

Determine the Scope of the GIS Applications

In beginning to plan a GIS implementation, management should define the scope of its GIS needs relating to the:

- number of anticipated users;
- number and types of decisions to be supported;
- geographic and programmatic areas to be covered; and
- types of data required.

These are among the crucial decisions which set the scope of the GIS application and determine the utility and versatility of the final product.

Identify Existing Data Sources

The geographic boundaries and scale of data required in the proposed GIS program need to be detailed. They must be considered in conjunction with the types of data that will be used in the system and the status of these data. Some of the data will probably already exist in computerized formats, while other data will be manual files in a variety of conditions (e.g., hand-drawn maps and technical reports). The manual files will have to be computerized using the GIS software/hardware (e.g., digitizer), while the computerized files will have to be converted to the GIS format. In addition, datasets must be reviewed to determine which files/fields need to be computerized and which ones, if any, can be eliminated. During this dataset inventory phase, identification of requirements for entirely new data should also occur. It is expected that the program will be able, in a parallel fashion, to describe these datasets in detail and provide a synopsis of their expected use.

Determine Staffing Requirements

The organizational environment in which a GIS will function depends on the existing ADP support services and potential for incorporating the GIS into an existing ADP support structure. For example, the choice between the use of a stand-alone dedicated system versus one that is "added on" to an existing computer system will change the staffing level and expertise required. Personnel required to operate the GIS may include computer system managers, computer operators, data analysts, programmers, supervisors, environmental scientists, cartographers, and specific program experts. Typically, full-time computer system managers and/or operators will be needed for mainframes and large minicomputers. The number of technicians required will depend on the amount of processing to be done, budget constraints, and time allocated for completion of the initial database.

It is extremely important to also have on hand computer-literate program management staff who are experienced with organizational responsibilities and requirements. GIS projects are multi-disciplinary in nature, and are most successful when developed by multi-disciplinary teams.

Another area requiring guidance may be GIS training. Centralized GIS training may prove to be a useful and cost-effective strategy for disseminating specialized GIS knowledge to organizational offices. In contrast, it might be more cost-effective to support sending staff to special training programs offered by the private sector and academia.

Establish Data Validation Measures

The issue of data validation must be addressed in the early phase of GIS data base planning. Program managers must determine if incorporation of existing QA measures for already existing data is sufficient. Furthermore, QA standards will also have to be established for newly acquired data. Data acquired from other data bases should always be thoroughly examined to reveal QA problems.

The quality assurance procedures for each GIS application must reflect a conscious decision on the part of management as to the level of data quality necessary to support decision making. Required levels of data quality can vary, depending on the decisions which the GIS will support. Quality indicators in the GIS data base or fields which identify data sources should be considered as a means of improving quality assurance.

Estimate Life Cycle/Staffing Costs

The implementation of a GIS system includes numerous costs associated with equipment purchase, installation, database development, etc. In estimating costs, the managers must pay particular attention to software and hardware prices and the additional costs of: upgrade of CPU or purchase of new CPU to support GIS applications; shipping of hardware; modifications to existing hardware or purchase of new hardware; site preparation and installation; training; quality assurance; data gathering and updating; supplemental utility programs; regular maintenance to both hardware and software; and system upgrades.

A realistic estimate of required staffing and associated budget costs is also necessary. It is helpful to convert staffing requirements to hourly costs. For example, a 40-man-year effort to create the working database can be accomplished over a four-year period with 10 programmers/analysts or over 10 years with 4 programmers/analysts. The total staffing costs will vary significantly between the two scenarios.

Establish GIS Standards

Another strategic step is the development of GIS standards. Whenever possible, previously established standards should be followed, but the unique characteristics of GIS technology will require establishing additional standards. Standards can be required for: digital spatial data organization; georeference definitions; interchange formats; feature type definitions; and data quality.

In some cases, it will not be appropriate to promote standards but rather provide guidance. A common practice is to use ANSI software standards to ensure long-term viability of GIS software in a dynamic technological environment.

APPENDIX 2. CRITICAL MANAGEMENT AND TECHNICAL GUIDANCE

A well-planned management approach for implementing GIS technology is necessary for ensuring successful GIS program applications. This series of questions and corresponding discussion is provided to help program managers focus on critical management and technical issues associated with GIS implementation.

1. *What types of data should be entered into the GIS, and what additional data should be collected?* Just because certain types of data have been collected does not justify their entry into a data base. Furthermore, the gathering of new types of data should not occur merely because a new tool is available to process that data.

2. *Should data base development be performed in-house or contracted*? Contracting has several advantages: the data base may be completed sooner, funds for contracting may be more readily available than manpower, and contracting the digitizing may alleviate the need for data entry hardware and/or software. However, when digitizing is performed by a contractor, any errors on the maps given to the contractor will find their way into the digital data base. If users familiar with the data do the digitizing, such errors may be caught prior to digitizing. Also, in-house digitizing produces trained operators, making the tasks of updating and editing less difficult.

3. *What type of data validation needs to be incorporated into the creation of the data base?* Data validation is a matter often confronted in the justification and implementation of a GIS. The process of computerizing information will often reveal data errors that may have been present, but unnoticed, for some time. For example, when maps of adjacent land parcels are overlaid by a computer for the first time, discrepancies in common boundaries may be noticed. The initial response to the discovery of such errors may be a costly attempt to improve the accuracy of the data. Some questions that should be asked first are:

- Are the data accurate enough?
- In the absence of a GIS, would the data be accurate enough?
- What costs might be incurred because of inaccurate data?
- Are inaccurate data better than none?
- What is the marginal cost of improving accuracy/precision?

In the above example, boundary line errors could be corrected by conducting a new land survey or redrafting the maps to a common base, solutions that are both costly.

4. *How important is accuracy, compared with consistency and appearance?* In order to accurately reference a map of a tract of land to known ground coordinates, the shape, orientation, or total area of the tract as mapped may change. A user may be forced to choose between keeping the appearance and acreage of a tract map consistent with legal records, or adjusting the map to gain locational accuracy.

5. *Should more time be taken to build a data base that can be accessed efficiently, or should the data base be completed more quickly at the expense of subsequent data analysis?* Because of technical considerations regarding file formats and database structures, shortcuts taken during data base development can lead to difficulty in the later access of that data. Conversely, digitization procedures that may seem tedious and time-consuming can enhance the efficiency of later processing steps.

6. *What is the desired spatial resolution of the database?* For example, in a map of water bodies, one may have many small map units representing small streams, or fewer large map units representing larger rivers. The choice of map unit size will influence the size of the resultant computerized data base as well as its variability, accuracy, and precision. The size of the minimum mapping unit should reflect the eventual use of the data. Generally, higher level managers are satisfied with information in a broader, more general form; lower level managers may require more detailed fine-resolution data.

7. *Is the data base anticipated to be static, or are additions and deletions anticipated?* The answer to this question will have a significant impact on the development of file-naming conventions and coding schemes used to

represent attributes associated with maps. It is important to devise a coding system that provides enough flexibility to accommodate changes while meeting the constraints of a particular GIS. For example, assigning code numbers or names to map features when digitizing will have a significant impact on the ease with which items may be later retrieved from the data base. Questions regarding coding systems will arise during pilot projects and are best resolved through consultation with vendors and other organizations experienced with the same GIS.

8. *How should the digitizing effort be prioritized*? Three general approaches should be considered. The first is the application-oriented approach, which involves digitizing data as specific analysis needs arise. In this way, a data base is built in pieces in response to certain projects or problems. A second approach is to build a comprehensive data base for the entire area to be managed, proceeding by geographic or administrative areas. This is especially useful when an organization has an administrative hierarchy that reflects geographic regions. This approach provides a useful set of data for each region in turn, allowing regional users to begin to use the GIS one at a time. The third approach is to build the comprehensive data base by categories. For example, transportation routes could be digitized for an entire region, then soils information, political boundaries, hydrology, etc., added in sequence. Using this approach, numerous users get access to a portion of the data base at the same time.

24

Advances in the Health Impact Assessment of Development Projects

Martin Birley and Genandrialine Peralta

INTRODUCTION

The wider objective of development activity is to promote a sustainable, high quality life for all communities and this implicitly includes good health. Development programs and projects derive their immediate objectives from an analysis of the constraints which include infrastructure, credit, markets, terms of trade, trained personnel and access to appropriate technologies. One important set of constraints is the indirect and unintended impact that a development in one sector may have on other sectors. Such impacts affect the community, its environment and its health.

SOME TERMS AND DEFINITIONS

In the following account of health impacts we need to make several distinctions at the outset.

We would like to thank the Rockefeller Foundation for initiating this book project and inviting our contribution. It was partially supported by the ODA through the Liverpool Health Impact Programme. The continuing support of the Joint WHO/FAO/UNEP/UNCHS Panel of Experts in Environmental Management is also acknowledged. Opportunities to develop these ideas were provided during consultancy to the Asian Development Bank, Office of the Environment, to whom we would like to express our gratitude. Responsibility for the ideas expressed remains solely with the authors.

- Health hazards are different to health risks. A health hazard has a potential for causing harm. In contrast, a health risk indicates the likelihood of harm occurring to a particular community group at a particular time and place. The identification of a health hazard does not imply that it is important in every development project. The importance is determined by the analysis of health risk.
- Development-related health hazards can be grouped into five major categories. *Communicable diseases* require relatively small doses of exposure to infective agents and then multiply in the human community. There are often many separate sources of infection. *Non-communicable diseases*, by contrast, may arise from the accumulation of toxic chemicals from a few point sources. *Malnutrition* occurs where communities are deprived of subsistence foods through changes in land use or farming systems, or through uneven economic development. *Injuries* occur through exposure to new technologies, poor working practices, poor dwelling design, improper use of machinery and poor machine maintenance. *Mental disorder* may be associated with the stress of new ways of living and the disruption of long-established communities. Box 24.1 illustrates the linkage between some of these health hazards and development projects (see p. 444).
- Health impacts refer to both positive and negative changes in community health that are attributable to a development project. Although it is important to consider both kinds of impact, we emphasize the negative impacts and seek procedures and methods by which the risks may be assessed and then effectively managed. We refer to these methods and procedures as Health Impact Assessment (HIA).

HISTORICAL PERSPECTIVE

Health impact assessment procedures have evolved independently in several development sectors. The principles used and the problems encountered share many similarities. There are additional similarities to methods and procedures used in environmental impact assessment and in more general development aid evaluation (OECD, 1986). In this section we briefly review the procedures that are used in water supply and sanitation, water resource development and the chemical sector. We also list some other current programs.

Water Supply and Sanitation

In the water supply and sanitation sector, WHO has published procedures for analyzing nonfunctioning or underutilized systems and for evaluating the positive health impacts of fully functioning systems (WHO, 1983a, WHO, 1983b). In this sector, health impact generally refers to the intended health improvements that are assumed to derive from safe water supply and sanitation. These consist of reductions in the prevalence of certain communicable diseases. It is relatively easy to install the "hardware" of well-engineered systems. It is harder to ensure the community participation required for appropriate use and maintenance. It is harder still to demonstrate a positive health impact.

Water Resource Development

Although water resource developments such as dams and irrigation have a long history of benefiting human health through improved nutrition, they have also had a deleterious effect through chemical pollution, poor drinking water quality and vector-borne diseases. One important group of health risks, the vector-borne communicable diseases, has received considerable attention. There have been many reviews (Oomen et al., 1988; Service, 1989). Such developments change the distribution and flow of surface waters, creating a favorable habitat for vector breeding. Human exposure to biting insects or contaminated waters provides the conditions necessary for an increased health risk. Expensive mitigation measures take the form of vector control through chemical application or environmental modification. In recognition of such increasing health risks a joint WHO/FAO/UNEP/UNCHS Panel of Experts on Environmental Management (PEEM) was formed in 1981. The panel members were aware that an important component of environmental management occurred at the design stage. Decisions about infrastructure, location and resettlement could help reduce vector populations or prevent exposure. This, in turn, would require an assessment procedure. The procedure was published as "Guidelines For Forecasting The Vector-Borne Disease Implications Of Water Resources Development," known as PEEM2 (Birley, 1991). It covered the sub-sectors of irrigated agriculture and multipurpose reservoirs and assisted the user to identify:

- the specific vector-borne disease hazards that occur regionally and in different environments;
- the vulnerable communities;
- the capabilities of the health service to monitor, safeguard and mitigate.

These three components of the assessment were then combined into a statement of health risk. In retrospect, PEEM2 omitted to distinguish between a health hazard and a health risk, reducing the logical flow of the procedure.

A recent report advocates a simpler procedure than PEEM2, for use by nonhealth specialists during the project screening phase of the development cycle. A set of vector-borne disease hazards was identified and a simple questionnaire was devised to determine whether the health risks appeared to warrant the project manager seeking specialist advice (Bolton et al., 1990).

Chemical Sector

In the chemical sector there are two main sources of health hazards:

- non-communicable diseases associated with poisoning by routine or accidental exposure to toxic chemicals;
- injury from fire, explosion, radiation and corrosive action.

Over 60,000 chemicals are in common use and adequate information about toxicity and reactivity is not available for all of them. A meeting in 1986 established principles and objectives for health and safety assessments (WHO, 1987). Health impact assessment was viewed as a component of environmental impact assessment (EIA), already a well-established procedure. A program of work was outlined to transfer knowledge and encourage debate to meet the perceived needs for health impact assessment. The meeting also reviewed the experiences of thirteen assessments of chemical plants spanning the period 1973–1983. A number of methodological issues were discussed that can be adapted to health impact assessments in other sectors. The three main tasks of health impact assessment were listed as: identification of hazard, interpretation of health risk and risk management.

A procedure referred to as Environmental Risk Assessment (ERA) has been developed to analyze the health hazards arising from chemicals used or produced in industrial projects (ADB, 1990). ERA focuses on discrete and relatively rare events, such as the unplanned release of toxic and reactive substances. The risks are effectively considered to be zero before construction commences. Impact frequency is tabulated against impact severity. Risk is defined as the probability that an identified hazard will cause harm of a specific severity. For example, there could be 10–7 events per year in which the number of fatalities exceeds 1,000. Quantification of this kind is not practical in most HIAs. ERA is described as a component of Environmental Impact Assessment (EIA). EIA identifies the hazards and the uncertainty; the more detailed process of ERA then replaces uncertainty by risk estimates. The normal outputs of EIA are viewed as risks with a high probability and an obvious need for mitigation.

Other Initiatives

In 1990, the Health Impact Programme was established at the Liverpool School of Tropical Medicine. It received financial support from the British Overseas Development Administration. Its immediate objective is to improve the analysis and management of the health impacts of development projects by developing a procedure for health impact assessment.

During 1992, the Asian Development Bank Office of the Environment, based in Manila, commissioned us to prepare a Guidelines for the Health Impact Assessment of Development Projects (ADB, 1992). During the preparation of these Guidelines we developed the operational procedure described below.

The Australian government has prepared a National Framework for Health Impact Assessment with emphasis on urban development projects (Ewan et al., 1992). It describes some other historical trends and proposes an HIA procedure for national use.

The World Health Organization has published various reviews of health and development and these are referred to below. An additional reference is "Environmental and Health Impact Assessment of Development Projects, A Handbook for Practitioners" (Turnbull, 1992).

PROBLEM ANALYSIS

The previous sections illustrate that while there is widespread concern about the need for Health Impact Assessment, there is no universal procedure. In order to illustrate what is required we have constructed the problem tree in Figure 24.1. The central statement in the figure poses the problem that health risks can increase as a result of development. The effects are listed above and the main causes are listed below.

The effects include reduced productivity, quality of life and educational achievement. These, in turn, will reduce project sustainability and transfer hidden costs to the health sector.

The main cause of the problem is identified as inadequate attention to health safeguards and mitigation measures during project design and operation. This, in turn, is postulated to be the result of no health impact assessment, no budget and no technical skills for the design of health safeguards and mitigation measures.

Figure 24.1 is deliberately framed as a set of negative statements to highlight the problem components. The problem analysis proceeds by converting all the negative statements into equivalent positive statements, referred to as an objectives tree. For example, as the result of a health impact program we expect health risks to decrease because there are adequate health safeguards. This, in turn, depends on health impact as-

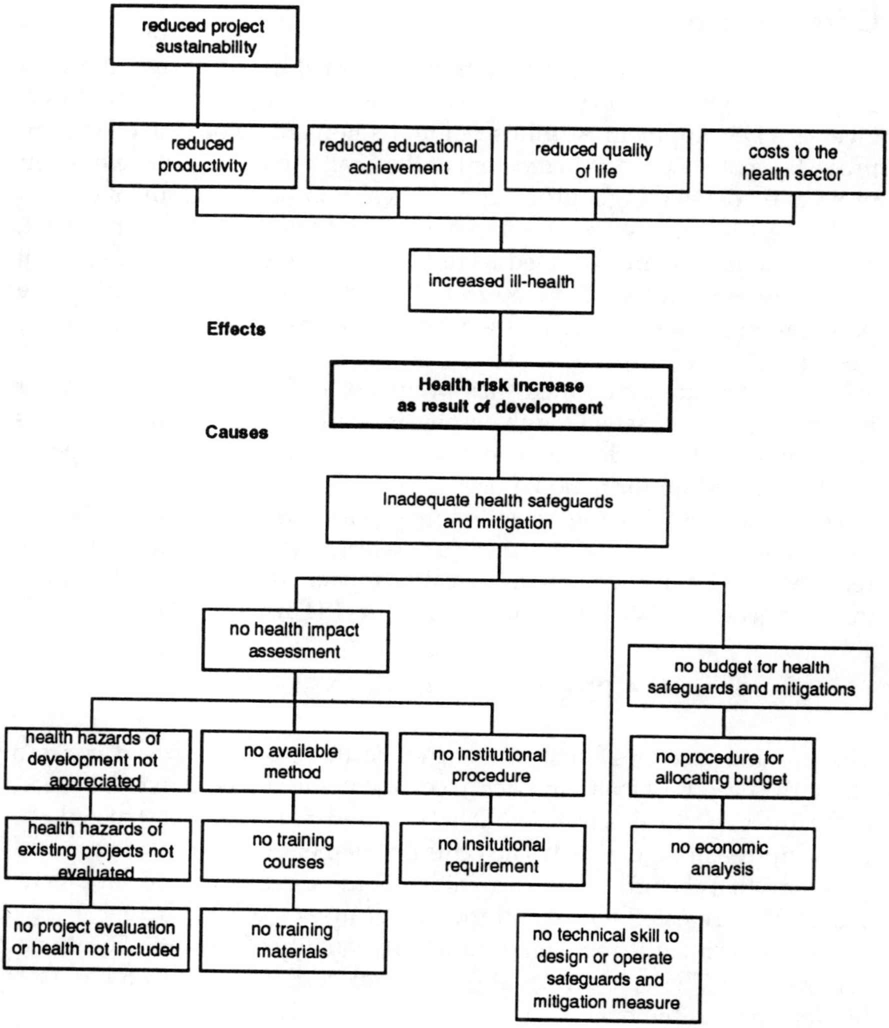

FIGURE 24.1 Problem tree for the health impact of development projects.

sessment being routinely applied and an adequate budget being available where necessary. To ensure this outcome we require health impact assessment methodologies, widespread appreciation of the health hazards of development and training programs.

The procedure for Health Impact Assessment should be integrated with the existing procedures for Environmental Impact Assessment in order to reduce or prevent health risks arising from the development project.

Environmental Impact Assessment (EIA)

In theory, EIA already includes a limited concern with health issues. In practice, health is often neglected. The reasons for this are complex. Policy makers are not yet as sensitive to health issues as they are to environmental issues. Or, if they are, they consider it a specialist subject that belongs to the health profession. On the other hand, the health profession is only trained and interested in matters of development that lie directly within the health sector. In this section, we review the experience and procedure of EIA and incorporate HIA.

Considerable experience of Environmental Impact Assessment has become available to donor agencies and governments during the last two, or more, decades. This has helped to clarify the nature of the impact assessment process. As well as a formal planning procedure, impact assessment is a process of communication between participants with different perspectives, objectives and requirements (Spellerberg & Minshull, 1992). There are three principal participants.

- Project proponents are primarily concerned with gaining consent in the most cost-effective manner. They are frequently line ministries responsible for building and operating infrastructures or relocating and employing labor.
- Consultants are employed by the project proponents to produce the impact statement under severe time and financial constraints.
- Planning authorities are concerned with effective application of planning policy. In many developing countries such authorities are called Environmental Protection Agencies. They require accurate statements of suitable detail to enable proposals to be assessed for permitting or regulatory purposes. Where they are of recent origin, they may not have functional procedures for either EIA or HIA.

Environmental Protection Agencies

Governments and aid agencies, such as the Asian Development Bank and the Overseas Development Administration, have been instrumental in establishing and strengthening in-country Environmental Protection Agencies. These agencies have a role in safeguarding, mitigating and monitoring the environmental impacts of development projects. This role includes safeguarding health. A critical appraisal of the capability of the agencies involved is essential to determine whether health safeguards, mitigation and monitoring measures are likely to be effective and where action is required to strengthen existing capabilities.

One of the largest practical obstacles to health impact assessment appears to be the planning delays which prevent health impact studies from starting at the same time as other studies. Studies that are left until the last minute or require long baseline data collection periods are unlikely to receive proper consideration during the final planning negotiations.

From the viewpoint of the line ministries responsible for design and implementation of a development project, intersectoral concerns add costs and delays. The objective of impact assessment is to assist agencies responsible for protecting the environment, or the health of the community, to participate in negotiations with the line ministries and the donor agencies in a timely and practical manner (Tiffen, 1991). The objective is not to block the development but to seek mutually acceptable solutions.

The following experience is typical. An Asian country recently created an Environmental Protection Agency. Legislation required all new projects to receive an EIA. As the agency had limited resources there was a large backlog of projects to review. Fears were expressed that unless a process could be found to separate projects with major and minor impacts, the whole development process could become paralyzed. The primary concerns of the agency were environmental issues, including pollution. The procedure was to establish a Commission within each line ministry to review project plans. In principle, representatives from other ministries could be invited to attend and be included in the review process. In practice, as there was no compulsion to do so, the health sector was often not represented. Similarly, there was no requirement to consider occupational health and safety.

HEALTH IMPACT ASSESSMENT PROCESS

A health impact assessment is an early warning to alert decision makers to possible health risks that may be reduced, but not totally eliminated, by incorporating safeguards and mitigation measures. It consists of three main steps:

- health hazards identification;
- interpretation of the health hazards as health risks attributable to the project;
- health risk management.

The first two of these steps are referred to as project screening. Screening is the process of determining whether a development project should be subject to an impact assessment (WHO, 1987). It depends on the perception of hazard by the decision maker, the politician and the general public. Screening is most likely to be conducted internally by administrative staff who need to decide quickly whether each project has a potential for undesirable side effects. The screening must be kept simple as the decision maker is unlikely to be a specialist in either environmental or health impact assessment. The principal decision is whether to call in specialist support. The additional information to be gained from such support must be offset against the cost and the delay.

For example, ODA uses a screening process to register "danger signals" and to avoid unnecessary investigation where impacts are likely to be minimal (ODA, 1989).

Health Hazard Identification

In most cases the screening process will be based on an identification of the health hazards that are associated with the category of project and its location. The decision maker will require a catalogue indicating the kinds of health hazards that have been experienced on similar projects and information about health-sensitive locations obtained from maps, health records and knowledge of disease foci. For example, irrigation is associated with schistosomiasis in parts of Africa but not in many parts of Asia because the snail host is absent.

The catalogue of health hazards is based on a review of known health impacts and should be carefully classified. Classification systems are important because they have predictive value. Similar projects are likely to share similar health hazards. Compiling such information provides a useful method of sensitizing the development community to the health issue. It is not, in itself, sufficient. The important next step is to make use of the compiled material within a procedure for health impact assessment.

WHO has published several reviews of the impact of development and environmental change on health (Cooper Weil et al., 1990; WHO, 1992a; WHO, 1992b). Such reviews are inevitably open-ended and relevant new material can always be added. We have compiled our own catalogue in a form readily accessible to project planners, by cross-referencing health hazards to development sectors (Birley, in press). Box 24.1 illustrates the material available.

The identification of a hazard does not imply that it is important. There is a range of health hazards between severe and trivial. For example, the odors from factories and piggeries, the drone from construction equipment, the taste of drinking water may pose inconvenience but do not constitute a significant health risk. Therefore, the next step is to identify the health risk associated with the health hazard.

Interpretation of Health Risks

Interpretation of health risks forms the core of the Health Impact Assessment. In order to expedite this procedure it is necessary to divide it into

Box 24.1—Examples of the Linkage between Health Hazards and Development

- Transport systems provide a conduit for the distribution of communicable disease such as occurred with HIV infection in truck drivers and women working in bars in Uganda in 1986 (Carswell, 1987). People who migrate in search of work are especially at risk from sexually transmitted diseases and may carry the infections to new areas.
- During the 1970s half the malaria cases in Amazonia were linked to the narrow area of influence of the Transamazon Highway (Coimbra, 1988). The malaria mosquito became more abundant because forest clearance provided new breeding sites. The parasite was transported to the region by migrants.
- Transport-related injuries are more common in developing countries where driving tests may be circumvented, roads are of poor quality and vehicles may be poorly maintained. In Papua New Guinea during the 1970s traffic injuries were estimated to cost 1% of (GNP) (Havard, 1987). In developing countries generally, the annual rate of disabling injuries to workers is 21–34%, compared to 3% in the UK (El-Batawi, 1981).
- Miners frequently work in confined spaces that are heavily laden with rock dust. Long-term exposure to this dust may induce permanent lung damage. Damaged lungs are more susceptible to infection with tuberculosis. Infection rates have been reported in South African mines of 800–1000 per 100,000 (Packard 1989). Miners are exposed to injury from rock falls and fast moving machinery. In Bolivia during the 1970s the population of 24,000 mineworkers in large mines had 5,430 injuries (El-Batawi 1981).
- Household cooking on an open fire may be the largest single occupational health problem of women. Burning biomass fuels produces large quantities of pollutants that may lead to respiratory or eye disease.
- In Sri Lanka, a rice development project created breeding sites for mosquitoes that transmit Japanese encephalitis. Pigs near the rice fields provided the virus. The mosquitoes acquired the virus by feeding on the pigs. The virus multiplied in the mosquitoes and was subsequently transmitted to people who were bitten by the mosquitoes. Consequently there was an epidemic of this often fatal disease (IRRI, 1987). Again in Sri Lanka, until the 1970s child labor was common on some tea estates,

Box 24.1—(*Cont.*)

education facilities were minimal and water supplies were inadequate. Chronic malnutrition and infant mortality rates were twice the rural average (Laing, 1986).

- Urban water supplies are often provided before drainage facilities. Consequently, large areas of polluted water form that are ideal breeding sites for the mosquito that transmits lymphatic filariasis (Macdonald, 1991). Manifestations of this disease are common in many Asian coastal cities.
- In Cubato, Brazil, during the 1980s there were 23 major industrial plants and many small operations. A high rate of respiratory disorders was associated with high levels of water and air pollution. Neonatal mortality and birth deformities increased (Findley, 1988; Pimenta, 1987; Thomas, 1981). Other examples include lung disease due to lack of face masks in fiber factories in Albania, birth defects associated with lead and zinc plants in Bulgaria and chronic ill health due to air pollution in Hungary (Carter & Turnock, 1993).

two steps: a rapid assessment followed as necessary by a detailed Health Impact Assessment.

The rapid assessment is also referred to as an initial health examination. This integrates with the Initial Environmental Examinations (IEE) used in EIAs. It uses secondary data, checklists and, sometimes, a factfinding mission. The output is a project classification (World Bank, 1991).

The detailed HIA is similar in content to the rapid assessment but normally employs specialists working to a term of reference and is based more securely on primary data (ADB, 1990, ADB, 1992, Tiffen, 1991).

The project classification usually consists of three classes.

A: Significant impacts, mitigation difficult or requires special budget, requires a detailed HIA.

B: Significant impact, mitigation practical without special budget component, may require a detailed HIA.

C: No significant impact.

In rapid assessment it is necessary to determine which geographical areas, project phases and communities to include in the analysis. It is also necessary to consider the environmental factors that determine exposure to the health hazard and the capabilities of the agencies responsible for protecting human health. Adequate consultation should be undertaken among potential stakeholders, including the affected community. Finally, the conclusions reached in each component of the analysis must be combined and presented to the decision makers in a format that will enable them to use the information effectively.

Geographical Areas

One important consideration is the geographic boundary, especially downstream and downwind. In the case of communicable disease it is necessary to consider whether migrants will import new diseases from distant localities. If the disease is transmitted by flying insects, it is necessary to consider the flight range of those insects. In the case of contaminated water, the downstream impacts may be important. For example, a large project was completed to supply a city with a new piped sewerage system. The engineering focus was on removing raw sewage from the city streets. The main sewerage pipes led to a primary treatment plant with settlement tanks. The septic fluid was then discharged into open drains that were beyond the bounds of the engineering project. The unfenced drains flowed through densely populated suburbs and the community had direct contact with the septic fluid, even extracting it for domestic use. In this example there was a clear case for the boundary of the health impact assessment to be larger than the boundary of the engineering problem.

Project Phases

The most important phases in the project cycle are: construction, early operation and late operation (after 10 years). Some health risks can increase rapidly when the environment is changed. Examples include malaria, traumatic injury and acute malnutrition. Other health risks increase slowly, as a result of prolonged exposure of the community to the environmental factor. Such hazards may be regarded as "time bombs," ticking away at the heart of the project. In the same way that there are environmental time bombs (Stigliani et al., 1989), there are health time bombs that are waiting to be set off within the project cycle. A chain of events may result in the delayed and sudden occurrence of harmful effects due to the mobilization of chemicals stored in soils and sediments. Examples of these are conversion of farmlands to forest requiring lime application that releases pesticides, fertilizers and heavy metals (Munn, 1992). Another example is dredging of coastal areas for reclamation freeing sulphides and bound heavy metals. In both cases, the harmful chemicals that are released may accumulate in food plants and animals. People who eat the contaminated food may then receive a harmful dose. Other examples of delayed effects include schistosomiasis, dust-induced lung disease and chronic malnutrition. Some forms of ill health, such as genetic defects and carcinomas, may be difficult to attribute to specific projects, because of long time delays and low prevalence rates (Eisenbud 1990).

Communities

There will usually be many different human communities affected by the project and they may have differing vulnerability to the health hazard. There are many procedures for classifying the community vulnerability.

For example, in a chemical plant development it may be appropriate to distinguish exposure through occupation, accident, consumption and residence (WHO, 1987). On a resettlement scheme, by contrast, it may be appropriate to distinguish: settlers chosen by government, self-selected settlers, displaced communities and temporary workers (Roundy, 1989). Large construction and mining projects sometimes require a workforce of single adult males. They may live away from their families for years at a time, in remote rural environments. Such communities attract large numbers of "camp-followers." These communities may live in temporary settlements without adequate water supply or sanitation and sell goods and services to the newly wealthy workforce. Sexually transmitted diseases may flourish under such conditions.

Environmental Factors

Environmental factors determine whether a health hazard could become a health risk through processes such as amplification, concentration, deprivation and exposure. The hazard may be restricted to point sources or widely distributed. Many industrial developments require the use and disposal of toxic and reactive substances. Exposure occurs through skin contact, inhalation or ingestion and can be classed by severity, extent and distribution (ADB, 1990; WHO, 1987). Concentration of toxins occurs by bioaccumulation, as they pass through the food-chain. Exposure depends on discharge dilution rates, land zonation policies, consumption rates and occupational safety procedures.

Agricultural projects are associated with vector-borne disease hazards (Birley, 1991). Exposure occurs through skin/water contact and arthropod bite. For example, the intermediate hosts of schistosomiasis are aquatic, or semi-aquatic, snails that may proliferate in flooded fields, irrigation and drainage canals, reservoir margins, or swamp. The amplification of exposure sites depends on factors such as rainfall, water velocity, temperature, chemical composition and fluctuation. Exposure depends on working, bathing, hunting or playing in infected waters. Construction of field latrines, as at Mushandike in Zimbabwe, may contribute to the interruption of the transmission cycle.

The mosquito-borne diseases associated with agricultural development include malaria, dengue, filariasis and viral encephalitis. The extension and modification of surface waters amplify the mosquito population by providing breeding sites. Exposure to mosquito bite depends on settlement location, house design and occupation. For example, in Thailand the rubber plantations provide shaded stream pools that are the habitat of the larval malaria mosquito. Rubber-tapping takes place at night providing occupational exposure to the biting, adult mosquitoes.

Determinants of childhood malnutrition include absolute and seasonal shortages and differential entitlements to food within the household. A switch from subsistence to cash cropping may paradoxically increase malnutrition as food purchases compete with other household priorities.

These examples demonstrate that the environmental factors which influence community vulnerabilities to health hazards are many and complex. They range from the most direct consequences of a development project, such as construction injuries, to the most indirect, such as variation in insect abundance or food security. The pathways may be described using causal modelling. However, conclusive proof linking cause and effect may not be obtainable.

Capabilities of Health Protection Agencies

The capability of national health services to contribute to health safeguards varies greatly between countries, as does the percentage of government income spent on health. National health statistics may contain little reliable information and there may be no functional health surveillance system. Health service capability may be restricted entirely to providing curative and supportive medical care. Preventative services may not have the authority, staff or other resources to act as watchdogs to developments in the non-health sector.

In the case of diseases such as malaria there may be a national control program that is already responsible for combating the disease. The disease may already be prevalent before the development commences but it is necessary to ensure that the development does not increase the health risk. There is a tendency to assume that such services have the existing capacity to manage any changes in the health risk that may occur. In reality, the health service may not be informed or consulted and valuable opportunities to safeguard health may be lost at the planning stage.

In cases of industrial development, a new health hazard is introduced by the development. However, plans and procedures to contain the release of chemicals from production plants may ascribe no role at all to the health service in relation to risk assessment and management (ADB, 1990; WHO, 1987). At the least, an adequately equipped and staffed casualty unit will be required if exposure cannot be averted.

Health protection is not only the responsibility of health ministries. The capacity of other agencies should also be considered. For example, occupational health and safety is often the responsibility of labor ministries while water supply and sanitation may be the responsibility of ministries of works. Many Non-Governmental Organizations (NGOs) also have a role in health protection, especially those working with local communities.

The Health Risk Summary

The final task of the assessment is to reach a conclusion regarding the change in health risk from examination of the components. In many cases there will be a health risk even if there is no project and only the risk attributable to the project should be included. A simple, nominal classification may suffice such as "risk increase," "risk decrease" or "no change." The summary should be accompanied by explanatory text and supported by detailed appendices, as necessary. The process can be repeated for each vulnerable community group, for each project stage and for each health hazard.

Because of the lack of data or the indirect nature of the pathways, the assessment is inevitably based on assumptions as well as sound scientific judgement. The process remains valid only so long as the assumptions are fully stated so that the reader is free to disagree.

HEALTH RISK MANAGEMENT

The health risk assessment is presented to an audience of decision makers who must evaluate the relative importance of the impacts that have been identified in a wider context. They will decide whether safeguards and mitigation measures are required, negotiate resources and assign monitoring tasks.

Health risk management consists of incorporating safeguards and mitigation measures in project design, construction and operation. Safeguarding entails modifications to project plans and operations. Mitigation may entail vigilant monitoring followed by appropriate and timely response to increasing health risks. Response depends on staff, management, supplies and distribution.

During the construction and operation start-up phase an environment and safety overseer may be hired to supervise the implementation of safeguards. Additional tasks could consist of co-ordinating the collection and reporting of health and environment information generated within the project. The cost of on-site supervision must be balanced against the risk of an adverse outcome.

It is always best to adopt a precautionary approach in the context of health risk management—a "no-regrets" policy. In other words, sufficient action should be taken to ensure that there should be no later stage at which regret is expressed that action was not taken. Certain actions or policies could be taken as insurance measures. Examples of these measures are:

- Basic medical examinations for construction workers as part of health surveillance;
- Environmental management measures for vector control;
- Creation of a formal linkage between environmental and health and safety plant personnel for regular consultation and joint monitoring;
- Training of community and health workers.

Monitoring and Surveillance

Surveillance is often defined as systematic measurement of variables and processes to establish a time trend. Monitoring, by contrast, is the process of collecting data for analysis and action. Monitoring depends on an adequate health information system. Routine health surveillance data is unlikely to be sufficiently accurate, sensitive or to have the coverage needed to indicate changes in health risk associated with a specific development project. It may be necessary to commission special surveys. However, the linkage between the project and community health may be so indirect that health change cannot be conclusively attributed to the project.

Direct monitoring of human health may be expensive, impractical, unreliable or unethical and there may be a need for proxy health indicators. For example, an urban drainage project might monitor the biting density of the common mosquito, Culex quinquefasciatus, as an indicator of drainage obstruction as well as a factor in filariasis transmission. The state of the ecosystem may provide another proxy indicator. For example, fish consumption is the major route of human exposure to hydrophobic toxic chemicals such as pesticides. If birds and other wildlife are unaffected by pollution, then it may be safe to say that humans are spared of any imminent danger (Mackay, 1992).

Monitoring systems are always perceived as additional costs with no direct link to productivity. Optimization of monitoring systems can be achieved through linkage with established environmental networks and health surveillance teams that are located within the project's focus. The public or community, especially in rural areas, could also provide an inexpensive but reliable option. Chemical accidents or spillage are best reported by those on the spot rather than by setting up an elaborate official surveillance network (Whyte & Burton, 1980). River or coastal pollution can be monitored by fishermen using indicators such as dead fish, algal bloom, smells, foam or colored discharges. Public complaints to an upsurge in vermin or mosquito bites could also be used. However, these monitoring systems rely on public education about the indicators of high risk and require an effective communication system between the public and responsible government officials. To the environmentally conscious public, environment is too important to be left to experts who are no longer seen as omniscient or incorruptible (Lowenthal, 1990). Therefore, public participation in matters of health concern could easily gain wide acceptance.

Monitoring is usually done by the project proponent while surveillance is by the regulatory agency. Where both parties agree on the objectives of monitoring and aim to share information regularly, they can be forewarned by certain trends or upsets in the system. In this way, preventive measures can be planned whenever possible. The municipal health officers and environment protection officials are both key persons to alert to possible disturbances.

Since monitoring has been proven to be a cost-effective measure to avoid adverse outcomes, it is important to invest time and expertise in developing and accomplishing the monitoring plan. Most often, monitoring becomes an afterthought and relegated to junior employees.

Environmental Management

Many health safeguards consist of physical modifications to the environment. These measures have been considered particularly important for limiting the breeding sites of disease vectors (WHO, 1982). However, similar principles apply to other health hazards. Three forms of environmental management are usually distinguished.

1. Permanent modification to the environment such as canal lining and land zonation.
2. Repetitive actions, such as weed removal and routine maintenance.
3. Changes in human behavior and habitation that are designed to reduce the hazardous conditions or limit exposure.

None of these measures is likely to be incorporated in project design or operation unless previously identified through health impact assessment.

FUTURE DIRECTIONS

At present HIA is a blunt tool with the rudiments of an accepted methodology. It requires progressive refinement through detailed substudies. Refinements are needed on two separate levels: managerial and technical. In developing countries the primary problem is not one of improving the technical capabilities to deliver accurate assessments, although this is a difficult enough task. Rather, we must convince decision makers that health impact should be undertaken and that the results can be used to modify project design and operations. For this latter task we need three kinds of studies. First, we need policy research to explain how health impact decisions are made. Second, we need economic research to ensure that the decisions are made in a forum where the economic costs and benefits of health are assessed alongside all other costs and benefits. Third, we need case studies that can be used as models that are specific to the needs of each country. In the longer term, our objective is to provide more quantitative assessments of more carefully defined accuracy.

CONCLUSION

HIA is applied unevenly in several development sectors. It is not yet a requirement for all development projects. However, recent World Health Assembly declarations and statements in Agenda 21 of UNCED have placed renewed emphasis on impact assessment of all kinds.

If HIA is to be applied widely and successfully it must have a structured approach. Experience of EIA and ERA suggests that long and costly procedures do not appeal to users. Donor agencies are already overburdened by requirements to consider issues such as gender, environment and poverty. They are unwilling or unable to absorb complex health assessment procedures. HIA must a have a simple entry point based on rapid assessment and project screening. In many cases a rapid assessment will suffice to strengthen the negotiations of the health sector within the multi-sector planning forum.

Health risk management is consistent with sound project management. Human health and the health of the environment are mutually interdependent. If the health of people is safeguarded then, ultimately, the ecosystem itself must be safe.

REFERENCES

ADB. 1990. Environmental Risk Assessment: Dealing with Uncertainty in Environmental Impact Assessment. Asian Development Bank. NTIS, 7.

ADB. 1992. Guidelines for the Health Impact Assessment of Development Projects. Asian Development Bank. NTIS, ADB Environmental Paper No. 11.

Birley, M. H. 1991. Guidelines for Forecasting the Vector-borne Disease Implications of Water Resource Development. World Health Organization. NTIS, WHO/CWS/91.3, second edition.

Birley, M. H. in press. *The Health Impact of Development Projects.* Norwich: HMSO.

Bolton, D., Imevbore, A. M. A., & Fraval, P. 1990. A rapid assessment procedure for identifying environmental and health hazards in irrigation schemes. *Hydraulics* Research Wallingford. NTIS, OD 120.

Carswell, J. W. 1987. HIV infections in healthy persons in Uganda. *AIDS 1*: 223–227.

Carter, F. W, & Turnock, D. 1993. *Environmental Problems in Eastern Europe.* London: Routledge.

Coimbra, C. E. A. 1988. Human Factors in the Epidemiology of Malaria in the Brazilian Amazon. *Hum Org 47(3)*: 254–260.

Cooper Weil, D. E., Alicbusan, A. P., & Wilson, J. F., Reich, M. R., Bradley, D. J. 1990. *The Impact of Development Policies on Health: a Review of the Literature.* Geneva: World Health Organization.

Eisenbud, M. 1990. The Ionizing Radiations. In *The Earth as Transformed by Human Action: Global and Regional Changes in the Biosphere over the Past 300 Years.* Edited by B. L. Turner, W. C. Clark, R. W. Kates, J. F. Richards, J. T. Matthews & W. B. Meyer. Cambridge University Press.

El-Batawi, M. A. 1981. Special problems of occupational health in the developing countries. In *Occupational Health Practice.* Edited by R. S. F. Schilling. 27–46. London: Butterworths.

Ewan, C., Young, A., Bryant, E., & Calvert, D. 1992. Australian National Framework for Health Impact Assessment in Environmental Impact Assessment. University of Wollongong.

Findley, R. W. 1988. Pollution control in Brazil. *Ecol Law Qtrly 15(1)*: 1–68.

Havard, J. D. J. 1978. World Health Organization Assignment Report. World Health Organization Regional office for the Western Pacific. NTIS, ICP/HSD/015.

IRRI. 1987. Vector-borne disease control in humans through rice agroecosystem management. International Rice Research Institute, Los Banos, Philippines: International Rice Research Institute and WHO/FAO/UNEP Panel of Experts on Environmental Management for Vector Control.

Laing, R. 1986. *Health and Health Services for Plantation Workers; Four Case Studies.* Edited by G. Walt. London: Evaluation and Planning Centre for Health Care, London School of Hygiene and Tropical Medicine.

Lowenthal, D. 1990. Awareness of Human Impacts: Changing Attitudes and Emphases. In *The Earth as Transformed by Human Action: Global and Regional Changes in the Biosphere over the Past 300 Years.* Edited by B. L. Turner, W. C. Clark, R. W. Kates, J. F. Richards, J. T. Matthews & W. B. Meyer. Cambridge University Press.

Macdonald, W. W. 1991. Control of Culex quinquefasciatus in Myanmar (Burma) and India: 1900–1960. *Annals of Trop. Med. 85(1)*: 165–172.

Mackay, D. 1992. *Multimedia Environmental Models: The Fugacity Approach*. Florida, USA: Lewis Publishers.

Munn, R. E. 1992. Towards Sustainable Development. *Atmospheric Environment (26A)15*: 2725–2731.

OD A. 1989. Manual of Environmental Appraisal. Overseas Development Administration.

OECD. 1986. Methods and Procedures in Aid Evaluation. 1 ed. Paris: Organization for Economic Cooperation and Development, Publications.

Oomen, J. M. V., de Wolf, J., & Jobin, W. R. 1988. Health and Irrigation: incorporation of disease-control measures in irrigation, a multi-faceted task in design, construction, operation. Wageningen: International Institute for Land Reclamation and Improvement.

Packard, R. M. 1989. Industrial production, health and disease in sub-Saharan Africa. *Soc Sci Med 28(5)*: 475–496.

Pimenta, J. C. P. 1987. Multinational corporations and industrial pollution in Sao Paulo, Brazil. In *Multinational Corporations, Environment and the Third World*. Edited by C. S. Pearson. 198–220. Durham: Duke University Press.

Roundy, R. W. 1989. Problems of resettlement and vector-borne diseases associated with dams and other development schemes. In *Demography and Vector-borne Diseases*. Edited by M. Service. 193–205. Boca Raton: CRC Press.

Service, M. W. 1989. *Demography and Vector-Borne Diseases*. Boca Raton: CRC Press Inc.

Spellerberg, I. F., & Minshull, A. 1992. An investigation into the nature and use of ecology in environmental impact assessments. *BES Bull. 23(1)*: 38–45.

Stigliani, W. M., Brouwer, F. M., Munn, R. E., Shaw, R. W., & Atonofsky, M. 1989. Future Environments for Europe: some implications of alternative development paths. *Science and Total Environment 80*: 1–102.

Thomas, V. 1981. Pollution Control in Sao Paulo, Brazil: Costs, Benefits and Effects on Industrial Location. The World Bank. NTIS, Staff Working Paper No. 501.

Tiffen, M. 1991. Guidelines for the Incorporation of Health Safeguards into Irrigation Projects through Intersectoral Cooperation. World Health Organization. NTIS, WHO/CWS/91.2.

Turnbull, R. G. H. 1992. *Environmental and Health Impact Assessment of Development Projects, A Handbook for Practitioners*. London and New York: Elsevier.

WHO. 1982. Manual on Environmental Management for Mosquito Control, with Special Emphasis on Malaria Vectors. Edited by WHO. Offset Publications. Geneva: WHO.

WHO. 1983a. Maximising Benefits to Health . . . An appraisal methodology for water supply and sanitation projects. World Health Organization. NTIS, ETS/83.7.

WHO. 1983b. Minimum Evaluation Procedure (MEP) for water supply and sanitation projects. World Health Organization. NTIS, ETS/83.1, CDD/OPR/83.1.

WHO. 1987. Health and Safety Component of Environmental Impact Assessment. World Health Organization. NTIS, 15.

WHO. 1992a. Health Dimensions of Economic Reform. Edited by WHO. Geneva: World Health Organization.

WHO. 1992b. *Our Planet, Our Health*: Report of the WHO Commission on Health and Environment. Geneva: World Health Organization.

Whyte, A. V., & Burton, I. 1980. *Environmental Risk Assessment.* John Wiley and Sons, New York.

World Bank. 1991. Operational Directive 4.01: Environmental Assessment. World Bank.

PART IV
Policy Considerations

25

Environmental Policy Options for Health: Social, Political, and Economic Considerations

Gurinder S. Shahi and Phillip W. Sarocco

INTRODUCTION

Societies in the process of development generally tend not to be particularly concerned with environmental issues or with dealing with pollution-related problems, often treating them as necessary evils in the process of development.

This was starkly obvious, for example, in the Eastern European Socialist states where inefficient and highly polluting production processes were tolerated in the name of "progress." Phenomenal changes have since taken place as the formerly state-controlled and environmentally-blinkered economies of Eastern Europe developed a new faith in democracy and the free market and now find themselves having to deal with major environmental problems created by their past lapses. As a result of previous exposure to pollutants and particulate matter, their populations suffer from major adverse health effects (for example, cardiorespiratory diseases) which are likely to continue to cause problems in these societies for at least the next several decades (Datsenko et al., 1988). Other developing societies have also tolerated higher levels of risk than are acceptable in "developed" societies today.

When people in more developed countries and regions rebel at the pollution and associated environmental degradation wreaked by industries, the "profitability" principle (by which an individual or corporation determines actions to be taken on the basis of the prospect of financial gain) has determined that it is often far more economical to relocate to areas that are still willing to put up with the problem than to reform the industry or to improve production processes. Hence, environmental problems often tend to be exported, usually to less developed communities hungry for investment and willing to pay the "price" for progress (that is, pollution and environmental degradation). The result, both within and across national boundaries, has been a tendency for polluting industries to shift their operations from areas with strictly enforced (and expensive) environmental protection measures to areas with less stringent environmental control.

Such considerations have undoubtedly played some part in the development of countries like Mexico, Brazil, and the Asian Tigers (Hongkong, Taiwan, South Korea and Singapore); the South in the United States (which has managed to attract industries from California and the northeastern states); and southern Europe (for example, Spain and Portugal). The increased industrial investment that these regions/countries have enjoyed can be attributed, at least in part, to the fact that they have tended to have laxer environmental rules (or less strict enforcement of existing rules) than the more developed countries (MDCs) and regions.

Countries and regions receiving such investment are slowly waking up to the fact that economic growth and jobs have often come at the expense of having to cater to industrial and other concerns which might operate at levels far less stringent and more polluting than would be the case in their home countries or regions. India's experience with Union Carbide in Bhopal is just one illustrative example (Shaikh, 1986). Only relatively recently have people become aware of the global nature of damage caused by unregulated pollution and the indiscriminate dumping of toxic wastes. This increased awareness has possibly been accentuated by scares surrounding the depletion of the ozone layer and its possible link to recent climatic changes.

Increasingly, we have to ask what price we are willing to pay for economic growth and development? Is "sustainable" development a realistic goal, or must environmental integrity (accompanied by increased risk to human health and well-being) always be sacrificed for industrial development?

POLLUTION AS AN EXTERNALITY

Pollution is generally considered, in the language of economists, an externality.[1] This is because the cost of pollution to society (arising from the

[1] An externality is said to exist when the production or consumption of a good directly affects businesses or consumers not involved in buying and selling it and when these spillover effects are not adequately reflected in the market price (Fischer et al., 1988).

release of byproducts or wastes of the production process into the environment) is usually not fully reflected in the price of products. Although externalities can be either positive or negative, most instances of pollution involve negative externalities[2] in the sense that changes in physical conditions occur that reduce the quality or the value of the environment.

Being regarded an externality, pollution is not usually taken into account in the producer's cost/benefit calculus so the price (private cost) of a product does not reflect the social cost incurred by environmental damage in producing the product. In some cases, since the emitting source does not generally have to pay for polluting, there is no financial incentive for it to reduce such pollution (Anderson et al., 1977). In fact, producers pass the "benefit" of their lower costs on to the consumers who generally respond to the lower prices by demanding larger quantity of product than they would if the price reflected the true social cost of environmental damage caused in generating the product (Hemenway, 1988). This, in turn, leads to an excess production of the product, the correction of which requires that the social cost of producing the product (and its associated pollution) be "internalized" into its price. Pollution can, hence, be viewed as a pricing problem. The production and consumption of the product are at price levels which do not reflect its social cost (Hemenway, 1988).

THE ENVIRONMENTAL PARADOX

We are faced with limited availability of resources (what the economists call a "scarcity" of resources) which must be used to fill virtually unlimited wants. Not everything desired by society can be provided and tough choices need to be made. To improve environmental quality (a desirable resource), society needs to invest in pollution control and must, therefore, forgo other goods and services. This is the opportunity cost[3] of pollution control and must be weighed against the value and benefit society derives from improved environmental quality.

Paradoxically, although people may be willing to give up some goods and services to get an improvement in environmental quality, the free market does not generally provide a mechanism for achieving this. In the

---

[2] An interesting example of a situation where pollution can, in fact, be a positive externality is the case of increased levels of atmospheric carbon dioxide secondary to industrial activity which has been predicted to result in a stimulation of photosynthesis and, consequently, an increase in agricultural yields (Tyler Miller, 1990).

[3] The opportunity cost of any good or service is the amount of other goods or services that must be given up to obtain it (Fischer et al., 1988).

interest of society, therefore, there is often the need for regulation to bring about appropriate environmental control, or the establishment of appropriate mechanisms whereby the market does take account of people's desire for a cleaner environment.

The issue of what can be done and how improvements in environmental quality can be achieved will be considered in the course of this chapter. This chapter also examines the various policy options available to any government or agency considering controlling environmental pollution and its associated risks.

HISTORICAL PERSPECTIVE (BASED LARGELY ON THE U.S. EXPERIENCE)

Prior to the 1960s, it was a common assumption that human activity could not impose permanent or widespread environmental damage. The environment was considered to have a massive ability to absorb the effect of any human activity (acting as a "sink"), the impact of which was generally assumed to be small. This conventional wisdom was forced to change when confronted with evidence to the contrary: for example, worsening smog in cities such as Los Angeles, and pollution and heavy contamination of rivers and lakes in the Great Lakes' states.

In the United States, the passage of the 1970 Clean Air Act and the 1972 Federal Water Pollution Control Act, together with the establishment of the U.S. Environmental Protection Agency (1970), marked a change in perspective and the realization that a serious approach to protecting the environment was needed (Reilly, 1991).

Early efforts at pollution control were aimed at controlling release of hazardous wastes into air and water since it was recognized that such wastes can eventually find their way into the food chain as well as contaminate drinking water (Downing, 1984). Land disposal of toxic wastes, because it isolates these materials from the air and water, was considered safer. However, experiences such as the Love Canal situation in Niagara City, New York (Brown & Pope, 1982), have shown that poorly designed or abandoned disposal sites can be associated with seepage of toxic chemicals into the ground and contamination of both the ground and surface water supplies.

Recognition of the need to regulate the design and operation of land disposal sites led to the 1976 Resource Conservation and Recovery Act. The desire of the American public for cleaning up accidental spills of toxic materials and past unregulated sites, such as Love Canal, led to the passage of the 1980 Comprehensive Environmental Response, Compensation, and Liability Act (commonly referred to as the Superfund Act) (Downing, 1984).

The most commonly used approaches to regulation of hazardous waste disposal have been characterized as "command and control" environmental management—wherein legal compulsion dictated the amount of waste emission allowable (Howe, 1991).

In recent years, there has been a trend towards the increasing use of market forces to find innovative approaches to solving environmental problems (Stavins, 1989). With this has come a notable change from a top-down implementation of rules towards the use of consensus-building and economic incentives prior to implementation, as envisioned, for example, by the EPA and which was legislated in the 1990 Amendment to the Clean Air Act (Reilly, 1991).

Another trend in environmental protection has been the increasing recognition of the need for pollution prevention and a reduction in the production and use of hazardous and toxic substances. The Pollution Prevention Act in May of 1993 seeks to shift away from the faults inherent in the previous environmental "command and control"-based laws in the USA (Browner, 1993). While such "command and control" measures tended to focus on cleaning up or treating wastes post-emission, pollution prevention approaches seek to have an "up-stream" impact in terms of minimizing waste generation or even eliminating waste generation without sacrificing production. Effective pollution prevention often involves the need for building consensus between potential polluters and regulators, and can be facilitated through the utilization of appropriate economic incentives to promote implementation.

MAINTAINING ENVIRONMENTAL QUALITY

Whatever approach to pollution control is taken, it is important to remember:

a) that environmental quality standards and objectives must be set;
b) that an effective system of monitoring needs to be worked out and enforced to ensure that standards are being met and that appropriate actions are taken if they are not.

Ambient Environmental Quality Standards

Pollution can be controlled by laws to establish desired standards and by technology to achieve these standards. The legislated standards, which can be described as ambient environmental quality standards, state the minimum level of environmental quality that the air or water should meet.

These standards can be set according to various criteria:

a) use-based criteria. Water quality standards might, for example, be set so that the water is suitable for swimming in (e.g., relatively free of potential infectious agents such as pathogenic bacteria, and meeting aesthetic standards of color, taste and smell) or, perhaps, of such a quality that game fish can thrive (so fishing becomes viable).

b) human health protection criteria. All pollution control efforts would, in this event, be pursued with the goal of maximizing the community's health. This appears to have been the goal of the 1970 U.S. Clean Air Act wherein consideration of costs in attaining the health-based standards was expressly forbidden (Stewart, 1985). If no thresholds are set, a strict interpretation of health protection criteria may require the elimination of all potentially harmful pollutants (Crandall, 1983).

Such a policy would require levels of control that may not be technologically feasible or which are likely to require very high capital outlays that are simply economically unattainable. Furthermore, there is always the possibility that such control levels would tend to drive industry from areas where they are strongly enforced to areas where enforcement is lax or where required standards are not so difficult or expensive to achieve.

Conversely, such regulatory criteria, if appropriately applied, might also serve to accelerate the development of new technologies, since setting a standard which is currently technically infeasible tends to create a driving force for industry to innovate and produce improved control technologies.

c) technological feasibility. Because of technological constraints, policymakers sometimes find themselves having to rely on setting environmental quality standards according to what is technically feasible. This requires an assessment of emissions and of control techniques.

If a technological process were available that reduced emissions to zero, the standard might then be set with emissions at the zero level. One obvious possible means to achieve zero emissions (in the absence of suitable technology) would simply be to shut down all polluting plants. Such an approach would, however, result in loss of jobs and, eventually, a decline in living standards in the region, a development which would not be economically or politically acceptable in most countries today. The determination of technological feasibility must, hence, be tempered by economic and political considerations.

d) economic feasibility. No country can escape the unavoidable fact that financial resources are limited. It may, therefore, prove necessary, due to economic constraints, to accept a lower standard than is technically feasible. The process of cost/benefit analysis takes account of health maximization, use, and technological feasibility considerations, while explicitly providing a mechanism for assessing the value of environmental standards to society (Downing, 1984).

An economically efficient standard would be one where the demand for environmental quality is in equilibrium with the supply or the feasibility of environmental quality. Economic feasibility standards have not, until recently, been much used in environmental regulation, but are being increasingly recognized as pragmatic and practical.

Effluent Standards

Ambient environmental quality standards recognize environmental quality as a goal in itself. They state the expected outcome of control policy implementation but are not particularly useful, in themselves, as they do not tell each pollution source how much to control its emissions.

More specific regulations must be drawn up to state specifically which sources must control their emissions and by how much. Effluent standards are typically the means by which this is achieved. Some combination of environmental quality standards and effluent standards would comprise the typical repertoire of pollution control strategies used by most agencies today.

Effluent standards essentially state the acceptable level of performance that an individual source must reach in controlling its emissions. There are two types of effluent standards:

a) prescriptive regulations
b) emission standards.

a) Prescriptive Regulations. A prescriptive regulation usually states the specific technical control actions that an emitting source should take. Such action may, for example, involve the installation of a particular control device (for example, an electrostatic precipitator) or the use of particular inputs (for example, the requirement that low-sulfur or lead free fuels be used). Such regulations presume that the prescribed action will help bring about the desired level of control.

Prescriptive regulations have the advantage that they are relatively easy to enforce. A source's compliance with the regulation can be verified by determining whether the required input is being used or the required device has been installed and is operational.

There are, however, some potential disadvantages to the use of prescriptive regulations. For one thing, technology is continually changing. When a more effective or less expensive device becomes available, it would be desirable to require its use. New devices must, however, be approved by the regulatory agency. The approval process is a time-consuming and uncertain process that can cause prescriptive regulations to become less flexible than emission standards.

A second problem is that installation and operation of control devices does not necessarily guarantee that emissions will be reduced to the desired level. Because prescriptive regulations often carry no other specific requirements or monitoring procedures, agencies often have no choice but to assume that the device is effective. This may not be a serious problem in simple setups but could prove severely wanting in more complex industrial situations.

b) Emission Standards. Emission standards require that emissions of a pollutant be controlled to a specified level and that a source not emit more than a specified amount over a certain period. In the 1960s, it was common to specify emission standards in terms of concentrations (for example, parts per million). The problem with such standards, as was quickly discovered, was that the source could meet the standard simply by diluting the effluent rather than actually reducing emissions. This is a rational and intelligent approach to complying with the letter of the law that would, unfortunately, lead to little or no improvement in environmental quality.

Realization of this loophole stimulated a move towards standards based on mass (for example, U.S. standards specifying that a 1982 car can emit no more than 0.05 grams of hydrocarbons per mile) (Downing, 1984). Such mass-based standards represented an improvement but still did not determine total emissions from the source since, if the car is driven more miles, for example, emissions would increase and air quality decline.

A third alternative, which is in common use today, is to state emission standards in terms of total emissions per hour, day or year (mass per unit time standards).

Advantages of emission standards include the fact that they allow greater flexibility in dealing with control technology since the standards do not specify the type of technology to be used, only the desired level of effectiveness. This allows a source to search for the least expensive measures or combination of measures to meet the standards. It also gives leeway for the source to innovate technologically and to implement effective new ideas immediately.

The major disadvantage of emission standards is that they are difficult to enforce since they require the measurement of actual emissions, which is often a technically difficult and expensive task. Once the appropriate emission standards are determined, it is necessary to ensure that each source complies with the standards.

Emission control is expensive and reduces profits so that firms will tend to avoid doing it unless the penalty for doing so (in addition to the benefits that accrue from being considered "green-conscious" by the general public) exceeds the cost of complying with the standards.

Monitoring and Enforcement

The emphasis in monitoring and enforcement actions by regulatory agencies tends to be on installation of control equipment (prescriptive regulations), while presuming appropriate operation of the equipment, self-monitoring, and compliance (Howe, 1991). Audits of effluent release into the air or water by industrial plants are generally conducted on a very infrequent basis and usually involve a review of company-provided records with no direct assessment of emissions by the regulatory agency (Howe, 1991). It comes, therefore, as no surprise that such self-reporting has uncovered very few violations of standards that were not discovered by other means (Russell et al., 1986).

With current state of the art technology, it should prove relatively inexpensive for regulatory agencies to monitor pollution sources directly at relatively low cost. Proper monitoring of ambient environmental quality and effluent discharges are necessary prerequisites to the successful operation of any control program, whether it uses a "command and control" approach, or economic approaches such as effluent fees or transferable permits for regulation (these various approaches are discussed overleaf).

Penalties for violation of standards also should be severe enough to "encourage" compliance. There would, otherwise, be little or no incentive for the polluting source to clean up since it may prove cheaper to pay small fines for violations rather than to pay for installing expensive control devices or other inputs.

Improved monitoring and enforcement would allow regulatory agencies to know how their programs are working as well as allow offenders to be readily identified and penalized. The threat of both having to pay fines and the associated adverse publicity can act as an effective spur for firms to conform with regulations.

Need for Comprehensive Control

A particular source may be emitting pollutants in more than one environmental medium (for example, into the air and water). In order to ensure effective control, it would, hence, be necessary to control releases into all media simultaneously.

An interesting example, in this regard, is that of paper and pulp manufacturing plants in Wisconsin in the 1950s (Downing, 1984). The implementation of strict water pollution laws caused paper plants to seek inexpensive control measures. They discovered that a relatively simple process would dramatically reduce the generation of water pollutants. Unfortunately, this process resulted in the release of sulfur-containing wastes into the air. Since air quality was not regulated at that time, these releases were not controlled. The sulfur-containing wastes smelled like rotten eggs and killed trees for miles around the plant. The state finally reacted by also adopting stricter air pollution laws (Downing, 1984).

The need for a comprehensive approach to monitoring and enforcement cannot be overemphasised. Regulations should cover all possible emitting sources and all possible pollutants. There should also be recognition of possible environmental interactions with effluents (for example, chemicals which are harmless in themselves may be converted in the environment to more toxic pollutants).

To avoid the possibility of neglecting pollution effects on one environmental medium when controlling pollution in another, emissions in all possible media should be monitored. The source should meet all emission and environmental quality standards simultaneously.

OPTIONS IN POLLUTION CONTROL

The various possible approaches to dealing with the risk associated with pollution include:

- no intervention
- regulate using strict standards
  - a) command and control approach
  - b) economic approaches:
    - 1) effluent fees (pollution taxes)
    - 2) subsidies
    - 3) tradeable pollution permits
  - c) integrated approach

No Intervention

The easiest but, perhaps, the costliest option (in the long term) would be to have no policy regarding pollution control and, therefore, no agency responsible for such control. Market forces would then probably rule.

As explained previously, since no attempt is made in this situation to take the social cost of pollution into account, producers would be unlikely to attempt to reduce output of pollutants. On the contrary, they are likely to produce larger quantities of product (and, hence, more pollutants) since the private cost of the product is now much lower than the true cost so society would demand larger quantities of the product than would be the case if the social cost had been internalized into the price of the product. Society would have to live in a dirtier environment. Incidence of respiratory ailments would probably rise because of higher levels of particulate matter in the air (Marth et al., 1989); and there is also likely to be a higher level of toxic chemicals and carcinogens (as pollutants) in air and water (Tyler Miller, 1990).

On the plus side, dirty industries will be attracted to the area and, although pollution would tend to increase, employment opportunities would probably be quite abundant. Society would need to decide which option it prefers.

Regulate Using Strict Standards

This is the approach taken by practically all responsible governments today. Pollution control agencies may be set up at the national as well as regional or state levels. These agencies establish standards for ambient environmental quality as well as prescribe regulations and emission standards for polluting industries and agricultural concerns.

There are several options, however, for an agency to choose from in deciding how to implement and regulate environmental quality. One constant for successful attainment of acceptable environmental quality appears to be the need for strong financial penalties and a realistic threat of litigation for violation of standards.

a) Command and Control Approach. This is the basic (or "traditional") approach to pollution control adopted by most countries. The government defines a desired goal, formulates specific rules or regulations that mandate the actions needed to meet that goal, and develops an enforcement program to ensure compliance. If a source does not comply with government regulations regarding control, civil and criminal sanctions can serve to bring compliance (Howe, 1991).

Prescriptive regulations (for example, that only low sulfur fuels be used) are probably best implemented using this approach. However, it should be borne in mind that requiring all producers to use the same control technology can have the negative consequence of discouraging innovation in the development of cheaper and better control strategies. Emission standards are generally also implemented using the "command and control" approach.

Another potential problem with using this approach (assuming, of course, effective implementation and good compliance) is that legislating blanket control levels can often mean that more stringent standards are applied than may be necessary—often at great cost to industry and society. As a result, actual program costs based on a "command and control" strategy may be several times higher than estimated least costs based on a more rational approach (Tietenberg, 1985). Also, requiring the same standard across a country fails to take account of the varying ability of local or regional environments to cope with different levels of pollutants. For example, Kathmandu, Nepal, already has higher ambient levels of most pollutants than, say, Bandung, Indonesia, and would require more stringent controls than are probably necessary in Bandung.

Recognizing the deficiencies and potential pitfalls of using a strictly "command and control" approach, the U.S. Clean Air Act of 1977 introduced some interesting ideas, in particular, the "bubble" concept and the idea of emission offsets.

The "bubble" concept allows all the processes in a factory to be treated as a group rather than process by process, thus allowing the utilization of less expensive control strategies. Previously, emission standards were set for each process in a plant. The "bubble" concept allows the regulatory agency to treat all the processes collectively as if they were one source, thus allowing the plant the freedom to choose the level at which it controls the emissions from each process and so reducing costs while ensuring that overall emissions generated do not exceed the accepted emission standards.

Emission offsets require a new source entering an area to negotiate with existing sources in the area for a corresponding reduction in their emissions (this approach has some similarity to that used with transferable permits). This applies particularly to new sources in heavily polluted areas which already exceed the national primary air quality standards (described in the United States as "nonattainment" areas, which are areas where ambient air quality standards are not being attained). The new plant must comply with emission standards applicable for new sources and obtain a reduction of emissions from existing sources equal to, or greater than, the increase in emissions resulting from its operations. To obtain this reduction, the new firm must generally pay an existing firm to reduce its emissions. Such payment must cover at least the additional costs for reducing emission from the existing source or it is unlikely to agree to the additional control. The new firm would, itself, prefer to control more stringently and purchase less control from existing sources if this could be done more cheaply. There would, hence, be a tendency towards each firm developing the most efficient solution for control (Liroff, 1980).

Other measures may be used in combination with the "command and control" approach. These include the provision of tax breaks, subsidies for purchase of pollution control equipment and the provision of nonfinancial incentives (such as, for example, "Environmentally Conscious Company of the Year" awards, etc.). These measures are often used to increase the likelihood of compliance and can serve to encourage a company to take pollution control action which it may not otherwise do. They can also serve to stimulate the move towards achieving the level of pollution control that the agency desires. Tax breaks for implementing control measures and the provision of subsidies for the purchase of pollution control equipment effectively serve to reduce the opportunity cost and the financial burden on the firm and, thus, make it more likely that the firm will control pollutant output.

Companies are finding it increasingly important to clean up their images and to be seen by the public as being environmentally conscious. Giving recognition (for example, National Environment Awards) to these cleanup efforts can go a long way towards making companies environmentally responsible.

b) Economic Approaches. Pollution is an externality for which the emitting source does not pay. Producers respond to this lack of costs by tending to release excess emissions. They do not, however, waste resources for which they have to pay. Costs cause them to weigh their use of resources carefully.

1) Effluent Fees. One solution to the pollution problem would be to make the emission of pollutants costly. In other words, there could be a charge for emissions into the environment. Such emission charges can also be referred to as effluent fees or taxes.

Causing producers to factor the effluent fees into their production costs would help stimulate them to economize on waste release, just as they normally economize on other costly resources. A recent study in the United States, for example, estimated annual savings of about $10 billion in air quality programs alone if benefit-costs assessments or emission charges are applied (Portney, 1990).

To save money and reduce having to pay high effluent fees, producers would be stimulated to seek innovative ways to reduce or prevent effluent output. They might, for example, change their production process or install control devices to reduce the output of effluent to save costs. An effluent fee system can, thus, generate the incentive to control emission output.

Producers which are unable to meet the cost increases as a result of having to pay effluent fees or to implement control measures may find that they have to cut their losses by stopping production.

The effluent fee reflects the value society places on environmental resources. Each source must analyze the desirability of continuing to produce the final product and the pollutant. If a firm cannot continue to produce and cover all costs, including environmental costs, it should cease production.

The effluent fee system can, hence, be seen as a mechanism for removing the least efficient and most environmentally damaging sources from the market. An effective and efficient effluent fee system will generate efficient market adjustments as relatively "dirty" sources reduce output or drop out, while relatively "clean" sources remain to produce in ways that lower environmental damage. Effluent charge systems have been used with good effect in several parts of the world including, for example, the Ruhr river area in Germany (Kneese, 1960).

It should be noted, however, that effluent fees can probably best and most easily be applied to point source pollution (where the polluter and the amount of pollution can be readily identified). There may be substantial practical difficulty in applying such fees when dealing with nonpoint source pollution (for example, water pollution arising from pesticide use by hundreds of farmers).

Effluent fees can effectively cause the price of a product to reflect its true cost to society (private cost plus social cost) if the fees are set at an optimum level. However, it may take some trial and error before this optimum level is attained. Because the polluter pays, an added benefit of the effluent fee is that it provides an incentive for innovation and process improvement since reduced pollution output saves costs.

Another major advantage of an effluent fee system is that it generates revenue. This might possibly be used for various efficiency- or equity-enhancing purposes. For example, the revenues could go toward environmental improvement measures or toward providing grant money to firms willing to implement control measures, so acting as a further incentive for pollution control.

Another way the funds generated can be used is in assistance of members of the public or workers who may have been adversely affected as a result of exposure to the pollutants. This approach has been used since 1973 in Japan where, for example, air and water pollution charges are applied to both stationary and mobile sources to finance the payment of compensation to individuals who suffer from pollution-related damage to health (Gresser, 1975).

2) *Subsidies.* Under a subsidy system, the source might, for example, be paid for the units of pollution it does not produce. Such a subsidy would have a somewhat different effect on the firms' output decisions than an effluent fee. Rather than increasing production costs, the subsidy reduces production costs. The initial impact of this would be to generate a profit.

A subsidy can bring profits to operations that would not otherwise be profitable. Also, because the subsidy is usually paid for every unit of pollution not released, it is necessary to determine how much pollution would have been produced without the subsidy and its accompanying control measures. A source could adopt a more polluting technology in order to gain a greater subsidy even though this dirtier technology increased pollution control costs. This could be a useful strategy (from the firm's perspective) since the firm would tend to increase profits if it is handsomely subsidized to control its emissions arising from the use of dirty technology.

An advantage of providing subsidies is that they keep production costs down and can lead to increased profits. This helps to keep the price of the product low and would, therefore, promote international competitiveness and provide goods to the public at lower prices.

There are, however, major problems with the use of a subsidy approach for pollution control. Because production costs are lower, and the product cheaper, the manufacturer tends to produce more to cope with demand. Increased production would lead to increased pollution.

Second, subsidies involve the use of government revenue resources rather than generating revenue as would be the case with emission fees or transferable permits. Taking resources away from other uses (such as provision of social services) to keep polluting industries viable is probably not the best or most cost-effective way to control pollution (or to use scarce public funds).

3) *Transferable Permits.* The concept of transferable permits has been advocated by policy makers and economists for many years (Dales, 1968; Noll, 1982). To begin with, the agency determines a desired level of environmental quality and sets a standard at that level. It then determines the number of units of a given pollutant per unit time that can be allowed in order to achieve that environmental quality standard.

Once the allowed total of emissions has been determined, permits to emit the particular pollutant might, for example, be auctioned on the open market. After the initial sale, permits can be traded when a buyer and seller agree on a price. The permit is transferred to the new owner who can increase emissions while the previous owner reduces emissions.

A major advantage of transferable permits is that they provide incentives to control and innovate in the same way that the effluent fee does. This would help guarantee that all sources are contributing toward an improvment of environmental quality at the lowest cost. When a source innovates, it will reduce its emissions and can sell permits to increase its profits. This allows other sources to increase emissions, saving resources in the process. A further advantage is that permits can be purchased by anyone. This would allow environmentalists, for example, to express their desire for an improved environment directly by purchasing permits and retiring them. This would reduce total emissions and help improve environmental quality.

A major potential pitfall with the use of transferable permits is the need for extensive and careful monitoring and enforcement to ensure that all players (permit-holders) do not produce more pollutants than they are allowed to.

Conversely, a major advantage of pollution permits is that the financial burden of monitoring emissions would tend to be placed on the polluting firm rather than the government regulatory agency, as the firm would have a vested interest in knowing how much pollution it emits, in order to minimize its expenses and potentially maximize its profit from the sale of permits it no longer needs.

Tradable pollution permits do appear to be an economically efficient way to decrease emissions while maintaining pollution control technology innovation. However, experience with the tradable permit system has shown that the market mechanism for trading is having trouble understanding what value to give permits. As a result, permits have been auctioned and purchased, but only a small percentage has been traded; the system then resembles more a purchased effluent fee.

c) Integrated Approach. An integrated approach, combining elements of command and control and economic incentives and adding negotiation and public disclosure, is an option which has become fashionable in recent years. Current efforts to encourage this approach seek to avoid some of the disadvantages of the other approaches. In the U.S. an effort to develop an integrated approach to pollution prevention has been embodied in the Pollution Prevention Act of May 1993.

The U.S. approach seeks to be nonprescriptive, allowing industries to innovate in their own way to, for example: reduce or substitute the toxics used as inputs to production; change production processes to reduce pollution; or recycle toxic inputs. The overall goal is, of course, to reduce total polluting emissions to all media and to reduce use of toxics. Encouraging such innovation is intended to stimulate greater interest in preventing pollution and the use of toxic substances "upstream," at the level of production inputs and processes, rather than at the "end of the pipe" (Browner, 1993).

One advantage of using such an approach is, hence, that it allows industries to plan for input and process toxic reduction and to incorporate the environmental externalities of pollution into the total cost of production.

Another advantage to the approach used in the U.S. is that it emphasizes the need for negotiation between industry, government, and the affected public communities. Negotiation can be less costly to all parties and more productive at getting improvements to environmental quality than confrontational litigation such as has been experienced in the U.S. in the past.

An interesting and important aspect of the integrated approach used in the U.S. is that it requires public disclosure of the type and quantity of toxic emissions and toxic inputs used by industry. This allows those companies which take the lead in innovation to reduce pollution to have the opportunity to gain recognition for their efforts. The requirements for public disclosure and negotiation is also beneficial in that it provides the public with an additional mechanism to voice concern over the environmental health and safety implications of the pollution outputs and toxic inputs in the production processes used by private firms (Geiser, 1991). A potential disadvantage of such disclosure is that it can lead sometimes to unwarranted public concern regarding the implications of the use of toxic substances which are unfamiliar to the public—hence, such disclosures should be made in the context of objective public education/knowledge of the relative potential harm of substances, and to reduce the amount of imperfect information for public decision making. Another major concern relating to the integrated approach used in the U.S. is that, as yet, it has not been given the sharp teeth of mandatory adherence and penalties for noncompliance.

IMPORTANT ISSUES

Several important issues need to be considered when evaluating the possible usefulness and applicability of the various environmental control measures discussed:

Environmental ownership rights
Politics, economics and the environment
Role of government
Imperfect information and risk uncertainty
Cost/benefit analysis in pollution control.

Environmental Ownership Rights

Each individual acts to maximize her own best interests (Anderson *et al*, 1977). This can lead individuals to seek government legislation that will make them better off. Firms and other polluters may find it in their interests to seek reductions in the effectiveness of pollution control laws.

Alternatively, they may seek subsidies for the costs they incur in controlling emissions. The general public (being the recipients of polluting effluents) may, on the other hand, find it in its best interests to seek more control over environmental quality and to require that the polluter pay for cleaning up.

The right to use property and the constraints on its use are termed property rights. It is the absence of well-defined and easily enforceable property rights that results in environmental quality being treated as an externality. Society needs to decide who owns the environment—for example, do factory owners have a right to emit wastes into the air and water as long as they own the land over which the air and water flow? Or does society at large own the environment (in other words, the environment is a public good[4]) and, therefore, has the right to determine what can or cannot be emitted into the air or water?

This question of property ownership over the environment is an important one as it is concerned with the issue of who should be responsible for paying for pollution control. Self-interest is very much tied to the question of who pays. I may prefer high environmental quality but the more I have to pay for this quality, the less environmental quality I will actually demand.

In other words, there exist individual and market demands for environmental quality just as for other goods. If, by political action, I could require someone else to pay for improvements in environmental quality, I would need to pay a lower price for the quality and would, therefore, demand more. Self-interest and the related issue of who pays are central to all political decisions on the environment. Everybody wants a cleaner environment, especially when someone else pays for it.

If, for example, society decides that the environment is the property of the general public and, perhaps, that it is a social right to expect clean and fresh air, it is then implicit that the environment is a public good and that potential polluters should be totally responsible for pollution control.

On the other hand, if society values industrial production above all else and considers environmental degradation to be a natural component of such development, this then implies that no one owns the environment and that the potential polluter is free to pollute at will.

If, as is sometimes the case, society subsidizes pollution control measures taken by factories, the implicit (and rather perverse) understanding in this situation is that the emitters are being paid to reduce pollutant output and that they, therefore, hold the property rights to the

---

[4] A public good is one that, if consumed by one person, is still available for consumption by others (Fischer et al., 1988).

environment while we have to pay them so that we can enjoy a clean environment.

Politics, Economics and the Environment

Society perceives environmental pollution and degradation to be of concern and hence, most countries have legislation to control pollution. There is a growing realization that economics and politics play a significant role in the development of environmental policy.

The goal of cleaning up the environment and of limiting pollution to the extent that there are no adverse effects is, at least currently, unrealistic and technically impossible. Economically speaking, the cost of such a massive effort would far outweigh the benefit society would derive from such a high level of environmental quality. Politically, policy is not made by unbiased analysts. The political process intrinsically involves a situation where compromise between competing interests has to be obtained before agreement is reached. The economics of environmental issues cannot be fully separated from the politics. Polluting firms act politically to influence control policy because such policy is costly to them. Environmentalists, on the other hand, act politically to try to influence politicians who control the means by which environmental improvements can be wrought.

Role of Government

Each society needs to decide what role government should play in determining environmental policy. Should free market forces be allowed to control environmental quality? Should government play an interventionist role by helping to reallocate resources toward improving environmental quality?

It is important to note that an uncontrolled free market which does not attach any cost to pollution emission is likely to overproduce polluting goods and to inefficiently degrade the environment. Government intervention may, in such situations, prove necessary and desirable. Having decided that there is a role for government in pollution control, we need to decide how that role is to be conducted.

One obvious role for government is in the provision of information (Zeckhauser & Viscusi, 1990). In public decision making, uninformed individuals are less likely to choose options that would be in their best interests than if they knew all the facts. Thus, providing information to the public in such areas as environmental quality, the effect of pollution, and the costs of control leads to a better informed public and more efficient public choices.

Another important role that government can play is in ensuring that the least well-off members of society (taking account not only of the economically weak but also the politically weak: the poor, the minorities, the women, and the children) benefit as much, if not more, from pollution control policies. Working to ensure equity would help correct historical imbalances in which the least well-off tend, in practically every human society, to be exposed to disproportionately higher levels of pollution and its attendent risks to health and well-being.

Imperfect Information and Risk Uncertainty

One serious problem in designing any system to control pollution is that there is inevitably uncertainty in the information used to generate public policy. For instance, even the estimates we use to ascertain risks associated with exposure to various pollutants are highly uncertain (Finkel, 1990). There are uncertainties, for example, in extrapolating dose-response data from animal studies to human populations; in determination of safe thresholds; and in exposure assessment studies (EPA, 1984).

Any analysis of whether or not to control emission of a particular pollutant, and at what level, needs to take account of the benefits and costs of risk reduction and prevention as well as the uncertainties involved in assessing that risk (Kunreuther, 1991).

It is almost inevitable, because of these uncertainties, that there will be some instances where strict control standards are decided which, in retrospect, prove unnecessary. Conversely lax control measures may be adopted that prove, in retrospect, to have serious public health and/or environmental consequences. Such is the nature of dealing with uncertainty.

Cost/Benefit Analysis in Pollution Control

a) The Cost of Preventing Pollution. Society generates unwanted by-products in producing, transporting, and consuming goods and services. Release of these by-products into the environment can cause damage. There are, essentially, four ways to prevent such damage:

1. The source could refrain from releasing waste. The simplest way to accomplish this would be to refrain from production—this is obviously not necessarily the best approach, especially if the product is very beneficial or desired.
2. The source could modify the form of the waste or the location of its release to reduce the damage it does to the environment.
3. The ability of the environment to absorb waste without adverse effects could be improved. For example, growing more trees to

metabolize increased industrial output of carbon dioxide may be one way of countering rising atmospheric carbon dioxide levels.

4. Use of approaches to pollution prevention (such as substituting less toxic material inputs, changing to cleaner production technology, or increasing internal recycling) could be implemented. Producers often find that they can keep the same product output level and reduce the pollutant output and hence not decrease environmental quality (in fact, some industries have actually found that such approaches can even improve environmental quality).

Prevention of environmental damage can be costly: capital must be invested in pollution control equipment; workers must be employed to operate this equipment; land must be used to locate the equipment or to hold wastes for future release. All of these inputs to production could have been used to produce other goods and services instead.

The cost of pollution control is, hence, the opportunity cost of the resources (land, labor, capital) used. This is the value of other goods that could have been produced using the same input resources.

The *total cost of pollution control* (TCC) depends on how effective the control process is at removing damaging wastes. TCC increases at an increasing rate because higher levels of emission control are more expensive than lower levels of control (Figure 25.1).

Essentially, a source of emissions will tend to select easy, and therefore, less expensive, controls to achieve small reductions. More sophisticated (and expensive) equipment would be required to reduce emissions to zero.

Marginal cost is the change in total cost for a unit of increase in environmental quality. It can be expressed as the slope of the TCC curve at any given level of environmental quality (Figure 25.1). The fact that TCC increases at an increasing rate implies that the marginal cost of control (MCC) increases as environmental quality improves.

b) Benefits from Controlling Pollution. Worsening of environmental quality as a result of emissions can cause damage to people, plants, animals, and physical assets. People may suffer from the effects of pollution on health; poor air quality can, for example, trigger asthma attacks or respiratory infections. Uncontrolled output of potentially carcinogenic pollutants could lead to increased incidence of neoplastic conditions such as cancers of the lung or bladder. People may also suffer from a reduction in the satisfaction they derive from consuming the environment: for example, they might lose the view of distant mountains. Pollution might also cause disease and lack of growth of plants and animals.

Benefit of pollution control would then include reduction of such losses when environmental quality is improved. Benefit or "utility" gain from consuming the environment represents the demand for environmental

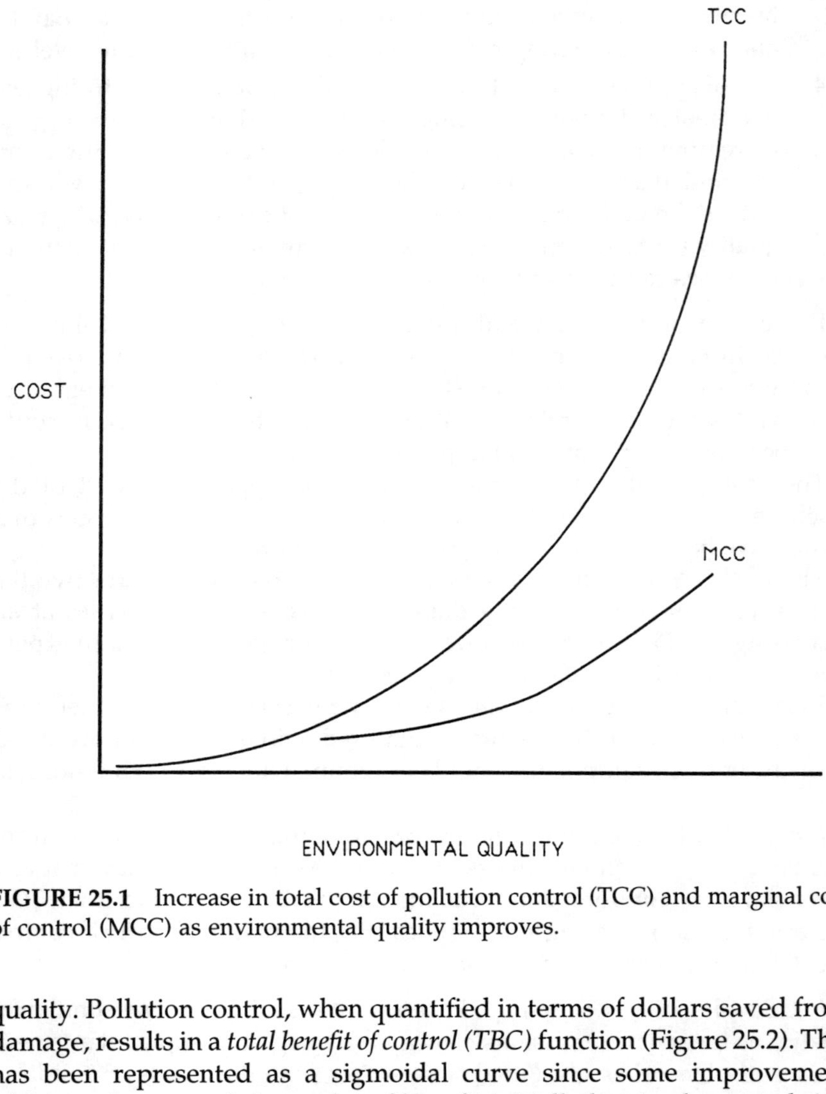

FIGURE 25.1 Increase in total cost of pollution control (TCC) and marginal cost of control (MCC) as environmental quality improves.

quality. Pollution control, when quantified in terms of dollars saved from damage, results in a *total benefit of control (TBC)* function (Figure 25.2). This has been represented as a sigmoidal curve since some improvement of the environment brings a lot of benefit initially but tends not to bring about much more benefit beyond a certain level of environmental quality.

The *marginal benefit of control (MBC)* is the slope of the TBC curve (Figure 25.2). The MBC curve generally has a negative slope because the marginal benefit (the benefit that would be derived from improving environmental quality by one more unit) is decreasing.

c) Efficiency of Pollution Control. To justify the expenditure of scarce resources to improve environmental quality, it is necessary to show that

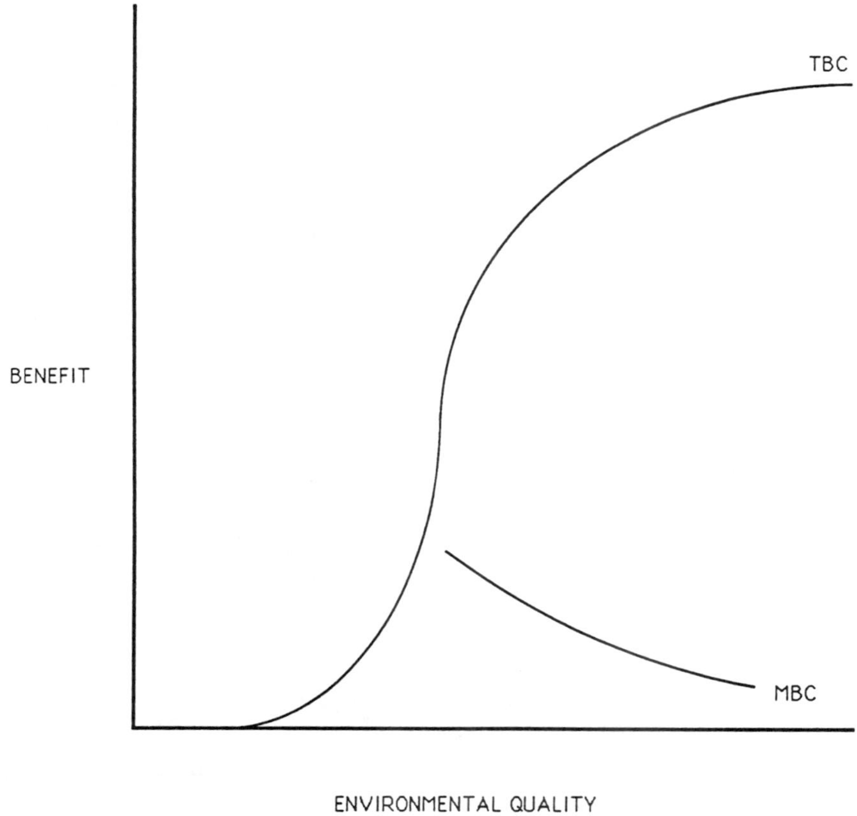

FIGURE 25.2 Increase in total benefit of control (TBC) and marginal benefit of control (MBC) as environmental quality improves.

the resultant improvements are more valuable than the foregone goods and services. This is often accomplished through cost/benefit analysis (Figure 25.3).

The MCC curve indicates the opportunity costs of controlling emissions and improving environmental quality. This is because the cost of land, labor, and capital employed in controlling emissions reflects the value these productive resources would have if they were used to produce other goods of value or services valued by society.

The MBC curve indicates the value to society of improvement in environmental quality and represents the demand for environmental improvement.

There are three basic criteria for efficient pollution control:

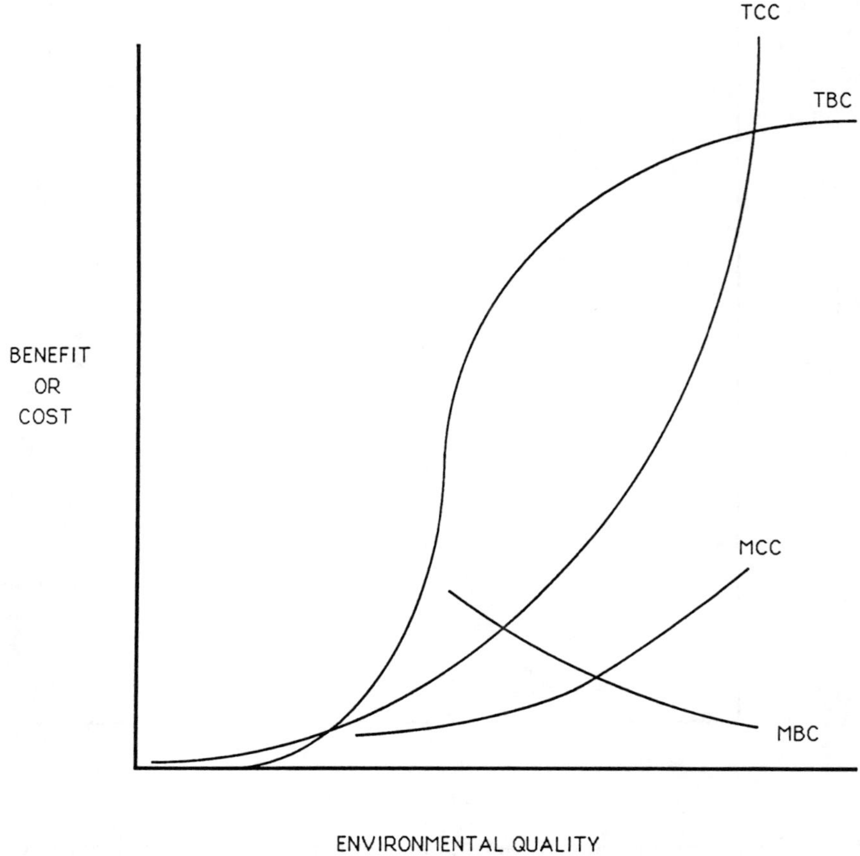

FIGURE 25.3 Cost/benefit of total cost of population control (TCC), marginal cost of control (MCC), total benefit of control (TBC), and marginal benefit of control (MBC) as environmental quality improves.

1. Total benefit must exceed total cost.
2. The optimal level would be the equilibrium point of the MBC and MCC curves (Figure 25.3).
3. The measures used should be cost-effective, that is, the measures should be those which bring about the most benefit at the least cost, since any cost in excess of the lowest possible cost is a waste of resources and therefore inefficient.

In deciding how much it is willing to give up to obtain improvement in environmental quality, a society should seek efficient solutions. Efficiency requires that any chosen level of environmental quality be achieved at the lowest possible cost. Efficiency also requires that the level of environmental quality sought should be the quantity at which net benefits are maximized (Downing, 1984).

CONCLUSION

When a control authority has perfect information about the costs and benefits of control, it is possible to develop efficient control policies using any one (or a combination) of the approaches described: "command and control" regulations, effluent fees, subsidies, transferable permits or integrated approaches aimed at negotiated pollution prevention and reduced use of toxic substances.

"Command and control" policies can be made efficient. They imply that property rights are shared by emitters and recipients. They are in use worldwide and are easier to implement and enforce than other regulatory policy options.

The effluent fee system can lead to efficient outcomes. It implies that recipients have a right to a perfectly clean environment. The damage that remains when emissions are controlled efficiently is compensated for by the payment of a fee. The revenue from this fee can be used to help clean up the environment, to administer the effluent fee system, and to compensate those who are damaged by the remaining emissions.

Subsidies can also be effective. They imply, however, that the rights to the environment are owned by emitters. They may not be very efficient since providing subsidies to polluting and inefficient firms may help keep the firms viable when the appropriate outcome, economically and environmentally speaking, would be to allow their closure.

Transferable permits have similar advantages and disadvantages as effluent fees and can serve effectively to stimulate innovation since the firms involved stand to benefit directly from being able to sell off permits if they can reduce their pollutant output.

Integrated approaches allow for negotiated pollution prevention and the reduced use of toxic substances. Such approaches attempt to take the concerns and considerations of all stakeholders into account (including, for example, governmental regulatory concerns, the best interests of the public, the concerns of workers who might be exposed to toxic substances, the concerns of environmentalists and public health professionals, and the economic realities faced by the polluting firm) to attempt to create win-win situations. In this way, integrated approaches can help to work towards human health and environmental protection and a reduction in the use and release of damaging pollutants, while ensuring minimal loss of economic prosperity for firms.

It is likely that on a local or national level, a society will chose a combination of the environmental policy approaches described. Whatever set of policy options is selected or used, there is a need for constant monitoring by state agencies as well as concerned members of society (for example, nongovernmental organizations). Environmental and emission standards must be met so that the desired level of environmental quality can be obtained, while seeing to the need for equitable socio-economic development and the generation of wealth.

REFERENCES

Anderson, F. R., Kneese, A. V., Reed, P. D., Stevenson, R. B., & Taylor, S. (1977). *Environmental Improvement through Economic Incentives*. The Johns Hopkins University Press: Baltimore.

Brown, L., Pope, C. (1982). *Hazardous Waste in America*. Sierra Club Books: San Francisco.

Browner, C. M. (1993). Pollution Prevention Takes Center Stage. *EPA Journal*, September 1993.

Crandall, R. W. (1983). The environmental control problem. In: *Controlling Industrial Pollution: The Economics and Politics of Clean Air*, pp. 58–98. The Brookings Institute: Washington, DC.

Dales, J. H. (1968). *Pollution, Property, and Prices*. University of Toronto Press: Toronto.

Datsenko, I. I., Denisiuk, A. B., Doloshitsky, S. L., Tolmacheva, E. I., Dychok, L. A., & Plastunov, B. A. (1988). Effect of pollution of the atmospheric air on the health of children. *Med. Profess., 4:* 112–113.

Downing, P. B. (1984). *Environmental Economics and Policy*. Little, Brown and Company: Boston.

Environmental Protection Agency (EPA) (1984). *Risk Assessment and Management: Framework for Decision Making*. EPA: USA.

Finkel, A. (1990). *Confronting Uncertainty in Risk Management. Resources for the Future*. Center for Risk Management: Washington, DC.

Fischer, S., Dornbusch, R., & Schmalensee, R. (1988). *Introduction to Microeconomics* (2nd Edition). McGraw-Hill Book Company: USA.

Geiser, K. (1991). The Greening of Industry: Making the Transition to a Sustainable Economy. *Technology Review. September 1991*, pp. 65–72.

Gresser, J. (1975). The Japanese Act for the compensation of pollution-related health damage: An introductory assessment. *Environmental Law Review, 5*: 502–529.

Hemenway, D. (1988). *Prices and Choices*. Harper Business: New York.

Howe, C. (1991). An evaluation of U.S. air and water policies. *Environment, 33*: 11–15, 34–36.

Kling, D., Schaeffer, E. (1993). EPA's Flagship Program. *EPA Journal*, September 1993.

Kneese, A. (1960). *The Economics of Regional Water Quality Management*. Johns Hopkins University Press: Baltimore.

Kunreuther, H. (1991). Managing hazardous waste: Past, present and future. *Risk Analysis*, 11: 19–26.

Liroff, R. (1980). *Air Pollution Offsets*. The Conservation Foundation: New York.

Marth, E., Moose, J. R., Bencko, V., Tichacek, B., Sixl, W., Koeck, M., & Sixlvoigt, B. (1989). Air pollution emissions and changes in lung function. *Zentralbl. Hyg. Umweltmed. 188*: 439–448.

Noll, R. (1982). Implementing marketable emission permits. *American Economic Review, 71*: 120–124.

Portney, P. R. (1990). Air Pollution Policy. In: *Public Policies for Environmental Protection* (Portney PR, ed), chapter 2. Resources for the Future: Washington, DC.

Reilly, W. K. (1991). The new Clean Air Act: an environmental milestone. *EPA Journal, Jan/Feb 1991*: 2–4.

Roy, M., Gray, H. (1992). Toxics Use Reduction: The Critical Issues. *Pollution Prevention Review. Spring 1992.*

Russell, C. S., Harrington, W., & Vaughn, W. J. (1986). *Enforcing Pollution Control Laws. Resources for the Future*: Washington, DC.

Russell, M. (1987). Environmental protection for the 1990s and beyond. *Environment, 29*: 12–15, 33–37.

Shaikh, R. (1986). The dilemmas of advanced technology for the Third World. *Technology Review, April 1986*: 57–64.

Speth, G. J. (1990). Toward a North South compact for the environment. *Environment, 32*: 16–20, 40–43.

Stavins, R. N. (1989). Harnessing market forces to protect the environment. *Environment, 31*: 5–7, 28–35.

Stewart, R. B. (1985). Economics, Environment, and the limits of legal control. *Harvard Environmental Law Review, 9*: 4.

Tietenberg, T. H. (1985). *Emissions Trading: An Exercise in Reforming Pollution Policy. Resources for the Future*. Washington, DC.

Tyler Miller, G. (1990). *Living in the Environment*. Wadsworth Publishing: Belmont, California.

Zeckhauser, R. J., & Kip Viscusi, W. (1990). Risk within reason. *Science, 248*: 559–564.

26

Policies to Protect and Promote Workers' Health Are Necessary for Sustainable Human Development

Barry S. Levy and Kathleen M. Rest

Sustainable human development is a new development paradigm that puts people at the center of development, regards economic growth as a means and not an end, protects the life opportunities of future generations as well as the present generation, and respects the natural systems on which all life depends. Sustainable human development, in turn, depends on many resources, processes, and commitments, ranging from adequate education and employment to appropriate trade policies, and from primary health care to appropriate investment and equitable tax policies.

To a large extent, sustainable human development also depends upon a healthy workforce and safe work environments. While this may seem obvious, many developing countries—even those that claim to place a heavy emphasis on sustainable development—do little to ensure a healthy workforce and a safe workplace. In many of these countries, low priority is given to occupational health, a multidisciplinary field that includes a broad range of activities, such as exposure assessment and hazard prevention in the work environment, preventive and curative medical services, disease and injury surveillance, safety and ergonomics, worker education, and other related functions. Even *developed* countries often give inadequate attention to these issues.

Critical to ensuring a healthy workforce and safe work environments is the development and enforcement of various policies, ranging from regu-

---

The authors acknowledge the helpful suggestions of Mrs. Bernice Goelzer of the Office of Occupational Health, World Health Organization, Geneva.

lation of exposure limits for hazardous substances, standards for safe work practices, and programs of effective worker training to policies for the provision of health and safety services and the allocation of human and other resources to provide these services.

Barriers: There may be many reasons why nations fail to place sufficient importance on or give a high priority to a healthy and safe workforce. For example:

- Other health issues, from AIDS to maternal and child health, are seen as more important and in need of more immediate attention.
- The private business workplace is seen, by some, as beyond the scope of public health activities.
- Heavy emphasis is placed on economic development and the creation or maintenance of jobs—regardless of their safety and impact on worker well-being.
- Some people may believe that special emphasis on occupational health and safety will deter investment and steer multinational corporations to establish facilities elsewhere.
- Some may believe that programs to prevent occupational disease and injury are too costly, requiring human and financial resources, technological sophistication, and an infrastructure that are not available in-country.

All of these factors may hamper the recognition that *workers* are integral contributors to economic development. This fact is most dramatically observable in developing countries where labor-intensive industries and jobs are common. In these countries, where there is less infrastructure, less automation and technology at work, and less affluence, most of the wealth in society is created by the value added by workers.

If workers are injured or ill, their absence reduces productivity and earnings, and negatively affects the economy—even if there are other workers waiting to take their jobs. As many large corporations in *developed* countries have come to realize, it is in their enlightened self-interest to preserve and protect the health of their workers. Thus, many employers provide both safety programs and preventive and curative health services for their workers, often onsite. These services:

- Prevent health problems, thereby preserving and protecting workers' well-being and saving the company money—not only the expenses of medical and rehabilitative services, but also the costs of replacing an injured or ill worker.
- Control occupational and environmental hazards, thus protecting not only the health of workers in the facility, but also the health of people living near it, as well as the ambient environment.

- Enable workers who are ill or injured—from both occupational and nonoccupational factors—to receive prompt medical care, the quality of which the enterprise can monitor and influence.
- Enable the enterprise to maintain productivity and promote good morale among workers.
- Provide workers and managers an opportunity to work together for occupational safety and health, an area of mutual interest.

POLICIES THAT PROMOTE A HEALTHY WORKFORCE AND A SAFE WORK ENVIRONMENT

Public policies that are well designed and well implemented can promote a healthy workforce and a safe work environment, as well as facilitate adequate provision of health and safety services in—or near—the workplace. These policies can be grouped into the following categories: personnel and services, collaboration and support, prevention, participation, and rights. Illustrative examples of policies in each of these categories are given below.

Personnel and Services

Policies to Facilitate Training of Health and Safety Personnel: To ensure a healthy workforce and safe work environments, there needs to be adequate numbers of health and safety professionals must be trained to meet the occupational health and safety needs of workers and employers. These needs include the recognition, treatment, and prevention of occupational (and nonoccupational) illnesses and injuries as well as the establishment, maintenance, and improvement of policies and programs in the workplace to support these activities.

To meet these needs, the health and safety workforce must reflect several disciplines and provide expertise in medicine, nursing, safety, industrial hygiene, ergonomics, engineering, economics, epidemiology, toxicology, workplace design, human factors, and human resource management. Thus, national policies should encourage and provide the necessary support and incentives for training and deploying professionals with expertise in these areas. These may include training stipends and scholarships as well as economic incentives for employment of such professionals.

Equally important, national, local, and enterprise-based policies should encourage interaction, collaboration, and cooperation among these professionals. Too often, these experts work independently when effective solutions require interdisciplinary problem-solving and collaboration.

At present, some developing countries have a modest number of people who are adequately trained in these areas. In these countries, training often takes place in programs organized by government agencies, academic institutions, business and labor groups, and external aid organizations. However, in most developing countries, the amount and extent of professional training in health and safety is insufficient due to inadequacies in resources, such as facilities, trainers, and materials. Efforts to provide this infrastructure are needed in order to meet the health and safety needs of employers and workers.

Policies to Support a Linkage of Occupational Health Services with Primary Care: Despite encouragement by the International Labor Organization, the World Health Organization, and other groups for linking occupational health services and primary health care, most developing countries have not sufficiently exploited this potential. For example, primary care physicians and community health workers could be better trained to recognize potential risk, recommend preventive measures that promote and protect workers' health, and interact with appropriate bodies to ensure intervention and remedial action in the workplace. An occupational illness and injury surveillance system, drawing on information from primary health care providers, could be helpful in this regard. When it is not feasible to offer occupational health services, as is the case for many small employers, community-based primary care programs could provide many services to workers and managers at these workplaces if public policies encouraged and supported these programs in doing so.

Collaboration and Support

Policies to Promote Intersectoral and Interministerial Collaboration: Many units of government have some responsibility for or have an impact on the health and safety of workers. Yet, these units may seldom communicate, cooperate, and collaborate. In most developing countries, intersectoral collaboration among these ministries is usually inadequate. The ministries that may contribute the most to worker health and safety include: Labor (which may have overall responsibility for occupational health and safety as well as other important labor policies); Health (which has major responsibility for the treatment and prevention of illnesses and injuries); Agriculture (which often regulates the use of pesticides and other agrochemicals); Environment (which has the responsibility for environmental protection and pollution control); Commerce (which has responsibility for promoting business and trade); and Finance (which sets and enforces tax and other monetary policies); and Education (which may have some responsibility for job training).

There are some instances, however, of positive, although limited, collaboration. For example, in some developing countries, the Ministry of

Health assigns some of its physicians and nurses to the Ministry of Labor on a permanent basis to provide occupational health services. More often, however, there seems to be less than adequate collaboration among the ministries of agriculture, labor, and health concerning pesticide safety—a major problem in many developing countries. One could also argue that the most important need for ongoing communication and collaboration exists among those ministries concerned with economic development and commerce, on the one hand, and those concerned with human health and well-being and the environment, on the other. In most countries (developed *and* developing) policies are needed to improve this type of intersectoral communication, collaboration, and problem-solving.

Policies That Encourage Externally Based Organizations to Support Worker Health and Safety: In developing countries, it is important to examine the multinational corporations, external aid organizations, and other externally based organizations, such as the World Bank, in order to determine how they can be encouraged to support worker health and safety.

For example, multinational corporations can be encouraged or even mandated to provide the same level of worker protection and types of health and safety programs and services that they provide in their home countries. This would help upgrade the standard of occupational health and safety in the host country for other enterprises as well.

External aid organizations account for much aid to developing countries, often in the form of education, training, and technical assistance—approaches that are also relevant for occupational health. However, very little of this external aid has been used to promote worker health and safety, in part because these organizations do not want to intrude into private industries and businesses in other countries. These aid organizations need to better understand the relationship between development, on the one hand, and worker health, workplace safety, and general public health, on the other. When they do so, they are likely to establish aid policies and programs that attend to and complement all of these factors.

Lending and other policies of the World Bank can have a profound impact on a nation's economy and, in turn, on the health and safety of its workers. World Bank policies, for example, could require recipient countries to take measures to promote worker health and safety as a condition of participating in projects that are funded by the Bank.

Many external organizations look to the host country government for direction on what projects to support and what policies are consistent with national goals and priorities. If a host country's government is forthright in communicating with the external organization about its occupational health and safety problems and needs, that organization is more likely to factor occupational safety and health into its projects and operate in a manner that supports workers' health.

Prevention

Policies to Ensure Adequate Provision of Resources for Preventive Services: In many developing (and developed) countries, inadequate resources are allocated to preventive services, especially for working, apparently healthy, adults. Because worker health is an essential factor in a country's development, preventive services are critical. Resources should be allocated not only to protect workers from workplace hazards, but also from such nonoccupational hazards as tobacco and motor vehicle risks.

Policies to Promote Primary Prevention in the Work Environment: Policies are needed to promote "anticipatory prevention" in the workplace in order to avoid unhealthy, unsafe, and polluting conditions up front. Accident and pollution prevention should be built into the planning and design stages of new equipment, work processes, and workplaces and into plans to change these production processes or work environments. Retrofitting existing facilities and processes is much more costly and less efficient. Anticipatory preventive actions, as described in the WHO publication *Hazard Prevention and Control in the Work Environment—Prevention and Control Exchange (PACE)* (1995), should include:

- Occupational and environmental health impact assessments, prior to the design and installation of any new facility . . . ;
- Selection of the most suitable and safest (least hazardous as well as least polluting) technology, as well as an environmentally appropriate location;
- Proper design, with the required control technology as an integral part of the project, including provisions for safe handling and disposal of the resulting effluent and waste;
- Elaboration of guidelines and training on the correct operation of processes, including on safe work practices and emergency procedures; and
- Creation of an effective joint health and safety structure involving workers and their representatives.

Policies That Promote Development and Enforcement of Appropriate Standards: Occupational health and safety standards must address the country's needs and be appropriately stringent to meet these needs. Moreover, they must be enforced adequately. Guidance for standards development can be obtained from many organizations, such as the International Labor Organization (ILO) and the European Union. For example, ILO has compiled and published *Occupational Exposure Limits for Airborne Toxic Substances* (Occupational Safety and Health Series, No. 37, 3rd Edition, Geneva, 1991). Policy makers must be trained to assess the need for specific standards—gathering appropriate surveillance and risk assessment data from within the country, obtaining needed technical information, eliciting information from the stakeholders, and following developments in other countries. Among a number of information sources that may be useful in this regard are the *Environmental Health Criteria Series* publications of the Geneva-based International Program for Chemical Safety (IPCS) that provide risk assessments on almost 200 individual chemicals.

The standards development *process* is also important; policy makers may need to learn how best to involve and obtain input from all concerned parties, especially those most likely to be affected by the standards—that is, workers and employers.

Enforcement is critical. It requires a sufficient number of adequately trained individuals; their access to workplaces; their freedom to intervene, assist, and issue appropriate penalties, if necessary; a judicial system that supports fair enforcement of laws and regulations; and, most of all, the political will to ensure that laws and regulations are enforced.

Policies That Focus on Prevention for Individual Workers: Clinical preventive services, screening programs, and rehabilitation and disability care all comprise the spectrum of preventive services for individual workers. Policies can be designed and implemented to provide these primary, secondary, and tertiary preventive services through the workplace and/or community-based care.

Policies to Facilitate Collection and Analysis of Surveillance Data on Groups of Workers: The identification of high-risk industries, occupations, employers, and workers requires the systematic collection and analysis of data. Without policies to establish and maintain surveillance systems to collect health and illness data on groups of workers, the data needed to design appropriate intervention strategies will not likely be generated. Data sources are varied, each with strengths and limitations. Surveillance systems should be designed to access multiple sources.

Policies That Regulate the Import of Hazardous Substances and Hazardous Industries: Government ministries can work together to prevent or restrict the importation of hazardous substances, technologies, and industries. This form of primary prevention can be highly effective, eliminating the need for costly—and perhaps unpopular—solutions later.

Many developing countries restrict the importation of extremely hazardous pesticides to some degree. However, most do not have a comprehensive policy on importation of hazardous substances. Many other countries, desperate for hard currency have been tempted to import hazardous substances, including hazardous and radioactive wastes, or very hazardous industries, against their better judgment. (See Chapter 17, by Joe LaDou.)

Policies That Provide Economic Incentives to Promote Worker Health and Safety: Many countries have found that economic incentives can supplement efforts to protect both worker health and the environment. Although traditional "command and control" policies, such as standards and regulations, are the backbone of these efforts, other economic strategies are available and may be effective supplements, especially in market-based economies. These include grants, loans, and tax credits to invest in prevention as well as charges and taxes on emissions and certain inputs or hazardous products. Experience in countries that are members of the Organization of Economic Cooperation and Development (OECD) has found that a mix of policy investments is most effective.

Participation

Policies That Promote Labor Organizations: Labor unions and other worker organizations have often been advocates of worker health, safety, and well-being. A country's labor policies should ensure that unions are free to organize workers and to campaign for safe work environments. The freedom of unions to organize workers, to help monitor workplace health and safety, and to work with appropriate authorities to identify, evaluate, and control workplace hazards can have a significant and positive impact on overall occupational health and safety in a country. Labor unions can also play vital roles in worker training and education, encouraging participation in screening and surveillance programs, monitoring the quality and acceptability of health services, and, as discussed below, participating in problem-solving, decision-making, and policy-development processes.

Policies That Promote Workers' Participation in Decision-Making Processes: Governments—as well as enterprises and individuals—are constantly confronted by many problems, needs, and demands. Prioritization of need and the appropriate allocation of resources are difficult problems. It is important that worker health and safety not be lost among the issues of concern in the prioritization and resource allocation process.

Decisions that affect workers, their families, and communities should be made with their involvement or the involvement of their representatives. However, in many developing (and developed) countries, policies that affect workers' health are determined by government ministry officials, company officers, and workplace managers, with little, if any, input from the labor community. Workers can greatly contribute to the recognition of workplace hazards and should participate in developing strategies to reduce or eliminate them. They have the most at stake in ensuring that a workplace is healthful and safe. Participation in decision making by workers or their representatives promotes a healthy and safe workforce.

Their active support of and participation in workplace safety programs is critical.

Worker participation can take many forms. In the workplace, it can include (a) joint labor-management health and safety committees; (b) collective bargaining, a process that can lead to agreements concerning occupational health and safety; (c) participation in developing hazard prevention and control programs; (d) participation in safety audits and inspections; and (e) worker input into other policies that affect health (policies on production, inputs, health care, disability, and social issues). Beyond the workplace, worker participation is needed in the development of regulatory policy, the enforcement process, the design and implementation of worker education and training programs and materials, and the development of other public policies that affect their health and well-being, including labor, development, and a variety of social policies.

Rights

Policies That Ensure Workers' Rights: Recognition and protection of workers' rights have an important bearing on their health and on the safety of the workplaces in which they work. These rights include, among others, a legally accepted right to know about the hazards of substances they use and the conditions in which they work, and a right to refuse hazardous work—rights that are increasingly commonplace in developed countries. In addition, workers need to know about their rights and the avenues open to them to secure these rights. Laws and regulations can also help to prevent workplace discrimination against and exploitation of women, minority group members, children, and the economically and socially disadvantaged.

ACTIONS TO SUPPORT POLICY DEVELOPMENT

It is much more difficult to develop and implement policies to promote workers' health and safety than it is to theorize about them. Policy development starts with a genuine commitment to improve workers' health and safety and/or to improve the health of enterprises, which, in most cases, requires a healthy workforce. Policy development also requires a genuine commitment to obtain the necessary information and gain the popular and political support for policies to accomplish these ends.

A number of actions can facilitate and promote policy development to improve and maintain workers' health. These include:

- Alerting government officials, investors, and employers to the links between a healthy workforce and a healthy business, between a healthy workforce and economic development, and between a healthy workforce and sustainable human development;

- Establishing and maintaining participatory processes through which workers, their representatives, and other advocates for their health can influence decision makers;
- Helping workers and their representatives enhance their knowledge of occupational safety and health and their ability to participate in the policy- and decision-making processes of public agencies and private enterprises;
- Working with the appropriate ministries and academic institutions to develop an adequate supply of health and safety professionals, with an emphasis on capabilities for hazard prevention and control;
- Reviewing surveillance and other data to better determine workplace health and safety needs and how these needs can be best addressed;
- Promoting awareness among other professional groups; and
- Establishing and maintaining international linkages—between and among universities, governmental agencies, labor unions, trade or business associations, and nongovernmental organizations (NGOs)—that can support individuals and organizations as well as improve the flow of information concerning policies, their implementation, and their impact.

CONCLUSION

These and other creative efforts can help ensure that strong policies to protect and promote worker health are developed, implemented, and enforced, and that sustainable economic and human development become more than just good intentions.

BACKGROUND READING

Africa and Asia-Pacific Newsletters on Occupational Health and Safety. Published by the Finnish Institute of Occupational Health, Helsinki, Finland.

Baker, E., & Matte, T. "Surveillance of Occupational Illness and Injury" in Halperin, W., Baker Jr., E. (Eds.) *Public Health Surveillance.* New York, Van Nostrand Reinhold, *1992*: 178–194.

Christiani, D. C., Durvasula, R., & Myers, J. "Occupational Health in Developing Countries: Review of Research Needs," *American Journal of Industrial Medicine 1990; 17*: 393–401.

Elgstrand, K. R. Occupational Safety and Health in Developing Countries, Editorial. *American Journal of Industrial Medicine 1985; 8*: 91–93.

Feachem, R. G. A., Kjellstrom, T., Murray, C. J. L. et al. *The Health of Adults in the Developing World*. Oxford: Oxford University Press, 1992.

International Journal of Occupational and Environmental Health 1995; *1*(2): 76–222.

"International labour standards" and "Training" in *World Labour Report: 2*. Geneva: International Labour Office, 1985.

Jeyaratnam, J. Health problems of pesticide use in the Third World. *British Journal of Industrial Medicine 1985; 42*: 505–506.

Jeyaratnam, J., editor. *Occupational Health in Developing Countries*. Oxford University Press, Oxford, 1992.

Levy, B. S., Kjellstrom, T., Forget, G. et al. Ongoing research in occupational health and environmental epidemiology in developing countries. *Archives of Environmental Health 1992; 47*: 231–235.

Levy, B. S., Wegman, D. H. (Eds.). *Occupational Health: Recognizing and Preventing Work-Related Disease, 3rd ed*. Boston: Little, Brown, 1995.

Phoon, W. O. *Occupational Health in Developing Countries of Asia*, Southeast Asia Medical Information Center, 1985.

PART V
Selected Case Studies

27

Developing a Global Professional Network to Strengthen Training and Research in Environmental Health

Tord Kjellström and Carlos Corvalán

INTRODUCTION

The development of national programs for the prevention and control of environmental hazards has not in general kept pace with the increase in environmental health problems brought about by rapid industrialization and urbanization. At the same time, in many developing countries, the traditional health hazards of poverty (lack of basic shelter, sanitation and safe water supply) remain as major causes of ill health (WHO, 1992). The introduction of new technology and the increasing use of potentially hazardous technologies, such as agrochemicals, create conflict between desired economic and social developments, and the achievement of environmental quality and good health.

In order to break this pattern, national programs for the prevention and control of environmental health hazards must be strengthened. This capacity building should be concerned with improvements in information exchange and methodology, promotion of policy formulation, improvements in national institutional capacities, and training at all levels. Effective activity in these areas will depend on environmental epidemiology as a means of securing the necessary information concerning the links between environment and health.

In addition, research in the field of environmental health, within the framework of technical cooperation, is required to encourage the sharing and exchange of skills, experience and resources. This will in turn increase the use of up-to-date technology and methods in studies carried out in developing countries.

In 1987 WHO prepared a strategy for technical cooperation with Member States on the control of environmental hazards. The Global Environmental Epidemiology Network (GEENET) was created by WHO's Division of Environmental Health to implement this strategy. The aims of GEENET are to assist professionals involved in the prevention and control of health problems arising from environmental hazards, by strengthening education, training and applied research in environmental epidemiology (WHO, 1994a).

The report of the WHO Commission on Health and Environment (*Our Planet, Our Health*; WHO, 1992) was WHO's main contribution to the United Nations Conference on Environment and Development (UNCED) and includes conclusions and recommendations concerning priority issues in environmental epidemiology. *Agenda 21*—the main report from UNCED—also includes a series of recommendations related to environmental health (UN, 1993). Based upon these recommendations and the accumulated experience of WHO, a *WHO Global Strategy for Health and Environment* was developed (WHO, 1994b). Training, education and research have a major role in this strategy, and the GEENET project is a key component of the implementation of the *WHO Global Strategy*. The Network activities implement several of the recommendations made by UNCED and are also contributing in an important way to the United Nations' *Capacity 21* program.

GOALS AND OBJECTIVES

The overall development objective of the GEENET project is to strengthen education, training and applied research in developing countries on health problems caused by environmental hazards, and in this way support sustainable development.

The specific objectives are:

(i) to create and maintain a Global Environmental Epidemiology Network of people in government institutes, universities, industry and nongovernmental organizations, who are involved in teaching and supervision of applied research (field studies of exposed humans) on the health effects of environmental hazards. The development of National Networks on a broader basis will also be encouraged and facilitated;

(ii) to identify and support in each Member State, one or several (in selected major cities) main libraries, willing to establish Environmental Health Reference Collections with "essential information" on environmental health hazards and their control;

(iii) to establish and strengthen, at the local level, education and training on environmental health hazards and their control; this will include the strengthening of programs and courses in universities, short training workshops for public health staff and seminars on specific problems. GEENET will provide standard "training kits," support for national workshops to test and demonstrate training materials and approaches, and opportunities for "training of trainers" in order to make the new local activities sustainable;

(iv) to encourage and facilitate new and improved applied research using epidemiology to study and resolve local environmental health problems; this will include provision of advice and information on methodology, funding, similar studies elsewhere and research recommendations; establishment of cooperative projects and promotion of environmental health hazard research to funding agencies.

HISTORICAL PERSPECTIVES

In 1987 the first plans for GEENET were developed including membership invitations and application forms. These were initially distributed through WHO regional offices and later invitations were sent to a variety of environmental and public health agencies and institutions.

1988 was the first full year of GEENET activities. Priority information materials were distributed, and a standard format for a national training workshop on Environmental Epidemiology was developed. In addition, an inventory of existing basic training materials was produced and the preparation of new training materials was initiated. A regional workshop using these materials was held in Kuala Lumpur for countries in the Western Pacific Region and a national workshop was held in Cuba. By the end of 1988 GEENET had about 500 members.

During 1989 membership reached 800 and the first list of members, their interest and experience was distributed. Microcomputer procedures for the management of GEENET were established and a manual for the standard software used in GEENET was prepared and printed. National training workshops were held in Chile and the People's Republic of China and the standard workshop curriculum and training materials were translated to Spanish. A training text on Basic Epidemiology was drafted and preparations for testing the text were made. A number of information materials on specific environmental hazards were distributed to GEENET members in accordance with their interests. This included relevant materials from Member States, and nongovernmental organizations.

The number of GEENET members increased to about 1,300 at the end of 1990. Network membership lists and microcomputer diskettes were distributed to members. The microcomputer procedures were further developed. Plans for development of "Environmental Health Reference Collections" (EHRCs) were consolidated in discussions with librarians and public health staff in Chile, Argentina, Brazil, Kenya, Mauritius, Malaysia and Viet Nam. Agreements were reached with UNEP, ILO and some other international agencies concerning provision of free materials for the reference centers.

The standard workshop curriculum was updated and a number of teaching examples were developed. National one-week training workshops were held in Argentina, Brazil, India, Kenya and Viet Nam. A collection of environmental epidemiology reviews on key teaching topics was published in the *World Health Statistics Quarterly*. An inventory of ongoing environmental and occupational epidemiology research projects was prepared. Priority research areas for each country were reviewed in conjunction with country missions to Argentina, Brazil, Chile, Kenya, Mexico, and Viet Nam.

By the end of 1991 GEENET had grown to 1,500 members. The EPIINFO epidemiological software was promoted and supplied on request to members. Libraries were provided with a printed listing of the "Environmental Health Reference Collection." An inventory of newsletters was prepared and existing inventories were updated and reprinted. A special newsletter for GEENET members was prepared.

National training workshops were held in 1991 in Bolivia, the Gambia, Indonesia, Mexico, Peru, Poland and Portugal. Several training materials were prepared and a consultation on environmental epidemiology training was held at WHO, Geneva. In terms of research promotion, a conference on the *Epidemiological, Social and Technical Aspects of Indoor Air Pollution from Biomass Fuels* was held and the proceedings distributed to members. In collaboration with the United States Environmental Protection Agency (USEPA) a review of the potential for environmental epidemiology in Asia was carried out and a similar more detailed review in Latin America was started.

By the end of 1992 GEENET membership had reached 1,700 members, representing over 100 countries. Microcomputer diskettes with the GEENET files and the accompanying minimanuals were provided on request. A GEENET document collection, consisting of all network documents, was prepared and provided to WHO regional offices, relevant WHO programs and other key institutions such as funding agencies.

The list of essential literature sources on environmental and occupational health titled "Reference Information for Environmental Health Training and Research" was sent to all GEENET members with an introductory letter to the librarian of their institutions. The members were encouraged to contact their library regarding the establishment of an "Environmental Health Reference Collection" (EHRC) which would give the GEENET members improved access to the reference materials from WHO, ILO, UNEP, UNESCO, etc. The librarians who responded that they were interested in establishing an EHRC were included in a new Global Environmental Library Network (GELNET).

A series of problem-based training exercises for environmental epidemiology was published with separate versions for tutors and students. In addition, a training manual for environmental disease outbreak investigations was published, and an anthology of training case studies of environmental disease episodes was also published. A training kit for a one-day workshop on chemical hazards was completed. Work started on a new specialized text on environmental epidemiology, to be used as the main teaching source in more advanced workshops on environmental epidemiology research methods.

National training workshops were held in Costa Rica, Venezuela, Philippines, Latvia, and Colombia. Additional national or provincial workshops (for which GEENET provided training materials only) were held in Argentina (2 workshops), Poland, Chile, Indonesia (2 workshops), and Viet Nam (3 workshops).

During 1993 electronic mail was tested as a distribution method for membership lists and other GEENET information. Membership had reached over 1,800 and information collected about members was used to better identify their expertise, and to separate them into "active members" and "observers." Plans and funding proposals for National Environmental Health Networks were developed. The principal aim of these networks is to maintain and support local and national environmental epidemiology activities initiated via the GEENET project. Initial efforts were made in Nicaragua, India, the Philippines and Viet Nam to set up such networks.

GEENET continued to supply libraries that had decided to establish EHRCs with key reference and promotional materials. Negotiations with other international agencies to add further useful free material to the EHRC were continued. Three issues of the *Environmental Health* newsletter and three issues of the *GEENET Update* newsletter were issued to members in the appropriate language (English, French or Spanish).

The final editing of the new training text *Basic Epidemiology* was completed and made available as a WHO monograph (Beaglehole et al., 1993a). A *Teacher's Guide to Basic Epidemiology*—including a "chart-book" with presentations in graph form of environmental health concepts and data for easy use as overhead transparencies in teaching—was also produced (Beaglehole et al., 1993b). National one-week training workshops were held in Ethiopia, Gabon, Venezuela, Nicaragua, and Thailand. Advanced and more specialized workshops were held in Viet Nam and Malaysia.

Collaborative research projects developed jointly by GEENET members with UNEP, IARC, the World Bank and other agencies were promoted. (Topics and countries covered included air pollution in China, air pollution and asthma in Chile and Mexico, water pollution and metal poisoning in Brazil and China, and solar UV radiation and cataracts in India.) A WHO/USEPA project to review environmental epidemiology research needs and opportunities in Latin America was completed. The report

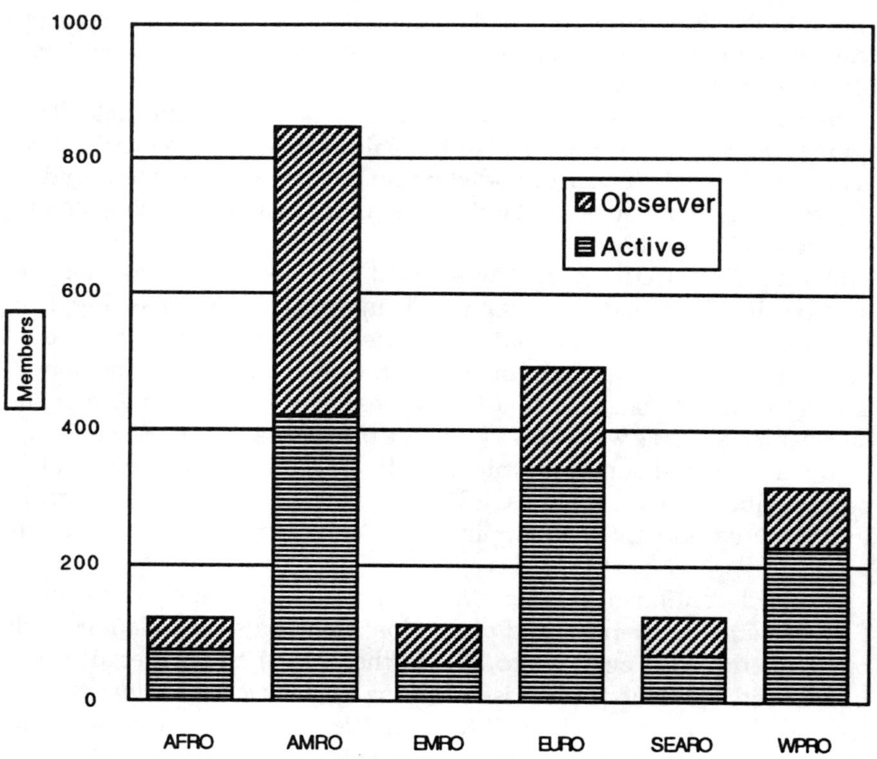

WHO Regions—AFRO: Africa; AMRO: Americas; EMRO: Eastern Mediterranean; EURO: Europe; SEARO: South East Asia; WPRO: Western Pacific.

FIGURE 27.1 GEENET members by WHO region, 1994.

highlights the need to study and remedy the effects of air pollution and contamination with metals, and basic sanitation deficiencies.

At the end of 1994, GEENET had over 2,000 members from more than 100 countries (Figure 27.1). Workshops were carried out in Africa, Asia and the Middle East. Electronic communications with and among members were intensified, and information dissemination via the Internet was further developed.

NETWORKS IN ACTION

In an increasingly complex world, where information grows exponentially, specialized networks of individuals provide a means to abstract, synthesize and link information which can then be shared among network members, and later disseminated outside the net.

Three simple schematic network linkages (Wallis, 1990) can be used to explain the functioning of the Global Networks (Figure 27.2a, b, c). During an initial stage, most networks function as a hub-and-spoke linkage (27.2a). This was the mode of operation of GEENET during the first two years. As information about activities in different parts of the world, as well as membership lists, distributed from the hub, the network began to establish links among members (27.2b). This stage (known as the rim-effect, where participants begin to collaborate with each other as well as with the hub), occurred around 1989. Later, sub-networks at the national and regional level were developed in some places, generating a new level of activities (27.2c). An example of a major sub-network is GEENET-*Euro*, which aims at establishing electronic linkages with all its members in Western, Central and Eastern Europe.

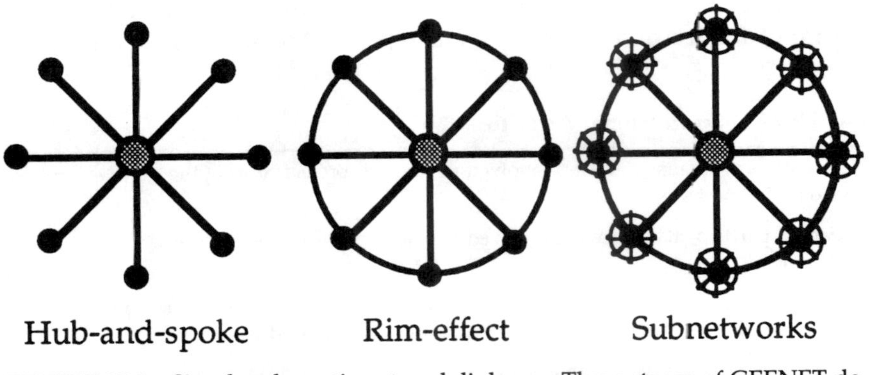

FIGURE 27.2 Simple schematic network linkages: Three stages of GEENET development. (Adapted from Wallis, 1990.)

Results of a GEENET Members' Survey

During 1992–93 a survey was carried out among GEENET members in order to evaluate the use and value of the Network. A total of 494 members were covered and approximately equal numbers of developed and developing country members returned completed questionnaires. Following is a summary of the major findings of this survey.

Professional Activities

The participants were asked about their professional activities. A large proportion of those surveyed reported that they had worked on one or more research projects during the previous 12 months, and that they had been involved in teaching during the same period. Also, a large proportion had published one or more reports or articles relevant to occupational and environmental health (Table 27.1).

Contact Among Members

Another important feature of the Network is the opportunities it provides for establishing new contacts. This is of particular interest to developing country members who often work in greater isolation than their developed country counterparts. Table 27.2 shows that nearly half of the participants used the Network to contact other members for joint activities and that the majority of contacts were made by participants from developing countries. Of those who established contact with other members, many had established contact with at least three other members, and some with more than ten.

The participants were asked about their principal reasons for contacting other members. The most common was information exchange, but others included seeking collaboration for research or training purposes and seeking input for research proposals and reports. About 90 specific projects

TABLE 27.1 Professional Activities

Percent of participants who were involved in research projects during the previous 12 months	84
Percent of participants who were involved in teaching during the previous 12 months	80
Percent of those participants who were involved in teaching during the previous 12 months, who taught at least 30 days during the same period	36
Percent of participants who published at least one report/article relevant to occupational and environmental health during the previous 24 months	78

TABLE 27.2 Contact among GEENET Members

Percent of participants who established contact with other GEENET members (n = 219)	44
Percent of participants who established contact who are from developing countries	61
Percent of participants who established contact who contacted at least 3 other GEENET members	62
Percent of contacts which aimed at information exchange	80
Percent of contacts which aimed at research	25
Percent of contacts which aimed at training	24

were listed, most often involving collaboration between members in a developing country and another in a developed country. Other reasons mentioned for contacting GEENET members included organization of workshops; fund raising; student, teacher and personnel exchanges; recruitment; sabbatical opportunities; improvement of library services, and distribution and exchange of documents.

GEENET Workshops

At the start of this survey, 21 national training workshops (based on the one-week training course *Introduction to Environmental Epidemiology*) had already been held. GEENET workshops aim to strengthen capacity in environmental epidemiology by:

- reinforcing and increasing the participants' knowledge of basic epidemiological principles and methods;
- reinforcing and increasing the participant's knowledge of environmental and occupational hazards and health effects, with emphasis on assessment, and prevention and control activities;
- encouraging and facilitating future collaboration among participants in order to assess, prevent and control environmental and occupational health hazards in their countries; and,
- encouraging participants who have teaching responsibilities to apply the knowledge gained from workshops in local training activities.

Sixty-eight of the survey participants (14%) had taken part in national training workshops. They commented that their technical skills in environmental health and epidemiology had improved as a result, that the workshop had offered a good opportunity for exchanging ideas and experiences in environmental health-related areas, had stimulated the creation of contacts with other researchers and research institutions, and helped initiate collaboration on research projects. The workshops also helped many participants to improve their teaching skills.

In some countries, additional training in related areas has been organized. For example, in Indonesia, the GEENET training workshop led to two additional environmental epidemiology workshops, organized by GEENET members within Indonesia, and paid for entirely by the Indonesian government. Another example comes from Chile, where a model project to strengthen training in environmental health in all university faculties was started in 1992 by GEENET members in Concepción. The results will be used to promote similar training in other Latin American countries.

Libraries

As mentioned earlier, the Network's objectives include identification and strengthening of libraries in developing countries. This involves improving the holdings of environmental health literature, and ensuring that these are readily accessible to health professionals and students. This is being carried out through the creation of *Environmental Health Reference Collections*. GEENET members have been encouraged to contact their libraries to promote these ideas. The survey asked members whether they had contacted their libraries as suggested.

About half of the participants reported that they had contacted their library to promote the GEENET document *Reference Information for Environmental Training and Research* (Table 27.3). Of those who had contacted their library, 71% reported that their library was planning to develop an EHRC. The collaboration with libraries has also resulted in other activities such as the creation of databanks or registers of available documents; translation of documents; creation of document centers within libraries; creation of epidemiological information centers; improved documentation distribution to environmental and occupational health professionals; and collaboration between libraries, research institutes and universities.

An example of new developments in this area came from Argentina, where a regional reference library of medical ecology and environmental health has been created with the collaboration of the central library of the

TABLE 27.3 Libraries

Percent of participants who had made contact with their libraries (n = 243)	52
Percent of contacts aimed at developing an *Environmental Health Reference Collection*	71
Percent of contacts aimed at additional new collaborative activities with libraries	55

Centro Medico de Mar Del Plata. Materials received from GEENET provided the stimulus for this collection, which is being used to support new training courses in environmental health and ecology for postgraduate students.

New Training Activities

GEENET members were asked if GEENET materials and/or activities had encouraged them to start any new training activities; 41 percent of the survey participants reported that they had done so. Those who had started new training activities had worked on adapting course content, arranging new training courses, modifying training courses (in accordance with recommendations made in GEENET documents and by incorporating training exercises distributed by GEENET), and developing training through provision of field experience.

About 54 percent of the participants who had initiated new training activities, mentioned that they had used GEENET documents as training materials, in particular the training exercises and the *Basic Epidemiology* textbook. This textbook and other training materials are now being translated into more than ten languages (including Chinese, Farsi, French, Hungarian, Indonesian, Polish, Portuguese, Russian, Spanish, Swedish, and Vietnamese), often with the assistance of local GEENET members. This is expected to further facilitate local training activities.

New Research Activities

The participants were also asked whether they had initiated new research activities after having received GEENET documents; 18 percent of the participants reported that they had done so.

Those participants who answered that they had initiated new research activities, mentioned areas such as collaboration on research projects (establishing collaboration between researchers, research institutions and universities); sharing of information concerning research methods, results and documents; and exchanging and commenting on research proposals and documents.

Future Activities

The participants were asked to make suggestions for future GEENET activities that could strengthen and support members' work. The most common suggestion was for a GEENET inventory of funding resources for research (59%). Nearly a quarter of the participants indicated that they would find it helpful if the Network produced research methods guidelines relating specifically to the epidemiology of pesticides. The next most common suggestion was for guidelines for the interpretation of epidemiological data (12%).

Willingness to Contribute to Future Network Activities

The participants were asked whether they were interested in participating in certain activities, to be promoted by GEENET in the future. Table 27.4 shows the proportion of the participants who reported that they were interested in the activities proposed.

Approximately two-thirds of the participants indicated that they would be willing to pilot test new training materials, and microcomputer software; the majority of the participants are willing to assist other members by reading and commenting upon research proposals and reports, and more than half indicated that they would be willing to prepare bibliographies and summary reviews.

Comments on how GEENET Could Further Promote Environmental Health Training and Research

Several participants asked whether GEENET could assist with publication of research findings in environmental epidemiology, particularly those of developing country researchers.

A number of participants described professional isolation as a major constraint, particularly in countries where postage and telephone charges are high or international travel restricted, or for whom the cost of international travel is prohibitively high. Several suggested that GEENET should include electronic mail addresses in its participants list and establish a bulletin board accessible by electronic mail, which members could use to contact one another and to access information about environmental health matters.

TABLE 27.4 Willingness to Assist with Future Network Activities

Percent of participants who are willing to pilot test new training materials ($n = 343$)	75
Percent of participants who are willing to pilot test microcomputer software ($n = 336$)	75
Percent of participants who are willing to assist other members by reading and commenting upon research proposals and reports ($n = 363$)	81
Percent of participants who are willing to prepare bibliographies and summary reviews ($n = 257$)*	59

*Referred mainly to subjects such as air pollution (mentioned most frequently); hazardous waste disposal; heavy metal pollution; industrial environmental hazards; occupational epidemiology; pesticide poisoning; and water pollution.

Some members suggested that GEENET should produce a document on how to respond to environmental health "incidents". Such a document would deal not so much with the investigation of causes (which is covered in training texts) but rather with how to manage acute episodes. Environmental health law was another area mentioned by a number of respondents as an important issue, and one with which GEENET could usefully become involved.

Discussion of Survey Results

Of all the materials distributed by GEENET, the training materials, particularly the problem-based exercises, were the best received. These have been used in a variety of settings, and according to respondents, more such training materials would be welcome.

This survey has also shown that the Network contributes to increased collaboration, both within and between research disciplines, and countries/regions. Members have often initiated activities that go beyond the immediate services offered. The survey results also demonstrate the willingness of members to get involved in additional GEENET activities.

Clearly GEENET has chosen an appropriate path for its activities, and has great potential for future strengthening of networking and collaboration among environmental health professionals in both developing and developed countries.

FUTURE NETWORK DIRECTIONS

The establishment of the electronic network brings about new challenges coupled with enormous possibilities. Fast and inexpensive linkages are already available to members connected to the Internet. As the Internet continues to grow, increasing access to GEENET materials, updates and ongoing information is achieved.

Electronic-based activities include further development of the Gopher server in order to include all materials available to GEENET members as well as materials belonging to the other Networks. These can be downloaded and printed locally by the users. The Gopher is accessible to all persons with Internet connection and thus not restricted to Network members. In addition, other forms of data dissemination, such as the World Wide Web, are under development.

Electronic mail-based training in environmental epidemiology is at a planning stage. This will allow the dissemination of short courses, of one- or two-week duration, to a wide audience, and at minimal cost. The basic setup consists of one or two teachers, sending daily information, via Email, to students who have registered by sending their E-mail addresses. During the course period, students need to have access to and log into their computers on a daily basis. Course materials and simple "tests" are E-mailed to the students. Completed "test" forms can be checked automatically (if multiple choice questions were included), and a correct answer sheet mailed the following day. Questions from students are encouraged and a selection is made by the teachers and E-mailed to all with answers. E-mail contact is also encouraged among students and a complete E-mail list can be made available during the course. If adequately advertised, such a course can cover hundreds or even thousands of students with similar effort.

An electronic-based journal, giving emphasis to research from developing countries can become operational as soon as the Internet covers a minimum number of cities within developing countries. The Internet is growing rapidly in most continents with the exception of Africa. The journal will allow the exchange of information, establish links among researchers, learning of ongoing research and getting fast feedback regarding their work. The Internet allows easy transfer of data as well, making possible the analysis of data by international experts, and the preparation of joint papers by researchers who have never met physically. It is expected that this journal will help increase and improve research in environmental epidemiology in many developing countries.

The growth of electronic networks will help disseminate useful information in many areas to remote parts of the world. However, one cannot rely on market pressure to extend the Internet to the least developed countries. An international effort should be initiated to extend electronic networks to all countries in order to obtain a global benefit of this technology.

It should be emphasized that, for the foreseaable future, information distribution and communication among many of the GEENET members will still depend on printed materials and traditional ways of communication. Those Network members who suffer from professional isolation and have very limited access to key information sources are least likely to be able to gain access to electronic mail and other forms of electronic-based communications in the near future. GEENET will continue to cater to their needs by distributing printed information.

CONCLUSIONS

The establishment of the Global Networks by WHO has been of importance for the strengthening of training and research in environmental health, and particularly so for developing countries. Training materials developed and distributed by GEENET have been very successful and have resulted in a large number of workshops and related training activities in many countries. At present, with over 2,000 members in more than 100 countries, GEENET continues to expand its activities, and continues to evaluate new ways of further developing its activities.

The Network has been indispensable in its contribution to increased collaboration, within and between the related research disciplines in environment and health, and between countries/regions.

There is still an enormous potential for future strengthening of networking and collaboration among environmental health professionals in both developing and developed countries, which will be greatly enhanced by the expanding effort toward electronic networking. However, there will still be an important role for more traditional means of communication and for information supply in printed form.

REFERENCES

Beaglehole, R., Bonita, R., Kjellström, T. *Basic Epidemiology*. WHO, Geneva, 1993a.

Beaglehole, R., Bonita, R., Kjellström, T. *Teachers' Guide for Basic Epidemiology*. WHO, Geneva, 1993b.

United Nations. *Agenda 21—The United Nations Programme of Action from Rio*. UN, 1993.

WHO. *Our Planet, Our Health*. Report on the WHO Commission of Health and the Environment. Geneva, WHO, 1992.

WHO. GEENET progress report. Doc. WHO/EHG/94, 19, 1994a.

WHO. Healthy and productive lives in harmony with nature: A WHO global strategy for health and environment. Doc. WHO/EHE/94.1, 1994b.

Wallis, J. A. N. Network experiences in development research, education and training. Economic Development Institute of The World Bank, 1990.

28

Leadership for Environment and Development (LEAD) International: A New Force in Environment, Development, and Health

Al Binger and Gurinder S. Shahi

INTRODUCTION

The concept of sustainable development integrates a range of important implicit concepts. For development to be sustainable, it should: cause minimal damage and destruction to the environment; lead to opportunities for individuals participating in it to generate sustainable livelihoods; promote the establishment of circumstances and patterns of behavior which minimize risk to individual and ecological well-being and health; and not occur at the expense of future options.

The problems and dilemmas facing humankind today call for creative, effective solutions which maximize broad-based participation in crafting these solutions. While developing countries need to find ways to deal with rapidly growing populations and rising consumption of natural resources, developed countries need to recognize and initiate the process of rectifying the fundamental unsustainability of current economic trends and consumption patterns. In many countries, the lack of a skilled human resource pool or an effective mechanism for the exchange of ideas impedes responsive action. Professionals who are committed to sustainable development face many challenges: difficult working conditions, inadequate information resources, resistance to changing "traditional" economic and social paradigms, and little contact with colleagues in related sectors and in other countries.

Recognizing the fundamental need for creative, imaginative leadership and activism to move the development process along in a sustainable, equitable fashion, the Rockefeller Foundation embarked in 1990 on establishing a global network of leaders in the arena of environment and development. The Leadership for Environment and Development (LEAD) program is unique in that it seeks to be a comprehensive capacity-building and professional support network. Starting with experienced and highly motivated mid-career professionals who demonstrate leadership qualities and have already achieved some distinction as movers and shakers in their chosen professional field, the LEAD formula involves providing them first with two years of a capacity-building program aimed at equipping them with a broad-based understanding of the political, social, economic, environmental, ecological and human factors intrinsic to the development process. After graduating from being Associates during this capability enhancement phase of the program, alumni of the LEAD program continue to form a part of the ever expanding LEAD network and can keep in constant contact with their fellow LEAD alumni and associates through a state-of-the-art computer network, LEADNet, which has been designed to meet the needs of LEAD programs globally. In addition to facilitating interactive communication with individual colleagues and with special interest groups, LEADNet provides access to a growing list of databases and other information resources (including geographical information systems (GIS) and case studies documenting advances in environmental protection, approaches to sustainable livelihoods, etc.), as well as opportunities for Associates to gain expert advice from an ever expanding range of experts and specialists who make themselves available for contact by E-mail.

It needs to be emphasized from the beginning that the LEAD program does not limit its focus specifically on health and the environment. Nor does it concentrate solely on examining the link between development and the environment. The vision which drives the LEAD program takes these perspectives into account but is much more comprehensive. Recognizing the limitations and restrictiveness inherent in traditional academic and professional training programs, the program encourages specialists and experts to step outside their familiar professional terrian and enter the exciting, if largely uncharted, territory of interdisciplinary space. In short, the LEAD program seeks to encourage the development of a global network of concerned, activist leaders with the ability to think across disciplinary and sectoral lines and whose agenda is no less than changing the world as we know it.

This chapter will describe the organization and governance of the LEAD program, the process by which individuals are selected to join the LEAD program, the nature of the training that they undergo at home and internationally, and the support they are given to assist them with their future activities.

HISTORICAL PERSPECTIVE

The period preceding the end of the 1980s brought with it historic changes in global geo-political realities including: the end of the Cold War era; growing concern at the impact that human activity was having on the vitality and long-term viability of the planet; and, most important, recognition that we can no longer pretend to be isolated nations and pockets of humanity but are, in fact, intimately connected within a global economy and ecology.

These changes opened up a window of opportunity that could have vital consequences for the future of this planet. For the first time in history, barriers were breaking down between nations and there seemed to be an optimistic, global sense that real change was imminent.

People were revolting against the shackles of ideology and conflict and seeking new ways to work toward greater individual development and freedom. The Tiananmen Square demonstrations in China, the fall of communist regimes in Eastern Europe, the bringing down of the Berlin Wall, were all part of a global wave of change. As democracy was breaking out all over the former Socialist Bloc, Africa and Latin America, the center of gravity of the global economy was rapidly shifting from what has been called the "North" to the Asia-Pacific region. For the first time, developing countries were beginning to take leadership positions in promoting economic and social change—many newly industrializing countries, for example, were standing up to take their place as equals to any.

These events could not be ignored—they offered an opportunity for action. There was talk of a "New World Order" but how to translate such thinking into reality seemed to be a problem.

The Brundtland Commission on Environment and Development had, in 1987, issued a report "Our Common Future" (World Commission on Environment and Development, 1987) which signalled the need to recognize and operationalize a new understanding of the links between individuals, populations, consumption patterns, attitudes and behavior. Increasing concern was being expressed on concerns of supranational and even global significance including global warming, ozone depletion, deforestation, desertification, degradation of agricultural lands, and pollution of the global commons.

At the same time, many "Southern" countries had been having a very bad decade in the 1980s. In many countries—particularly in Africa and Latin America—economic and social development was hard pressed to keep pace with rapid population growth—in fact, many countries were actually experiencing declines in average quality of life. There was, additionally, growing disparity between rich and poor—within countries and between countries (the so-called "North–South divide"). The strongest indicator that something needed to be done to correct this imbalance was the fact that net outflow of development assistance funds from more developed countries to less developed countries actually reversed during the decade and the MDCs found themselves receiving, annually, as much as US$50 billion more in 1989 than they provided as aid—largely in the form of interest repayments from previous loans (United Nations Development Programme, 1992).

Another thread in the changing fabric was that the United Nations (UN) system, which might ostensibly have played a leadership role in promoting change, was increasingly seen as unwieldy and even out of touch with changing global needs. To be correct, the UN was moving in the right direction but this was perceived as occurring very slowly. Rather than providing leadership and vision, the UN was generally seen to operate reactively, and was being increasingly peripheralized.

Similarly, government bureaucracies have traditionally not been designed to respond to the needs of individuals within societies. Too often, the attitude has been one of top-down management—this being relatively easier and not requiring input and feedback from the people but, consequently, often resulting in the government being completely out of touch with the needs of individuals at the grassroots. People's priorities were often not met and government simply lacked the resources, in many countries, to meet even the basic needs of people.

The nongovernmental organizations (NGO)—whether community-based, or concerned with issues of supranational consequence, came, in the 1980s, increasingly to lead where government had failed. Their efforts were often spurred by the increasing transparency engendered by the increased availability of information in the form of publications such as the Human Development Report, State of the World, World Development Report, World Resources, the numerous reports of Amnesty International, and by the reporting of such broadcast networks as CNN and the BBC. Concerned individuals with the knowledge and skill to understand the events of moment happening all around them were coming to terms with the need to take a more activist role in promoting change.

While individuals were acting singly and in groups, there did not exist a mechanism for breaking down barriers of race, religion, culture, politics, and nationality in seeking ways to understand problems of others and to find means by which people could work across these barriers to seek and find solutions that would have global moment.

These events, coming together as they did, led The Rockefeller Foundation to the inevitable conclusion that there was an urgent need to evolve new paradigms and to develop mechanisms for concerned, skilled and knowledgeable people throughout the world to initiate dialogue focused, fundamentally, on radically changing the way we view ourselves and our interactions with other inhabitants of this planet (animal, vegetable and human) and the life-support mechanisms that sustain us all.

The Rockefeller Foundation's response to its analysis of global trends was untried and high risk but potentially very promising: to initiate a global network of mid-career individuals and potential leaders, from as varied backgrounds as possible, who are interested in bringing about the necessary changes to society as we know it (especially in relation to issues of global significance), provide opportunities for them to learn and understand the complexities and problems affecting global issues; give them appropriate fora to discuss and dialogue and learn from each other and to develop action agendas to change the status quo; and then to provide them with backup resources and institutional support to translate their ideas and vision into reality. This idea was germinated and nurtured by the Global Environment Program (now a full Division of the Foundation) and evolved to become the LEAD program.

THE LEAD PROGRAM

The LEAD program seeks to achieve its goal through the following strategy:

1. Identify talented professionals who will play key roles in the fields of environment and development.
2. Sponsor a continuing series of fellowships to provide these professionals with the training, resources, and technical support necessary to design and implement effective development and environment protection strategies.
3. Support collaborative efforts by providing resources and opportunities for participants within and among LEAD countries to work together on national, regional and global initiatives.

The LEAD program was initially launched in the following countries/regions: Brazil, China, India, Indonesia, Mexico, Nigeria, and the Commonwealth of Independent States. These countries/regions were selected on the basis of their current and potential impact on the global environment and development agenda.

The LEAD program has, at least until recently, focused on less developed countries and regions. The decision to focus initially on the "South" was a conscious one. The trend through much of the post-World War II era has been one of continued intellectual and financial dominance by the more developed countries (MDCs); development efforts in less developed countries (LDCs), for example have tended to be funded by loans from international lending institutions deriving their funds from MDCs; expertise in international development tends to be predominantly "Northern" in origin and LDCs depend often on consultants from the North. Additionally, the issues of global concern which were discussed in international fora and which were disseminated by "Northern"-dominated media services carried a decidedly Northern perspective—with the LDC perspective not often being heard. It was, therefore, perceived as necessary, for the dialogue to be truly on an equal footing, that a priority of the LEAD program should be the establishment of an effective voice for the South. [N.B. Based on experience with the first cohorts of LEAD Associates, the next generation of leaders in LDCs is quite vocal and able to express its concerns and commitment to changing the world as we know it. In fact, the Associates have shown themselves to be so competent, and the dialogue process so constructive, that it quickly became apparent that, while the Associates were empathetic to the situation and concerns of the "North," the absence of "Northern" Associates meant that a truly global perspective and discussion of concerns was not yet possible. As a result, LEAD has accelerated the second phase of its operationalization—during which LEAD National programs in MDCs are being instituted and brought into the LEAD fold. Hence, in addition to expanding developing country representation to include Southern Africa and Pakistan, LEAD programs have also been established in Canada and Europe. Efforts to establish programs in Japan, the United States, and the newly industrializing countries of the Asia Pacific region are expected to lead to operational LEAD programs in these countries and regions by 1997 or 1998.

LEAD Country/Regional Programs

In each participating country or region, a Host Institution, such as a university or research institute, hosts the LEAD Program Secretariat. In addition, a National or Regional Steering Committee comprising senior level professionals from a range of sectors and disciplines oversees program administration, curriculum development, and the selection of associates.

Each Program is coordinated under the auspices of a Program Director who is responsible for day-to-day management of the Program, including overseeing the selection and training of LEAD Associates.

LEAD Program Governance

The global focus, scope and direction of the LEAD program are determined under the guidance and supervision of an International Steering Committee consisting of respected international luminaries and authorities in the fields of environment and development. The respective Chairperson of each National Steering Committee also serves on the International Steering Committee.

LEAD International

LEAD International has recently been incorporated as an international nongovernmental organization independent of the Rockefeller Foundation. LEAD International, which is governed by an independent Board, works closely with the International Steering Committee and the various National programs to coordinate and oversee international activities of the LEAD program. It also houses the LEADNet database and serves as the nerve center for network communications.

LEAD Participants

In each participating country, a diverse and varied group of successful mid-career professionals with demonstrated leadership capability in at least one aspect of environment and development, is selected as two-year LEAD Associates. Usually, between 12 and 15 Associates are selected per country/region per year. Participants come from such backgrounds as:

- academia and research;
- government and policy-making;
- non-governmental, community organizations, environmental action groups;
- media;
- the commercial and private sector.

Although Associates continue to meet their professional obligations, they must secure eight weeks of leave annually to participate in LEAD activities. These seminars, workshops, and field visits are scheduled in two- to three-week programs throughout the year. Associates are also expected to devote additional time to completing individual projects, contributing to the development of case studies of environment/development dilemmas, and preparing for upcoming sessions.

In addition to a total of 10 weeks of intensive, in-country sessions, LEAD Associates also receive 6 weeks of international training in common with their colleagues of the same cohort from the other countries/

regions during their 2-year stint as LEAD Associates. While national languages and English are used in the in-country sessions, all international events are conducted in English.

Upon successful completion of the two-year program, Associates graduate and become part of the international community of LEAD Alumni. They also become eligible to qualify to become LEAD Fellows. As Alumni and Fellows, they are encouraged to take on leadership roles in their respective sectors—within their own countries as well as working across national and regional boundaries to advance sustainable development.

LEAD Alumni whose projects are selected for funding support are appointed as LEAD Fellows and may receive up to 2 years of funding during which they may be provided with seed capital to start new training, educational, research or even commercial initiatives with a focus on promoting a sensible and sound approach to environmental protection and development.

The global network of LEAD Associates and Alumni continues to expand each year. For example, after only four years, a participating country will have at least 50 Associates and Fellows who are, in turn, linked to a wider network of their colleagues worldwide.

The LEAD Curriculum

During the course of the program, the Associates undergo an extensive training program which involves opportunities to think through—from local, national and global perspectives—a range of global themes which are summarized in Table 28.1.

LEAD Activities

Activities conducted by the LEAD program—internationally as well as within host countries—include:

1. *Training and Educational Activities*

The LEAD program undertakes an extensive training program for individuals selected from a wide array of nations and professions and develops curricula and materials for use in training seminars and practical activities (see Table 28.1). These training efforts serve to advance science and education on an individual and regional level and help build-up "human capital" in the LEAD countries—LEAD Associates help provide their respective countries and the international community with the necessary technical capabilities and knowledge base essential for equitable development and environmental protection.

TABLE 28.1 The Two-Year Curriculum for LEAD Associates (1992–1994)

1. **Population and Natural Resources**
   a. *Population*
      i) urbanization*
      ii) migration*
      iii) employment/livelihoods
      iv) quality of life
   b. *Natural Resources*
      i) open access/common property*
      ii) resource degradation*
      iii) management under subsistence conditions
      iv) water/land use planning
      v) food production planning
      vi) fuel availability
2. **Energy, Trade, and Debt**
   a. *Energy*
      i) energy policies*
      ii) energy-related environmental degradation*
      iii) energy efficiency
      iv) energy technology (including alternative and traditional sources)
   b. *Trade*
      i) trade barriers and protectionism (internal and external)*
      ii) trade policies and the environment*
      iii) international, regional, bilateral and commodity trade agreements
   c. *Debt*
      i) debt and aid (multilateral and bilateral)*
      ii) forms of debt servicing and conversion*
      iii) structural adjustment plans—their design, operation and environmental/trade effects
      iv) the major multi-lateral financing institutions

*The topics marked with asterisks (*) are covered during the first year of the LEAD Program, while unmarked topics are covered in the second.

The LEAD program bridges cultural and academic boundaries by bringing together qualified individuals from diverse national and professional backgrounds. LEAD Associates and Alumni will be able to increase their contribution to their professional fields with their advanced technological skills and access to extraordinary resources (such as LEADNet), continuing contact with other participants, and the ability to share ideas and discoveries with individuals all over the world.

Human capital is often undervalued, but well-trained and highly skilled professionals can be of great benefit to their respective nations. This is particularly so for less developed nations facing inadequate resources and facilities. The inclusion of a variety of academic disciplines and professions allows scientists, business leaders, government officials and others to share information which might not otherwise be disseminated beyond their respective professional disciplines but which clearly has broader relevance.

2. *LEADNet*

LEAD International operates a global computer information system which enables LEAD Associates and Alumni to communicate and disseminate information on an international level, sharing research, new technologies, data, and information on local project development efforts. This network allows important information to be widely and rapidly disseminated among nations and individuals involved in many disciplines. For example, a LEAD Fellow working on an energy efficiency project in Brazil could share information with a regional planner in Indonesia, enabling both individuals to benefit from the related experiences of their colleagues. Too often, difficulties in disseminating information have prevented valuable data and knowledge from being shared among nations and especially among individuals working in different professions, and on different aspects of the same problem. The creation of a single network will do much to improve the communication of relevant information which might otherwise never be shared.

The advanced computer and telecommunications technologies developed by LEAD provides a range of information resources, including databases, and analytical and educational tools. LEAD provides hardware, software, technical expertise, and training needed to utilize and manage these technologies. LEAD also works with LEAD Associates to develop new technologies and applications relevant to environment and development.

The benefits of this network extend far beyond LEAD International and the individual participants and will result in increased knowledge and capabilities in planning and development efforts generally in less developed countries. Access to the information system is intended to be made as widely available as possible. More important, sustainable development efforts can lead to significant improvements in living and environmental conditions throughout the world.

3. *Continuing Educational Activities*

LEAD International supports the efforts of LEAD Associates and Fellows in research, publishing, education, and policy development. Such efforts are likely to have wide application across political and cultural boundaries and give special emphasis to:

- utilizing the interdisciplinary approaches which are fostered by LEAD's training efforts;

- strengthening institutional capacity in less developed countries; and
- promoting a spirit of cooperation and collaboration among LEAD Associates and Fellows.

Through these activities, the LEAD program hopes to create greater public awareness of environmental and development issues, provide governmental and nongovernmental organizations with valuable advice and data, combat poverty and contribute to sound development on a global basis.

The LEAD Experience

Although each Associate selected for the LEAD program has expertise in a field related to development and the environment, none is proficient in every area. Through a series of activities overseen by the program's International and National Steering Committees, LEAD Associates can reasonably be expected to:

1. *Gain an appreciation of the complexities and scope of environment/development issues.* The LEAD curriculum covers an array of topics, including energy efficiency, natural resource management, population dynamics, public health, resource degradation and pollution, climate change, economics, ethics, policy tools, and intervention strategies.
2. *Become familiar with major environment and development issues in other participating countries.* LEAD provides opportunities for Associates from different countries to interact and collaborate, and to access a computer network linking them with one another and with a variety of information resources. In addition, Associates benefit from the opportunity to exchange ideas and to work with their international colleagues during the International Session each year.
3. *Keep abreast of key international developments.* Associates have access to the most up-to-date information concerning treaties and protocols, trade and investment patterns, scientific collaboration, technological advances, and new political and financial initiatives and institutions.

The LEAD curriculum and activities are designed to help Associates develop a more interdisciplinary, global approach to environment/development issues. For example, an Indian public health officer who has worked in preventing respiratory infections would, with participation in the LEAD program, begin to view urban disease patterns from the broader perspective of environmental economics, industrialization policies, atmospheric science, renewable energy opportunities and demographic pressure. She also has the benefit of viewing these issues not just from an Indian viewpoint, but also from the perspectives of her colleagues in other countries. LEAD provides similar experiences for the Mexican ecologist, the Indonesian energy planner, the Chinese engineer, and Associates from other countries and nations.

It is important to note that LEAD is not about ideology. LEAD is not interested in imposing a view of the world—whether from a "Northern" or "Southern" perspective—on its Associates. It is, however, about transparency and the dissemination of unbiased facts and data to concerned individuals. It is also about breaking down the barriers of discipline and specialization that tend to divide us all. It seeks to provide an environment for a common language aimed at finding effective and equitable solutions to global problems.

LEAD also does not seek to provide a prescription or formula for problem solving. It recognizes that the circumstances operating in each country and in each problem are sufficiently varied as to require different approaches to their solution. Still, while uniquely local actions should be taken, the process of coming to an understanding of the extent and scope of problems in collaborative discourse and in a spirit of free exchange of information and ideas, is seen as an important contribution that LEAD can make to developing solutions.

LEAD's not-so-hidden agenda is to provide:

1. a mechanism for individuals with potential to break out of traditional limitations imposed by professional, political, geographical or social barriers;
2. an opportunity for intelligent and committed individuals from all over the world to participate in a true dialogue—seeking to understand and empathize with the problems and difficulties that others face and to work together, through sharing of ideas, experiences and insight to develop new and innovative approaches to dealing with problems and obstacles to ecological and human well-being;
3. a forum for continued debate and consideration of priorities for action and a workable action agenda at the individual, local, national, regional and global levels;
4. LEAD Associates with the necessary skills, knowledge and resources to bring about requisite change.

More than just an attempt to raise awareness that most fora or conferences tend to be, the LEAD program is a long-term, sustained commitment. The program will aid and nurture the work that its Associates embark on while providing them with opportunities to continue putting their knowledge, skills and resources into aiding the equitable development of their societies and of future generations of Associates.

PROGRAM SUPPORT

The LEAD program is designed to benefit not only individual participants, but their employers as well. The skills and contacts that Associates acquire during the two-year program can make a rich contribution to the universities, government ministries, businesses and organizations which employ them. Associates' supervisors are also kept abreast of LEAD activities and are invited to key events. In exchange, employers are expected to provide eight weeks of annual leave to allow Associates to participate in LEAD activities. National Steering Committee members are available to help Associates make arrangements with their employers or home institutions when necessary.

FUTURE LEAD DIRECTIONS

With the successful launch of the first phase of the LEAD program in the largest and most important developing countries and regions, the program has entered phase II. This involved expansion of the program to include additional developing countries, newly industrialized countries, and the developed countries of North America, Western Europe, and Japan.

This expansion will ensure that the LEAD program becomes truly global. It is anticipated that the dialogue and cross-fertilization of ideas—particularly between Associates from developing and developed countries—will lead to very useful and constructive new insights and approaches to dealing with the problems and issues confronting mankind.

COLLABORATIVE LINKS

The LEAD program and its activities cut across all spheres from the macro, global to the local grassroot. Several international agencies have already recognized the potential that LEAD offers as an agent for change. Besides the Rockefeller Foundation, the program receives funding support from a range of donors from North America, Western Europe, and Asia. Additionally, it has strong institutional links with such agencies as the United Nations Environment Programme, the United Nations Development Programme, and the World Bank—all of which have expressed strong interest and support for the activities of the LEAD program.

At the national levels, the program has support at the highest levels of government in most countries in which it operates. It has a network of contacts with leading environmental and development agencies, governmental agencies, and nongovernmental organizations—and the network grows as new Associates introduce their institutions and range of contacts, professional and social, to the activities of LEAD. These links are beginning to pay off with LEAD Associates becoming recognized for the special skills and knowledge they bring to their respective communities. In the Commonwealth of Independent States, for example, the Altai Republic requested that the Regional LEAD Program work with government and policymakers to make the Republic the "World's First Sustainable Republic." This exciting experiment in sustainable development has been coordinated by the first cohort of LEAD Associates for the region.

LEAD AND HEALTH

The astute reader will no doubt note that health was hardly mentioned in the preceding discussion. Yet, the work of LEAD is all about health—in the very broadest sense referred to at the start of this book. Let us quickly review the links to health implicit in the work of LEAD. A quick survey of the curriculum (see Table 28.1) with consideration of some illustrative examples will make this obvious:

1. **Population and Natural Resources**
   a. *Population*
   The links between considerations of population and health have generally been well recognized. In general, the more rapidly population grows, the greater the pressure on expanding land use for housing, commerce and agricultural purposes. As the most fertile areas are generally already being utilized, this often means that marginal lands come into cultivation—with the consequence often being rapid degradation of the soil. Rapid population growth also often implies the need for economic development at a rate high enough to keep pace with population growth if quality of life is to improve. Rapid population growth can therefore have a very significant impact on ecological well-being and biodiversity, causing acceleration of devegetation and desertification, and leading to a reduction in quality of life and well-being. Societies with high population densities are particularly at risk at times of political or social turmoil, famines and droughts. Finding effective ways to ensure that population growth rates do not exceed a region's ability to provide for rising populations, developing rational and sustainable land use practices, and helping to ensure that individuals are able to escape from poverty and to enjoy a

decent quality of life are therefore prerequisites to ensuring and maintaining human and ecological well-being and health.

b. *Natural Resources*

Natural resource utilization patterns determine the rates at which we are likely to consume nonrenewable resources as well as often dictate the manner in which we utilize the global commons. Excessive rates of consumption, and industrial activity associated with this rising consumption and desire for material possession have been largely responsible for the major problems which we now recognize in terms of global warming, the hole in the ozone layer, and pollution of the land, air and water. All of these increase the risks and hazards to health of exposed individuals (while also devastating the ecological environment). Finding ways to make our production processes less damaging and maintaining quality of life while substantially reducing the stress we place on our limited stocks of natural resources is vital to ensuring human and ecological well-being in the long-term.

2. **Energy, Trade, and Debt**

a. *Energy*

Energy issues can also have significant direct and indirect implications for health. Close to 70 percent of the world's population is dependent on the utilization of biomass as their principal source of energy. It is being increasingly recognized that the indoor air pollution arising from the use of wood, dung and crop residues for fuel in peasant homes throughout the less developed world is strongly associated with such health consequences as acute respiratory infection (the most common cause of death in children under five), chronic respiratory disease in women (including bronchitis, pneumonia and even tuberculosis), malignancies of the lung and even adverse pregnancy outcomes. Finding less polluting fuels and improved stoves can be one very effective intervention that can greatly minimize exposure to the risks associated with indoor air pollution.

b. *Trade*

Issues of concern when considering global trade and terms of trade can have very significant impacts on health and well-being. For example, farm subsidies to farmers in MDCs often result in price distortions on global markets that make it untenable for farmers in LDCs to produce and sell their products in their markets because MDC produce can be obtained at a significantly lower price. While city dwellers benefit, the subsidies given to MDC producers also result in very significant social disruptions in the LDCs. Firstly, valuable foreign reserves need to be used to pay for importing food from overseas. Secondly, farmers (who make up about 75 percent of the population of most LDCs outside Latin America) find themselves with no means of livelihood, are often forced to migrate to overcrowded cities to find work, and often constitute the bulk of the world's population which is today described as living in absolute poverty. Nutritional, social and health status of such individuals is appallingly poor. Finding more equitable mechanisms for promoting fair trade between countries can help significantly in improving the lot of the agricultural workers in less developed countries.

c. *Debt*

Many developing countries are heavily indebted. Countries like the Philippines, for example, were using more than 30 percent of their GDP to repay development assistance loans in the early 1990s. Such large loan repayment burdens can severely restrict the ability of these countries to invest in infrastructure development (including health) and to provide for the future needs of people. Working to develop strategies for ensuring that emphasis is placed on human, social and economic development as priorities—with the recognition that greater economic viability of a country makes it a lower risk for loans and investment—is one possible way in which LEAD Associates and Fellows can contribute to improving the future quality of life, health and well-being of people in their respective countries.

CONCLUSION

We cannot restrict our thinking to our traditional professional and disciplinary training. We need to review and start the process of changing the way we view ourselves, our relationships with other living creatures on this planet, and our links to its future inhabitants. But we need to go far beyond the lofty words of Rio and *Agenda 21*. We need to put action where before there were words. We need to begin the work of change for the future. Bringing about the sort of cultural and social revolution intrinsic in a transition to sustainable development is not easy.

The LEAD program has begun the process by identifying individuals who have already started to distinguish themselves as respected leaders in their fields of environment and development. These workers have tremendous potential to impact on future investment in drinking water, food security maintenance (for example, sustainable agriculture), water security maintenance, socioeconomic development, human development, social service infrastructure (including educational facilities, primary health facilities, etc). Their potential impact on human and ecological health—direct and indirect—will be substantial.

More than mere dialogue, the program equips Associates with knowledge, skill and understanding across sectoral concerns and goes on to assist them in the work they perform in promoting improved quality of life and sustainable livelihoods. LEAD is an approach to train and support the next generation of world leaders to be responsible and accountable—not only to their constituents, but to the constituents who are yet to be, and to all other inhabitants of this planet.

Programs like the LEAD program—and the knowledge, skills, access to resources, and support that they place at the fingertips of Associates—will help ensure that actions which these future leaders take will be as broad-based as possible and that they will impact positively on the health and well-being of those they touch.

REFERENCES

United Nations Development Programme (1992). *Human Development Report*. Oxford University Press: New York.

World Commission on Environment and Development (1987). *Our Common Future*. Oxford University Press: Oxford.

29

INCLEN: A Global Network with Potential to Confront Issues of Environment and Health in the Developing World

Howard Frumkin, Arturo Morillo, and Seth Berkley

INTRODUCTION

In 1982, the International Clinical Epidemiology Network (INCLEN) was formed, with major support from the Rockefeller Foundation (Halstead et al., 1991). INCLEN was designed to equip clinical faculty members at leading medical schools in developing nations with the insights and methods of clinical epidemiology. Initially, 27 medical schools in 16 nations were selected as the sites of Clinical Epidemiology Units (CEUs) (Table 29.1). Over about a decade, faculty members from each of these medical schools were identified and trained at centers in the United States, Canada, and Australia. Trainees are mid-career faculty members from the full range of major clinical specialties. When a CEU's full complement of faculty is trained, there are between five and ten clinical epidemiologists, as well as at least one biostatistician, a social scientist (Higginbotham, 1992), and a health economist (Eisenberg et al., 1979).

What is "clinical epidemiology?" In general, epidemiology is defined as the study of "the distribution and determinants of disease frequency" in human populations (MacMahon & Pugh, 1970). The concept of clinical epidemiology as a separate entity arose in the 1960s. This discipline is defined as:

> the application of epidemiologic principles and methods to problems encountered in clinical medicine. It is a science concerned with counting clinical events occurring in intact human beings, and it uses

TABLE 29.1 Locations of INCLEN Clinical Epidemiology Units

Latin America
Mexico City, Mexico (General Hospital, Institute of Nutrition)
Santiago, Chile (University of Chile)
Temuco, Chile (Universidad de la Frontera)
Bogotá, Colombia (Pontifica Universidad Javeriana)
São Paulo, Brazil (Escola Paulista de Medicina)
Rio de Janeiro, Brazil (Universidad Federale do Rio de Janeiro)
India
New Delhi (All India Institute of Medical Sciences)
Vellore (Christian Medical College)
Trivandrum (Medical College Trivandrum)
Nagpur (Government Medical College)
Lucknow (King George Medical College)
Madras (Madras Medical College)
Africa
Yaounde, Cameroun (University of Yaounde)
Ismailia, Egypt (Suez Canal University)
Addis Ababa, Ethiopia (Addis Ababa University)
Nairobi, Kenya (University of Nairobi)
Harare, Zimbabwe (University of Zimbabwe)
Kampala, Uganda (Makarere University)
Asia
Shanghai, PRC (Shanghai Medical University)
Chengdu, Sichuan, PRC(West China University of Medical Sciences)
Yogyakarta, Indonesia (Gadjah Mada University)
Manila, Philippines (University of the Philippines)
Khon Kaen, Thailand (Khon Kaen University)
Bangkok, Thailand (Mahidol University, Chulalongkorn University)
Europe
Lyons, France (Claude Bernard University)

epidemiologic methods to carry out and analyze the count. (Fletcher et al., 1988)

The unique features of clinical epidemiology, as opposed to epidemiology, are not always clear; some wags have suggested that clinical epidemiologists are simply epidemiologists who wear white coats and take care of patients from time to time.

What do clinical epidemiologists study? Sample presentations from the 1994 INCLEN meeting included: "Risk Factors for Severe Liver Disease in Childhood: A Case-Control Study," "Screening of Rheumatic Heart Disease Among High Risk Primary School Children," and "Design of a Double-Blind Randomized Trial of Dexamethasone in Tuberculous Meningitis." Like most work in clinical epidemiology, these presentations each focus on a specific disease; they address etiology, diagnosis, and treatment, respectively. One is hospital based, one is community based, and one is both. It is easy to appreciate the appeal of these topics to the medical specialists who will investigate them, a gastroenterologist, a cardiologist, and an infectious disease specialist.

Recent trends within INCLEN have emphasized the importance of prioritizing research issues and assuring that research results are used to influence policy decisions. The fusion of epidemiology, social science and economic methods allows INCLEN researchers to approach these decisions broadly and effectively.

The goals of INCLEN are realized through the activities of the CEUs. First, CEUs are expected to carry out high-quality research using the methods of clinical epidemiology. Second, investigators should strike an appropriate balance between hospital-based and community-based research, focusing on questions that are relevant to medical practice and public health in their countries. Third, the research performed at CEUs should be disseminated appropriately, in both national and international journals. Fourth, the research should have an impact on national health policy. Fifth, the CEU is expected to provide consultation to those conducting clinical research within the institution. Sixth, the CEU is expected to play an active role in teaching, including courses in clinical epidemiology and critical appraisal of medical literature for medical students, postgraduates, and other members of the faculty. In fact, CEUs are expected to mature to the point that they can assume a regional training function themselves, preparing others in their regions to pursue clinical epidemiology research.

The Rockefeller Foundation had a long legacy of program-building in schools of medicine, public health, and nursing, both in the United States and abroad, that preceded INCLEN by many decades (Fye, 1991; Abrams, 1993; Brown, 1976; Donaldson, 1976; Solórzano, 1992). However, INCLEN represented an ambitious new initiative. The Foundation had previously supported much health research in schools of public health, but INCLEN signalled a shift toward those working in clinical departments of medical schools. These faculty members—pediatricians, surgeons, internists, gynecologists, and so on—were moved to the center stage of health research. A particular research paradigm—that of clinical epidemiology—was actively promoted, rather than the medical research enterprise more generally.

The early progress of INCLEN has been summarized elsewhere (Halstead et al., 1991). In its first decade INCLEN nearly completed the task of training and staffing CEUs at its member medical schools. Many of the CEUs became productive research units, publishing regularly. In several instances members of the CEUs assumed senior leadership positions in their medical schools and/or in government health agencies. Several made important contributions to health policy in their countries. An important feature of INCLEN is the tradition of close follow-up and collaboration that was established early. Faculty from training centers make frequent visits to CEUs, and an annual INCLEN-wide meeting brings together substantial numbers of CEU members for research collaboration, discussion, and networking. (In 1994, these decreased in frequency to biannual, with regional meetings held in alternate years.) Therefore, INCLEN has produced not only objective research accomplishments, but it has also become a truly interactive network of clinical epidemiologists in developed and developing nations.

ENVIRONMENTAL AND OCCUPATIONAL HEALTH IN INCLEN

Interest in Environmental and Occupational Health (EOH) first surfaced in INCLEN in 1989, at the seventh annual meeting. At that time a small group of participants, including faculty from training centers and members of CEUs in several developing nations, met to discuss their interests. This group included three physicians, from the U.S., Australia, and Brazil, all with primary interests in EOH. They wrote a short position paper that defined the scope of EOH and identified several unique features: the unique kinds of populations that are studied, the focus on exposure variables, the sometimes unique diseases that are studied, and issues of ethics, equity, and development policy that pervade EOH research. They also emphasized the need for multidisciplinary approaches in EOH research. The group proposed a role for EOH within INCLEN.

Shortly after that meeting all INCLEN CEUs were surveyed to assess their interest in EOH. Eight CEUs responded, including those in Trivandrum, Vellore, Manila, Yogyakarta, Shanghai, Rio de Janeiro, Temuco, and Nigeria (which had a CEU at the time). The respondents reported concentrations of textile, chemical or petrochemical, and other industries in their vicinities, as well as agriculture. The EOH concerns identified as priority issues spanned a broad range (see Table 29.2).

At this point INCLEN's possible options in EOH began to emerge through group discussions and letters. These included fellowship training to establish a "specialty" within INCLEN (the approach used to train social scientists and health economists), collaborative research involving several CEUs, seed grants to stimulate EOH research at individual CEUs, and short courses offered in either developing nations or at training centers. The importance of collaborating with other organizations and agencies was also stressed in these discussions, and links were made with the World Health Organization, the Field Epidemiology Training Programs of the U.S. Centers for Disease Control, and other groups.

TABLE 29.2 EOH Concerns Identified by INCLEN CEUs in 1989 Survey ($N = 8$)

Exposure	Responses
Chemical pollution of air and water	5
Heavy metal poisoning	5
Pesticide poisoning	8
Workplace accidents	6
Noise exposure	4
Occupational dermatoses	5
Asbestos	3
Occupational musculoskeletal disorders	7
Occupational respiratory diseases	5
Occupational cancer	3
Ionizing radiation	2

In late 1990 a decision was made to move ahead with a program of EOH seed grants to investigators at CEUs, with support from the Rockefeller Foundation. These grants, first offered in 1991, were in the range of $10,000 each. Applicants were encouraged to identify important EOH problems in their geographic areas, and to design short research projects building on their clinical expertise and training in clinical epidemiology. Announcements were distributed widely throughout INCLEN. In the first year, three applications were received. All were evaluated by a committee drawn from the training centers, and were felt to be promising. All were funded. The project names and locations are shown in Table 29.3.

The 1992 annual INCLEN meeting in Bali included several sessions dedicated to EOH. This was possible because the meeting was held jointly with the FETP; the two groups cooperated in holding EOH sessions, and lively dialogue resulted. That year, based on the promising results of the 1991 seed grant program, funds were again offered for EOH seed grants. This time there were no fewer than 18 applications, of which five were funded (see Table 29.3). Of the remaining applications, many were quite strong, and showed potential for subsequent funding. All applicants received detailed feedback on their applications, consisting of at least three separate critiques by members of the review committee. All were encouraged to reapply during the next grant cycle.

The large number of applications, and the active interest in EOH evident at the 1992 meeting, were considered extremely promising. Discussions were held about expanding EOH initiatives within INCLEN. A consensus emerged among leadership in INCLEN, at the Rockefeller Foundation, and those in INCLEN responsible for the EOH effort, that a short, intensive training course in EOH would be the appropriate next step. Such a course would be intended to equip clinical epidemiologists

TABLE 29.3 EOH Seed Grants Funded by INCLEN, 1991–1994

Project	Location
1991 (3 applications received, 3 funded)	
Risk factors for bladder cancer in Egypt	Egypt
Assessment of the respiratory health profile of families living in and around the Makiling-Banahaw geothermal power generation plants	Philippines
Repetitive strain injuries in keyboard operators: A cross-sectional study	Brazil
1992 (18 applications received, 5 funded)	
Ambient air pollution and respiratory disease in infants and preschool children	India
An epidemiologic study of mushroom workers' lung	China
Frequency, types, causes, outcomes, and hospital cost of head injuries in Addis Ababa	Ethiopia
Longitudinal study of transmission of hepatitis B in dental professionals in Chengdu	China
The neurotoxic effects of methyl bromide on exposed workers in Region V: A cohort study	Chile
1993 (5 applications received, 1 funded)	
Maternal exposure to lead and neonatal birth weight	India
1994 (13 applications received, 4 funded)	
Longitudinal study of transmission of hepatitis B in dental professionals in Chengdu (year 2)	China
Childhood lead poisoning	India
Lead exposure in children and its effect on cognitive functions affecting scholastic performance	Egypt
Risk factors for burn injuries in children in south India	India

with special knowledge and skills in EOH. The syllabus included topics such as exposure measurement techniques, air pollution, heavy metals, and other specific hazards, database searching, and proposal preparation. Students would also meet with colleagues at key U.S. and international agencies, helping to network them in the EOH field.

In 1993, the annual INCLEN meeting in Cairo featured several formal presentations that addressed EOH. Some results from the 1991 seed grants were presented. A third cycle of EOH seed grants was then offered, but surprisingly, only five applications were submitted, of which one was fundable. Based on this decline in applications, a decision was made to defer the investment in a training course.

However, the fourth cycle of EOH grant applications, in 1994, demonstrated a return to previous high levels of interest. Of 13 applications submitted, four were selected for funding, including three new projects and a continuation of an ongoing project (see Table 29.3).

By 1994, some assessment of the outcome of the EOH initiative was possible. Although there was a long delay between the funding and

TABLE 29.4 Summary of INCLEN EOH Seed Grant Applications, 1991–1994 (N = 32)

Environmental vs. occupational:	
Environmental	19
Occupational	11
Combined	2
Exposures of interest:	
Ambient air pollution	4
Indoor air pollution	3
Pesticides	5
Motor vehicle accidents	2
Occupational biomechanical stress	3
Occupational mental stress	1
Hepatitis B virus	1
Lead	3
Radiation	2
Work in specific industries (mushroom growing, fishing, coir manufacturing, forestry)	4
Occupational carcinogens	1
General environmental exposures	1
Tannery emissions	1
Outcomes of interest:	
Respiratory disease	9
Infectious disease	3
Multisystem chemical toxicity	4
Musculoskeletal illness	2
Injury	2
Cancer	1
Neurotoxicity	2
Burns	1
Mental health	1
Adverse reproductive outcomes	1
Carboxyhemoglobinemia	1
Multiple outcomes	5
Geographic distribution:	
India	14
Asia (other than India)	5
Latin America	6
Africa	7

Note: Applications submitted more than once counted only once.

completion of projects, the early projects were showing promising results. For example, the Philippine investigation of the health effects of geothermal power generation plants played a major role in a national debate on this power source, and the investigator became an active participant in the government's health assessment process. The Egyptian project on bladder cancer demonstrated a previously unrecognized relationship between pesticide exposure and bladder cancer (Khedr et al., 1995), and the Brazilian project documented occupational upper extremity disorders for the first time in Latin America (Ferraz et al., 1995). The Indian study of air pollution resulted in two presentations at international meetings, extensive press coverage in India, and a manuscript submitted to an international journal. Overall, although it is too early to make a long-term assessment, the marriage of EOH with clinical epidemiology in INCLEN appears to be productive and useful.

DISCUSSION

Several factors suggest that INCLEN can make major contributions to research in EOH. First, hazardous environmental and workplace exposures are ubiquitous in developing nations, including those that contain INCLEN CEUs (Forget et al., 1993; Hardoy et al., 1992; Reich & Okubo, 1992; and World Bank, 1992). Motor vehicles, manufacturing, and power generation foul the ambient air, while indoor air is polluted by primitive cooking and heating fuels such as crop residues, low-grade coal, and wood. Industrial waste and inadequately treated sewage contaminate waterways. Solid and hazardous waste is disposed of improperly. Pesticides are used excessively without adequate safeguards. Technologies to prevent and remediate may be unavailable or prohibitively expensive, and technical expertise scarce.

Second, the human health effects of these exposures arouse more concern than any other effects. However, because of traditional divisions between health and environmental concerns—the two have different academic and career pathways, different university departments and research institutes, different government agencies, even different books and journals—few health researchers have focused on environmental issues. This has resulted in major data gaps, and in lost opportunities for health workers to influence environmental policy and prevent disease.

However, a substantial number of INCLEN clinical epidemiologists are interested in the health effects of environmental exposures, as the experience of 1990–1994 makes clear. Accordingly, INCLEN CEUs comprise a unique resource; they form a network of skilled medical researchers in major medical centers in developing nations, capable of performing high-quality investigations of EOH problems.

In fact, clinical epidemiology has some unique attributes that make it a very promising approach to EOH research. Clinical epidemiologists, based in medical centers, see and treat patients with diseases and injuries associated with workplace and environmental exposures. They have their fingers on the pulse of disease trends, and are well positioned to recognize increases in certain diagnoses, to raise questions about possible causes, and to exploit clinical data bases in seeking answers. At the same time, they are accustomed to considering the whole range of possible diagnoses, and are unlikely to implicate environmental exposures in a reflexive or alarmist manner. Involving clinical epidemiologists in EOH research brings the health sector and the environmental community together, linking two constituencies that can effectively contribute to policymaking that protects both human health and the environment.

A wide range of questions can be addressed by clinical epidemiology. Consider several of the 1994 applications. One proposed a clinical trial to test the standard antidote for pesticide toxicity against placebo. The investigator argued that this imported medication is expensive but of unproven benefit; if it proved no more effective than placebo, considerable cost savings could be realized without compromising patient care. Another application was based on the observation that women in India commonly carry large loads on their heads. The applicant hypothesized that this practice increases the risk of cervical spine injuries. If true, the investigator noted, modifications in carrying methods and/or prior training might help prevent these catastrophic injuries. A third application noted that indoor air pollutants such as smoke from dirty cooking fuels increase children's risk of respiratory diseases. The application proposed to implement several interventions, such as changing cooking practices, and to evaluate their ability to lower respiratory disease incidence. These examples illustrate the application of rigorous research methods to practical clinical problems, an awareness of social and economic issues, and an ability to extend medical research from the medical center to the community, all hallmarks of clinical epidemiology.

Another advantage of combining clinical epidemiology and EOH lies in risk communication. Workplace and environmental hazards are complex, and policymakers and members of the public have great difficulty in evaluating them. Research results that quantify risks, especially those that embody considerable uncertainty, must be explained with care and sensitivity. Clinicians are accustomed to risk communication; every day they must explain uncertainties to their patients. Clinical epidemiologists with an understanding of EOH are in an ideal position to explain the health hazards of air pollution, pesticides, and other hazards, interpreting complex science to patients and the public.

On the other hand, several factors might limit INCLEN's role in EOH research. First, INCLEN investigators are generally more oriented toward conventional clinical research topics than toward environmental or occupational exposures. Second, and related, EOH research requires interdisciplinary and intersectoral collaboration; epidemiologists must work closely with exposure assessment experts such as engineers and industrial hygienists, with corporate managers, and with others not commonly encountered in the halls of medical schools. For INCLEN members, the necessary relationships may not be in place. Third, there is considerable EOH research already under way in some areas, and INCLEN efforts there might be redundant. For example, several state governments in India have recently supported EOH research, the School of Public Health in Manila has a well established occupational health program, and the National Institute of Public Health in Mexico has an active research program in environmental health. The marginal contribution offered by INCLEN in such settings may be small.

Overall, the application of clinical epidemiology to EOH problems in developing nations, as implemented by INCLEN, appears extremely promising. In carefully selected locations, with adequate training and support for researchers, and with encouragement for clinicians to team with colleagues in related professions, this research can provide essential insights into the nature and magnitude of EOH problems in developing countries. In the mid-1990s INCLEN will seek independent funding to allow continued support, and expansion, of its EOH research program.

REFERENCES

Abrams, S. E. Brilliance and bureaucracy: Nursing and changes in the Rockefeller Foundation, 1915–1930. *Nurs Hist Rev 1993;1*:119–137.

Brown, E. R. Public health and imperialism: Early Rockefeller programs at home and abroad. *Am J Public Health 1976;66*:897–903.

Donaldson, P. J. Foreign intervention in medical education: A case study of the Rockefeller Foundation's involvement in a Thai medical school. *Int J Health Serv 1976;6*:251–270.

Eisenberg, J. M., Freund, D., Glick, H., Hall, J., Halstead, S., & Labelle, R. Clinical economics education in the International Clinical Epidemiology Network. INCLEN Economics Faculty. *J Clin Epidemiol 1989;42(7)*:689–695.

Ferraz, M. B., Frumkin, H., Helfenstein, M., Gianeschini, C., Altra, E. Upper extremity musculoskeletal disorders in keyboard operators in Brazil: A cross-sectional study. *Int J Occup Env Health 1995;1*:239–244.

Forget, G., Goodman, T., & de Villiers, A., Eds. *Impact of Pesticide Use on Health in Developing Countries* (Ottawa: International Development Research Centre, 1993).

Fletcher, R. H., Fletcher, S. W., & Wagner, E. H. *Clinical Epidemiology: The Essentials*, 2nd Edition (Philadelphia: Williams & Wilkins, 1988).

Fye, W. B. The origin of the full-time faculty system: Implications for clinical research. *JAMA 1991;265*:1555–1562.

Guess, H. A., Goldsmith, C. H., Henry, D., & Strom, B. L. Pharmacoepidemiology as a focus for clinical epidemiology in developing countries. *J Clin Epidemiol 1991;44 Suppl 2*:101S–105S.

Halstead, S. B., Tugwell, P., & Bennett, K. The International Clinical Epidemiology Network (INCLEN): a progress report. *J Clin Epidemiol 1991;44(6)*:579–589.

Hardoy, J. E, Mitlin, D., Satterwaite, D. *Environmental Problems in Third World Cities* (London: Earthscan Publications, 1992).

Higginbotham, N. Developing partnerships for health and social science research: the International Clinical Epidemiology Network (INCLEN) social science component. *Soc Sci Med 1992;35(11)*:1325–1327.

Khedr, M. S., Frumkin, H., Samy, A. Quantitative assessment of the risk factors for bladder cancer in Egypt. *Sci Med J Cairo Med Synd 1995;7*:131–144.

MacMahon, B., & Pugh, T. F. *Epidemiology: Principles and Methods* (Boston: Little, Brown, 1970).

Reich, M. R., & Okubo, T., Eds. *Protecting Workers' Health in the Third World* (New York: Auburn House, 1992).

Risk factors for cardiovascular disease in the developing world. A multicentre collaborative study in the International Clinical Epidemiology Network (INCLEN). INCLEN Multicentre Collaborative Group. *J Clin Epidemiol 1992;45(8)*:841–847.

Schilling, R. S., & McDonald, J. C. Occupational health at the London School of Hygiene and Tropical Medicine. *Brit J Ind Med 1990;47*:125–137.

Solórzano, A. Sowing the seeds of neo-imperialism: The Rockefeller Foundation's yellow fever campaign in Mexico. *Int J Health Serv 1992;22*:529–554.

World Bank. *Development and the Environment: World Development Report 1992* (New York: Oxford University Press, 1992).

30

Field Epidemiology Training Programs: Continuing Innovation in Epidemiologic Training

Heidi Lyn Holt and Daniel B. Fishbein

DEFINITION

Field Epidemiology Training Programs (FETPs) are training programs in applied epidemiology and public health for health professionals located in different countries around the world. They are established to provide a continuous supply of epidemiologists who learn about epidemiology and public health by applying it to disease prevention and control at national, provincial and local levels.

FETPs are loosely modeled after the Centers for Disease Control and Prevention's (CDC) Epidemic Intelligence Service (EIS) Program.[1] The EIS and FETP trainees are primarily physicians, but dentists, veterinarians, laboratorians, and pharmacists have also participated. The EIS Program has trained almost 2,000 physicians, veterinarians, dentists, nurses, statisticians, and behavioral and social scientists since it began in 1951 and now provides a continuous supply of epidemiologists to local, state, and national health departments in the United States. However only a relatively small number of these EIS graduates work in other countries.[1]

FETPs were developed to fill this gap. The main goal of the FETPs is the same as for the EIS Program: "To foster the professional development of epidemiologists who are competent in the practical application of epidemiologic methods to a wide range of contemporary public health problems".[1]

BACKGROUND

In 1979, the Kingdom of Thailand approached the CDC and asked for assistance in establishing its own in-country training program in applied epidemiology. A shortage of trained epidemiologists was recognized in several national five-year health plans, and continues to be strongly re-emphasized in the current five-year plan (1992–1997).[2] The decision was made to model this training program after the CDC's EIS Program. The Thailand program began as a national endeavor to build up a progressive center for supplying highly trained and experienced epidemiologists who were needed at the central, regional, and provincial levels.

In June 1980, in collaboration with the World Health Organization (WHO), a long-term CDC consultant epidemiologist was assigned to Thailand, and the first FETP was formally inaugurated.[3] Within two years, the improvement in epidemiological services was visible. Outbreak investigations became more detailed and new diseases were investigated. By October 1982, reporting of sexually transmitted diseases and tuberculosis had improved, reporting and publication of data were more timely, and the first stage of a computerized surveillance system was in place.[4] The long-term consultant was replaced in 1983 by a second consultant epidemiologist who remained through 1986. At that time, the Thailand FETP became autonomous, and Thailand became fully responsible for the coordination of the program.[5]

The success of the FETP in Thailand generated strong interest from other countries. The popularity of this first national training program was the impetus to negotiations for the next FETP, which began in Indonesia in 1982. As of March 1996, 14 FETPs and two "Public Health Schools Without Walls" have begun. Nine are autonomous programs (Tables 30.1 and 30.2).

ESTABLISHING AN FETP

FETPs are begun in response to national and sometimes international interest in increasing capacity to apply epidemiology to public health problems of a country. Programs in countries with low-income economies have required the financial support of an international donor, most often the U.S. Agency for International Development, but also the World Health Organization, the Rockefeller Foundation (in collaboration with its "Public Health Schools Without Walls" program), the World Bank, and the Pan-American Health Organization. The Rockefeller Foundation has played a key role in the establishment of a new type of Field Training Program, "Public Health Schools Without Walls." However, all the programs in countries with high-income economies and one program in a country with a middle-income economy (Colombia) have been implemented entirely with national resources.

TABLE 30.1 Directory of Field Epidemiology Training Programs and Public Health Schools Without Walls, March 1996

Name of Program and Director	Mailing Address	Phones, FAX and E-Mail
Australia Field Epidemiology Training Program Christine Roberts	National Centre for Epidemiology Population Health, Australian National University ACT, 0200, AUSTRALIA	Ph 51-62-49-2378 (NCEPH) Ph 61-62-49-5609 (direct) FA 61-62-49-0740 (NCEPH) email: Christine.Roberts@nceph.anu.edu.au
Canada Field Epidemiology Training Program Jamic Hockin, MD, MSc Program Director	Field Epidemiology Devision Laboratory Centre for Disease Control, Health Tunney's Pasture Postal Cocator 0603E1 Ottawa ON, CANADA K1AOK9	Ph 613-957-1764 FA 613-998-6413 email: JHOCKIN@HPb.Hwc.CA
Colombia Programa de Adiescramiento Avanzado en Spidemiologia Aplicada Fernando de la HOE, MD, Director	Instituto Nacional de Salud Avenida Eldorado y Carrera 50 Santafe de Bogotá, COLOMBIA	Ph 57-1-2220577 FA 57-1-2220194 email: ins@itece5.Telecom-co.Net
Egypt Field Epidemiology Training Program Dr. Esmat Manscur, Program Director Dr. Farouk Abdeen, Egyptian Counterpart	Ministry of Health Child Survival Project I Abd el Mageeb el Rimali St. Bab el Loug, Cairo EGYPT	Ph 20-2-354-5102 ext 241 (OFFICE) Ph 20-2-355-1598 (OFFICE: Farouk/Hatch)
Hungary Field Epidemiology Training Program Dr. Peter Rudnai, Dr. Tamas Angelus	National Public Health Center Public Health Program Unit P. O. Box 64 Budapest, H-1966, HUNGARY	Ph 36-1-215-5438 (office) Ph 361-215-5435 (fax) email: 72054.344@compuserve.com
Indonesia Field Epidemiology Training Program Hudoyo Hupudio, MD, MPH, FETP Director Yuwono Sidharta, MD, Assistant Director	FETP Dit EPIM Dit-Jen PPM & PLP—Kotak Pos 223 Jalan Percetakan Negara No 29 Jakarta 10520 INDONESIA	Ph 62-21-420-1511 (FETP) FA 62-21-420-7807 (DITJEN-PPM-PLP)

Program	Address	Contact
Italy Reparto Malattie Infettive Laboratorio di Epidemiologia e Biostatistica Dr. Donato Greco, Director Glasepe Salaminia, M. D.	Instituto Superiore Di Sanita' Largo Degli OSCI 22 00785 Rome, ITALY	Ph 39-6-445-4617 FA 39-6-446-8380 FA 39-6-445-6686 (or 6741) FA 39-6-446-0120
Mexico Epidemiologia Aplicade (PEA) Dr. Pablo Kuri Morales Director Ejecutiva	Dirección General de Epidemiologia FCO De P. Miranda 177, 3er Piso Col. Lomas de Plateroe Delegación Alvaro Obregon DF 01480 MEXICO	Ph 525-651-6970 FA 525-651-8700 email: CONYER@SERVIDOR.UNAM.MX
Peru Programa de Especializaoión en Epidemiologia de Campo [PREC] Dr. Mario Chuy Chui, MBP	Oficina General de Epidemiologia Ministerio de Salud Jr Camilo Carrilo 402 Jesus Maria, Lima, 11—PERU	Ph 51-14-335859 Ph 51-14-335428 FAX 51-14-336140 FAX 51-14-330081
Philippines Field Epidemiology Training Program Manolet M. Dayrit, M. D., M. Sc. Director	Dept. of Health, San Lazaro Compound, Sta. Cruz, Metro Manila, PHILIPPINES 597391	Ph 6-32-741-7048 FA 6-32 741-7048 email: 72054.332@compuserve.com
Saudi Arabia Field Epidemiology Training Program Nasser Al-Hamdan, M. D.	EPITRAIN, JECOR Unit 61306 APO AE 09803-1306	Ph 966-1-479-0726 (FAX x419) FA 966-1-478-1424 (FETP) FA 966-1-454-5076 (Nasser) FA 966-1-464-4870 (JECOR) email: 72054.345@compuserve.com
Spain Programa Epidemiologia Aplicada de Campo J. Fernando Martinez Navarro, Director Designate	Centro Nacional de Epidemiologia Sinesio Delgado, 6 28029 Madrid, SPAIN	Ph. 34-1-3141654 ext 22 FA 34-1-3147970

TABLE 30.1 *(Continued)*

Name of Program and Director	Mailing Address	Phones, FAX and E-Mail
Taiwan Field Epidemiology Training Program Chen Kow-Tong, M. D., MPH FETP Director	Department of Health P. O. Box 91-103 Taipei, TAIWAN	Ph 886-2-396-7764 (Day) Ph 886-2-928-5226 (Night) FA 886-2-321-0110 email: 72054.327@compuserve.com
Thailand Field Epidemiology Training Programme Kumnuan Ungchusak, M. D., Director Narumol Silarug, M. D., MPH, Deputy Director	Division of Epidemiology Permanent Secretary Office, Bldg. 6-F Ministry of Public Health Muang District, Nonthaburi 11000 THAILAND	Ph 66-2-591-8581 FA 66-2-591-8581 or 8579 email: nxs3@health.moph.go.th
Uganda Fred Wabwire-Mangen, M.B.Ch.B., M.P.H. Senior Lecturer and Head	MPH Program Institute for Public Health Makerere University PO Box 7072 Kampala, UGANDA	Ph: 256-41-531807 FAX: 256-41-531-807
Zimbabwe MPH Training Programme Ministry of Health & Child Welfare Dr. Paul Sikosana, MBBS, MPH (MOH) Dr. Reginald Matchaba, Chairman Department of Community Medicine	Ministry of Health & Child Welfare Kaguvi Bldg, Room 3-62 P. O. Box CY1122, Causeway Harare, ZIMBABWE University of Zimbabwe School of Medicine P. O. box A178, Avondale, Harare ZIMBABWE	Ph 263-4-738048 (MOH) Peterson ext 175; Sikosana ext 229 FA 263-4-793634 (MOH) FA 263-4-792145 (MOH) Ph 263-4-791631ext. 277 (UZ) FA 263-4-795019

TABLE 30.2 Structure of Field Epidemiology Training Programs, March 1996

COUNTRY	Cumulative Graduates	Location of Trainees	Concurrent 1st & 2nd Year Class	Program Inception	Program Autonomy*	Epidemiology Bulletin
Australia	14	States	Y	1991	1993	Bi-weekly
Canada	52	Central/ Province	Y	1975	1975	Bimonthly
Colombia	5	Central	Y	1992	No	No
Egypt	6	Central	Y	1993	No	No
Hungary	†	Central	Y	1995	No	No
Indonesia	58	Districts	Y	1982	1990	Monthly
Italy	5	Areas	N	1992	1993	No
Mexico	84	Central	Y	1984	1991	4 each Monthly
Peru	40	Central	N	1989	1995	Weekly
Philippines	40	Central	Y	1987	1994	Quarterly
Saudi Arabia	36	Central	Y	1989	No	Quarterly
Spain	‡	Central (2nd year in autonomous communities)	Y	1994	No	No
Taiwan	58	Central and local	Y	1984	1988	Monthly
Thailand	62	Central	Y	1980	1986	Weekly
Uganda**	†	Provinces	N	1994	No	No
Zimbabwe**	4	Provinces	Y	1994	No	No

*Autonomous, with regard to the FETPs, signifies the removal of a long-term, CDC-sponsored consultant, and removal of any external funding previously received. The usual period for an FETP to gain autonomy is 5 to 7 years.
†Will graduate 1st class in 1997.
‡Will graduate 1st class in 1996.
** Public Health Schools Without Walls.

The formal establishment usually begins with a visit of a one- or two-person assessment team from CDC and other international partners. Public health officials are interviewed and a country planning document is prepared for country evaluation. Certain commitments must be made by all parties involved in developing the program. The Ministry of Health (MOH) usually makes the commitment to support trainees in the performance of their investigations. Also, trainee positions by their nature should be full-time positions committed to epidemiology, without conflicting responsibilities. The Ministry of Health agrees to provide permanent local support staff, office space, and an FETP director to run the program once it is autonomous.

The basic model is designed to be flexible and responsive to the specific epidemiologic needs of its host country. Class size, training requirements, location of apprenticeship, and trainee certification all vary according to these needs. The names of the programs vary widely; a number of programs are not called FETPs. The Zimbabwe and Uganda training programs, which lead to a Masters of Public Health degree, are called "MPH programs" and are begun in close affiliation with local universities. However, the general goals and curriculum structure are similar, the main variation being in the quantity of didactic training and academic credits, and the location of trainees (in a single national office or in regional or local health departments) [Table 30.2].

To ensure quality as a program is being established, the first classes are usually small (three to five trainees per year). Trainees are selected from various sources. Recruiting is usually focused toward national, regional, and local public health program staff, recent graduates of medical schools, and public health school graduates, in an attempt to recruit persons with the potential to become leaders at regional and national levels. Competition may be keen, particularly when training is accompanied by special stipends.

The development of an FETP is a long process. The average time from assessment to the beginning of the first class is two years. This requires commitment and persistence on the part of many people within the host country and CDC. It is crucial that each FETP work toward a sustainable, institutionalized program. A strong relationship with the Ministry of Health is important to the FETP's future sustainability. The MOH should be willing to accept a long-term advisor to its program for the period of 2 to 8 years. The staff at CDC work with the long-term consultant and his or her counterpart to ensure a strong relationship between the FETP and the MOH exists before removing the long-term consultant. Also, once a program is autonomous, the CDC is then able to better focus efforts on assisting in the establishment of new FETPs and expanding the network of training programs.

Once the FETP program is established and the trainees are selected, the training begins with several weeks of didactic lectures, case studies, and computer training to provide trainees with a basic foundation in epidemiologic methods and statistics. The introductory course usually concludes with a field survey, a number of which have been of sufficient importance and quality to have been published in the national and international scientific literature.[11,12] The introductory course is followed by a minimum of 18 months of supervised, on-the-job field work, which is supplemented with additional didactic training and exercises.

The apprenticeship nature of the programs supports the goal of training in applied epidemiology. Although the location and type of apprenticeship varies between and within country programs, it serves the common goal of training public health professionals to be competent, applied epidemiologists by actually practicing epidemiology. The course work and CDC consultant serve to reinforce and direct trainee behaviors toward correct and appropriate directions.

Upon completion of the training, graduates may be certified in a variety of manners. The criteria and method of certification is determined by the Ministry of Health during the planning stages. Options include special diplomas, specializations, Masters of Public Health degrees from a cooperating university, a Certificate of Completion from the CDC and/or the training program, and other masters degrees or credit toward other credentials for work accomplished during their training. These mechanisms are constructed on a country-by-country basis, depending on available resources, collaborative efforts, the cultural norms for particular credentials, and public health infrastructure needs.

The final step of a program is institutionalization, or being considered an established part of the public health system. Institutionalization is achieved when there is:

- leadership by a national director who is most often (or is assisted by) a graduate of the training program;
- organizational identity within the Ministry of Health;
- operational budget and authority; and
- self-sustaining cycles of recruiting, training, and graduation.

Through experience, the satisfaction of the above criteria has proven to be a great determinant of sustainability and institutionalization within countries.[6] Other items which may be useful in ensuring the sustainability of the FETP include:

- certification or credentialing of graduates;
- career paths for graduates;
- publication of an epidemiology bulletin;
- annual epidemiology conferences; and
- periodic external evaluations.

SCIENTIFIC MEETINGS

The directors and selected trainees of the programs meet each year at the Directors' Meeting and Scientific Conference held in the spring in conjunction with the Epidemic Intelligence Service (EIS) Conference at the CDC facilities in Atlanta, Georgia. Representatives of the FETP programs also meet every other year in a joint conference with International Clinical Epidemiology Network (INCLEN) and the International Epidemiologic Association (IEA). Both meetings include lectures by international authorities on various aspects of epidemiology and public health, presentations by FETP trainees, and formal and informal discussions of administrative and program development issues.

Accomplishments and Public Health Contributions of FETPs

FETPs have never been established to meet a clearly defined and measurable public health goal, such as control of a specific disease. The contribution of FETPs to their host countries is, therefore, much more difficult to quantify than programs aimed at specific public health goals. This section will use three criteria to evaluate the accomplishments and public health contributions of FETPs.

1. *Success at building sustainable epidemiologic capacity in their host countries.* Although the location and type of apprenticeship varies between and within country programs, all programs share a common goal of increasing the number of competent, applied epidemiologists. Since the 1980 inception of the first FETP, the programs have graduated over 350 epidemiologists. At least 90 percent of these graduates receive or return to a public health position at national, regional, or local levels. Indonesia, for example, has 41 percent of graduates working at the central Ministry of Health (MOH), 28 percent at the regional (provincial) level, and 28 percent at the local (district) level. As of March 1996, all FETPs but two (Italy and Peru) continue to enroll and train new classes of epidemiologists.

2. *Contributions to the public health of their countries.* While it is not possible to quantify the contribution that the FETPs have made to their ministries of health, the FETPs have responded to and addressed numerous public health problems in their respective countries.[6] Some more

TABLE 30.3 Excerpts of External Evaluations of FETPs

Mexico, 1988: The FETP is a successful program which deserves continued support. A number of significant problem areas and recommendations for improvement were listed.

Philippines, 1990: The FETP is remarkable for its achievement of very strong support from the secretary, Department of Health (DOH), and his undersecretaries. It has good relations with DOH program managers, and important institutions (outside the DOH). One of the outstanding achievements of the FETP is the hospital-based Sentinel Surveillance System.

Thailand, 1990: The FETP was well accepted within the health services and academic community, and was meeting the goals of the Ministry of Public Health in producing specialist epidemiologists and strengthening epidemiologic capabilities at central, provincial, and district levels.

Kingdom of Saudi Arabia, 1993: The FETP is contributing significantly to the public health needs. Numerous successes of the program have defined an on-going role for epidemiology.

recent accomplishments of FETPs are presented in Table 30.4, Many of these investigations are communicated to the epidemiologic community at national and international conferences (above), and numerous investigations and studies have been published in the peer-reviewed scientific literature.

3. *Results of external evaluations of the FETP programs.* The FETP program, sometimes in conjunction with the bilateral donor that supports the FETP, periodically conducts evaluation of individual programs. These evaluations have almost always been laudatory, although they are frequently accompanied by suggestions for improvement (Table 30.3).

FUTURE DIRECTIONS

There are two dimensions of FETPs that have yet to be evaluated and that are important in assessing the contribution of these programs. One is the appropriateness and effectiveness of the EIS model and the CDC support of the programs. An evaluation of the CDC component of these programs will be conducted in 1995 and 1996, and any definitive comments about the CDC model should await the results of this evaluation.

A second dimension in need of evaluation is the ability of FETPs to respond to changing needs of their ministries of health, countries, and the international community. FETPs must be successful not only in terms of a public health model that was established in the late 1950s (at CDC) and in the 1980s (in Thailand), but also in terms of the international public health priorities of the 1990s. Measurement of the ability to respond to changing needs is difficult, but the selected accomplishments of the FETPs (Table 30.4) suggest that the programs continue to address new public health problems. The ability to address new and emerging problems of importance to their countries may be one of the great strengths of the FETP programs. For example, in Peru, the prompt response of the FETP to the cholera epidemic may partially be responsible for the low case-fatality rates seen in that country.[13]

The above questions notwithstanding, the long-term goal for the International Branch at CDC is to continue to develop a global network of sustainable, national epidemiology training programs that will provide a group of trained, competent epidemiologists and increase the capacity of nations to prevent and control disease. In addition to improving and guiding established programs, the CDC continues to assist with the development of new FETPs. There are currently three FETPs in the planning stages: the Dominican Republic, Guatemala, and South Africa. Preliminary negotiations with other countries are also in process.

TABLE 30.4 Selected Public Health Contributions of the FETPs and Public Health Schools Without Walls

Egypt: Identification of additional unreported polio cases through active surveillance helped guide polio eradication activities, and led to increased recognition in the Ministry of Health that the quality and accuracy of data are useful to guide decisions.

Colombia: The program has addressed public health problems neglected by the Ministry of Health. One of these is the epidemic of violence in Colombia, which is being assessed in terms of the costs and amount of services required as a result of injuries. The program has participated in a national effort to make an epidemiological surveillance network for injuries. Other issues that have been addressed include immunopreventable diseases like pertussis, a disease of previously unrecognized seriousness.

Thailand: Establishment of HIV/AIDS surveillance; weekly surveillance report and annual epidemiologic summary, and an annual national epidemiology seminar.

Zimbabwe: Having trainees assigned to provinces has increased the use of operational research to address new and longstanding problems. Investigation of outbreaks now goes beyond the simplest description of the problem, instead following more proper epidemiologic approaches and working systematically to make new recommendations for disease control.

Philippines: The FETP has produced 40 highly skilled field epidemiologists currently serving in various capacities at the central, regional, provincial, and city health offices nationwide. A national sentinel surveillance system has been set up which collects data on 14 infectious diseases and injuries. Outbreak investigations, surveys, and surveillance activities conducted by FETP trainees and graduates have helped achieve a better understanding of the dynamics of several public health problems, such as cholera, red-tide poisoning, and fireworks-related injuries, resulting in more effective prevention and control programs.

Several obstacles exist to the development of FETPs. One is funding. The cost of developing a program often varies according to funding source, infrastructure needs, and qualifications of the consultant epidemiologist. Since many of these countries that need epidemiologic capacity building have limited discretionary funds, the need to look for alternative methods of funding arises. One possible mechanism is to use graduates of FETPs to establish programs. The use of such graduates decreases the largest single component of the above financial requirements, the salary and support of an American on official duty overseas. Colombia has been extremely successful in establishing a program using graduates of the Mexican FETP as consultants.

It is expected that a global network of training programs will exist in the future. Continuous sharing of knowledge and the combination of efforts toward the common goals of disease prevention and control are crucial to improved global public health. The health of one country is not isolated from that of another. With this in mind, CDC hopes to network these programs together with telecommunications equipment, epidemiologic bulletins, continuing participation in scientific conferences, and regular direct interaction, thereby reducing the communications isolation that currently affects many countries.

REFERENCES

1. Thacker, S. B., Goodman, R. A., & Dicker, R. C. Training and Service in Public Health Practice, 1951-90-CDC's Epidemic Intelligence Service. *Public Health Reports. 1990; 105*: 599–604.
2. External Evaluation of the Thailand Ministry of Public Health Field Epidemiology Training Programme (FETP), October 29–November 16, 1990. Unpublished.
3. Field Epidemiology Training Programme. *Weekly Epidemiological Record 1981; 7*: 49–56.
4. Field Epidemiology Training Programme: Annual Report 1981–1982. *Weekly Epidemiological Record 1982; 41*: 313–320.
5. Autonomous, with regard to the FETPs, signifies the removal of a long-term, CDC-sponsored consultant, and removal of any external funding previously received. The usual period for a FETP to gain autonomy is 5 to 7 years. CDC maintains an ongoing relationship with all autonomous FETPs, including meeting at least once a year as a large group to discuss sustainability and programmatic issues.
6. Music, S. I., & Schultz, M. G. Field Epidemiology Training Programs: New International Health Resources. *JAMA. 1990; 263*: 3309–3311.
7. Field Epidemiology Training Programme: Annual Report 1980–1981. *Weekly Epidemiological Record 1981; 41*: 321–325.
8. Field Epidemiology Training Programme: Annual Report 1982–1983. *Weekly Epidemiological Record 1983; 45*: 345–352.
9. Field Epidemiology Training Programme. *Weekly Epidemiological Record 1983; 9*: 61–68.
10. Field Epidemiology Training Programme: Monthly Report July 1981. *Weekly Epidemiological Record 1981; 42*: 334.
11. Brandling-Bennett, A. D., Jatanasen, S., Maturosapas, W., Kunasol, P., & Brachman, P. S. *World Health Forum 1983; 4*: 344–347.
12. Anonymous. AIDS-related knowledge and behaviors among teenagers in Italy—1990. *MMWR 1991; 40*: 214–215, 221.
13. Anonymous. Use of seat belts in front seat occupants—Madrid, 1994. *MMWR 1995; 44*.
14. Anonymous. Cholera—Peru, 1991. *MMWR 1991; 40*: 108–109.

31

Urban and Rural Planning: Impact on Health and the Environment

Roberto Luís Monte-Mór

URBAN-REGIONAL PLANNING IN THE BRAZILIAN AMAZONIAN FRONTIER

In recent decades, the transformation of parts of Amazonia into an agricultural and mining frontier has followed a pattern of territorial expansion that has characterized the Brazilian economy since colonial days. Although efforts to occupy Amazonia have been present since Portuguese domination, it was only in the early 1970s that public and private investments truly changed the face of that region. The opening of major roads linking the new national capital—Brasilia—to northern states paved the way for the sale of cheap land to cattle-ranching enterprises and agro-colonization projects. In fact, the contemporary Amazonian frontier responded to the military governments' multi-purpose efforts to fuel Brazil's resource-oriented economic model, to lessen social conflicts and land-tenure pressures in both agricultural areas and overcrowded metropolises in southern regions, and to enforce the geo-political strategies aimed at guaranteeing sovereignty and control over that un(der)populated territory. "Land without People for People without Land" was the official slogan ratifying Brazil's nonagrarian reform policies in the overpopulated southern regions.

Attempts to promote and control the occupation of the new frontier led to public policies based on economic incentives for cattle ranching, mineral research, public infrastructure, and colonization schemes. Land price differentials between Amazonia and other regions, mineral findings and timber affluence attracted a variety of productive and speculative capitals. It also attracted thousands of landless workers and small farmers interested in acquiring free or low-priced public land.

Colonization projects occupied stretches of land one hundred kilometers wide along the main highways, and the former Federal Territory of Rondonia (a state since 1981), in Western Amazonia, became a major experiment in public colonization conducted by the National Agency for Agrarian Reform—INCRA.

Planning schemes from federal to municipal levels placed the state at the center of frontier expansion in most areas. Federal and state agencies for regional development (communications, energy, transportation, agricultural support and research, mineral activities, banking and financial activities, etc.) produced a myriad of local and regional plans for the region. City planning was financed for medium and large cities, and most public and private colonization schemes incorporated town and country planning in their attempts to organize the social space.

Those multiple experiences in regional and urban-rural planning did not, however, prevent a wide spectrum of serious social and environmental problems brought about by poverty, sociopolitical violence and tropical diseases. At first, pilot experiences produced encouraging results, as dormant soils put to agricultural use responded well to traditional farming methods. But it soon became clear that INCRA could not cope with the avalanche of migrants demanding farming land in public colonization projects. Concurrently, private colonization projects, mostly concentrated in Southern Para and Mato Grosso, did not guarantee profitable returns, often complicated by property invasions by *garimpeiros* (placer miners) and/or landless settlers, and did not entice the overflow demand of INCRA. In addition, good soil plots in Amazonia were much less prevalent than expected, and the creation of necessary infrastructure throughout the region required more effort and funds than the agonizing "Brazilian Miracle"—annual GNP growth rates over 10 percent from the late 1960s to the mid-1970s—could support.

Problems of transportation and storage of agricultural goods, limited regional and local markets, high transport costs to the southern markets, insufficient technical and financial support and limited infrastructure all contributed to determine the relative failure of the colonization model and the further impoverishment of the majority of migrants. By the late 1970s, intense health problems revealed the impacts of the socioeconomic failure and of the environmental disruption caused by deforestation and mining.

EXTENDED URBANIZATION AND THE CONDITIONS OF PRODUCTION

The sociospatial and environmental conditions generated in Amazonia by agricultural settlements, cattle ranching, mining and forest extraction are quite different when compared to older frontiers in Brazil. This is partly due to the rather unique natural conditions of the tropical jungle, and to the fact that patterns of production and occupation of social space in that frontier are closely linked to the dynamics of contemporary urban-industrial capitalism.

In fact, contrary to what is commonly expected, Amazonia is much more complex a region than a pristine jungle occupied by native inhabitants and poor migrants from all over Brazil in search of land and gold. Indeed, dispossessed rural workers were among the most willing to move into such a hostile region, coping with its pervasive precarious conditions of (re)production.

However, this is only part of the picture. The scenario also includes the spatial dynamics of Brazil's late urban-industrial capitalism. Such an extension to Amazonia implies a twofold movement of capital, commodities, services, and labor that redefines the socio-spatial relations between the new frontier and the industrialized regions.

The occupation of Amazonia must also, and perhaps primarily, be examined from the perspective of Brazil's urban-industrial development model and of the extension of its general conditions of production. The spread of those conditions is based on *extended urbanization,* a vital and pervasive socio-spatial network that links Amazonia to the rest of the country. It constitutes a privileged perspective from which to grasp the nature of urban and rural settlements, the organization of micro-regional space and the environmental conditions there produced. It also sheds light on the health implications derived from such a socio-spatial pattern.

Before moving further it is necessary to clarify what is meant by *extended urbanization* in this context. This concept derives from Henri Lefebvre's work (1968a, 1968b, 1972, 1974, 1976) in which the terms *urban tissue, urban nucleus-i,* and *urban process* refer to a theoretical perspective that looks at urbanization as a particular socio-spatial form generated within late industrial capitalism and defines *urban* as the locus of the mobilization, production, appropriation and absorption of social surplus.

Extended urbanization reaches beyond city limits, though encompassing it. It spreads throughout regional space as capitalist relations produce the socio-spatial conditions necessary for continuing accumulation. The resulting socio-spatial forms respond to the urban-industrial conditions of production, circulation and collective reproduction of labor demanded by late capitalism. It derives from what Lefebvre calls *the urban process,* a result of the merge/clash between the capitalist industry and the pre-existing city. The political and/or mercantile city, taken over by capitalist industrial production, is radically transformed: the city, traditionally the locus of power and surplus, becomes also the locus of production itself. The political foundations of the traditional city are partially lost, and depoliticization is a consequence of its recreation under direct dominance of production. Submitted to the immediate needs of capitalist industrialism, the city itself is transformed from *work* (oeuvre)—use value—into *product*—exchange value. The result is a new dialectical unity organized in two relational parts emerging from the *implosion/explosion* of the city: on one hand is the locus of power, the *urban nucleus* imploded into the historical core redefining the "downtown" area; on the other is the locus of industrial production (and reproduction) exploded upon the periphery in the form of an *urban tissue,* i.e., a socio-spatial network spreading beyond the city to reach regional scale.

In Amazonia, extended urbanization is more prevalent than most of the literature is willing to perceive or accept. "Two faces of a same coin" (Becker, 1985), urbanization and frontier expansion represent the penetration of capitalism in areas that were internally organized under pre-capitalist relations, though externally integrated to capitalism through export-oriented production. This integration has allowed for large transnational and national investments in mining, cattle ranching, timber, and electronics production to coexist with peasant colonization and small farm production by southern and northeastern migrants, and rubber and nut extraction by native inhabitants. Extended urbanization integrates all levels—territories and scales—mediating local and international forces, national and regional interests, amidst the intense circulation of capital and labor.

Social Production of Space and Urban-Rural Relations

The micro-regional and urban-rural social space produced in the Amazonian frontier is significantly different from both traditional extractive Amazonia and other agricultural frontiers in Brazil. Geopolitical and socio-economic concerns led to a vast network of communication and transportation services covering most of the region's occupied area: local television stations transmit everywhere, changing the face of the region as bulldozers and chain-saws (not to mention fire) dramatically produce a new "nature." Different times and spatialities co-exist as late capitalist integration carries commodities everywhere, generalizing consumption, restructuring traditional forms of production, and revealing a surprising contemporary synchronicity. Extractive activities, cattle ranching and agriculture, transferred surplus, personal savings, and public investment assure the existence of widespread urban-industrial relations.

The process of territorial (and economic) integration in Brazil has its roots in the 1930s when President Vargas's nationalist dictatorship—"Estado Novo"—consolidated a strong central government that invested heavily in industrialization and its required conditions: transportation and energy, organized labor, and the search for natural resources. Those import substitution policies were strengthened during the War and magnified during Kubitschek's "fifty-years-in-five" term (1956/60). Concentrated investments in hydroelectric plants, automotive industries, the construction of Brasilia and the opening of federal highways across Amazonia defined the major lines along which the "miraculous" economy of the late 1960s and early 1970s would develop.

The opening of the country to foreign capital increased and redefined the process of urbanization during the 1950s and 1960s. Metropolises grew fast, for only they reunited the necessary conditions of production for the durable goods industry. An organized labor force, investments in infrastructure, a rationalized state apparatus and a financial market guaranteed, in major state capitals, Brazil's selective "Welfare State." In the interior, resource-oriented industries produced their own urban-industrial space building new towns or attaching themselves to existing ones.

Intensive rural-urban migration, Brazil's major trend in the recent decades, brought nearly 30 million net migrants to cities between 1960 and 1980, when urbanization reached 68 percent of the total Brazilian population (Monte-Mór et al., 1992). The urban-industrial tissue was extended in the metropolitan areas as population concentrated: Brazil's nine Metropolitan Regions (MRs) comprised 25.7 percent of the country's population in 1970, and 29.1 percent, in 1980. The new conditions of production were then extended into the country as a whole, to include Amazonia as new resource areas.

Investments in urban services and infrastructure did not keep pace with urbanization, nor did the capital-intensive industrialization produce the necessary jobs to incorporate the new contingent of migrants who demanded those selectively localized conditions of (re)production. Instead, collective reproduction deteriorated in the country's major urban areas and diseconomies of agglomeration led to deconcentration tendencies that impacted upon medium and small towns and their hinterlands.

In the same period, the countryside experienced two major transformations: the modernization of export-agriculture (particularly mechanized soybean farming) and the destruction of low-productivity market and/or subsistence-oriented small-scale agricultural production. As a result, petit-agricultural land was taken over by export crops or by sugarcane plantations to supply Brazil's ethanol-fueled automobile industry. Small farmers and peasants were displaced, having for options migration to urban-industrial areas or to the frontier.

The result of this dual process was both the concentration and exclusion of poor populations in metropolitan areas, as well as land tenure concentration and the displacement of workers and small proprietors from traditional rural areas. This contingent of disenfranchised workers constituted part of the families who migrated to Amazonia. The other part is composed of merchants, small capitalists, state functionairies, professionals and middle-class semi-qualified workers in search for better conditions to compete.

In the context of extended urbanization, urban and regional planning efforts were redirected to systems of cities and their market areas. The "urban tissue" brought everywhere electricity, communications and production services, financial and commercial networks, and a widespread bureaucratic order that redefined time, space and social life itself. These new conditions allowed for those economically integrated high levels of collective consumption based on private cars, durable goods in general, and an ample consumption basket, reaching even remote areas such as Amazonia.

The extension of selective urban-industrial conditions of production to the Amazonian frontier produced an environmental milieu that combined the undeveloped and isolated situation of quasi-peasants occupying a continental jungle with the mobility and capitalist competition that characterizes urban areas in developed regions of Brazil. This spatial combination stresses the particular dialectic relationships between nature and socially produced space thus redefining, at various scales, the ecological possibilities and forms of (re)production in Amazonia.

URBAN AND RURAL PLANNING, MALARIA AND THE ENVIRONMENT

From the beginning, the Amazonian frontier was thought of as an extension of Brazil's urban-industrial space. Regional policies, urban planning, and rural urbanism (Monte-Mór, 1980) were applied at various scales and levels: regions and micro-regions, states and territories, towns and hamlets, public and private colonization projects.

Spontaneous economic processes and activities have produced "proto-urban" concentrations throughout the frontier: camps and mining communities (often transforming into towns), large timber industries and capitalist farms with housing and social services, storage facilities, cooperative services, urban nuclei for rural support, etc. Communication networks link local to international contexts while transportation systems integrate the occupied areas with the rest of the country. Furthermore, extensive bus services connect urban nuclei and rural settlements, producing crowded bus stations in almost every town. The proliferation of trucks, vans, cars, airplanes, motorboats, machinery for road construction, timber extraction and mining (water-pumps, chain-saws) produce a network of industrial services that reaches even distant localities. Rather sophisticated commerce and services networks in towns and villages infuse mass TV-culture into "primitive" social environments. The patterns of accessibility within the frontier have currently reached levels not seen before in other frontiers, bringing Brazil's national space integration to a new threshold.

It is not surprising, in this context, that migrants maintain close connections with other regions. Migration to Amazonia does not simply mean population displacement from a region to the other, it also gives rise to a series of intense population movements between the newly settled region and the migrants' areas of origin. At the same time, the frontier displays rather unexpected internal mobility of commodities, information, labor, etc., despite the difficulties posed by limited resources, enormous distances and hostile natural conditions.

These widespread urban-industrial conditions of production—extended urbanization—produce new forms of socio-spatial organization that impact social and environmental problems, including disease transmission and health control in Amazonia. Ecological disequilibrium, man-made disruption and precarious conditions of reproduction have generated problems of malnutrition, insufficient sanitation in crowded, unequipped urban areas, accidents in timber and mining activities, and the reappearance of endemic infectious diseases, of which malaria is the most widespread.

In the case of malaria, the production of the environment and social space lies at the basis of disease control, since the favorable natural and socially built environmental conditions determine local levels of transmission. In fact, malaria control has proved to be a much more difficult task in Amazonia than in other parts of the country. The high density of mosquito vectors and the precarious socio-environmental conditions in settlement areas (low income, poor housing, insufficient services and environmental disruption) have greatly increased the levels of malaria infection. Migration and internal mobility make it difficult to control treatment itself and the various forms of risk contacts.

As the frontier is rapidly deforested and urban-industrial space is socially produced, malaria outbreaks claim thousands of victims in both urban and rural areas, the disease following the precarious implementation of the extended conditions of production. The number of malaria cases in Brazil multiplied by ten between 1970 (54,644 cases) and 1990 (560,396 cases), while the Annual Parasite Index (API) increased from 0.6 to 3.9 per thousand. Since virtually all malaria transmission in Brazil is restricted to Amazonia, the API for the region surpassed 30 in 1990 (Sawyer & Monte-Mór, 1992). Microregions that had historically registered low levels of malaria eventually became "contaminated" by infected individuals, be they miners moving from site to site in search of gold or agricultural settlers moving back and forth between "old" colonization areas and new ones.

On the other hand, Brazil's traditional control method of DDT spraying in the houses did not prove effective in Amazonia due to housing conditions (in mining camps or early colonization projects, huts actually lack walls on which to spray the poison), high exposure to the forest and breeding areas, and changes in the assumed vectors' habits, i.e., from endophilic and endophagic to exophilic and exophagic, among other factors (Sawyer et.al., 1987). Absence of experience with the Amazonian environment among migrants and the mutant and varied nature of the disease itself has added to rapid dissemination and high levels of infection.

Given the ubiquitous environmental conditions for reproduction of the malaria vector (adequate climate, multiple water breeding sites partially shaded and containing organic matter), the central transmission factor is the encounter of contaminated human beings with vector populations. This time-spatial determination is related to the forms in which work and living spaces (and environments) are produced and organized, as well as to the patterns of inter- and intra-regional population movements. It is also related to the spatial distribution and efficiency of malaria treatment services.

Many characteristics are found in the Amazonian frontier that increase risks of contamination, as compared to other traditional rural areas, even in Amazonia itself. On one side, the very nature of the work done by settlers and/or *garimpeiros* constitute a high-risk exposure to vectors within the natural environment, i.e., in the various forms of jungle (meaning the pristine forests), and the secondary forests (meaning deforested areas restored to natural conditions). In both cases, the destruction of habitats provokes malaria outbreaks and men who do the forest-clearing belong to the highest risk group.

On the other side, production of space and built environment itself can increase the risks of contamination by changing the local ecology and producing new conditions for mosquito breeding. Road construction, for example, produces a series of artificial water collections (side borrowing pits, small bridges and dams, dirt fills)—man-made breeding sites throughout the settlements. The same effect can be caused by town construction, timber mills, mining and newly cleared pasture and agricultural areas.

Other urban spatial forms include electricity, motor vehicles, modern lighting and flash-lamps that allow people to be outside longer and more often after dark, thus increasing exposure. Similarly, recreational practices including parties and community television in forested areas contribute to additional exposure and risk.

The various stages and timings of the occupation of the jungle also shape patterns of spatial mobility and consequent risks of disease transmission. The migrant, whether coming from Brazil's northern regions (therefore with more experience and adaptability to local conditions) or from southern regions, very rarely possesses the requirements to move directly to the acquired rural lot. Instead, settlement includes stages in which parts of the family might live in a town, in a friend's or relative's rural lot, or in another previously acquired lot before completely relocating. The "urban base" (meaning a house in town) is a common device to allow for both access to social services and to urban jobs and temporary work responsible for cash to maintain the family in the beginning years (Monte-Mór, 1980). In short, a myriad of situations have in common a pattern of circular movements between the new settlement area and locales of temporary settlement. The interactions between these spatially mobile and socially heterogeneous groups greatly increase contamination risks.

In mining communities, the scenario is tinted by the extremely high mobility of *garimpeiros*. They enter the forest in search of new mineral findings, living in precarious and densely populated huts. Working almost naked in water collections and building their villages near clear forest waters (perfect breeding sites) and degradated mining areas, these ill-treated infected miners concentrate by the dozens, hundreds or thousands (Monte-Mór, 1986). Mining camps are, therefore, areas where the urban and rural environments combine to produce privileged conditions for malaria infection. In addition, miners constantly move from site to site, from one mining hamlet to the other and back to towns for supply and/or to rural areas to visit relatives.

Miners' way of living does not encourage obedience to adequate and/or complete malaria treatments. Lost work days are economically, socially, and ideologically undesirable. Therefore, levels of drug resistance and asymptomatic infection contribute to endemic contamination. Although tap-miners and (agricultural) settlers might present strong differences and oppositions, they are by no means mutually exclusive, both familiarly and individually, and these interrelationships also add to the transmission risks.

Even in more stable agricultural and cattle-ranching areas, permanent settlement in a rural lot or a town (most commonly, both) does not imply immobility: circular movements do not cease (Monte-Mór, 1986). Instead, they are part of the frontier: *regular* movements result from the socio-spatial organization of the family or economic group. They include interactions (complementary or not) between distinct activities such as agriculture and gold-mining, jobs in close-by towns, timber-mills, construction companies, etc., and, therefore, various work bases can be located in different mining camps and/or rural lots. Trips also are for health treatments, education, business purposes and other situations that characterize the urban-rural integrated space of frontier Amazonia. In addition, there are *seasonal* movements: trips to other regions when rainfall drastically reduces activities in Amazonia and temporary work in forest-clearing, harvesting, and nut collection.

Spatial and Environmental Planning and Malaria Control

The high levels of mobility confronted with the primitive work and living conditions contribute both to the spread of malaria and to the difficulties in controlling its transmission in Amazonia. Although it is possible to recognize common aspects of malaria transmission, risks of exposure and difficulties of control are not uniform. It depends greatly on the levels of the settlements' socio-spatial organization. Construction, research and mining companies, for example, who allocate their personnel in protected areas (with broad forest clearing, surrounding wooden walls, and malathion spraying), provide adequate and fast malaria treatments, and offer proper housing (solid walls, screens) and better environmental handling manage to avoid high levels of infection. Modern individual care using mosquito-nets, proper clothing, repellents, and chemical spraying also protect from contamination, as research teams have empirically shown. On the other hand, the older the settlement, the more likely it contains better working and living conditions, larger distances to vector habitats, reflected in lower infection rates.

Local conditions and levels of infection and transmission express a combination of factors: (a) vector contact including density and risk exposure; (b) environmental factors at the macro-environment and the micro-environment at the levels of the peri-domicile and intra-domicile; (c) population characteristics such as degrees of immunity, knowledge of the disease, levels of education, community values, and spatial mobility; (d) institutional features, such as health services, technical support, transportation facilities, and educational campaigns.

Analyses of data collected on the socio-economic and environmental aspects of malaria transmission and control in three Amazonian micro-regions—Southern Para, Rondonia and Northern Mato Grosso—by the CEDEPLAR research team since the early 1980s have shown differentials related to various geographical, social and environmental risk factors (Sawyer et. al., 1987; Sawyer & Monte-Mór, 1992). Rural activities, in general, and those that demand contact with the forest, in particular, are important risk factors that can be reduced through improvements in the macro- and micro-environments. Furthermore, increased health education and community mobilization has been shown effective in lowering risks.

Several control measures related to urban-rural relations have been identified in new settlements (Sawyer & Monte-Mor, 1992). The use of urban lots for settlement, for example, can avoid higher risks to families at the first stages of occupation. This implies that project design should require the establishment of multiple urban nuclei to allow for proximity to work areas while maintaining considerable distance from forests and breeding places. In fact, our data (Sawyer et al., 1987; Sawyer & Monte-Mór, 1992) also show that the greater the eco-social stability of the population (meaning time of arrival and regional acquaintance, amount of land cleared, and peri-domicile control), the lower the malaria risks. Houses located farther from the jungle or secondary forest, greater distance from water collections, vegetation clearance and control in the peri-domicile, topographical location of houses (hill tops show risk differentials as compared to low areas) and housing quality are some of the factors that can help reduce risks.

MACHADINHO D'OESTE, RONDÔNIA: TEN YEARS OF EPIDEMIC MALARIA

The Machadinho Settlement Project, state of Rondonia, whose occupation began in 1984, incorporated in its design and planning some of the socio-spatial and environmental characteristics that seem helpful in preventing malaria infection. Roads were located on water basin dividers, thus minimizing local bridges and man-made water collections (although the luxurious local hydrography still required over 600 bridges) while providing for house location near the roads and, consequently, far from streams and rivers on the rear part of the rural lots. Urban lots in the newly built small town provided settlers with the possibility of choosing a more protected area (theoretically) to live in. Small urban nuclei were built to offer urban housing conditions and health and education services throughout the project. Wooden boards given to early settlers for house construction attempted to guarantee better living conditions. Technical support from federal and state agencies should help develop production methods and provide adequate services.

However, those efforts did not prevent malaria outbreaks nor succeed in avoiding epidemic malaria transmission throughout the first ten years in the project area. Two years after settlement began, Machadinho registered the highest malaria infection rates in Brazil, more so in the town itself. Among other factors, the relatively high population density and strong urban-rural mobility within the area were responsible for the disease concentration.

Many are the reasons for the failure of the Machadinho Project concerning malaria control. They range from the settlers' economic weakness and socio-cultural limitations regarding the Amazonian environment to insufficient social, technical and financial support by public agencies, of which health services are the major example. On the other hand, strong interactions with nearby mining areas, high internal and external mobility of the population, lack of information about the disease itself and low levels of education added to the failure in controlling malaria in the area. Instead, malaria became the central reason for the high levels of attrition found in Machadinho's early years of settlement.

Although the town eventually grew to become a new municipality—Machadinho D'Oeste—and the settlement project developed towards socio-economic stabilization, the lack of more thorough and effective planning can be identified as one of the causes of Machadinho's socio-economic difficulties and persistent malaria problems.

Among various traits of such a misguided planning experience is the weakness of social development programs. In accordance with Brazil's traditional urban and regional planning paradigms, emphasis rested on economic efficiency expecting better socio-environmental conditions to be its necessary byproduct. Given that economic determinants were not controlled at the local level, depending instead on national and international factors (markets, credit, public investments), economic weakness generated a scenario of severe social and environmental disruption.

Participatory planning was also neglected and community action was only marginally encouraged by the public health agency—SUCAM (today, FNS—National Health Foundation), and it only happened after the epidemic scenario had already become entrenched. Given its technical and economic limitations to conduct actions beyond the traditional malaria control methods (DDT sparying), SUCAM's induced communitary action was restricted to selective breeding site control and health education.

Ten years later, malaria control in Rondonia shows significant improvements. Spatial zoning and updated information allow FNS to rapidly identify areas of high transmission. Zonal monitoring helps to implement control measures that also include malathion spraying, active search for rapid treatment, and community participation in the identification and notification on infected individuals and in providing preliminary treatments. In fact, levels of infection decreased significantly in the early 1990s only to raise again last year due to new forest-clearings in the surrounding area and to administrative and institutional crises in FNS.

The Machadinho case illustrates how urban-rural relations in settlement areas in Amazonia helped redefine and integrate contemporary tendencies in urban and rural planning with health control measures. It also dramatically shows that control strategies must follow a tight program if new epidemics are to be avoided. Any loosening in control action might lead to new outbreaks, both in urban-rural areas and in large towns, such as Porto Velho and Manaus, where malaria has recently reappeared with surprising virulence. Other examples could be drawn from Para and Mato Grosso.

Little has yet been done to replace the technocratic planning schemes of the past decades with participatory actions involving local communities in the planning process. As for health and environmental control, it is worth stressing the growing importance of civil society's participation (NGOs, unions, professional and neighborhood associations) in planning efforts conducted by the state at its various levels. It also appears tantamount to be very explicit about the need to incorporate environmental and health perspectives within the concerns of the urban-rural and regional planners themselves.

On the other hand, it also seems clear that attempts to control malaria transmission in the Amazonian frontier must increasingly take into consideration the socio-spatial and environmental problems brought about by the encounter of ecologically disruptive human activities with "hostile" nature. Micro-determinations suggested by specific local conditions are to be evaluated within the broader context of the extension of urban-industrial conditions of production that have characterized contemporary Brazil.

REFERENCES

Becker, B. (1985). Fronteira e Urbanização Repensadas. *R.Bras. Geogr.*, Rio de Janeiro, *47(3/4)*: 357–371, jul./dez.

LeFèbvre, H. (1968a). *La vie quotidienne dans le monde moderne*. Paris: Galimard.

LeFèbvre, H. (1968b). *Le droit à la ville*. Paris: Anthropos.

LeFèbvre, H. (1972). *La Revolución Urbana*. Madrid: Alianza.

LeFèbvre, H. (1974). *La production de l'espace*. Paris: Anthropos.

LeFèbvre, H. (1976). *The Survival of Capitalism: Reproduction of the Relations of Production*. London: Allison & Busby.

Monte-Mór, R. L. (1980). *Espaco e Planejamento Urbano: o caso de Rondonia*. Rio de Janeiro: UFRJ/COPPE. (M.Sc. Thesis).

Monte-Mór, R. L. (1986). Malaria e meio-ambiente na Amazonia Brasileira. In: SEMINARIO SOBRE POPULACAO E SAUDE. *Anais*... Campinas: Unicamp, Clacso.

Monte-Mór, R. L., Sawyer, D. R, & Sawyer, D. O. (1992). *Economic Development and Population Movements*. Paper presented in the Interregional Meeting on Malaria. Brasilia: Pan American Health Organization.

Sawyer, D. O., & Monte-Mór, R. L. (1992). *Malaria Risk Factors Assessment in Brazil*. Paper presented in the Interregional Meeting on Malaria. Brasilia: Pan American Health Organization.

Sawyer, D. R., et al. (1987). *Malaria on the Amazon Frontier: Economic and Social Aspects of Transmission and Control*. Belo Horizonte: CEDEPLAR. (Research Report).

32

The Partnership for Child Development: An International Program to Improve the Health and Education of Children Through School-Based Services

Donald Bundy and Andrew Hall

"Enough is now known to recommend health and nutrition programmes among efforts to increase school enrollment and learning."[1]

"The school setting itself offers opportunities to correct health and nutrition problems of public health and educational significance."[1]

In 1990 the World Summit for Children set a target of achieving basic primary education for at least 80 percent of children by the year 2000. If these children are to take full advantage of the education they are offered, their ability to attend school and to learn must not be compromised by ill health. The Partnership for Child Development was established in January 1992 to examine ways in which schools themselves can play a more active role in improving the health of school-aged children.

INTRODUCTION

As a result of the success of child survival programs almost 90 percent of the world's children now live to their fifth birthday. The school age population has increased by 42 percent between 1965 and 1985, and the educational authorities of the developing world have responded to this challenge by increasing school enrollments by 62 percent over the same period. Increasingly strong evidence indicates that this expansion of schooling increases national rates of economic growth and improves household income and welfare.[2]

These successes have, however, given old problems a new prominence. While child mortality rates have declined, there is evidence that levels of ill health and malnutrition have failed to decline as quickly: many children still face health problems that compromise their attendance at school and their ability to learn.

Although more children now survive to attend school, their ability to benefit from education is limited by ill health. It may now be time to expand the scope of child health programs to include the school-age child as well as the preschool child, and to seek new ways to improve the quality of life of their lives.

The increasing recognition of the link between health and the ability of a child to participate in school has spurred many countries to seek to address the most prevalent health problems of the school-aged child. These attempts are compromised, however, by a lack of resources in the health sector and by the extraordinary stresses on the educational sector that have followed the dramatic rise in enrollment. The increasing perception of the need for "healthy schools" has not been accompanied by the development of sustainable and cost-effective approaches by which that need can be satisfied.

Many countries are already employing the school system as a mechanism for improving the health of schoolchildren. However, there have been few attempts to evaluate the effectiveness of this approach, or to develop ways of improving its efficiency.

The school system provides an existing structure by which health services can reach school-age children. Not all health problems of schoolchildren can be dealt with in this way, but a series of recent meetings held by the Rockefeller Foundation with the United Nations Development Program,[2,3] have identified parasitic infections and micronutrient deficiencies as highly prevalent and important conditions which can be dealt with effectively and inexpensively through school health programs. Indeed, the 1993 World Bank Development Report[4] has identified intestinal parasitic infection as a major but soluble constraint on the health of school-age children. Many other conditions are important, but the potential to deliver anthelmintics and micronutrient supplements at low cost, and at very infrequent intervals, makes these interventions particularly attractive for initial efforts to improve the health of school-aged children.

Such an approach also provides a focus for participatory health education, and the opportunity to address a broader range of health problems. This approach may even provide, and here perhaps is the greatest challenge, the opportunity to help to alleviate other "non-health" constraints on the effectiveness of school systems, for example by attracting children into school or in helping them learn while here.

The meetings[2,3] recommended the development of a partnership of donor agencies, participating governments, and technical agencies, to develop or improve means to deliver these interventions on an operational scale, and to assess their benefits and value in different regions of the world.

STRUCTURE OF THE PARTNERSHIP

The Partnership for Child Development was formally established in January 1992 in order to investigate the ways of strengthening school-based health services as a means of improving the health and educability of school-aged children. The Partnership perceives the development of school-aged children as an essential sequel to the success of child survival programs, and aims to improve the quality of life of school-aged children by improving health, by encouraging individual responsibility for health, and by enhancing the capacity of children to participate in education.

The Partnership is supported internationally by the United Nations Development Program, the World Health Organization, and the Rockefeller, Edna McConnell Clark and James S. McDonnell Foundations. The Clark Foundation provides core support and specifically targets the programs in Africa. The McDonnell Foundation supports activities related to education and learning. Other agencies with a continuing interest in the Partnership include the World Bank and the British Overseas Development Administration. The national offices of the UNDP and UNICEF support some programs at the national level.

The Partnership is both an organizational structure and a concept. In terms of organizational structure the major donors provide the focus for policy development and serve as the Secretariat. The Scientific Coordinating Centre (SCC) has both technical and administrative functions, but its major roles are to develop a horizontal coordinating structure for the many technical agencies within the Partnership and to make this expertise available to countries which support the aims of the Partnership and which implement and evaluate the school-based programs. The first countries to become partners are Ghana, Tanzania, Colombia and Indonesia.

Technical assistance to develop programs in partner countries is being provided through technical panels (see p. 579) by agencies and organizations with specific interests and expertise including: the IRC International Water and Sanitation Centre in The Netherlands in the field of health education, the Program Against Micronutrient Malnutrition based at Emory University, Atlanta, in the field of iodine and vitamin A, the

Institute of Child Health in London in the field of growth monitoring and iron deficiency, and the Swiss Tropical Institute in Basel in the field of cost-effectiveness analysis.

In terms of concept the Partnership aims to develop or strengthen national and international relationships between agencies and institutions. Many of these relationships are typically "new" partnerships, crossing traditional boundaries between the health and education sectors, for instance, or between government agencies, NGOs and the private sector. These include partnerships with national NGOs, such as the *Centro de Investigaciones Multidisciplinaria* en Desarrollo in Colombia, with international NGOs such as INMED, and with private sector companies such as SmithKline Beecham.

AIMS OF THE PARTNERSHIP

The major aims of the operations research programs of the Partnership include:

- to test and evaluate methods to improve the affordability and sustainability of school health programs;
- to strengthen the ability of the education sector to participate in school health programs;
- to develop mechanisms to promote the health of groups which are underserved by current approaches to health delivery, including absentee and non-enrolled children, older preschool children, and young women; and
- to build national capacity by promoting intersectoral collaboration, particularly between the education and health sectors.

APPROACH AND STRATEGY

The Partnership is intended to provide a collaborative structure which is responsive to the needs of individual countries, while at the same time providing an international framework to standardize procedures for monitoring the programs.

The main activity of the Partnership consists of operations research projects to investigate how a package of interventions, initially to include anthelmintics, micronutrient supplements and health education, can be delivered most effectively and at lowest cost to children via the educational system. These core programs typically involve populations of some 100,000 school-aged children and are implemented and monitored by the country partners themselves, with technical support and resources from the Partnership as a whole.

Core Interventions

A number of simple and effective treatments for common causes of ill health have been identified which offer great potential benefit at a low cost.

Anthelmintics

Over a third of the world's population is infected with one or more species of parasitic worm, and in most communities these infections are most prevalent and intense in school-aged children. Figure 32.1 shows, for example, that although the prevalence of infection with whipworm in a typical community is high in all age groups after the age of 5 years, the mean intensity of infection shows a pronounced peak among children aged 5 to 15 years old. Intense infection with parasitic worms is associated with compromised physical growth and school performance, while treatment has been shown to stimulate catch-up growth and enhance performance in tests of cognitive function.[5,6]

Treatment given to all children in areas where the prevalence of infection is high reduces the intensity of infection and thereby virtually eliminates morbidity due to heavy infections. Periodic mass treatment, at intervals of 6 months to 2 years depending on the species of parasite, serves to keep mean worm burdens low. This approach also has benefits for the community at large as it serves to eliminate major sources of infection by treating heavily infected children.[7]

These benefits can be achieved using safe, single dose, oral treatments, and only two different drugs are required to treat the common infections worldwide: albendazole or mebendazole is effective against all the major nematode species, while praziquantel acts against the major schistosome species.

Micronutrient Supplement

Another group of widespread and chronic conditions in developing countries for which some simple and effective treatments are also available are micronutrient deficiencies. A diet deficient in vitamin A, for example, can lead to night blindness, permanent damage to the eye, and may increase susceptibility to infections, while a deficiency of iodine leads to goiter, impaired intelligence and hearing, and may cause young women to give birth to cretinous children if they have poor reserves of iodine when they become pregnant. Regular oral capsules of iodine and vitamin A during childhood at intervals of 6 to 12 months can prevent these deficiency diseases from occurring during a crucial period of growth and development.

Participatory Health Education

The major aim of health education is to encourage and promote behaviors which can lead to improvements in health. School teachers provided with appropriate educational materials can encourage children to play an active and responsible role in improving their own health and the health of other children by means of action-orientated health education. The context of the health education will concern the general prevention of infectious diseases including those caused by parasitic infections, and will promote an awareness of dietary measures to improve health and growth as well as ways to prevent micronutrient deficiencies from reccurring.

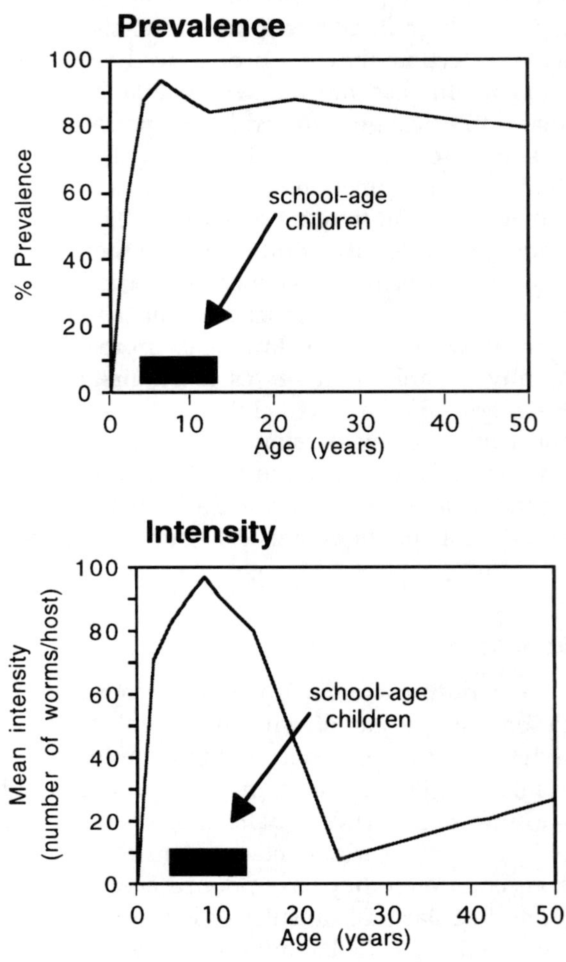

FIGURE 32.1 The prevalence and intensity of infection with *Trichuris trichiura* by age in St. Lucia.

Each partner country will identify which of the package of treatments is appropriate depending on the local occurrence and prevalence of parasitic infections and micronutrient deficiencies. It is intended that the package of interventions will provide a basis on which to establish or strengthen school health services with the potential to add further interventions based on local needs as the programs become established.

Delivery and Monitoring of the Core Program Interventions

Since a major aim of the Partnership is to strengthen the capacity of governments to assess the feasibility and sustainability of their own school health programs, it is essential that the health delivery system is developed and implemented by the partner countries themselves and that the delivery system reflects local practices and resources and builds on existing infrastructures. The process of delivery will be monitored by a national coordinating group in order to assess the cost and feasibility of the delivery system developed by each partner country.

The development of these delivery systems has already suggested a range of practical questions to be addressed which could improve the efficiency or scope of delivery. For example: Are there interactions between anthelmintics, or between anthelmintics and micronutrients, if given together? Can a school-based delivery system also reach absentee, non-enrolled and preschool children? Can the delivery system respond to the special need of female children of child-bearing age? Can the delivery system be targeted affordably at populations at special risk of intense infection and severe deficiency?

These questions are being addressed by a series of specific research studies being undertaken by the Technical Panels of the Partnership (see p. 579). These panels of international and national technical expertise also serve as a technical resource for the development and improvement of the core programs.

Monitoring the Outcomes of the Core Programs

The outcomes of the interventions are monitored by a consortium of international and partner country research institutions. Outcome monitoring focuses on the prevalence and intensity of parasitic infection, micronutrient status, simple measures of illhealth, growth, behavior change, and educational achievement.

These monitoring activities are undertaken by local governments in collaboration with research institutions and provide an opportunity for national capacity strengthening and technical cooperation between developing countries.

CURRENT STATUS

Since the establishment of the Partnership in January 1992, the first group of four countries has begun to develop core programs, while a second group of countries are actively exploring the benefits of the Partnership concept or are undertaking research studies.

Partner Country Core Programs

The Ghana Partnership for Child Development

The program in Ghana evolved from the Ghana Expanded Program of Chemotherapy, which was initiated by the Task Force for Child Survival and which aimed to provide anthelmintic treatment to schoolchildren nationally. The Government of Ghana has now decided to adopt the Partnership approach, and is to evaluate a school health program in one region before making a decision to upscale to a national program.

The program in Ghana involves a partnership between the Ministries of Education and Health, and, most important, with the Ghana Education Services (GES), the executing arm of the education sector. The GES is the delivery mechanism for the current National School Health Education Program. The preexisting interagency National Committee for School Health serves as the policy focus, while the local Partnership Coordinating Centre seeks to strengthen the implementing and planning activities of the existing School Health Education Program based within the GES. A range of government technical institutions, academic institutions and NGOs provides technical support for monitoring and evaluation.

The core program is based in three districts of Volta Region and contains 85,000 school-going children. A regional coordination group has been established which mirrors the interagency composition of the central policy group. Didactic health education materials have been designed and piloted. A survey of some 900 schoolchildren in the target districts has indicated that the prevalences of both hookworm and urinary schistosomiasis exceed 50 percent, and that goiter is present in 30 percent. A preliminary evaluation of a questionnaire approach to identifying schools where urinary schistosomiasis is a problem indicates significant correlations between questionnaire responses and observed prevalences of hematuria.

A program for training in health education evaluation, conducted jointly with WHO/TDR, was planned for September 1993. A program for obtaining baseline and comparison data on health and nutrition was implemented at the start of the school year in September 1993 after which the first treatments with albendazole, praziquantel and iodine were administered.

Cognitive psychologists from the University of Ghana have participated in the Cognition Panel Program in Jamaica (see p. 579) and have adapted materials for cognitive testing to be locally appropriate and are using them in a study of the effects of urinary schistosomiasis on cognitive development. The first results were available in September 1993.

Finally, a research proposal has been developed to evaluate the social, economic and cultural factors influencing school enrollment and attendance by females. This project, which aims to promote the access of young to school health services, was expected to be implemented in Volta Region late in 1993.

Ushirikiano Wa Kumwendeleza Mtoto Tanzania (The Tanzania Partnership for Child Development)

The Tanzania government invited members of the SCC to participate in a national workshop on the health of school children in September 1992, and hosted a workshop to establish a partnership program in February 1993. The Tanzania partnership involves the Ministries of Health, of Education and Culture, of Local Government, and of Community Development, Women Affairs and Children. The preexisting interagency National Committee for School Health acts as the national focus for policy. An equivalent Regional Committee in the Tanga Region will serve as the local coordinating and implementing body. A plan of action is currently being developed through the facilitating actions of a representative of the Muhimbili Medical Centre, and with the oversight of the national UNDP office.

The Nutrition and Growth Panel of the Partnership is examining the health and nutrition of absentee and non-enrolled children. A protocol has been approved by the SCC, and a planning visit has been made to the Tanzania Food and Nutrition Center and the study site. A visit for developing a health education program was planned for July 1993.

Kemitraan Dalam Perkembangan Hidup Anak (The Indonesia Partnership for Child Development)

Discussions have been held with a broad range of governmental and nongovernmental agencies and the Partnership concept has been endorsed by the national planning agency (BAPPENAS) for implementation in Central Java. The national UNDP Office has been an active participant in these discussions.

The Cognition Panel and the Growth and Nutrition Panel have developed a research proposal with King's College, London, and with the Departments of Psychology, Parasitology and Nutrition at the University of Indonesia, Jakarta, to undertake a project of iron deficiency, hookworm infection and cognition. Support for this project will be provided by the Cognition Panel, by the British Council and by the local UNDP office. Work is currently under way to identify suitable study sites.

Desarrollo de la Poblacion en Edad Escolar en Colombia (The Colombia Partnership for Child Development)

The National Program in Favor of Children (PAFI), a multinational-agency coordination committee based in the Office of the President of the Republic, hosted a national workshop which defined the need for a national health program for school-aged children, and delegated to CIMDER (Centro de Investigaciones Multidisciplinarias en Desarrollo) the responsibility for coordinating a Core Program in the Cali Region. A subsequent workshop involving representatives of the President's Office, the Ministries of Health and Education, the Institute for Family Welfare, and the national UNICEF office has further refined areas of responsibility. A planning workshop was held in Cali, Colombia, in March 1993. Assessment of community responses to the program is currently under way.

Other Activities

Several other countries have expressed interest in the Partnership model, are evaluating existing programs with assistance from the Partnership, or are undertaking research studies.

- The use of schools as a delivery point for anthelmintics is being explored by the USAID-supported Schistosomiasis Research Program in Egypt.
- The WHO Communicable Diseases Division is assisting the Government of Myanmar to explore a similar approach to geohelminth control, with assistance from the local UNDP office.
- The State Government of Gujarat, India, is implementing a package of health interventions—based on the Partnership model—for three million children. This program is being evaluated with support from the Partnership.

- The Partnership is beginning an evaluation of a national school-based program in Guatemala, which was facilitated by INMED, a U.S.-based NGO.
- The Partnership has established research programs in China, Ghana, Indonesia, Jamaica, Kenya and Tanzania.

Partnership Technical Panels

The design, monitoring and evaluation of the core programs involves a broad range of issues and is technically complex. In order to support national governments and institutions in undertaking these activities, the Partnership has developed Panels of Expertise to serve as a technical resource. These technical panels also provide a central monitoring group for the development of specific research projects. The existing panels are listed below, and panels to consider other important issues, such as women's health and the health of non-enrolled children, are being developed.

Growth and Nutrition Panel

In collaboration with the SCC, technical guidelines are being prepared on iodine and vitamin A by the Program Against Micronutrient Malnutrition based at Emory University and CDC, Atlanta, and for growth monitoring and iron by the Institute of Child Health, London (ICH). The latter document is currently undergoing technical review.

Protocols for research into issues related to micronutrients are being prepared with PAMM and the ICH. These studies include the development and field evaluation of new, simple technologies for assessing micronutrient status in the field. Studies of micronutrient deficiency and parasitic infection are being implemented in Tanzania (with ICH), and in Indonesia (with King's College, London, and the University of Indonesia).

Economics Panel

Technical guidelines on cost analysis are being prepared in collaboration with the Swiss Tropical Institute, Basel. An Epidemiology and Economics Research Consortium has been established, and dynamic models of the cost-effectiveness relationships of geohelminth and schistosome control by chemotherapy have been developed. This group has contributed to the WHO/TDR informal consultation on schistosomiasis modeling. Three representatives of the Consortium held an economics workshop at the USAID-Schistosomiasis Research Program in Egypt in early 1993. The panel is a participant in the initiative to estimate the global burden of

Disease, and was a contributor to the 1993 World Development Report of the World Bank [4].

Cognition Panel

The activities of this panel are supported by the James S. McDonnell Foundation. Guidelines for the assessment of cognitive ability are being developed. The Panel has held workshops in Jamaica and New York, and has established a research project in Jamaica which is examining the relationship between geohelminth infection, cognition and educational achievement. The project in Jamaica also serves as a focus for piloting new approaches to cognition assessment, in which scientists from the Massachusetts Institute of Technology and the Universities of Yale, Cornell, McGill and Cambridge are involved, and for technical cooperation between developing countries. The results were reported at a workshop in Jamaica in September, 1993.

Other research projects have been established in Ghana with the University of Ghana and the Ministry of Health, in China with Brown University and Nanjing Medical College, in Kenya with the University of Cambridge and the Kenya Medical Research Institute, and in Indonesia with Kings College and the University of Indonesia.

A workshop to examine the mechanisms involved in the interaction between infection and cognition was organized for October, 1993.

Education Panel

Guidelines for the evaluation of educational outcomes are being developed. A workshop was held in London and a program to raise awareness of the relevance of health to education was developed. A document relating health to the active learning capacity of children is currently being published and distributed by UNDP/DGIP. A rationale for including educational interventions in the partnership package is being prepared by a process which has included visits to the Escuela Nueva program in Colombia. A meeting to define educational outcome measurements and to develop a strategy for assessing educational achievement is planned for October 1993.

Health Education Panel

Guidelines for the preparation and evaluation of participatory health education approaches are being prepared by the IRC International Water and Sanitation Centre, the Hague. This Panel has maintained close coordination with the Education and Cognition Panels, and there has been reciprocal representation at all workshops so far. A collaborative network is being developed.

The activities of this Panel are focusing initially on Ghana, to which planning visits have been made and a plan of action prepared. The Child-to-Child Trust has indicated an interest in this project. A workshop on health education is being planned in collaboration with the WHO/TDR.

The UNDP-World Bank Water Supply and Sanitation Program for Low Income Communities has indicated an interest in linking with the PCD Health Education activities particularly in Indonesia, and opportunities are being examined through the East African and Asian regional offices.

Parasite Control Panel

The activities of this panel are principally being undertaken as WHO initiatives in which the Partnership has been invited to participate. WHO/TDR is examining the interaction between praziquantel and albendazole through clinical trials in Kenya, China, Brazil and the Philippines. Preliminary results were presented in August 1993 and the SCC will participated in this meeting. WHO/CDS has undertaken a trial of the comparative efficacy of albendazole and mebendazole against geohelminths in Pemba. The trial has been completed and preliminary results are be available. The SCC has linked with an NGO in Jakarta, Indonesia, and with the University of Caracas, Venezuela, to evaluate experiences of school-based parasite control in both these countries.

The SCC has negotiated preferential rates for the purchase of albendazole and praziquantel with the manufacturers, and is currently investigating other ways in which the private sector could participate in PCD activity.

Study Design and Data Management Panel

A guideline on the sampling design for the core program assessment is currently being prepared by Imperial College, London. A sampling protocol is being prepared for the Ghana program, and McGill University is examining issues relating to cluster sampling.

DISCUSSION

The Partnership approach to school health programs has been rapidly adopted by many developing countries. The reasons for the popularity of this approach are undoubtedly complex, but the following have been identified as being of particular importance.

The Focus on School-Aged Children

International health programs have in recent years tended to focus on the survival of the pre-school child and on maternal and child health. There is, however, a growing awareness that the 90 percent of children in developing countries who now survive past the age of five also deserve and require good health care, not least because the female school child of today is the mother of tomorrow. Moreover, ensuring the physical health and mental alertness of the school-aged child will allow that child to take fuller advantage of what in many developing countries is the only formal education it will ever receive.

Child-Centered Approach

This approach, which is the mainstay of community medicine, is rarely reflected in the organization structures of the international health sector. Instead, individual diseases and conditions are often targeted, often by different specialist organizations. The division is most sharp between intellectual and physical development, where health and education are usually perceived as separate issues, rather than two interactive components of child development.

Education Sector as a Health Implementor

In developing countries there are more schools than clinics, more teachers than nurses. The school and teacher are a major focus within communities, yet their role in community health has hardly been explored or developed. The development of simple, effective and safe treatments for widespread causes of ill health will enable teachers to become involved in promoting the health of children.

Development of New Partnerships

Community development involves an interaction between a broad range of governmental, nongovernmental and private sector organizations, but health is often perceived as the responsibility of a single government agency. The development of new partnerships has the potential to release untapped potential in developing countries.

Combination of Research and Control

The Partnership Technical Panels play an important role in bringing new advances in health and education research to the attention of developing country policymakers. Importantly, however, the Partnership then empowers the local institutions and government agencies to assess the value of these research findings to the local context by supporting operations research under local conditions.

REFERENCES

1. Summary report of the 16th Session of the Subcommittee on Nutrition of the United Nations (ACC/SCN); Feb. 19th 1990, UNESCO, Paris.
2. Berkley, S., & Jamison, D. (1991). *A Conference on the Health of School-age Children in Bellagio, Italy*. Summary report available from the Rockefeller Foundation, 1133 Avenue of the Americas, New York, New York.
3. Bundy, D. A. P., & Hall, A. (1992). Summary report of the Next Steps Meeting, New York, New York. January 7–8, 1992.
4. World Bank (1993). *Investing in Health*. World Development Report, 1993. Oxford: Oxford University Press.
5. Hall, A. (1993). Intestinal parasitic worms and the growth of children. *Transactions of the Royal Society of Tropical Medicine and Hygiene 87*: 241–242.
6. Nokes, C., Grantham-McGregor, S. M., Sawyer, A. W., Cooper, E. S., Robinson, B. A., & Bundy, D. A. P. (1992). Moderate to heavy infections of *Trichuris trichiura* affect cognitive function in Jamaican school children. *Parasitology 104*: 539–547.
7. Bundy, D. A. P., Wong, M. S., & Horton, J. (1990). Control of geohelminths by delivery of targeted chemotherapy through schools. *Transactions of the Royal Society of Tropical Medicine and Hygiene 84*: 115–120.

PART VI
Diverse Opinions and Perspectives

33

Health, Economics, and Development: Working Together for Change

Rosalia Rodriguez-Garcia

INTRODUCTION

Over the last two decades, the world has witnessed profound changes in the socioeconomic, political, demographic and environmental fabric of societies in industrialized and developing countries alike. These changes have increased expectations about individuals' basic right to health and governments' responsibility to provide for better education, higher per capita income, and better quality of life for all segments of their population. These higher expectations call for a re-examination of the processes and goals of development, for an expansion of the definition of health to include human rights, and for a better understanding of the relationship between health and development.

Because how a problem is defined determines what will be done about it, we propose that health be defined as per WHO's definition in terms of "physical, mental and social well-being," including people's welfare and human rights. In this context, public health would seek to ensure the conditions in which people can achieve a state of physical, mental and social well-being. Further, I propose that health is central to the development process and essential to socioeconomic development—"the process of improving the quality of life." In this context, improved health status ought to be a central objective of national development policies.

The author thanks Diane Kuntz, Barry Levy, James Macinko, and John Williams for their comments on a previous version of this manuscript.

Although the factors that contribute to the determinants of health status—physical, mental and social well-being—vary within and among societies, it is clear that societal factors constitute the major set of determinants of health status. To promote and protect public health, the societal determinants of health must be identified and understood as a prerequisite to informed action. In the past, the major approach to the societal determinants of health has been based on a socioeconomic analysis. To grasp fully the importance of development for health requires familiarity with economics. Yet, the traditional socioeconomic approach is, by itself, insufficient. Among the major advances in thinking about public health in recent years have been the identification of a fundamental linkage between health and population, health and the environment, health and development, and health and human rights.

This chapter is intended to stimulate discussion and debate regarding a coherent and coordinated approach to influencing the underlying societal conditions which are acknowledged to be the major determinants of health status. To strengthen this debate, information is provided about health and socioeconomic development, population and health, and health and human rights. In order to advance in our thinking about health, however, it will be essential to become more informed and knowledgeable about socioeconomic development and health as a basic human right. Ultimately, the goal is to help public health, development, and other organizations to recognize their commonality and their critical relationship in the effort to improve the human condition.

This chapter is divided into the six following sections. Section 1 discusses briefly some of the basic concepts of health and economic growth. In section 2, the chapter examines some of the issues and experiences that attest to the link of health to development and development to health, in order to provide a broad framework within which to consider courses of action. Section 3 identifies some of the linkages and barriers to the relationship between health, economics and development. Section 4 considers the role of intersectoral dialogue and action as a key vehicle for health and development. Section 5 calls on Public Health Associations (PHAs) to take a leadership role to protect, promote and maintain people's health and well-being and to place health on the political agenda. In section 6, the chapter concludes by putting forward some of the strategic areas—policy, programs, participation—that PHAs can consider when formulating their national action agendas.

HEALTH AND ECONOMIC GROWTH

Recognition of the centrality of health to development has not been a cornerstone of traditional development policies. Rather, since the "discovery" of economics in the 18th century, development has been considered nearly synonymous with economic growth: "a rise in national or per-capita income and product."[1] Economic growth is said to translate into a general improvement in living standards with economic development being defined as "economic growth that involves fundamental changes in the structure of the economy which are likely to result in changes in the way society is organized".[1]

In most countries, economic growth has helped build the health infrastructure by facilitating the expansion of primary health care and the strengthening of secondary and tertiary care. National economic policies and development strategies accompanied by parallel social policies in such areas as health, education and housing have contributed significantly to improvements in health status. Better health status coupled with increased education and improved living and working conditions has resulted in higher life expectancy and quality of life, as well as a decrease in infant mortality around the world.[2] In the context of fighting poverty, this is the strategy recommended in The World Bank 1990 World Development Report on poverty: a combination of labor-intensive growth and the provision of basic social services, with health having a fundamental role.[3] Whether this recommendation has been implemented and with which results remains to be determined.

Economic growth generates demand for social services and a surplus which can be distributed to the social sector. Indeed, economic surplus, equitably distributed, would be necessary in order to improve health. For economic growth to result in improvements in the quality of life, governments should play a regulatory role to foster markets for health services while assuring the provision of services to the poor and other vulnerable groups.

The private sector provides some examples where the presence of industry has produced enclaves of socioeconomic and human development. In Uruguay, for example, an urban industrial cooperative that manufactures thermos bottles includes a broad social program that encompasses medical and dental care, and a development fund to finance coverage of the extension of clinical primary health care to poor residents of an urban slum adjacent to the cooperative.[4] In rural areas, there are cases in which large-scale private mining companies do establish similar programs to cover the basic health care, education, and housing needs of their employees, and the surrounding communities.[5] These efforts, however, are by and large short-term and unlikely to be sustainable without the presence of the specific company.

Conversely, some aspects of economic growth have produced ill health. Rapidly changing lifestyles brought about by changes in the economy and the emergence of new markets and patterns of consumption are an important part of the disease burden of industrialized countries (manifested in chronic disease, alienation, substance abuse, violence and suicide) and are becoming a burden in developing countries as well[2] (see Figure 33.1). The next century might face the reality of a society where social values and health development have not grown at the same rate as market opportunities—a society where people are living longer but not better.

Industry, power plants and transportation can cause air and water pollution as is the case in industrialized countries. In some parts of the developing world, air quality is rapidly deteriorating in large part due to the use of inexpensive and sometimes inappropriate technologies. Many countries around the world find themselves in a situation where they must use cheaper fuels and technologies in order to meet the demand for increased economic activity, even though these fuels may be polluting the environment enough to adversely affect the health of local populations. However, better technologies to protect the air and water supply often cost more than developing economies can afford. The unintended by-product of economic growth achieved on these bases is ill health. Polluted water is known to cause a myriad of illnesses ranging from diarrhea to cancer. Around the world, more than 1 billion city dwellers breathe unhealthy air and only 40 percent of urban dwellings are connected to sewers.[6]

This situation is caused by a combination of economic growth with simultaneous population growth and increase in urban population size. In developing countries, the urban population is growing by an average of

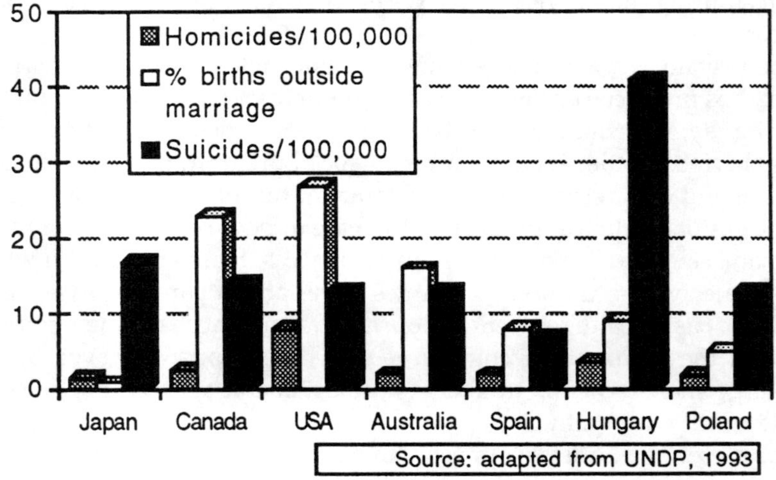

FIGURE 33.1 Weakening social fabric.

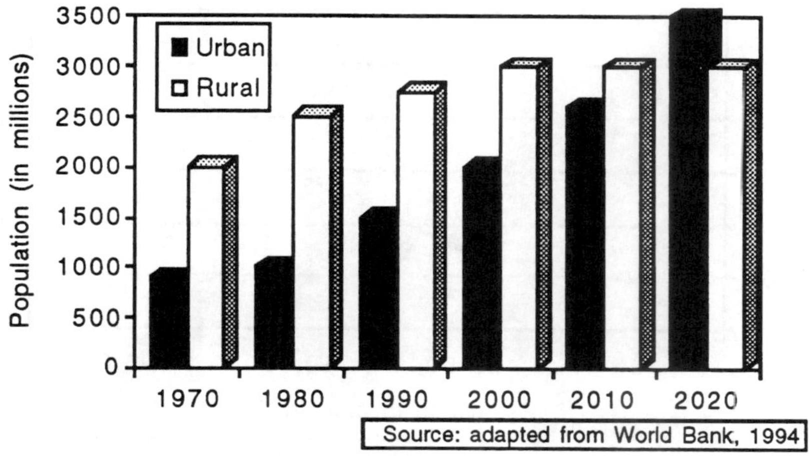

FIGURE 33.2 Urban-rural population trends in developing countries.

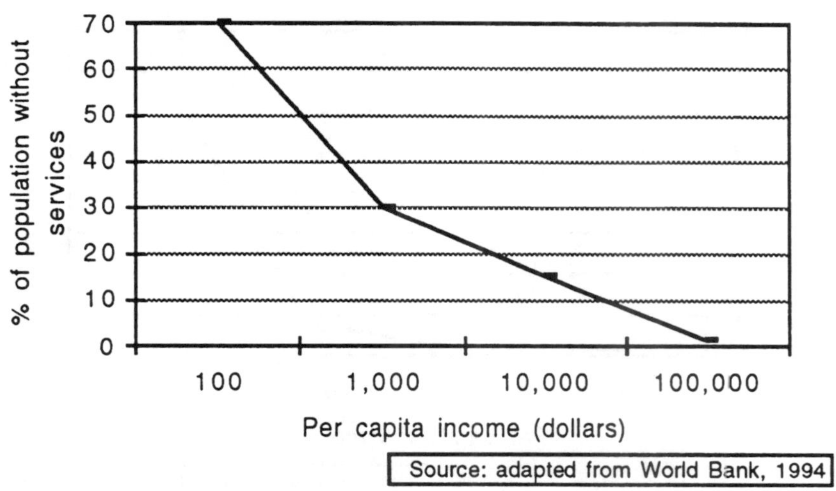

FIGURE 33.3 Urban population without adequate sanitation.

3.8 percent per year (see Figure 32.2). By 2005 the number of people living in cities will exceed the number of those living in the countryside.[6]

Cities in both industrialized and developing countries share similar environmental problems. Sanitation improves with income, but municipal waste and carbon dioxide emissions also increase (see Figures 33.3–33.5). Problems such as air and water pollution in cities have great immediate impact on people's health. Nearly 70 percent of people in most

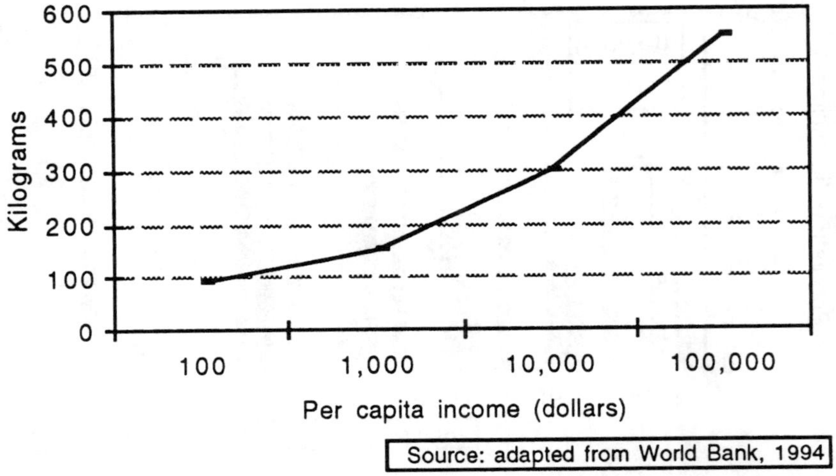

FIGURE 33.4 Municipal wastes per capita.

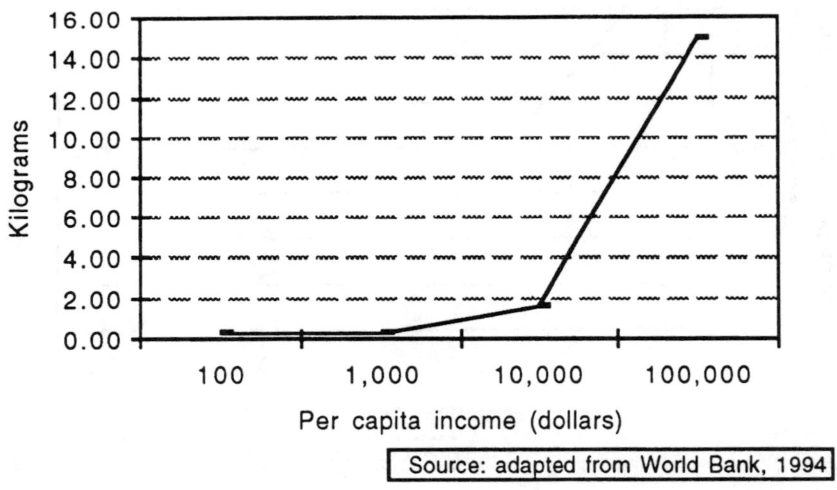

FIGURE 33.5 Carbon dioxide emissions per capita.

parts of the world, including the developing world, agree that environmental protection should be given priority over economic development when such development threatens their environment. This has yet to influence policy-makers. Ideally, the objective should be to promote both environmental protection and economic development.

Although overall economic growth has occurred and aggregate levels of poverty were reduced in many regions of the world in the 1980s, striking social and economic disparities remain within as well as among nations, and have, in many cases, worsened.[7–9] There is evidence that many large-scale development projects have had important human and ecological costs. In fact, a number of World Bank-funded projects have actually created greater impoverishment among the people they were intended to benefit, and have caused disastrous environmental degradation.[10]

One of the most striking findings in the development field of recent years is that higher levels of employment do not necessarily follow higher rates of economic growth. According to the 1993 Human Development Report,[11] employment growth has consistently lagged behind output growth since 1975 (see Figure 33.6). In many countries in Africa, despite economic improvement in a few areas, there has been a decline in formal sector employment as well as in the extent and quality of education and health care.[12] This gap is projected to widen during the 1990s.

These disparities reflect the inequitable societal distribution of resources and benefits gained from development that is based solely on economic growth. Worldwide economic data show a strong link between economic growth and inequality, particularly for the post-1980 period[13,14] with some economists arguing that inequality is the single greatest constraint to economic growth.[15] In situations such as urbanization or rural development planning where measures for economic growth have been undertaken without simultaneous social development measures, planning for and managing the health-development link becomes critical.

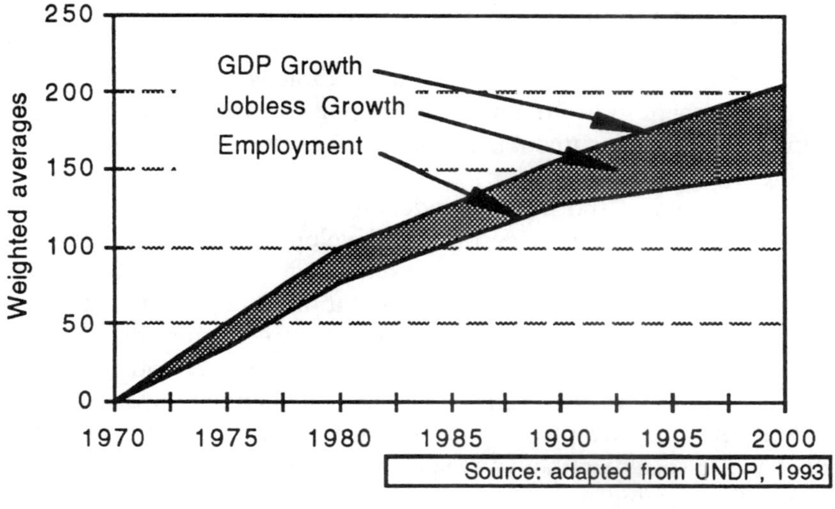

FIGURE 33.6 GDP growth has not resulted in equal growth in employment.

After almost 50 years of a largely one-dimensional approach to development based on economic growth, it is evident that economic growth might be a necessary condition but is not a sufficient condition for improving the quality of life of the world's population, including its most vulnerable groups.

Most important, because of the market failures, the beneficial effects of this intrinsic health-development link will not happen automatically, but would require explicit policy and program actions.

THE INTER-DEPENDENCY BETWEEN HEALTH AND SOCIOECONOMIC DEVELOPMENT

In the late 1970s, The World Health Organization brought to the attention of health and other professionals the vital relationship that exists between health and development. The Alma-Ata Conference and its Declaration defined primary health care as the main strategy for health development.[16] This Conference also emphasized that development involves a progressive improvement in the living conditions and quality of life enjoyed by society and shared by its members. Economic development is necessary to achieve social goals, and social development is necessary to achieve economic goals. Thus any separation between economic and social development, they stated, is no longer tenable.[16] It is in this context that the critical relationship that exists among health, economics, and development, and this relationship's effects on the individual, are being reexamined.

Health is intrinsically linked to social, economic, political, and human development (see Figure 33.7).[17] In this light, the concept of development must be broadened from a strictly economic dimension to include qualitative improvement in health and well-being. Accordingly, the underlying assumption of this document is that health is central to the socioeconomic development process.[2]

An awareness of the interdependency between people's health and well-being and national socioeconomic development has been present in the development field for quiet some time. However, despite their awareness of this link, major development institutions and governments have, by and large, viewed health in isolation from economic development strategies, and as a responsibility of the health sector. Both the health and economic sectors often believe that "the interaction between development and health takes place by itself, that the benefits of the interaction will accrue to society without any special interventions and that the negative health outcomes can be dealt with as and where they emerge in specific projects and activities".[2] Yet, ignoring the health-development

FIGURE 33.7 The health-development link. Health is central to the development process. *Source*: Rodriguez-Garcia, R. and Goldman, A. (1994).

link can result in important losses to health and other components of development.

In this chapter, development, which is understood as socioeconomic development, is defined as "the process of improving the quality of life through changes that result in (1) higher standards of living, (2) increased purchasing power, (3) greater political participation, and (4) access to basic goods and services".[18] This chapter also subscribes to the World Health Organization's definition of health as "the state of complete physical, mental and social well-being, and not merely as the absence of disease or disability"[16,19]—a definition which sees the individual as a social being, not merely a biomedical entity. Further, it sees health as a human right as well as "a societal issue as the conditions which promote health or cause ill health are being produced by society and the economy as a whole".[2]

Socioeconomic development, as defined in this way, would require that governments apply policies of equitable redistribution with growth to ensure that all of their citizens and their most vulnerable groups benefit from economic expansion. These socioeconomic policies would also need to ensure that economic growth is balanced with socioenvironmental protection. Unbalanced distribution coupled with an unprotected environment and unbalanced population growth can hamper the capacity of societies to cope with increasing populations.[20] "Population growth is an acknowledged engine of socioeconomic growth . . . but imbalances in both population growth and resource distribution are exacerbating land and food shortages, leading to environmental degradation and outpacing the provision of needed health, education and housing services".[20] Redistribution policies that result in shared growth would ensure that basic social services such as primary health care, nutrition, family planning, housing or primary education are accessible to all segments of the population.[4]

The above definition of socioeconomic development defines the goal of development in social as well as economic terms. The first outcome of development included in this definition—"higher standards of living"—has an implicit economic orientation. However, the standard of living is not determined by economics alone—health is essential. Investments in health interventions can contribute to economic development because health is an integral component of human capital. Children who are healthy and well-nourished are both more likely to attend school and to perform better in the classroom.[21] Children who have done well in school become workers who tend to earn more than relatively low achievers. Healthy workers lose fewer work days due to illness, are more productive on the job, work more years and thus make greater individual contributions to aggregate GNP than do those who suffer poor health.[22] Moreover, preventive health interventions reduce the incidence of disease, which can translate into major savings in foregone treatment costs, both for individuals and among a population as a whole.[22] In this manner, public health services have been historically, and still are, crucial to national socioeconomic development.

Investment in the health sector can also result directly in economic gain. First, expansion of the health sector affords employment opportunities to health care providers, managers, researchers, unskilled workers and others, and generates income.

Second, the health sector is essential to the development of other profitable sectors of the economy such as transportation, business, and tourism (lodging and restaurants). The increasing accessibility of long-distance travel for business, conventions, and leisure and the related difficulty of national authorities to control the spread of diseases such as AIDS, cholera, bubonic plague or Legionnaire's disease have highlighted the linkages among the transportation, tourism, business, and health sectors.

Adequate health services, trained health personnel, and health policies that provide guidance for the effective prevention and management of epidemics constitute a necessary part of the business and leisure tourist industry infrastructure.[23] In many countries such as those in the Mediterranean basin or the Caribbean, Switzerland or Indonesia, business and leisure travel and health tourism—travelling for health reasons—are among the most profitable sectors of the economy. In the Bahamas alone, tourism accounts for 53 percent of gross domestic product and more than a third of all exports. In Barbados, it accounts for 29.8 percent of gross domestic product, in Jamaica for 16.5 percent[24] and in Martinique for 7.3 percent (Office of Tourism, personal communication, 1992). Business and leisure tourism not only requires preventive and curative health infrastructure for its sustainability; it also creates jobs, income and wealth which increase the possibility of improving the host country population's health in general.[25]

Third, the health sector is in itself a development sector. In the context of intersectoral collaboration, the health sector can be developed and strengthened with the resources required to achieve outcomes that result in improved health.[25] As the World Bank asserts "good health is a crucial part of well-being, but spending on health can also be justified on purely economic grounds".[22] The health sector is not a recipient sector but can be an important contributor to the national economy. At the local level, the expansion of the health sector can create a demand for skilled health care workers and can encourage investment in the indigenous production of pharmaceutical and medical technology.

Since the Alma-Ata Declaration, works by independent scholars and international agencies attest to a growing understanding and acceptance that both health development and economic growth are essential components of the development trajectory. Four essential lessons can be drawn from the socioeconomic development and health experiences of the past few decades as collected in these works.

First, health and development efforts are interconnected and continuously feed from and build on each other's strengths. Economic development contributes to health, and health is a cornerstone of the human development process, and, therefore, essential for achieving the long-term goal of sustainable development (see Figure 33.8). Second, multisectoral and intersectoral cooperation is vital to building a strong constituency to deal with the health-development link. Third, nongovernmental organizations constitute a central locus through which the various development sectors and grassroots mobilization efforts can work and collaborate in each country to protect and promote the health and human development of their most vulnerable groups. Fourth, regional and international organizations and agencies can bring together individuals from around the world—whether they are professionals, policymakers, community leaders or advocates—to ensure that development and health projects attend to the health-development link.

Although these lessons may be well known, efforts by agencies such as the World Health Organization have not yet been generally followed by development institutions. Much work remains to be done in order to shift the economics-dominated development paradigm and transform the value systems which sustain it. Nongovernmental and private voluntary

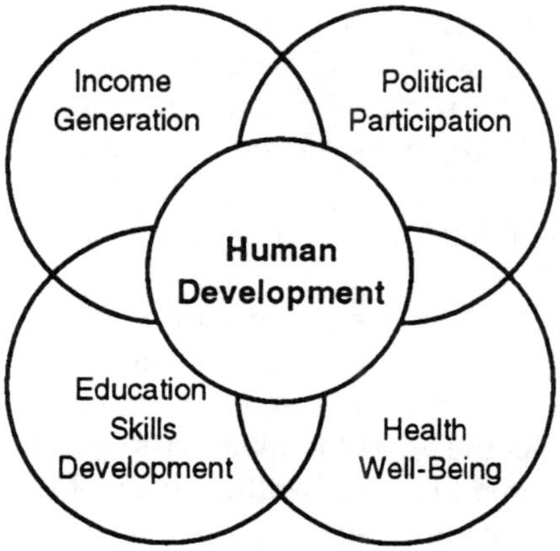

FIGURE 33.8 The health-development link. A building block for human development. *Source*: Rodriguez-Garcia, R. and Macinko, J. (1994).

organizations, such as public health associations (PHAs), international agencies, private-sector volunteer organizations and government agencies can work together to synthesize and apply these lessons to achieve sustainable development in the context of renewed attention to the individual and to vulnerable groups. An international movement is needed to advocate for health as central to the development process and for managing the health-development link.

LINKAGES AND BARRIERS: HEALTH, ECONOMICS, AND DEVELOPMENT

Though the economic benefits that health interventions bring may be well understood and appreciated, there are practical obstacles that hinder their realization. Due to the vested interests of ruling groups in many countries, health ministries are chronically underfunded and are often subject to greater reductions during periods of economic crises than are other parts of the government budget.[17] Proposals to reallocate expenditures and provide services to disadvantaged segments of the population are invariably met with questions concerning who will underwrite these interventions. Unfortunately, solutions based solely on the market—though often proposed—are not always viable alternatives to government-funded programs for there is no incentive for private markets to provide services on a long-term basis to those unable to pay. Moreover, a traditional function and fundamental "raison d'être" of the state in most societies is to finance public goods. Public goods are not limited to interstate highways, police forces and educational systems, but also include services that have an impact on individuals' and society's health, such as potable water, safe sewage disposal, women's health, child care, and universal immunization.

Although some totally public funded systems (e.g., Canada and Cuba) seem to perform relatively well, there can be disadvantages to health care delivery that is financed only with public funds. Shortages of supplies and inefficiencies in distribution can result from systems which have no relation to the marketplace.[26] Therefore, as the government fulfills its duty to provide public goods and services it must do so in an appropriate mix with market-based services—a mix determined through careful analysis of the market for such services and of specific capabilities and needs at local, district, provincial, and national levels. When public health services and basic health care for the disadvantaged are funded primarily by the government without private sector support, policymakers should actively solicit input from grassroots organizations and associations, and thereby decide who will be required to pay for preventive and curative services.

So far, this discussion of health and socioeconomic development has focused on only the first two of the four factors which comprise our definition of socioeconomic development. Although (1) higher living standards and (2) improved purchasing power generally accompany economic growth, they do not necessarily translate into human development.[11] In fact, economic growth that does not pay attention to the health-development link can result in the emergence of new vulnerable groups and the reinforcement of factors which keep certain population groups in a state of vulnerability.[27]

Now, we turn our attention to the last two factors in our socioeconomic definition of development—greater political participation and access to goods and services which are not explicitly addressed in the traditional economic development perspectives. When there is unequal access to goods and services, whether in the health care system or in the economy as a whole, certain segments of the population are not benefitting from economic growth as much as other segments. This situation is exacerbated if the distribution of health services "does not take account of the heterogeneous (and constantly changing) distribution of needs among the population".[28]

The allocation of resources which determine people's access to basic goods and services is a political decision often based on historical antecedents. In many countries, there is a need to devote a larger proportion of the health budget and health personnel to comprehensive primary health care (and women's health care) including preventive, promotive, protective, curative and rehabilitative services in both rural and urban areas. But power structures within a society often allow the special interests of the elite to override the general welfare of the public at large, and allocations for the health sector still tend to respond to a social elite whose demand is predominantly for curative care.[29] This type of allocation leads to a distortion in the health care delivery system, with tertiary hospitals absorbing an inordinate amount of the health budget. Further waste is created when public health and clinical interventions, which could be provided through lower-level facilities, are instead provided through facilities at higher levels of the health services delivery pyramid, resulting in higher costs without significantly improving the quality of care, or the accessibility of services.

Since a status quo rarely changes without pressure from groups with interests that diverge from those of the political system's sustainers, broader political participation at the grassroots level is needed, whether through nongovemmental organizations, community alliances, or professional associations. To foster this participation, fundamental changes are required in the political decision-making process of many countries where only the political, economic or professional elites have a real voice in matters of state. Only then will local initiatives be able to thrive and effectively sway inequitable allocations of financial, technical, and human resources in their favor. Broader political participation, particularly when oriented toward specific goals that can be shown to have benefits to the society at large, is thus likely to improve overall access to the basic goods and services essential to human development.

This discussion has emphasized, albeit succinctly, the relationship of health and socioeconomic development, with health being seen as central to the development process. Health is an integral component of human capital, but, while economic considerations are important and cannot be ignored, it is important to emphasize that health is fundamentally an ethical concern and, for many, a basic human right, not a commodity. Expenditures for health can be justified if they can be shown to reduce the toll of human pain and suffering brought about by poor health and living conditions, and social, economic and political marginalization.

Ethical considerations have long been subordinated to pragmatic concerns but are slowly being introduced into public policy discourse. Many recent developments such as the trend toward emphasizing public health and preventive care over private practice and curative care would indicate a shift in prevailing values. Yet, technological innovations that benefit but a few , and the values rooted in the market model that are permeating the health system in many countries have created a new awareness of the need to "ensure that ethical safeguards are put in place to guarantee that the safety and rights of both individuals and communities are adequately protected in health-related areas".[2]

INTERSECTORAL ACTION

One of the most effective vehicles to move us toward the goals of social and economic development is intersectoral action.[30] Intersectoral action requires a multidisciplinary dialogue which entails active and dynamic exchange between all relevant development sectors and at all levels of society. At the grassroots level, nongovernmental and volunteer organizations play a central role in initiating this dialogue by working with communities to identify and voice their basic needs, conveying those needs to local and national governments, and providing logistical support for health and development activities.[31] By obtaining input directly from disadvantaged populations, health programs can be designed to address the heterogeneous needs of communities and provide truly viable and sustainable solutions to public health challenges. Democratic efforts that focus on promoting grassroots participation, above and beyond the promotion of market interventions, are more likely to affect national political processes worldwide.

The lines of communication between donor and recipient countries, or between local groups and government agencies are essentially vertical. But, effective intersectoral dialogue is horizontal as well as vertical, and exchanges among communities and among nations with similar needs, vulnerabilities and constraints, are equally important for maximizing the use of scarce resources and promoting health and sustainable socioeconomic development. Horizontal dialogue must occur not only in a political sense, but also in a functional sense—so that different sectors of the government, the economy and society act jointly to achieve development goals. At the national level, dialogue among different government sectors and the private sector can yield more comprehensive health and development initiatives and enhance efficiency and equity in the distribution of resources. Dialogue between donor countries and agencies and recipient countries is equally crucial.

However, while this dialogue is truly the key to integrated health and development efforts, perhaps the single greatest obstacle has been the lack of recognized health-development economists in the health sector and of health leaders in the development sector. The development and health sectors interact but they do not necessarily communicate. This problem manifests itself at both national and international levels. Many Ministers of Health do not have development economists on their staff, and, until recently, development banks had few health experts in their ranks. This situation has seriously hindered the establishment of interdisciplinary dialogue. Thus, the next step—the call to change—will require a concerted effort to develop or recover within the health sector an interlocutional capacity, a widely accepted authority to call to the table leaders of other sectors to discuss issues involving health, socioeconomic, and human development. The current shift that moves global support for health initiatives from bilateral to multilateral agencies may encourage genuine dialogue among the different national and international actors.

Intersectoral cooperation can be promoted among countries and within countries by national governments and international agencies as well as grassroots organizations. Initiatives by multilateral agencies, such as UNICEF, UNDP, WHO, UNFPA, PAHO and the development banks have influenced the distribution of basic health services. They have done so both directly, when loans and grants are made contingent upon a government's efforts to allocate funds for the health sector more equitably and responsibly, and indirectly, through their perceived moral authority and leadership status.

Public Health Associations with their wealth of public health experts are in a unique position to see that vertical and horizontal lines of communication among all these actors remain open and are strengthened. PHAs can be the fundamental loci through which health concerns could be addressed and intersectoral action and cooperation can be mobilized within and among countries.

LEADERSHIP ROLE OF PUBLIC HEALTH ASSOCIATIONS

Public Health Associations have great potential to provide the leadership needed to safeguard and improve the public's health. PHAs are multidisciplinary in nature and understand that health improvements encompass much more than providing health care services. They have a commitment to call attention to inequalities with respect to health, protecting the environment, and guarding the most vulnerable population groups. PHAs are in a position to influence national policies to ensure that the needs and desires of local people be taken into consideration. Their member-based organizational capacity enables PHAs to bring about judicious change. Associations in industrialized countries can join forces with those in developing countries to support efforts for social change.

A central debate runs throughout most contemporary health care systems: the medical establishment, by and large, advocates individual-based health care and is supported by the professional and other elites who can afford such care. The public health profession, on the other hand, tends to espouse population-based policies which seek to improve the human condition by addressing the entirety of individuals' well-being.

Historically, private practice medicine has won out. But as the debate continues, public health interests and approaches have made important advances.

With well-informed citizens as members—particularly in nations where civic associations are relatively rare—PHAs are often in a key position to influence health policy-makers and health programs at the local, provincial, and national levels. In an advocacy role, PHAs can become a critical intermediary between the most vulnerable and poorest segments of the population and the government and organizations that represent the elite and their status quo.

If PHAs are to assume a leadership role in (1) shifting the medical-based health model to primary health care and (2) shifting the economics-based development model to a public health-development orientation, they will need to develop and propose specific and detailed health and development policies, strategies, and programs. One concept that public health brings to health care and the education of health personnel is a population-based approach. Another key concept is equity, which can be defined as universal coverage and care according to need, which necessitates the full range of health-related disciplines—epidemiology, clinical sciences, economics and other health sciences, and health system planning and management. Equity is a moral and technological imperative for both health sciences education and health system development.[32]

Groups such as the International Network of Community-Based Health Sciences Educational Institutions—with leadership from Suez Canal Medical College, Ismalia, Egypt; McMaster University, Canada; and Maesterich University in the Netherlands—have been promoting development oriented education of health professionals with reasonable success over the past 15 years. These programs stem from community-based and problem-based learning so that the skills and knowledge of public health practitioners are immediately useful within the constraints and environment in which they work. More recently, The George Washington University, in the United States, developed and is using, since 1989, a health-development framework to prepare public health, international affairs, and international development students for work in international and cross-cultural settings.[33] Programs formulated in consultation with PHAs in other nations as well as with international health organizations take advantage of the benefits that arise from intersectoral dialogue and action. At the same time, PHAs can leverage the prestige of international organizations to pressure their governments into eliminating health policies that impede development, and likewise, development policies that may jeopardize the public's health.

One of the most pervasive—and intransigent—problems affecting health and development in many nations is that of the prevailing educational policies in medicine and public health. Schools of public health and medicine are often a part of the problem more than of the solution, for the link between health and development is rarely, if ever, addressed in their curricula. To assume a leadership role in protecting the public's health, PHAs must begin to work on these two educational fronts: medical education and public health education.

The training of medical doctors is of particular importance due to physicians' direct and immediate influence on health care delivery. Most medical curricula in developing nations are based on the models of the U.S., Canada and Europe and, consequently, tend to emphasize diseases prevalent in the West with little discussion of the health problems endemic to developing countries. Few medical schools offer courses that examine the relationship between health and socioeconomic conditions and few medical schools require coursework in public health.[34,35] PHAs should press for the incorporation of such coursework into the medical curriculum since physicians are central actors in how health is defined and how health services are provided. This is essential not only in developing countries but also in the West, where health promotion, protection, and preventive services have been somewhat neglected, and avoidable public health problems are becoming increasingly prevalent among certain segments of the population.

The second educational front on which PHAs can have an impact is the curricula of graduate programs in public health; for, just as economic development must take health into account, health must take socioeconomic development into account. When we treat the health sector as if it were exogenous to social, economic and political concerns, we operate at a disadvantage in our decision-making and are doing a disservice to the public we hope to serve. Courses in public health should address, for example, the social and economic determinants of health; the impact of health on development; the ways in which different development strategies can affect health policy formation and implementation; and the means by which social and cultural factors influence health in each nation. If we expect public health concerns to be understood as part of, and essential to, social, economic, and political development by community members at the bottom, and by policy-makers at the top, we must begin with the training of public health practitioners, managers, and researchers at the center.

The need for public health education reform has been acknowledged as the cornerstone necessary for advances in health and social development since the late 1980s by groups such as the Institute of Medicine in the United States (1988) and the Pan American Health Organization and its member states.[35] The Pan American Health Organization/WHO advocates the preparation of public health leaders who understand the present-day health circumstances that exist in their countries. This "health circumstance" has changed in recent years due to the growth of sciences and technology; the realignment of power based on changing patterns of production and trade; ethnic and religious disagreements; social disparities among nations and within nations; the fragile balance of societies to the environment; and global challenges of geopolitical changes and conflict.

In order for public health to meet these challenges, we urgently need public health educational institutions to produce effective leadership.[35]

In addition to improving the quality and content of public health education, it is vital to increase the number of training programs in public health policy, planning and management. The public health profession is generally underrepresented in most countries, if not by its numbers, then, by its powerlessness, relative to the influence of physicians. Public health specialists, including policy analysts, health and development specialists and management personnel, are in short supply the world over. This imbalance between medical practitioners and public health practitioners—in number, power, or both—has serious implications for the type and the location of care available, and the distribution of health services among different populations.

PHAs can further an agenda that includes health together with socioeconomic and human development by supporting and initiating research that examines the economic and social benefits of health and economic investments. "Investments in research have been the source of the enormous improvements in health in this century".[22] Research has led to improvements in medical technology and the introduction of public health measures has contributed to the decline of child mortality in the late 19th and early 20th centuries. But perhaps the most important breakthrough in public health came when scientific knowledge was used to show people how to reduce dangers to their own health and the health of their children through such measures as hygienic food preparation, sanitary living conditions, appropriate waste disposal, and the elimination of disease-bearing insects.[20] While research findings are crucial to policy formation and implementation, they must be disseminated beyond the ivory towers of political corridors and university hallways. Public Health Associations are one important mechanism for such dissemination.

Data show that, prior to the dissemination of this information, educational level and affluence made little difference in the risk of child mortality. It was not so much the scientific information itself, but the dissemination of that information that was essential in bringing about dramatic changes in health status. While further biomedical research is needed, research on health and development is equally important. PHAs can serve as the mechanism to disseminate research results and inform the public about their application. PHAs can increase the public's understanding of the synergy of multisectoral activities in health and development, thereby encouraging the participation that is necessary to harness that synergy, in order to make the individual health care consumer the central locus of action and decision-making, and effecting true change.

Finally, PHAs can play a vital role in improving the public's health by calling attention to society's accountability for health, and encourage governments, local groups, and individuals to work together to promote healthier lifestyles. In fact, the individual must be recognized not only as a beneficiary, but also as a key contributor to the prevention of disease, the protection of health and the environment, and the promotion of health-seeking behaviors to ensure the success of health policies. Once this is realized, the ineluctable conclusion is that education about health and development should begin in primary school where children are the most curious and impressionable about their lives and their surroundings, and when they in turn provide a bridge to their families and communities.

Although great strides have been made in public health throughout the world, we must now refine our vision, redirect our efforts and renew our vigor in order to confront the challenges that face us today: new and reemerging diseases, increasingly vulnerable population groups, HIV/AIDS, poverty, environmental degradation, lack of health security, and general impairment in the quality of life. After all, it is the single human being—the child, the man, the woman, the elder—who is the central locus through which the components of health, economics, and development interact and have meaning; by whom and with whom public health and development associations can act to advance human development and social progress.

CONCLUSION: A CALL TO ACTION

The premise of this chapter has been fourfold: (1) health is central to the socioeconomic development process; (2) economic growth per se does not assure human rights, health or the equitable distribution of goods and services particularly to the most vulnerable groups in society; (3) human development and well-being is the rightful objective of socioeconomic development; and (4) both development and health efforts must attend to the health-development link to assure human development.

This chapter has examined the relationship of health, economics, and development. Through this examination a new multifaceted vision of health has taken shape. In this vision of health, health is best seen as:

- A basic human right
- A societal value
- A condition for and result of sustainable development
- A sensible investment
- An integral component of human development
- A shared responsibility
- A bridge for peace
- A tool for political dialogue
- An ethical imperative.

This vision demands a reorientation of public health and other professions so that they may provide the leadership that is needed to labor for people's health and human development. This reorientation will include establishing professional mechanisms for international collaboration and information sharing; attracting and incorporating diversity in their membership in terms of age, gender and ethnicity; and placing health in the national and international political agendas. The protection and promotion of health will be successful in so far as human rights and human dignity are respected, that health is recognized as different from healthcare and from health services, and that health is not viewed as a commodity but as a social value.

This broader vision challenges us to become catalysts for the experiences and resources of public health and other professional associations around the world and facilitators of a unified effort to better address the health and development needs of our populations. To achieve this new vision of health for human development, we need to strategically place health in the broader political agenda. The following recommendations contribute to this goal.

Strengthening National Public Health Associations to be more effective in public health advocacy, education, practice, and research:

- Update public health education to include subjects such as development economics, the sociology of development, and the health-development link.
- Strengthen existing institutional capabilities to advance the national public health agenda.
- Strengthen institutional capabilities to advocate for vulnerable groups.
- Advocate the introduction of education about health and development in primary and secondary schools' curricula.
- Adopt measures to better represent each country's diverse populations.

- Translate research results into public health programs and public information efforts.
- Provide for the training of physicians and other health workers in public health.
- Develop a scientific knowledge base to define public health issues and action areas.

Promoting a New Vision of Health for Human Development by raising political awareness about the multifaceted nature of health.

- Review relevant publications and manuals and adapt them by adding new information that calls attention to the health-development link.
- Raise political awareness about the centrality of health to socioeconomic development.
- Ensure that public health and development programs, both national and international, address the needs of vulnerable groups and the health-development link.
- Promote health as a central component of socioeconomic development.
- Sponsor resolutions and legislation to promote the new vision of health.
- Promote the concept of health as a tool for political dialogue.
- Build a constituency to support, call attention to, and better manage the health-development link.
- Keep decision-makers and the public informed on emerging issues and concerns in public health.
- Provide leadership in a systematic manner to define a new public health paradigm.

Building Intersectoral Bridges as mechanisms for dialogue and action.

- Take advantage of regional and international fora to advance the public health agenda, and emphasize the role of health in development.
- Support health activities that can improve people's welfare and contribute to conflict avoidance and resolution around the world.
- Strengthen relationships and forge new ones with grassroots, nongovernmental and civic groups, as well as with international agencies and national leaders.
- Establish mechanisms for information-sharing within the organization, with the local, regional, and national communities, and with other national and international organizations.
- Disseminate findings from research to other advocacy organizations, interest groups, and decision-makers, and the public.

Public health and other professional associations will need to galvanize the experiences and resources provided by their members to break these recommendations down into specific and quantifiable actions that can be implemented and evaluated to better address the health and development needs of populations around the world. The call is to build an international health and development movement that is active, dynamic, representative, participatory and effective in achieving more sustainable gains for people's health.

REFERENCES

1. Gillis, M., Perkins, D., Roemer, M., & Snodgrass, D. (1987). *Economics of Development*. New York, NY: Norton Publishing Co., p. 7.
2. WHO (1994). *Health in development: Prospects for the 21st century*. Background paper for the Task Force on Health and Development Policies. Geneva: World Health Organization, p. 5.
3. World Bank (1990). *World development report*: Poverty. New York, NY: Oxford University Press.
4. Mesa-Lago, C. (1992). *Health care for the poor in Latin America and the Caribbean*. Scientific Publication No. 539. Washington, DC: Pan American Health Organization/WHO.
5. Mazur, J. L. (1994). The "new order" in South America. A Bolivian Case Study. Paper presented at the conference of International Oil, Gas, and Mining Development in Latin America. Sponsored by the Rocky Mountain Mineral Law Foundation. Houston, TX: April 18–19, 1994.
6. World Bank (1994). *World development report: Infrastructure for development*. New York, NY: Oxford University Press.
7. PAHO (1994). *Health conditions in the Americas*. 1994 Edition, Vol 1. Washington, DC: Pan American Health Organization/WHO. Scientific Publication No. 549.
8. PAHO (1994). *Health, equity and changing production patterns in Latin America and the Caribbean*. Volume 28 of the complete collection of the 113th meeting of the Executive Committee of the Director's Council. Washington, DC: Pan American Health Organization.
9. Harpham, J., & Stephens, C. (1991). Urbanization and health in developing countries. *World Health Statistics Quarterly 44*, 62–69.
10. Rich, B. (1994). *Mortgaging the earth: The World Bank, environmental impoverishment, and the crisis of development*. Boston, MA: Beacon Press.
11. UNDP (1992, 1993, 1994). *Human development report*. United Nations Development Programme. New York, NY: Oxford University Press.
12. Adepoju, A. (Ed.) (1993). *The impact of structural adjustment on the population of Africa: Implications for education, health, and employment*. UNFPA. London, U.K.: James Curry, Ltd.
13. Waldmann, R. (1994). *Inequality and growth in a cross-section of countries* (Working paper).

14. Persson, T., & Tabellini, G. (1994). Is inequality harmful for growth? *American Economic Review.* June 1994.
15. Birdsall, N., & Sabot, R. (1994). Virtuous circles: Human capital growth and equity in East Asia. Paper presented at Northeastern University Development Conference. Yale University, October 14, 1994.
16. WHO/UNICEF (1978). *Declaration of Alma Ata.* Statement issued at the International Conference on Primary Health Care, Alma Ata, Sept. 12, 1978. Geneva: World Health Organization.
17. Rodriguez-Garcia, R., & Goldman, A. (Eds.) (1994). *The Health-development link.* Washington, DC: Pan American Health Organization/WHO.
18. Rodriguez-Garcia, R. (1992). Health and development. *Healthlink.* August; pp. 2–3, 10. Washington, DC: National Council for International Health.
19. WHO (1977). *Provisional guidelines for evaluating strategies for health for all by the year 2000.* Geneva: World Health Organization, PDWG/REP/3.
20. Sadik, N. (1991). *Population policies and programmes: Lessons learned from two decades of experience.* United Nations Population Fund. New York, NY: New York University Press.
21. Schuftan, C. (1985). The Role of health and nutrition in development. *IFDA Dossier 49.* Washington, DC: International Fund for Development Assistance.
22. World Bank (1993). *World development report 1993: Investing in health.* New York, NY: Oxford University Press.
23. Alleyne, G. (1990). Health and tourism in the Caribbean. *Bulletin of PAHO. 24(3)*, 291–300.
24. Harrison, D. (1992). *Tourism and the less developed countries.* London, U.K.: Belhaven Press.
25. PAHO (1992). *Health and tourism.* Provisional agenda for the Inter-American Conference on Food Protection and Tourism. Washington, DC: Pan American Health Organization/WHO.
26. Akin, J. S. (1987). *Financing health services in developing countries: An agenda for reform.* World Bank policy paper. Washington, DC: World Bank.
27. WHO (1991). *Health: A conditionality for economic development? Breaking the cycle of poverty and inequity.* Background paper for the World Health Organization Accra Conference, Ghana, December 4–6, 1991.
28. de Kadt, E., & Tasca, R. (1993). *Promoting equity: A new approach from the health sector.* Health and Development Series. Washington, DC: Pan American Health Organization.
29. Green, R. H. (1991). Politics, power and poverty: Health for all in 2000 in the Third World?. *Social Science and Medicine. 32(7)*, 745–755.
30. WHO (1991). *Promoting health through women's functional literacy and intersectoral action.* Report of the World Health Organization Annual Intercountry Meeting, December 8–11, 1991, Accra, Ghana.
31. Rodriguez-Garcia, R., & Macinko, J. (1994). The role of NGOs in community health and development. *International Journal of Health Education/Health Promotion.* December 1994.
32. Bryant, J. H. (1993). Educating tomorrow's doctors. *World Health Forum 14.* Geneva: World Health Organization.

33. Rodriguez-Garcia, R., & Chandra, P. (1991). The health-development link: Teaching international health within a health-development framework. *Health for all: Strengthening the role for public health.* Selected Proceedings from the Sixth International Congress of the World Federation of Public Health Associations and the 119th Annual Meeting of the American Public Health Association. Washington, DC: American Public Health Association.
34. U.S. Institute of Medicine (1988). *The future of public health.* Washington, DC: National Academy Press.
35. PAHO (1992). *The crisis of public health: Reflections for the debate.* Washington, DC: Pan American Health Organization/WHO. Scientific Publication No. 540.

34

Health, Economics, and Development: An Economist's Perspective

Emil Salim

The theme of the 7th International Congress of the World Federation of Public Health Association was "Health, Economics, and Development: Working Together for Change." The choice of this theme implied that health, economics, and development are not working satisfactorily together. This needs to be corrected, especially facing the challenge of change in the future.

Let us therefore elaborate further why health, economics, and development should be working together. What is the situation today? And what change do we envisage in the future?

CURRENT SITUATION

Health

The World Health Organization has defined health as a state of complete physical, mental, and social well-being, and not merely the absence of disease or infirmity.

During the last 40 years since WHO has been established, the world's health situation has improved. Life expectancy has increased, and the infant mortality rate has decreased. While these changes are generally applicable, people in developing countries still suffer from preventable diseases, premature death, relatively short life expectancy, and high infant mortality rates. It may not be possible to reach the WHO goal of "Health for all by the year 2000."

Economics

Economics is the social science concerned with the production and consumption of goods and services and the analysis of societal activities in satisfying its needs.

A person's preoccupation in life is to obtain means to satisfy his needs. While the means are limited, human needs are unsatisfiable, especially if these needs are transformed into human wants.

In order to fulfill a humane life, certain basic needs must be satisfied, such as nutritious food, essential clothing, housing, means of transportation, basic health and educational services, and a healthy environment.

Many developing countries have still to struggle to meet these basic needs. And this has brought economics to the center of the attention.

Development

"Development" has to do with allocating resources, natural, human, manmade, and organizational, to obtain goods and services needed to meet an increased standard of living.

Since resources are limited and the demand for goods and services tends to increase because of population increase and rising aspirations, the developmental efforts are preoccupied with economic models, theory, and methodology.

Health, economics, and development are focused on the same objective: human beings. Each of them has different approaches, stressing a particular aspect of human beings.

Health stresses aspects of physical, mental, and social well-being. Economics stresses the ways of production and consumption to satisfy human beings' need at a particular period of time. Development stresses the process of resource allocation in raising living standards.

In the attempt to achieve their respective objectives, each of them develops its own paradigm, methodological approaches, and models, which make it possible for each of them to grow independently into a separate sector.

In the early stages of human development, with efforts to satisfy these limited essential needs, far-reaching specialization was not necessary.

But when human needs are growing and life becomes more complex, it gives life to further specialization in health, economics, and development. Each of them has their own domain and activities that makes possible the emergence of specialized sectors of health, economics, and development.

Since both economics and development are dealing with the allocation of resources to satisfying human needs through production and consumption, economics and development become inseparable. Economics is the driving force of development. And development for the past several decades has been synonymous with economic development.

In economic development, human resources are considered an important factor of production. With human resources, it is possible to raise the value added to natural and man-made resources, and make the product or service more valuable.

Health is embodied in the human factor of production. Its role is considered as raising the productivity and quality of human resources as a factor of production.

As such, health is treated as a subsystem of economic development, which stands at the periphery and not in the mainstream of development.

If development proceeds and income increases, either personal or national income, this allows the spending on health to increase. Health improvement is necessarily a byproduct of economic development.

Development is basically an economic issue, all others are treated as supporting sectors, including health. The role of health is important insofar as it contributes to raising productivity and reducing costs, as the successful indicators of development.

Working together among health, economics, and development is therefore not something new. It has been going on already for quite some time. Health has worked together with economic development, but on the terms set by the latter.

In development, it is economics which will set the pace, conditions, and directions to be followed by all other sectors.

Economics-centered development has created wide repercussions in other fields, giving rise to the need to reexamine the concept of development, especially to make it more viable to meet the challenges of change in the future.

CHALLENGES OF CHANGE

After decades of development since 1900, the world has changed considerably. People's standard of living has changed dramatically as revealed in the total Gross World Product, which in 1990 was 20 times that of 1900. This has been made possible by the increase of industrial output in 1990 to 30 times the output in 1900. Industrial production has been driven by energy use in 1990, which was 50 times the total energy use in 1900.

While these increases of output have raised the standard of living in most parts of the world, they have, however, also reduced the quality of the global environment.

Forests and their biological natural resources suffer depletion in their capital resource stock. When the depletion rate reached an alarming level, the world responded by agreeing to a global convention on saving biodiversity (1992).

The development process has a wide negative impact on nature, by polluting the air, water, land, rivers, and seas all over the world. Most dramatic is the impact of development on depleting the ozone layer and increasing global temperature. This development necessitated the world to launch the global convention on climate change (1992) in order to reduce jointly the use of products that produce the greenhouse gases.

While these efforts are necessary, they are dealing only with the symptoms rather than the cause of environmental degradation, which lies in the concept of development.

The concept of development thus far is too narrowly centered on economics only, and treats natural resources apart from their ecosystems and human resources separate from social systems.

Environment is merely treated as an item in the appendix. Environmental problems are considered "at the end of the production pipe."

Such an attitude explains why development has taken place with environmental degradation as a byproduct to be handled later. This attitude is, of course, costly, and may not reverse damage to the ecosystem.

This kind of development has taken place in the industrialized countries with only 20 percent of the world's population, but the environmental damage is already disastrous.

What will happen if the same pattern of development is followed by the 80 percent of the world's population who are inhabitants of the developing countries?

This is then one of the major reasons why there is a strong urge to develop a new pattern of development, namely, development with environmental consideration, or sustainable development.

In this concept of development, the characteristics of the respective ecosystems from which the resources are drawn for development are specifically considered.

By considering the nature of the ecosystems on these resources, development can take place sustainably, supported by the sustainability of these development resources.

Sustainable development is the course of development as set in the Earth Summit of June 1992 in Rio de Janeiro. The task now is to elaborate further this concept of sustainable development and implement this in the world at large.

This concept of sustainable development has broadened the focus of development, not only limited to issues of economics, such as economic equilibrium, but also to issues of ecology, such as ecological equilibrium.

Such an evolution of development concept does not stop here. There are currently attempts to broaden the focus of development to include social development.

The Social Summit in Copenhagen in 1995 developed further refinements within the context of social development. This development is a continuum of the Cairo Summit on Population and Development (1994). This brand of social development will necessarily also embrace health issues.

Already 80 percent of the world's people are suffering diseases that can be traced to waterborne and airborne factors.

The 1993 *World Development Report* of the World Bank lists six strategic health services that deserve high priority to eradicate disease in developing countries to improve the quality of life:

1. Immunization, which inexpensively can reduce many communicable diseases, such as tuberculosis and measles
2. Improving diet and nutrition, including iodine, iron, and vitamin A supplementation, where necessary
3. Decreasing fertility as attempts to reduce population growth and improve maternal health
4. Reducing abuse of tobacco, alcohol, and illegal drugs
5. Reducing negative environmental influences on health, both outdoors and indoors
6. Combatting AIDS.

The World Bank's proposal is consistent with the prevailing knowledge that the following four factors affect public health, namely: the physical, social, and ecological environment; social behavior and lifestyle factors; quality of and access to health services; and genetic factors.

The average developing country spends, however, three-fourths of its health budget on the development and construction of urban hospitals instead of focusing on efforts of prevention rather than cure. Some countries have tried to stop this trend. For example, Pakistan froze all hospital construction for 5 years, during which time it increased its childhood immunization coverage from 5 percent to 62 percent.

Health can be decoupled from economic concerns. For example, although Sri Lanka and Zimbabwe have lower per-capita income than Brazil, both of these countries have better indicators of health status than Brazil does. Development is no assurance for reaching complete physical, mental, and social well-being. One need only to look to developed countries to see the truth of this statement.

The state of complete physical, mental, and social well-being is no more a subsystem to be reached through development, but it now stands on its own as part of the quality of life, to be recognized as a goal of development.

The industrialized countries are still suffering poor quality of life as the result of noncommunicable diseases linked to sedentary lifestyle, stress, and harmful behavior patterns.

In the process of change, the developing countries face a double burden; the existence of communicable diseases linked to inadequate hygiene and other factors, and the emergence of noncommunicable diseases linked to development—to lifestyle, consumption, and behavioral factors giving rise to cardiovascular disease, diabetes, cancer, and other diseases. This strengthens the need for health as a focus of development, offering a better quality of life.

The development concept has broadened its focus. From structural economic development, emphasizing changing economic structures; to development with quality of environment; to development with quality of life and social dimensions such as eradication of poverty, employment, and physical, mental, and social health. Development that gives meaning to life. "Add life to years, rather than merely years to life" (Professor D. Sampoerno).

THE RESPONSE TO CHALLENGES

All countries of the world face five challenges today.

1. Development causes structural changes not only economically but also socially, creating new social groupings such as industrialists, entrepreneurs, professionals, and a new middle class;
2. The world has become borderless in terms of trade, production and investment and introduces new work, lifestyle and consumer patterns;
3. The introduction of new technologies which affect the production pattern and structure of employment;
4. Population growth accompanied by increased mobility creates potential social conflicts and social disintegration;
5. Rapid and basic economic and social changes have uprooted many fundamental value systems, while new value systems are not yet forthcoming.

These challenges require new responses. The environment and human behavior are changing. This requires a new development-cum-health paradigm. Health must be considered embodied in the quality of man, and become as such the focus of development.

Development-cum-health needs to tackle simultaneously the two primary factors affecting health, namely, environment and human behavior.

Health, economics and development are focussed on human beings and their quality of life, which embodies health. Therefore health may not be considered as an afterthought by putting it "at the end of the production pipe" but it must be considered already at the planning stage, at the start of production.

Health must shift from a subordinated subsystem to a focus of development. Health must be incorporated already in the design phase of development to strive for the goal to enrich the quality of life and quality of person through efforts that encounter the double challenge of health: communicable and emerging non-communicable diseases.

In coping with these diseases we need to focus on environment and human behavior as the primary cause of disease, which bring to bear the various fields of endeavor and expertise, including medicine, psychology, anthropology and economics.

To incorporate health into development, we must embody in development the system of handling its negative impact on health through polluted water, air, noise, loss of habitats and degrading ecosystems.

The value of wildlife and ecosystems for the future and affecting health need to be raised by arranging the discount rate.

Health must be treated as a valuable resource having "opportunity cost," meaning that the cost is determined by the loss of health. In a way health's value in economic terms is more than nothing, since without health anything useful for a healthy person means nothing.

Health, economics, and development must work together to meet the challenge of change. We must go a step further and merge health, economics and development into the comprehensive concept of *sustainable development*.

Such development does not only assure the sustainability of natural resources to enhance welfare, but it also assures the sustainability of human beings in raising the quality of people's lives.

The concept of sustainable development that incorporates environmental consideration into the development to ensure sustainability of ecosystems has been widely discussed and elaborated.

The concept of sustainable development needs to incorporate now the aspect of quality of life. It is through the quality of life that health plays a crucial role.

In order that incorporation of health into sustainable development is possible we need to create new economic instruments to analyze the development-cum-health process.

In the development process it is necessary to tackle not only the diseases but also the causes of the diseases which are rooted in the broadly defined environment covering natural, man-made and social environment, human behavior and lifestyle. This requires the need to broaden our knowledge and our capability to utilize various fields of study, including anthropology and psychology, to better understand human behavior and its linkage to disease—and in a broader scope to understand the linkages between health, environment, economics and development.

Health and environment can no longer be treated as externalities, we need to internalize the cost of negative impact of development on health into the cost structure of production—to internalize the costs of environmental pollution and environmental degradation.

We need to place a higher value, than we do now, on life in the future. Politicians have short-term vision, but health is a long-term phenomenon. With a high discount rate, we discount the value of the future and have an incentive to exploit resources now. A lower discount rate puts more value on the future. We must manipulate factors that affect the discount rate.

We need to treat health as a valuable resource by giving meaning to health as a basic element of the quality of life. Health must also be treated as having "opportunity cost" meaning that a lot of life has to be foregone if there is no health. Quality of life is a goal of development, and we need to make health an essential ingredient of the quality of life.

To enhance the concept of sustainable development-cum-health, we must mobilize all medical and relevant scientific endeavors that deal with the twin issues of health and development.

We must put more emphasis on communication, information, training and education to raise the awareness and understanding of sustainable development-cum-health.

Health leaders, such as ministers, director-generals, health managers, need to understand the interdependence between development and health. They must be able to understand the impact of development policies on health and the impact of health policies on development. They need to have the capacity to translate public health into the language of policymakers.

We must develop institutions that is capable to develop and monitor sustainable development-cum-health.

We must build a global network to strengthen the position of health in development and be able to apply global thinking into local action.

Health, economics and development must not only work together. They must also be merged into a common endeavor in order to meet the challenge of change.

35

Environmental Health: Sound Science or Intellectual Self-Indulgence?

Jim Listorti

This chapter is an unscientific, renegade presentation aimed at opening a discussion on the worth and direction of environmental health as it currently is practiced. How much is sound science; how much intellectual self indulgence? Given a vast array of health problems that span different fields from agriculture to industry, are environmental health practitioners building bridges or falling between the cracks? Are governments, foundations, and international agencies getting the message? Are environmental epidemiologists unrealistically reciting a litany of research requests, redefining problems but not suggesting solutions? Is environmental health research influencing public policy, or, more important, improving the quality of life? In spite of public concern expressed in the Gallup poll, public health issues are *not* influencing policymakers nor receiving budgets concomitant with their importance. Part of the problem lies directly with the environmental health community itself.

First a definition—not an easy task, since it is hard to avoid a literal alphabet soup of components and connections. Environmental health can be defined as the full range of parameters affecting human health and an equally broad range of interrelated factors prescribing remedial measures. The key concept separating it from other disciplines revolves around a wide multidisciplinary view of cause and effect that serves as a point of departure. Wearing an environmental health hat to analyze broad-based programs or highly focused projects yields a radically different identification of problems and solutions than wearing an engineer's, epidemiologist's, or physician's hat. In particular, the *relative* importance of multiple, simultaneous sources of morbidity and mortality plays a much greater role in devising remedial measures. Environmental health analyses must deal with a broader set of interlinkages, often seemingly insignificant, which could preclude health improvement if neglected, or conversely, can exert an enormous positive impact if addressed.

Trying to influence public policy to respond to environmental health problems is challenging precisely because the notion of environmental health spans so many professions, each with different definitions and differing emphases related to the same or similar problems. Five professions are especially important in influencing public policy: health, environment/ecology, engineering, economics/finance, and the law. Others like sociology/anthropology should also be included, but currently do not have enough professional clout outside their own field. Bridging the gaps among these fields is vital, but is not being done effectively by the health community. Indeed, environmental health specialists are being left behind in the dust by ecology groups with the inadvertent result of having green issues deflect much needed attention to problems that are not necessarily the most important for the well-being of society as a whole.

Why is this happening? Largely for four interrelated reasons:

a) many decisions impinging on human health are made *without* the input of health specialists at the earliest stages, or are tacked on as afterthoughts;
b) many decisions, even those made by health specialists, are made out of context or with incomplete information, but, nonetheless, considered as comprehensive analyses;
c) many environmental health practitioners are far too inward looking to be understood or even considered pertinent outside their specialty;
d) big-bucks research, relatively speaking, ignores the environmental health problems of the bulk of the world's population.

All these factors have had an adverse effect on effective advocacy of the environmental health community. If you define only half a problem, chances are you will devise only half a solution.

Absence of Participation of Health Specialists

Increasing professional specialization since the end of World War II has produced countless scientific advances in combatting disease, but not without opportunity costs, i.e., lack of communication and coordination among different specialists. Indeed, probably over three-fourths of decisions ultimately setting environmental health policy are now made mainly by people who have little or no health training, i.e., economists, engineers, and environmental assessment specialists, and lawyers. Economists generally play a major role in overall planning and budgeting. Pollution is largely considered the purview of engineers who accentuate the technical rather than the social setting; and when they do deal with human health, they focus more on sources than on diseases. (The field of public health engineering is an exception, but it has gradually diminished in popularity.) Similarly, environmental impact assessment specialists tend to favor natural resource management issues, with health considered most likely under the engineering-type pollution control or in occupational settings. Laws, standards and other such regulatory measures fall within the domain of lawyers who concentrate on the mechanics of legal enforcement rather than health outcomes.

Even though these key professions are slowly changing, most notably in university training, they are, nonetheless, still not competent to judge on multidisciplinary environmental health issues. Indeed, when such issues are accentuated, the result is often misdirected hysteria rather than useful proposals for remedies. (Recall the stir created over the use of the pesticide alar on apples in U.S. school lunches, at the same time that the paraffin lining of the milk cartons was more hazardous to children's health.) Even with these changes on the horizon, the tendency for specialization still dominates, reducing appropriate environmental health inputs. For example, among the 300 program titles of the 1992 annual meeting of the International Association of Impact Assessment (IAIA), many dealt with pollution, but only three contained the word health; two of these were dropped; the third dealt with cosmic influences on personal health and psychological well-being. The agenda of two events held in tandem is equally salient. A Social Impact Assessment workshop preceding the IAIA meetings did not have even one topic on health in its three-day program; and a conference examining 20 years of urban development contained a full afternoon on urban environmental problems but never mentioned cholera, even though Latin American capitals were regularly discussed.

Incomplete Information About Health Repercussions

Health improvement interventions are often based on an incomplete picture of important, identifiable health parameters at play, effectively analyzing out of context from public health. The engineering and environmental assessment approach, for example, tends to focus on "end-of-pipe" problems, such as smokestacks, vehicle exhausts, and sewer outlets, often ignoring intermediate pollution sources, which collectively are often greater than end-of-pipe sources. A similar situation exists in occupational and environmental health, which are often lumped together.

Both still concentrate on workplace safety and pollution, with relatively little consideration of health impacts in surrounding airsheds and watersheds.

This incomplete analysis occurs for several interrelated reasons:

a) the 20–30-year lag between exposure and clinical manifestation of symptoms is too far from most planning/budgeting exercises which focus on 5–10-year horizons;
b) because of statistical significance, research methodologies tend to focus on a single disease or pollutant, limiting the breadth of variables studied;
c) pollutants whose accurate measurement is considered too costly or too complicated (e.g., 0_3 and PM_{10})[1] are often dropped from analyses;
d) pollution measurement flaws cannot adequately compensate for peak exposures over a 24-hour period or the percentage of time spent indoors when measuring ambient air quality, etc.; and
e) political and social pressure often forces attention to aspects of a problem that is not epidemiologically significant relative to more serious health issues (e.g., alar in apples).

Consequently, data gathering and other forms of monitoring inputs that subsequently lead to planning and budgeting focus on the most statistically significant *measured* sources of risk or exposure, while underestimating other sources that were not or cannot be measured, but which can be of equal or greater importance. To oversimplify: air pollution is not monitored at nose level.

Take an example, such as lead. In Mexico City, well known for its air pollution, lead absorption from traditional glazed dishes and cooking pots can be greater than that from vehicular emissions, but gets nowhere the same attention or funding. Such frequently under- or unmeasured sources could affect a large but broadly dispersed segment of the population, such as lead poultices used by women for cosmetic and religious purposes in India. They could also be localized to neighborhoods or exist as citywide pockets, such as cottage industries recycling jeweler's wastes in West Africa. This type of information tends often to fall between the bureaucratic cracks by the time it passes from health agencies to policymakers and budget planners. The scenario could be repeated for the

[1] Ozone, O_3, is a form of oxygen, common in smog; PM_{10}, particulate matter less than 10 microns in diameter, describes a physical characteristic of the size of pollutants which are small enough to penetrate deep into the lungs.

most common and epidemiologically important pollutants[2] which require different monitoring equipment and laboratory procedures.

INWARD FOCUS

Health professionals often assume that, because they deal with potentially life-threatening issues, others attribute the same importance to their work. Regrettably, like so many other fields, the language of health reports tends to be incomprehensible to those outside the field, seldom presenting an abstract in simple language explaining why the reports, research proposals or work plans are useful. For example, why should governments or foundations respond enthusiastically to a proposal to study the neurotoxicity of organochlorines? They might, however, respond generously were they asked to fund research on the adverse health effects of commonly used pesticides which accumulate in the body and cause cancer (and possibly lead to a class action law suit).

It seems that even epidemiologists, the most interdisciplinary mavens of the health field, have gone the way of the family doctor. At conferences one hears of risk assessment, exposure assessment, toxicology, and statistics as fields separate from epidemiology. Similarly, environmental impact reports, which should be multidisciplinary, in practice are prepared mostly by environmental assessment specialists who tend to study vehicular or industrial emissions rather than air that winds up in the lungs. For example, a recent analysis establishing environmental priorities in Eastern and Central Europe, conducted by an exposure assessment specialist, identified three of the four most important problems as related to industrial air pollution (the fourth was water), but never mentions indoor residential air pollution nor cites smoking habits as predisposing or complicating factors.

OMISSION OF BULK OF THE WORLD'S POPULATION

The unintended focus—indeed, control—of environmental health on pollution and research methodologies excludes most of the world's population in setting policy. Admittedly, many research and pollution issues are

[2]Suspended particulate matter (of various sizes with different equipment for monitoring indoor and separate analysis of lead), carbon monoxide, oxides of sulfur, oxides of nitrogen, ozone, and volatile organic compounds (with separate analysis of formaldehyde).

self-contained in the industrialized countries. But, would it not make more sense to consider global problems in a global context? Yet, collectively, water-related and respiratory illnesses, coupled with malnutrition, are the single greatest cause of morbidity and mortality in the world today. In developing countries, which comprise the bulk of the world's population, about 30 percent of the people still lack safe drinking water and 50 percent lack basic sanitation. The situation in impoverished areas of the industrialized countries is similar with diarrheas, malnutrition, and pneumonia replaced by other poverty-related diseases. Nonetheless, pollution of the ambient external environment currently seems to dominate public agendas concerned with environmental health, while professional agendas concerned with these issues seem to concentrate on occupational health. The result has been to displace the traditional problems related to deficiencies in water supply, waste disposal, drainage and housing, which are often no longer even viewed as pollution under conditions of heavy emissions from industry, transport, and energy.

Moreover, the voice of the bulk of the world's population in formulating environmental health policy is almost systematically excluded, albeit inadvertently, by circumstance. For example, membership in most professional societies or a subscription to a technical journal, about US$75–100, represents a month's pay for senior staff in developing countries, severely curtailing their contributions to publications, if not effectively eliminating their attendance at conferences. In Bobo-Dialasso, a regional capital of Burkina Fasso (formerly Upper Volta), the national nursing school had a US$100 budget for all external events. Two years ago, nurses in Guyana went on strike to increase their monthly salary from US$27 to US$30. In discussions for future meeting sites, a member of an environmental health organization queried why Africa should even be included on a short list since it had so few environmental problems. A Harvard exercise at combining a broad range of variables to define environmental health priorities for Kenya found radon exposure to be among the top ten health problems.

LITERATURE REVIEW

This presentation draws heavily on personal observation and in particular on two recent, extensive literature reviews which look at environmental health in a broad context: "A Review of Environmental Health Impacts in Developing Country Cities," by the London School of Hygiene and Tropical Medicine, and "The Impact of Development Policies on Health," published by the World Health Organization (WHO), based on a WHO/Harvard/World Bank investigation. They demonstrate the difficulty in devising a comprehensive yet manageable system satisfactory to health specialists, economists, and ecologists, each of whom needs to analyze and justify projects on different grounds in their roles as specialists and as project managers.

The "Review of Environmental Health Impacts in Developing Country Cities" was especially helpful in showing the repetition of investigations on nutrition, water supply and sanitation, diarrheal diseases, children, and the technical aspects of popular tropical diseases, such as malaria and schistosomiasis. More important, by their omission, it implies the relative neglect of other pertinent topics, such as indoor air pollution, or the proliferation of new synthesized chemical pollutants, etc. All these factors collectively contribute to poor health.

In this vein, the WHO/IBRD/Harvard literature review is especially useful as an indicator of literature gaps, covering about 400 publications on general macroeconomic planning, agriculture, industry, energy and housing.[3] The Review implies, by extension, the limitations of programs and projects to respond to environmental health problems dealing specifically with interventions concentrating on a single sector. Two overriding conclusions stand out:

a) health repercussions have generally not played an important role in policy decisions outside the health sector—except where a high level of understanding about health linkages already exists, e.g., water pollution, and;
b) macroeconomic policy decisions appeared to be based more on technical factors within a sector, rather than on their application in broader context, e.g., on the manufacture and immediate use of chemicals rather than on their accumulation in watersheds and food chains.

Cross-Sectoral Linkages that Tend to Fall Between the Cracks

Without looking at environmental health in a broad perspective, many cross-sectoral linkages fall between the administrative cracks of agencies charged with protecting and maintaining human welfare, largely because clear lines of responsibility and budgets are not spelled out. The forthcoming selection presents a common range of examples with emphasis on developing countries since their views have been underrepresented.

---

[3]In macroeconomic policy, 88 publications; agricultural policy, 78; industrial policy, 94; energy policy, 75; housing policy, 56.

AGRICULTURE

In the agriculture sector, three linkages are vitally important: (1) the misuse of pesticides as an occupational hazard, (2) the reuse of contaminated water in irrigation, coupled with the potential penetration of pesticides, heavy metals and pathogens into the food chain, and (3) the extension of the habitat of insect vectors.

Agriculture policies tend not to look at health repercussions except for water resource development, "where an association with vector-borne disease is now recognized, after two decades of prompting by a number of agencies." Nonetheless, few projects actually measure before and after levels of specific diseases. Pesticide subsidies aimed at improving productivity have not been examined for health consequences, despite well documented cases of poisonings (workers and consumers), increased resistance of disease vectors, and "over-reliance on chemical pest control strategies." More work is needed on the adaptation of pesticide use to local conditions. Moreover, land tenure policies have rarely been examined as a factor for the spread of endemic diseases among migrants, where water supply plays a key role. Agricultural researchers are only beginning to consider the repercussions of new technologies and policies on farmers and consumers.

The combination of overall population growth and continuing migration to cities has placed drinking water supply in competition with irrigation. Developing new water sources to meet demand, increasingly farther away from the ultimate point of use, has added to the cost. Added cost, in turn, leads to pressures to cut corners and compromise on environmental issues, such as additional funds for drainage, chemical and biological runoff, waste disposal, and especially for programs to operate and maintain the drinking water supply or irrigation systems in sound working order.

Pesticides are often considered primarily an occupational hazard and direct threat to rural populations and the natural environment subjected to pesticide application and runoff. Nonetheless, they have a direct bearing on water contamination to the population at large because of the high levels of illiteracy in developing countries, and the large share of the population which earn their living in agriculture. Take, for example: (1) pesticide buildup in the food chain, (2) improper transport and storage from ports to fields, (3) reuse of containers for water storage or makeshift housing parts in slums and squatter settlements, (4) seasonal variations in concentration of pollutants in the receiving waters used for drinking or watering/washing vegetables, and (5) resistance of water-related insect vectors (mosquitoes and snails).

Additional analysis is needed in devising specific types of irrigation policy to mitigate against negative health effects. Pesticide analysis has focussed on documenting causes of poisoning, rather than on examining policies that promote and subsidize pesticide use, or on identifying incentives and regulations that promote safer alternatives. Similarly, analyses on land tenure have not focussed on health repercussions, except, for example, in large-scale transmigration projects, or the spread of malaria in the Amazon.

INDUSTRY

The industrial sector is linked to others by five factors: (1) pollution of drinking water; (2) contamination of the food chain; (3) occupational hazards and air pollution; (4) the tendency of slums and squatter settlements to grow around industrial sites, with a propensity for accidents and the all-to-familiar range of diseases; and (5) generation and improper disposal of toxic waste.

Governments have emphasized industrial growth and social welfare by considering types of industrial specialization, ownership and siting, e.g., industrial zones, "with relatively little attention to the consequences for health." This has been due in part to the lack of clear-cut understanding of the cause and effect of pollution and health deterioration. Similarly, promotion of small-scale industries has also disregarded low-income factory workers or the inhabitants near industries. Current emphasis in this regard is being directed inside factories, while the surrounding communities remain a low priority. The deleterious effects of water and air pollution and hazardous waste control have been receiving increased attention. Nonetheless, more work is needed on understanding the health consequences of heavily polluted areas. (Some of the latter are currently being dealt with in industrialized countries under the umbrella of "environmental justice.")

Research on industry has dealt primarily with occupational health and accidents, rather than their underlying causes. Researchers have emphasized needs for adjustment in health policy where potential for change seems greatest—standards, availability of health services, training, and safe equipment—rather than overall strategies. Literature on air and water pollution is still too inconclusive to permit precise determination of cause and effect by industry or pollutant on a given population. Several factors have hindered research, e.g., inadequate data on populations, absence of monitoring equipment, poorly understood theoretical effects applied to defined topographical conditions or applied to the siting of pollution-intensive industries. While enormous amounts of data have been generated on the existence of industrial pollutants, especially heavy metals, by comparison very little has been done on contamination of the food chain.

ENERGY

The links with the energy sector are mainly four: (1) extension of habitats for disease-causing vectors (snails and mosquitoes) in hydro-power; (2) deterioration of health in general due to the physical stress of gathering fuelwood; (3) household air pollution from poorly ventilated combustion-type stoves and other heating/cooking sources; and (4) pollution from generation of power.

Energy policies in developing countries have not given adequate attention to the health consequences of the different stages of energy production, i.e., extraction, consumption and pricing. Deforestation has led to added stress and threatens to reduce nutrition in poor households, where women spend ever increasing amounts of time for gathering firewood. When coupled with daily demands to fetch water, this places considerable physical stress on women and children. Policies to increase wood fuel reserves rarely touch the households suffering from "fuel poverty." Efforts have been directed at increasing domestic fuel efficiency, but only recently has attention been devoted to improving housing and cooking stoves in the context of health risks associated with chronic in-house exposure to fumes from biofuels. Fuel subsidies have not taken health and pollution into consideration, nor have they promoted nonpolluting, safe fuels. Pricing policies tend to favor urban areas, where air pollution is generally greater, over rural areas. Hydropower, especially large dams, remains high on development priority lists. Yet, associated health risks "still do not figure predominantly" in project preparation and implementation.

A growing literature has documented the relationship between domestic fuel use, respiratory infections and low birthweights, identifying biofuel use as a major hazard. Yet, this information has not yet been integrated into energy policies mitigating urban or rural indoor air pollution. Similarly, developing countries need better analysis of the effects of fuel gathering, its shortage, fuel substitution, and food preparation. Epidemiological evidence is increasing on the links among energy use, outdoor air pollution and the incidence of respiratory illness and cancer. Yet, few studies have recommended regulatory measures or identified high-risk populations or areas for special attention.

HOUSING

The housing sector has three important linkages: (1) deficiencies of water and sanitation services, especially in low income settlements; (2) inadequate waste disposal, and (3) physical stress from household air pollution.

A considerable literature exists on health and housing. Urban policies, however, rarely pay adequate attention to the targeted low-income populations, nor do they assess changes in health status of the beneficiaries. This may be due in part to the large number of confounding socioeconomic and behavioral variables (e.g., income, employment, education, sexually transmitted diseases, alcohol/drug abuse, child abuse, stress, nutrition, or expenditure on patterns, alcohol or luxuries). Nonetheless, specific recommendations are available in a number of reports linking housing, water and health.

Even though links between poor housing and health exist in the literature, researchers have not explored the underlying policy factors, such as building restrictions, tenure, allocation of public services, etc. Increased costs due to improved government housing have been linked to diminished food expenditures in low-income populations, possibly lowering nutritional intake. (Excessive cost of housing in sites-and-services schemes was singled out.) More analysis is needed on this association in view of reducing trade-offs between housing and food budgets. Nonetheless, health authorities "have not been actively engaged in the design or implementation of urban housing policies. . . . On the whole, housing policy has paid little attention to disease control or public health programs, and health services are often treated as secondary objectives . . ."

REFERENCES AND BIBLIOGRAPHY

Abt Associates; "Human Health Risk Assessment for Municipal Sludge Disposal: Benefits of Alternative Regulatory Options" (prepared for the USEPA, Office of Water Regulations and Standards, PB89-136626); Springfield, Virginia: U.S. Department of Commerce, National Technical Information Service; February, 1989.

Ashford, Nicholas A., & Claudia S. Miller; *Chemical Exposures: Low Levels and High Stakes*; New York: Van Nostrand Reinhold; 1991.

Barnum, Howard & Robert Greenberg; "Health Sector Priorities Review: Cancers"; World Bank (Population, Health and Nutrition Division, HSPR-01); January, 1991.

Bartone, R., Smith, J., & Wilson, D., Eds.; *The Safe Disposal of Hazardous Wastes: The Special Needs and Problems of Developing Countries* (IBRD Technical Paper No. 93); Washington: World Bank/WHO/UNEP (in 3 vols.); 1989.

Berry, Brian, J. L., & Frank, E. Horton, Eds.; *Urban Environmental Management: Planning for Pollution Control*; Englewood Cliffs, New Jersey: Prentice-Hall, Inc.; 1974.

Bertaud, Alain, & Mary Young; "Geographical Pattern of Environmental Health in Tianjin, China: The Development of an Environmental Health Data Base"; (Urban Development Division, Sector Policy and Research [INURD] Working Paper #13); Washington: World Bank; February, 1991.

Biggar, James, W., & James, N. Seiber; *Fate of Pesticides in the Environment: Proceedings of a Technical Seminar*; Oakland, California: University of California, Division of Agriculture and Natural Rsources (Pub. No. 3320), 1987.

Bradley, David, et al.; "A Review of Environmental Health Impacts in Developing Country Cities"; World Bank (Urban Management and the Environment, Discussion Paper), July, 1992.

Brimblecombe, Peter; *The Big Smoke: A History of Air Pollution in London since Medieval Times*; London: Methuen; 1987.

Burke, T., et al.; "Role of Databases in Risk Management;" in *Archives of Environmental Health, Vol. 47, No. 6*, Nov./Dec. 1992.

Cairncross, Sandy, & Richard Feachem; *Environmental Health Engineering in the Tropics: An Introductory Text*; Chichester (U.K.): John Wiley; 1983.

Clark, R. B.; *Marine Pollution*, Third Edition; Oxford: Clarendon Press, 1992.

Cooper Weil, D. E., & Alicbusan, A. P. Wilson, J. F. Reich, M. R., & Bradley, D. J.; *The Impact of Development Policies on Health*; Geneva: WHO; 1990.

Draggan, Sidney, & Cohrssen, J. J., & Morrison, R. E.; *Environmental Impacts on Human Health: The Agenda for Long-Term Research and Development*; New York: Praeger; 1987.

Esrey, Steven, et al.; *Health Benefits from Improvements in Water Supply and Sanitation: a Survey and Analysis of the Literature on Selected Cases*; USAID (Water and Sanitation for Health [WASH] Project, prepared for the Office of Health, Bureau of Science and Technology, Task No. 35); July, 1990.

Feachem, Richard, et al., Eds.; *The Health of Adults in the Developing World*; World Bank, pre-publication draft, May, 1991.

Fisch, A., et al.; "A New Approach to Combatting Iodine Deficiency in Developing Countries: The Controlled Release of Iodine in Water by a Silicone Elastomer;" *American Journal of Public Health, Vol. 83, No. 4*, 1993.

Gallup International Institute; *Health of the Planet Survey*; Princeton, N. J.: Gallup International Institute; July 1992.

Ginzburg, Lev. R.; *Assessing Ecological Risks of Biotechnology*; Boston: Butterworth-Heinemann, 1991.

Goldman, L. R., et al.; "Use of Exposure Databases for Status and Trends Analysis;" *Archives of Environmental Health, Vol. 47, No. 6*, Nov./Dec. 1992.

Graham, J., et al.; "Role of Exposure Databases in Risk Assessment;" *Archives of Environmental Health, Vol. 47, No. 6*, Nov./Dec. 1992.

Hutchison, T. C., & Meema, K. M. Eds; *Lead, Mercury and Arsenic in the Environment: SCOPE 31*; New York: John Wiley & Sons, published on behalf of the Scientific Committee on Problems of the Environment (SCOPE).

IBRD/UNDP/UNCHS; "Urban Environmental Indicators Questionnaire"; Urban Management Program; January, 1992 (draft).

IBRD; *Environmental Assessment Sourcebook: Volume II—Sectoral Guidelines*; World Bank Technical Paper No. 140; August, 1991.

IBRD; "Measuring Health Benefits of Investments in Water Supply"; Public Utility Notes PUN 20; 1975. (out of print)

IBRD; *World Development Report 1992: Development and the Environment*; New York: Oxford University Press (Published for the World Bank); 1992.

IBRD; *World Development Report 1993: Investing in Health*; New York: Oxford University Press (Published for the World Bank); 1993 (pre-publication draft).

Kreimer, Alcira & Mohan Munasinghe, Eds.; *Managing Natural Disasters and the Environment*; Washington: World Bank; 1991.

Krupnik, Alan, & Iona Sebastian; "Issues in Urban Air Pollution: Review of the Beijing Case Study"; World Bank (Environment Department Working Paper No. 31), May, 1990.

Listorti, James A.; *Environmental Health Components in Water Supply, Sanitation and Urban Projects*; (IBRD Technical Paper No. 121); Washington: World Bank, Sept., 1990.

Manatoski, G., et al.; "Role of Exposure Databases in Epidemiology;" *Archives of Environmental Health, Vol. 47, No. 6*, Nov./Dec. 1992.

Margulis, Sergio; "Back-of-the-Envelope Estimates of Environmental Damage Costs in Mexico;" World Bank, Policy Research Working Paper (WPS No. 824), January, 1992.

Mooney, Gavin, & Andrew Creese; "Health Sector Priorities Review: Priority Setting for Health Service Efficiency—the Role of Measurement of Burden of Illness;" World Bank (Population, Health and Nutrition Division, HSPR-23); October, 1991.

Norberg-Bohm, Vicki, & William C. Clark, et al.; "International Comparisons of Environmental Hazards: Development and Evaluation of a Method for Linking Environmental Data with the Strategic Debate Management Priorities for Risk Management;" Cambridge, Massachusetts: Kennedy School of Government, Harvard University (CSIA Discussion Paper 92-09); October, 1992.

Olivio, Jaylyn; "Environmental Health Agenda for the 1900s: Summary of Workshop, October 1–6, Santa Fe, New Mexico"; *Environmental Research, vol. 63, 1993*; pp. 1–15.

Ostro, Bart; "Generic Estimates of the Economic Effects of Criteria Air Pollutants: A Review and Synthesis;" World Bank (Country Economics Department), draft, March, 1992.

Over, Mead; *Economics for Health Sector Analysis—Concepts and Cases*; World Bank, EDI Technical Materials, 1991.

Paul, John, E., & Josephine A. Mauskopf; "Cost-of-Illness Methodologies for Water-Related Diseases in Developing Countries (Technical Report No. 75)"; Washington, D.C.: USAID (Water and Sanitation for Health [WASH] Project, prepared for the Office of Health, Bureau of Science and Technology, Task No. 083); October, 1991.

Rom, William, Ed.; *Environmental and Occupational Medicine*, second edition; Boston: Little, Brown & Co.; 1992.

Samiullah, Yusaf; *Prediction of the Environmental Fate of Chemicals*; London: Elsevier Applied Science; 1990.

Scrimshaw, Nevin, S., & Gary, R. Gleason, Eds.; *RAP—Rapid Assessment Procedures: Qualitative Methodologies for Planning and Evaluation of Health Related Programmes*; Boston: International Nutrition Foundation for Developing Countries, 1992.

Sebastian, Iona; "Issues in Urban Air Pollution: Ankara Diagnostic Report;" World Bank (Environment Department Working Paper No. 38), August, 1990.

Sebastian, Iona; "Issues in Urban Air Pollution: Mexico City Diagnostic Case Study;" World Bank (Internal Environment Department Working Paper), March, 1990.

Sexton, K., et al.; "Estimating Human Exposures to Environmental Pollutants: Availability and Utility of Existing Databases;" in *Archives of Environmental Health, Vol. 47, No. 6,* Nov./Dec. 1992.

Shin, Euisoon, et al.; *Economic Valuation of Urban Environmental Problems—With Emphasis on Asia*; IBRD (Urban Development Division, Infrastructure and Urban Development Department) January 28, 1992. (pre-publication draft)

Singh, Udai, P., & Otto, J. Helweg, Eds; *Supplying Water and Saving the Environment for Six Billion People*; New York: American Society of Civil Engineers, 1990.

Stansfield, Sally, & Donald Shepard; "Health Sector Priorities Review: Acute Respiratory Infections;" World Bank (Population, Health and Nutrition Division, HSPR-30); October, 1991.

Treiff, Norman M.; *Environmental Health*; Ann Arbor, Michigan: Ann Arbor Science Publishers; 1981.

United States—Eastern Europe Exchange for Occupational and Environmental Health; "Environment and Health in Eastern Europe: Proceedings of the 'Symposium on Occupational and Environmental Health during Social Transition in Eastern Europe'", Pecs, Hungary, June 22–27, 1990; Management Sciences for Health, Boston, Massachusetts, 1990.

USAID; "Ranking Environmental Health Risks in Bangkok, Thailand"; USAID (Office of Housing and Urban Programs Working Paper; prepared by Abt Associates [Bethesda, Md.] and Sobotka & Co. 2 vols.); Washington: USAID; December, 1990.

Vernet, J. P.; Ed.; *Heavy Metals and the Environment: Trace Metals in the Environment 1*; Amsterdam: Elsevier, 1991.

WHO; *Compendium of Environmental Guidelines and Standards for Industrial Discharges*; WHO (Doc. No. EFP/83.49), 1983.

WHO; *Drinking-Water Quality and Health-related Risks: a Framework for Developing Data Reliability*; WHO Environmental Health Series No. 23; Copenhagen: WHO, 1987.

WHO; *Report of the WHO Commission on Health and Environment, Panel on Urbanization*; Geneva: WHO, 1992.

WHO; *Report of the WHO Commission on Health and Environment, Panel on Energy*; Geneva: WHO, 1992.

WHO; *Report of the WHO Commission on Health and Environment, Panel on Industry*; Geneva: WHO, 1992.

WHO; *Report of the WHO Commission on Health and Environment, Panel on Food and Agriculture*; Geneva: WHO, 1992.

WHO; *PCBs, PCDDs and PCDFs: Prevention and Control of Accidental and Environmental Exposures*; WHO Environmental Health Series No. 23; Copenhagen: WHO, 1987.

WHO; *Rapid Assessment of Sources of Air, Water, and Land Pollution*, (WHO Offset Publication No. 62), 1982. [Updated by *Management and Control . . .*, above.]

WHO; *Management and Control of the Environment* (Doc. No. WHO/PEP/89.2); Geneva: WHO; 1989.

WHO; *Urban Air Pollution in the Megacities of the World*; Washington: Pan-American Health Organization; March, 1992.

WHO; *Toxic Oil Syndrome: Current Knowledge and Future Prospects*; WHO Regional Publications Series No. 42; Copenhagen: WHO, 1992.

WHO; *Revision of the WHO Guidelines for Drinking-Water Quality* (Doc. NO. PEP/IPCS/EURO/92.1); Geneva: WHO; 1992.

WHO; *Our Planet, Our Health: Report of the WHO Commission on Health and Environment*; Geneva: WHO, 1992.

PART VII
Research and Intervention Priorities

36

Health Research and International Development

Scott B. Halstead

Beyond the emergencies which press for the immediate attention of the world are the slow, silent and sustained medical disasters, largely out of view, the dark plight of humankind. The lives of 8 million children under five were lost last year; one of three children born will suffer some level of mental or physical impairment due to malnutrition. There are an estimated 120 million women who do not want to become pregnant but are not using family planning—about one in every five babies born are unwanted; in much of Africa the chance that a woman will die during childbirth is nearly one in ten; in 28 countries of the world girl babies are subjected to genital mutilation. Through neglect or worse, female babies fail to survive at the same rates as male babies in 20 countries.

It is readily apparent that there will never be enough money or human resources to cure diseases in all developing countries to achieve levels of health attained in industrialized countries, at least not in the immediate future. We simply cannot allow these diseases and poor health conditions to continue. They must be prevented.

How do we do this? The prevention of epidemics, overt and silent, requires careful long-term planning with the full participation of all involved. It is necessary to train leaders and build institutions. A significant fraction of total effort must be directed to disease prevention and primary health care. Disease prevention is the responsibility of the public health system. A system is needed which can identify priority health problems, frame questions which deal with solutions to these problems, assemble the research resources needed to answer these questions and mobilize the funds to get the research done. Attempting to mobilize the world community around the need for health research has been the goal of a movement which has come to be known as Essential National Health Research (ENHR).

ESSENTIAL NATIONAL HEALTH RESEARCH

The Commission on Health Research for Development, an independent international initiative, was launched in 1987 to study the status, effect and needs of research on the health problems of developing countries. After three years of site visits and conferences, the deliberations of the Commission were presented at a Nobel symposium and subsequently published. This report, *Health Research: Essential Link to Equity in Development*, provides a useful catalog of international health research resources. It also presents the Commission's key finding, that although the problems of developing countries are the focus of only 5 percent of the world's expenditure on health research, those countries suffer 93 percent of the burden of premature mortality, as measured in potential years of life lost. For example, acute respiratory infections, including measles and whooping cough, are responsible for 7.4 million deaths a year; diarrheal diseases for 5 million.

Recognizing that behavioral, cultural, ecologic and economic conditions added to various technical or scientific considerations play a part in defining the unique health profile of every country and region, the commission labeled such research as "essential national health research." It was the Commission's recommendation that every country, no matter how poor, must engage in essential national health research to guide health policy and management decisions; otherwise, precious health resources will be wasted. Central to the concept of essential national health research is a critical but often neglected link between health research and policymaking.

The Commission's report addresses the issue of the inadequate transfer and adaptation of scientific knowledge and technology from the First World to the Third World. But it also examines the reality that such transfers are constrained by lack of capacity, the understanding of the essential role that research plays in the design and management of health systems and by the political will needed to allocate resources to health research. The Commission determined to help build the capacity of developing countries to conduct and act on their own research in the areas most pertinent to the health of their own citizens. With that capacity on hand, countries can address their own health priorities in a strategic and ongoing way and can contribute importantly to the world's ability to cope with the health issues that transcend national borders.

To carry out ENHR, the Commission recommended that each country specify at least 3 percent of its health budget for health research. Further, it was suggested that those development agencies which deal with health issues should allocate 5 percent of their annual budgets for health research. The Commission called for the creation of an international support system which might help developing countries strengthen their capacity for country-specific health research. In the Commission's view, such a system would include coordination of the efforts of the existing international programs; a facilitating unit; an annual meeting of scientists, health leaders and donor representatives and international awards for distinguished contributions to country-specific health research.

To operationalize its vision, the commission gave birth to a Task Force on Health Research for Development, chaired by Professor V. Ramalingaswami. The Task Force established a headquarters in Geneva with Dr. Richard Wilson directing its activities from 1991 to 1993. Information-sharing meetings and workshops were held in a number of countries, while serious health research programs were created by health ministries in Mozambique and the Philippines.

In 1993, the Task Force created a Council on Health Research for Development under the chairmanship of Dr. Jaime Sepulveda. The Task Force and Council have worked with more than 20 countries wishing to begin an ENHR process. The day-to-day work is being carried out by Dr. Yvo Nuyens. Close links have been established with WHO, UNICEF, UNDP and with international networks such as INCLEN, IHPP, and the Community-Based Health Educational Institutions. The Council publishes a monthly newsletter, the ENHR Forum. Sponsors of the Task Force and Council include IDRC, SAREC, the Edna McConnell Clark Foundation, the Rockefeller Foundation, The Ford Foundation, the Aga Khan Foundation, the Carnegie Corporation, Gesellschaft für Technische Zusammenarbeit, and the Pew Charitable Trusts.

THE ROLE OF EPIDEMIOLOGY

Of the skills needed to carry out ENHR, epidemiology is foremost. A problem which the countries of the world have yet to solve, independently or collectively, is how to identify silent health crises, prioritize them in terms of cost and impact, design appropriate interventions and learn how to judge the effectiveness of solutions to health problems, whether curative or preventive. These are the kinds of concerns which led to the creation of the three programs being described in this chapter. There are two important components in this chain of problem identification, problem solving and intervention: the National Epidemiology Boards (NEBs) are structured research institutions designed to manage high-priority research. The NEBs attempt to operationalize ENHR by building institutions which are specifically designed to identify health problems, to test interventions and to recommend program and policy changes to decision makers. Other programs which contribute to this process and which also contribute to training research-caliber epidemiologists are the International Clinical Epidemiology Network (Chapter 29), the Field Epidemiology Training Network (Chapter 30), and Public Health Schools without Walls.

What Is Epidemiology?

Epidemiology is the science used to define the prevalence and incidence of disease, to measure the impact of diseases on populations, to study the causation of disease, to establish the priorities for implementing public health programs, to design interventions and, finally, to test the outcome of interventions. These tasks very nearly describe the whole of public health practice.

How Are Epidemiologists Created?

The skills required by an epidemiologist are not always naturally or easily acquired in every culture. The nature of epidemiology is to acquire new knowledge, to find new causes of disease and to observe new relationships between biological phenomena. In other words, the information required in epidemiology is not to be found in textbooks. This creates an immediate problem because many educational systems base education on rote learning. The opinion of authorities is important. The concept of causation or the treatment of disease may be traditional and not susceptible to challenge.

New Ways of Creating Epidemiologists

The field of epidemiology is relatively young. Formal training programs were not generally available until after the creation of schools of public health early in this century. Most students, particularly those from developing countries, have regarded epidemiology as a research field and not as a powerful and practical discipline which could help them do a better job at home. As a result, epidemiological skills are not widely available where they are needed most.

Several innovative programs may change all that: the Field Epidemiology Training Project (FETP); the International Clinical Epidemiology Network (INCLEN); National Epidemiology Boards (NEBs) and Public Health Schools without Walls (PHSWOW). Descriptions of the history, organization, purpose and effectiveness of these initiatives follow:

FETP

Begun in 1980, FETPs are post-graduate training programs in applied epidemiology. These are organized by national ministries of public health, usually with the assistance of officers from the Centers for Disease Control and Prevention (CDC). FETP trainees are usually physicians, but dentists, veterinarians, pharmacists and laboratorians have also participated. The

FETPs are modeled after CDC's two-year training program in applied epidemiology known as the Epidemic Intelligence Service Program (EIS). The EIS has operated continuously since 1951; its more than 1,800 graduates serve in public health, academic and health positions all over the world.

CDC has assisted 13 countries to start FETPs (Thailand, Indonesia, Mexico, Taiwan, Philippines, Saudi Arabia, Peru, Australia, Italy, Colombia, Egypt, Zimbabwe and Spain).

Seven of these programs have a national teaching cadre and are self-sustaining. In Zimbabwe, the FETP is one component of a larger program supported by the Rockefeller Foundation, called Public Health Schools without Walls (PHSWOW). Programs exist in all six WHO Regions and training is conducted in six languages, Arabic, Chinese, English, Indonesian, Spanish and Thai.

The typical FETP begins with several weeks of didactic lectures, case studies and computer training. These are often given by collaborating university faculty members. The purpose of this component is to provide the trainee with a basic foundation in epidemiologic methods and statistics. This is followed by two years of supervised, on-the-job field work which is supplemented with additional classroom training. The main approach in training is to learn by doing, just as in most medical or surgical residency programs. Training is centered on the study of outbreaks or unusual disease occurrences. This teaches the student the use of controls, the value of statistics in assessing probability, the definition of causation and above all, a practical working knowledge of his or her own country. During the two-year on-the-job experience, the trainees participate in surveillance and epidemiological field investigations, in conducting laboratory procedures, evaluating control and prevention measures, public health administration, oral and written scientific communication, the application of microcomputers and teaching other trainees. On completing the training program, most students have a new sense of resourcefulness and confidence in their ability to solve work-related problems.

Public Health Schools without Walls

Ever since the first school of public health was founded at Johns Hopkins University in 1918, public health education has lacked the kind of practicum which is essential to medical and surgical training. Internship and residency training programs are designed to build upon a knowledge of the basic sciences of medicine and provide the graded clinical experiences necessary to master the skills to practice medicine and surgery. Originally, public health training was designed for physicians who were already performing public health work. Over time, public health graduate degrees have been awarded to students who were contemplating a public health career. These students had little or no prior preparation for this profession. Unfortunately, public health training has become progressively academic, research oriented and often, theoretical. Worse, many developing countries lack their own public health training programs and opt to send students to schools in industrialized countries. This results in an academic exposure to irrelevant health systems, a focus on developed country diseases and over-reliance on high technology solutions. For poor countries this is a particularly inappropriate preparation for the day-to-day realities of administering public health programs. Competence in that job requires an ability to distinguish between affordable and nonaffordable, workable and unworkable solutions. This requires an ability to recognize and prioritize health problems and prioritize solutions in terms of effectiveness. These approaches to problem solving require epidemiology.

Over the past several years, the Rockefeller Foundation has funded demonstration projects in Zimbabwe and Uganda which apply the lessons learned from the FETP experience to a broader kind of public health training. These lessons include selection of young or mid-career candidates who are already serving in the public health service and providing a rigorous on-the-job training experience designed to attain academic and field competencies which relies on problem-based learning. The program in Zimbabwe which is up and going is two years in duration and is jointly taught by public health officers, and faculty from the University of Zimbabwe who are supplemented with expatriate lecturers from time to time. A full-time officer from the Centers for Disease Control is stationed in Zimbabwe to oversee the field training component. The early experience with this program is that it provides useful and reality-based training which nonetheless has a good academic standing. Students have uniformly expressed a favorable opinion. The dividend of the program is the enhanced field and problem-solving competence of the faculty from both the ministry of health and the university. By working in the field and on real problems, the ivory tower attribute of public health training has been replaced by a curriculum that matches the students' exact needs.

NATIONAL EPIDEMIOLOGY BOARDS

One of the biggest challenges to developing countries is to mobilize all available human resources to pursue societally valuable goals. In most developing countries there is a sharp division between the goals and activities in the public health sector and those of medical practitioners and educators. The latter hold responsible positions in tertiary health care institutions; they are patient oriented, hospital and city oriented, rather than population or nation oriented. There is little incentive for them to adopt any other behavior. Yet it is these capable and prestigious groups which generate new knowledge through health research, educate future generations of health professionals and create the standards which serve as models for professional behavior.

When governments in developing countries opt to create a biomedical research program the model often selected is the United States' National Institutes of Health (NIH) which funds research through investigator-initiated grants. This may be an unfortunate decision. For many developing countries there is an urgent need to identify important disease burdens, to relieve those burdens using preventive or curative health interventions and to assess their effectiveness. Each of these responsibilities, but particularly the first and third, require epidemiological studies. Classical investigator-initiated research is not often epidemiological and less often is it directed to practical health programs. What is needed is another strategy.

Developing countries encounter a situation not unlike that which confronted industrialized societies in the last century or the first half of this one. At that time infant mortality rates, life expectancies and the burden of infectious disease in northern countries were similar to health indices in the poorest countries today. Under these circumstances medical research, as it began to come into existence, was very practical. Once organisms were identified and the mode of transmission established, vaccines were developed or sanitary measures devised and adopted. Just before the outbreak of World War II, the United States created a unique institution designed specially to cope with the burden that infectious and tropical diseases were expected to exact on American military personnel during the war. In all previous wars in history, deaths due to infectious diseases greatly exceeded those due to battle injuries. Curative and preventive measures against most severe infectious diseases were not generally available in 1940; indeed, causative agents were not known for many of these diseases. To meet this huge research challenge the military had virtually no human resources. The assistance of the civilian health research sector was essential.

To meet the needs of an applied preventive medicine program, the Armed Forces Epidemiology Board was created. Its central feature were: (1) the use of an advisory panel of distinguished civilian scientists who, together with representatives of the military services, identified priority health problems, (2) the formation of specialized Commissions which kept the AFEB current on emerging health problems, (3) the provision of funds to the Commissions and Board to organize and administer a contract research program and (4) sponsorship of regular meetings between military and civilian health workers.

During its existence, the AFEB greatly strengthened infectious and tropical disease research in the United States, particularly in the medical schools. The contract research system served to focus health research on preventive measures. The AFEB was extremely effective; curative and prophylactic antibiotics were developed, their disease range discovered and their effectiveness determined, DDT was found to prevent typhus and malaria; chloroquine could be used to prevent or treat malaria; vaccines against influenza and hepatitis were developed; preventive regimens were developed which sharply reduced the incidence of meningococcal disease and acute rheumatic fever. The net effect was to make recruit training camps relatively safe and bring down infectious disease deaths in military personnel to about the same level as battle casualties. By the Korean War, deaths due to infection fell below those due to battle, where they have since stayed.

Over the past 10 years, three developing countries have experimented with establishing National Epidemiology Boards (NEBs). They all have as a central feature the use of contract research which funds non-health ministry biomedical researchers to take on public health problems. NEBs are in Thailand, Mexico and Cameroon.

Each of these countries is in a different stage of evolution in its public health program. Mexico is a relatively affluent developing country with strong public health leadership, a commitment to apply epidemiological research to health policymaking and a cadre of well-trained and gifted researchers. In Mexico, a goal of the Advisory Board on Epidemiology has been to build epidemiological research capacity in the various states outside of Mexico City.

Thailand, which is approaching middle income status, has underinvested in epidemiological research. The National Epidemiology Board of Thailand (NEBT) has worked creatively through a combination of consensus conferences and has used contract research to identify and study important new health problems, to conduct pioneering national health surveys, to define the burden of illness and to frame specific as well as general solutions to the country's ills. The NEBT has convened committees which have reorganized the health ministry and created a Health Systems Research Institute. It has developed a strong advocacy program and sought to educate Thai citizens on personal health measures as well as on their role in bringing about change through the political process. The unusually gifted young men and women who staff the NEBT have used epidemiology as a springboard for health reform.

Cameroon is the least developed country of the three. Its health research resources are very limited. The National Epidemiology Board of Cameroon (NEBC) has established Commissions on communicable diseases, non-communicable diseases, environmental health and health systems research. Their chief task is to identify the burden of illness in these fields, design and test preventive strategies and to assess the effectiveness of components of the national health system. Each of the research projects awarded by the Board provides opportunities for academic researchers to work on the applied aspects of important health problems while improving and exercising their research skills.

The programs described in this paper are among the few contemporary efforts to redirect at least some resources from curative interventions into preventive services. A critical requirement is people who are capable of problem recognition, problem solving and management. Epidemiology is central to attaining these self-sufficiency skills.

Do we have any choice except to help people help themselves? Compassion dollars should and must be allocated to this valid and worthy goal.

REFERENCES AND BIBLIOGRAPHY

1. Music, S. I., & Schultz, M. G. Field Epidemiology Training Programs. *JAMA 263:* 3309–3311, 1990.
2. Halstead, S. B., Tugwell, P., & Bennett, K. The International Clinical Epidemiology Network (INCLEN); A progress report. *J. Clin. Epidemiol. 44:* 579–589, 1991.
3. Woodward, T. E., *The Armed Forces Epidemiology Board, its first 50 years.* Office of the Surgeon General, Department of the Army, Falls Church, Virginia. 1990.
4. Commission on Health Research for Development. *Health Research: Essential Link to Equity in Development.* Oxford University Press, New York, 1990.
5. Task Force on Health Research for Development. *Essential National Health Research: A Strategy for Action in Health and Human Development.* Geneva, 1991.

37

From Environmental Health to Health and the Environment: Research That Focuses on People

Gilles Forget

INTRODUCTION

The environment in which people live is acknowledged as a major determinant of their health.[1] For many people *Environmental Health* is still identified with issues relating to clean drinking water and adequate sanitation (both the disposal of human feces and solid wastes). In order to remedy the existing health hazards in relation to water and sanitation, a number of multilateral agencies participated in the *International Drinking Water Supply and Sanitation Decade* from 1981 to 1990.[2] The activities undertaken during the decade generated valuable information but met with mitigated success as they did not achieve their stated goal of providing the 100 percent water and sanitation coverage to urban and rural populations.[3]

However, it is increasingly recognized that there are many other determinants of ill health in the home/living environment which cannot be attributed directly to unsafe drinking water or inadequate sanitation. Although the latter are still pressing issues, other environmental hazards, however, such as indoor air pollution, atmospheric pollution, inadequate housing, vector-borne diseases, and communicable diseases, are attracting attention as environmental factors of concern.[1]

In 1990, according to World Bank data,[1] Disability-Adjusted Life Years (DALYs) loss caused by communicable diseases in the South still represented on average 48.1 percent of the total DALYs lost for the region, compared to an average 9.7 percent for countries in the North. Diseases which can be directly ascribed to environmental determinants such as diarrhea and respiratory infections caused 7.8 percent and 9.5 percent of the DALYs lost in the South, respectively, compared to 0.3 percent and 2.6 percent in the North. In Africa, malaria—a disease linked to the presence of infective mosquitoes in the environment of most of the continent—still results in 10.8 percent of the total DALYs lost for that demographic region.

The United Nations Conference on the Environment and Development (UNCED) confirmed many problems which were seldom recognized in the *Environmental Health* lexicon. Among those were the interrelationship of health and development, of poverty and environmental degradation. *Agenda 21*[4]—the blueprint for action derived from this *Earth Summit*—also highlighted the need for community-health education, and that of confronting the management of communicable diseases for which environmental control strategies are fundamental.

Agenda 21 recognizes the broader precepts of human health in relation to the environment. It outlines five major areas of action:

1. Meeting Primary Health Care Needs;
2. Control of Communicable Diseases;
3. Protecting Vulnerable Groups;
4. Meeting the Urban Health Challenge; and
5. Reducing Health Risks from Environmental Pollution and Hazards.

Thus, it confirms the need to promote and protect health by the provision of primary health care, and it identifies the need to protect and educate vulnerable groups—infants, youth, women and indigenous people—as a necessity if the goals of health and sustainable development are to be met.

Public policy reports earlier in this decade were harbingers of such a concern for a focus on people through participation and education.[5,6] There was an understanding that greater participation by those who stood to benefit from interventions was a key to successful development.[7] The principle of investing in people is a sound one, and very relevant to issues of a healthy environment. The term *Health and the Environment* will be used here to encompass issues of human health in the context of a more participatory, people-centered approach as opposed to the technology orientation often identified in the past, perhaps unjustly, with the term *Environmental Health*. These concerns were articulated in 1991 at the Sundsvall Conference on Health Promotion,[8] where the concept of supportive environments for health was articulated by delegates from 81 countries. The conclusions of the conference were that the social, economic and political dimensions of environmental health were inextricably linked.

Fundamental points in the promotion of Health and the Environment will be discussed here:

- the importance of research as a tool for the generation of new knowledge leading to community empowerment;
- the significance of community participation in all aspects of project development, implementation and evaluation, and a proposed model of action which could facilitate this process;
- the suggestion of a new paradigm of "research at the interface" as a means of promoting interdisciplinary research in *Health and the Environment;* and
- the description of an iterative research strategy for improving community health by *empowerment through knowledge.*

THE RESEARCH APPROACH

Championed by development agencies like Canada's International Development Research Centre (IDRC) and the Swedish Agency for Research Cooperation with Developing Countries (SAREC), research has slowly gained respectability on the international scene as a vital element of the development equation. In 1987, the Commission on Health Research for Development was created with a mandate to assess the state of research in health in developing countries. The group underlined the importance of health research, while recognizing that many developing countries did not utilize research efficiently to inform policy. Furthermore, the Commission recommended that countries adopt an *Essential National Health Research* strategy allowing researchers, policy makers and communities to jointly establish national priority research needs.[9] This recommendation was ratified by the 14th World Health Assembly,[10] which invited member states to define national health research policies and to institute strategies for their implementation. The World Health Assembly further recommended that bilateral and multilateral development agencies increase their support to Essential National Health Research.

By allowing people to generate knowledge pertinent to their own situation, research promotes appropriate programs leading to healthy and environmentally friendly development. Research is a powerful tool, because:

- it allows communities to identify health hazards arising from the environment, and
- it allows them to devise sustainable solutions to mitigate the effects of these health hazards.

Through support for *research,* international agencies can assist developing countries in creating their own long-term solutions to pressing development problems. In its brief to the fourth preparatory conference to the *UNCED,* IDRC stated:[11]

> Research can be a powerful tool in assisting the world's poorest peoples to develop solutions for coping with environmental health risks. It is of prime importance to focus on both the physical dimensions of environment and on the human dimensions of development. Health, population, poverty and environmental degradation are highly interdependent and tightly linked.

The *International Development Research Centre* (IDRC) is a research organization, focusing on issues of international development and whose stated mission is *Empowerment through Knowledge*. Its approach is thus centered on people and on their participation in their own development. The Centre additionally believes that the promotion of development in the South must be predicated on principles of equity and sustainability. Following the Earth Summit in 1992, IDRC was chosen by the Government of Canada to be one of the key implementing agencies for *Agenda 21*. The announcement offered IDRC a challenge compatible with its mandate in the areas of research and capacity building for sustainable and equitable development. The fundamental principles contained in *Agenda 21* blend well with the aims and philosophy of IDRC. One area of particular emphasis identified by the Centre in this follow-up is *Health and the Environment*.

Research projects which aim at investigating a particular environmental determinant of human health must consider the problem in its totality. The environmental determinants of health exert effects which can be modulated by many factors. The sociocultural, economic and behavioral characteristics of a given community are some of the most critical modulators of the environmental health risks experienced by that community.

Figure 37.1 illustrates some of the major issues which need to be considered in planning a study which aims at the remediation of an environmental health risk. A community identifies a particular health issue of concern. Trained health specialists can identify the condition which has a known environmental etiology. The appropriate specialists (toxicologists, entomologists, ecologists, nutritionists, microbiologists, etc.) carry out a study of the environmental hazard. At that point, the scientists will often take the lead, although as indicated in the figure, the community can often contribute to the understanding of the risk, for instance through traditional knowledge.

The environmental health risk can be modulated by human activity. The nature of this activity is strongly influenced by human behavior sets of the community, which are in turn derived from the inherent sociocultural and socioeconomic context of the group. Research must also be conducted into how human activity either exacerbates or reduces the environmental risk; however, modifying behavior which causes a specific

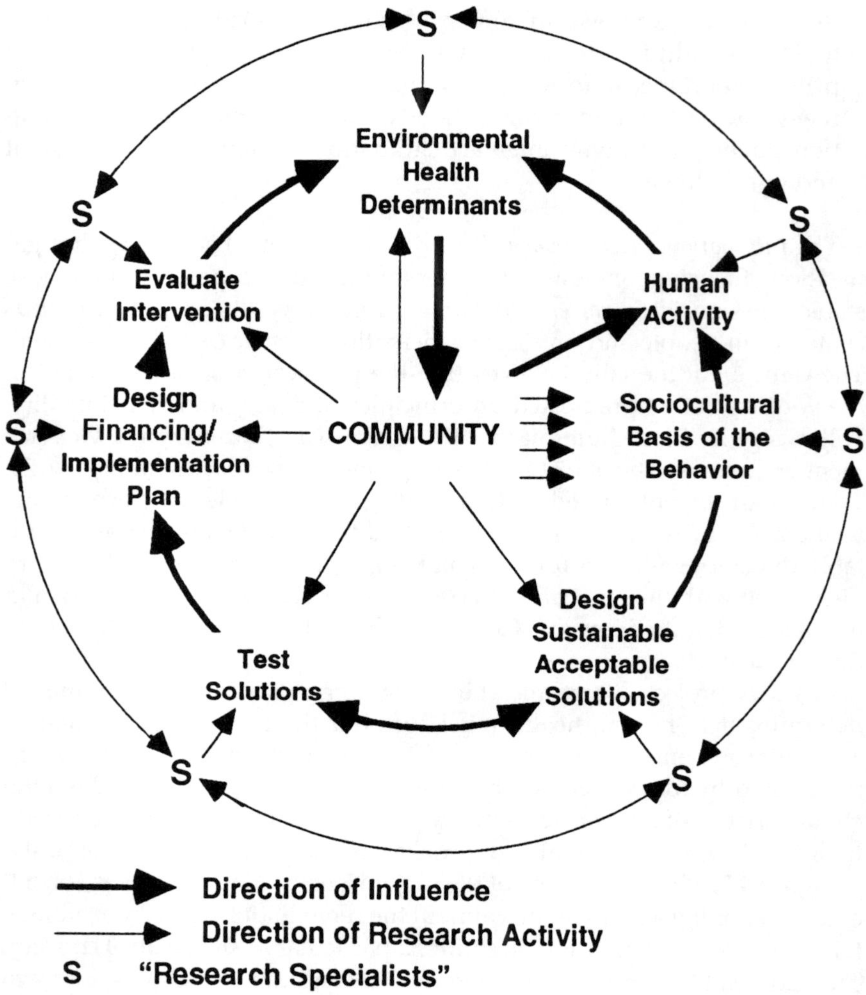

FIGURE 37.1 Holistic research strategy for health and the environment. This model describes the distribution of research effort responsibilities between the community and the scientific establishment ("Specialists"—outer gray circle). The research commitment of the community and of the scientific establishment can be seen to change with a given domain (as indicated by the relative sizes of the grey arrows): For example, the study of the environmental health determinant will likely fall mostly (but not all) to the scientists, while the design or testing of the solutions may be shared equally, and the evaluation of the intervention package will often rest more heavily on the community.

aggravation of the health risk can only be achieved after the sociocultural or socioeconomic bases of the behavior are clarified. This is the work of other specialists (health anthropologists, sociologists, behavioral scientists, economists) and the work can usually be enhanced by participatory research methods involving the community.

Once these key environmental and human parameters have been elucidated, elements of solution to the original health problem can be formulated and elaborated. At this point, the extent of the community participation in the overall research effort often matches that of the science establishment. This maximizes the acceptability of a solution by the people. Original solution-design is followed by an initial evaluation of its efficacy. Again, the participation of the community in the evaluative process is imperative.

No solution is effective if it cannot be sustained. Operational research must be conducted to investigate financing and maintenance options which are available to the community in order to guarantee that the intervention becomes part of the societal response to the environmental health risk.

Once the solution has been integrated into the community response, it is important to evaluate it in that context, including all aspects of the intervention (sustainability, health protection, acceptability and affordability). Such a strategy complies with the admonition of *Agenda 21* to use intersectoral cooperation and coordination in protecting and promoting human health in relation to environmental hazards.[4] In order to carry out such holistic research efforts, however, interdisciplinary teams of research specialists *and* community participants are essential. Constant sharing and evaluation of information among the different specialists as well as community participants are an indispensable ingredient of a successful *Health and the Environment* research project.

PROMOTING INTERDISCIPLINARY HEALTH AND THE ENVIRONMENT RESEARCH

How can true interdisciplinarity be promoted? As noted previously, the consequences of environmental health determinants can be influenced by human activity, which in turn is more or less regulated by sociocultural, and socioeconomic factors. All three facets of the equation must be studied in order to formulate viable interventions. Some of the most promising areas of *Health and the Environment* research can in fact be found at the interface of the three domains: Production activities, environmental determinants of health and sociobehavioral/sociocultural/socioeconomic determinants of health (Figure 37.2). This paradigm is useful, because it helps us to visualize the multiple interactions and their consequences.

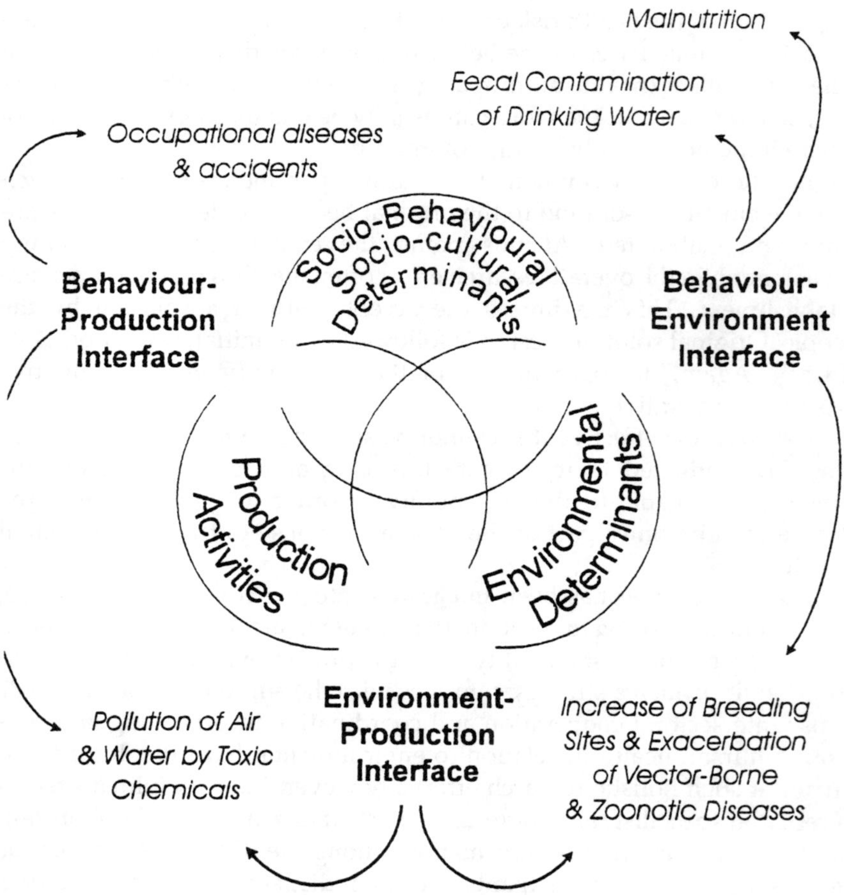

FIGURE 37.2 How three important groups of determinants interact to modulate health in relation to the environment. Environmental health risks (Environmental Determinants universe), human behavior (Sociobehavioral, Sociocultural Determinants universe) and risks arising from productive (or development) activities (Production Activities universe) are three key sets of forces which act on health in a synergistic fashion. It is at the interface between these sets of determinants that some of the most useful research can be carried out, often yielding sustainable societal responses leading to improved health and well-being. For example, existing environmental threats (such as the vector-borne yellow fever) are often exacerbated by human behavior (littering with empty containers, multiplying breeding sites for the vector), and understanding the determinants of this behavior may provide long-term solutions to the problem. Occupational accidents are often the results of faulty equipment which in turn ensues from lack of maintenance (human practices) or unavailability of parts (economic issue). Understanding the interactions occurring at the interfaces between these domains is likely to lead to some of the most exciting solution opportunities in Health in the Environment.

The Behavior–Environment Interface

Where the environmental determinants set overlaps with the behavioral determinants set, research aimed at understanding how people either exacerbate or minimize environmental health risks can be profitably studied to foster sustainable interventions.

For example, when community practices favor indiscriminate disposal of solid wastes, how does the behavior influence the environmental density of container-breeders like the *Aedes sp* mosquitoes which transmit yellow fever?[12,13] What is the impact of this rise on the actual number of cases of yellow fever? (People's behaviors and practices could also reduce the actual rate of transmission.) Understanding why people do what they do is the first step in devising a solution to the environmental health risks which affect them. Thus research in this case should concentrate on behavioral determinants, as well as on operational studies of alternative solid waste management which would meet with societal expectations.

How do human behavior and practices influence drinking-water contamination? Is water contaminated at the source through indiscriminate human defecation practices (behavioral determinant) or by animal feces (environmental determinant)? Is drinking water—which was clean originally—contaminated after collection either because of the contamination of the container used for transport or by the contamination of the storage containers in the home (sociocultural, sociobehavioral determinants)? Such possibilities are often well-known facts, but rarely do research teams endeavor to integrate all aspects of the cycle into comprehensive research projects. It would be, by the same token, an error to overlook research into the actual environmental hazard. Only a thorough perception of the etiology of the health risks will allow a precise understanding of the global interaction between the environment, people and health, and permit the design of an effective and sustainable intervention.

Another good example of holistic research opportunities which are fostered by examining the *Behavior—Environment* interface is issues related to malnutrition. Are the children of a particular community suffering from a deficiency in iodine because the substance is absent from the locally grown food (environmental determinant), or because the traditional diet contains goitrogenic substances (environmental and/or cultural determinants)?[14] Is iodized salt available but not used because people do not associate the problem with a deficiency in iodine which could easily be resolved by the consumption of this enriched salt (behavioral determinant—education) or because they can only afford the cheaper, locally produced alternative (behavioral determinant—economic)? In such a study, nutritionists, food biochemists, health-anthropologists, agricultural scientists and economists must all participate with community members to bring about an understanding of the health determinant and to find viable solutions. Such a project may need to include feasibility studies of building and operating salt iodization factories, organizing the distribution infrastructure, and examining the cost of such a national intervention. What about the needs for national policies which would ensure the sustainability of this intervention?

There are some very complex issues at this interface which are not always evident. If people use CFCs to cool their home or preserve their food, and these compounds make their way to the upper atmosphere where they destroy the ozone layer, how does this impact on seemingly unrelated health issues like vaccination? The thinning of the ozone layer increases the intensity of UV irradiation at the planet's surface. There are indications that UV rays could reduce the activity of the immune system in mammals.[15,16] What will be the overall effect of their increased intensity on the success of Extended Programmes of Immunization (EPI)? What will be the compounded effect on UV-induced skin cancer?

The Environment–Production Interface

Production activities are defined here as all the human activities which lead to community development and livelihood, be they at the cottage industry, sustenance farming or agro-industrial, industrial, mining, and construction industry levels.

Human productive activities can also exacerbate existing environmental health risks.[17,18] The implementation of new irrigation systems may intensify the risk for contacting schistosomiasis if the new conditions are favorable to the snail host (environmental determinant). This same irrigation scheme may influence the risk of contracting malaria because of increased breeding sites for the anopheline mosquitoes (environmental determinant). The increase of sandy areas brought about by road construction and mining activities increases the likelihood of contracting leishmaniasis (environmental determinant). Colonization and migrations influence the appearance of diseases in regions where they were previously unknown. Although much is already known about the transmission of these diseases, the biology of the vector and clinical treatment, a great deal of information is often missing on the behavior of the disease transmission systems in the context of these new environmental conditions. Thus, research can play an invaluable role in the development of sound productive activity practices or remedial actions to forecast and mitigate the new health threats that they bring about. How may agricultural practices affect health?[19] Concern is now being raised in the South about the contamination of the underground water table by agrochemicals.[20]

Similarly, large-scale animal husbandry (intensive pig and poultry farming) results in substantial fecal contamination of the surface waters in certain areas.

How does increased production of goods impact on the quality of the environment, and thus on human health? This is an area which more people easily identify with environmental health research: the contamination of the air and water by toxic substances. Much research is needed in this context on remedial measures to help communities cope with new environmental health threats. Most agree that development is a desirable aim, but the delegates from the South at the UNCED emphasized how they would find it (rightly so) untenable to simply curtail their development programs in order to protect the global environment. Thus the development and transfer of appropriate technologies must be carried out in the context of environmental safety and human well-being. To reach this aim, it will be necessary to promote research which will investigate all acceptable remedial programs leading to environmentally friendly development.

The Behavior–Production Interface

Air pollution may be caused by industrial activity, but it is also generated by motor vehicle emission, an origin more directly related to human practices than to actual production activities. Although research in this area can be profitably undertaken to look at some of the biomedical effects of given pollutants or their mixtures (environmental determinants), behavioral and socioeconomic studies to understand the barriers to reducing vehicular traffic may be of even more pressing relevance (sociobehavioral determinants). Research on acceptable alternatives to the use of private vehicles would be of major pertinence.

Most of our waking time is spent at work. However, the working environment often holds health hazards not normally found in the home (toxic chemicals, dangerous procedures, etc). In developing countries, this is also true, but can in certain cases be magnified by the fact that the industrial processes may be farther outside of the normal living experience of the workers who may be less prepared socioculturally or intellectually for them. Furthermore, in the South, cottage industries bring the working environment to the home, eliciting greater risks for children and women, even if they do not participate in the actual production.

While it is true that the hazards particular to the working environment are real, people's working habits and practices can greatly amplify its actual health impact. Many accidents at work are more related to dangerous work practices and faulty or ill-maintained equipment. In agricultural production, for instance, mechanization and agrochemicals can be the source of serious injuries or diseases. In developing countries, most externally funded research projects in occupational health focus on chemical hazards.[21] The following subjects which are amenable to research, are often not specifically understood to be the purview of occupational health specialists. What is the actual impact of work practices and cultural beliefs related to them on the actual intoxication incidents? What is the impact of equipment maintenance on occupational accidents? How are the maintenance schedules affected by the unavailability of parts which need to be ordered overseas? What alternatives exist? What is the potential impact of healthier labor laws and regulations?

These are only examples of the advantages of using the interface approach suggested here to foster true interdisciplinary research. Moreover, this approach if linked to community participation may in many instances lead to sustainable, long-term solutions to environmental health threats. Understanding all the parameters of the risk arising from the environment allows the communities to choose a societal response, to try it out, and to adopt it if successful and appropriate to their sociocultural and socioeconomic circumstances. Truly innovative research will often arise from such "interface" research, as long as the appropriate mix of specialists is brought in from the start to ensure that the investigation protocol meets the scientific prerequisites of the various fields which must be involved.

AN ITERATIVE RESEARCH STRATEGY FOR IMPROVING HEALTH BY EMPOWERMENT THROUGH KNOWLEDGE

Health and the Environment research should lead to sustainable and practical solutions (societal responses) to threats to health arising from the environment. One global strategy which could facilitate the process is an iterative research strategy for improving health by empowering communities through the generation of relevant knowledge on these threats, their etiology and exacerbating factors.

In order to achieve the objectives of this strategy, four complementary tactical approaches should be considered:

- Promoting the discovery, creation, exchange and use of health knowledge;
- Developing innovative and appropriate tools and methods for improving health;
- Mobilizing and improving management of resources for health, and
- Strengthening capacity for multidisciplinary and participatory research for health.

This strategy identifies two major axes of health and development which allow interdisciplinary research to lead to such societal responses (Figure 37.3). The articulation of these two axes—*understanding the determinants of health and human development* and *societal response to health and human development needs*—is predicated on the empowerment of communities through knowledge.

New knowledge generation leading to the understanding of the determinants of health and human development will necessitate the study of environmental factors, of sociobehavioral factors and of existing health services, for instance. In agreement with the interface model of *Health and the Environment* research, this strategy promotes interdisciplinary research. On the other hand, the optimization of interventions for change (the societal response) will need to focus on "downstream" issues such as capacity building, policy development and resource management. This side of the equation is regrettably often lacking in practice from the protocol of research projects in *Health and the Environment* in developing countries.

The generation of new knowledge about the disease risks and determinants of human health is a necessary prerequisite to identifying opportunities for change. This knowledge must include all the factors which may be associated as causative factors of ill health in relation to the environment. Holistic studies should also focus on the existing health systems in the community participating in the research, and evaluate their effectiveness, affordability and sustainability in the prevailing context, as well as their relevance to the environmental health risk under scrutiny.

The principle behind this strategy is to optimize the societal response to a given set of environmental health risks through the identification of intervention opportunities (new knowledge) arising from research aimed at understanding the determinants of health. Issues such as capacity building, resource management and healthy policy development are crucial determinants of success in the elaboration of optimal societal responses. This strategy has the potential to ensure that the people most at risk of ill-health will be given the tools to improve and sustain their own health.

CONCLUSION

In this brief overview of research strategies for *Health and the Environment*, a number of issues were raised: the value of research for development, the importance of community participation, the importance of setting health research priorities, the need for the interdisciplinary nature of the re-

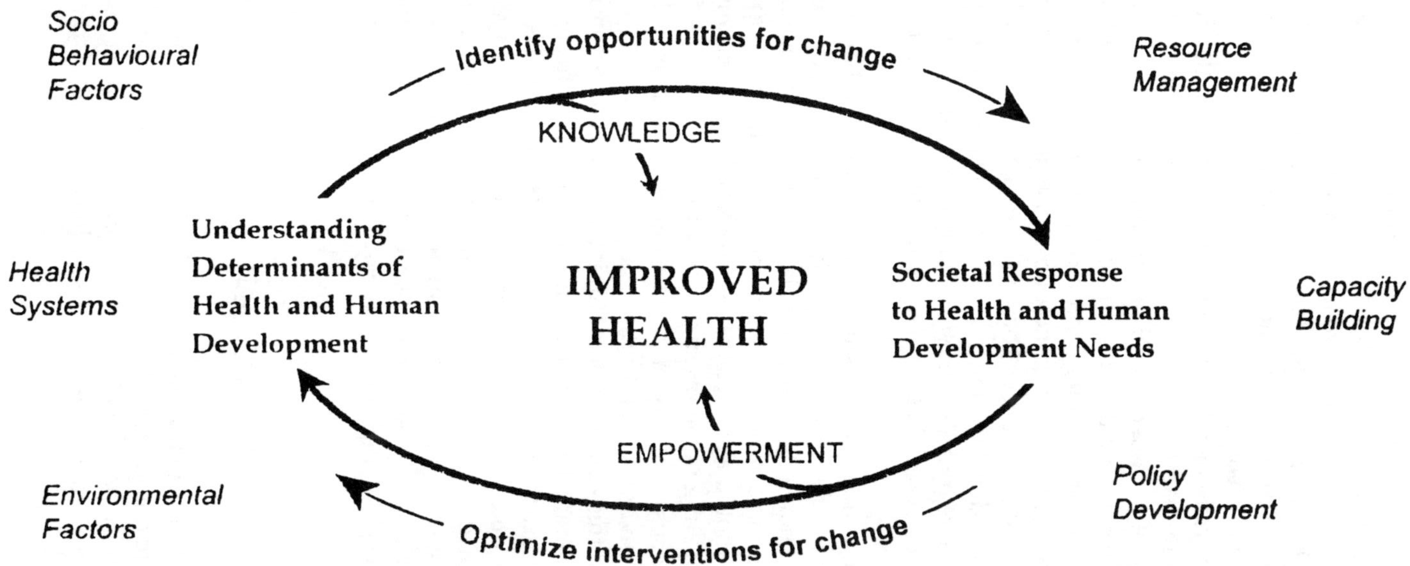

FIGURE 37.3 Iterative research strategy leading to improved health by the empowerment of communities through knowledge. The strategy proposes an iterative process predicated on a two-pronged approach: (1) identifying opportunities for change through research leading to an understanding of the determinants of health (sociocultural/behavioral factors, environmental factors and the existing systems of health care) promoting *knowledge*; (2) optimizing interventions for change through research on existing societal responses to the health risks, as well as the design and evaluation of solutions. Ideally, the latter research effort would emanate from the knowledge obtained in the former, leading to *community empowerment*, the only true measure of sustainability and equity.

search, the necessity for the kind of practical research which can lead to acceptable, affordable and sustainable solutions.

Research can be a very powerful tool in the hands of communities to empower them to effect their own development. When the generation of new knowledge for change is carried out in close collaboration with the community, the potential for empowerment and sustainability is enhanced.

The ENHR process[9] is rapidly making headway in the South. In 1992, over 32 countries were already considering, planning or implementing the strategy.[22] The strong signal that countries in the South are sending to the North is that they believe research in health is an important tool; more, that it is a prerequisite to the amelioration of public health. More to the point, they are manifesting in no ambiguous way that they should control the research agenda. *Agenda 21* also encourages research for development, with an emphasis on the development of sustainable, environmentally friendly solutions.

Environmental health threats are mostly grounded in a complex set of environmental, behavioral and economic realities. Sustainable solutions cannot be developed without a clear understanding of all these factors. Holistic, participatory health research offers the means to this end, because it promotes an approach which links the community to the search for knowledge and its evaluation for fitness in the prevailing circumstances. Furthermore, it ensures that all relevant science specialists will contribute their particular brand of scientific expertise in collegiality, thus ensuring the optimal generation of insight and innovation.

Innovative approaches to health research may ultimately hold the key to understanding both old and new environmental threats to health. Many communities, naive to conventional Western thought-patterns, often hold to a paradigm of disease causation which is quite different from the conventional wisdom of Western medicine. Traditional beliefs until recently lessened the impact of environmental hazards on health could hold the key to more appropriate, sustainable societal responses leading to improved community health. Uncovering this knowledge cannot be achieved in the absence of an intimate community participation, nor of the right mix of scientists in the research team from the onset (including in the planning stage). It cannot be sufficiently emphasized that empowering communities to design and implement their own effective response to health and development needs is the surest way to ensure viable solutions to environmental health risks.

Thus one of the surest ways to foster this new approach to *Health and the Environment* research is to support capacity-building for interdisciplinary research and to emphasize the need for behavioral and social scientific inquiry in the context of a participatory approach to community empowerment through knowledge.

REFERENCES

1. World Bank (1993). *World Development Report 1993: Investing in Health, World Development Indicators.* Oxford University Press, p. 90.
2. United Nations (1983). *Yearbook of the United Nations 1980.* Volume 34. New York: United Nations.
3. The World Bank (1980). *Water supply and waste disposal: Poverty and basic needs series* (World Bank, Washington).
4. United Nations (1993). *Earth Summit Agenda 21: The United Nations Programme of Action from Rio.* Chapter 6, pp. 42–51.
5. Organization for Economic Cooperation and Development (OECD) (1990). *Towards a green development strategy. In:* 1990 Report on Efforts and Policies of the Members of the Development Assistance Committee, OECD, Paris, pp. 29–43.
6. World Bank (1990). *World Bank Development Report, 1990.* Oxford University Press, New York.
7. United Nations Development Programme (UNDP) (1990). *Human Development Report, 1990.* Oxford University Press, New York, NY, p. 189.
8. (1991) *Supportive Environments for Health: The Sundsvall Statement.* Health Promotion International *6:* 297–300.
9. (La) Commission sur la recherche en santé au service du développement (1991). *La recherche en santé: Elément essentiel d'un développement équitable,* Centre de recherches pour le développement international, Ottawa, Ontario. p. 121.
10. Fourteenth plenary session of the World Health Assembly, Resolution 43.19, May 17, 1990.
11. Forget, G. (1992). *Health and the Environment—A People-Centred Research Strategy.* Searching series #3. IDRC, Ottawa, p. 36.
12. Bang, Y. H., Brown, D. N., & Onwubiko, A. O. (1981). Prevalence of larvae of potential yellow fever vectors in domestic water containers in south-east Nigeria. *Bull. World Health Organ. 59:* 107–114.
13. Slosek, J. (1986). Aedes aegypti mosquitoes in the Americas: a review of their interactions with the human population. *Soc. Sci. Med. 23:* 249–257.
14. Lamberg, B. A. (1991). Endemic goitre—iodine deficiency disorders. *Ann. Med. 23:* 367–372.
15. Rivas, J. M., & Ullrich, S. E. (1992). Systemic suppression of delayed-type hypersensitivity by supernatants from UV-irradiated keratinocytes: An essential role for keratinocyte-derived IL-10. *J. Immunol. 149:* 3865–3871.
16. Harriott-Smith, T. G., & Halliday, W. J. (1986). Circulating suppressor factors in mice subjected to UV irradiation and contact sensitization. *Immunology 57:* 207–211.
17. Coosemans, M., & Mouchet, J. (1990). Consequences of rural development of vectors and their control. *Annales de la Société Belge de Médecine Tropicale, 70:* 5–23.
18. Walsh, J. F., Molineux, D. H., & Birley, M. H. (1993). Deforestation: effects on vector-borne disease. *Parasitology (England) 106 supp:* S55–S75.

19. Forget, G. (1991). Pesticides and the Third-World. *J. Toxicol. Environ. Health 32 (1):* 11–31.
20. Jamall, I. S., & Davis, B. (1991). Chemicals and environmentally caused diseases in developing countries. *Infect. Dis. Clin. North Am. 5:* 365–375.
21. Levy, B., Kjellström, T., Forget, G., Jones, M. R. D., & Pollier L. (1992). Ongoing Research in Occupational Health and Environmental Epidemiology in Developing Countries. *Arch. Environ. Health 47:* 231–235.
22. Task Force on Health Research For Development (1992). Essential National Health Research (ENHR) Country Status Report—(31 December 1992). In: *Plan of Work and Budget for the Council on Health Research for Development*, pp 1–7.

38

Women, Environments, and Health: Overview and Strategic Directions for Research and Action

Rebecca Peterson

The task of looking at gender in relationship to environmental health issues is a daunting one, because of the need to look at the overlap of many disciplines, and to have a clear understanding of both gender, and environmental health. In undertaking this task, I work out of assumptions that I have developed while teaching for 21 years in a faculty of environmental studies where we have been asking questions about environments, about research process in relationship to policy, and about gender. I bring the following assumptions to this task. There are four central issues that we need to address. One issue is the need for innovation in paradigms to incorporate broader concepts of "environment" into health research questions. The second issue is the need for incorporation of environmental approaches into women's health research priorities. The third issue is related to a need for new approaches to defining research agendas which interrelate them with grassroots action agendas of women. A fourth and related issue is the need for collaborative work across disciplines by researchers to define research agendas in participatory processes so that we can become a learning system of collected individuals and groups, rather than isolated researchers in isolated institutions. All of these issues relate to the underlying assumption that we are in a state of rapid change in environmental systems, that gender issues are central to our understanding of environmental health problems, and that in order to move rapidly into effective modes of research and action in this area we need to create new processes and opportunities for cross fertilization of ideas and people in order to meet the challenges to women's health on a global level.

I am advocating that we should look at the overlap of three fields of research and policy intervention: (1) women and environments, (2) women and health, and (3) health and environments, and begin to cross boundaries in our conceptual frameworks and action strategies. This requires that we look at our assumptions about research and action in complex systems, so this chapter will address these issues as well. In recent years, there has been increasing focus upon the relationship of women to their environments in the (1) women and development literature and in (2) North America and Europe. These burgeoning bodies of literature have not been synthesized in any systematic way; however, they have been developing in tandem, and some people have been working across the boundaries. Emerging books in the field have identified a number of issues that must be addressed in order to begin to look at women from an environmental perspective. The concerns that are beginning to emerge include issues such as women's roles in contributing to and alleviating problems of environmental degradation, both in the developed world and the developing countries.

At the same time, a political process has been unfolding, initiated by women, and targeted toward international organizations which make decisions about global environmental issues. Women have become more powerful in stating their concerns in these global forums, and they have begun to stake a claim to their right to be heard in the important decisions about the global environmental future.

This chapter will address the concern for the convergence of issues of women and environments and health at a global level. Concerns with women's health issues have begun to be expressed in global terms. The authors taking a global perspective on women's health issues have seldom addressed them in conjunction with analysis of women's environments. It is the contention of this author that we should begin to systematically work across the boundaries in the political processes, and the research processes, to begin to identify research and action priorities that adequately conceptualize women's health issues that are directly related to our analysis of women's environments. In order to undertake such a massive task, it is the author's view that we must utilize new processes, based on new paradigms that are only now beginning to emerge, and that participation should be central to this task, at all levels of the enterprise. The World Health Organization has addressed questions of health and environment, and there are individuals and groups there who are beginning to articulate approaches which go beyond the traditional health research paradigms of prediction and control of variables. But again, they have not yet set out a systematic analysis of the integration of this work with the viewpoint that women's experience of environments is fundamentally different from that of men in most cases, and that we should have a different conceptual framework for addressing these issues. Because this task questions the very core assumption of some health researchers, i.e., that we can identify single variables that will predict health status, it is seen as lacking in direction or focus by some groups.

WOMEN AND ENVIRONMENTS: THE EMERGING ISSUES AS THEY COME FROM NORTH AMERICA AND EUROPE AND THE DEVELOPING COUNTRIES

North American and European Research: Focus on Design and Planning

The literature on women and the environment has expanded rapidly from the early edited volumes (Wekerle, Peterson, Morley, 1980) through the most recent edited volume (Altman & Churchman, 1994). In the North American and European literature on women and environments, the home has been identified as an environment that deserves scholarly and activist attention (Andrew & Milroy, 1988; Peterson, 1987; Weisman, 1992; and Wekerle, Peterson, & Morley, 1980). The increasing sophistication of the analysis in the field has contributed not only to our understanding of women and their environments, but also to the wider field of environment and behavior studies. It is my assumption that this careful attention to gender issues in relationship to the home, neighborhood, and the urban environment (in short, to the context of the everyday lives of women), can make a contribution to the definition of gender issues in environmental health.

Studies of men and women in the home have demonstrated that even when women work outside the home, they carry the primary responsibility for work in the home. Innovations in home design have moved toward incorporating services into homes and neighborhoods that would simplify the lives of working parents, or single parents. Some of the recent literature on innovations in home design focuses upon the design of collaborative communities (Fromm, 1991).

Horelli and Vepsa (1994) have described the innovative approach taken by the project called the New Everyday Life. This group of Scandinavian women from various countries has focused upon the evaluation of built environment initiatives in terms of how they contribute to the ability of women to continue to work outside the home while carrying out domestic life experiences. The purpose of these initiatives is to make more visible the private work of women in the home, to provide intermediate level "neighborhood" environments where collective work and leisure activities can occur, and to in various ways transform both homes and neighborhoods to be more supportive of women's changing roles. These kinds of initiatives may have direct impact on the health of women, both mental and physical, and could be linked to some form of health planning and assessment. It is the effort to include this level of environmental analysis in the discourse about women's environments and their health that I would like to see proceed.

Also of note is the research on health hazards in the home environment which acknowledges the role that the home plays as a workplace in women's lives (Luxton, Rosenberg, & Sedef Arat Koc, 1990). In addition, new research is emerging which examines the impact that home-based employment is having on the lives of men and women, but in this literature there is a particular emphasis upon the role conflicts that are developing for many women who must combine working in the home with childrearing responsibilities on a 24-hour basis. Christensen (1994) points out that increasingly the question may be one of combining employment roles at home with elder care responsibilities. The questions to be addressed here, in my opinion, are ones of whether these home-based employment experiences are contributing to the health and well-being of the women in question, or are instead leading to new environmental health problems for women that are up to now undefined. There are here, as in other areas of inquiry, questions about how innovative design and social solutions might enhance the quality of life for the individuals and groups engaged in these home-based activities.

Issues of urban design have been addressed in this literature as well. Central to these are issues of land use, the relationship of home to work, and transportation between those two points. All these issues are related to questions of income and access to resources such as automobiles or public transit. In addition the location and availability of services for addressing the stresses of the double and triple days that women experience as workers in the home, and workers in paid employment have been addressed in this literature. All these are couched in the language of issues of design and planning, and the need for information about the impacts of these environmental arrangements on women's lives as they are now lived in developed countries in the 1990s. Michelson (1985) has carried out a substantial study of children in the city, which included an analysis of environmental stressors on parents. One finding which has particular relevance to this analysis is that women find transitions between work and home as particularly stressful parts of their environments, especially when they are parents and schedules are tight for picking up children from child care situations. One explanation for this which is supported by the research literature is that women are more likely to be carrying out their travel with fewer resources since they are more likely to take transit rather than have access to an automobile. All these and other issues are addressed in detail in Peterson (1987).

Public spaces have also been the focus of much research in this area. The research agenda has been combined with action approaches to address questions of women's access to and levels of comfort in public spaces. A recent focus of research in this area is the concern that women have for safety in the urban environment (Whitzman & Wekerle, 1992). Here the concern is with changing design of public spaces to reduce the fear of violence that women carry with them in many environments in their lives. Redesign of parks, and parking garages, and assessment of unsafe areas in public transit systems have all been addressed in this research area. This links closely with the emerging concerns in the women and health research area about women's exposure to violent behavior over the life span, and further research and action is needed in this area.

One of the cultural shifts that has occurred in the last 30 years in North America is the move toward increased work outside the home in the area of paid employment for women. The workplace is increasingly a space which has impacts on women's health and well-being.

> Topics that have been of great concern in recent literature include VDT's ergonomics and health; air quality in sealed office environments; and the impact of the open-plan office on workers. As in other areas, researchers have only recently begun to analyze the impact on women as a special user group. Much is yet to be done in this field. Of special concern are (1) the questions of user control over design decisions; (2) the relationship of women users to the management decision-making processes in regard to air quality; (3) the possible biases in perception of women users by the largely male building-management specialists; (4) the differences in physiological response of male and female users to office environments; and (5) the relationship of female job categories that are lower in the status hierarchy to behavior patterns that influence use of office environments, i.e., less freedom to leave the desk, etc. This list could be expanded, but it is illustrative of the types of problems that are in need of further attention. (Peterson, 1987, pp. 210–211)

All of the above research, and other research on women and shelter in North America and Europe have acknowledged the problems that women face in having a lower income than men, and having less access to all types of environmental resources (Wekerle, Peterson, Morley, 1980). A second premise is that women have not been involved in environmental decision making at the levels required for changing some of the problems that have been identified in the literature. A third premise is that women are a diverse group, and that race and class issues and life cycle stages play a role in the impact of environments on women's lives. A fourth premise of this research is that women are particularly time-pressured in their daily life experiences. In this regard, I am in agreement with

Michelson's recent article which states that we should view women and environment issues as issues of everyday life in contextual perspective. The type of concern that he is articulating, is that we should have a deeper understanding of just how the daily lives of women are linked to both opportunities and constraints in the structure of their wider contextual environments. Michelson (1994) argues that we need to pay attention to how the structure of our macro environmental context influences time and space concerns of women, and I would argue indirectly has a potential impact on the health of women.

Women and Environments in Developing Countries: Basic Needs Predominate

Certainly there is much overlap in the issues addressed in the North American and European literature and the issues being addressed in the developing countries' literature. Lack of time and the stresses of multiple roles in women's lives are central assumptions in this research. In addition, income is even a more critical issue in these countries since overall incomes are lower, and access to resources is dwindling as environmental degradation increases with development pressures. Women's access to decision-making roles is a central issue in this research area, and participatory processes are advocated in all areas to redress the power imbalances between men and women that have developed over the centuries, and increased with development processes. Work environments of women are rapidly changing as women move into paid employment, many times in dangerous roles such as prostitution, and low paid industrial jobs where they are exposed to hazards such as violence, AIDS, and long hours, low pay, and other occupational stressors.

One contribution of this research approach, whether it is in North America and Europe, or in developing countries' literature, is the focus upon women's lives as they are lived every day, and the specific impacts of the combination of environments that they experience on their quality of life. Kettel (1993) has completed an impressive review of literature on women, health and environment which primarily focuses upon the biophysical environment in developing countries. She advocates the focus upon women's spheres of activity, i.e., a clear analysis of "understanding where and how women actually live in the biophysical environment, and the implications of their use of certain arenas of the biophysical environment for their health" (Kettel, 1993, p. 12). This is a gender sensitive approach which would allow us to focus upon women's daily activity patterns which have implications for exposure to environmental health hazards, and the approach would allow researchers to explore differences in actual life experience between women.

In contrast to the work in North America and Europe, the work on women and environments in developing countries has focused more often upon the relationship of women to the natural environment. There are clear reasons for this since environmental degradation and access to basic resources play such an important role in the lives of many women living at a subsistence level in these countries. The primary focus of a recent book on women and environment issues in development has been upon the issue of access to basic resources such as water, wood, and the impact that environmental degradation has on the lives of women (Rodda, 1992). These are critical issues for the planet and for the lives of these women. However, increasingly, the lives of women in developing countries are urban lives as well, so the focus of the research will possibly shift in the direction of addressing built environment issues. Kettel (1993) has identified issues of urbanization in her overview paper, as have authors such as Satterthwaite (1993).

Adekanye (see chapter 10) has pointed out that the major environmental issues for women in developing countries include urbanization; water and sanitation problems which require many hours of female labor, and cause many health problems for all family members; and problems with fetching fuel for cooking, heating and lighting. Women are also exposed to the pollution and health hazards associated with burning fuel wood, charcoal, dung or crop residues since they are responsible for tending the cooking fires. Of particular concern to Adekanye are issues related to agriculture since women provide some 60–80 percent of the labor input in agriculture in Africa; but she indicates that they are often left with the marginal and degraded lands after men have followed policies which lead to erosion and over-exploitation of land resources. She recommends policies which include promoting sustainable development through development education that is economically useful and through the provision of appropriate technology for relieving the incredible burdens upon women's time and energy.

WOMEN'S HEALTH RESEARCH: THE LACK OF CONCERN WITH ENVIRONMENTS

Questions of women's health have been systematically addressed in a number of publications. Researchers in women's health have focused upon issues relevant to women's reproductive health, women's occupational health needs, women's needs as consumers of health care, women and addiction, specific mental health issues related to women (Chavkin, 1984; Dhruvarajan, 1990; Frankenhauser, Lundberg & Chesney, 1991; Leppa, 1988, 1989, 1990; and Miles, 1991). In addition, a massive literature is emerging which addresses questions of variables having an impact on women's health specifically focusing upon particular disease processes such as cardiovascular disease, cancer, HIV, chemical dependency, etc. (American Psychological Association, 1994). Noticeably lacking from most of this analysis is any emphasis upon environments as a systematic factor in women's health. Even though epidemiologists have addressed questions of women's incidence of disease across environments, a focus upon the systematic analysis of women's daily environments as predictors or potential indicators of their health status has not been prevalent in the women's health literature.

In a recent book summarizing global research on women's health, Koblinsky, Timyan and Gay (1993) have addressed a broad variety of issues, but environmental health issues are addressed only briefly in a section on environmental degradation and the status of women. In the book on *Women and the Environment* by Rodda (1992) there are references to health issues that affect women, but only in a relatively small section of the book. Shiva (1994) has edited a volume which addresses issues of the reconnection of ecology, health, and development as viewed through the eyes of women. This volume is a useful contribution to the emerging concern with the connection between environment and health. In particular the chapters which have special relevance to the issues discussed in this chapter are those which deal with toxic wastes, environmental degradation and the health of women. There is no doubt that large-scale accidents such as Chernobyl, and Bhopal, and toxic exposures to chemicals and radiation are increasing health concerns for women around the globe. Many people are beginning to address the threat to health that these pose, and they are of particular concern to women. There are now many documented cases of tragic impacts on women's lives of these accidents and similar toxic long-term exposures. The connection to socioeconomic status and particularly to poverty is clear in much of this research and documentation. Adler et al. (1994) have documented the clear connection between socioeconomic status and health. If we take this another step further and connect the lack of income to lack of choice in environments, then you have a clear connection between health and environments because many women must live in situations where they are exposed to environmental health hazards due to lack of economic resources. A number of people are beginning to make this connection.

There is an emerging literature on environmental justice which addresses questions of the differential impact of environmental hazards on the poor in developed and developing countries. All these threads contribute to the clear picture that is beginning to emerge about the impact of environments on health, but the point that I have tried to make is that some health researchers have so narrowly defined their research objectives and variables, so as to exclude any possibility of investigating environmental impacts on health in either men or women.

HEALTH AND ENVIRONMENTS ISSUES: THE NEED FOR A FOCUS ON GENDER

There is a significant literature on the impact that environments have on the health of individuals and groups. Satterthwaite (1993) has produced a comprehensive review of the literature on the impact on health of urban environments. In this article he has identified seven hazards to health within the urban environment including biological pathogens; chemical pollutants; the availability and cost of food, water and fuel; physical hazards such as flooding; built environment problems such as overcrowding, noise, etc.; natural resource degradation caused by waste from cities; and national/global environmental degradation with more indirect, but long-term influences on human health (Satterthwaite, 1993, p. 88). He explores the inequality inherent in the health impacts of the environment on individuals in the city, confirming the greater impact of environmental hazards on the poorer inhabitants of cities. In addition, he identifies women as a vulnerable group, both because of their biology, and their gender roles. He links women's greater vulnerability to reproductive biology, and to the activities that they are responsible for such as cooking, provision of water and sanitation, caring for children and the sick, subsistence crop and livestock production, and firewood gathering. He also includes domestic violence as an environmental hazard for women. So within the literature on health and environment, some authors have identified women as a particularly vulnerable and important group. Satterthwaite has also suggested strategies for intervening at the level of the neighborhood or the small city, through involving the inhabitants, since he perceives that outside experts find it more difficult to do the integrative thinking necessary to identify all the important environmental hazards or problems in a particular area. He advocates that inhabitants have the knowledge that allows them to identify the critical problems in an area. This is congruent with my own analysis and thinking.

Jordan and Wagner (1993) have looked specifically at the question of meeting women's needs and priorities for water and sanitation in cities. This is an especially important issue for women since they take on most responsibilities for household management and childcare. They describe how the lack of consultation with women leads to problems in water and sanitation projects, and they advocate involving women in planning and implementing water and sanitation projects in order to use their expertise in creating a good fit between the problems and the solutions. The provision of safe and convenient water supplies affects women in important ways. The authors summarize the points made in the paper in the following way:

that the lack of clean and accessible water dooms women to poverty and sickness;

that the time and energy required to obtain water for basic daily needs consumes time which could be well spent on economic pursuits;

that women throughout the world are anxious to improve their

situations when not limited by social and technological restraints. (p. 144).

In the Sundsvall conference report, *Creating Supportive Environments for Health,* gender perspectives were summarized in the following way:

> Gender interacts with other dimensions of oppression. Low-income women, indigenous women, women from minority ethnic groups, disabled women, all carry the major burden of creating healthy environments with the least resources. If a gender perspective was applied to the analysis of disadvantage and health promotion, a whole range of different choices would be made regarding the allocation of resources. Similarly, if a gender perspective was applied to the social construction of epidemiology we might well get a different data base for the development of health promotion programs. Valuing women's experiences would lead to the development of an infrastructure for supporting women's community-based organizations and giving them a much stronger voice in the development of health promotion policies and structures to create supportive environments. (Pettersson & Tillgren, 1993, p. 43)

STRATEGIC DIRECTIONS FOR RESEARCH AND ACTION: BRINGING TOGETHERPARADIGMS AND APPROACHES IN INNOVATIVE WAYS

In reviewing these various literatures that have relevance to questions of women, environments and health, we can draw the following conclusions. First of all, there is a strong emphasis in North America and Europe on the analysis of changing roles of women as they intersect with environments that are culturally unsupportive of the present conditions that women experience in their daily lives. These concerns have led to a literature which focuses upon the redesign of homes, neighborhoods, and urban environments to better meet the needs of women as they are presently defined. In addition, concerns with toxic contamination and pollution have brought many groups of women together to analyze the connection between environments and health, with a clear focus upon political action and change needs. In developing countries, the concerns expressed in the literature are with basic issues of water, sanitation, fuel and food. In addition, the impact that development has had on women's connection to the natural environment, particularly women's tendency to loose access to quality land and natural resources as development proceeds, has been of concern. The increasing impact of urbanization and the feminization of poverty also are prevalent themes in the literature. In the women's health research domain, emphasis upon environment has not been central. Rather issues that relate to specific disease states, and issues of particular concern to women, such as reproductive health, have been more central to these research agendas.

Some new work is emerging which tries to reconnect ecology, health, and women, and this is being widely recognized as important work. Finally, in the international literature on health and environments, gender has become an important category in some research efforts, and attempts are being made to identify issues which are particularly of concern to women.

Based on this analysis, and coming from my own understanding of the need for multiple approaches to intervention in bringing about changes in paradigms, and new approaches to defining problems, I suggest the following items should appear on a research agenda concerning women, health and environments.

1. *The need to determine the present state of environmental analysis in the area of women's health research, and to contribute to the incorporation of environmental issues into their research paradigms.* As was stated earlier in this chapter, most research projects on women's health have not incorporated environmental analysis into their conceptual frameworks, rather they have been working from the single or multivariate predictive models which often times exclude environmental analysis. Social support, and stress, have been used as concepts to incorporate environmental influences into the research analysis, and some attention to lifestyle variables and poverty as barriers to health and well-being have been utilized. However, much of health research still lacks environmental content. There are exceptions to this in the health promotion literature, and in the international conferences which have focused upon creating supportive environments for health and the healthy cities projects. Here, the need is for a more comprehensive look at women's needs within these approaches.

2. *The need to analyze the contribution that environmental innovations such as those proposed by women and environments researchers might have toward*

improving the health of women. In North America and Europe, the field of environment and behavior has focused upon changes in the built environment which might facilitate and fit more closely with women's changing lifestyles. Proposed innovations include attention to housing design; incorporation of services into housing and neighborhoods to support working families; redesign of urban land use to lessen the separation between work and home, and the needed commercial services for everyday life; and redesign of transportation systems to take into account the particular needs of women users, including the need for multiple trips, safety at night, and the need to bring baby carriages and shopping carts onto transit vehicles. These kinds of proposed innovations and others may have an impact on the health of women, if we assume that as environments become more supportive, stress is decreased, and women feel more able to accomplish their goals in life. Health researchers might compare health perceptions and outcomes for various groups of women in different environmental contexts to evaluate the impact that these types of innovations might have.

3. *The need to further develop the focus upon women, environments and health in the healthy cities movement, the supportive environments approach, and other WHO-related initiatives that address environmental health questions.* The *WHO Global Strategy for Health and Environment* identifies a number of action strategies for achieving the goals stated in the document. Under the heading of "research" the document outlines the need for "the support of a new research agenda on matters affecting the environment, health and development concentrating on the promotion and conduct of applied research on environmental factors, physical and social, affecting human health, determining in particular how development and environmental degradation affect health" (WHO, 1993, p. 17). The issues identified in this paper in relationship to women's particular environmental health issues are ones which deserve more research attention, and more attention in action strategies as well. In addition in the *WHO Global Strategy for Health and Environment*, there is a call for creating supportive environments for health. "The promotion of healthy life-styles and the fostering of supportive environments require the joint efforts of policy-makers, decision-makers, and those active in the community (p. 21)." Already there is a focus upon women as a vulnerable group in many of the WHO initiatives; however this focus would benefit from expansion and linking with women and environments analysis in order to better define the issues that particularly affect women in these programs.

4. *The need to develop participatory research processes which involve researchers from the three named areas (women and environments, women's health,*

and environmental health) in an exercise which focuses upon changing paradigms, sharing conceptual strategies, and moving toward shared goals in the area of women's environmental health. There are many innovations in process which have been developed and are being implemented in a number of domains. For example, there is a field of study called action learning which focuses upon the ways in which complex domains can be intermeshed in participatory processes (Wright & Morley, 1989). Action learning approaches are participatory based approaches which utilize an open conference format to bring together individuals representing a number of networks and organizations in order to deal with complex issues of futures planning (Morgan, 1983; Weisbord, 1992). In addition, an even more recent approach has been developed by Owen (1992) called "open space technology." This approach to large meeting management allows a large group to create its own agenda in a short period of time, carry it out, produce a document, and move forward in a spirited manner from a new vantage point. Excellent results have been achieved in the use of this approach, and it would seem to have direct application to the kind of need that is identified in this action objective.

5. *The need for researchers and women in communities to work in participatory modes to define critical environmental issues for women's health.* There are already many good examples of participatory processes which have included women in the international domain (Srinivasan, 1993). However, they have not focused upon defining critical environmental issues for women's health. In some cases, like the water projects, women have been involved in specific concerns that are environmental health concerns, but I know of no studies where they have been involved in defining their own critical environmental health issues.

6. *The need to network women from different communities, and from different income groups within communities, to compare environmental health issues that are central to their well-being, in order to increase awareness of inequity in distribution of health impacts on women in different race and class categories.* Again, focus upon good process is important in this arena. Women Plan Toronto is an organization which has worked to create a participatory planning process for women within the city of Toronto (Women Plan Toronto, 1986). Other participatory processes have occurred in London, i.e., Women Plan London. These efforts have brought together diverse groups of women within the city to identify built environment issues affecting the quality of life for women. Similar approaches could be used in regard to environmental health issues.

7. *The need for frequent opportunities for women from developed and developing countries to gather around the definition of environmental health issues*

that are critical to creating sustainable, and healthy environments on a global scale. The role that women have played in global environmental decision making has been less than that of men in the past. Women are becoming more politically active in regard to environmental issues, witness such events as the Women's Conference for a Healthy Planet (WEDO, 1992). These types of global gatherings of women should be encouraged to occur with some frequency, since the input of women into issues of global health is essential.

8. *The need for the inclusion of a wide variety of nongovernmental organizations in a dialogue around women's environmental health issues on a global scale.* Women's input into the dialogue around *Agenda 21* has been vital to the process (United Nations Development Fund for Women, 1993). There are numerous recommendations coming out of *Agenda 21* which have clear relevance to women, and the above mentioned document highlights those. Organizations such as UNIFEM, WEDO, and many others perform a vital function in creating the dialogue around women's issues. Issues of environmental health are particularly appropriate ones for women's participation as non-governmental organizations.

SUMMARY

In summarizing the points made in this chapter, there is a need for an integration of the efforts of women's health researchers, women's environment researchers, and environmental health researchers. This integration should be achieved through processes generated by the participants, in order to move toward a clearer understanding of the relationship between women's environments and their health. This understanding should be developed in conjunction with women in communities and nongovernmental organizations as well, and the hope would be that the paradigms developed would make for more relevant research, and more effective action toward a healthy future for all women around the globe.

REFERENCES

Adler, N. E., Boyce, T., Chesney, M. A., Cohen, S., Folkman, S., Kahn, R. L., & Syme, S. L. 1994. Socioeconomic status and health: The challenge of the gradient. *American Psychologist, 49, 1,* 15–24.

Altman, I., & Churchman, A. 1994. *Women and the Environment*. New York: Plenum Press.

American Psychological Association. 1994. *Psychosocial and Behavioral Factors in Women's Health: Creating an Agenda for the 21st Century: Book of Abstracts.* American Psychological Association, Washington, D.C.

Andrew, C., & Milroy, B. 1988. *Life Spaces: Gender, Household, Employment.* Vancouver: University of British Columbia Press.

Chavkin, W. 1984. *Double Exposure: Women's Health Hazards on the Job and at Home.* New York: Monthly Review Press.

Christensen, K. 1994. "Working at Home: Frameworks of Meaning." In I. Altman and A. Churchman (Eds.) *Women and the Environment.* New York, Plenum Press, pgs. 133–166.

Dean, K., & Hancock, T. 1992. *Supportive Environments for Health.* World Health Organization, Regional Office for Europe, Copenhagen.

Dhruvarajan, V. 1990. *Women and Well-Being.* Montreal: McGill-Queen's Press.

Frankenhaeuser, M., Lundberg, U., & Chesney, M. 1991. *Women, Work and Health: Stress and Opportunities.* New York: Plenum Press.

Fromm, D. 1991. *Collaborative Communities: Cohousing, Central Living and Other New Forms of Housing with Shared Facilities.* New York: Van Nostrand Reinhold.

Hancock, T. 1993. Health, human development and the community ecosystem: three ecological models. *Health Promotion International, v. 8, no. 1.*

Horelli, L., & Vepsa, K. 1994. "In Search of Supportive Structures for Everyday Life," in I. Altman & A. Churchman (Eds.) *Women and the Environment.* New York: Plenum Press, pgs. 201–226.

Jordan, S., & Wagner, F. 1993. Meeting women's needs and priorities for water and sanitation in cities, *Environment and Urbanization, v. 5, no. 2,* 135–145.

Kettel, B. 1993. Women, Health and the Environment. The Fourth Meeting of Commonwealth Responsible for Women's Affairs. Divison of Women and Youth Affairs, London: Commonwealth Secretariat, England.

Koblinsky, M., Timyan, J., & Gay, J. (Eds.). 1993. *The Health of Women: A Global Perspective,* Westview Press, Boulder, CO.

Leppa, C. J., & Miller, C. 1988. *Women's Health Perspectives: An Annual Review.* Volume 1. Phoenix, Arizona: Oryx Press.

Leppa, C. J. 1989. *Women's Health Perspectives: An Annual Review.* Volume 2. Phoenix, Arizona: Oryx Press.

Leppa, C. J. 1990. *Women's Health Perspectives: An Annual Review.* Volume 3. Phoenix, Arizona: Oryx Press.

Luxton, M., Rosenberg, H., & Arat Koc, S. 1990. *Through the Kitchen Window: The Politics of Home and Family.* Toronto: Garamond Press.

Michelson, W. 1994. "Everyday Life in Contextual Perspective," in I. Altman and A. Churchman (Eds.) *Women and the Environment.* New York: Plenum Press, pp. 17–42.

Michelson, W. 1985. *From Sun to Sun: Daily Obligations and Community Structure in the Lives of Employed Women and Their Families.* Totowa, New Jersey: Rowman & Allanheld.

Mies, M., & Shiva, V. 1993. *Ecofeminism.* Fernwood Publications, Halifax, Nova Scotia.

Miles, A. 1991. *Women, Health and Medicine.* Milton Keynes: Open University Press.

Morgan, G. 1983. *Beyond Method: Strategies for Social Research.* Beverly Hills: Sage Publications.

Owen, H. 1992. *Open Space Technology: A User's Guide.* Abbott Publishing, Potomac, Maryland.

Peterson, R. 1987. "Gender issues in the home and the urban environment." In E. H. Zube & G. T. Moore (Eds.), *Advances in Environment, Behaviour, and Design*. Plenum Press, pp. 187–218.

Peterson, R. 1986. "Feminist critique of the built environment: reflections on cultural change in North America." In David G. Saile (Ed.), *Architecture in Cultural Change: Essays in Built Form and Culture Research*. University of Kansas Press, pp. 129–134.

Reterson, R. 1986. "Ten active years: a review of women and environments research," *Women and Environments, Vol. 8, No. 3*, 9–11.

Reterson, R. 1986. "Women as a special user group in a changing North American cultural context," *Environments, Vol. 18, No. 3*, 64–73.

Peterson, R., Morley, D., & Wekerle, G. 1978. "Women and environments: an overview of an emerging field," *Environment and Behaviour, Vol. 10, No. 4*, 511–534.

Pettersson, B., & Tillgren, P. (Eds.) 1991. *Creating Supportive Environments for Health: Report from the 3rd International Conference on Health Promotion*, Sundsvall, Sweden, June 9–15.

Rodda, A.1991. *Women and the Environment*. Zed Books, London and New Jersey.

Satterthwaite, D. 1993. The impact on health of urban environments, *Environment and Urbanization, V. 5, no. 2*, October, 87–111.

Shiva, V. (Ed.) 1994. *Close to Home: Women Reconnect Ecology, Health and Development Worldwide*. New Society Publishers, Philadelphia, PA.

Srinivasan, L. 1993. *Tools for Community Participation: A Manual for Training Trainers in Participatory Techniques*. Prowwess/UNDP-World Bank Water and Sanitation Program.

United Nations Development Fund for Women. 1993. *Agenda 21: An Easy Reference to the Specific Recommendations on Women*.

WEDO 1992. *Official Report: World Women's Congress for a Healthy Planet, November 8–12, Miami, Florida, U.S.A.* Women's Environment and Development Organization, New York,

Weisbord, M. R. 1992. *Discovering Common Ground*. San Francisco: Berrett-Koehler.

Weisman, L. K. 1992. *Discrimination by Design: A Feminist Critique of the Man-Made Environment*. Urbana: University of Illinois Press.

Wekerle, G., Peterson, R., & Morley, D. 1980. *New Space for Women*. Boulder: Westview Press.

Whitzman, C., & Wekerle, G. 1992. *A Working Guide to Planning and Designing Safer Cities*. Toronto: City of Toronto Planning and Development Department.

WHO Commission on Health and Environment. 1992. *Our Planet, Our Health*. World Health Organization, Geneva.

Women Plan Toronto. 1986. *Shared Experiences and Dreams*. Toronto, ON.

World Health Organization. 1993. *WHO Global Strategy for Health and Environment*. World Health Organization, Geneva.

Wright, S, & Morley, D. 1989. *Learning Works: Searching for Organizational Futures*. Toronto: The ABL Group, York University.

39

Population, Environment, and Development: A New Method for Research, a Starting Point for Action

Daniel Taylor-Ide and Carl E. Taylor

> Grandparents in Nepal watch their children's children walking hours to bring firewood that the grandparents in their youth could gather near their mud home. The parents, as they look to the future, confront tough decisions. Is it better to send children to school—or to expect children to meet immediate family needs by taking a porter's job carrying loads? Looking at their environment, parents ask: How can fields produce more food? Can they bring to their homes electricity, an outside tap with running water, glass in the windows?

The above example happens to be taken from the Himalaya, but the problem is universal. In an era of degenerating environments, how can outsiders help village parents who want to pass along a better life to their children and their grandchildren? Our answer has three parts. First, families and concerned officials need to understand, in a way they all can agree on, what the local problems, priorities and options are. Second, growing out of such pragmatic problem identification, action is needed, community specific action that uses local resources both to optimize development for the people and also to ameliorate impacts on the environment. Third, the role of both governments and international agencies should be to empower sustainable local action not to impose outside interventions, especially in an era when donors (national and international) recognize the limitations of their resources.

A NEW METHOD FOR UNDERSTANDING COMMUNITY-LEVEL INTERACTIONS

Understanding how local communities function is a process of understanding diversity. A conceptual framework is needed to integrate understanding of local interactions between population, environment and development. Increasing research worldwide on the dynamics of these interactions has moved toward increasing sophistication of computer modeling to accommodate the complex multiple variables (Meadows, 1992). While these models may become more representative, their increasing sophistication requiring larger data sets makes them ever more difficult to use, a tool too sophisticated for regional or local application (IIASA, 1992) and with little relevance to families where ultimately action must take place. For practical solutions the need is not for increased complexity, but rather for simplicity.

By contrast, in searching for simple solutions to these problems decision makers responsible for practical programs have repeatedly attempted simple, hopefully broadly relevant conceptual frameworks for action. This SIMPLE → SIMPLE quest assumes there are straightforward answers. The problems are recognized to be urgent. But, simple relationships do not exist at the population-environment nexus. The highly sophisticated modeling alluded to above (which is still criticized because it is not sophisticated enough) demonstrates that any specific environmental consequence of population and development dynamics is the interactive product of multiple forces affecting permutations of both human and environmental variability and adaptibility. To seek a simple solution the analytic process must move through a SIMPLE → COMPLEX → SIMPLE sequence. Starting with simple observations, the analysis should evolve to accommodate all critical aspects of system complexity (biological, cultural and politico/economic) in order to arrive at simple solutions. (To illustrate the diversity of environmental and economic interrelationships in the Himalaya, see Figure 39.1.)

How can such complex dynamics of a whole interacting system of environmental and socioeconomic factors be analyzed accurately and efficiently? In the Himalaya (as in any community) this complex analytical task is made more difficult because there are finite limitations of time, labor, finances, natural resources, and access to decision-making influence. For programmatic problem solving the analysis must balance the complexity of the task against the limited resources that can be brought to the solution.

Figure 39.2 simplifies the complexity of Figure 39.1 and structures the association between population-development and population-environment interactions to illustrate the centrality of the values, priorities and practices of local people. Two sets of adaptive variables mediate between

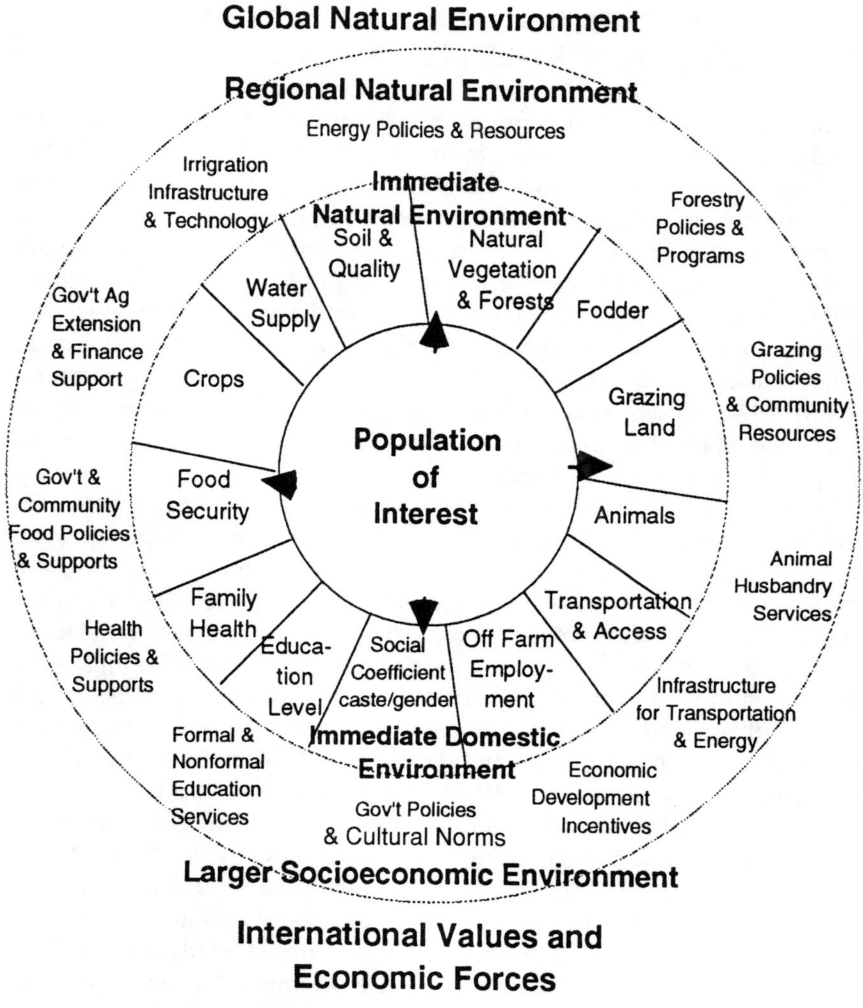

FIGURE 39.1 Primary relationship dynamics; population and land use.

these forces with the people at the center. For a presentation of these variables see Figure 39.3.

The usual field research techniques are both too time consuming and too costly for the involvement and interests of policymakers and local people. Recent analytical advances, however, have evolved a variety of Rapid Assessment Procedures (RAP) that demonstrate the efficacy of

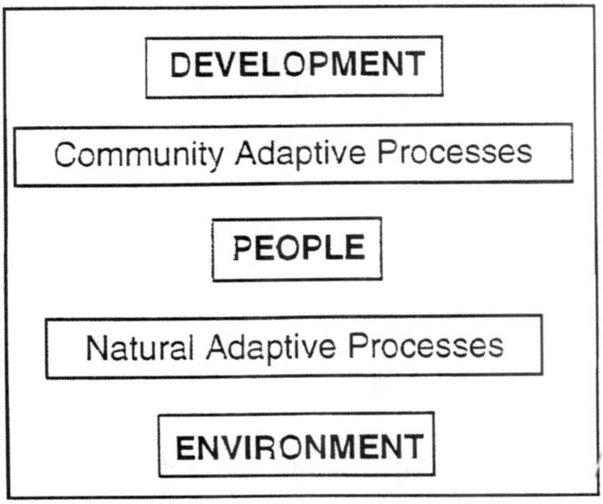

FIGURE 39.2 The association between population–development and population–environment.

quick integrated analyses of local problems (Scrimshaw, 1987, 1992). A RAP (as commonly used) depends on experts who draw on personal experience to make intuitive judgements. The RAP method proposed here is different in that it allows communities to administer the process themselves. This participation creates a broader awareness and ownership of the data so that they are less likely to dismiss the conclusions as they often do with data presented to them by experts and government officials.

The proposed RAP also differs because it spans the complex variables of population, environment and development. To cover these fields using standard scientific techniques, multisectoral ecosystem study and a complex socioeconomic profile would be prohibitively time consuming and expensive. In the proposed RAP this complexity becomes manageable by using key indicators for each variable to allow a Self-Evaluation using Essential Data (SEED) by accurate yet simple objective, quantifiable measures. For example, in seeking demographic data, the traditional population profile (age/sex distributions, marital/economic status, etc.) is not described; but rather, only that information that defines population change. For many variables data about individuals are not needed and aggregate household or community data are sufficient.

Central to the SEED process is to avoid overvaluing any one sector. Prior research tends to give preeminence to specific variables. These can

Population
- **Demographic Characteristics**
  - Population Numbers and Age Distribution
  - Mortality and Fertility
- **Situational Characteristics**
  - Health Status
  - Education Status
  - Housing Status
  - Equity Status

Environment
- **Geophysical**
  - Soil
  - Water
  - Energy Potential
- **Biological**
  - Plant Communities
  - Domestic Animal Communities
  - Wild Animal Communities
  - Energy Potential
- **Societal**
  - Historical Self-Perception
  - Trade and Tourism
  - Transport and Communication
  - Industry
  - Family Planning Use
  - Government and Foreign Aid
  - Administrative and Political Structures

Community Adaptive Processes
- Migration
- Technology and Energy Use
- Animal Husbandry Practices
- Forest Uses (Wood Use and Medicinal Plants)
- Attitude to Change and Hope for Future (Qi/Brahma)
- Local Participation In Decision Making
- Consumption and Wealth

External Adaptive Processes
- Health Services
- Formal Education
- Administrative and Financial Infrastructure
- Food Security Supports
- Outside Business and Industry
- Institutions Supporting Change

FIGURE 39.3 Population, environment, and development variables for which SEED key indicators are needed.

range from the atmospheric to the zoological and from economics to culture; from remnant endangered organisms to interactions of whole ecosystems; and from fertility and conception to life goals parents have for the old age of their children. The amount of data in any one of these areas can be enormous. Across sectors, aggregated data may consume millions

Search for Simple Indicators—Example One

An illustration of the utility of simple indicators is in the sequence that led to improved diagnosis of childhood pneumonia.

Formerly a sick infant was examined with the tools of temperature, chest percussion, stethoscope and intuition. Often the diagnosis was missed.

Then came sophistication with blood tests, X-rays, and lung punctures to identify invading organisms. A reliable diagnosis resulted—but was hospital dependent and expensive while the disease progressed and babies died in 3–5 days.

Now algorithms simplify the process. A neonatal infant having difficult breathing at a rate of 60 per minute has high probability of pneumonia; babies 2 to 12 months old the rate is 50/minute; babies 1–3 years, 40 times/minute. When the lower ribs are retracted, pneumonia is critical. With this technique diagnosis can be done in homes by an auxiliary health worker and accuracy is high. Mortality can be cut by half. The simple technique required complex analysis to develop.

of data points—and become incomprehensible as a whole integrated system. The intent of the SEED approach is to eliminate detail and to focus on key representative indicators for each variable.

Preliminary tests suggest that such minimum data sets are valid and can be surveyed. Protocols outlining this approach in pilot studies in Nepal and China's Tibet are presented in Appendices A through E at the end of this paper. An outline of the general categories of variables is in Figure 39.3. Out of this long list in each region the variables that are most relevant to local problems can be selected and SEED indicators identified.

The SEED process is not a single survey but rather it uses multiple methods to get the following data: (a) household and agriculture surveys, (b) in-depth leader interviews, (c) review of available documentation, and (d) observation and direct measurement. Some information is quantifiable. Much of the most valuable data, however, must be based on the judgment of knowledgeable persons—another reason to use local people from the community. Pre-tests of this methodology have affirmed the complementarity of using qualitative and quantitative techniques that fit

The Utility of Simple Indicators—Example Two

Nature has provided simple yet sensitive indicators to monitor her complexity. Himalayan birds (more than 1,000 species) reveal the ecosystem change of Himalayan slopes.

- In undisturbed Himalayan forests, one indicator is pheasants. Their calls chronicle a healthy habitat.
- As habitat is degraded under 2,000 meters the Spiny Babbler indicates the forest is no longer pristine.
- When people take ownership, the indicators become: Common Myna, Sparrow and House Crow.

local cultural practices. But the process of opening to local people must go even further. The local people must *own* the data.

The SEED methodology links data from otherwise disparate environmental and societal disciplines to create a holistic portrait balancing variables that stress validity more than precision. It has four advantages.

1. In a streamlined and highly selective form it will enable communities to determine what is happening in their local situation.
2. It allows comparisons from one local situation to another with the expectation that variables and indicators can be standardized for a region.
3. It permits comparisons against global standards to judge what can be expected for sustainable improvement.
4. The SEED method enables comparisons over time so that communities can monitor their changing population and environmental status and the results of their own actions.

Once the SEED indicators are selected, it is anticipated that students can do much of the data gathering, perhaps as part of school activities. A Nepal pretest of this method showed that trained local high school graduates were in some instances more effective in obtaining answers than professional interviewers from the capital city. With clear procedures no one has more ready access to some types of information than local people—and the student population may come as close as any group to having universal access within homes. However, it is essential to have close supervision, cross-checking of data, rewards for accuracy, and an atmosphere in which the process is enjoyable as well as a learning experi-

The Usefulness of Simple Indicators—Example Three

In the Himalaya, as population size doubles, how can communities monitor if water quality, the most basic of all resources, is declining? Determining microbial contamination usually requires laboratory support.

Recent tests proved effective a simple, all-in-one-piece plastic container for culture media which is incubated in an even simpler, totally no cost, incubator (a human armpit). As a result, villagers can use an effective technique to monitor their water quality directly and not depend on indirect evidence.

ence. The presence and proper utilization of school teachers may be a vital resource.

FROM RESEARCH TO ACTION

Conducting SEED surveys is the first step to guide action by communities. The second step is for community members, policymakers and experts to meet together, analyze the data, and then, decide collectively what actions should be taken and how resources should be allocated. The key is for government officials to share control with the local people (Arole, 1988). UNICEF calls this the Triple-A process, Assessment, Analysis, and Action.

The assumption is that once communities become informed they will more responsibly select their future directions. As awareness, options and confidence grow it is expected that their limited resources will be allocated more efficiently and community willingness to take risks may increase. A second assumption is that equity (not the personal interests of those in power) should guide the implementing of interventions. Giving a priority to surveillance for equity has been shown to work in several field demonstrations (Taylor, 1992). Pursuing equity for the whole community means focusing on people among whom the greatest needs are concentrated. Specifically, the involvement of women in a focus on equity is essential.

Numerous examples can be given of success in developing community participation in locally specific solutions. For instance, 20 years of effective Asian primary health care has evolved successful, low-cost health care alternatives. Such projects often incorporate effective fertility control that rapidly lowers birth rates. Similarly, other effective demonstrations have shown that the status of women can be improved and their economic opportunities expanded and this has direct implications for successful conservation programs (Jacobson, 1992). Effective community afforestation projects also fit well with the locally specific approach proposed here. Formal and nonformal literacy education also seems a powerful mobilizing mechanism—and through much of the world the infrastructure of schools is now in place.

The assumption cannot be made that people will spontaneously be ready to take action. In village life experimentation is hazardous; there is a thin margin for error. To start with communities should be asked if they want to participate in the SEED process, and whether they are prepared to uncover new understandings in order to identify entry points for change? No meaningful action will be possible unless key questions come into the open: How can development assistance produce sustainable change? What is the ownership of economic power? What are sociocultural patterns of collective decision making and barriers between groups with contradictory goals? What are the shared cultural values, the symbols and myths all know and believe that provide a mutual sense of place, common past and hope for the future? (For example, it may be that Hindu and Buddhist belief in incarnation can contribute to a helpful holistic view of ecology.)

To prepare for action that will follow the SEED research, it must be determined how the community makes decisions. In most Asian societies, especially in rural areas, decisions are made not by individuals but by a mix of social groups. Different people need to be consulted on different subjects. Our fieldwork in Nepal showed communities to be highly stratified according to ethnicity as well as economic group. In Tibet, communities tend to be more homogeneous. A sociogram may be useful as a nonverbal tool to open discussion about decision making. Outsiders must learn how local dialogue functions. Anthropological communication and assessment approaches are probably the optimal methods to determine patterns of group dialogue. To support the ongoing need for feedback, there may be need for a new category of folk anthropologists to function in parallel with community workers.

The above steps must be conducted without creating unrealistic expectations of forthcoming outside assistance. However, trust needs to develop. Most communities have now seen enough research that has not led to action that some confidence-building assistance may be useful to establish credibility that in this instance there will be results. The character and amount of help, however, should neither create expectations that cannot be sustained nor should it be given with strings that usurp community-driven leadership.

Trusting Local Capacity

Himalayan rivers run narrow and fast. To cross these rivers a suspension bridge is needed anchored to the rocks and cantilevered out from concrete abutments, a complex engineering task.

Several years ago, Nepal tried an experiment. With one 700,000 rupees they sent government engineers to one district to build bridges. Another 700,000 rupees they gave to a different district with the provision that the people build their own according to official engineering specifications. When both were finished, the government built 2 bridges; the local people, 62.

The whole process should build collective action. The focal point for continuing action, our experience suggests, is best done around a major annual meeting for each community, and where possible for all communities in a region. There should also be periodic meetings. At all such meetings data and experiences are presented and options explored. It is absolutely critical that a range of involved parties participate, especially the poor and needy. Out of their collective input all should agree to follow the same development strategy. Such meetings will help evolve community-specific solutions and partnerships.

THREE-PARTNER COLLABORATION

Effective research followed by effective action will require interactive partnership among three groups: research scientists, government officials and local people. The needed partnership is not the traditional process of getting permission from officials, then information and labor from local people and sophisticated analysis from scientists. Rather, this process is one of creating a low-cost interactive dialogue among three parties who previously had each tended to see themselves as gatekeepers judiciously bestowing permits or control over other groups.

Local people need to be included as partners. Involvement of local residents in the past has usually been as informants, field assistants, or coolies. Such restricted involvement isolates the work from both reality and practical implementation. Thoughtful and observant local persons accumulate significant data in a lifetime—not to mention the wisdom from lifetimes handed down to them. The need is to integrate what local people know with what local people can never know—to combine tradi-

Local Leadership Within Appropriate Systems

Amma was chosen as health volunteer in Tulo Bharka Village in central Nepal because she was smart and articulate. During training five years ago, she was promised Rs100/month but after four months her salary stopped. She continues today because her neighbors do not let her stop.

Ward 5 has 42 households. When Amma started half the babies died; now only 2–3 out of the 10–12 born each year. Most deaths used to be from diarrhea but now mothers use oral rehydration. Deliveries were assisted by a female relative but now Amma delivers all babies. The Rs45 per day Amma gets for her annual five days training she uses to create a fund to buy medicines for which she charges those who can pay and gives free to the poor.

Amma reports that the greatest change is acceptance of family planning. Fifteen women get injections of depoprovera. Fifteen couples use condoms. Now that they trust her care for their baby, women start family planning postpartum. These women say that their families have better health, more time, less work, and more food. Amma also reports that "family planning brings peace in the home because there are fewer reasons for conflict."

tional knowledge with information that must be uncovered through research or brought in from outside experience. Involving local people is not simple—or such involvement would have happened more often. They often lack linguistic and conceptual skills. Village viewpoints about environment are wrapped in local world views that, when expressed, sound more superstition bound than factual (Muller-Boker, 1991). Involving local people becomes more complicated when a voice is given to the poor, the women and others who are often discriminated against.

If local people and officials are to own the data, *and make decisions based on the data,* they need to be involved in data analysis. Community involvement in the analytical process sometimes appears beyond the capacity of local villagers and too time consuming for officials. Specialists can assist through systematizing a variety of techniques. One approach is participatory discussion groups of knowledgeable persons that combine a review of available data and experience to set priorities among problems and consideration of options for solutions. Other tasks such as coding and entering of data can involve local people. Public discussions of data can use the many options in graphic presentation that do not require high levels of literacy. A positive spin-off is that the intuitive understanding of local people provides a useful accuracy check since they know whether "the numbers make sense."

Involving policymakers and administrators in a substantive fashion is also frequently overlooked. Politics affects virtually all research even though it is often disparaged as detracting from solid science. For the issues of concern here it will be pragmatically essential for science to adapt to political reality. The proposed work intentionally engages political processes because it is apparent that policymakers and administrators are the individuals most able to facilitate the movement from research to action. Three steps will be taken:

1. Incorporating policymakers in research design to focus on their known needs.
2. Special meetings with leaders, local people and experts to share research findings.
3. Joint formulation of recommendations for development interventions.

Involving scientists in a process is also fundamental—but it is also expensive since their salaries and expenses must be paid. However, involving them is critical since they perform two tasks. First, careful research is needed to select accessible and representative SEED indicators. Such selection must be based upon regionally specific parameters and must also cross, discipline-by-discipline, the whole spectrum of population, environment and development sectors. Several months spent in selecting the right SEED indicators will avoid the usual pattern of comprehensive research on a few variables at a time. Second, once the survey is started, scientific research is needed to validate the SEED process and findings. Maybe errors are creeping in? Periodic spot checking with more precise scientific methods will determine both bias and variability.

While SEED has practical significance for determining and guiding services, it will be useful to have parallel scientific validation for independent corroboration and to get wider professional recognition of the findings (especially since the method is new). This can be achieved through selected professionally conducted surveys on scientifically valid sample populations and detailed in-depth scientific research using more sophisticated techniques than the SEED format. Perceptions and practices can be assessed through survey questions such as:

a. Has there been change in understanding of the interactions of population, environment and development?
b. Have new patterns of community dialogue emerged?

Local Ecosystems—Community-Initiated Action

Steep Himalayan slopes that were forested had many more springs than there are now after deforestation. As broad-leaved forests disappear with them natural springs tend to dry up. Rain is then the annual hope for a maize crop.

The village of Madanpur realized that to protect their springs, they had to protect their forests. Doing so would ensure, not just water, but fodder for animals and fuel wood for homes. Thus, Madanpur protected their slope between 1,500 and 2,000 meters. Indigenous *Schima* and *Castanopsis* trees are regenerating well. A forest guard was hired from village funds. In the words of a local woman, "This is our forest, we pay this guard. Every year we feast together in the forest to remind ourselves of community solidarity for conservation."

c. Have family planning techniques become more accepted?
d. Have changes been initiated in environmental management?
e. Are development services now more effective?

More sophisticated analytical steps, while useful, tend to retain control by professionals. The ultimate judgments about the SEED methodology will be subjective, not scientific. The policymakers and government officials who are now enthusiastic may or may not find the method useful and will decide whether to continue to support the process. Most important in evaluation of the methods are the local communities. Do they think it works? Since local people are to be involved in all aspects of project implementation, they will be heard throughout in an ongoing tale told in muddy streets when people with issues on their minds make judgments about outside influences, or in dry fields waiting for rain, and in gossip between neighbors where they report all the mistakes and sometimes appreciate benefits. Listening to such local feedback will be a continuing process that should produce incremental adjustments in patterns of work and refinement of interventions.

REFERENCES

Arole, R. S., & Arole, M.; A Comprehensive Approach to Community Welfare, *Indian Journal of Pediatrics*, 55, 100–105, 1988.

Barlow, R., Clay, D., Ness, G., Norman, K., & Stycos, J. M.; "Population & Environment: What Do We Know? What Do We Need To Know?" (unpublished manuscript); University of Michigan Population & Environment Team; Ann Arbor, MI; 1992.

CIESIN, *Pathways of Understanding, The Interactions of Humanity and Global Environmental Change,* University Center Michigan, The Consortium for International Earth Science Information Network, 1992.

IIASA, International Institute of Applied Systems Analysis; *Population, Environment & Development,* Laxenburg, Austria, 1992.

Jacobson, J. L.; *Gender Bias: Roadblock to Sustainable Development;* Worldwatch Paper 110; Washington, D. C.; 1992.

Meadows, D. H., Meadows, D. L., & Randers, J.; *Beyond the Limits: Confronting Global Collapse, Envisioning a Sustainable Future;* Chelsea Green Pub; Post Mills, VT; 1992.

Muller-Boker, U.; Knowledge and Evaluation of Environment in Traditional Societies of Nepal; in *Mountain Research & Development; Vol 11, No 2;* May 1991.

National Research Council; *Report on Population Change and Land Use;* Committee on Population & Commission on Geosciences, Environment & Resources; National Academy of Sciences, Washington, D. C.; 1993.

Population Information Program, *Population Reports, The Environment and Population Growth,* Johns Hopkins University, Baltimore, Vol XX, No. 10, May 1992.

Scrimshaw, N. S., & Gleason, G.; *Rapid Assessment Procedures: Qualitative Methodologies for Planning and Evaluation of Health Related Programs,* INFDC, Boston, 1992.

Taylor, C. E.; Surveillance for Equity—Policy Implications from International Experience, *International Journal of Epidemiology; Vol 21;* 1992.

APPENDIX A—EXISTING RECORDS AND PRIOR SURVEYS

The data for this survey will come primarily from three sources: (1) existing government agencies, surveys and publications; (2) specific outside, primarily academic, research; and (3) local archives, particularly those associated with temples or monasteries.

SEED Variable	*Measurement Method*
Environment Related—Geophysical	
Maps of Region	Acquire all available
Environment Related—Societal	
Administrative & Political Structures	Describe
Historical Services Environment	Research history of development efforts
External Adaptive Processes	
Health Services	Describe government and private services
Formal Education	Describe government services
Financial Systems Supports	Describe available credit Describe financial incentives
Food Security Supports	Community or government food supports
Government & Foreign Aid	Describe available services
Community Adaptive Processes	
Health Services	Describe traditional services
Institutions for Change	Institutions available to support change
Religious and other Community Agencies	

APPENDIX B—HOME AND CHILDREN SURVEY

Population Related—Demographic Variables (for Brass techniques)

Ages	*Question 1*[1]	*Question 2*[2]	*Question 3*[3]	*Question 4 & 5*[4]	*Question 6 & 7*[5]
0–4					
5–9					
10–14					
15–19					
20–24					
25–29					
30–34					
35–39					
40–44					
45–49					
50–54					
55–59					
60+					

[1] Question #1 asks how many females are currently alive in the household in each of the listed five-year age groups?

[2] Question #2 asks how many males are currently alive in the household in each of the five-year age groups?

[3] Question #3 asks how many live births in the household since this time 12 months before. The number enters the form by 5-year age groups of mothers.

[4] Question #4 asks how many males been *ever born* to the mothers in the household who are currently in the identified 5-year age groups.
Question #5 asks how many of these males have died. Deaths under 5-years of age are recorded by exact age at death; deaths over 5 are recorded by 5-year age groups.

[5] Question #6 asks how many females have been *ever born* to the mothers in the household who are currently in the identified 5-year age groups.
Question #7 asks how many of these females have died. Deaths under 5-years of age are recorded by exact age at death; deaths over 5 are recorded by 5-year age groups.

SEED Variable	*Measurement Method*
Population Related—Situational	
Health Status	
5 Major Causes Death	Symptoms & history of each household death
Nutritional Status	Arm circumferences of every child under five
People's Perceptions[6]	Describe five major illnesses in community
Education	
Literacy	Who in home can read the sample pamphlet
Male/Female School Attendance	School attendance by children
Family Planning Use	What methods known? What methods used?
Community Adaptive Processes	
Migration	
Permanent	Question regarding family members away
Seasonal	Question regarding family patterns
Internal/External	
Attitudes Change & Hope (Qi/Brahma)	
Hope	What gives you greatest hope for future
Concern for Others	Discuss to see what they do for others
	What are their concerns about their neighbors
Cultural/Religious Activities	What percent time devoted to such activities

[6] People's perceptions of health seek to determine the five locally perceived priority health problems. For this, a scientific diagnosis of what this condition might be is neither assumed nor appropriate.

APPENDIX C—AGRICULTURE AND FORESTS SURVEY

SEED Variable	*Measurement Method*
Environment Related—Biological	
Wild Animal Communities	Report animal types found in area
	Query regarding identified indicator species
Fuel	
Fuelwood	How far to walk now
	How far to walk thirty years before
	How many hours/week in energy acquisition
Other fuels	Identify types and amounts used
Fodder	Identify types & sources (distance)
	Amounts used by season
Environment Related—Societal	
Agriculture	
Crops	Types of crops
	Frequency of crops
	Distance of fields from home
Management	Irrigation (what crops & how much used)
	Fertilizer
	Technology use
	Whether produce is sold
Domestic Animals	
Types	Identify types & numbers
Feeding Practices	Stall feeding practice
	Grazing practice & areas
Trade & Communication	
Percent Income from Trade	Question each household
Trade Commodities & Volume	Question each household
Percent Population Receiving Media	Question each household
Percent Radios Ownership	Question each household
Consumption	
Farm Produce	What food is purchased
Clothing	Clothing purchased each year

APPENDIX D—LEADERS SURVEY

SEED Variable	*Measurement Method*
Population Related—Situational	
Equity Status	
Poverty	Income & wages? Differ by age/gender?
Land Ownership	Create simple village map, who owns what
Environment Related—Societal	
Historical Self-Perception	What are main problems of village Main groups (ethnic & economic) Most successful development programs Why? Least successful development programs Why? Major environmental changes you remember? Groups in village with chronic needs What has population growth done to valley? What technology was most helpful so far?
Transport & Communications	Frequency of travel outside village Mechanization of travel
Tourism	Number of nights tourists stay Number of tourists passing through

APPENDIX E—OBSERVATIONAL SURVEY

SEED Variable	*Measurement Method*
Population Related—Situational	
Equity Status	
Age	How are children & elderly treated?
Consumption	
Manufactured Goods	Check what in each home
Non-local Materials in Shelter	Itemize
Environment Related—Geophysical	
Air	
Indoor Air	Measure
Outdoor Air	Measure
Soil	
Texture	Measure
Organic Matter	Measure
Rooting Depth	Measure
Core Samples for Pollen	Measure
Water	
Biological Indicators	Fly larvae to sludge worms Coliform culture the drinking water sources
Chemical/Physical	Sediment, pH
Supply	Seasonal stream flows, Watertable
Energy Potential	
Solar	Measure
Hydro	Measure
Wind	Measure
Environment Related—Biological	
Plant Communities	
Diversity of Species	Measure from sample plots
Change Among Most Sensitive	Same as above
Energy Potential	
Fuel Wood	Photograph community's wood lots (distinguish community, private, government)
Fossil Fuels	What is for sale in shops

SEED Variable (Cont.)	*Measurement Method (Cont.)*
Environment Related—Societal	
Agricultural Practice	Terracing, irrigation, etc. Observe harvest rates
Community Adaptive Processes	
Wealth	Observe for indicators such as jewelry
Participation in Decision Making	Describe community decision making (consensus or hierarchical)

40

Realizing Sustainable Public Health: Implications for Public Health Training

Gurinder S. Shahi, Frank Hartvelt, and Michael Sacks

Public health in the context of sustainable human development is based on an expanded understanding of health to include recognition that human health is tied, in the broadest sense, to our ability to maintain environmental and ecological integrity. Building on the 1978 Alma Ata definition of health, the conceptual basis for sustainable public health might be phrased as follows: "not merely the absence of disease but a state of complete physical, mental, social, environmental and ecological well-being" (see also chapter 1, Box 1.2). Sustainable public health practice integrates health, environmental, and developmental concerns. It recognizes that human security and health are built on a foundation of economic, social, and human development in a milieu of sustainable stewardship of natural resources and the environment. It is, in consensus with other emerging perspectives on public health, focused on "people and communities as key actors for their own health . . . and a health systems concept that seeks to integrate prevention, promotion and cure and that relates actively to other sectors for the purpose of joint action. (Modegal, 1994)"

In sustainable public health, the principles of preventive health care and the encouragement of health-promoting behavior would be holistically expanded to the wide range of activities and interactions between people, the environment, and health. Individuals working to promote ecological integrity and environmental protection have long recognized the similarity between their work and that of primary health care professionals—they have even coined the phrase "primary environmental care" which, analogously to primary health care, seeks to identify and implement approaches based on prevention of environmental degradation rather than "therapeutic" correction of damage after it has occurred (secondary or tertiary care) (Bajracharya, 1993).

Implicit in the consideration of any new conceptual framework is the recognition that current ways of thinking and acting are inadequate to meet the challenges of the present and the future. We are able to deal with some inadequacies by "tinkering" to make the existing approaches more responsive to changing needs. We appeared until recently, for example, to have been fairly successful in using industrialization and ever-rising consumption as the engine for development. Now, we are becoming increasingly aware that we cannot continue indefinitely along such a course—and that a fundamental change in our understanding and approach to development, sustainable human development, is required. Similarly, achieving sustainable public health will require fundamental changes in the way we view ourselves and the world around us, and the way we approach health and health-services delivery.

Bringing about change requires a careful rethinking of our approaches to capacity building for health, and reengineering of the way we operate at several levels—from the policy and legislative framework that provides the context and environment in which we operate; to the institutions through which we operate; to the technical, financial and infrastructural resources at our disposal; to the way we support and train people who work to achieve our health objectives. Unless we develop effective strategies for change at all these levels to achieve a holistic, internally consistent, and integrated approach to achieving sustainable public health, our efforts will likely fail. Box 40.1 addresses some of the key issues which need to be considered.

PARAMETERS OF SUSTAINABLE PUBLIC HEALTH

Fundamentally, any area of human endeavor and of human interaction with the world around us that might have a direct or indirect impact on human health and well-being would be of interest to the sustainable public health practitioner. At the urban community level, this might involve:

- understanding and contributing to the nature and strength of family relationships;
- taking an active interest in support services for child care, the elderly, the handicapped, the invalid, the mentally ill;
- working to ensure that the community deals effectively with crime, violence, alcoholism, drug addiction, or homelessness;

Box 40.1—Some Issues in Capacity Building for Sustainable Public Health

1. Policy and legislative framework
—Do existing health, social, environmental and developmental policies and laws promote sustainable public health?
—What changes, if any, are needed to ensure that our policies and laws encourage the achievement of sustainable public health?
(A particular challenge will undoubtedly be to ensure that our policy and legislative framework encourages integrative and comprehensive thinking and implementation. This will require a fundamental reversal from current thinking which tends to give greater credence, for example, to "specialist" than "generalist" perspectives.)
2. Institutional framework
—Are existing institutions and management structures conducive to the establishment of sustainable public health?
—What reforms to existing institutions (or, perhaps, new institutions) are needed to facilitate the achievement of sustainable public health?
(A major challenge will be devolution of power and decentralization of decision-making responsibility through, for example, giving the power and authority to allocate funds for priority needs to local communities and their representative councils.)
3. Technical, financial, and infrastructural resources
—Have sufficient (and appropriate) resources been allocated to encourage the establishment of sustainable public health?
—What additional resources will be needed—and how can they be obtained?
(Major challenges will include the need to reallocate resources from excessive military budgets in favor of development and social service (including health) priorities, and the need to explore such resource-mobilizing approaches as cost-recovery and fee-for-service.)
4. Human resources
—Are doctors, nurses and other health practitioners ready to take on the challenges of implementing and encouraging the achievement of sustainable public health?
—What changes in training (methodology of training, curriculum, etc.) would be necessary to ensure that future health professionals have the requisite skills and knowledge for sustainable public health?
—How can health professionals who are already in service be equipped for sustainable public health?

- dealing with questions of equity of access (especially of the poor) to social services and support;
- working to promote the status of women and of minorities;
- seeking to promote social hygiene through encouraging improvements in community waste disposal, and water and sanitation practices;
- working to ensure that pollution and potential sources of pollution are well regulated and do not pose undue risks to the health and well-being of community members.

The urban health professional might, for example, take an active interest in promoting the establishment of community-support groups for crime prevention, for dealing with the homeless, for raising awareness and prevention of AIDS, or for preventing domestic violence.[1]

In rural communities, the health professional might additionally work to promote understanding and awareness of the impact of pesticide use and the intrinsic dangers of exposure to pesticides, to encourage the implementation of more sustainable land-use practices that allow for soil fertility to be maintained without degradation, or to help ensure that tourist activities do not degrade the land or contaminate water resources. In rural areas of the poorer developing countries, the focus might include, besides perennial concerns regarding water and sanitation, reducing the risk of health-threatening exposure to indoor smoke arising from biomass fuel use.[2]

At the international and global levels, health professionals might work to promote sustainable human development and to recognize and respond to threats to its establishment. Areas of concern might include promoting peace and human security, working toward better allocation of resources, encouraging environmentally and ecologically sound economic activity, and promoting respect for human rights. Sustainable pub-

[1] While some health professionals today already do take on such activities, most such "nontraditional" work is conducted on an ad-hoc basis—those who do take on such responsibilities do so with little or no professional training or support.

[2] Approaches for dealing with exposure to indoor smoke which the health practitioner might usefully encourage the use of cleaner, less polluting fuels and better designed stoves. Community initiatives for plantation of fire-wood producing trees could be particularly beneficial since farmers would not then have to resort to using soil-fertility enhancing dung and crop residues as poor quality, highly polluting fuels for cooking—as is currently the case in rural areas of many poor developing countries.

lic health professionals might, for example, take an active interest in issues of international trade and their implications for equity,[3] and the encouragement of international peace-making and peace-keeping efforts.[4] The work of groups such as the International Physicians for the Prevention of Nuclear War (IPPNW), Physicians for Social Responsibility (PSR) and Physicians for Human Rights (PHR) has been significant in helping to raise awareness of some of these issues and concerns.

DEALING WITH EXISTING REALITIES IN PUBLIC HEALTH

Conventional approaches to medicine and public health in developed countries have tended to focus on curative medicine and to encourage specialization and hospital-based practice.[5] Unfortunately, this "modern" approach to health care provision has also been largely transplanted into developing countries—many of which have wanted to be able to provide similarly sophisticated, state-of-the-art health care to their societies (at least to privileged members of their societies!). The impact of such a focus has been disastrous, especially in the poorest countries where disproportionately more resources are spent on maintaining and upkeeping expensive tertiary care facilities than on providing life-saving primary health care (which has therefore suffered and seems, in many cases, to have been provided for almost as an after-thought).

The World Development Report 1993 (World Bank, 1993) helped raise awareness, in both developed and developing countries, that consider-

---

[3] Falling prices of commodities and agricultural products have resulted in lower income and massive increases in debt for developing countries despite higher levels of production. This, in turn, has reduced the ability of these countries to deal effectively with the concerns of the poor and the unreached—with consequent implications for health and well-being.

[4] Health practitioners can, for example, provide an important voice encouraging "preventive" development—working in partnership with governments and non-governmental organizations to encourage the establishment of civil society and investment in socio-economic and infrastructural development. Such investment could help reduce the likelihood of social disorder and civil war.

[5] An interesting recent trend in developed countries, especially the United States, has been the increasing recognition of the importance of primary health care and the need to strengthen preventive service delivery and health promotion—this "post-modern" perspective has been fueled by a recognition that too many individuals were falling between the cracks of the conventional approach. This change in perspective has gained added impetus in connection with the World Development Report 1993 (World Bank, 1993).

ably more attention needs to be placed on preventive medicine and on health promotion. It has raised recognition of the cost-effectiveness of primary health care. And it has helped countries recognize the need to prioritize and determine their health care provision needs based on epidemiological data. Implementation of these ideas would greatly rationalize resource allocation for public health and contribute to the eventual establishment of sustainable public health.

While developed countries, and middle- and high-income developing countries, are likely to be able to provide adequately for the human development and health care needs of their populations, low income developing countries are likely to continue to require international assistance and support for developing their primary health care infrastructure and for investment in preventive service delivery (for example, immunization or AIDS prevention). Such assistance has, in the past, come from bilateral and multilateral donors, as well as development banks, foundations, or religious organizations. It is critical that such investment be made according to sound principles—resources should, as far as possible, be preferentially allocated to preventive services and investment in health and human development-related activities. As far as possible, the use of public funds (or international development assistance) for expenditure on tertiary care facilities (including the building and operation of modern hospitals and state-of-the-art diagnostic equipment) needs to be carefully considered in the context of cost-effectiveness and primary health care needs.

UNDP's and UNICEF's concept of the 20/20 vision (an increase in public expenditure on socio-economic development and the provision of health and social services (including education) to at least 20 percent with at least 20 percent of this being used for health improvement) is well worth encouraging. Currently, expenditure on weapons and defense take an inordinate proportion of spending in many developing countries. Money should, wherever possible, be diverted from military expenditure to social and infrastructural investment. The government itself should commit to providing the majority of resources for health and human services—rather than expecting the international development community to pick up the tab. In particular, there is need to actively avoid situations where a government might use all its resources to build up its military or to provide perks to its political elites, and then turn to the international community to provide funds for education and health because these are "priority" areas that need investment.

There is considerable need to sensitize policy-makers to the broader implications of the need for change and to obtain their commitment to bringing about appropriate change. The benefits of working toward redistribution and reallocation of resources to ensure more equitable access to health services and greater cost-effectiveness of health care delivery should also be emphasized. Also, to ensure sustainability of the health care system, fee-for-service and other mechanisms for cost recovery need to be explored and implemented where appropriate.

As many as 1 in every 5 individuals living in the world today continues to live lives of abject poverty—they have insufficient access to food and shelter, social services, education or employment opportunities. This group deserves special attention since the highest fertility and infant mortalities are concentrated in this group. The poor and the illiterate will account for a disproportionate share of global population growth as numbers rise over the next century to over 8 billion and, possibly, as many as 11 billion.

As many as 36 percent of individuals living in developing countries do not have adequate access to health care (defined as access within one hour to appropriate local health services on foot or by local means of transport) (United Nations Development Programme, 1992). In sub-Saharan Africa, more than 50 percent lack such access.

Major disparities in access to health services exist particularly between urban and rural areas of developing countries. The proportion without adequate access varies, on average, from about 10 percent in developing country urban centers to about 50 percent in rural areas. In sub-Saharan Africa, the comparable numbers range from about 20 percent in urban centers to nearly 65 percent in rural areas (UNDP, 1992). This urban/rural disparity is caused largely by the lack of infrastructure and development in rural areas of most developing countries. Many areas remain remote and difficult to access. Additionally, the political realities in many developing countries have tended to make rural development difficult—for example, many countries spend an inordinate amount of their resources on military-related expenditure; also, many politicians have found that their political power bases tend to be the educated, middle-class urban elite, and they have often chosen to direct resources to keeping this group satisfied (usually at the expense of the rural poor).

There is need to focus on the individuals who do not currently have access to services and to develop effective mechanisms for ensuring access for them. The reasons for lack of health services access in developing countries are myriad—isolated, remote communities; lack of trained physicians and other health practitioners; and lack of infrastructure and technical resources.

There are approximately 10 times more doctors and 12 times more nurses per capita in developed countries then in developing countries (Table 40.1). The discrepancy is even greater when seen from a sub-Saharan African perspective where there are 1/50 doctors and about 1/18 nurses per cap compared to developed countries (UNDP, 1992).

If sustainable public health is to be achieved, the health care system must be more responsive to local community concerns and needs than it has traditionally been. This would require a major reorientation from the top-down hierarchies that tend to characterize public health systems throughout the world to decentralization of the decision-making and resource allocation responsibilities to local communities. The traditional hierarchical organization of health systems has not been very successful at providing universal health care coverage—significant proportions of the population (especially the very poor and the remotely located) continue to have little or no access to primary health care. The current trend toward decentralizing health-related decision making to the district level is likely to lead to more rational allocation of resources and improved access to primary health care. Additionally, the establishment of nontraditional, community-generated approaches to health care should be encouraged where possible. These might, for example, include the establishment, encouragement, and linking up of the public-sector health service delivery with the work of nongovernmental organizations, community action groups or health volunteers.

There is considerable need for technical back-up and service support to health practitioners—especially those posted to remote or inaccessible areas where they have little likelihood of support from field hospitals or specialists within easy reach. Public sector health care provision must be modernized to take account of new developments in information technology and to work toward integration of health service delivery within the broader context of striving for sustainable human development. Technical support should, if possible, reach all levels of the public health

TABLE 40.1 Comparison of Population per Doctor and Nurse in Developed and Developing Countries

	People/Doctor	People/Nurse
Developed Countries	460	150
Developing Countries	4,590	1,910
Sub-Saharan Africa	22,930	2,670

Source: UNDP, 1992.

system including the community health workers operating at village health posts. Such support might be as simple as the provision of a telephone hot-line (or, where this is not feasible, radio communication links). Provision of telecommunications support to health workers is likely to be cost-effective and beneficial in many ways. Besides serving as a means for providing health workers with access to advice and more timely logistic supplies, such support can assist greatly in coordinating immunization and community outreach activities, providing valuable epidemiological data, serving as an early warning system for disease outbreaks, and integrating health care delivery with other services including agriculture, education, and literacy programs. Additionally, it could provide an invaluable life-line to members of isolated communities at times of disaster or, during better times, enable them to communicate with relatives who have migrated to urban areas. Provision of such facilities can help make the local health facility a natural community focal point—a fact which the astute health worker might utilize effectively for outreach and information dissemination purposes.

The common practice for health workers (especially physicians) has been to encourage members of the community to attend clinics and such activities as immunization sessions as the principal points of contact between health workers and the community. It is increasingly being recognized that community outreach can be critical for such efforts as ensuring universal immunization coverage, reducing infant mortality, fighting the spread of HIV and AIDS, and promoting concepts of birth spacing and family planning.

It seems certain that future efforts to deal with the challenges posed by epidemic diseases, to prevent exposure to environmental hazards, and promote sustainable human development and a broader understanding of health and the role of the health worker will require a more "activist" approach for the health worker than has previously been the norm. In addition to performing the work traditionally associated with health workers, sustainable public health workers (who would often be among the most literate and highly educated members of their community) could play central roles in helping to collaborate with teachers, agricultural extension workers, water and sanitation engineers, community development officers, and local entrepreneurs to promote integrated and holistic community development approaches aimed at promoting human, environmental and ecological well-being. In all these activities, the health worker in the community can bring together the different groups and help to coordinate their activities so they complement each other and help accelerate the achievement of common health care and development goals.

REALIZING SUSTAINABLE PUBLIC HEALTH

Ensuring the establishment of sustainable public health would require significant innovation in the way in which public health and development workers operate.

Public health practitioners as catalysts for development. Efforts at promoting public health can often serve as an effective mechanism for stimulating socioeconomic and human development. The public health practitioner concerned for the health and well-being of her community can often help identify economic and developmental needs and concerns of her community and help ensure that public attention is directed to dealing effectively with such concerns.

Promoting social equity. The argument for investing in the poor and illiterate is not just a humanitarian or ethical one—our ability to eradicate poverty and to provide equity of access to education and social services for these individuals will do much to keep population numbers globally in check and reduce the pressure of rising human population on global life-support systems. This, together with efforts to reduce runaway consumption in developed countries and to prevent such wastefulness in developing countries, will be critical if we are to achieve sustainable development.

Meeting environmental health challenges and integrating primary health and environmental care. Public health practitioners can greatly facilitate and catalyze environmental and ecological protection efforts through raising awareness of the public health consequences of not working simultaneously to achieve both human and environmental well-being in their local community (The Independent Task Force on Community Action for Social Development, 1995). Efforts are only now beginning to get under way to emphasize the complementarity of efforts to promote primary health and environmental care. Such work is proceeding at many levels—from the global level (through, for example, the work of UNDP, UNICEF, WHO, and international non-governmental organizations) to the local community level where approaches taking integrated, holistic perspectives such as Taylor-Ide and Taylor's work on "Going to SCALE" and developing local markers of sustainability of local community activities are being assessed (Taylor-Ide & Taylor, 1995).

Meeting the challenge of AIDS and other emerging diseases. Health workers need to be ever vigilant in detecting changes in the pattern and incidence of different diseases in their community, and in recognizing the potential for outbreaks of epidemics. To do this effectively requires at least a basic understanding of research methodology and of epidemiology.

With regard to AIDS, there is urgent need for effective prevention, prophylaxis and cure. Efforts to generate effective preventive strategies need to be stepped up. There is, for example, need for better understanding of social mores and cultural behavior in our different societies, and for developing strategies for preventing spread of the epidemic which do not infringe on human rights.

Working toward population and demographic sustainability and ensuring that societies are prepared for the epidemiological transition. It is necessary to ensure, over the long term, that population growth levels off in time and that human resource consumption does not occur at such levels as to be unsustainable.

There is need for health practitioners to prepare for post-transitional concerns. After population growth levels off and societies approximate zero population growth, the proportion of young people in a population tends to decrease while the aged represent a growing proportion of the population. In Japan, for example, it has been estimated that the proportion of the population aged over 65 years will nearly double from 12.6 percent today to about 25 percent in 2020 (Han, 1994). Societies need to prepare for such epidemiological changes and to take account of them in social and community planning.

Coalition building and encouraging community involvement and participation. The public health practitioner is uniquely placed to bring the members of her community together to deal effectively with issues of common concern. This is because she is usually well respected and her views are sought after because of her special knowledge and understanding of disease and illness.

Health workers need to work closely with community leaders and opinion-makers to ensure that they are involved and committed to the effort. The community should also be actively encouraged to contribute to decision making, design, and implementation of any program that impacts on them. This sort of participation is critical for the sustained impact of any activity—from encouraging family planning and birth spacing, to changing agricultural practices, to nutritional education and dissemination of information on the use of oral rehydration salts.

Promoting intersectoral, interdisciplinary collaboration. Ensuring sustainable public health will require the coming together of practitioners and expertise from the widest range of disciplines to develop effective strategies for dealing with problems and concerns of common interest. The players will vary depending on such variables as the nature of the problem. Training of health practitioners on how to network and to function effectively as members of teams with colleagues from other professions or disciplines can greatly facilitate acquisition of this capacity.

NEED FOR INNOVATION IN TRAINING

Institutional public health, which is focused on university-based teaching or postgraduate training of public health practitioners, has generally been shaped by the experience and needs of developed countries. The focus has been on specialization and often on academic research that tends to have more to do with keeping pace of developments and rigid scientific requirements in developed countries than on real needs in developing countries.

The training of public health practitioners should, fundamentally, be responsive to the needs of society. In the context of training physicians and paramedical personnel, the focus should not be just on training them to function effectively but also on sensitizing them to the problems and concerns that threaten the well-being of the communities they serve and on equipping them with the knowledge and skills to help bring about appropriate change. Achieving this requires recognition of the existing realities and constraints to public health in developing countries, and the implementation of innovative approaches to overcome such constraints.

Most public health practitioners in developing countries (especially those running public-sector primary health care facilities) are relatively junior physicians/nurses working rotations within a few years of completing their hospital-based internships. They are relatively inexperienced and often in considerable need of furthur education and support.[6]

Most public health training programs tend to focus on post-qualification training for the physician or paramedical professional with several years of experience. They generally do not address the public health education needs of these health workers when it is most

[6] Programs such as Public Health Schools Without Walls (PHS-WOW, an initiative of the Rockefeller Foundation) have been designed to help meet this sorely felt need.

necessary—before they get posted to run primary health care centers. The best time for such training is probably while they are still attending medical or nursing school (or, possibly, during their internships or apprenticeships).

Physicians who have completed master's-level public health training tend, in developing countries, to become too valuable to deploy in the field and are often pulled back to Ministries of Health to serve as policy makers, or take up academic appointments at universities. Hence, public health training often takes experienced professionals out of field appointments—tending to exacerbate the already acute shortage of knowledgeable professionals in the field. Also, senior health practitioners tend, as a general rule, to gravitate toward urban centers. Attention needs to be given to providing incentives that would encourage practitioners to continue working in rural and remote areas (for example, subsidized housing, posting allowances, or preferential opportunities for career advancement).

In general, we have been slow to innovate and meet the changing health care needs of our populations. Relatively innovative programs such as the Field Epidemiology Training Program operated by the Centers for Disease Control (USA), the International Clinical Epidemiology Network (INCLEN) initiated by the Rockefeller Foundation, or the Public Health Schools Without Walls (PHS-WOW) program, have come into operation in recent years to deal with perceived deficiencies in public health systems and their service delivery. These programs focus, respectively, on training physicians to deal more effectively with disease outbreaks, on getting them more interested in dealing with community health concerns, or on providing distance learning and/or field-based opportunities for public health professionals. While useful and important, such programs do not directly address the fundamental societal and infrastructural problems associated with relative scarcity of physicians and other trained public health personnel in many countries; nor have they been particularly effective in developing appropriate mechanisms and strategies for helping to meet the public health needs of the large segments of society which remain unreached.

Clearly, there is need to consider not only the nature and quality of training but also the quantity (and type) of personnel trained. How do we ensure adequate health care to populations in regions facing severe shortages of trained personnel? Questions need to be asked, for example, regarding whether the traditional university- and/or hospital-based approaches to training health care professionals are appropriate for all developing countries and should continue to be followed—or whether, especially in the more deprived areas, greater emphasis should not be placed on deploying nurse aides or community health workers to meet the basic health care needs of community members—at least for the short- to medium-term while capacity for better trained individuals is being built up.

There is need to educate health workers to recognize that large segments of the populations they serve are currently not being reached. The unreached, who are often the poor, the illiterate, and the remotely located, are often in greatest need of preventive services and of health education and should be specifically targeted for service delivery. Public health professionals will require the knowledge and skills to characterize who the unreached are, according to such characteristics as age, gender, geographic location (urban/rural, remoteness, accessibility of terrain, etc.), and socioeconomic status (which has strong correlations with such issues as access to safe water and sanitation, quality of housing, degree of overcrowding, nutritional status, or likelihood of substance abuse). They will, additionally, require training to enable them to develop appropriate strategies for providing basic services and support to the unreached.

Health workers also require training and support in issues of human rights and equity as they are faced, for example, with the HIV epidemic and find themselves having to deal effectively, but with sensitivity, to contain the spread of the HIV epidemic; or to consider the social and developmental needs of HIV orphans and of communities which have been devastated by the epidemic.

As we develop a more comprehensive understanding of the issues in sustainable human development, we are recognizing more and more that efforts to promote human, environmental and ecological well-being are complementary and that the health worker can play a fundamental and catalytic role in helping to achieve such development in her community. There will be increasing need to bring consideration of environmental and ecological concerns into the curriculum of the health workers and to equip them with the knowledge and skills to take on "activist" roles in identifying and helping to rectify threats to human, environmental or ecological well-being. Health concerns should be viewed within the context of sustainable human development concerns of the people. For example, sustainable public health practitioners should recognize that many approaches currently used, such as the provision of health care using immunization as the initial point of contact and basis for expanding health care provision to communities, without due consideration to meeting education and development needs of communities, and to ensuring that resources will subsequently be available to continue to support and expand such effort, are unlikely to be sustainable—especially if externally funded.

The need to actively encourage the participation and involvement of communities in promoting their own development and well-being is critical. Health workers need training and support to encourage them to take on the roles and responsibilities of social organizers and coordinators who can play a vital role in helping to mobilize the community in efforts to promote its own development and to contain any threats to its survival or well-being. In this context, health workers might gain from instruction on how to maximize the use of their resources (including, where appropriate, the mass media) for greater cost-effectiveness and maximum impact.

In all the work that is done, it is important to realize that determination of local priorities for human, environmental and ecological well-being, or tracking disease outbreaks in the community, cannot be adequately conducted without the ability to collect and analyze data (either epidemiological or even laboratory). Hence, basic training in the methodologies of laboratory and field epidemiological research is also critical. Health workers should be capable of (and encouraged to) conduct their own situational analyses and to perform simple studies. Additionally, training to enable consideration of the cost-effectiveness of health-related interventions (including, perhaps, instruction on how to conduct and understand simple cost-effectiveness analysis) should be incorporated within the training curriculum of health workers. Hence, essential community health research (community-level information gathering and research leading up to essential national health research or ENHR) should, wherever possible, be encouraged.

Bruce (1994) (see Box 40.2) provides an excellent summary of the basic knowledge and skills that innovative programs in public health training need to equip health practitioners with before they complete their formal training. Such skills, together with a basic understanding of the issues in sustainable human development would help ensure that these practitioners are ready to take on the challenges of striving for sustainable public health practice.

MEETING THE AFRICAN AND SOUTH ASIAN CHALLENGE

It will not be easy to achieve sustainable public health anywhere in the world but Africa (especially sub-Saharan Africa) and South Asia offer particular cause for concern. These regions hold the highest concentration of the absolute poor and the unreached. In many countries in these regions, it would appear that things would almost have to get worse before they start getting better.

Box 40.2—General Competencies for Public Health Workers

1. *Analytic skills*—defining a problem, evaluating data, making relevant inferences from available information.
2. *Communication skills*—communicating effectively orally and in writing, presenting information for professional and lay audiences, advocating for public health programmes and resources, interacting with the media.
3. *Policy development/program planning skills*—collecting and summarizing data relevant to an issue, stating policy options, deciding on appropriate courses of action, developing mechanisms to monitor and evaluate programs for their effectiveness.
4. *Cultural skills*—understanding the dynamic forces which contribute to cultural diversity, interacting sensitively with persons from different socio-economic and educational backgrounds, and with persons of all ages and lifestyle preferences, identifying the role of cultural, social, and behavioral factors in determining illness and disease.
5. *Human/community development skills*—understanding that needy communities have strengths as well as weaknesses and that one usually builds from the strengths, ability to work effectively as partners with those who live in environments of poverty and social devastation, ability to understand and motivate individuals and groups to concerted action, effectiveness in building coalitions and organizing groups to advocate for healthier opportunities for children and the elderly.
6. *Basic health sciences skills*—defining, assessing, and understanding the health status of populations, applying behavioral/social/biomedical sciences.
7. *Financial planning and management skills*—developing and presenting a budget, determining fiscal priorities, monitoring program performance, applying basic human relations skills for managing organizations, resolving conflicts.

Source: Bruce, T. A. (1994). Public health principles in the regeneration of medical education. In: *World Federation for Medical Education*. Proceedings of the World Summit on Medical Education (Walton H, Ed). *Medical Education*, Vol. 28, Suppl. 1, pp 68–70.

Sub-Saharan Africa and other developing countries should not blindly mimic MDC health systems. The relative lack of infrastructure and trained personnel means that in these regions, more than anywhere else in the world, innovative approaches based on community involvement and participation and the cost-effective use of limited resources are likely to pay off in terms of new ideas and approaches to health care delivery that will undoubtedly impact greatly on approaches to health care delivery elsewhere in the world. They should make use of the experience and knowledge gained from the past to promote the establishment of innovative and cost-effective strategies for risk reduction and health promotion—appropriate to the resources they have available and to local customs and culture. For example, training of health workers who come from remote communities or minority or tribal groups to provide services within their communities is likely to prove more sustainable and effective than placing individuals who have no local knowledge and no desire to be posted to remote areas.

CONCLUSION

A consensus view appears to be emerging in the international environment, development and health communities of what it will take to achieve sustainable development and sustainable human development. Working toward sustainable human development will undoubtedly alter our understanding of health and of public health along lines similar to those outlined in this chapter.

Present-day institutions are not structured to support interdisciplinary or holistic work that brings together wide-ranging expertise to solve problems that they cannot individually tackle. There is, in the near future, likely to be considerable need for institutional and organizational reform as we come to terms with operationalizing sustainable human development and an expanded understanding of health within the context of such development (sustainable public health).

The need for such fundamental reform should not, however, prevent the introduction into the public health training curriculum of the conceptual basis for integrated and holistic perspectives for health promotion and disease prevention. Neither should it delay introduction into the curriculum of instruction on helping health workers become more effective communicators, coordinators of integrated approaches, and activists for stimulating the establishment of sustainable human development and human, environmental, and ecological well-being.

The road ahead will not be easy. Public health workers have the opportunity to take the lead in engaging society in a dialogue to incorporate new thinking on health to include environmental and ecological health and on the prerequisites for sustainable human development. Introducing these ideas into the public health curriculum today will increase the likelihood that public health workers will be able to increase their own effectiveness in promoting health and, by stimulating development, ensure that such gains are sustainable.

REFERENCES

Advisory Committee on Health Research (1993). Chapter 3—Relevance of the economic environment to health. In *Research for Health: Principles, Perspectives and Strategies*, pp 20–23. World Health Organization: Geneva.

Bajracharya, D. (1993). UNICEF and the Challenge of Sustainable Livelihood—An Overview. New York: UNICEF.

Bruce, T. A. (1994). Public health principles in the regeneration of medical education. In *World Federation for Medical Education.* Proceedings of the World Summit on Medical Education (Walton, H., Ed.). *Medical Education, 28,* Suppl. 1, pp 68–70.

Han, S. T. (1994). Health in the Western Pacific in the 21st Century. In *World Federation for Medical Education.* Proceedings of the World Summit on Medical Education (Walton, H., Ed.). *Medical Education, 28,* Suppl. 1, pp 77–78.

Modegal, S. (1994). Learning from the community: implications of a new approach to public health for medical education. In *World Federation for Medical Education.* Proceedings of the World Summit on Medical Education (Walton, H., Ed.). *Medical Education, 28,* Suppl. 1, pp 126–129.

Mosley, W. H., Bobadilla, J., & Jamison, D. T. (1993). The health transition: Implications for health policy in developing countries. In *Disease Control Priorities in Developing Countries* (Jamison, D. T. & Mosley, W. H., Eds.). Oxford: Oxford University Press.

Rothermel, T. (1994). Opening session. In *World Federation for Medical Education.* Proceedings of the World Summit on Medical Education (Walton, H., Ed.). *Medical Education, 28,* Suppl. 1, pp 16–18.

Taylor-Ide, D., & Taylor, C. (1995). Community-based Sustainable Human Development: A proposal for going to scale with self-reliant social development. Children, Environment and Sustainable Development—Primary Environmental Care Discussion Papers No. 1, February 1995. New York: UNICEF.

The Independent Task Force on Community Action for Social Development (1995). Partnerships for Social Development: A Casebook. Franklin, WV: Future Generations.

United Nations Development Programme (1992). Human Development Report 1992. Oxford University Press: New York.

Concluding Remarks

This book has sought to provide some insights into how we might begin to deal effectively with the environment, development and health challenges which confront us, and to promote a holistic, integrative approach to dealing with such challenges.

The human species has not been very long on this planet. Yet we have managed, in this short time, to have had a tremendous impact on almost all aspects of life. We have changed local environments and landscapes, bred and genetically modified other plant and animal species to meet our food and social needs, and produced and released thousands of synthetic chemicals which do not exist in nature into the environment with scant regard for their potential impact on environmental, ecological and human well-being.

Warning signs that our manipulations and alterations in the name of progress and development are placing considerable stress on global life support systems and homeostatic mechanisms abound. We cannot run away from the fact that we are ourselves, collectively, responsible for the many concerns and threats documented in this book. This is as true for the population crisis (see chapter 1) as it is for the massacres we have witnessed in Rwanda and Bosnia or the destruction of ecosystems and the hole in the ozone layer. We must, therefore, find solutions to these problems. Yet, the history of human social responsibility is not good. We are quite adept at blaming others for our problems and concerns—pointing fingers, for example, at the industrialists, immigrants, foreigners, the Communists, or whatever other scapegoat happens to be the "flavor" of the day.

Rather than take obviously needed actions, national governments are quite happy to point fingers at each other. More developed countries (MDCs) may, for example, point to projections that energy consumption and carbon emission from less developed countries (LDCs) are likely to rise rapidly as they develop and demand, therefore, that LDCs curb rising consumption. LDCs, on the other hand, point to already excessive consumption and emission in MDCs, and ask that they take steps to curb their output so LDC increases can be offset. In any event, such discussions end with little or no resolution and no country agreeing to any of the voluntary curbs.

So long as we do not move beyond our short-term, self-interest perspective to take long-term, socially responsible perspectives that focus on the common good, we will continue to remain indecisive. This is as true of our work in the environmental sphere as it is in economics, in health, and in population. It is, therefore, unsurprising that we find ourselves in near-crisis situation in so many spheres (see chapter 1, Introduction)—many drumbeats are sounding yet too many of us continue to turn a deaf ear. It seems inevitable, given the prevailing insularity and self-interested climate prevalent in so many arenas and so many countries, that we may have to experience the tragic consequences of major global catastrophes before we recognize that actions to alleviate constantly worsening problems need to be taken.

There is need for radical reform in our political and social systems to reward long-term community perspectives rather than short-term self-interest perspectives. There is need to create a culture supportive of environmental and ecological conservation. And there is need for people to think more about the implications of their actions for the others who share this planet with us, and for future generations.

As we approach the end of this millenium and contemplate our roles during the next, the critical challenge facing us is how we choose to utilize the window of opportunity that currently exists to influence the direction and shape of future human development and well-being. This book has attempted to consider what we know and what we need to know if we are to achieve sustainable public health. It is clear that there are many gaps in our knowledge and understanding, and that developing a holistic, integrative framework for appropriate action will require considerably more research and analysis. We can wring our hands and stand aside claiming that our current approaches and practices are so deeply entrenched that rethinking and reorientation are too difficult or impossible. We would then become increasingly irrelevant and continue to operate in a reactive mode as bystanders in a global crisis of development. Or we can proactively work to contribute effectively and constructively toward the future establishment of sustainable development and sustainable public health. The choice is ours.

The Editors

Index

G

H

O

P

Q

R